Visual Basic 5 SECRETS®

by Harold Davis

IDG Books Worldwide, Inc.
An International Data Group Company

Foster City, CA ♦ Chicago, IL ♦ Indianapolis, IN ♦ Southlake, TX

Visual Basic 5 SECRETS®
Published by
IDG Books Worldwide, Inc.
An International Data Group Company
919 E. Hillsdale Blvd., Suite 400
Foster City, CA 94404
www.idgbooks.com (IDG Books Worldwide Web Site)

Library of Congress Catalog Card No.: 97-70654
ISBN: 0-7645-8019-1

Printed in the United States of America
10 9 8 7 6 5 4 3 2 1
IB/TR/QT/ZX/FC

Distributed in the United States by IDG Books Worldwide, Inc.

Distributed by Macmillan Canada for Canada; by Transworld Publishers Limited in the United Kingdom and Europe; by WoodsLane Pty. Ltd. for Australia; by WoodsLane Enterprises Ltd. for New Zealand; by Longman Singapore Publishers Ltd. for Singapore, Malaysia, Thailand, and Indonesia; by Simron Pty. Ltd. for South Africa; by Toppan Company Ltd. for Japan; by Distribuidora Cuspide for Argentina; by Livraria Cultura for Brazil; by Ediciencia S.A. for Ecuador; by Addison-Wesley Publishing Company for Korea; by Ediciones ZETA S.C.R. Ltda. for Peru; by WS Computer Publishing Company, Inc., for the Philippines; by Unalis Corporation for Taiwan; by Contemporanea de Ediciones for Venezuela. Authorized Sales Agent: Anthony Rudkin Associates for the Middle East and North Africa.

For general information on IDG Books Worldwide's books in the U.S., please call our Consumer Customer Service department at 800-762-2974. For reseller information, including discounts and premium sales, please call our Reseller Customer Service department at 800-434-3422.

For information on where to purchase IDG Books Worldwide's books outside the U.S., please contact our International Sales department at 415-655-3023 or fax 415-655-3299.

For information on foreign language translations, please contact our Foreign & Subsidiary Rights department at 415-655-3021 or fax 415-655-3281.

For sales inquiries and special prices for bulk quantities, please contact our Sales department at 415-655-3200 or write to the address above.

For information on using IDG Books Worldwide's books in the classroom or for ordering examination copies, please contact our Educational Sales department at 800-434-2086 or fax 817-251-8174.

For press review copies, author interviews, or other publicity information, please contact our Public Relations department at 415-655-3000 or fax 415-655-3299.

For authorization to photocopy items for corporate, personal, or educational use, please contact Copyright Clearance Center, 222 Rosewood Drive, Danvers, MA 01923, or fax 508-750-4470.

ABOUT IDG BOOKS WORLDWIDE

Welcome to the world of IDG Books Worldwide.

IDG Books Worldwide, Inc., is a subsidiary of International Data Group, the world's largest publisher of computer-related information and the leading global provider of information services on information technology. IDG was founded more than 25 years ago and now employs more than 8,500 people worldwide. IDG publishes more than 275 computer publications in over 75 countries (see listing below). More than 60 million people read one or more IDG publications each month.

Launched in 1990, IDG Books Worldwide is today the #1 publisher of best-selling computer books in the United States. We are proud to have received eight awards from the Computer Press Association in recognition of editorial excellence and three from *Computer Currents*' First Annual Readers' Choice Awards. Our best-selling *...For Dummies*® series has more than 30 million copies in print with translations in 30 languages. IDG Books Worldwide, through a joint venture with IDG's Hi-Tech Beijing, became the first U.S. publisher to publish a computer book in the People's Republic of China. In record time, IDG Books Worldwide has become the first choice for millions of readers around the world who want to learn how to better manage their businesses.

Our mission is simple: Every one of our books is designed to bring extra value and skill-building instructions to the reader. Our books are written by experts who understand and care about our readers. The knowledge base of our editorial staff comes from years of experience in publishing, education, and journalism — experience we use to produce books for the '90s. In short, we care about books, so we attract the best people. We devote special attention to details such as audience, interior design, use of icons, and illustrations. And because we use an efficient process of authoring, editing, and desktop publishing our books electronically, we can spend more time ensuring superior content and spend less time on the technicalities of making books.

You can count on our commitment to deliver high-quality books at competitive prices on topics you want to read about. At IDG Books Worldwide, we continue in the IDG tradition of delivering quality for more than 25 years. You'll find no better book on a subject than one from IDG Books Worldwide.

John Kilcullen
CEO
IDG Books Worldwide, Inc.

Eighth Annual Computer Press Awards 1992

Ninth Annual Computer Press Awards 1993

Tenth Annual Computer Press Awards 1994

Eleventh Annual Computer Press Awards 1995

IDG Books Worldwide, Inc., is a subsidiary of International Data Group, the world's largest publisher of computer-related information and the leading global provider of information services on information technology. International Data Group publishes over 275 computer publications in over 75 countries. Sixty million people read one or more International Data Group publications each month. International Data Group's publications include: **ARGENTINA:** Buyer's Guide, Computerworld Argentina, PC World Argentina; **AUSTRALIA:** Australian Macworld, Australian PC World, Australian Reseller News, Computerworld, IT Casebook, Network World, Publish, Webmaster; **AUSTRIA:** Computerwelt Osterreich, Networks Austria, PC Tip Austria; **BANGLADESH:** PC World Bangladesh; **BELARUS:** PC World Belarus; **BELGIUM:** Data News; **BRAZIL:** Annuário de Informática, Computerworld, Connections, Macworld, PC Player, PC World, Publish, Reseller News, Supergamepower; **BULGARIA:** Computerworld Bulgaria, Network World Bulgaria, PC & MacWorld Bulgaria; **CANADA:** CIO Canada, Client/Server World, ComputerWorld Canada, InfoWorld Canada, NetworkWorld Canada, WebWorld; **CHILE:** Computerworld Chile, PC World Chile; **COLOMBIA:** Computerworld Colombia, PC World Colombia; **COSTA RICA:** PC World Centro America; **THE CZECH AND SLOVAK REPUBLICS:** Computerworld Czechoslovakia, Macworld Czech Republic, PC World Czechoslovakia; **DENMARK:** Communications World Danmark, Computerworld Danmark, Macworld Danmark, PC World Danmark, Techworld Denmark; **DOMINICAN REPUBLIC:** PC World Republica Dominicana; **ECUADOR:** PC World Ecuador; **EGYPT:** Computerworld Middle East, PC World Middle East; **EL SALVADOR:** PC World Centro America; **FINLAND:** MikroPC, Tietoverkko, Tietoviikko; **FRANCE:** Distributique, Hebdo, Info PC, Le Monde Informatique, Macworld, Reseaux & Telecoms, WebMaster France; **GERMANY:** Computer Partner, Computerwoche, Computerwoche Extra, Computerwoche FOCUS, Global Online, Macwelt, PC Welt; **GREECE:** Amiga Computing, GamePro Greece, Multimedia World; **GUATEMALA:** PC World Centro America; **HONDURAS:** PC World Centro America; **HONG KONG:** Computerworld Hong Kong, PC World Hong Kong, Publish in Asia; **HUNGARY:** ABCD CD-ROM, Computerworld Szamitastechnika, Internetto online Magazine, PC World Hungary, PC-X Magazin Hungary; **ICELAND:** Tolvuheimur PC World Island; **INDIA:** Information Communications World, Information Systems Computerworld, PC World India, Publish in Asia; **INDONESIA:** InfoKomputer PC World, Komputek Computerworld, Publish in Asia; **IRELAND:** ComputerScope, PC Live!; **ISRAEL:** Macworld Israel, People & Computers/Computerworld; **ITALY:** Computerworld Italia, Macworld Italia, Networking Italia, PC World Italia; **JAPAN:** DTP World, Macworld Japan, Nikkei Personal Computing, OS/2 World Japan, SunWorld Japan, Windows NT World, Windows World Japan; **KENYA:** PC World East African; **KOREA:** Hi-Tech Information, Macworld Korea, PC World Korea; **MACEDONIA:** PC World Macedonia; **MALAYSIA:** Computerworld Malaysia, PC World Malaysia, Publish in Asia; **MALTA:** PC World Malta; **MEXICO:** Computerworld Mexico, PC World Mexico; **MYANMAR:** PC World Myanmar; **NETHERLANDS:** Computer! Totaal, LAN Internetworking Magazine, LAN World Buyers Guide, Macworld Netherlands, Net, WebWereld; **NEW ZEALAND:** Absolute Beginners Guide and Plain & Simple Series, Computer Buyer, Computer Industry Directory, Computerworld New Zealand, MTB, Network World, PC World New Zealand; **NICARAGUA:** PC World Centro America; **NORWAY:** Computerworld Norge, CW Rapport, Datamagasinet, Financial Rapport, Kursguide Norge, Macworld Norge, Multimediaworld Norge, PC World Ekspress Norge, PC World Nettverk, PC World Norge, PC World ProduktGuide Norge; **PAKISTAN:** Computerworld Pakistan; **PANAMA:** PC World Panama; **PEOPLE'S REPUBLIC OF CHINA:** China Computer Users, China Computerworld, China InfoWorld, China Telecom World Weekly, Computer & Communication, Electronic Design China, Electronics Today, Electronics Weekly, Game Software, PC World China, Popular Computer Week, Software Weekly, Software World, Telecom World; **PERU:** Computerworld Peru, PC World Profesional Peru, PC World SoHo Peru; **PHILIPPINES:** Click!, Computerworld Philippines, PC World Philippines, Publish in Asia; **POLAND:** Computerworld Poland, Computerworld Special Report Poland, Cyber, Macworld Poland, Networld Poland, PC World Komputer; **PORTUGAL:** Cerebro/PC World, Computerworld/Correio Informático, Dealer World Portugal, Mac*In/PC*In Portugal, Multimedia World; **PUERTO RICO:** PC World Puerto Rico; **ROMANIA:** Computerworld Romania, PC World Romania, Telecom Romania; **RUSSIA:** Computerworld Russia, Mir PK, Publish, Seti; **SINGAPORE:** Computerworld Singapore, PC World Singapore, Publish in Asia; **SLOVENIA:** Monitor; **SOUTH AFRICA:** Computing SA, Network World SA, Software World SA; **SPAIN:** Communicaciones World España, Computerworld España, Dealer World España, Macworld España, PC World España; **SRI LANKA:** Infolink PC World; **SWEDEN:** CAP&Design, Computer Sweden, Corporate Computing Sweden, Internetworld Sweden, it.branschen, Macworld Sweden, MaxiData Sweden, MikroDatorn, Nätverk & Kommunikation, PC World Sweden, PCaktiv, Windows World Sweden; **SWITZERLAND:** Computerworld Schweiz, Macworld Schweiz, PCtip; **TAIWAN:** Computerworld Taiwan, Macworld Taiwan, NEW ViSiON/Publish, PC World Taiwan, Windows World Taiwan; **THAILAND:** Publish in Asia, Thai Computerworld; **TURKEY:** Computerworld Turkiye, Macworld Turkiye, Network World Turkiye, PC World Turkiye; **UKRAINE:** Computerworld Kiev, Multimedia World Ukraine, PC World Ukraine; **UNITED KINGDOM:** Acorn User UK, Amiga Action UK, Amiga Computing UK, Apple Talk UK, Computing, Macworld, Parents and Computers UK, PC Advisor, PC Home, PSX Pro, The WEB; **UNITED STATES:** Cable in the Classroom, CIO Magazine, Computerworld, DOS World, Federal Computer Week, GamePro Magazine, InfoWorld, I-Way, Macworld, Network World, PC Games, PC World, Publish, Video Event, THE WEB Magazine, and WebMaster; online webzines: JavaWorld, NetscapeWorld, and SunWorld Online; **URUGUAY:** InfoWorld Uruguay; **VENEZUELA:** Computerworld Venezuela, PC World Venezuela; and **VIETNAM:** PC World Vietnam. 2/14/97

Credits

Managing Editor
Andy Cummings

Acquisitions Editor
Gregory S. Croy

Software Acquisitions Editor
Tracy Lehman Cramer

Developmental Editor
William P. Sullivan

Senior Copy Editor
Barry Childs-Helton

Copy Editor
Deborah A. Craig

Technical Reviewer
Jeff Bankston

Project Coordinator
Susan Parini

Graphics & Production Specialists
Vincent F. Burns
Andreas F. Schueller
Mark Schumann

Quality Control Specialist
Mick Arellano

Proofreader
Jenny K. Overmeyer

Indexer
Mark Kmetzko

As always, for Phyllis

Acknowledgments

To acknowledge means to give thanks. Since a book like *Visual Basic 5 SECRETS* is never really the work of one person, I have much thanks to give. Here are some of the "thanks" that I owe!

Thanks are due to the excellent staff at IDG Books, particularly Walter R. Bruce III, Gregory S. Croy, and William P. Sullivan.

Deborah Craig did her usual excellent job as manuscript editor. Deborah: thanks for your care, your English, and your kindness.

Without Matt Wagner, my agent, it is unlikely that this book would have been written (at least by me).

I am also deeply grateful to those who provided software for inclusion on the *Visual Basic 5 SECRETS* companion CD-ROM. In this connection, I'd particularly like to thank Marylin Guarino of Blue Sky Software; Dan Appleman and Roan Bear of Desaware; Don Williamson of FarPoint Technologies; Bill Muscato of ImageFX; Ruth James, of Mabry Software; Sam Patterson of MicroHelp; Christi Westphal of Sax Software; Kimberly Schreuders of TVObjects; and Gustavo Eydelsten of VideoSoft.

A very special thanks is due to Jon Roskill at Microsoft Corporation for his continued support.

The real heroes of this operation are the unsung developers at Microsoft, who did such an incredible job with Version 5 of Visual Basic. Without them, of course, there would be no *Visual Basic 5 SECRETS*.

In every sense but officially receiving the credit, *Visual Basic 5 SECRETS* was as much authored by my wife, Phyllis Davis, as by me.

(The Publisher would like to give special thanks to Patrick J. McGovern, without whom this book would not have been possible.)

Contents at a Glance

Contents

Visual Basic: An Overview

Chapter 1

Read This First

Visual Basic 5 SECRETS fills a yawning need that has yet to be met. Programmers and developers need a book that they can use to quickly find the tools, techniques, and tricks they need to solve problems that come up when writing real-world Visual Basic applications for 32-bit Windows. You'll find this information here — for the first time in one place — with no nonsense, developer to developer. In this chapter you'll learn how to best use this book and quickly find the information you need.

Version 5 is the first entirely 32-bit version of Visual Basic. (This means you can't use it to create legacy 16-bit applications.) There are numerous new and exciting features in this release that you will learn to use in *Visual Basic 5 SECRETS*, including

- The option of creating fully compiled executables
- The ability to create ActiveX controls
- Support for easily creating Web applications (and deploying ActiveX controls created in Visual Basic 5 on the Web)
- Enhanced ability to create extensions to the Visual Basic environment

This chapter contains background information about Visual Basic 5 and this book. You'll learn

- Why a book like *Visual Basic 5 SECRETS* is needed
- How to quickly find the information you need in *Visual Basic 5 SECRETS*
- How this book is structured
- How to find the "good parts" of the book
- Where to get more information about Visual Basic
- What the various editions of Visual Basic Version 5 are and what is different about them
- How to install Visual Basic Version 5
- What's new in Version 5 of Visual Basic
- An introduction to OLE
- What's on the companion CD-ROM

Why *Visual Basic 5 SECRETS*?

The roots of Visual Basic are — forgive the pun — "basic." But around the humble core of Visual Basic has grown a vast system of extensions, techniques, and third-party tools. It is undoubtedly easy to get Visual Basic to do "easy" things, but much harder indeed to release its full potential. Particularly with the widespread adoption of Windows 95 and Windows NT 4.0, there is a very apparent need for one book that reveals all the tricks of the trade from the view point of the working developer.

Programming is — at its best — one part art, one part science, and one part lore. As programming languages go, Visual Basic is extremely easy to program, but only up to a certain point. Learning the secrets that lie beyond that point, sometimes referred to by developers as the "VB Wall," is a matter of obtaining access to arcane techniques passed by word of mouth from programmer to programmer, browsing on-line forums, assimilating documentation from myriad sources, and practical real-life experience. In *Visual Basic 5 SECRETS*, I draw on my experience as a developer and my extensive collection of Visual Basic tricks and techniques to take you behind the scenes of Visual Basic. This book collects — in one place for the first time — everything the Visual Basic programmer needs to create sophisticated professional applications.

How to Use This Book

If you are an experienced programmer and have used an earlier version of Visual Basic, probably the best strategy is to start with Chapter 5, "What's New in Visual Basic 5." You can then continue with topics that specifically interest you.

If you are looking for information on programming with the look and feel of the Windows 95 interface (which is included in NT 4.0) and its impact on Visual Basic, Part II, "Programming 32-Bit Windows," is for you. You should also make a point of having an early look at Part VIII, "Third-Party Tools, Setup Programs, and Help Files," which covers some of the hottest new 32-bit ActiveX-based products (such as OLE controls) and how they are best used with Visual Basic 5.

The world of Windows component programming is, to a great extent, the world of ActiveX and OLE. Programming ActiveX applications is easy and exciting in VB5. For information on this topic, turn to Part V, "Using ActiveX."

Visual Basic 5 includes far more OOP (object-oriented programming) features than previous versions of Visual Basic. If you'd like a jump start on the concepts involved in OOP — and how Visual Basic implements them — you should start with Chapter 3, "Event-Driven Programming," continue with Chapter 4, "The Visual Basic Language," and proceed to Part III, "Coding Secrets."

Combining the use of OLE and the concepts behind OOP, you can now create true ActiveX controls using Visual Basic 5. You can use these ActiveX controls as components in other development environments such as Visual C++,

Delphi, and FoxPro. You can also easily add them to Web applications, making dynamic executable content on the Web a present reality. For information on creating ActiveX controls, turn to Part VI, "Creating ActiveX Controls."

Now, more than ever, it is easy and fun to extend the Visual Basic environment. ActiveX documents are Internet forms. Add-ins are ActiveX components, which you can write in Visual Basic, that modify the Visual Basic Integrated Development Environment (IDE) and the current Visual Basic project. Wizards are applications that guide a user through a task. In Part VII, "Extending the VB Environment," I'll show you how to create Internet applications in VB, how to create ActiveX documents that can be viewed in an Internet browser, and how to create your own Visual Basic add-ins and Wizards.

Finally, if you are one of the few advanced programmers out there who has never experienced the joys of Visual Basic, by all means start at the beginning: After this chapter, go straight to Chapter 2, "Exploring the Visual Basic IDE." You'll catch on to the Visual Basic syntax and way of doing things in no time — and will be on to building great applications before you know it.

This Book's Overall Structure

Visual Basic 5 SECRETS is divided into eight parts.

Part I: Visual Basic: An Overview

This part summarizes the Visual Basic IDE (Integrated Development Environment) and language. It covers the basics of event-driven programming and OOP in Visual Basic and describes what's new in Visual Basic 5.

Part II: Programming 32-Bit Windows

This part covers the Windows 95 and NT operating systems and what you need to know to create successful Visual Basic applications for them. Topics include Windows 95 components and common dialogs, the Registry, the Win32 API, the Windows messaging system, and using Visual SourceSafe.

Part III: Coding Secrets

In this part you'll learn the secrets of the Visual Basic programming masters. The part covers scoping, OOP and inheritance, class modules, creating custom properties, using the API in the real world, handling errors, conditional compilation, and optimizing your programs for speed and size.

Part IV: Display Secrets

The impression your programs make comes largely from how you handle the display. This part of the book is about creating incredibly, impossibly wonderful dynamic displays. It contains many "secret" display techniques that you can use immediately in your own projects.

Part V: Using ActiveX

Using exposed OLE methods of existing objects and creating your own ActiveX component — OLE server — applications are among the most exciting things you can do in any Windows programming environment. This part explains everything you always wanted to know about ActiveX, OLE and Visual Basic 5 but were afraid to ask.

Part VI: Creating ActiveX Controls

Poor Visual Basic! Invited to the party, but never able to roll its own — until now. You used to be able to use a Visual Basic form as an OLE container for any ActiveX component by adding the ActiveX control to your Toolbox then placing it on a form. But you could not create your own components. Well, now you can! This part explains everything you need to know to create industrial strength ActiveX controls — for your own internal use or for deployment on the Web.

Part VII: Extending the VB Environment

It's easy to create Internet applications in VB5 using new controls. In addition, you can use VB to create ActiveX documents, which are applications that run in Explorer — and can be used to extend the VB environment itself. I'll show you how this works, and how to use Visual Basic to create powerful add-ins and Wizards that extend the VB environment. I'll demonstrate how to program your own — for internal use or as a tool to distribute to others.

Part VIII: Third-Party Tools, Setup Programs, and Help Files

This part covers the secrets of effectively using the most important Visual Basic third-party tools in their new incarnation as ActiveX controls. It also includes material on creating professional setup programs and help files.

Finding the Good Parts

To help you find what you are looking for, I've listed the most important topics of the chapter at the beginning of every chapter. I've also included a slightly more detailed summary at the end of each chapter.

In addition, I've used some specialized icons in the margin to help you quickly identify important material. If you wish, you can just jump from icon to icon, reading the surrounding material for background information. Here are the icons I've used:

The New to Visual Basic 5 icon indicates that the concept or technique being illustrated is important, and is new to Visual Basic 5.

When you see the ActiveX icon, I'm covering something important to understanding ActiveX or creating ActiveX controls.

The OOP icon points out important aspects of Visual Basic's implementation of object-oriented programming.

I've used the Inside Scoop icon when there is something you really should know. In other words, reading *Visual Basic 5 SECRETS* text flagged with the Inside Scoop icon may save you many hours of hard labor. Inside Scoops contain especially useful information and insights that are not easily found elsewhere.

The High Risk icon indicates pitfalls that you should often keep an eye out for.

Besides providing these helpful icons, I'll often give you step-by-step instructions explaining how to carry out a specific task. My intention is to provide a way for you to accomplish the task even if you are not familiar with the underlying theory. (Of course, if you do want to understand the hows and whys, I include this kind of material as well.)

For Further Information

Visual Basic ships with extensive product documentation in the form of manuals and on-line help. This documentation is the first place to look for answers to your questions. (See "Quickly Finding Information in the Documentation" in Chapter 4 for more details.)

You can access the multivolume Visual Basic books on-line through the Search Master Index item on VB5's Help menu.

Microsoft Developer Network (MSDN) provides a quarterly CD-ROM with its Level 1 subscription service that contains a wealth of technical information on all of Microsoft's development products. (See "Quickly Finding Information in the Documentation" in Chapter 4 for more about MSDN.) You can contact MSDN at 800-759-5474, or you can find more information on the Web at *http://www.microsoft.com/MSDN/*.

Microsoft's Web Site

Microsoft's Web site includes a great deal of information about Visual Basic programming, and about using Microsoft programming tools in general. This information tends to be both more up-to-date and authoritative than that available elsewhere. (Remember the old saying about straight from the horse's mouth?)

The URL for information on Visual Basic is *http://www.microsoft.com/vbasic/*. You can find information about ActiveX programming and Internet technologies at the Site Builder Workshop, *http://www.microsoft.com/workshop/*.

CompuServe

If you can't find what you need in the documentation, on Microsoft's Web site, or on the MSDN CD-ROMs, there are several other places to hunt for the information you need.

CompuServe has a number of forums with a great deal of technical information about Visual Basic. Either use a keyword search to find what you are interested in, browse the forum library by library, or download an index file, go off-line, study the index for what you want, and then go back and grab it.

The two most interesting CompuServe forums from the viewpoint of the experienced Visual Basic developer are the MS Basic Forum (Go MSBASIC) and the Visual Basic Programmer's Journal Forum (Go VBPJ). The file ***Msbasic.Txt***, located in Library 1 of the MS Basic Forum, contains an index of the newest files in the forum (usually, the last month or so of uploads).

Magazines

There are currently two rather good monthly magazines aimed at Visual Basic developers.

Fawcette Technical Publication's *Visual Basic Programmer's Journal* is highly recommended and features programming techniques, tools, and tips. For subscriptions, call 303-684-0365. VBPJ maintains a Web site with much valuable Visual Basic information: *http://www.windx.com*.

Oakley Publishing's *VB Tech Journal* is entertaining, but focuses more on reviews of third-party Visual Basic tools than hard-core development issues. Recently, *VB Tech* has announced a change of emphasis to focus more on corporate development issues. VB Tech's business phone is 800-234-0386.

Books

The following two books provide general background information on important topics. They should be on the bookshelf of every serious programmer.

Gary Entsminger's *The Tao of Objects* (2nd ed., M&T Books, 1995) is the best general introduction to the concepts of OOP. The book includes coverage of object-oriented programming in Visual Basic 4.

Steve McConnell's *Code Complete: A Practical Handbook of Software Construction* (Microsoft Press, 1993) is exactly what the subtitle suggests. This invaluable book is a broad yet detailed guide to the software development process from a technical point of view, written by a Microsoft Project Leader.

The Learning, Professional, and Enterprise Editions

There are three editions of Visual Basic 5 on the market. All three are 32-bit applications (meaning they run under Windows 95 or NT, but not Windows 3.*x*) that produce only 32-bit programs.

The Learning Edition is the least expensive of the three editions. It includes the core Visual Basic controls, sometimes called the *intrinsic* controls, and grid, outline, and bound controls (but not the other controls included with the Professional Edition). The Learning Edition lacks some functionality that is required for the creation of professional applications. Printed and on-line documentation consists of the *Programmer's Guide*.

The Professional Edition includes everything in the Standard Edition. It also ships with an extensive collection of additional controls, including 3D controls, an animated button control, a communications control, a ListView control, a MAPI control, a ProgressBar control, a Toolbar control, and many more, including Internet controls. In addition, it ships with Crystal Report Writer.

The Professional Edition has the important capability — which the Learning Edition does not — of creating ActiveX component applications and ActiveX controls.

In addition to the *Programmer's Guide*, the Professional Edition includes printed versions of these manuals: *Language Reference*, *Professional Features*, and *Crystal Reports for Visual Basic Users*.

The Enterprise Edition is intended to help professional teams of programmers produce robust applications — including client/server applications — in an enterprise environment.

The Enterprise Edition includes everything in the Professional Edition plus an object Repository (used for organizing components in an enterprise environment), the Automation Manager, the Component Manager, Visual SourceSafe (a versioning tool), database management tools, client/server development tools, and more. One particularly exciting feature of the Enterprise Edition is that it enables you to create Remote Automation OLE servers that can be executed remotely over a network.

Of course, the Enterprise Edition ships with documentation for its various parts (as well as the Professional documentation set).

To keep things simple, this book assumes that you are working with at least the Professional Edition. As an advanced-level development tool, the Learning Edition just doesn't hack it. The additional controls alone in the Professional Edition are well worth its additional expense. In addition, many of the most exciting VB5 features — such as the ability to create ActiveX controls — are not available except in the Professional and Enterprise Editions.

I'll be covering some of the features specific to the Enterprise Edition. (For example, Chapter 12, "Using Visual SourceSafe," discusses the versioning tools that are supplied only with the Enterprise Edition.) When I do so, I will clearly indicate that the discussion only applies if you are working with the Enterprise Edition.

Windows 95 and Windows NT

How time flies! It seems but a blink of an eye since Windows 95 was released and Windows users at large were introduced to a 32-bit operating system — and its exciting new interface. Visual Basic 5 focuses on 32-bit development and firmly leaves Windows 3.1 and 16-bit applications behind.

Although there are considerable differences under the hood between the two 32-bit versions of Windows — 95 and NT — with the release of NT 4.0 the interfaces are essentially the same. By and large, programs that work under one of these operating systems will also work just fine under the other. (I'll note in the text any specific issues that require coding to handle differences between NT and 95.) You should know that one of the key requirements for Windows 95 certification is that an application also perform well under Windows NT.

Installing Visual Basic 5

To run the Professional Edition of Visual Basic 5, you'll obviously need a system that is running Windows 95 or Windows NT 4.0. Microsoft suggests a minimum of 8MB of RAM for 95 and 16MB for NT. I suggest more, particularly for OLE application development. I programmed and tested the sample OLE server applications in *Visual Basic 5 SECRETS* on a Windows 95 Pentium 90 with 32MB of RAM and a Windows NT 4.0 Pentium Pro with 32MB of RAM. Performance was acceptable, but I wouldn't have wanted to be doing it on much less.

A full installation of the Enterprise Edition requires about 110MB of hard drive space; you'll need at least 35MB free on your boot drive to successfully install it.

As a general rule, it's a good idea to test your application on a wide range of hardware, from slow to fast. Programs that run acceptably on your machine may be intolerably slow on your users' (slower) systems.

When you run the Professional or Enterprise setup program from the CD-ROM, you'll get an initial menu where you decide what you want to install, as shown in Figure 1-1. For most users, the Typical setup option will do just fine.

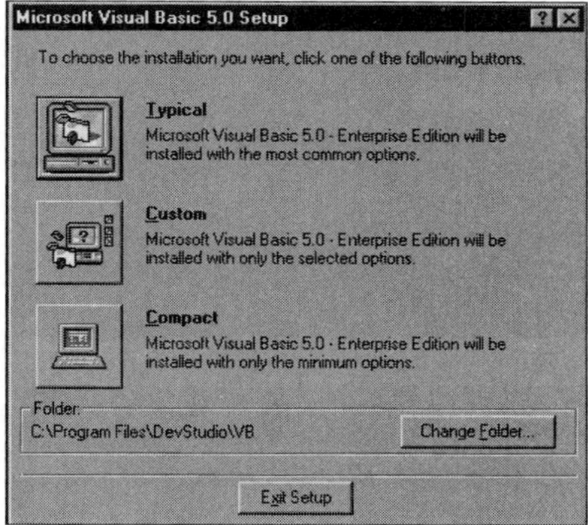

Figure 1-1: The Enterprise Edition CD-ROM: Choosing setup options.

What's New in Version 5: An Overview

Even a casual glance at Version 5 of Visual Basic will disclose that much has changed. Some of the changes have to do with the full shift to 32-bit programming, and the increased importance of Web programming. (In the latter category, note that ActiveX is vital to Microsoft's Web strategy.)

Others more simply have to do with enhancing the Visual Basic IDE (Integrated Development Environment) and making it easier and more fun to use. These IDE enhancements add up to a programming language and tool set that can deliver a lot more power — provided that you know how to take advantage of the new facilities. That's where *Visual Basic 5 SECRETS* comes in.

Significant new features of Visual Basic 5 include

- A native code compiler. You can now create true executables (although, in some circumstances, you may prefer to stick with Visual Basic's traditional p-code).
- The ability to create ActiveX controls that can be run in any ActiveX host environment, including VB5 itself, Visual Basic 4, Delphi, and Visual C++.
- The ability to create ActiveX documents that behave like Web applications within Internet Explorer.
- Easy deployment of VB-created ActiveX controls and applications over the Internet.
- Enhanced class support.
- The ability to add debugging assertions.
- Subclassing of windows.

- Win32 API callbacks.
- Many new included controls.
- The possibility of greatly customizing the IDE.
- Wizards to help you with many tasks.
- A Wizard manager to help you create your own Wizards.

For more information on what's new, see Chapter 5, "What's New in Visual Basic 5."

OLE: An Overview

Microsoft OLE expert Kraig Brockschmidt has defined OLE, object linking and embedding, as follows:

OLE is a unified environment of object-based services with the capability of both customizing those services and arbitrarily extending the architecture through custom services, with the overall purpose of enabling rich integration between components.

By programming exposed OLE objects or OLE enabled applications — for example, Microsoft Excel — you can easily gain access to the capabilities of the OLE server.

By creating your own OLE objects, ActiveX applications, and controls, you can:

- Build a library of standard components that allow code to be shared and reused
- Create applications that are made up of components written in a variety of languages using different tools
- Access objects you've created from OLE supporting macro languages — for example, from the Word for Windows macro language
- Create applications that you can maintain and update by replacing selected OLE objects with newer versions that keep access routines unchanged
- Create ActiveX controls that can be used in other programming environments and across the Web

OLE programming will be covered throughout *Visual Basic 5 SECRETS* as it comes up and in detail in Part V, "Using ActiveX." I'll show you how to make good use of OLE programming techniques you've learned in Part VI, "Creating ActiveX Controls," and Part VII, "Extending the VB Environment."

What's on the CD-ROM

The companion CD-ROM contains all the source code for projects developed in *Visual Basic 5 SECRETS*, organized by chapter. You can use this code in your own projects, and you can open the projects on the CD-ROM in order to study them fully.

In addition, the CD-ROM contains demonstration versions of most of the third-party tools discussed in Part VIII, "Third-Party Tools, Setup Programs, and Help Files." These are 32-bit ActiveX controls (OCXs). By and large, they are fully functional at design time. At runtime they are fully functional as well, except for an initial banner stating that your program is using a demonstration version of the control in question.

I've made every effort to include only top flight, cutting edge third-party tools on the CD-ROM. You won't waste your time exploring these controls. I've only included material from the first tier of Visual Basic tool vendors, including Blue Sky Software, Desaware, ImageFX, MicroHelp, Sax Software, Sheridan, TVObjects, and Videosoft.

For further discussion of these tools, see Part VIII. Appendix A contains a complete list of the third-party tools on the CD-ROM.

If the CD-ROM disc that comes with this book is damaged, by all means contact IDG Books Worldwide, which is committed to providing you with a CD-ROM disc in perfect condition.

Unfortunately, it is a truism that all Windows application code contains bugs. Although I have made every effort to write accurate and bug-free code in *Visual Basic 5 SECRETS*, neither I nor IDG Books can make any promise or warranty about the code from the book that I have placed on the CD-ROM other than that I have done my best. I will not provide technical support for this code, but I am interested in learning about any significant bugs. You can reach me by e-mail at the following address: *harold@bearhome.com*. You may also be interested in the sample programs and development ideas that I post to my Web site from time to time. The URL is *http://www.bearhome.com*.

Neither I nor IDG books are familiar with all the details of the third-party tools on the CD-ROM. We do not provide any technical support for these products. Typically, the vendor of the product will provide support, but only if you first purchase and register a copy.

Summary

Visual Basic is the world's best-selling programming language. With Version 5 and the ability to create ActiveX controls, its power has been greatly expanded. The manuals are fine, up to a point. But there are many hidden techniques and tricks that will help you create better programs faster. That's what *Visual Basic 5 SECRETS* is all about.

In this chapter, I

- Explained why a great deal that the experienced developer needs to know is not covered in the product documentation
- Discussed how to quickly find where you need to go in *Visual Basic 5 SECRETS* to track down the answer to a specific question
- Showed you the icons I use to identify particular kinds of information

- Told you where else to go for the best technical information on Visual Basic 5 programming
- Described the differences between the Learning, Professional, and Enterprise Editions of Visual Basic 5
- Provided an overview of features that are new to Visual Basic Version 5
- Defined OLE and explained why it is important
- Described the contents of the companion CD-ROM

Chapter 2

Exploring the Visual Basic IDE

Visual Basic has come a long way since those early days when it was code named "Thunderbolt" and ran under Windows 3.0. In this chapter, I'll start with an overview of the Visual Basic Integrated Development Environment (IDE). If you're not familiar with Visual Basic — or are new to Version 5 — this will give you a sense of how to accomplish basic tasks before you go on to more advanced topics. The chapter is, roughly speaking, organized in the order in which you'd work with a programming project: First you open it (or start a new project), next you use the tools provided in the IDE to work with it, and, finally, you compile the program.

In this chapter, I'll show you how to

- Open existing VB projects and start new projects
- Decide which kind of VB project you should use
- Save VB source files and projects
- Set Environment, Project, and Editor options
- Add the different kinds of modules to a project
- Use the Edit menu
- Use the Toolbox to add controls to forms
- Add new controls to your Toolbox
- Use the Project Explorer to navigate through projects and source code
- Make effective use of the Code window
- Move quickly through source code with the Object Browser
- Use the Menu Editor to add menus to a form
- Use the context-sensitive menus that appear when you right-click various items on the screen
- Use the VB debugging tools
- Create compiled executable files

Although the core language and the purpose of most of the IDE tools have not changed significantly since Visual Basic 4, you'll find a great deal that is new in this release. There are many enhancements to the way the IDE works. As just two examples, a Visual Basic project group can now contain more than one project, and the enhanced Code window automatically suggests proper language syntax elements when you enter code. (This last enhancement makes me feel like a kid in math class with a calculator who doesn't have to do arithmetic by hand: "What, you mean I don't have to remember the argument orders and constant names?")

Chapter 5, “What’s New in Visual Basic 5,” covers the totally new IDE features, including the ability to create ActiveX controls, your own Wizards, and Internet documents.

The IDE: An Overview

The Visual Basic development environment is rather straightforward and easy to use once you become acquainted with it. When you launch Visual Basic, by default you’ll see the New Project dialog shown in Figure 2-1. You can use this New Project dialog to open an existing project or a new project. A third tab makes it easy to open projects you have worked on recently.

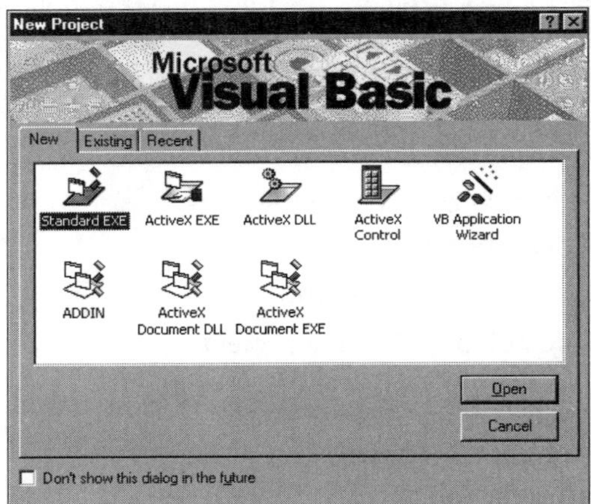

Figure 2-1: You’ll see the New Project dialog the first time you start Visual Basic 5.

When you choose New from the main Visual Basic File menu, the New Project dialog you see consists of only the New Project tab; it does not include the Existing or Recent tabs shown in Figure 2-1.

If you check the Don’t Show this Dialog in the Future option on the initial New Project dialog, you won’t see this dialog the next time you start Visual Basic. Instead, VB will automatically create a default Standard EXE project when it starts. To toggle the initial New Project dialog back on, choose Options from the Tools menu, choose the Environment tab, and select the option Prompt for Project when Visual Basic starts.

The New Project Dialog

By default, the New Project dialog presents eight options:

- Standard EXE is for creating a standard executable project.

- ActiveX EXE is for creating an out-of-process OLE server application.
- ActiveX DLL is for creating an in-process OLE server application.
- ActiveX Control is for creating an ActiveX control (an ***.Ocx*** file). For more information, see Part VI, "Creating ActiveX Controls."
- VB Application Wizard guides you through the initial design choices regarding the interface of a standard application.
- ADDIN helps you to construct your own Visual Basic add-in (see Chapter 29, "Creating a VB Add-In").
- ActiveX Document DLL is for creating an in-process ActiveX document application (see Chapter 28, "Creating Internet Applications in VB").
- ActiveX Document EXE is for creating an out-of-process ActiveX document application (see Chapter 28).

Projects that you add to Visual Basic's ***Templates\Project*** directory appear as template options in the New Project dialog. I'll show you how to add your own template projects to the available choices in Chapter 5.

In-process OLE server applications execute as part of the same thread as the client application that has invoked them, while out-of-process OLE servers require their own execution thread. For more information, see Part V, "Using ActiveX."

IDE Elements

Once you've opened a project in VB5, you'll see something along the lines of what is shown in Figure 2-2. (Note that you can configure the appearance of most IDE elements; your actual screen appearance will depend upon the settings you have selected and how you have arranged things.)

At the top of the screen is the *title bar* (also called the *caption bar*), which displays the name of the open project and indicates whether you are working in design, run, or break mode.

Below the title bar is the *menu bar,* which gives you access to the commands that let you build your projects. The Visual Basic menu bar consists of the File, Edit, View, Project, Format, Debug, Run, Tools, Add-Ins, Window, and Help menus.

Below the menu bar is the *toolbar*. The toolbar contains buttons that let you quickly perform common programming tasks, including adding a new project; adding a new module; opening the Menu Editor; opening an existing project; saving the current project; cutting, copying, pasting, finding, undoing, and redoing; starting, pausing, or stopping the execution of an application; showing the Project Explorer; showing the Properties window; showing the Form Layout window; showing the Object Browser; and showing the Toolbox.

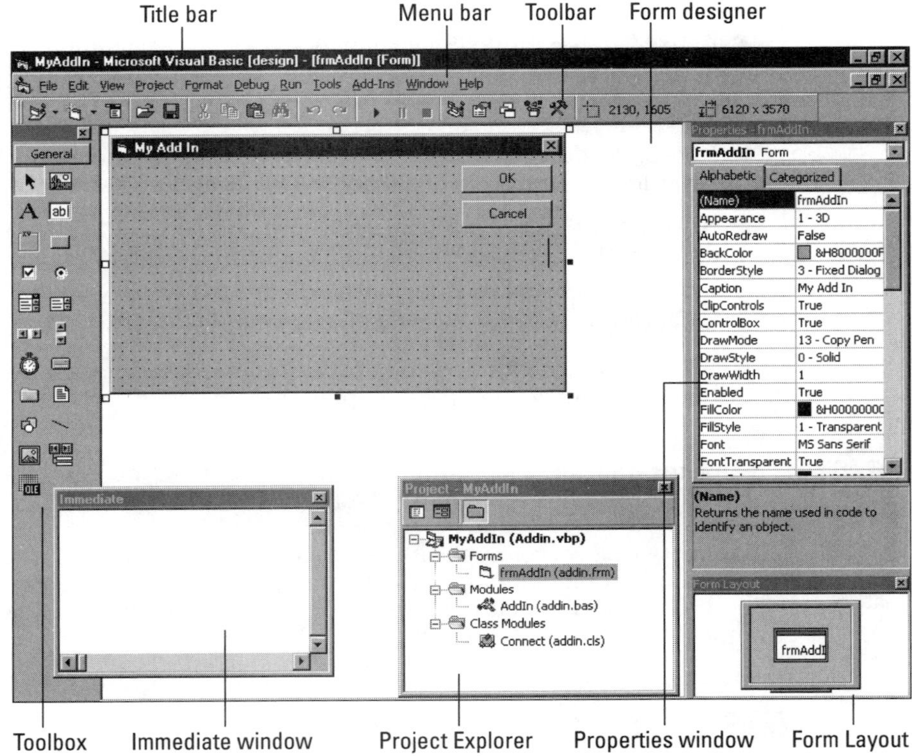

Figure 2-2: You can see that the VB5 IDE packs a lot of power.

Some of the toolbar buttons now invoke list boxes of options. For example, you can choose what kind of module you'd like to add from the drop-down list that appears when you click the Add Module button.

Other IDE elements shown in Figure 2-2 (and which appear by default when you open a new Standard EXE project) include:

- The Toolbox, which displays currently available ActiveX controls (and other objects that can be inserted in your VB form)
- The Immediate window, which is used in debugging to show information that results from debugging statements in your code, or that you request by typing commands interactively into the window
- The Project Explorer, which you can use to navigate between the modules in a project (and the projects in a project group)
- The Form Layout window, which you can use to position forms on the screen
- The Properties window, which you can use to set form and control properties at design time
- A Form designer, which you can use to manipulate the appearance of a form

You can use *designers* to manipulate the appearance of other kinds of modules besides forms. For example, you can use a User Control designer to create the runtime appearance of an ActiveX control. ActiveX control applications are built around User Control modules in the same way that standard executable applications are built around form modules. There is no essential difference between the various kinds of designers — except that they are operating on different kinds of modules.

In previous versions of Visual Basic, the function of the designer and the Form Layout window was accomplished in one window, which was the primary VB workspace.

Some Important New IDE Features

Visual Basic 5 includes myriad exciting new features. Some that deserve special mention include

- When making an executable, you can choose between creating true compiled stand-alone programs or traditional Visual Basic pseudocode executables.
- You can add a project to an existing project, forming a project group. This is particularly useful when creating ActiveX controls, because you can create a project to test the control without having to first compile it. (See Part VI for more information.)
- Wizards make many tasks easier. There's even a "Wizard Wizard" to help you create your own Wizards. (See Chapters 8 and 30 for more information.) It's easier than ever to customize instances of the Visual Basic IDE (VBIDE), using add-ins and Wizards. You can use these extensions to Visual Basic to increase your own productivity, or can distribute them as tools to others.
- The Code Editor features comment blocking, automatic syntax completion, and Auto Quick Info, which dynamically displays a syntax chart of the possible correct conclusions to code lines as you enter them. The Complete Word option — which you can access at any time by right-clicking in the Code window — offers a dynamically updated pop-up list of everything known to the environment that can logically be entered at the point it is invoked.
- You can now run the Visual Basic compiler from the command line, which is useful for automating unattended project builds.
- Last, and certainly not least, you can now use the VB environment to create additional kinds of projects — including ActiveX control projects and ActiveX document (Internet form) projects.

These enhancements, and more, are discussed in this chapter and, in more detail, later in *Visual Basic 5 SECRETS*. New Code Editor features are covered in Chapter 3, "Event-Driven Programming," and Chapter 4, "The Visual Basic Language," as well as Part III, "Coding Secrets." True native code compilation — and its advantages and disadvantages compared with p-code compilation —

are discussed in Chapter 5, "What's New in Visual Basic 5," and Chapter 16, "Optimizing Secrets." You'll find material on creating your own ActiveX controls in Part VI, "Creating ActiveX Controls," and on ActiveX documents in Chapter 28, "Creating Internet Applications in VB."

Starting a New Project or Opening an Existing One

Remember, when you start Visual Basic, a dialog that allows you to open a new or existing project appears by default. If you have turned off the environment option that displays this dialog at startup, or already have VB open, it's still easy to start a new project in VB. Just choose New Project from the File menu. To open an existing project, choose Open Project from the File menu (or press Ctrl+O), use the common dialog box that appears to move to the directory where the project lives, choose it, and then click the Open button.

For your convenience, the Open Project dialog now provides a Recent tab, from which you can open any project that you recently worked on, as shown in Figure 2-3.

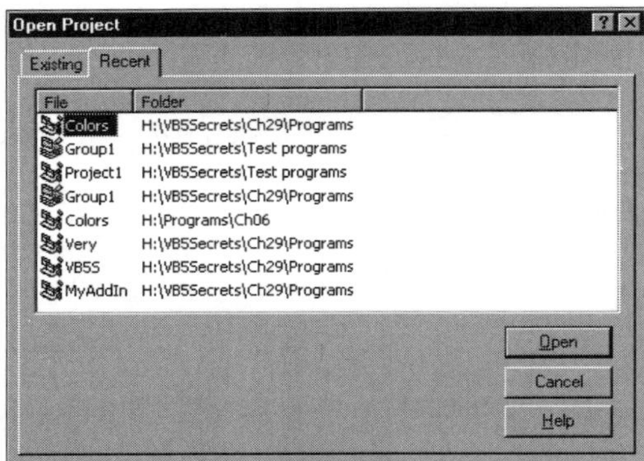

Figure 2-3: You can use the Recent tab of the Open Project dialog to open any project that you've worked on recently.

Saving Your Projects

When you save a Visual Basic project, or project group, the VB environment moves you through a series of Save common dialogs (depending upon the types of modules your project contains). To save a project and its associated files, choose Save Project (or Save Project As) from the File menu or click the Save toolbar button. If you're saving a project group — which is defined simply as more than one project open in the workspace — the items on the File menu will change to Save Project Group and Save Project Group As.

The dialog boxes move you through the contents of your entire project or project group, first letting you save form (***.Frm***) files, then module (***.Bas***) files, class modules (***.Cls***), ActiveX documents (***.Dob***), user controls (***.Ctl***), Property Pages (***.Pag***), and finally the project file(s) (***.Vbp***) themselves and the project group (***.Vbg***), if applicable. Each kind of file can have the same name — with a different extension — if you'd like.

Many of the kinds of modules — and their associated filename extensions — are new to VB5. The project group, and ActiveX document, user control, and property page modules are particularly significant enhancements. Table 2-1 lists all the types of files (with their extensions) that can be part of a Visual Basic project or project group.

Table 2-1 File Types That Constitute a VB Project

Extension	*Purpose*
.Bas	Code source module
.Cls	Class source module
.Ctl	User control file
.Ctx	User control binary file
.Dca	Active designer cache
.Dep	Setup Wizard dependency file
.Dob	User document form file
.Dox	User document binary form file
.Dsr	Active designer file
.Dsx	Active designer binary file
.Frm	Form file
.Frx	Binary form file
.Log	Log file for load errors
.Oca	Control Typelib cache
.Pag	Property page file
.Pgx	Binary property page file
.Res	Resource file
.Swt	Visual Basic setup Wizard template file
.Tlb	Remote automation Typelib files
.Vbg	Visual Basic group project
.Vbl	User control licensing file
.Vbp	Visual Basic project
.Vbr	Remote automation registration files
.Vbw	Visual Basic project workspace
.Vbz	Wizard launch file

You may be interested to know that Visual Basic project groups (*.Vbg* files) cannot be nested. In other words, your project group can contain numerous projects, each containing numerous modules, but cannot contain another project group.

Setting Environment, Editor, and General Options

You can customize the Visual Basic IDE in many ways. To do so, start by choosing Options from the Tools menu. A multitabbed dialog box appears, as shown in Figure 2-4. Using the tab pages in this dialog box you can set options as described under each tab.

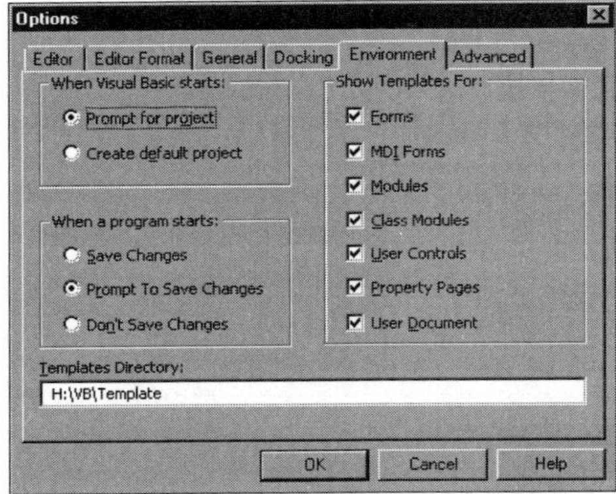

Figure 2-4: Here's the Options dialog box with the Environment tab on top.

Environment Tab

You use the Environment tab to specify the attributes of your Visual Basic development environment. Changes you make here are saved to your Registry file. They are loaded every time you start Visual Basic.

If Prompt for Project is selected, you are given a choice about the kind of project you want to open each time you start Visual Basic (see "Starting a New Project or Opening an Existing One" earlier in this chapter).

If Create Default Project is selected, a default executable (standard EXE) project is opened each time you start Visual Basic.

If Save Changes is selected under When a Program Starts, running a project automatically saves any changes made to it since the last save. If you are running a new file that has not been saved, the Save As common dialog box appears so you can give a name and location to your project. If Prompt To Save Changes is selected, running a project displays a dialog asking if you want to save unsaved material. If you select Yes, you can save the project and its files. If you select No, Visual Basic runs the project using the memory image, but does not save any changes. If Don't Save Changes is selected, when you run your project, Visual Basic runs the memory image of the project and does not save the changes.

Prompt To Save Changes is the best setting for this option. The danger of running unsaved projects is that you may lose some of your work. This setting reminds you to save your work before running your projects, without requiring you to do so in situations where its a nuisance.

The Show Templates For box lets you determine whether you want templates for modules to be available when you add modules to a project. Here's how this works, using a form module as an example. To add a form module, choose Add Form from the Project menu. If Forms has been checked in the Show Templates For box, all ***.Frm*** files in the ***\Template\Forms*** directory will be displayed as possible templates for a new form, as shown in Figure 2-5.

Obviously, being able to use the templates that VB provides is a major convenience. You can take this one step further and add customized templates — for example, all class modules might include boilerplate code for properties you like to use, and all form modules might be based on particular color choices.

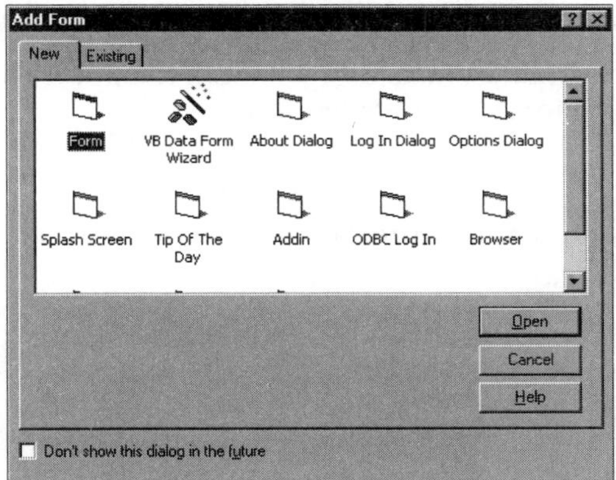

Figure 2-5: You can use the templates feature to add new modules that include many features "out of the box."

By the way, you can also use the Environment tab of the Options dialog to change the location of the default template structure. (The default template directory is installed beneath the directory in which VB was installed.)

Table 2-2 shows the kinds of modules that can be based on templates and the default location of the related templates.

Table 2-2 Modules and Related Template Locations

Module Type	***Default Template Location***
Forms	***Template\Forms***
MDI Forms	***Template\MDIForms***
Modules (***.Bas*** files)	***Template\Modules***
Class Modules	***Template\Classes***
User Controls	***Template\UserCtls***
Property Pages	***Template\Proppage***
User Documents	***Template\UserDocs***

It's possible that not all of these Template subdirectories were created when you installed VB5 — in which case you'll have to create them if you want to add custom module templates.

In addition to modules, you can place Wizards (***.Vbz*** files) in a template directory. The Wizards will display in the Add dialog. If the user selects one, it will start running and help the user create a specific kind of module. (For example, the VB Data Form Wizard shown in Figure 2-5 guides users through the process of creating a data form.)

In the same way, you can add projects that you wish to appear as templates in the New Project dialog to the ***Template\Projects*** directory.

Editor Tab

You use the Editor tab, shown in Figure 2-6, to configure the behavior of the Code Editor.

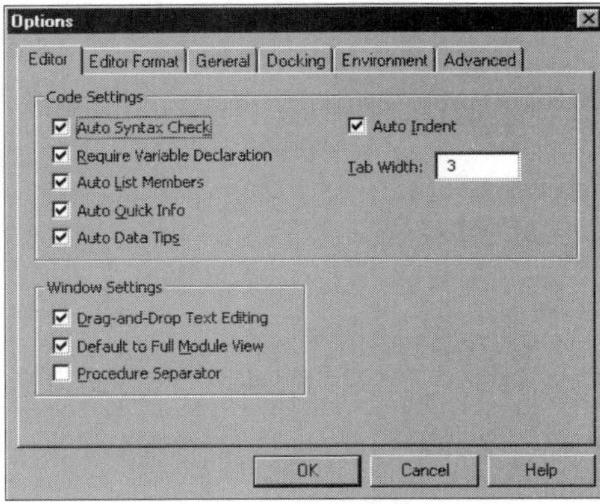

Figure 2-6: You can use the Editor tab to modify the behavior of the Code Editor.

The Code Settings box allows you to control important aspects of the functionality of your Code Editor:

- Auto Syntax Check enables automatic syntax checking after you complete each line of code.
- Require Variable Declaration adds the Option Explicit statement to the beginning of each module. This requires that all variables you use be explicitly declared. It is good coding practice to enable this option, and require variable declaration.
- When Auto List Members, Auto Quick Info, and Auto Data Tips are enabled, you'll interactively receive real-time syntax information as you enter code.

In addition, you can use the Editor tab to enable drag-and-drop code editing; set the number of spaces used by a tab; set auto indentation; set code viewing to full module view as opposed to procedure-by-procedure viewing; and, if you are using full module view, add or remove procedure separators.

Editor Format Tab

You use the Editor Format tab, shown in Figure 2-7, to configure the appearance of the Code Editor. This is where you set the Code window's font and font size and specify code colors for different sorts of text — for example, Syntax Error Text, Keyword Text, and so on.

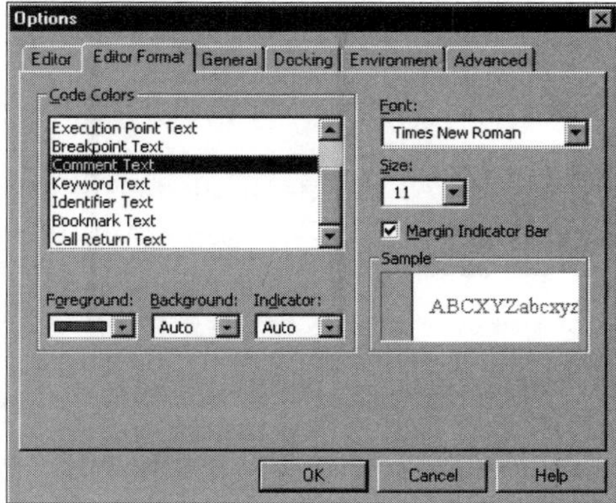

Figure 2-7: You can use the Editor Format tab to determine how code is displayed.

General Tab

You use the General tab, shown in Figure 2-8, to specify grid settings, error handling settings, and compile settings for your current Visual Basic project.

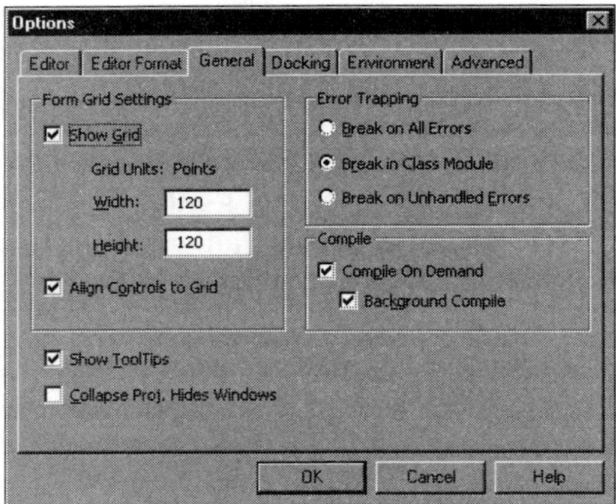

Figure 2-8: You can use the General tab to specify grid behavior and compile settings for the current VB project.

If Show ToolTips is selected, balloon help is displayed for toolbar and Toolbox items. If Collapse Proj. Hides Windows is selected, module windows are hidden when a project is collapsed in the Project Explorer.

Error Trapping settings control how errors are handled in the Visual Basic development environment. These settings are not saved for each project so setting this option affects all instances of Visual Basic started after you change the setting. You can choose between three possible error trapping settings:

- If Break on All Errors is selected, any error causes the project to enter break mode.
- If Break in Class Module is selected, any unhandled error produced in a class module causes the project to enter break mode at the line of code in the class module that produced the error.
- If Break on Unhandled Errors is selected and an error handler is active, the error is trapped without entering break mode. If there is no active error handler, the error causes the project to enter break mode.

For more information on error handling, see Chapter 15, “Handling Errors.”

If you are debugging an ActiveX server project by running an ActiveX client test program in another project, set error trapping in the server project to Break in Class Module. This will help you accurately pinpoint the problem.

The Compile On Demand and Background Compile options speed up compilation time.

Docking Tab

You can use the Docking tab, shown in Figure 2-9, to determine which Visual Basic interface elements can be "docked" — that is, attached to a specific location rather than floating.

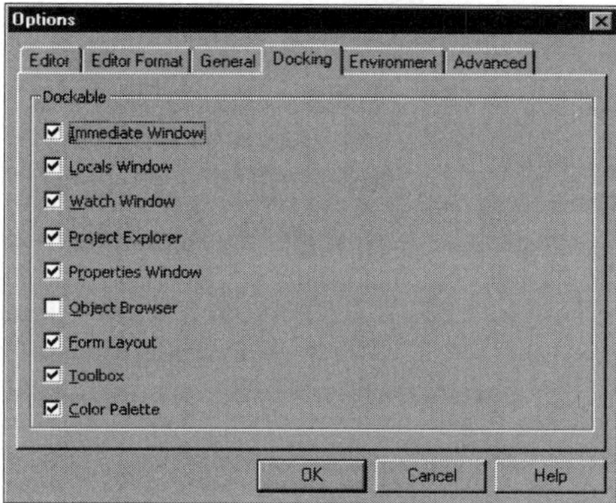

Figure 2-9: The Docking tab lets you set which Visual Basic interface elements can be docked.

Advanced Tab

The Advanced tab, shown in Figure 2-10, lets you enable background project load and notification when shared project modules are modified. It also allows you to toggle Visual Basic's IDE between multiple document interface (MDI) and single document interface (SDI).

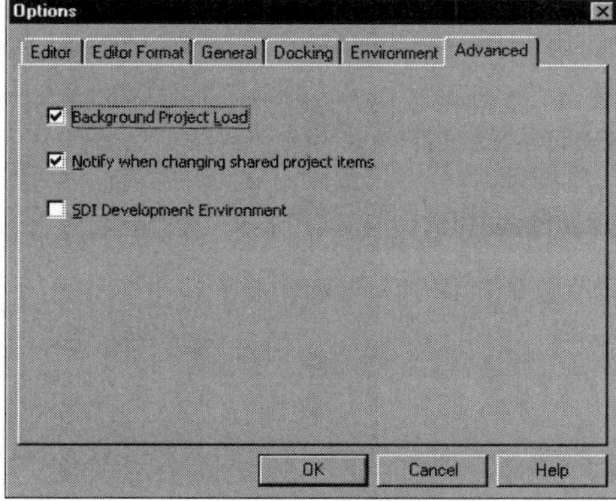

Figure 2-10: You can use the Advanced tab to set background project load, notification when shared project items are changed, and SDI or MDI development environment.

Loading code in the background increases the speed with which VB loads.

Visual Basic project files store references to the location of modules that are included in the project, rather than the modules themselves. Two or more projects can include references to the same module. If you're not careful, changing the module in one project will inadvertently change other projects as well. If you select Notify When Changing Shared Project Items, you will be alerted when you change a shared project item such as a form or module and try to save it.

Several projects can share the same items. Shared items are loaded into memory and each project has its own copy. If you change a shared item in one project, the other projects retain the copy of the item that was loaded until you save the projects. Then, the last project you save determines what the shared file is. When the Notify When Changing Shared Project Items option is selected, you are asked if you want to synchronize all copies of the item before you save.

Earlier versions of Visual Basic used a single document interface, meaning that you could only open one project at a time. By default, VB5 uses a multiple document interface. If you wish, you can toggle VB between SDI and MDI by using the SDI Development Environment check box on this tab.

In previous versions of VB, you set some compilation options related to a specific project — for example, command-line arguments — using the Options dialog. This was possible because you could only load one project at a time. You now make this kind of setting in the Project Properties dialog, which you access via the Project menu. For more information, see the section "Compiling Executables" later in this chapter.

Adding Different Modules to a Project

A Visual Basic module is an object that corresponds to a file that can be included in a project. The raw source code for a VB project primarily consists of module files. In VB5, there are six generic kinds of modules:

- Form (*.Frm*) files
- Class (*.Cls*) files
- Standard code module (*.Bas*) files
- User control (*.Ctl*) files
- Property page (*.Pag*) files
- User document (*.Dob*) files

Module files are ASCII text files that include code that is encapsulated within the module. If the module includes controls, descriptions of the controls are included in the file. Some kinds of modules are also linked to binary files that contain data about the appearance of the module — for example, *.Frm* files can be linked to ***.Frx*** files that have the same name other than the file extension. The ***.Frx*** file contains binary information about the appearance of the form, while the ***.Frm*** file contains module code, referenced to controls used on the form, and information about property settings of controls used and the form itself. You'll find more information on the internal structure of ***.Frm*** files in Chapter 19, "Runtime Display Secrets," in the section "The Secret Life of Forms."

There are a few ways to add different modules to a VB project:

- You can use the drop-down list under the Add Form button on the toolbar, as shown in Figure 2-11.
- You can add new modules using the Project menu.
- You can choose Add from the context menu in the Project Explorer.

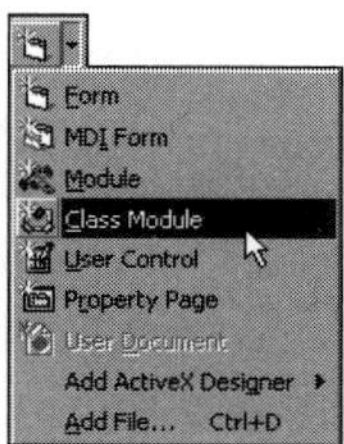

Figure 2-11: You can use the drop-down list under the Add Form toolbar button to add new modules to a project.

When you add a module to a project, that module is automatically added to the list of files hierarchically associated with the project in the Project Explorer.

The Edit Menu

In Visual Basic 5, the Edit menu has been revised to make life easier for us developers, as shown in Figure 2-12. The top half of the menu hasn't changed; however, there are some very significant additions to the bottom half of the menu.

Table 2-3 lists most of the items on the Edit menu and describes their purpose. (In addition to the items in the table, the menu includes the standard text editing tools such as Cut, Copy, and Paste.)

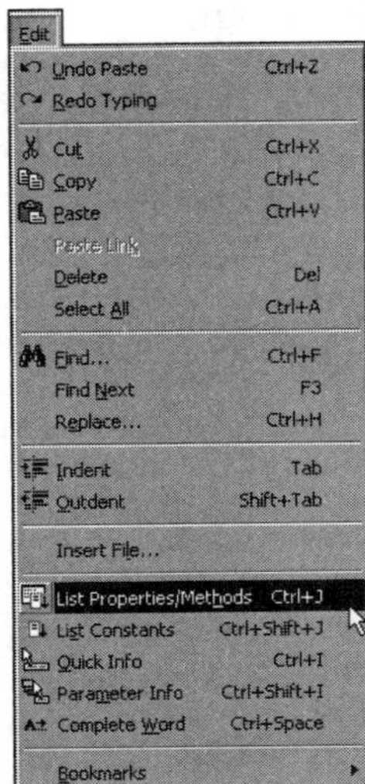

Figure 2-12: The Edit menu now contains a number of options that can make your life easier.

Table 2-3 The Edit Menu

Edit Menu Item	*Purpose*
Undo	Reverses the last editing action. Twenty levels of undo and redo are available.
Redo	Restores the last text editing if no other actions have occurred since the last Undo.
Find	Searches for the specified text in a search range specified in the Find dialog box.
Find Next	Finds and selects the next occurrence of the text specified in the Find What box of the Find dialog box.
Replace	Searches code in the project for the specified text and replaces it with the new text specified in the Replace dialog box.
Indent	Shifts all lines in the selection to the next tab stop.
Outdent	Shifts all lines in the selection to the previous tab stop.
Insert File	Opens the Insert File dialog box so that you can insert text from an existing file at the current position in the Code window.

(continued)

Table 2-3 (Continued)

Edit Menu Item	***Purpose***
List Properties/Methods	Opens a drop-down list box in the Code window that contains the properties and methods available for an object as it is entered in the Code window preceding the dot operator (.). Activated by the Auto List Members option in the Editor tab of the Options dialog.
List Constants	Opens a drop-down list box in the Code window that contains the valid constants for a property that is entered in the Code window preceding the equal sign (=). Activated by the Auto List Members option in the Editor tab of the Options dialog.
Quick Info	Provides the syntax for a variable, function, statement, method, or procedure selected in the Code window. Activated by the Auto Quick Info option in the Editor tab of the Options dialog.
Parameter Info	Displays information about the parameters of the first function or statement entered.
Complete Word	Completes the word you are typing once you have entered enough characters for Visual Basic to identify the word you want.
Bookmarks	Displays a menu that you can use to create or remove bookmarks in the Code window, move to the next or preceding bookmark, or clear all bookmarks. When you toggle a bookmark on, its position is represented on the left margin of the Code window by a blue oval.

The Toolbox

You use the Toolbox to add controls to containers such as forms while in design mode. Figure 2-13 shows the Toolbox with the "out-of-the-box" Enterprise Edition tool set.

The Toolbox includes standard controls that are always there. These standard controls — sometimes called the *intrinsic controls* — are the pointer tool, text box control, command button, option button, image control, and so on. The pointer does not really represent a control; it is used in the design environment to select objects.

Custom controls are those that exist in separate files with a ***.Ocx*** file extension and can be added to the Toolbox as needed.

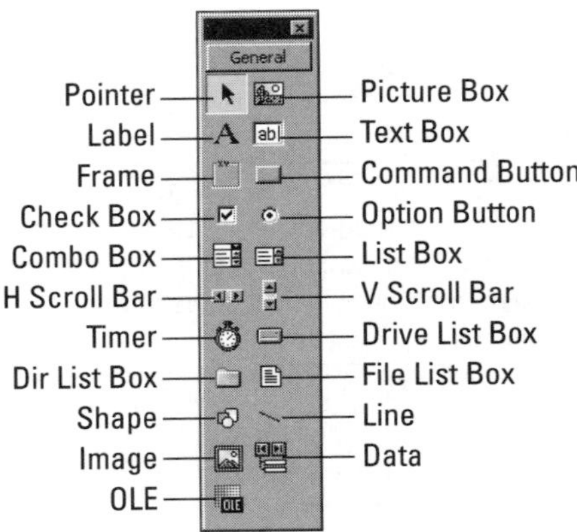

Figure 2-13: You can use the Visual Basic Toolbox to add controls (such as user controls) to forms and other containers.

You can add tabs to the Toolbox, and use these tabs to organize the controls that the Toolbox contains. Figure 2-14 shows the process of adding a tab to the Toolbox. To access the New Tab Name dialog, right-click an existing tab, and choose Add from the context menu.

To move between Toolbox tabs, simply click the button representing the tab.

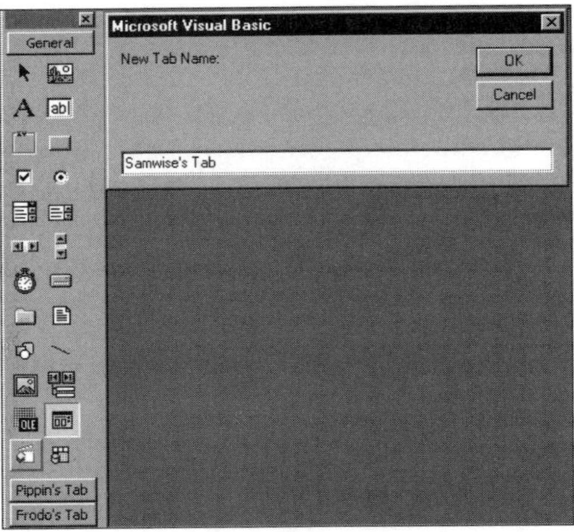

Figure 2-14: You can easily organize your ActiveX controls by adding custom tabs to the Toolbox.

Adding Controls to Forms

There are two ways you can add a control to a form (or other container). First select the form to which you want to add the control. Now, do one of two things:

- Double-click the desired control. A default-sized control appears in the center of the form. Move the control where you want it and resize it, if necessary.
- Choose the tool you want to use by clicking it once, point to the appropriate location over the form (your mouse pointer will turn into a crosshair), and then drag to create a control of the desired size.

If you need to add controls to an object that itself has been positioned on a form — such as a frame, which groups controls within itself — simply select the frame (rather than the form), and then add the control using either of the methods just described. When you move the frame around on the form, notice that the controls contained within that frame move with it.

To quickly create an array of controls — for instance, an array of option (radio) buttons — drop the first option button on the form where you want it to reside. Set its properties (setting properties is discussed later in the chapter under "The Properties Window"). Next, select it, copy it using the Edit menu, and then choose Paste from the Edit menu. A dialog asks if you want to create an array. Choose Yes and VB automatically names it using an array index. Continue to paste in as many option buttons as you need. (An alternative is to use the Name properties of the option buttons to create an array.)

Adding Components to the Toolbox

To add a component to the Toolbox, choose Components from the Project menu or press Ctrl+T. You will see the Components dialog shown in Figure 2-15.

To add a custom control, find it on the list and check the box by clicking it. (If you have installed a custom control and it is not on the list, use the Browse button to find it.) The control's name and path appear at the bottom of the dialog. Then click OK. The dialog disappears, the new control is added to the Toolbox, and the Toolbox automatically resizes itself to accommodate the new control.

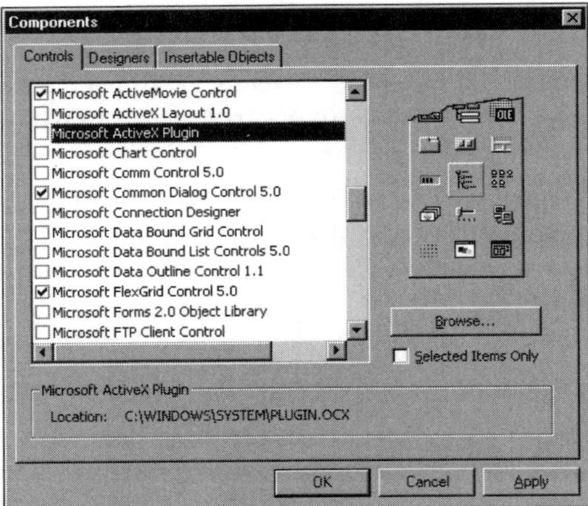

Figure 2-15: You can use the Components dialog to add custom controls to the Toolbox.

Insertable Objects

You might have noticed the Insertable Objects page tab in the Components dialog shown in Figure 2-15. *Insertable object* means any exposed OLE object — for example, an Excel spreadsheet or a Word document. Once you have added the object to the list in the dialog, you can add it to your Toolbox, and then add it to any VB form in the normal fashion.

This is an extraordinarily convenient way to add the power of other applications to your VB projects; I'll be discussing it in detail in Part V of this book.

Designers

You'll notice that a third tab of the Components dialog allows you to add designers. ActiveX designers are a way to extend the Visual Basic environment in a custom fashion. A number of designers are built in to the VB environment — for example, the Form designer and the User Control designer. These built-in designers provide visual interfaces for tasks that would otherwise require a great deal of code.

ActiveX designers produce classes from which you can create objects. These classes appear in the Project window, just like form classes. An ActiveX designer's design window is fully integrated into the development environment. You can size and arrange it just like built-in design windows such as the Form designer.

The Professional and Enterprise editions of Visual Basic include the ActiveX Designer Software Development Kit (SDK), which you can use to create new ActiveX Designers for use with Visual Basic. The ActiveX Designer SDK requires a C++ compiler, such as Microsoft Visual C++. You cannot write ActiveX designers using Visual Basic. For more information, see Part VII, "Extending the VB Environment."

You won't find Designers in the Toolbox. Once you have added a designer using the Components dialog, you access it via the ActiveX designers item on the Project menu.

The Properties Window

You use the Properties window, shown in Figure 2-16, to view and change the properties of a selected object, such as a control or module.

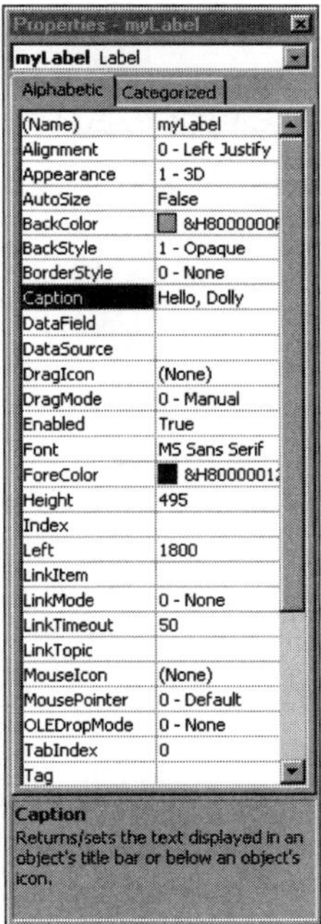

Figure 2-16: You can use the Properties window to set properties at design time. (Here are the properties for a Label control.)

There are several parts to this window. At the top is the Object Box, which displays the control's name and type. (In this case, the name of the control is myLabel and the type of the control is, of course, a label.) Clicking the down arrow to the right of the box enables you to select any object that is available on the selected form. The long list of items on the left-hand side of the figure contains the label's properties. (The length of the list depends on how many properties the object has — some are quite short.) The column on the right shows the properties' present settings.

Changing Control Properties

To change a property's setting, select the property and then click the corresponding box (the "settings box") in the right-hand column of the Properties window. If the property takes a string or integer value, a blinking cursor appears in that settings box. If the property can hold a set list of values, a button displaying either a drop-down arrow or an ellipsis (...) appears to the right of the settings box. Also, custom dialogs are often attached to property settings (also indicated by ellipses). Most often, custom dialogs are accessed from the Custom property. To access these settings and select what you want, click the button containing the down arrow or ellipses.

Categorizing Properties

As you can see in Figure 2-17, you can choose to view an object's properties sorted by categories. To make this so, select the Categorized (rather then the Alphabetic) tab in the Properties window.

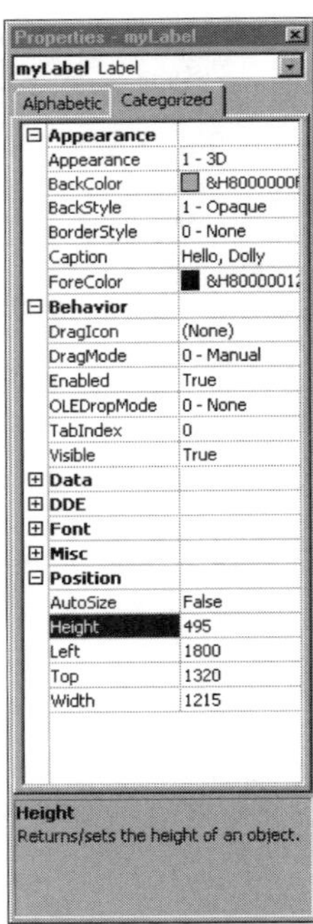

Figure 2-17: You can choose to view properties sorted by category.

You can contract or expand each major category to show the properties in the category. This is indicated by the plus (for there's more here) and minus (meaning, contract so you don't have to see these) icons on the left-hand side of the Properties window (see Figure 2-17).

The Project Explorer

A Visual Basic group file (*.Vbg*) is simply an ASCII file containing a list of all the Visual Basic projects associated with the group. Similarly, a Visual Basic project file (*.Vbp*) is simply a file that contains a list of all the files associated with a project.

The Project Explorer is a window that provides a hierarchical view of groups, projects, and the source modules associated with the projects, as shown in Figure 2-18. The Project Explorer provides you with an easy way to navigate between the parts of projects and project groups.

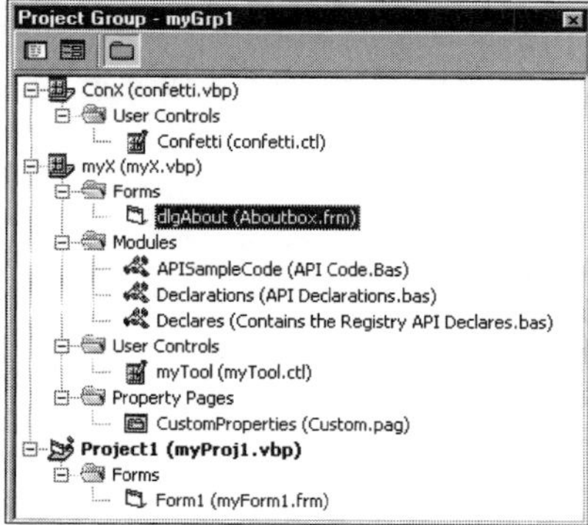

Figure 2-18: You can use the Project Explorer to navigate between different modules in a project and different projects in a group.

When you launch Visual Basic using a group file or project file (or open an existing group or project from VB), source files that are associated with the group or project are displayed in the Project Explorer window. When you add or remove files — for example, forms, modules, and so on — from a project, these changes are reflected in the Project Explorer.

Two "names" appear in the Project Explorer for each form or module. The name on the left is the property name that was given to the form when the programmer created it — for example, dlgAbout. The name on the right (in parenthesis) is the source file name with which the module was saved — for example, Aboutbox.frm.

You can use the buttons on the toolbar at the top of the Project Explorer (see Figure 2-18) to view code for any source module, view a module such as a form in a Designer, and contract (or expand) the Explorer tree.

In addition, you can use an extensive context menu, which changes dynamically depending on what is selected, to quickly manipulate the selected object.

The Form Layout

You use the Form Layout window to position forms on the screen. As shown in Figure 2-19, when you pass your mouse pointer over a form in the Form Layout window, it turns into a drag icon. You can then position the form by dragging.

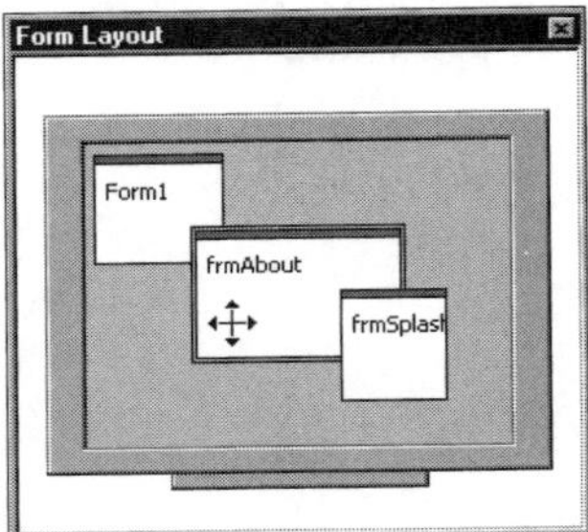

Figure 2-19: You use the Form Layout window to position forms on the screen.

In the Visual Basic 5 IDE, forms are locked to the upper-left corner of the Designer workspace. Although you can resize them in the Designer (by dragging the bottom or right borders of the form), you cannot move them in relation to the screen without using the Form Layout window.

Normally, the runtime position of forms on the screen is changed by the actions of the user — for example, when the user resizes a window — and in code as the program executes. Therefore, the primary impact of changes made in the Form Layout window is on the initial positions of forms.

The Format Menu

You use the items on the Format menu to manipulate the appearance of forms and other containers such as controls and property pages.

Table 2-4 shows how you can use the items on this menu to change the appearance of the active form. (Some of these menu items bring up dialogs, which you use to select options before applying the formatting.)

Table 2-4 Format Menu Items

Item	*Purpose*
Align	Aligns selected objects with each other.
Make Same Size	Makes the selected objects the same size — in the dimension(s) you choose — as the most recently selected object.
Size to Grid	Adjusts the height and width of the selected object to fit the nearest grid lines in your form.
Horizontal Spacing	Changes the horizontal space between selected objects.
Vertical Spacing	Changes the vertical space between selected objects.
Center in Form	Centers selected objects either vertically or horizontally on the form.
Order	Changes the design time back-to-front order of selected objects on a form. (To manipulate this setting at runtime, use the ZOrder property of objects you wish to affect in code.)
Lock Controls	Locks all controls on the form in their current positions so that you don't move them by mistake.

Making Effective Use of the Code Window

The Code window is, of course, where you enter Visual Basic code. (See Chapter 3 for information on how code interacts with objects and Chapter 4 for the details of programming in VB). Figure 2-20 shows a Code window for a form with a command button named cmdOK placed on the form.

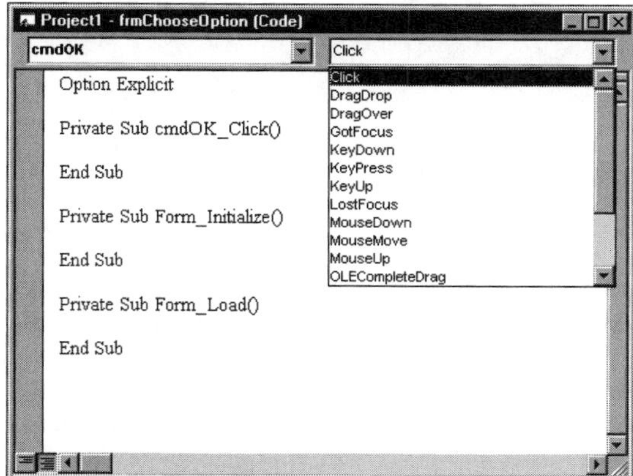

Figure 2-20: This VB Code window shows the Procedure list dropped-down.

You can quickly move to any procedure for any available control on a form by choosing the control from the Object drop-down list box and then selecting the procedure you want from the Proc drop-down list box, shown on the upper-right side of Figure 2-20. Navigating through procedures works the same way in a module's Code window.

Artificial Intelligence

No, Visual Basic 5 doesn't really come with an artificial intelligence engine — although the tools that are always available in the Code window with a click of the right mouse button may seem pretty darn smart to you. As you can see in Figure 2-21, there is an extensive arsenal of available coding aids.

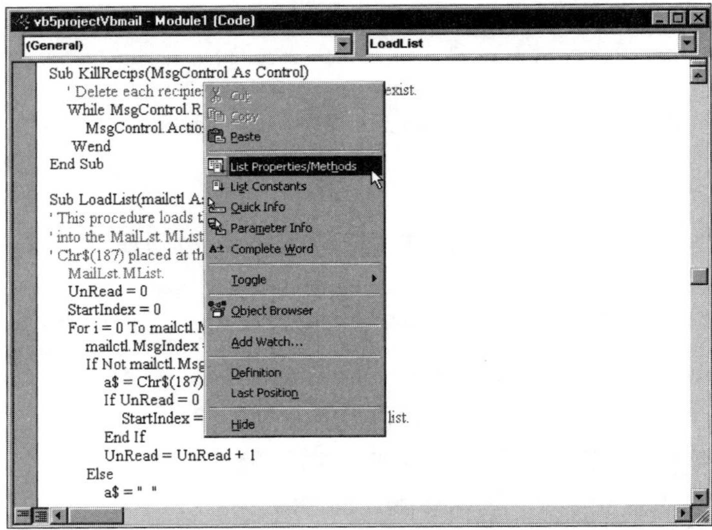

Figure 2-21: You can access some pretty intelligent programming aids just by right-clicking.

What this boils down to, if you get in the habit of using these tools, is never having to remember syntax or look it up in a manual again. I suppose that some curmudgeonly types may not appreciate this, and may even take to going around muttering under their breath, "I remember when...." For my part, I'm not going back to a typewriter, and any help that a development environment can provide, if it saves me time, is always welcome.

Programming aids available include List Properties/Methods, List Constants, Quick Info, Parameter Info, Complete Word.

List Properties/Methods displays a drop-down list of all properties and methods available for the object at the insertion point, as shown in Figure 2-22.

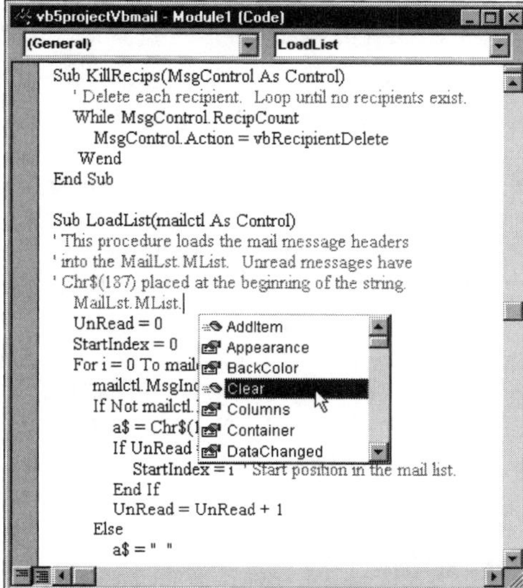

Figure 2-22: You can use List Properties/ Methods to quickly find the valid properties and methods for an object.

Lists Constants displays a drop-down list of all valid constants for a property you have entered in the Code window.

Quick Info provides the syntax for a selected variable, function, statement, method, or procedure.

Parameter Info displays a pop-up window that contains information about the parameters of a function or statement.

Complete Word fills in the rest of the word you are typing once you have entered enough characters for Visual Basic to identify the word you want. Most of the time, it gets this right. I fully expect that if they take this one step further, I can leave the computer on, get a good night's sleep, and come back to find my programming work done without me!

The Object Browser

You use the Object Browser to display the classes, properties, methods, events, and constants available in object libraries and the procedures in your project. You can use it to find and use objects you create, as well as objects from other applications.

To open the Object Browser, either press F2 or choose Object Browser from the View menu. You can use the top drop-down list box to display a particular library, as shown in Figure 2-23.

Shortcut Keys and the Code Window

Many shortcut keys can make life easier when you're using the Code window. For instance, you can move either up or down one procedure at a time by pressing Ctrl in combination with either the up- or down-arrow key, respectively.

Another shortcut that is a lifesaver in a large project is Shift+F2. If some code in the Code window makes a call to a routine and you don't know what module in the project it's located in, you can place your cursor within the name of the routine and press Shift+F2. This shortcut automatically opens a Code window displaying that routine.

For an extensive list of keyboard shortcuts that you can use in a Code window, look in Visual Basic's on-line help under the topic "Code Window — Keyboard Shortcuts."

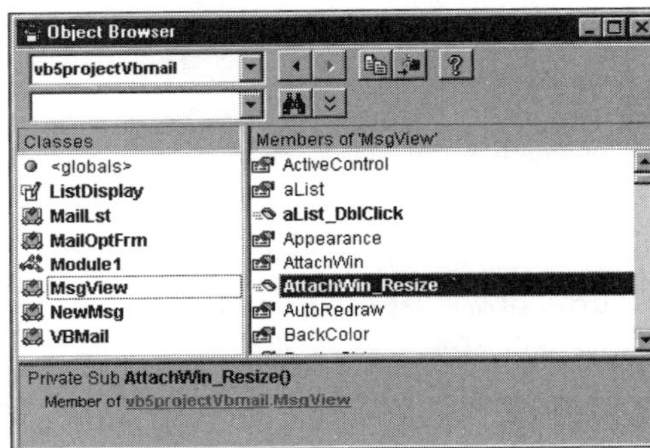

Figure 2-23: You can use the Object Browser to view classes and their members.

You use the drop-down list box below the object library list to enter text to find (you can also select it from a list).

The Classes pane — on the left in Figure 2-23 — displays all of the available classes in the selected library. If there is code written for a class, that class appears in bold. The list always begins with <globals>, a list of globally accessible members.

The Members pane — on the right in Figure 2-23 — displays the elements of the class selected in the Classes pane by group and then alphabetically within each group. Methods, properties, events, or constants that have code written for them appear in bold.

The Details pane — at the bottom in Figure 2-23 — shows the definition for a selected member.

The Menu Editor

You can easily add menus to any of your project forms by using the Visual Basic Menu Editor. To do so, select the form that you want to add the menu to, and then either press Ctrl+E or choose Menu Editor from the Tools menu. The Menu Editor window appears, as shown in Figure 2-24.

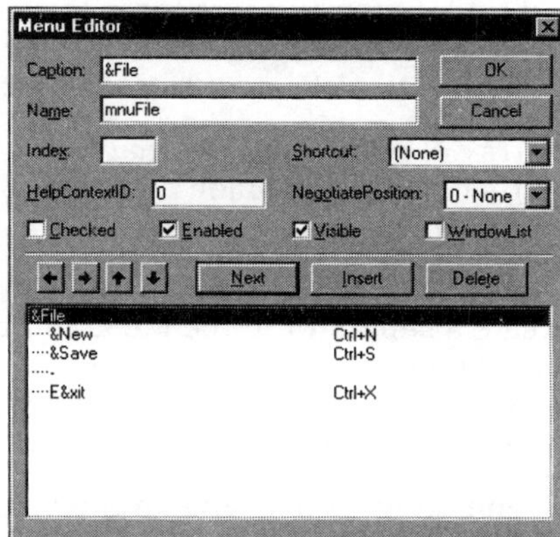

Figure 2-24: You can use the Menu Editor to add menus to forms.

As you can see in the figure, I've added a few entries to the Menu Editor: a File menu title, and three menu items under that title, New, Save, and Exit. Figure 2-25 shows the form with this mini-menu displayed.

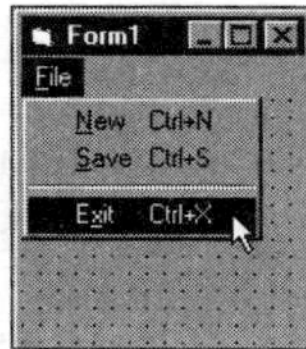

Figure 2-25: Here is a menu created using the Menu Editor.

As you can see in Figure 2-24, the entries for the menu title, File, are straightforward. First, I typed the name of the title in the Caption text box. Notice that I added an ampersand (&) before the F. This creates an access key, meaning that the program's user can access this menu using the keyboard shortcut Alt+F. Next, I gave the menu title a name, mnuFile, just as I would name any Visual Basic control. Then, I clicked the Next button to enter that menu title and move on to the first menu item.

The menu items shown in Figure 2-24 — New, Save, and Exit — are all preceded by dotted lines, indicating that they are subitems of the menu title. To make an item a subitem of the previous entry in the Menu Editor, select the item in the list box at the bottom of the window and press the right-pointing arrow button. Visual Basic allows four submenu levels. To move a menu item up one level, press the left-pointing arrow button.

Using the appropriate check boxes in the Menu Editor, you can make a menu item appear checked, enable or disable any menu item, or make it invisible or visible. You can also assign a shortcut key to each menu item — for example, Figure 2-24 shows the New menu item with a shortcut key of Ctrl+N.

You could also set up a control array of menu items — that is, an array of menu items with the same name that share a common click event — using the Index text box, as well as set a help ID number for each menu item.

The menu shown in Figure 2-25 also includes a separator bar between the Save and Exit menu items. To create a separator in the Menu Editor, enter a hyphen (-) in the Caption text box, and then give it any name you wish. Although it really doesn't matter what you name these separators, I usually name them something descriptive like mnuSep1, mnuSep2, and so on.

Detailed documentation of the Menu Editor is available in the Visual Basic *Programmer's Guide* and Chapter 18 of *Visual Basic 5 SECRETS*, "Managing MDI Applications and Menus."

Debugging Tools

When debugging an application, you are, of course, looking for the source of errors. Visual Basic offers several tools that can make this often tedious process easier. (Needless to say, it is better to create programs that don't contain bugs in the first place. If you cannot achieve this — impossible — goal, your programs should at least gracefully trap any errors and tell you what they are!)

First, VB can operate in three modes: design mode, run mode, and break mode. These modes are just what you would expect. Design mode is for doing most of the work of creating an application. Run mode is for running the application in the VB debug environment so that you can interact with your program the way a user would (possibly with some differences since the compiled version of the application is not being run). Break mode occurs when the execution of a running program is suspended. You can access any of these three modes by using the Run menu or the appropriate toolbar button.

You access VB's debugging tools through the Debug menu. Table 2-5 lists the options available on this menu. Only breakpoints and watches can be set at design time. The rest of the debugging tools run in break mode.

Table 2-5 Debugging Tools

Debugging Tool	*Description*
Step Into	Executes the next executable line of code and steps into routines.
Step Over	Executes the next executable line of code without stepping into routines.
Step Out	Executes the remaining lines of a function in which the current execution point lies.
Run to Cursor	With the application's execution halted, lets you place the cursor further down the code where you want to stop execution.
Add Watch	Set at design time, lets you watch expression values.
Edit Watch	Displays the Edit Watch dialog in which you can edit or delete a watch expression.
Quick Watch	Lists an expression's current value.
Toggle Breakpoints	Set at design time, lets you set a specific code line where execution will suspend. ("Toggle" refers to removing or adding a breakpoint.)
Clear All Breakpoints	Removes all the breakpoints in your project.
Set Next Statement	Lets you set the next code statement to be executed, even one that has already executed.
Show Next Statement	Lets you move the cursor to the next code line that will execute when program execution continues.

You can also select three error-trapping options — Break on All Errors, Break in Class Module, and Break on Unhandled Errors — on the General tab in the Options dialog box (choose Tools | Options). In addition, you can right-click over an open Code window to quickly gain access to these three options.

Debugging is discussed in detail in Chapter 15, "Handling Errors."

Compiling Executables

To compile an executable in Visual Basic, choose Make from the File menu. A dialog box like the one shown in Figure 2-26 appears. As you can see in the figure, you can save the executable under any name, and can place it in the default folder or in a folder of your choice by moving to that folder.

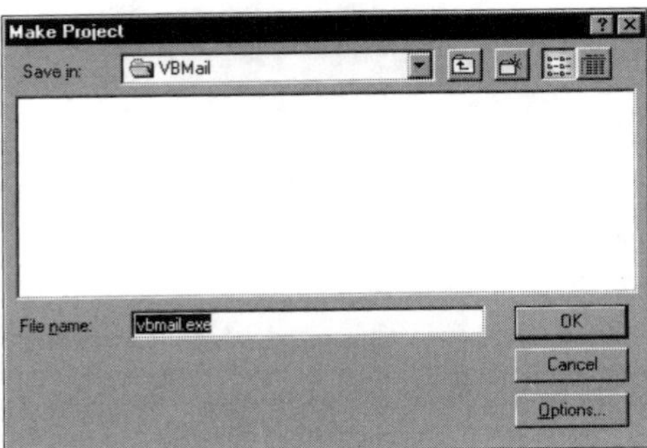

Figure 2-26: You can use the Make Project dialog to create an executable.

What's really interesting about the Make Project dialog is the Options button. Clicking this button displays the Project Properties dialog shown in Figure 2-27. Here you can specify version information about the executable, including major, minor, and revision numbers. If you check the Auto Increment box, VB automatically increments the revision number every time you create an executable for a project. You can enter other version information as well, including comments about the executable, the company that created it, the file description, the copyright, any trademarks, and the specific product name.

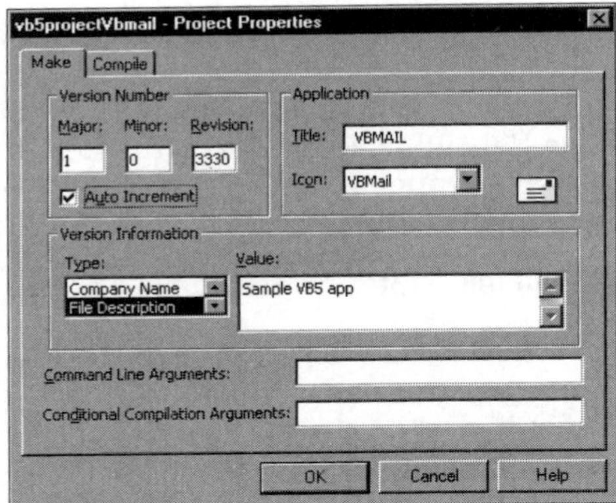

Figure 2-27: You can use the Project Properties dialog to set version information, command-line arguments, and conditional compilation arguments.

This embedded information — the version number, copyright, and so on — is what a user of your program will see when she right-clicks your compiled executable and selects the Version tab of the program's Properties Sheet.

You use the Compile tab of the Project Properties dialog, shown in Figure 2-28, to determine whether the executable is compiled to p-code or as a native stand-alone. (For more information on the consequences of this decision, see Chapter 16, "Optimizing Secrets.")

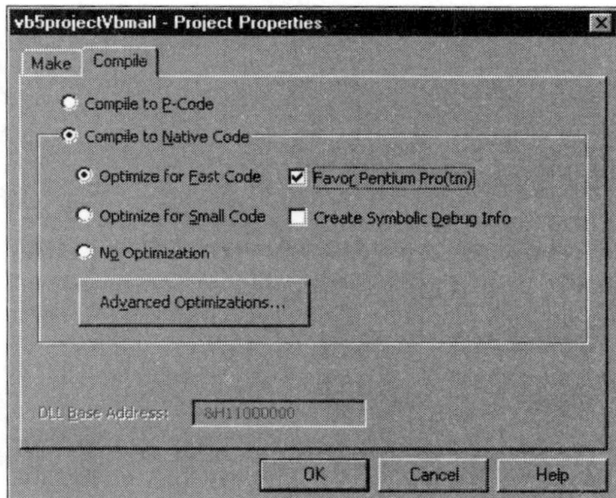

Figure 2-28: You can use the Compile tab of the Project Properties dialog to set compilation to p-code or to stand-alone.

Summary

This chapter presented an overview of the tools available in the Visual Basic IDE that will help you easily create polished VB applications. It emphasized features new to Version 5.

Topics covered included

- The IDE: the title bar, the menu bar, the toolbar, the Toolbox, the Project Explorer, the Properties window, the Form Layout window, and the Code window
- Opening existing VB projects and groups and starting new ones
- The different kinds of Visual Basic source files
- Using module and project templates
- Adding modules to an application

- Adding controls to forms using the Toolbox and adding custom controls and insertable objects to the Toolbox
- Using the Edit and Format menus
- Using the Project Explorer to navigate quickly through projects
- Taking advantage of the "artificial intelligence" built into the Code Editor
- Creating menus for your forms
- Setting Environment, Project, and Editor options
- Taking advantage of Visual Basic's debugging tools
- Creating compiled executable files

Chapter 3

Event-Driven Programming

This chapter discusses some important background information regarding Visual Basic 5. The topics covered include

- Working with Visual Basic source files
- Event-driven programming
- Properties and methods in Visual Basic
- Form event firing order
- Using the MsgBox function
- Adding code to form and control events
- Basic concepts of object-oriented programming (OOP)
- An effective technique for modularizing and encapsulating Visual Basic forms and dialogs
- Understanding class modules
- Creating, firing, and handling custom events
- Where to find further information in this book on the topics introduced in this chapter

Working with Visual Basic Source Files

Chapter 2, "Exploring the Visual Basic IDE," explained the numerous file types that can make up a Visual Basic project (Table 2-1 includes some 26 file types). Programmers working with Visual Basic source file don't really need to know more about many of these files types other than that they exist. However, you need to understand a bit more about the Visual Basic source files you work with.

The source code for a Visual Basic program that can be compiled "lives" in an arbitrary number of files of several different types. A small project could consist entirely of one Visual Basic form module (***.Frm*** file). If the project were slightly more complex, it might also include VB code modules (***.Bas*** files) and class modules (***.Cls*** files). These source code files are linked in one Visual Basic project (***.Vbp***) file, which also points to project-related resource (***.Frx*** and ***.Res***) files, controls (***.Ocx*** files), and required dynamic link libraries (DLLs).

VB5 features a new kind of overall file, the Visual Basic group (***.Vbg***) file. VB group files include references to VB project files in the same way that project files include references to modules that are part of the project. It's particularly useful to use groups of projects when testing controls.

The ability to create controls is new to version 5 of Visual Basic. Source code for a control is contained in a Control (***.Ctl***) module. Property pages that are part of the control require ***.Pag*** source files. Creating your own controls is covered in depth in Part VI, "Creating ActiveX Controls."

Each Visual Basic source project — a source project contains the code and symbolic information on which a final executable is based — must contain a ***.Vbp*** project file. (If you've been programming in Visual Basic for a while, you'll remember that in Versions 3 and earlier this file was called a ***.Mak*** rather than a ***.Vbp*** file.) A project file is created when you start a new project by choosing New Project from the File menu, and then save the project. Also, you open an existing Visual Basic source project by selecting its ***.Vbp*** file. I'll show you more about the anatomy of ***.Vbp*** files in Chapter 19, "Runtime Display Secrets."

At a minimum, in addition to a ***.Vbp*** file, a Visual Basic source project must contain either a ***.Bas*** (code module) file and/or a ***.Frm*** (form) file. As you learned in Chapter 2, you can add ***.Bas*** or ***.Frm*** files to a project by using the IDE's Project menu.

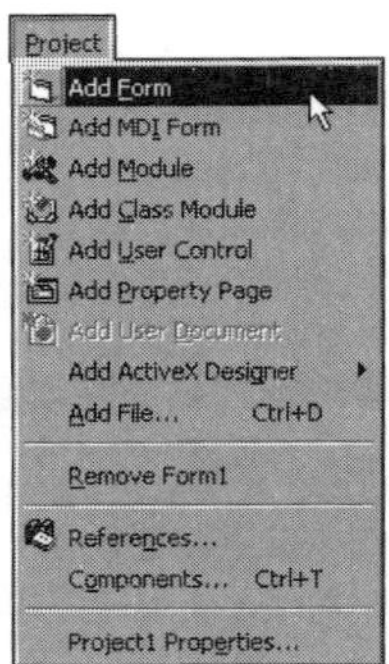

Figure 3-1: You can use the Project menu to add a form or other module to a Visual Basic source project.

What Is a Visual Basic Form?

A Visual Basic *form* is a window created in the Visual Basic IDE using the tools and techniques discussed in Chapter 2. Forms are like the "windows" that you are familiar with in standard Windows applications. However, VB forms come complete with an event and property scaffolding that greatly eases your task as a programmer. I'll discuss form events and properties later in this chapter.

Once you have more than one module or form in a project, you'll need to tell Visual Basic where to start code execution when it loads the project. You can designate any form as the startup form, in which case that form's event code is executed in the order discussed later in this chapter. The other possibility is to start code execution from a procedure named Main, which you must first add to a ***.Bas*** code module.

To choose your startup form — or Sub Main — open the Properties dialog for the project. You can access a project's Properties dialog from the Project menu, or you can right-click the project in Project Explorer. Select the General tab, and choose the startup form from the possibilities available in the drop-down list box.

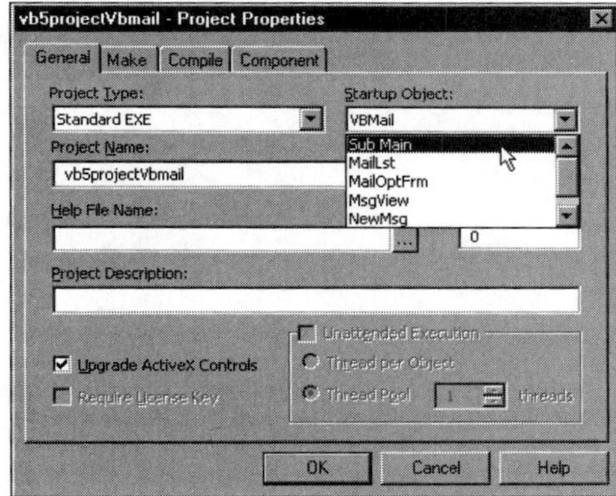

Figure 3-2: The Sub Main procedure is being selected as the startup object.

You also need to know how to add a procedure to a code module or a form. In particular, you can't start a project from a Sub Main unless you have first created the Sub Main by adding it to a module. In addition, it's hard to imagine a VB program of any complexity to which you don't add numerous procedures. I'll discuss the proper organization of these procedures later in this chapter — in particular under "Basic Concepts of Object-Oriented Programming" and "Encapsulating VB Dialogs" — and throughout Part III of this book, "Coding Secrets."

To add a procedure to a form or module, first open the form or module in *code view* (see Chapter 2 for an explanation of viewing code in the Code window). Next, choose Add Procedure from the Tools menu. (Note that Add Procedure is grayed out and not available on the Tools menu unless a module or form is open in the IDE in code view.)

The Add Procedure dialog will appear, as shown in Figure 3-3. You then give the procedure a name; decide whether it's a subroutine, function, or property procedure; and select scoping. (You can also set all local variables within the procedure to static using the appropriate check box.) Ramifications of these choices will be discussed in detail in Chapter 4, "The Visual Basic Language," and in Part III.

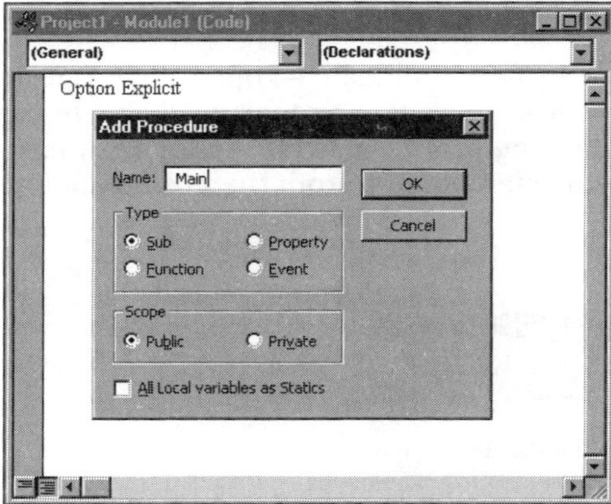

Figure 3-3: You use the Add Procedure dialog to add a Sub Main to Module1.

To summarize this section, Table 3-1 lists the files that make up a Visual Basic source project.

Table 3-1 Visual Basic Source File Types

File	*Extension*	*Purpose*
Group file	***.Vbg***	Links a group of VB projects; particularly useful for running controls in the design environment without having to first compile them.
Project file	***.Vbp***	Links all files in a VB source project. A project file is mandatory. In earlier versions of VB it was designated as a ***.Mak*** file.
Form file	***.Frm***	Contains event code and property information related to a VB form.
MDI form file	***.Frm***	Contains event code and property information related to a MDI (multiple document interface) form.
Code module	***.Bas***	Contains a group of procedures, meaning subroutines and functions.
Class module	***.Cls***	Visual Basic 5 class source code file.

File	*Extension*	*Purpose*
User Control	***.Ctl***	Source module that an ActiveX control is based on.
Property Page	***.Pag***	Contains event code and property information related to a control's property page.
User Document	***.Dob***	Source module that an ActiveX document is based on.
Form resource file	***.Frx***	Contains information related to a binary form, such as icons and other visual information that have been added to a form.
External resource files	***.Res***	Contains external resources such as text strings and bitmaps in standard Windows formations.
OLE custom control	***.Ocx***	A compiled ActiveX control that may be required by a VB project.
Dynamic link library	***.Dll***	An external compiled library that may be required by a VB project. Visual Basic executables compiled as p-code require the Visual Basic DLL runtime module. With VB5 executables, this file is ***Vbrun500.Dll***. Your projects may also require additional ***.Dll*** files.

Event-Driven Programming

Events are procedures (subroutines) that are *fired* (if any code is in the event, the code is executed) in response to specific conditions. All Windows programs are constructed around events, and Visual Basic applications are no exception. However, VB makes it very easy to program events and the response to these events. (In traditional Windows programming without a premade event scaffolding, programmatic response to event activation is a tedious affair indeed.)

What is an event? The concept is intuitively obvious: An event is fired (started) when something (the event) happens. You're already quite familiar with user actions that fire many common events. Some examples include

- Clicking the mouse, which fires a Click event
- Using the keyboard to enter text, which fires KeyDown, KeyPress, and KeyUp events
- Closing a window, which fires a QueryUnload and then an UnLoad event

As these examples show, one event can — simply by firing — trigger other events. You should also know that many events are fired without user intervention. One event can fire a cascade of other events. Under many circumstances, code, software, operating systems, and hardware can also fire events.

Event-driven programming has been presented as radically different in concept from traditional linear programming. The idea is that in the old days before the conquest of GUIs (graphical user interfaces), most program code went in a straight line. Possibly, the code allowed for branching depending on user input, but otherwise everything was precisely one directional.

In essence, you cannot take this one-track approach in an event-driven environment for three reasons:

- Program execution generally waits for events to be fired.
- The order of event execution is complex and not always entirely predictable.
- There are a great many possible events that can be fired.

This means that event-driven program code must be set up to respond to events as they are fired. You can think of this — it's an oversimplification but conceptually valid — as the program waiting on the actions of the user rather than doing anything independently.

In traditional Windows programming, the internal scaffolding is something like a giant case statement where each option in the case selection responds to a possible Windows message. (For example, selecting a menu item sends a WM_COMMAND message. Your case statement would have a branch for receipt of WM_COMMAND messages with a subbranch for the actual menu item selected. Visual Basic and the Windows messaging system are discussed further in Chapter 11, "The Win32 Software Development Kit (SDK), the Win32 API, and the Windows Messaging System.")

Obviously, this is an unwieldy approach. It produces programs that are impenetrable and difficult to debug. For better or for worse, Visual Basic is a high-level programming environment. It insulates you from having to understand the details of the Windows messaging system.

What Visual Basic does is present template events with its forms and controls. Also, forms and controls are bare-bones functional out of the box, so you don't have to worry about many kinds of details. For example, when you add a new form to a project, without further work on your part it can be resized or closed, and it comes with minimize and maximize buttons and a control box.

If you base a new project on the VB Application Wizard, it will build a great deal of the initial functionality of the user interface for you, based on the options you select.

An out-of-the-box form comes with many predefined events. Firing these events mostly doesn't *do* anything, however, unless you add code to them. If you open the code associated with one of these template events, you'll find a procedure beginning and end, and nothing in between. For example, here is the out-of-the-box template code for a Form_Click event:

```
Private Sub Form_Click()

End Sub
```

In and of itself, this event handler doesn't do anything, even though it is fired when the user clicks on the form when the project is running. Let's make it do something to further demonstrate the concept of the event-handling scaffolding.

Using the MsgBox Function when an Event Is Fired

The MsgBox function is very easy to use and is a surprisingly flexible way to pass messages to your program's users. It also enables you to retrieve simple answers to any query you may need to have your users answer.

You can also use this function as a debugging tool. It's easy to place a simple MsgBox function — which you can code as a statement rather than a function if you don't need any return values — in an event-handler to see if the event has actually been fired. For example, you might add

```
MsgBox "I was Fired!"
```

to a Form Paint event if you wanted to verify that the Paint event had been triggered.

For complete information on the MsgBox function, your best bet is to look it up in VB's on-line help. You can also effectively use the Object Browser to find all possible values of an icon and return constants that you can use in the MsgBox function. Use the Object Browser to check under VBA | Interactions. Because these constants are predefined in VBA (Visual Basic for Applications), you can use the listed word equivalents without defining the description to be equal to the required numerical value. (For example, vbCancel is predefined to be equal to 2. It is better programming practice to use the descriptive constant term rather than the less readable numerical equivalent. The only reason for using numerical values is to maintain backwards code compatibility with VB3 and prior versions.) You can add MsgBox constants; for example, you might want Yes, No, Cancel buttons *and* an exclamation icon.

Actually, with VB5's new "artificial intelligence" features, you don't really have to look anything up. Just type **MsgBox** in the Code window, press the spacebar, and VB pops up the complete syntax for the MsgBox statement. As you move to the parameters in the MsgBox statement that take constants as their arguments, VB produces a drop-down list of the valid possibilities. Double-click on a constant in the list, and VB pops it into the statement.

Adding Code to a Form Click Event

To add a MsgBox statement to a form click event, open the Code window with the form active. Use the Object drop-down list on the upper-left corner of the Code window to select the form. Once you've selected the form, use the Procedure drop-down list on the upper-right side of the Code window to select the click event. When you select the click event, VB automatically creates template handler code:

```
Private Sub Form_Click()

End Sub
```

Add the MsgBox statement (or any other code you want) within the handler procedure:

```
Private Sub Form_Click()
   MsgBox "Gadzooks, I've been fired!", vbExclamation, Me.Caption
End Sub
```

Now, when the user runs this sample program and clicks on the form, a message box will be displayed, as shown in Figure 3-4. (The Me.Caption keyword causes the caption of the current form to be displayed.)

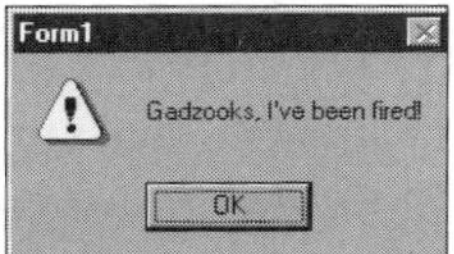

Figure 3-4: Any code you place in an event handler is executed when that event is triggered, including MsgBox statements like this one.

This chapter, and chapters to come, will demonstrate many more event-driven programming techniques. In the meantime, I'd like to conclude this overview of event-driven programming with a comment from my personal point of view.

I started programming back in the days when you passed a deck of punch cards through a reader into the behemoth in the next room. (Does anyone else remember the age of the dinosaurs?) These were surely non-event-driven linear programs. Not only was no user response involved, it took hours (or days) to get output back, and that output might only consist of a syntax error message.

This model of programming seems very different from current GUI standards, in which a programmer runs up her interface and then, typically, waits for the user's action. (As a side note here, the overwhelming popularity of Windows

95 and other GUIs among users clearly demonstrates the superiority of this style from the user's point of view, albeit with a trade-off of greater programming complexity.)

My real point here is that I don't actually believe event-driven programming is, in abstract theory, qualitatively different from the old style of programming. Rather, it is more complex but is no less linear in a logical sense. There are simply many more possible things (read "events") that the code needs to anticipate a response to. I believe that it is helpful to keep this in mind when designing event-driven programs: An event-driven program is merely a much more complex linear program. Not anticipating every possible event in this context is as mortal a sin as allowing illegal user input in a non-event-driven program. Fortunately, as you'll see, the Visual Basic event scaffolding provides a straightforward and easy way to manage events.

Properties and Methods in Visual Basic

In addition to events, most Visual Basic objects — such as forms and controls — come supplied with properties and methods. Methods and properties are fundamental conceptually to the way objects work; they are the basic building blocks for working in VB.

Properties

A *property* is a setting that describes something about an object such as a form. Depending on the property, you can set it at design time using the Properties window (see Chapter 2 for more information) and/or at runtime programmatically. For a full list and explanation of form properties, methods, and, for that matter, events, look up "Form Object" in Visual Basic's on-line help.

Here are two examples of Visual Basic form properties:

- MinButton. This property can be set to True or False. Depending on the setting, the form has (or does not have) a minimize button.
- BackColor. Setting this property to a value expressed as a RGB hexadecimal or a constant changes the background color of the form. You can look up the constants using the Object Browser in the VBRUN library under "ColorConstants" and "SystemColorConstants." The Object Browser is a very important Visual Basic tool that has been significantly enhanced in Version 5 of VB, as discussed in Chapter 5, "What's New in Visual Basic 5."

For example, to add a line of code to a form's double-click event at runtime, you'd simply modify the event handler as follows:

```
Private Sub Form_DblClick()
   BackColor = vbRed
End Sub
```

By the way, the hexadecimal equivalent is:

```
BackColor = &HFF&.
```

You can set the same color change — although not in response to an event firing — using the Properties window at design time. If you click the BackColor property, you'll get a color palette like the one shown in Figure 3-5. (The appearance of this palette depends on your graphic device settings and the settings in your Windows Control Panel.)

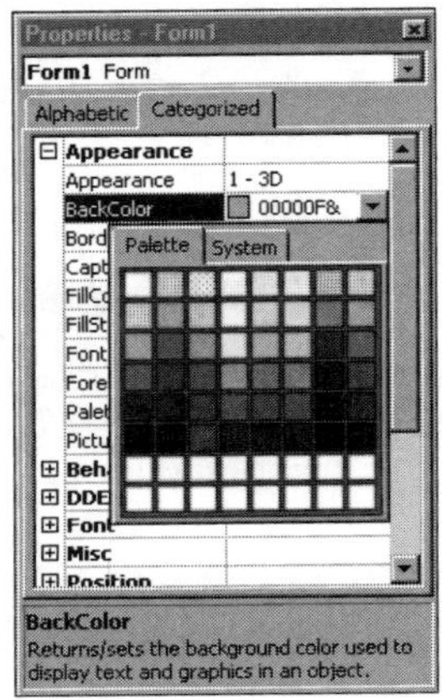

Figure 3-5: You can set a form's BackColor property using the Properties window.

Methods

Methods, as opposed to properties and events, are procedures that act upon an object. (Internally, methods are written as functions.) In general, they can only be executed at runtime, not at design time. Some examples of form methods are the Move method, which moves a form in two-dimensional space on the screen, and the ZOrder method, which positions the form in front of or behind other windows.

Methods are invoked by naming the object whose method is being called, listing the period operator (.), and then listing the name of the method. Like any routine, methods can take arguments. For example:

```
Form1.Zorder 0
```

As an example, I'll add a call to the Form.Move method to center the form when it loads. Listing 3-1 contains the code required to do this, placed in the Form Load event:

Listing 3-1: Centering a form on the screen

```
Private Sub Form_Load()
   Me.Move (Screen.Width - Me.Width) \ 2, _
      (Screen.Height - Me.Height) \ 2
End Sub
```

In addition to the Form.Move method, this code snippet uses a few simple VB techniques that you should know about to center any form on the screen. The keyword Me in VB refers to the currently executing instance of a form (or class module). The Screen keyword refers to a VB object that controls the runtime placement of forms on the screen (as well as the appearance of the cursor). .Width and .Height are two of the properties of the Screen object. (For a full list of its available properties, look it up in on-line help.) Finally, in VB5, a space followed by an underscore character (_) is used to continue a line of code to a subsequent line. The primary purpose of using this line continuation is to increase the readability of code.

You can easily add your own properties and methods to forms. This topic is discussed in Chapter 13, "Secrets of Good Programming Practice."

Event Firing Order

To successfully control the runtime appearance and behavior of forms (and controls as well), you must understand the order in which events are fired. Considerations of event firing order generally decide for you where a given bit of event response code should be placed. Form events can be divided into the following groups:

- Starting up
- Response to (user) action
- Linking
- Shutting down

I'll discuss linking events when we get to OLE Automation in Part V of *Visual Basic 5 SECRETS*. Right now let's look at the birth (startup), life (response), and death (shutdown) groups of events: what they do and when they are fired. (You should note that a given control will have a different set of events than a form. This means that while the event concepts discussed in this section often apply to controls as well as forms, the mapping is not always complete. However, this section should give you a feeling for the kind of behavior you can, in general, expect from events, no matter what object fires them. In addition, when creating your own controls you'll need to be clear about the difference, in a control, between receiving and firing an event. This topic is discussed in Chapter 24, "Understanding ActiveX Controls."

It is also important to understand that one event will often automatically fire another event, causing a cascade effect. For example, a KeyPress event cannot be fired without also firing KeyUp and KeyDown events. The secret to working with this kind of situation is a clear understanding of what fires each event in the sequence; the coding danger is starting an endless chain of circular recursive event calls.

Form Startup Events

You can set a form's birthing (or startup) events in motion either by naming the form as the startup form for the project, as described earlier in the chapter, or by invoking the Form.Show method, for example:

```
Form1.Show
```

The Show method loads and displays a form — two distinct actions that are both part of the birthing process. (Running the startup form also first loads the form and then shows it.) The Show method (for a non-MDI form) can be invoked as *modeless* or *modal*. Modal means that no subsequent code is executed until the form is hidden or unloaded. When a modal form is displayed, no user input (keyboard or mouse clicks) can occur except to objects on the modal form. Modeless forms, in contrast, do not necessarily monopolize the action!

Modality invocation is done with a *style* parameter following the Show method call. If the style is left off or is 0, the form is modeless (as above); if it is 1, the form is modal. For example:

```
Form1.Show 1
```

starts up Form1 modally.

In order, when the Form starts up, the following events are fired:

1. **Initialize** Used to initialize data used by an instance of the form so that it will already be present in the form — and visible to the user — when the form is loaded.
2. **Load** Used for further initialization code. It starts loading the form into memory and displaying it. You must be careful not to place potentially circular (recursive) calls to other form methods such as Activate, Resize, Paint, and GotFocus within this method.
3. **Resize** Occurs when a form is first displayed. It is also fired whenever the form is resized (so it, as well as Paint, could be considered a life as well as a birth event!).
4. **Paint** Occurs when part or all of a form is uncovered after it has been moved or enlarged or after a window that was covering the object has been moved. The Paint event is also invoked when the Refresh method is called at runtime. If the form's AutoRedraw property is set to True, repainting or redrawing is automatic, so there is probably no reason to add code to the Paint event.

Form User Response Events

By the very nature of event-driven program design, there is most often no way to predict exactly what user runtime actions will cause specific events to be fired. In other words, these events can't be ordered as neatly as the form startup sequence, but, to some degree, they can be grouped. (I'll cover how mouse-related events work in much greater depth in the sections on drag-and-drop programming in Chapter 21, "Creating Applications that Support OLE.")

Many user response events return parameters that contain important information about the event that has been fired — for example, the location of the mouse when it is clicked, or which key has been pressed. I'll discuss these events in greater detail in the appropriate places.

Mouse Events

The form-level mouse events (in alphabetical order) are

- **Click** Fired when a mouse button is clicked.
- **DblClick** Fired when a mouse button is clicked twice within the time limits set in the Control Panel. Note that firing this event actually fires a sequence of events: MouseDown, MouseUp, Click, DblClick, and MouseUp.
- **DragDrop** Occurs when a drag-and-drop operation is completed.
- **DragOver** Continuously fired when a drag-and-drop operation is in progress. You can use this event to monitor the mouse pointer as it enters, leaves, or rests directly over a valid target object, such as a form. The mouse pointer position determines the target object that receives this event.
- **MouseDown** Fired when a mouse button is pressed.
- **MouseMove** Fired when the mouse is moved.
- **MouseUp** Fired when a mouse button is released.

Keyboard Events

Here are the form-level keyboard events:

- **KeyDown** Fired when a key is pressed.
- **KeyPress** Fired when a key is pressed and released.
- **KeyUp** Fired when a key is released.

Miscellaneous Events

The miscellaneous events include the Paint and Resize events I've already discussed (under "Form Startup Events"). In addition, you should be aware of these events:

- **Activate** Fired when a form becomes the active window. Occurs before the GotFocus event is fired.
- **DeActivate** Fired when a form stops being the active window. Fired before LostFocus.
- **GotFocus** Occurs when a form (or control) receives the *focus* — that is, becomes the sole window that can receive mouse and keyboard input at that time. Normally, you can identify when a form gains the focus because its title bar changes color. When an object such as a command button gains the focus, the appearance of its caption changes. For example, a dotted line appears around the command button's caption. For an object to receive the focus, its Enabled and Visible properties must be set to True.
- **LostFocus** Fired when a form (or control) loses the focus.

Form Shutdown Events

Here are the events fired by a form as it shuts down, in order:

1. **QueryUnload** Fired by a form's Unload event, before any code in the UnLoad event is executed. QueryUnload gives you the chance to stop the form from being unloaded from memory when appropriate — for example, when the user has changed values in the form without saving her changes. The form will not be unloaded if the Cancel variable is set to True in the QueryUnload event procedure. It's common practice to set this variable to True following a user query along the lines of "Save Changes? Yes, No, Cancel" when the user responds by canceling. You can easily use the MsgBox function to give the user a chance to cancel an unload; see the next section for an example of how to do this. It's also useful that a UnloadMode parameter returned by the event procedure tells you the source of the QueryUnload event being fired. (Has the user clicked the close button? Has the Unload event been executed in code? Is the Windows Task Manager closing the application?) This allows you to possibly take different actions depending on what is shutting down your application.
2. **Unload** Fired when a user closes the form using the Close command on the Control menu or when an Unload method is executed in code. Unload immediately fires a QueryUnload event as just described. You can use the Unload event (as well as QueryUnload) to perform closure tasks such as saving and validating data. As with QueryUnload, you can also stop the Unload by setting the event's Cancel parameter to True. However, it is usually better practice to perform this action in the QueryUnload event, because you cannot stop Windows itself from closing from an Unload event.
3. **Terminate** Fired when all references to an instance of a form are removed from memory.

The MsgBox Function and QueryUnLoad

Listing 3-2 demonstrates how you might implement a MsgBox function that checks whether the user wants to save changed data — or not exit at all by canceling — in a Form QueryUnLoad event (this concept was explained in the previous section). Figure 3-6 shows the warning it displays.

Listing 3-2: Using the QueryUnLoad event

```
Private Sub Form_QueryUnload(Cancel As Integer, _
   UnloadMode As Integer)
   Dim Response As Integer
   Response = MsgBox("Your data has changed. Save it now?", _
      vbYesNoCancel + vbExclamation, _
      "Visual Basic 5 Secrets Warning!")
   Select Case Response
      Case vbYes
         MsgBox "Save the data and unload!"
      Case vbNo
         MsgBox "Don't save the data and unload!"
      Case vbCancel
         MsgBox "Don't Unload!"
         Cancel = True
      Case Else
         MsgBox "Internal Error!"
   End Select
End Sub
```

Figure 3-6: You can use the MsgBox function to display warnings to the user.

Adding Code to Form and Control Events

This chapter has already shown the general ways in which you add executable code to event-handling procedures. It's important, however, to explicitly review how to reach the proper event framework in which to place this code. This will let you pick the speediest and easiest way to get to the event-handling framework you need to add your code to. Once you reach the proper event-handler procedure, you attach code simply by typing it into the Code window, as I've shown you in the examples in this chapter. VB5's handy-dandy language tools help you find the right syntax in any situation.

It's important to realize that code attached to an event-handling procedure will often consist simply of procedure calls. The called procedures will in this case contain the actual executable code. One reason for designing a program in this fashion is that the same procedure can be called from many different event-handlers, thus simplifying, shortening, and clarifying program architecture. A common technique is to pass a procedure called from an event-handler a parameter indicating which handler has called it. Execution in the called procedure can then branch depending on which procedure called it (as determined by the parameter).

Here are the three ways to "reach" an event-handler procedure framework:

- Make sure the Project Explorer is open (if necessary, choose Project Explorer from the View menu). Select the form you wish to add event code to. (If you are adding an event to a control that has been placed on a form, select the form that is the control's "parent.") Click the View Code button. (Alternatively, right-click the form icon and choose View Code from the context menu.)

  In the Object list box, select the form or other object (for example, a control) to which you want to add event code. Next, from the Procedure list box, select the event-handler that you'll be adding code to. Note that event-handler procedures with code attached are boldfaced in the Procedure list box, whereas those with no code attached are not bold.

- Double-click the form to which you want to add code. Make your selection from the Object list box and Procedure list box as just described.

- Right-click the form. Choose View Code from the pop-up menu (see Figure 3-7). Make your selection from the Object list box and Procedure list box as just described.

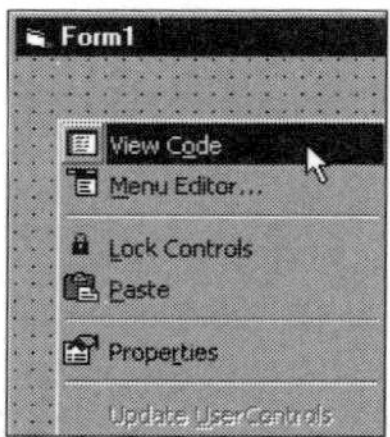

Figure 3-7: Right-clicking a form displays a context menu with options relevant to the form.

Basic Concepts of Object-Oriented Programming

Object-oriented programming techniques (OOP, for short) are among the most important tools that have become available to mainstream developers this decade. Programs that are designed with OOP in mind tend to be much more consistently reusable and maintainable. Sophisticated OOP programs can also be highly extensible, meaning that they potentially can simulate lifelike change and growth, and are appropriate for the implementation of expert systems and artificial intelligence (AI) constructs. The professional developer simply cannot afford to ignore OOP.

However, there is no consensus OOP standard, and the OOP tools available to developers depend on what programming environment they are using. Current languages offer a great range of OOP facilities. The spectrum ranges from relatively pure OOP languages such as Ada and Smalltalk (which are not, however, mainstream development languages) through mainstream languages such as versions of C++ and Borland's Delphi for Windows, which include powerful built-in OOP facilities.

Visual Basic is, of course, the world's best-selling programming language. There's good reason for its popularity: It's an incredibly easy to use yet powerful environment. As such, Visual Basic is definitely mainstream. Each successive release of Visual Basic has become more object oriented. Although Visual Basic is a hybrid language, VB5 provides extremely significant OOP facilities. The spirit of Visual Basic is essentially nondogmatic, but with Version 5 the OOP aspects of the environment — particularly the ability to create ActiveX controls without leaving VB — have become world class.

A number of additions to Version 5 of Visual Basic have made it substantially more OOP-friendly. As I'll demonstrate, enhanced class support, the ability to fire *custom* (meaning your own) events, and the ability to create your own ActiveX controls without leaving the environment — among other exciting new features — powerfully increase the OOP vocabulary available to VB developers.

There are three basic concepts involved in OOP programming techniques:

- **Inheritance** Inheritance means having the ability to create a new object that is based on an existing object. Some of the new object's events, properties and methods might be slightly different from the old object's. Or, a few new items might be added to the old events, properties, and methods.
- **Encapsulation** Encapsulation covers a range of concepts. At its simplest, it means bundling implementation details of objects so that the objects are only accessible to other parts of the program through predefined access procedures. The use of encapsulated objects fosters appropriate levels of "coupling," or connection, between parts of a program. This is very important if you wish to build "bulletproof" applications. The goal is to create encapsulated objects with strong internal integrity — known as "strong cohesion" — and obvious, direct, and flexible access between objects — known as "loose coupling."

- **Polymorphism** According to the dictionary, the term "polymorphism" applies to an object "having, occurring in, or passing through several or various [incarnations]." The idea is that polymorphism allows you to differently implement events, properties, and methods in subclassed objects. (A *subclassed* object is an object that inherits from an object conceptually located higher up in the class structure.) You can call a method, but the polymorphically inherited object does not know how the method is going to be implemented until it is "bound" at runtime.

  To better understand the concept, consider as a metaphor the "Turn it on" method which could apply to Television and Tractor objects, both belonging to the class of Powered Machines. Each of the machines handles the implementation of the "Turn it on" method differently — and we really don't care. In OOP lingo, one could say that the class Powered Machines has a "Turn it on" method that is inherited by each of its subclasses — Television and Tractor — and overridden by each with its own implementation.

Encapsulating VB Dialogs

The techniques of proper coupling and encapsulation dictate that programmers make every effort to avoid using global variables or hard-coding values. Avoiding these mistakes makes your programs easier to maintain and your objects easier to reuse. Most procedures within a properly encapsulated form object should be private in scope, and therefore inaccessible from outside the module. (The *scope* of a procedure or variable indicates how widely it is accessible to the other modules in a program.)

The problem is how to populate and return values to and from a dialog in a reusable way without adding public procedures to the object — which defeats the purpose of proper coupling. (Scoping in VB and its implications and consequences is discussed in Chapter 13.)

Here is one possible way to handle this issue:

1. Create a companion ***.Bas*** code module with the same name as each ***.Frm*** form file that you create. Use the ***.Bas*** file to put values in and retrieve them from the form. Because both modules have the same name — only their extensions are different — it will be easy to transfer them together to other projects and reuse them later.
2. Use an invisible label control (set the Label's Visible property to False) to pass information back and forth between the ***.Bas*** module and the .Frm module. The label control does not use Windows resources and can be given a name that clearly identifies it.

Another point this technique drives home is that a VB form is just a rather special kind of object. Visual Basic creates an instance of a form object for you, without being asked. But there's nothing to stop you from creating and destroying instances of forms yourself.

I'll run through how this works with an example. I've started by created a Bet Placing dialog like the one depicted in design mode in Figure 3-8.

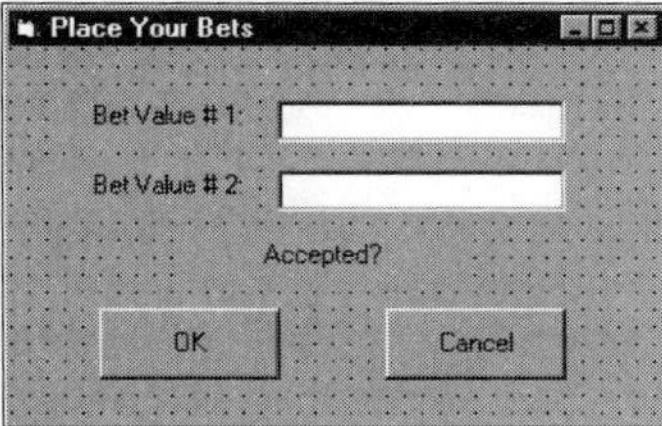

Figure 3-8: This Bet Placing dialog demonstrates how encapsulated parameter passing can work.

For that certain stylish *je ne sais quoi,* be sure to set the form's border style to 3-Fixed Dialog. Name the first text box txtBet1 and the second one txtBet2. Add a label named Accepted, and make sure to set its Visible property to False. (This label will be used to pass information back and forth about the form state, indicating whether the user has accepted the values.)

Next, add a command button named cmdOK with OK for its caption and another button named cmdCancel with Cancel for its caption. You can set the Default property of the OK button to True; this causes the Enter key to activate its click event. Also set the Cancel button's Cancel property to True; this causes the Escape key to activate the control's Click event.

Name the form frmEncap and save the form module as Encap.Frm. Add the following code to the cmdOK and cmdCancel buttons:

```
Private Sub cmdCancel_Click()
   Accepted = vbCancel 'predefined VBA constant value
   Me.Hide 'Hide the form but don't unload
End Sub

Private Sub cmdOK_Click()
   Accepted = vbOK  'predefined VBA constant value
   Me.Hide  'Hide the form but don't unload
End Sub
```

The next step is to add a new ***.Bas*** code module and save it as ***Encap.Bas***. Then add the function to ***Encap.Bas*** that will actually populate and retrieve information from the form (see Listing 3-3):

Listing 3-3: Encapsulating a form

```
Private Function PlaceBets(ByVal Bet1 As String, _
ByVal Bet2 As String)As Integer
   Dim X As New frmEncap 'Create new instance of frmEncap
   X.txtBet1 = Bet1      'Populate initial values
   X.txtBet2 = Bet2
```

```
    X.Show 1 'modal
    If X.Accepted = vbOK Then
        'If OK was pressed, return current values
        Bet1 = X.txtBet1
        Bet2 = X.txtBet2
    End If
    PlaceBets = X.Accepted 'Return whether OK pressed
    Unload X     'Unload instance of form from memory
End Function
```

That does the trick! I can test whether this code actually works by adding a Sub Main to the ***.Bas*** module and starting the project from it. Here's code in Sub Main that will populate the dialog — you can substitute whatever string values you choose — and return the contents of the dialog text box fields if, and only if, the user validates the values by selecting OK:

```
Public Sub Main()
    Dim RetVal As Integer
    Dim Bet1, Bet2 As String
    Bet1 = "$1,000"
    Bet2 = "$2,000"
    RetVal = PlaceBets(Bet1, Bet2) 'initialize values
    If RetVal = vbOK Then 'User accepted values
        MsgBox "First Bet Placed: " & Bet1 _
            & " ; Second Bet: " & Bet2
    Else 'User is not a gambler today!
        MsgBox "No Bets Were Accepted!"
    End If
End Sub
```

Understanding Class Modules

A *class module* is the template for an object without a visible interface, much as a form module is the template for an object that displays a window on the screen. Think of the class module as the cookie cutter and the class object as the cookie. Working with class modules is discussed in detail in Chapter 14, "Visual Basic and OOP." VB5's VB Class Builder utility is discussed in Chapter 5.

Properties

You can add properties to a class module using Public Property paired Get and Let Procedures:

```
Public Property Get myProp() As Variant
...
End Property

Public Property Let myProp(ByVal vNewValue As Variant)
...
End Property
```

You can add Property procedures to a class module using the Add Procedure dialog on the Tools menu (make sure that Property is selected as the type of procedure).

Once you have added a Property procedure to the class, you can change its attributes — which you can view using the Object Browser — using the Procedure Attributes dialog, which you also access via the Tools menu.

If you want a property to be used internally to a class module only, you don't have to use Property Gets and Lets: You can implement it simply as a module-level variable.

To implement the new property you have added to the class module, you need to create a class-level variable that will keep track of the value of the property:

```
Private thisVal As String

Public Property Get myProp() As String
   myProp = thisVal
End Property

Public Property Let myProp(ByVal vNewValue As String)
   If vNewValue <> thisVal Then thisVal = vNewValue
End Property
```

Methods

Class methods are implemented simply as public functions or procedures. For example, you could implement a method that tested the property myProp (defined a moment ago) by displaying a message box including it:

```
Public Function myMeth()
   MsgBox myProp, vbInformation, "Classy!"
End Function
```

Using Class Properties and Methods

To invoke the custom class property myProp and method myMeth that I just showed you how to create, you first need to create an instance of myClass. (Remember the cookie cutter and cookie analogy.) Then, you can assign property values and call methods using the dot operator. Here's the code required, placed in a form's click event:

```
Private Sub Form_Click()
   Dim X As New myClass
   X.myProp = "This is a test!"
   X.myMeth
End Sub
```

If you run the project containing the form and the myClass module, and click on the form, you'll get a message box like the one shown in Figure 3-9.

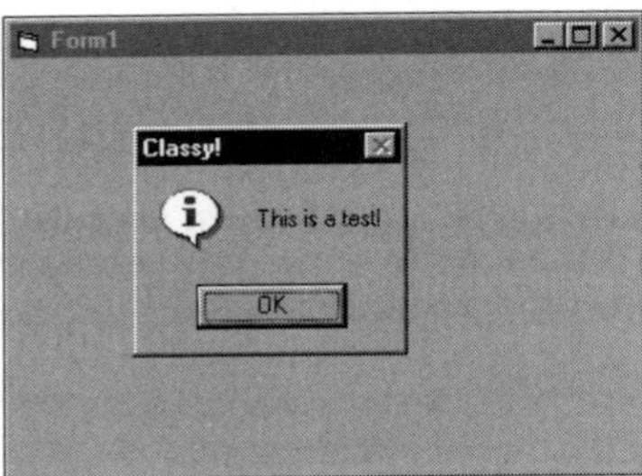

Figure 3-9: You can easily invoke class properties and methods, but first you must create an instance of the class.

Creating, Firing, and Handling Custom Events

To add an event to the myClass module, use the Event statement to declare an event with whatever arguments you'd like. Events must be declared as Public. Fire the event, again whenever you'd like, within the class module using the RaiseEvent statement. Be sure to supply any required parameters.

As an example — you could say, for the sake of science — I'll add an event named Frodo to the myClass module. Frodo is triggered by the invocation of myMeth, following the display of the myMeth message box.

Here's the revised code for the myClass module with the Frodo event added:

```
Option Explicit
Public Event Frodo()
Private thisVal As String

Public Property Get myProp() As String
   myProp = thisVal
End Property

Public Property Let myProp(ByVal vNewValue As String)
   If vNewValue <> thisVal Then thisVal = vNewValue
End Property

Public Function myMeth()
   MsgBox myProp, vbInformation, "Classy!"
   RaiseEvent Frodo
End Function
```

The next step is to access the event-handler in the form module that uses an instance of this class module.

In the Declarations section of the form module, declare a private variable of the class type, using the WithEvents keyword:

```
Private WithEvents X As myClass
```

You can now use the Object drop-down list to access the X object. With X selected in the Object drop-down list, you can access its Frodo event in the Procedure drop-down list, as shown in Figure 3-10.

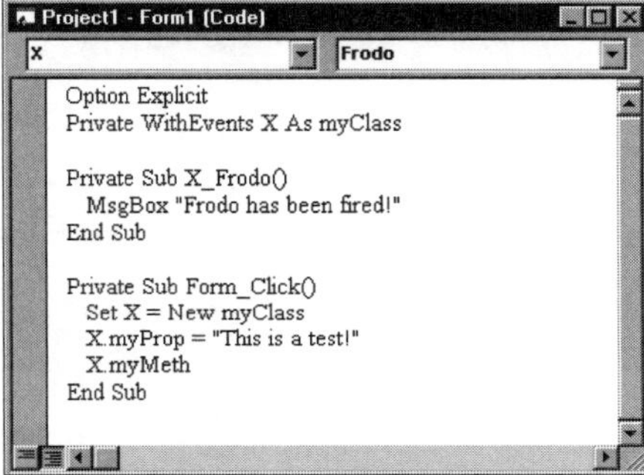

Figure 3-10: You can use the template event-handler generated by VB to add whatever code you want.

When you click the Frodo event in the Procedure drop-down list, VB creates template event-handler code:

```
Private Sub X_Frodo()

End Sub
```

You can add whatever code you want to this event to test that has really been fired. For example:

```
Private Sub X_Frodo()
   MsgBox "Frodo has been fired!"
End Sub
```

You cannot create an instance of an object variable declared using the WithEvents keyword using the Dim...As New syntax (called *implicit* creation). Instead, you must create it *explicitly*, using the Set statement.

Here's the revised code for the form module that creates a WithEvents instance of myClass and responds to the firing of Frodo:

```
Option Explicit
Private WithEvents X As myClass

Private Sub X_Frodo()
   MsgBox "Frodo has been fired!"
End Sub
```

```
Private Sub Form_Click()
   Set X = New myClass
   X.myProp = "This is a test!"
   X.myMeth
End Sub
```

If you run the project and click the form, first you'll see the myMeth message box. Next, you'll see the message box invoked in the Frodo event-handler, as shown in Figure 3-11.

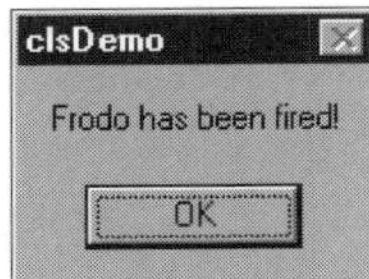

Figure 3-11: To be invoked successfully, objects declared using the WithEvents keyword must be created explicitly.

Summary

This chapter has covered a lot of ground. Among other things, I have

- Detailed the different kinds of source files that go into a Visual Basic 5 project
- Discussed event-driven programming; introduced events, properties, and methods
- Provided detailed information on form events and their firing order; showed you how to use the MsgBox function
- Demonstrated how to add code to form and other object events
- Provided an overview of object-oriented programming and VB's place in the OOP world
- Demonstrated an effective technique for creating a reusable, encapsulated, and loosely coupled parameter passage back and forth to a dialog form
- Explained class modules
- Demonstrated how to create and handle your own event

Along the way, I've let you know where in *Visual Basic 5 SECRETS* you'll find more detailed information on these topics. I've also, in passing, demonstrated

- Adding modules and procedures to a project; designating a project's startup form or procedure
- Changing a form's BackColor property either in code or in the Properties window
- Constructing a method call that centers a form on the screen

Chapter 4

The Visual Basic Language

In this chapter, I'll:

- Explain the details of some of the most important features of the Visual Basic language
- Tell you how to quickly find information in the VB documentation regarding language features that are not covered here
- Explain the syntax of working with objects
- Show you how to call a procedure located in an external library from a Visual Basic program
- Demonstrate how to call a Windows API function

Language Definition Overview

As you probably know, the Visual Basic language is a descendant of BASIC (Beginner's All-Purpose Symbolic Instruction Code). BASIC was originally specified in 1963 by John G. Kemeny and Thomas Kurtz of Dartmouth College. Kemeny and Kurtz intended BASIC as a teaching language. They were more concerned with intuitive ease of use — meaning that they designed the language to be as close to English as possible — than with optimizing feature sets and hardware implementation.

One major flaw of the early versions of the Basic language, from the point of view of the serious developer, was its lack of *structured* capabilities. Structured program design is characterized by systems that are divided into objects and routines that have well-defined, narrow interfaces whose implementation details are hidden from each other (see my remarks on "coupling" in the previous chapter). In contrast, unstructured programs tend to be recognizable by control flow that uses GoTo statements and logical jumps to specific destinations (sometimes derogatorily referred to as "spaghetti code").

Visual Basic in its fifth version has come a very long way from its humble BASIC roots. Although it retains much of the user-friendly, easy-to-use feeling of the earlier Basics, by now it has added an immensely rich and powerful feature set with an incredible capability for extension. It is now certainly possible to design complex Visual Basic applications in a highly structured and rigorous fashion. These characteristics have helped to make Visual Basic the world's best-selling programming language.

Before I get into the details of the Visual Basic language, I want to add another comment about VB programming technique in general. Visual Basic, as implemented, lets the developer do almost anything in almost any way. Particularly with all the third-party tools that are available, there are a tremendous variety of ways to do almost anything. (A substantial part of the work of developing in VB is keeping up with what's available.) This means that you can do things in the right way, or the wrong way (or almost any which way). VB won't stop you from designing systems badly. Therefore, it's critical to learn and make a habit of using correct programming and design techniques. This statement applies to many aspects of VB programming. For example, getting in the habit of using the

```
Option Explicit
```

statement in your projects (it causes the compiler to require explicit variable declarations and reject implicit typing) will save you hours of debugging time in the long run. (See the section "Using Option Explicit" a little bit later in the chapter.)

In keeping with its "do it your way" philosophy, Visual Basic lets you write code that is structured, or — the powers that be help you — highly unstructured. Of course, unstructured code is difficult — if not impossible — to debug and maintain. If you do not structure your code, it is much harder to be clear about what is fundamentally going on in a program. Perhaps nothing is more important to becoming a master Visual Basic programmer than internalizing and always using the techniques you need to properly structure your program design. Fortunately, the greater object orientation of Version 5 of Visual Basic makes it far more natural to write programs in a structured fashion.

VB Code Lines and Comments

Normally, you enter a Visual Basic statement on one line, meaning that the end of the physical line indicates the end of the statement. Thus, you can think of the end of the line as the usual implicit end-of-statement marker. This stands in contrast with usage in more highly structured languages. For example, in Object Pascal, you generally have to make the end of statement explicit with a semicolon (;).

There is essentially no limit to the theoretical length of a Visual Basic statement entered this way on a single line. However, it is a poor coding practice to create statements that don't fit on one line in either a printout or the Code window. With the Code window sized in the way you normally use it, you should be able to read each statement without having to scroll hidden code into view. The reason for this is, of course, that prime directive of programming style: "Thou shall write code that is clear." If you can see a statement all at once, it will be much clearer and less likely to contain mistakes.

Breaking Up Long Lines

In Visual Basic 5, you can, in the interests of clarity, break up long statements into multiple lines. A statement continuation on the next physical line is indicated by a space followed by the underscore character (_). (Obviously, the line continuation characters should not be placed within a string literal.) For example:

```
Dim Response As Integer
Response = MsgBox("Is this a Ring of Power?", _
    vbAbortRetryIgnore + vbQuestion, _
    "Line Break Demonstration", _
    "Frodo.Hlp", _
    23)
Rem Response = MsgBox (Prompt, Buttons, Title, _
    Helpfile, Helpfile context ID)
```

is much easier to read than it would be if the MsgBox function (and comment explaining it) were stretched out on one line (see Figure 4-1).

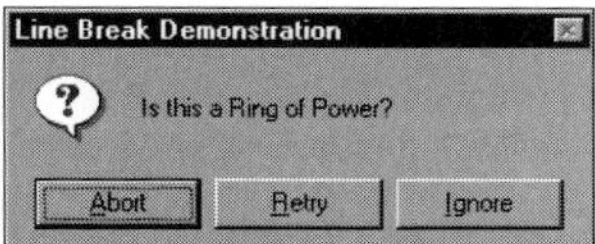

Figure 4-1: Frodo's message box is created with code that uses line continuations.

There is another option regarding VB statement termination. If you wish to place several (short) statements on one line, you can use a colon (:) to terminate, and separate, multiple statements (other than the final one) on a physical line. This example combines three statements on one line:

```
txtFrodo.text = "Not Orc" : MyColor = vbRed : Samwise = "Hobbit"
```

Including comments along with your code is an important way to make your work clearer to others. Commenting your code can even make it easier for you to understand when you come back to it later. However, the best advice is to create programs that are *self-documenting*. This means that — to a knowledgeable reader — the code's purpose should be clear because of the structural design, the clarity of statement and control exposition, and the choice of variable names. When you write code in this fashion, you should only use comments for two purposes:

- To clarify something that is otherwise not obvious — an example might be the expected value range of a parameter
- To provide a routine header that indicates author, date, purpose, and coupling for an entire project, module, or procedure

In these two contexts, not commenting code is a manifestation of one of the deadly sins: sloth.

In VB, you can create comments in one of two ways:

- With a single apostrophe
- With the Rem reserved word

In both cases, the rest of the line following the comment indicator is considered a comment and is ignored by the VB interpreter/compiler.

The apostrophe indicator can start a line, or appear anywhere within it. The Rem reserved word must start a line or must be preceded by a colon (breaking the line as just described).

By the way, an anomaly regarding Rem is that you can branch to a labeled line containing Rem using a GoTo or a GoSub statement. For reasons I've briefly touched on earlier in this chapter (that is, "spaghetti code"), doing so is not a particularly smart practice.

Here are examples of each comment style:

```
'Watch the counter on the next line!
OverFlowCount = NextMule + 1 'OverFlowCount > hdTop causes error
Rem hdTop is a global constant currently set to 20000.
Response = 3: Rem Response = MsgBox (Prompt, Buttons, Title, _
   Helpfile, Helpfile context ID)
```

The example shown in Listing 4-1 is a good way to use comments to create routine headers. A trick used by many professional developers is to save templates (in a small VB project) of the handful of routine headers that are likely to be used in various contexts and projects. (For example, a module header should be somewhat different than a subroutine or function header.) You could also save the headers in a directory as text files with a ***.Txt*** extension, and use Notepad to create and edit them.

You can use the Insert File facility (found on the Edit menu) to easily add the contents of a text file to code. The contents of the text file are inserted at the cursor position when the Code window is open.

There are a number of ways to make it easy to copy and paste the header templates into your code when you need them! (One of my working principles is to make practices that are good habits easy to follow. That way, I tend to practice them more often — to my long range benefit.)

Listing 4-1: A sample module header

```
'*   *   *   *   *   *   *   *   *   *   *   *   *   *   *   *   *
'*   *   *   *   *   *   *   *   *   *   *   *   *   *   *   *   *
'*   Module:   DataAccess.Bas
'*   Author:   Josephine Coder   Date Created:
'*
'*   This code module contains all data access routines and
'*   utilities for the entire project.
```

```
'*    All routines are intended for internal use only
'*    except:  GetData, PutData, ValidateData.
'*    See these routines for parameter explanations.
'*
'*
'*    *    *    *    *    *    *    *    *    *    *    *    *    *    *    *    *
'*    *    *    *    *    *    *    *    *    *    *    *    *    *    *    *    *
```

Identifiers, Constants, and Variables

Identifiers are used to name things. Constants and variables are things that need to be named. Constants represent fixed values in a program whereas variables represent variable values.

Identifiers

The term *identifier* refers to any element in your VB program that you have to give a name to. This includes constants, variables, subroutine names, and function names. Identifiers

- Must begin with a letter.
- Cannot contain embedded spaces, periods, or type-declaration characters. (Type-declaration characters must appear at the end of the name.)
- Cannot be keywords that are reserved by Visual Basic. For example, *For* is not a valid VB identifier because it conflicts with the reserved use of the For...Next statement.
- Identifiers that refer to variables, constants, and procedures can, in theory, be up to 200 characters long. Those that refer to controls, forms, classes, and modules cannot exceed 40 characters. As a matter of good coding practice, identifiers should be no more than about 25 characters. In particular, you want to be able to clearly read object and procedure names in the space available in the Code View Object and Procedure drop-down list boxes; using names that are too long can make this difficult.

Constants

Constants are identifiers used in place of values that either occur in many places in your code or whose functionality is not clear from the value. It is easier to understand at a glance the meaning of a properly named constant that refers to, for example, the maximum number of records in a search routine, than to make heads or tails of the meaning of a numerical value that is the equivalent of the constant. For example:

```
Const MaxSearchRecs = 20964
```

defines a clear value for your code. It will subsequently be much easier to understand the intention behind a comparison with MaxSearchRecs than a comparison with 20964.

Using constants also makes it much easier to maintain code if the constant values have to be subsequently changed. It is particularly helpful to place all constant declarations at the beginning of a module so that you can easily "nudge" them. Many languages require this is as a matter of syntax. You should structure your VB projects in this way, with maintainable blocks of constants, as a matter of sound coding practice.

Predefined Constants

Visual Basic comes with many predefined constants. You can use these constants in your code without any kind of declaration. One good way to find these constants is to use the Object Browser. You can enter text in the search field of the Object Browser, and it will find related constants. For example, if you enter the word "abort," the browser will come up with two relevant constants, as shown in Figure 4-2: the vbAbort constant that is a member of the vbMsgBoxResult class of the VBA library, and the vbAbortRetryIgnore constant that is a member of the vbMsgBoxStyle class of the VBA library.

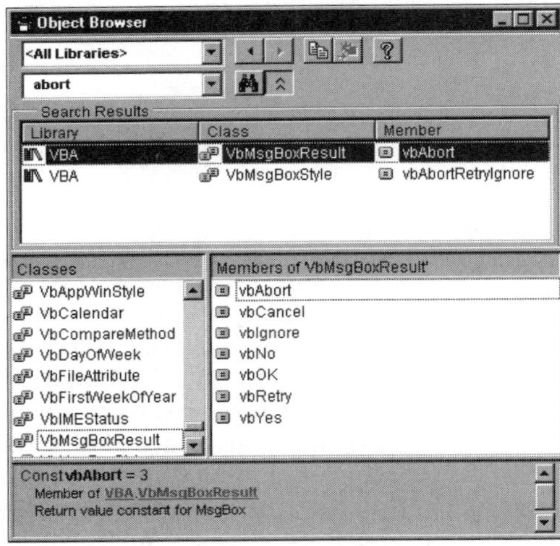

Figure 4-2: You can use the Object Browser to quickly find available predefined constants.

By the way, when you select a constant in the Object Browser, it will indicate the constant's numerical equivalent. (Using the enhanced features of the VB5 Object Browser is discussed in Chapter 5, "What's New in Visual Basic 5.")

The enhanced features of the VB5 Code window make it easy to ascertain available predefined constants — and add to your code. For example, after entering the first argument of a MsgBox statement, you can select List Constants from the Code window's context menu to display a drop-down list of the constants that are syntactically correct for the context, as shown in Figure 4-3. Double-clicking one of the constants adds it to your MsgBox statement.

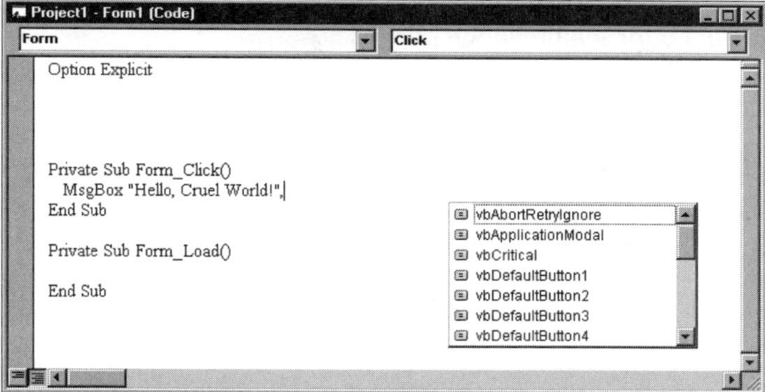

Figure 4-3: You can use the Code window's List Constants facility to easily find appropriate predefined constants.

Although you can certainly use the values instead of the predefined constant, it is a good idea to code with constants because they make it much clearer what the values represent.

Constants from the VB and Visual Basic for Applications libraries are prefixed with the letters "vb." For example:

```
vbShapeRoundedRectangle '=4, from the VB ShapeConstants library,
                        'meaning a rectangle rounded with curves

vbFormFeed  'ASCII character 12, equivalent to Chr$(12), from the
            'VBA constants library, used to force a form feed.
```

In versions of VB prior to Visual Basic 4, predefined constants were styled with all capitals and underscores, as in TILE_VERTICAL. (The VB5 equivalent is vbTileVertical.) You can, of course, still declare and use the old style constants.

User-Defined Constants

As discussed earlier in this chapter, it's good programming practice to use constants in place of values that will be used repeatedly. The primary reason for this is that it's easy to figure out the meaning of a well-named constant in the context of an application.

Your constants should all be defined in one place. Global constants should be declared in one module, not spread across a number of different modules. Module-level constants should go at the beginning of the Declarations section of the module. Procedure-level constants should be placed at the beginning of procedure code. Any constants whose meaning is not perfectly clear from their names should be commented.

If your constants are spread out between different modules and procedures, you might want to prefix all your constant names with a unique identifier — such as your initials — to make it easier to find them. For example:

```
Const hdTop
Const hdMaxPrice
```

Following these practices will make it much easier to modify constant values when needed for maintenance purposes.

You create your own constants using the Const keyword followed by a constant identifier and the equivalence with the constant value:

```
Const MyAppVersion = "1.02a"
```

You can place multiple constant declarations on one line, separated by commas. Also, constant values can be expressions that evaluate to a number or a string, provided that the expression does not include function calls. You can even include one constant in the definition of another. For example:

```
Const MyAppName = "Bear Games"
Const NameAndVersion = MyAppName & ", Version: " & MyAppVersion
```

When defining constants using other constants, be careful to avoid *circular* constant references, in which two or more constants are defined in terms of each other.

You can explicitly type constants using an As directive:

```
Const NewApp As String = "Panther Games"
```

For reasons I discuss in the next section, explicit typing is usually a good idea.

A final point is that user-defined constants have *scope*, just as variables do. You can think of scope as referring to the extent to which variables (or constants) are visible and can be referenced throughout a program. A variable or constant that is only visible in one procedure has limited scope, while one that can be used throughout a program is of broad scope. Scope is discussed further later in this chapter and in Chapter 13, "Secrets of Good Programming Practice."

Optionally, you can add a Private or Public keyword to the beginning of a constant declaration. For example:

```
Public Const CryptKey = "A56789C"
Private Const UltimateAnswer = 42
```

Using these keywords, the rules of scoping constants are as follows:

- To declare a constant local to a procedure, declare it in the procedure with no keyword or with the Private keyword.
- To declare a constant local to module — meaning available to all procedures within the module, but not to those in any other module — declare it in the General Declarations section of the module with no keyword or with the Private keyword.
- To make a constant globally available, declare it with the Public keyword in the General Declarations section of a form or standard module. Note that you can't declare a public constant in a class module.

Variables

Variables are identifiers that store values. They are *declared* — that is, made known to the VB compiler — as described in the next section of this chapter, "Using Option Explicit."

Table 4-1 lists the different kinds of VB variables, along with their permissible contents, and the type indication character that can be used for the particular type of variable when declaring it implicitly.

Table 4-1 Different Kinds of Visual Basic Variables.

Type	*Storage Size*	*Contents*	*Identifying Character*
Byte	1 byte	Numerical: 0 to 255.	N/A
Boolean	2 bytes	Logical: True or False.	N/A
Integer	2 bytes	Numerical: -32,768 to 32,767.	%
Long (long integer)	4 bytes	Numerical: -2,147,483,648 to 2,147,483,647.	&
Single (single-precision floating-point)	4 bytes	Numerical: -3.402823E38 to -1.401298E-45 for negative values; 1.401298E-45 to 3.402823E38 for positive values.	!
Double (double-precision floating-point)	8 bytes	Numerical: -1.79769313486232E308 to -4.94065645841247E-324 for negative values; 4.94065645841247E-324 to 1.79769313486232E308 for positive values.	#
Currency (scaled integer)	8 bytes	-922,337,203,685,477.5808 to 922,337,203,685,477.5807.	@
Date	8 bytes	January 1, 100 to December 31, 9999.	N/A
Object	4 bytes	Any object reference (actually stores a pointer to an instance of an object).	N/A
String (variable-length)	10 bytes plus string length	0 to approximately 2 billion characters (as opposed to approximately 65,400 for Microsoft Windows version 3.1 and earlier).	$
String (fixed-length)	Length of string	1 to approximately 65,400 characters. `Dim Frodo As String * 20` is an example of a declaration of a fixed-length string containing 20 characters.	$
Variant (with numbers)	16 bytes	Any numeric value up to the range of a Double.	N/A
Variant (with characters)	22 bytes + string length	Same range as for variable-length String.	N/A
User-defined	Number required by elements; total is therefore the sum (using Type) of that required by the elements. The range of each element is the same as the range of its data type.		N/A

Public and Private Keywords

Variables can be scoped as local to procedures, available to all procedures in a module, or available globally to all modules. Here's how it works.

- Variables declared within a procedure are local to that procedure. The following two declarations are equivalent within a procedure:

```
Private Meriadoc As String
Dim Meriadoc As String
```

- You cannot use the Public keyword in declarations that are within a local procedure.
- Variables declared in the General Declarations section of a module with the Private keyword are available to all procedures within the module but not to other modules. Declaring a module-level variable using Private is exactly equivalent in scoping impact to declaring it with Dim.
- Variables declared in the General Declarations section of a module — other than a class module, where it is not allowed — using the Public keyword are available to all procedures in all modules. For example:

```
Public MyObject As New Form1
```

- Note that the Global keyword, which has the same purpose as Public, has been retained from VB3 for purposes of backwards compatibility.

As you probably know, variables with the same name but different levels of scope can exist within one project. For example, there is certainly no reason you can't have two local variables declared

```
Private Pippin As Long
```

in one procedure within a module and

```
Private Pippin As String
```

within another. The two Pippin variables are, of course, completely independent and different.

The issue becomes somewhat more complex when you have several variables with the same name and overlapping scope. For more information on this topic, see Chapter 13 of this book.

In addition to scope, variables have a *lifetime*. The lifetime of a variable is the period for which it retains its values. By default, module- and public-level variables in VB *persist* — that is, live — as long as an application is alive and loaded into memory. Private (local) variables, on the other hand, only persist while the procedure they are within is executing.

To make private variables persist even when the procedure they are in is not executing — also known as *preserving* their value — use the Static keyword in place of Dim or Private. Here's a function that uses a static declaration to preserve a running value count:

```
Function TestStatic(NumVal As Integer)
   Static TestCount As Integer
   TestCount = TestCount + NumVal
   TestStatic = TestCount
End Function
```

You can test this function by calling it repeatedly — for example, from a form click handler:

```
Private Sub Form_Click()
   MsgBox Str(TestStatic(1))
End Sub
```

If you run this code, you'll see that the return value increments by 1 each time you call TestStatic. By contrast, had TestCount been declared as nonpersistent using Dim or Private, the TestStatic function would return 1 each time and never increment.

To make all local variables static within a procedure, add the Static keyword to the procedure heading. For example:

```
Static Function TestStatic(NumVal As Integer)
```

You can automatically create procedures and functions all of whose local variables are static by checking All Local Variables as Statics in the Add Procedure dialog (see Figure 4-4).

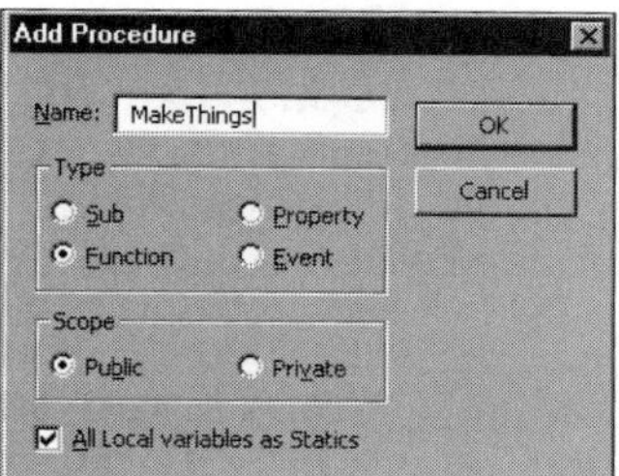

Figure 4-4: If you select All Local Variables as Statics when you use the Add Procedure dialog, your procedure will be defined using the Static keyword.

Using Option Explicit

Variables can be *implicitly* declared or *explicitly* declared. You implicitly declare a variable simply by using the variable in code.

Variant Variables

If the implicitly declared variable used has no type declaration character at the end of its name, VB assumes that it is a variant. Here are two examples of nonvariant implicit usage:

```
FlukeCount% = 1
'FlukeCount is an integer
HobbitName$ = "Frodo"
'HobbitName is a string
```

Here is an implicit variant usage (note that the same variable is storing string and numeric information):

```
WhatEver = "I like to sing!"
WhatEver = 42
```

You should not think of a variant variable as a variable with no type. Rather, a variant is a variable capable of being various types that generally converts its stored values between these types automatically. VB encapsulates the internal storage of variants and can automatically change the type of the variant that has been stored. It's important to know that objects — including forms, controls, and OLE automation objects — can be stored in a variant variable. (Actually, what is being stored is a pointer to the object!)

You should usually require explicit variable declarations as a matter of good coding practice to help minimize misspelled variable name errors. Explicit variable declaration is required in a module when you add the

```
Option Explicit
```

statement to the Declarations section of a class, form, or standard module. You can set up the IDE to automatically add the Option Explicit declaration in new modules (although you must add it manually to any preexisting modules), and I suggest you do so (see Figure 4-5). Choose Options from the Tools menu and make sure Require Variable Declaration is checked on the Editor tab of the Options dialog.

Once you have required explicit declaration, you can only use variables that have previously been declared using the Dim, Private, Public, and Static statements. (If you try to use a variable that has not first been declared with Dim or another keyword, you'll get a compiler error message when you try to run your source code.) Here are some examples of explicit declarations:

```
Option Explicit
Dim Whatever   'Variant
Dim OrcName As String 'String
Dim BodyType As Integer 'Integer
Dim MyName, HobbitName As String '2 strings
Dim EntName As String, Dim IdNum As Long 'string and long
Dim X As New Form1 'pointer to instance of Form1
```

Using implicitly declared variables can be convenient. The problem is that it is all too easy to introduce a new variable that is spelled slightly differently from an existing variable. Your intention was to change the contents of a variable and instead you created a new one. For example, TempVal, TempVl, TemVal, and Tempval1 all look surprisingly similar at a passing glance. The possible resulting bugs from confusion between these slightly different variable names — which never would occur if explicit declaration were required — can be difficult and time-consuming to pin down. The serious developer should bite the bullet and explicitly declare!

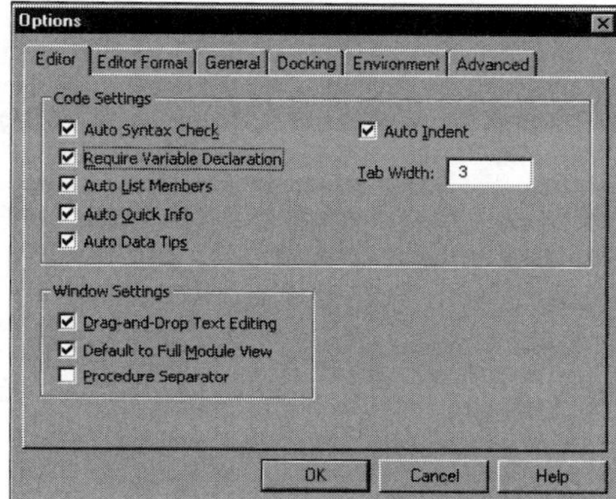

Figure 4-5: Check the Require Variable Declaration check box on the Editor tab of the Options dialog to require explicit variable declarations in all new modules.

By the way, suppose you *had* intended TempVal, TempVl, TemVal, and Tempval1 as different variables and explicitly declared them. Although there is nothing technically wrong with this, it does represent bad variable naming practice on three counts:

- These names provide no real information about the contents of the variables.
- The names are too similar to one another. Even if this doesn't lead to a bug as just described, it will make your code harder to read and less clear.
- Misspelled words in variable names — such as "Va1" in "TempVa1" — should be avoided.

Numbers

Most of the time you'll program using decimal numbers (base 10). You can also use hexadecimal numbers (base 16), which are represented with a prefix of &H, and octal numbers (base 8), which are represented with a prefix of &O. For example, in VB notation, 255 (decimal) equals &O377 (octal) equals &HFF (hex). An important technique when you want to use a large octal or hex number is to append the long type character (&) to the number. This strategy causes the number to be correctly stored as a long integer. For example, to store &HFF10F9CC as a long integer, you'd enter it:

```
&HFF10F9CC&
```

Operators

There are four general categories of operators in VB: Arithmetic, String Concatenation, Comparison, and Logical. Table 4-2 lists these categories with their elements.

Table 4-2: The Precedence and Categories of Visual Basic Operators.

Arithmetic	*String Concatenation*	*Comparison*	*Logical*
Exponentiation (^)	String Concatenation Operator (&) or (+)	Equality (=) Don't confuse with Assignment	Not
Negation (-)		Inequality (<>)	And
Multiplication and division (*,/)		Less than (<)	Or
Integer division (\)		Greater than (>)	Xor (Logical exclusion)
Modulo arithmetic (Mod), concerned with remainders		Less than or equal to (<=)	Eqv (logical equivalence)
Addition and subtraction (+,-)		Greater than or equal to (>=) Like (used to compare two strings using pattern matching) Is (used to compare the equivalence of two object references)	Imp (logical implication)

Dot Operator

In addition, you should certainly become friends with the dot operator (.). The dot operator is used

- To connect objects with child objects (such as controls)
- To connect objects with properties and methods
- To retrieve and store values of variables that have been defined within a user-defined structure

For example, you can use the dot operator to connect properties, controls, and forms:

```
Form1.BackColor = vbRed 'sets BackColor property to Red
```

and

```
Form1.txtUserId.text = "Finnegan's Wake"
'sets the text property of the control txtUserId, which is located
'on the object Form1, to the given string
```

If you leave the property of the control off an assignment that uses the dot operator, VB will, if it can, use the default property for the object. For example, .caption is the default property of a Label control. The following code assigns the value of Label1.caption into a variable (if there is no caption, an empty string is assigned):

```
Dim Contents As String
Contents = Form1.Label1
```

In a similar vein, Form1.Label1, of course, refers to the Label1 that is a child of (think of it as living on) Form1, whereas Form2.Label1 refers to the Label1 that is a child of Form2. For example,

```
Form1.ZOrder 1
```

uses the dot operator to invoke the form's ZOrder method. And

```
Form1.Text1.Move 0,0
```

moves Text1 to the upper-left corner of the client area of Form1.

Finally, if you have a user-defined structure such as

```
Type Animal
   Name As String
   Weight As Integer
End Type
```

you can use the dot operator to assign and retrieve values from the structure:

```
Animal.Name = "Bulgy Bear"
Size% = Animal.Weight  'Size is declared implicitly. Bad!
```

I'll discuss user-defined structures in more detail later in this chapter, under "Programmer-Defined Structures."

Assignment Operator

Visual Basic uses the equal sign (=) both as a comparison operator and as an assignment operator. When used as a comparison operator, = tests for equality; when used for assignment, as in the earlier examples, = transfers a value from the right side of an equal sign to the identifier on the left side.

It is important to understand which use of the = operator is involved when you look at a VB statement. To avoid confusion, some other languages only use = for comparison and have a different assignment operator. Thus, := means assignment in Object Pascal, and == (two equal signs) means assignment in C. In these languages, = is only used for comparison.

There is something to be said for separating the two functions, although, on VB's behalf, one might argue that it's faster to simply enter one equal sign rather than two characters, and that the context usually makes clear what is going on.

Collection Operator

The objects in a collection object are all the members of a collection — for example, all the controls on a form. The collection operator (!) is used to refer to specific object members of a collection. For instance:

```
Form1.Controls!Label1
```

addresses the Label1 member of the Form1.Controls collection. There are two other equivalent ways to address a member of a controls collection without using the ! operator: You can use the object's name directly, or you can use the index number of the collection member. If the control named "Label1" is the first member of the Form1.Controls collection (with an index value of 0), you can access it as follows:

```
Form1.Controls("Label1")
Form1.Controls(0)
```

You'll find more material on the syntax of referencing objects and collections of objects later in this chapter in the section "Speaking the Language of Objects," and in Part III of this book, "Coding Secrets."

As you'll notice in Table 4-1, ! is also used to designate that a variable is of type Single. Make sure to be clear about what ! is doing in a given context, and eschew obfuscation.

Operator Precedence

Table 4-2 presented most of the common operators in a left-to-right and top-to-bottom order of precedence, meaning that those in the leftmost column are evaluated first, and so on. Within each category, precedence goes from top to bottom. You can change the order of evaluation by adding parentheses to an expression. Operations within parentheses are always performed before those outside parentheses. Most of the functionality of the operators in this table should be pretty apparent; if not, they are all explained quite well in VB's on-line help.

String Concatenation

To concatenate two strings means to create a third string consisting of the first string plus the second string. You concatenate strings using the string concatenation operator, represented by either an ampersand (&) or a plus sign (+). Here's an example:

```
Private Sub Form_Click()
   Dim Msg As String
   Msg = "Tomorrow"
   Msg = Msg & vbCrLf & "    is"
   Msg = Msg & vbCrLf & "another"
   Msg = Msg & vbCrLf & "  DAY!"
   MsgBox Msg
End Sub
```

The example creates the string value of the variable Msg by repeatedly concatenating new strings with itself. This trick also uses the predefined constant vbCrLf (whose value is a concatenated ASCII character 13 and ASCII character 10). vbCrLf is concatenated into the Msg string to create line breaks. Finally, the MsgBox function is called to display the string (see Figure 4-6).

Figure 4-6: Here is the concatenated string with line breaks generated by the preceding code.

Concatenating strings is an important part of fluidly manipulating them. One of Visual Basic's great strengths is its incredible ease of string manipulation and wealth of string manipulation functions. I'll show you more about string manipulation as we go along in *Visual Basic 5 SECRETS.* (Although many of the demonstration projects in this book contain useful string handling techniques, specific string manipulation methods are discussed in Chapter 13, "Secrets of Good Coding Practice.")

Control Loops and Conditional Statements

Control loops and conditional statements enable you to manipulate the order in which program statements are executed. Without these statements, program *flow* — the order in which program statements are executed — would be unchangeable. The flow would be from top to bottom and left to right, which would be inadequate except for the very simplest programs.

If Statements

If statements are used to execute statements conditionally, depending upon the evaluation of an expression. The test expression must evaluate to True or False, and is often a comparison. (Numerical expressions meet this condition because VB considers a zero numeric value False and any nonzero value True.)

There are three kinds of If statements:

- The “single-line” If statement, in which the statement is executed if the condition evaluates to True.
- The “multiline” If statement, in which a block of statements are executed if the condition is True. The statements are concluded with the End If keywords.
- The “multiline” If statement, possibly containing many blocks of statements. Flow control is achieved through the evaluation of the original expression and through the evaluation of ElseIf and Else optional evaluations.

Here is an example that uses the three kinds of If statements. It also demonstrates the use of three string manipulation functions: Left, Len, and UCase. Left returns characters from the left of a string, Len returns the length of a string, and UCase returns the passed string in uppercase. To find out more about these and other string functions, look them up in VB’s on-line help.

To set up this project, add a text box control named txtUserInput, a label named lblOutput, and a command button named cmdDoIt to a form. (Note that the code refers to txtUserInput.text, the default property of this control, as txtUserInput; similarly, lblOutput.caption is referred to as lblOutput.)

The program will output a message when the command button is clicked in lblOutput’s caption, depending on the first letter and length of the input in txtUserInput (see Figure 4-7). Add the following code to cmdDoIt’s click event-handler:

```
Private Sub cmdDoIt_Click()
    lblOutput = ""
    If Left(UCase(txtUserInput), 1) = "A" Then
        If Len(txtUserInput) < 4 Then
            lblOutput = "Smerdyakov"
        Else
            lblOutput = "Dimitri"
        End If
    ElseIf (Left(UCase(txtUserInput), 1) > "A") And _
        (Left(UCase(txtUserInput), 1) < "D") Then
        If Len(txtUserInput) < 3 Then
            lblOutput = "Alexei"
        Else
            lblOutput = "Raskolnikov"
        End If
    ElseIf (Left(UCase(txtUserInput), 1) > "E") And _
        (Left(UCase(txtUserInput), 1) < "Q") Then
        If Len(txtUserInput) < 2 Then
            lblOutput = "Fyodor"
        End If
    Else
        If Left(UCase(txtUserInput), 1) = "T" _
            Then lblOutput = "Pasha Bear: "
        lblOutput = lblOutput & " That's all, folks!"
    End If
End Sub
```

Create Control Structure Framework First

You're less likely to produce syntactically wrong control structures — or worse, control structures that are correct in terms of syntax, but don't do what you think they do — if you first create the correct control statements. You can next add simple statements — for example, using the MsgBox function — to make sure that the flow is correct based on the test expressions. Only after you are satisfied with the framework should you add the actual execution statements.

Figure 4-7: Here is the output generated by If statements when the user input a string starting with "T."

Select Case Statements

The cmdDoIt If statements appear kind of complex to a casual reader, although the functionality it encapsulates is really pretty straightforward and no big deal. Nested control structures — and in VB there is no limit to the level of nesting allowed — can become much more complicated. One important way to simplify the resulting structures is to place single procedure calls in execution areas rather than including multiple execution statements within one branch of a control structure. The procedure that is called by the execution flow can then contain all of the statements necessary for program logic.

Another technique that can simplify decision structures is to use Select...Case...Else structures as an alternative to If structures. Select...Case works with a single test expression that is evaluated once at the beginning of the structure. Here are the demonstration If structures from the previous example rewritten using Select structures. I think it's much easier to see the flow control logic when the structure is written this way! (Of course, there is nothing to stop you from replacing internal If statements with nested Case statements.) I've added this code to the form click event so that it can be run in the same sample project as the previous code.

```
Private Sub Form_Click()
   lblOutput = ""
   Dim TestLet As String
```

```
   TestLet = Left(UCase(txtUserInput), 1)
   Select Case TestLet
      Case "A"
         If Len(txtUserInput) < 4 Then
            lblOutput = "Smerdyakov"
         Else
            lblOutput = "Dimitri"
         End If
      Case "B" To "D"
         If Len(txtUserInput) < 3 Then
            lblOutput = "Alexei"
         Else
            lblOutput = "Raskolnikov"
         End If
      Case "E" To "Q"
         If Len(txtUserInput) < 2 Then
            lblOutput = "Fyodor"
         End If
      Case Else
         If TestLet = "T" _
            Then lblOutput = "Pasha Bear: "
         lblOutput = lblOutput & " That's all, folks!"
   End Select
End Sub
```

Another Visual Basic trick that helps to clarify selection flow based on user input is to call a subroutine with a passed parameter that indicates the user selection. A Select...Case statement in the called routine can then be used to execute the proper statements. (Often, the decision structure in the called subroutine should itself have the sole purpose of calling appropriately named routines.)

To demonstrate this technique, add a list box (named lstSelect in the example) and a command button (named cmdPass in the example) to a form. Populate the list box in the startup form's load event with a selection of possible user choices using the list box's AddItem method. (Note that for the example to work, the first letter of each selection must be unique. There are, of course, many ways to change the parameter call should this not be the case. You could use the first two letters, not just the first one. You could use the entire string. You could use the list box's index number.)

Because lstSelect's Sorted property is set to True, the list will initialize in alphabetical order no matter which order you add the item in.

```
Private Sub Form_Load()
   lstSelect.AddItem "Waffles"
   lstSelect.AddItem "French Toast"
   lstSelect.AddItem "Pigs in a Blanket"
   lstSelect.AddItem "Granola"
   lstSelect.AddItem "Berries"
End Sub
```

Next, add code to the command button's click event that tests whether an item has been selected and then calls the decision structure subroutine, here named DoStuff, with the proper parameter:

```
Private Sub cmdPass_Click()
    Dim Choice As String
    If lstSelect.ListIndex = -1 Then
        'Check to see that something is selected
        MsgBox "Nothing is Selected!"
    Else
        Choice = lstSelect.List(lstSelect.ListIndex)
            'Gets the selected string
        DoStuff Left(UCase(Choice), 1)
        'Calls the decision structure with the first
        'letter of the string as a parameter.

        'This makes the assumption that each string
        'is first-letter unique.

        'The UCase call is not really needed since each
        'string was added to the list with an uppercase
        'first letter anyhow, but why not build in redundant
        'safety?
    End If
End Sub
```

Returning the String Value of a Selected Item

In the cmdPass procedure just listed, the statement

```
Choice = lstSelect.List(lstSelect.ListIndex)
```

returns the string value of the selected item in lstSelect. This is the general way to retrieve the contents of the current selection in a list or combo box, with lstSelect replaced with the object name of the specific control:

```
ListorComboObject.List(ListorComboObject.ListIndex)
```

The final step is to add the DoStuff code, where the flow control decisions are actually made. Obviously, in a real application you'd probably branch to other (appropriately named) routines within the Select...Case statement rather than merely sending up a MsgBox (see Figure 4-8).

```
Private Sub DoStuff(Which As String)
    Select Case Which
        Case "W"
            MsgBox "You selected waffles today!"
        Case "F"
            MsgBox "You selected French toast today!"
        Case "P"
```

```
            MsgBox "You selected pigs today!"
        Case "G"
            MsgBox "Granola is good for you!"
        Case "B"
            MsgBox "Which kind of berry will you have today, Sir?"
        Case Else
            MsgBox "Internal Error in DoStuff; call the developer!"
    End Select
End Sub
```

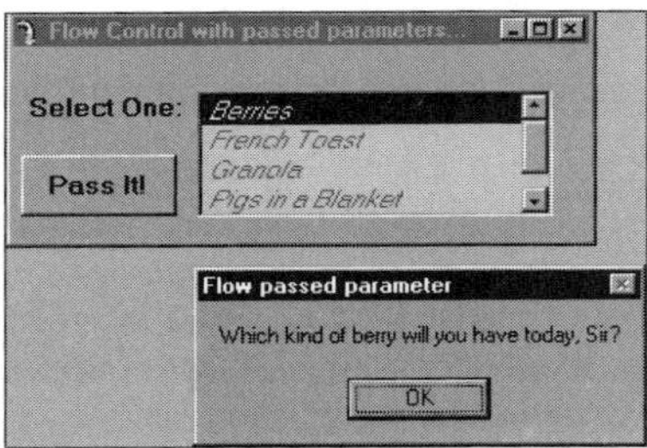

Figure 4-8: This user is having berries for breakfast today.

Watch Those "Dog Breath" Messages

In the DoStuff procedure, there is really no reason why the Case Else contingency should ever be executed. No one will ever see the "Internal Error" message box because we know the items added to the list box, and we know that we have enumerated all the possible choices before the end of the Select...Case statement.

Even so, it's good programming practice to add an error message, just in case something weird (along the lines of a typographic error in code entry) has occurred. If you do this, debugging the problem will be a snap should the message ever appear. Error handling in VB is discussed in detail in Chapter 15, "Handling Errors."

I think of the kind of ad hoc contingency error message that I added to the DoStuff procedure as a "Dog Breath" message. Supposedly, a developer got a call from a client who had received the error message, "Mis-allocated pointer error, Dog Breath!" Fortunately, as the story goes, the client had a good sense of humor. I suppose that the moral of the "Dog Breath" error message story is that you should make sure that all diagnostic error messages are phrased in a way that you could live with if a client saw one.

One nice thing about organizing a decision structure with a passed parameter is that it becomes extremely easy to add equivalent functionality to other event-handlers in a program (you just call DoStuff again). For example, the user should be able to make that crucial breakfast decision by double-clicking the lstSelect list box when an item is selected without having to click the cmdPass button. Just add the code that calls DoStuff to lstSelect's DblClick event-handler.

```
Private Sub lstSelect_DblClick()
   Dim Choice As String
   If lstSelect.ListIndex = -1 Then
      'Check to see that something is selected
      MsgBox "Nothing is Selected!"
   Else
      Choice = lstSelect.List(lstSelect.ListIndex)
      'Gets the selected string
      DoStuff Left(UCase(Choice), 1)
   End If
End Sub
```

Another way to do the same thing that uses less code — and may therefore be preferred — is to add a call to one event-handling procedure from within another. This is an easy way to include the functionality of the second event-handler within the first. Suppose you want the form's click event to behave like cmdPass's click handler (and call the DoStuff decision structure). You can simply add a call to the cmdPass click event from Form1's click event:

```
Private Sub Form_Click()
   cmdPass_Click
End Sub
```

Loop Structures

Structures that loop are designed to facilitate execution of one or more code statements repeatedly. You use Do loops most often when you don't know precisely how many times the controlled statements should execute, but do know the exit condition. You use For loops, on other hand, when you know precisely how many times a block of executable code should execute. In general, loop structures can be nested within each other to as many levels as you'd like. However, in the interest of creating readable code, I'd suggest you not nest more than two levels. If logical flow requires deeper levels, use subroutine calls (with your subroutines named intuitively), and place the deeper level structures with the subroutines.

I'll give an overview of the concepts involved in loop structures here, but for the precise syntax you should look in on-line help or the Microsoft Visual Basic 5.0 *Programmer's Guide*. Some issues of sophisticated loop optimization are covered in Part III of *Visual Basic 5 SECRETS*.

Do Loops

Visual Basic Do loops come in several varieties. You can loop Until a condition is True or While a condition is True. You can place the test expression in a Do Until or a Do While loop either at the top or bottom of the decision structure. When the test expression is placed at the top of the structure, it is evaluated before the statements in the structure are executed for the first time. This means that the statements might not get executed even once. On the other hand, when the conditional test is placed at the end of the structure, you are guaranteed at least one execution pass through the structure's statements.

Actually, there is no real need for VB to have both kinds of Do structures because, logically, Do Until is equivalent to Do While Not. Then again, Visual Basic lets you do it your way!

You can exit a Do structure from within the execution code at any point by using an Exit Do statement, which causes flow to jump to the first executable statement following the structure. Although there are occasionally valid reasons for using an immediate exit from a loop, better structured programming practice is to establish your test expressions so that this is not necessary.

For Loops

The For...Next loop structure includes a built-in counter variable. Using this structure, you can control exactly how many times the structure's statements are executed. VB's For statement is very flexible, allowing you to set the beginning counter value, its final value, and its increment using any (positive or negative) numeric value. You specify the increment using the Step keyword; if you leave it off, the increment defaults to 1.

As with Do, Exit For causes an immediate execution jump outside the control structure.

A variation on the For loop is the For Each...Next loop, which repeats execution statements for each element in a collection of objects or in an array.

Modules, Subroutines, and Functions

VB project source code is divided into modules, which are themselves comprised of subroutines. Another word for subroutine is *procedure*. One important kind of procedure is the *function*, which returns a value.

Modules

Visual Basic source code projects are made up of modules, which come in three flavors: form modules, standard modules, and class modules.

Form Modules

Form modules have an ***.Frm*** filename extension and contain information about forms that are visible to users at runtime. They can contain:

- Graphical descriptions of form properties and of form controls and their properties
- Form-level declarations
- General procedures
- Event-handling procedures

For more information about the actual contents of an ***.Frm*** file, see Chapter 19, "Runtime Display Secrets."

Form modules come in two varieties, depending on the user interface characteristics of the form: the *single document interface form* (SDI) and the *multiple document interface form* (MDI). When the term "form" is used by itself, it generally refers to SDI forms. (Note also that an MDI application can have only one MDI form.) MDI applications are discussed in Part IV of this book, "Display Secrets."

To add a new form module to a project, choose Form or MDI Form from the Insert menu.

Standard Modules

Standard modules have a ***.Bas*** filename extension. ***.Bas*** files contain libraries of source code. They can include global or module-level declarations, and global procedures. To add a ***.Bas*** module, choose Add Module from the Project menu.

Class Modules

You use class modules, which have a ***.Cls*** filename extension, to create new objects. Class modules are standard modules that can contain properties, methods and — with Version 5 of Visual Basic — events. You can use the New keyword to create a new instance of an object based on a class module (and a pointer to the instance). The section "Speaking the Language of Objects" later in this chapter covers some of the nuts and bolts of syntax related to classes; Chapter 14, "Visual Basic and OOP" covers object-oriented programming and creating class modules in detail.

To add a class module to a project, choose Add Class Module from the Project menu.

Long Filenames in VB5 Projects under 32-bit Windows

In 32-bit versions of Windows (for example, 95 and NT), you can use long filenames that include embedded spaces for your project and module names. This should mean an end to those "I have no idea what this module does" blues brought on by cryptic filenames (see Figure 4-9).

Although it's a good thing to be able to name modules in a way that makes clear what they contain, there are still some reasons for adhering to the bad old DOS 8 + 3 file naming system. For instance, the ISO9660 CD-ROM standard, which is the current state of the art, does not support long filenames.

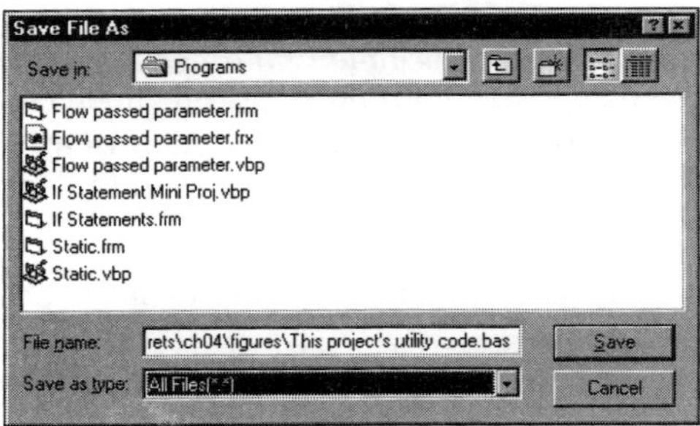

Figure 4-9: In Visual Basic 5, you can use long filenames for your modules.

Procedures

As you can see from the description of each kind of module, in general, the code portions of the three kinds of source modules are made up of declarations, which I discussed earlier in this chapter, and procedures. There are three kinds of procedures: Sub, Function, and Property:

- *Sub* procedures are *subroutines*. The code within a Sub is intended for execution when the Sub is called. Sub procedures do not have a return value.

  Sub procedures can optionally be declared using the Private/Public keywords. (Leaving the keyword off is equivalent to using Public.) Private means that the Sub procedure is only visible in its own module; Public means that it is visible globally in a project.

  Optional use of the Static keyword means that the Sub procedure's local variables are preserved between calls to the procedure.

- *Event* procedures are a specific kind of Sub procedure. They are used to store an event-handling procedure (see Chapter 3, "Event-Driven Programming"). Event procedures are always Sub procedures declared Private, and with an underscore separating an object and its event, for example:

  ```
  Private Sub Form1_Click ()
  ```

- *Function* procedures are like Sub procedures, except that they return a value. (Note that VB supplies many system functions for your use; you don't have to write them, you can just call, use, and enjoy them. Some of these premade functions are discussed later in this chapter.)

  By the way, as a matter of terminology, the words "procedure" and "routine" are generally used to refer to either subroutines or functions. You should think of a function simply as a kind of procedure, one that returns a value.

- *Property* procedures are used to create and manipulate form and other module properties. They are discussed in Chapter 14 and elsewhere along the way.

To add a procedure — of any of the three kinds — open the module you want to place the procedure in using the View Code button in the Project Explorer. (Chapter 3 described some other ways to open a module's code in the Code window.)

With the Code window activated, choose Add Procedure from the Tools menu. The Add Procedure dialog appears, and lets you specify the name and characteristics of the procedure you want (see Figure 4-10).

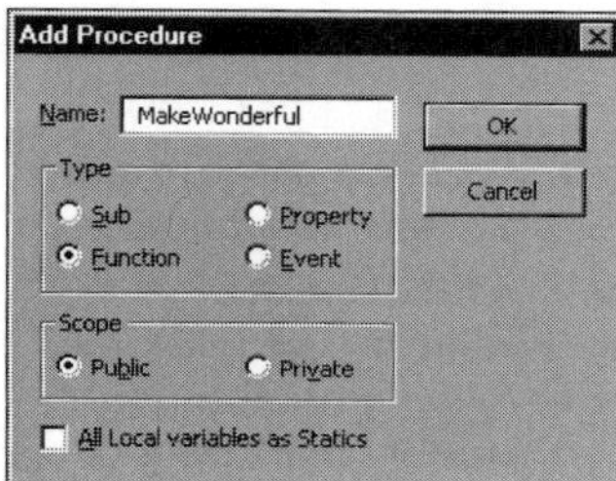

Figure 4-10: You can use the Add Procedure dialog to create a wonderful public function!

Here is the template code that the selections made in Figure 4-10 create:

```
Public Function MakeWonderful()

End Function
```

You can now go ahead and enter an argument list for the function you just created by typing it between the parentheses. (At this point you can also give your new function an explicit type.)

```
Public Function MakeWonderful(Orpheus As String, _
   Eurydice As Variant) As Integer

End Function
```

By the way, the argument list for a procedure or function is sometimes referred to as the *formal* parameters, distinguishing this list from the one provided when the procedure is called, which includes the *actual* parameters.

Passing Arguments

Values that are passed to procedures are known as *arguments* or *parameters*. Arguments can be passed *by value* or *by reference*.

When arguments are passed by value, only a copy of the passed variable is sent to the procedure. In this case, any changes made to the variable in the called procedure are not also made to the original. You use the ByVal keyword to specify that a parameter is passed by value.

When arguments are passed by reference, a pointer to the memory address of the variable is passed to the called procedure. In this case, changes made in the called procedure to the value of the passed parameter will change the value of the variable in the calling procedure as well. In VB, arguments are passed by reference by default if you don't specify a passing mode; you can also use the ByRef keyword to explicitly designate by reference arguments.

By the way, a procedure's formal parameter list could perfectly well include a mix of by reference and by value parameters. In other words, a routine's parameters don't all have to be the same in this respect. (The phrase "formal parameter list" means the list of parameters declared in a procedure heading, as opposed to the list of actual variables passed in the procedure call.)

To demonstrate the difference between passing by reference and by value, I am going to create two simple procedures — one statement that adds 42 to the passed argument — that differ in only one respect: DemoRef accepts its argument by reference, and DemoVal accepts it by value. DemoRef and DemoVal will be called with variables that have been set identically using an assignment statement before calling the routines. Following program return from DemoRef and DemoVal, the arguments will be displayed, demonstrating how DemoRef added 42 to the variable in the calling procedure (see Figure 4-11) and DemoVal did not.

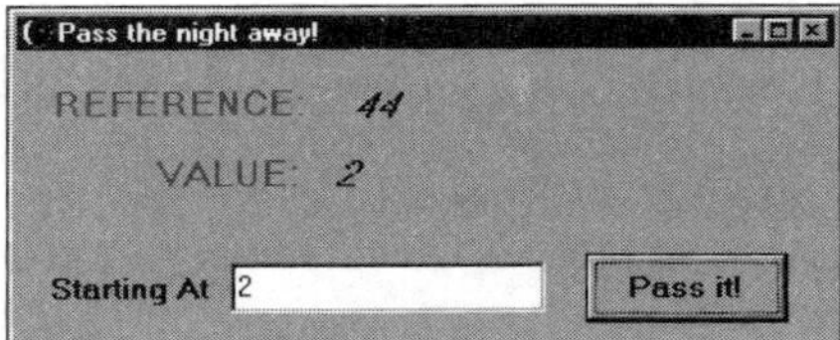

Figure 4-11: Passing parameters by reference or by value can lead to different results.

Use of Variant Variables Causes Proper Type Conversions

In this example, using variables declared as variant causes the correct conversions to take place automatically from the string content of the txtStart text box to a numerical value and back to a string label caption. Had I typed the variables as, for example, integer, I would have had to use the Val function, which converts strings to numbers, to get the starting input, and then the Str function, which converts numbers to strings, to display the result.

To set up the project, add two labels, lblRef and lblValue, to its form to display the demonstration results. Next, add a text box, txtStart, in which the user can enter a starting value for the subroutine call, and a command button, cmdPass, to start the demonstration. Note that I have not bothered with *input validation*. There is no check that the user has actually entered a number in txtStart. In a real-life program, you'd want to write input validation code to make sure that users could not input illegal values.

Here are the DemoRef and DemoVal subs:

```
Private Sub DemoRef(Argument) 'Passed by reference
   Argument = Argument + 42
End Sub

Private Sub DemoVal(ByVal Argument) 'Passed by value
   Argument = Argument + 42
End Sub
```

Here is the cmdPass_click code that runs the demo:

```
Private Sub cmdPass_Click()
   Dim ArguRef, ArguVal
   ArguRef = txtStart
   ArguVal = ArguRef 'Both are the same
   DemoRef ArguRef
   DemoVal ArguVal
   'Now they are not, although the DemoRef
   'and DemoVal routines are identical except
   'for parameter mode!
   lblRef = ArguRef
   lblValue = ArguVal
End Sub
```

I think, after this, it's pretty hard not be clear about the difference between passing by reference and value!

Here are some other important parameter passing techniques:

- Using optional arguments. If you use the Optional keyword in a parameter list, subsequent variant formal parameters don't have to be passed, but can be if you wish.
- Using an indefinite number of arguments. The ParamArray keyword in a formal parameter list allows you to specify that the procedure will accept an indefinite number of arguments.
- You can use a colon equal sign equivalence operator (:=) to pass and accept parameters by the formal name of the parameter, regardless of its order in the parameter list.

Programmer-Defined Structures

Programmer-defined structures, also called *user-defined types*, let you create your own data types made up of a combination of existing variable types. User-defined types can greatly clarify program logic. It is hard to imagine a well-written program of any complexity that does not make at least some use of them.

A user-defined type is defined in a module's Declaration section using the Public or Private keyword, followed by the keyword Type, followed by the user-defined structure's name, followed by a list, one per line, of the variables that make up the type, and concluding with the End Type keywords. To use a variable based on a user-defined type, you must take one more step: declaring the variable, in the normal fashion, as being based on the type.

Here is a very simple example of a user-defined type and some variable declarations based on it:

```
Option Explicit

'Declarations section of Form1
Private Type Employee
   FullName As String
   SSN As Long
   Rating As Integer
   DOB As Date
End Type
Private JacksonW, HopperB, EggertM As Employee
```

Storing and retrieving values from the elements of a user-defined structure is done with the dot operator (.), much as an object's properties are loaded and accessed. For example:

```
Dim HopperB As Employee
HopperB.Rating = 99
If HopperB.Rating > 80 Then MsgBox "Very Good!"
```

Everything but the Kitchen Sink...

All kinds of things can go in a user-defined type, including variant variables, arrays, and objects. Such inclusion can create very flexible and powerful structures. For example, one element could be an instance of a form:

```
Private Type RolePlay
   UserInput As Form
   dbUserList As Database
End Type
```

However, there are resource consumption trade-offs involved, particularly when defining a variant array as part of a structure. I'll discuss these issues, and related programming techniques, as I go along.

Arrays

As you probably know, an *array* refers to a series of variables with the same name that use an index or indices. Arrays can be single-dimensional or multidimensional. They can, themselves, be populated with arrays, if they are of type variant. They can include, and be included in, user-defined structures.

Later in *Visual Basic 5 SECRETS*, you'll learn how to work with arrays of controls and arrays of forms, as well as collections of objects. (Actually — and I'm going to continue to belabor this point until I'm certain it has really sunk in — object variables are *really* pointers to objects.)

The fundamental difference between arrays and collections is that an array's index number can be used to reference specific elements of the array.

If you're interested in more information on working with arrays and collections of objects, turn to Chapters 13 and 14.

The syntax of VB array declaration and manipulation is both flexible and easily understood. I'd suggest you have a look at the section on arrays in the Visual Basic *Programmer's Guide*. I'll also be covering some of the finer points of array handling and performance optimization later, particularly in Part III.

There is one aspect of array-handling in VB that is so fantastic — and fantastically easy to use, even for the fantastically wonderful development platform that Visual Basic is — that it's worth emphasizing.

Preserving the Contents of Dynamic Arrays

If you use ReDim to resize an array at runtime, all current values are cleared from the array. If you want to change the size of an array while keeping the current element value, you must use the Preserve keyword in the ReDim statement. For example:

```
Dim TheArray() As Integer    ' Declare dynamic array
Redim TheArray(5)            ' Allocate 5 elements.
For I = 1 To 5               ' Loop 5 times.
   TheArray(I) = I           ' Initialize array.
Next I

Redim TheArray(10)           ' Resize to 10 elements, erasing values
                             ' for all elements
For I = 1 To 10              ' Loop 10 times
   TheArray(I) = I           ' Initialize array
Next I

Redim Preserve TheArray(15)  ' Resize to 15 elements, preserving
                             ' the values of existing elements
```

VB lets you create arrays that are *dynamic* at runtime, meaning that you can change the size of your arrays — possibly depending on user input — as your program executes. Wow! You do this by originally declaring the array with an empty dimension list and using the ReDim keyword when you first, or subsequently, want to allocate the actual number of elements.

Speaking the Language of Objects

Objects, objects, objects! Everything — almost — is an object.

With Version 5, Visual Basic has, conceptually, become an environment that revolves around objects. You use objects to extend the power of the VB environment and structure your applications; in addition, you can use VB to create objects that others can pluck from the broad ocean of OLE-based ActiveX components and use in their own applications or on the Web.

All but the very simplest and least sophisticated applications will involve some interaction with objects. As a VB programmer, you can think of your interactions with objects as falling into the following general categories:

- Using ActiveX controls in your applications
- Using ActiveX components — OLE server objects — in your applications
- Internally creating and using objects — such as forms and objects based on classes
- Creating ActiveX components — OLE server applications — for your use — or for others to use
- Creating ActiveX controls and documents for your own use, for others to use as components, or for use on the Web

This section will provide information on the basic syntax for working with ActiveX controls, ActiveX components, OLE servers, and object libraries. For further information, you should have a look at Chapter 14, "Visual Basic and OOP," and Chapter 23, "Creating ActiveX Applications." You'll also find information on creating a very special kind of ActiveX component, one that manipulates instances of the Visual Basic environment itself, in Chapter 29, "Creating a VB Add-In."

Rolling out your own ActiveX controls is covered in detail in Part VI, "Creating ActiveX Controls." You'll find information on ActiveX documents in Chapter 28, "Creating Internet Applications in VB."

Using ActiveX Controls

To use an ActiveX control, add the control to your Toolbox using the Components dialog (accessed through the Project menu), as shown in Figure 4-12. Once you've added a control to your Toolbox, you can double-click the control to add an instance of it to a form. When the control instance has been added to the form, you can reference its properties and methods in code.

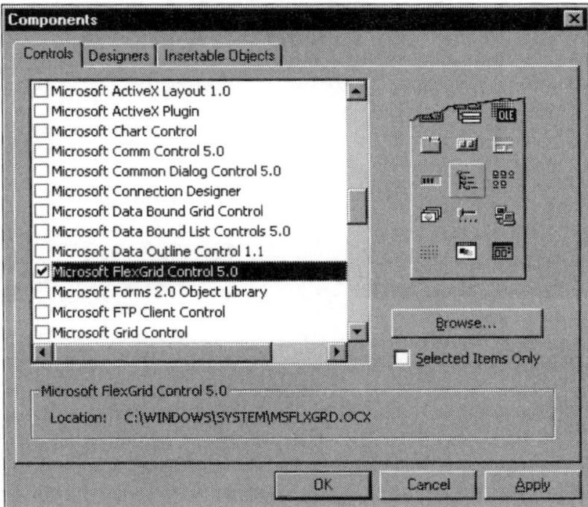

Figure 4-12: You use the Controls tab of the Components dialog to add ActiveX controls to your project.

The Object Browser is an excellent tool for finding available properties and methods of a control instance you have inserted.

Property assignments can be made using the dot operator. For example, if myTool1 is the name of a control with a caption property:

```
Dim OldCaption as String
OldCaption = Form1.myTool1.caption
Form1.myTool1.caption = "Frodo"
```

Note that within a given module — in the example, it would be Form1 — you don't really need to use the module name to invoke a control property:

```
myTool1.caption = "Frodo"
```

would work just as well, as long as you enter the code within the module that is the container for the control.

You can use the With...End With statement to write cleaner code involving objects through an extended implicit reference to the object. For example, if you have a command button named cmdDemo on a form, placing the following code in the Form load event changes the properties of the button by using an implicit reference so that

```
cmdDemo.caption
```

and so on doesn't have to be explicitly stated each time. This becomes even more helpful when you have nested objects within objects that you are manipulating. Here's the example code (with results shown in Figure 4-13):

```
Private Sub Form_Load()
   With cmdDemo
      .Caption = "Miss Piggy"
      .Font.Size = 12
```

```
      .Height = 620
      .Width = 1400
      .Default = True
   End With
End Sub
```

Figure 4-13: You can use With... End With to simplify code that references objects.

Methods are internally implemented within ActiveX controls as functions. They are called in the same way: as functions with arguments. For example, the control myTool might have a method DoSomething with one argument, a string. If an instance of myTool were placed on Form1, you would invoke the method as follows:

```
Form1.myTool1.DoSomething ("Take this string!")
```

ActiveX controls added to a container — such as a form — trigger events. (These events are not to be confused with events *received* by a control.) You respond to control events in the same way you respond to form events: by placing code that handles the event in the framework created for you by Visual Basic.

Using ActiveX Components

Many ActiveX components — OLE server applications — provide objects that you can insert into an OLE container. You use the Insertable Objects tab of the Components dialog — which you access via the Project menu — for this purpose, as shown in Figure 4-14. As an example, you could add a Word document.

When you double-click the icon for the insertable object in your Toolbox and add it to a container, normally the toolbars for the OLE server are displayed (in the example, Microsoft Word).

You can access properties, events, and methods of the inserted OLE object just as you would those of an ActiveX control. For example, you could display a message to the user when she finished editing an inserted Word document, by placing code in the object's LostFocus event (which is fired when an object loses "focus"):

```
Private Sub Document1_LostFocus()
   MsgBox "Are you finished for real?"
End Sub
```

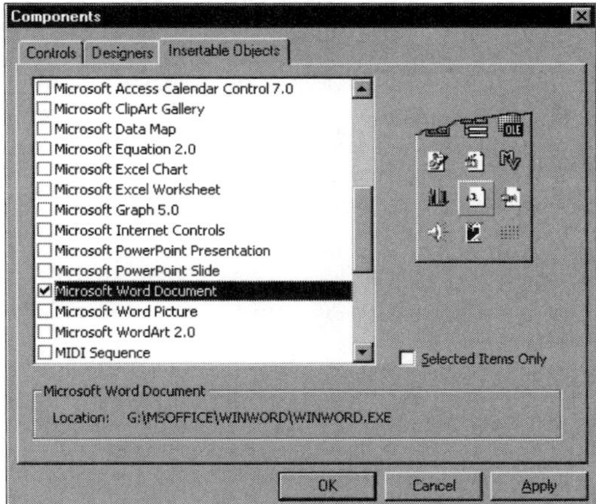

Figure 4-14: You can add OLE insertable objects to your Toolbox.

In addition to OLE objects that provide objects with visible interfaces for you to add visually to containers, you can create an instance of any OLE object — and use it in your code. You can create an instance of an OLE object (also known as an ActiveX object) using the CreateObject function. For example:

```
Dim ExcelSheet As Object
Set ExcelSheet = CreateObject("Excel.Sheet")
```

The variable ExcelSheet now holds an instance of an Excel.Sheet object. (This is known as *late binding*, because the VB compiler does not know what kind of object will go in the object variable until it is actually assigned.)

You can manipulate the exposed properties and methods — also called *members* — of this object in code as you'd like.

It's important to ultimately free up the memory reserved for objects you create. This happens automatically when the variable storing the reference to the object goes out of scope — for example, a procedure-level variable is no longer within scope when execution leaves the procedure. You can also do it explicitly, using the Nothing keyword:

```
Set ExcelSheet = Nothing
```

Using the References dialog (found on the Project menu) you can add a reference to an object library (see Figure 4-15).

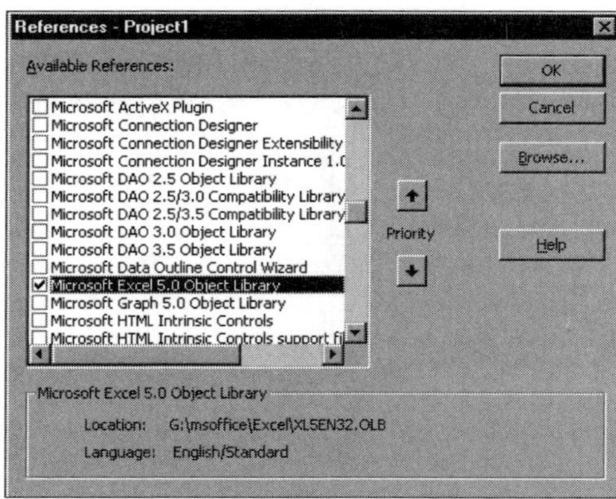

Figure 4-15: You can use the References dialog to add a reference to an object library to your project.

Without further ado, you can use objects that are part of the referenced library in your code:

```
Dim X As Excel.Sheet
```

Quickly Finding Information in the Documentation

There are, of course, a great many more Visual Basic 5 language features and capabilities than could possibly be included in this chapter. Particularly important among these are some broad categories of functions that are built in to VB:

- String manipulation functions. This chapter demonstrated how to use three string manipulation functions: Left, Len and UCase.
- Data-type conversion functions. In this chapter, I've briefly discussed two of the data-type conversion functions: Chr and Val.
- File manipulation functions. File manipulation functions are used to obtain and change information about, open, retrieve from, manipulate in, store to, and close files. As such, they are a vital part of your tool set. I'll be showing you effective ways to use these functions in examples as I go along.

If you don't find the information you need here, and you don't find it in your printed Visual Basic documentation, the next step is to use on-line help. (Actually, depending on your predilections, this step might come first.)

I have two suggestions about using the help system. The first is that there are a number of extensive Visual Basic on-line help topics that themselves consist of well-organized hypertext links to all possible subtopics and related topics. These hypertext topics are, thus, excellent starting places for carrying out a quick search if you have a ballpark starting area.

In the context of the Visual Basic programming languages, its statements, and what it can do, you should investigate the following hypertext topics:

- Statement Summary
- Programming Language Summary
- Keywords By Task

My second suggestion, if you haven't already done this, is to join the Microsoft Development Network (MSDN) in order to obtain the MSDN Development Library CD, which is Microsoft's comprehensive reference on programming for Windows (including Windows 95). MSDN is truly a good investment; the amount of information on the Development CD is incredible, and it is quite well organized. The CD appears quarterly, so that it stays reasonably up to date. It includes

- The complete printed Visual Basic documentation in electronic form
- An extensive collection of information about Visual Basic, including tips and tricks, white papers, sample code, journal articles, conference proceeding, Microsoft technical implementations, and much more
- Tools, utilities, and descriptions of important techniques
- Coverage of many other topics important to the VB developer, including Web development, Windows 95, 32-bit programming, database and client/server development, and much, much more
- A sophisticated search and query engine for quickly finding exactly what you need

MSDN can be reached at 800-759-5474. (And, no, they don't pay me a commission. *Tant pis.*)

Calling External Procedures

One of the most important ways to start extending the power of VB beyond its own impressive core facilities is through calling procedures (and functions) located in external compiled libraries. Generally, these are *dynamic link libraries*, referred to as DLLs, but a compiled library need not have any particular filename extension. (For example, a dynamic link library could be saved with an ***.Exe*** extension.)

It's very easy to use external procedures. There are two steps involved:

1. Use the Declare statement (in a module's General Declarations section) to identify the external library, procedure, procedure parameters, and scope of the references to the external procedure. External Subs or functions that are declared using the Private keyword are available within the module of declaration; those declared with Public are available to an entire project.

2. Using properly typed parameters, call the procedure normally from within your code at any place that the Declare's scope extends to. Using the external procedure — once it has been declared — is exactly the same as using a procedure or function that you have written in Visual Basic.

Although the actual syntax of the external declaration is not difficult, it is a bit complex because of all the different possibilities involved. I'll be showing you many, *many* examples of external declarations. For now, your best bet for a complete understanding of the syntax is to look it up in VB's on-line help under "Declare Statement."

Some other issues may come up at times when the language of the external procedure defines variables in a different way than Visual Basic. For instance, strings are represented internally in C in a different way than in VB. This means that string values returned from an external C function or procedure must be converted into a format that will be correctly recognized by VB. This issue is particularly important, because Windows is largely written in C. Therefore, the Windows *Application Programming Interface* (API) — the extensive set of procedures and functions designed to give programmers consistent access to internal Windows functionality — uses C variable typing. I'll be covering this and related issues in greater detail in Chapter 11, "The Win32 Software Development Kit (SDK), the Win32 API, and the Windows Message System." Here's an example of an external function declaration that would be placed in the General Declarations section of Form1:

```
Option Explicit

Private Declare Function Hobbit Lib "Mydll" _
   Alias "#1" (Which As Integer) As String
```

This would indicate that the function named Hobbit has been declared so that it can only be used within the Form1 module. The library that contains the Hobbit function is named ***Mydll.Dll*** (if the filename extension were other than ***.Dll***, it would have to be included). The Hobbit function has been supplied by ***Mydll*** with an ordinal index number, also known as an *entry point*, as specified in the Alias clause of the Declare statement. The Hobbit function accepts an integer value by reference and returns a string.

You should also realize that an external library cannot be loaded unless it is found. The best thing to do is usually to place DLLs in the execution directory. Alternatively, you can place them in the ***Windows\System*** directory, in any directory referenced by the Path variable, or with an explicit path statement:

```
Private Declare Function Hobbit Lib _
   "C:\VbSecrets\Programs\Mydll.Dll"
```

An example in Chapter 16, "Optimizing Secrets," explains how to set up a VB project to search for a file — such as a DLL — that is missing from its proper place. In the example project, I'll show you how, if the software cannot find the right file, you can give the user the chance to find it and try the project again.

Here's how the Hobbit function might be called from within Form1's click event-handler:

```
Private Sub Form_Click()
   MsgBox Hobbit(1)
End Sub
```

When the event is fired, the MsgBox function should display whatever the string return value of Hobbit is when passed the parameter 1.

Calling the Windows API

Calling one of the procedures or functions that is part of the Windows API involves exactly the same steps as calling any other external procedures. First, you must formally declare the external procedure at the module level. Next, you use the procedure with a proper argument list. Fortunately, VB5 comes with a tool that makes adding API declares a complete snap.

The procedures and functions that make up the core Windows API are located in three library files, which happen to have ***.Exe*** extensions. Table 4-3 lists the 32-bit Windows API files, along with the corresponding 16-bit Windows 3.*x* API library names for (historical) reference.

Table 4-3 32-Bit and 16-Bit API Library Files

Windows 95 and NT	*Windows 3.x*
User32.Exe	*User.Exe*
Gdi32.Exe	*Gdi.Exe*
Krnl32.Exe	*Krnl386.Exe*

To make it easier to add API declarations, Microsoft has included an application with VB5, the API Text Viewer. To open the API Text Viewer, use the Windows Start menu to locate the Visual Basic 5 program menu. You'll find the Viewer in the next nested menu level.

Visual Basic ships with an add-in that allows you to access the API Text Viewer from within the VB environment. For more information, see Chapter 29, "Creating a VB Add-In."

The first time you open the API Text Viewer, you must load it with an API data file. You have a choice here — namely, you can set the API Viewer to work with a straight text file or with an Access ***.Mdb*** database file. The trade-off is initial configuration time, because the database option can take quite a while to set itself up the first time. (If you are working on a system that is less powerful than a Pentium with 8 megabytes of RAM, you may wish to pass on the database option. I have actually heard developers with rings under their eyes wandering the halls muttering things under their breath like, "all night to configure the API database....") Of course, for subsequent uses, the database option is quite a bit faster.

Maintaining One Body of Source Code for Use with Windows 3.*x*, Windows 95, and Windows NT

You probably know that the declarations are different for the 16-bit Windows 3.1 API and the 32-bit Windows API. The 32-bit Windows API works pretty much the same way under NT and 95 — but there are some differences.

Of course, 16-bit programs that use the older API calls will still run under Windows 95. (Indeed, this was one of Microsoft's primary objectives when designing Windows 95.) But they will be using the 16-bit and not the 32-bit libraries. 16-bit programming is no longer supported in Visual Basic 5.

However, it's possible using VB5 to target the Win32s API, a subset (hence the "s") of the Win32 API. The Win32s APIs run on top of Windows 3.*x* enhanced mode. With Win32s you can take an executable file built for 32-bit Windows and run it under Windows 3.1. Generally, only modest source-code tweaking is required.

If you wish to have one source program that will run properly in the different operating systems — for example, 32-bit Windows 95, 32-bit Windows NT, and the Win32s API for 16-bit Windows — you must include multiple versions of the API declares (and calls) that you will need. Your program will start by checking what operating system it is running under. *Conditional compilation* will be used to include the correct API versions depending on the results of the test. This topic will be covered in Chapter 16.

Once the application has been set up, you can select from Windows Constants, Declares, or Types. The process is to add items you'll want to the Selected Items window and then use the Copy button to place them in the Windows Clipboard. In Figure 4-16, the Declarations for BitBlt, CascadeWindows, and ConnectToPrinterDlg APIs have been selected.

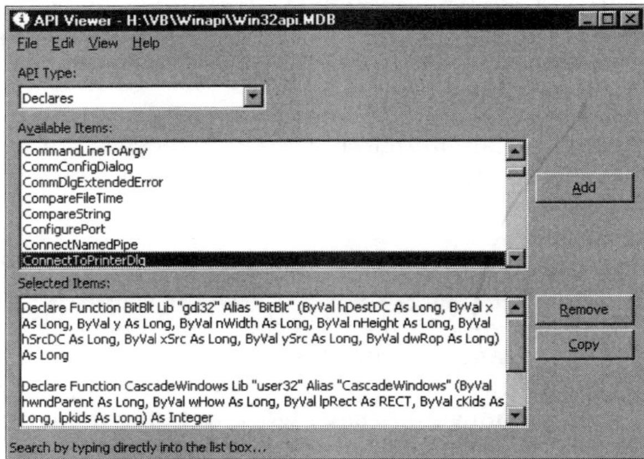

Figure 4-16: You can use the API Text Viewer to copy API declarations, types, and constants.

If you click the Copy button, the declarations for these procedures are copied to the Clipboard. The next step is go to the Declarations section of a module in your VB project and paste — using the Paste option on the Edit menu, or CUA (Common User Access) interface keystrokes.

Here are the resulting declarations, ready to use, as they appear after pasting (I've added line continuation characters and split the lines):

```
Option Explicit

Declare Function BitBlt Lib "gdi32" _
   (ByVal hDestDC As Long, ByVal x As Long, _
   ByVal y As Long, ByVal nWidth As Long, _
   ByVal nHeight As Long, ByVal hSrcDC As Long, _
   ByVal xSrc As Long, ByVal ySrc As Long, _
   ByVal dwRop As Long) As Long
Declare Function CascadeWindows Lib "user32" _
   (ByVal hwndParent As Long, ByVal wHow As Long, _
   ByVal lpRect As RECT, ByVal cKids As Long, _
   lpkids As Long) As Integer
Declare Function ConnectToPrinterDlg Lib "winspool.drv" _
   (ByVal hwnd As Long, ByVal flags As Long) As Long
```

If you tried to run a project into which you'd pasted these particular declarations, you'd get a syntax error based on an undefined type: "User-defined type not recognized." It turns out that RECT is Windows-defined type, specifying a rectangle, that must be defined if you plan to use procedures that use the type.

You could look up the right type definition, but it is easier to go back to the API Text Viewer. This time, select Types in the API Type drop-down list box. Next, scroll down until you locate RECT. Add it to the Selected Items list, copy it, and paste the definition into your project:

```
Type RECT
   Left As Long
   Top As Long
   Right As Long
   Bottom As Long
End Type
```

That's really all there is to adding API declares using the Text API Viewer. (Again, there is nothing to stop you — except the waste of time — from looking up the proper syntax for the declares and entering them by hand in your VB project.)

One final way to simplify calling APIs in your projects is to create an out-of-process OLE server in Visual Basic that encapsulates Windows API calls, thus simplifying programs that use the API. There's nothing much to this process once the OLE fundamentals have been explained. There is a demonstration in Chapter 10, "Programming the Registry in VB."

Summary

Although it's not a formal language definition, this chapter has covered the Visual Basic language from the point of view of the experienced programmer. I've assumed that the underlying concepts are familiar and have only gone over them briefly. The emphasis has been the wonderful, intuitive, and powerful Visual Basic 5 language. I've particularly tried to explain language elements you'll need to know to create professional programs.

Along the way, I've illustrated language concepts with code samples you can use directly in your projects. In this chapter, I've demonstrated how to

- Break a single message box string into multiple lines
- Add module and routine comment headers, and save them for reuse
- Find the string value of the selected item in a list box control
- Branch in a modular fashion depending on the item selected in a list box
- Use the default properties of controls
- Understand the difference between passing parameters by reference and by value
- Use the syntax necessary for working with objects
- Declare and call a procedure located in an external function
- Declare and call the Windows API

Chapter 5

What's New in Visual Basic 5

Version 5 of Visual Basic is the VB4 wish list come true. The developers at Microsoft worked hard and waved their 32-bit wands. Just about everything you could desire is included.

VB5 is the most exciting upgrade ever of the world's most popular programming environment. The most significant new features include the ability to create native code executables, to fire custom events, to create ActiveX controls, and to create applications that support OLE compound storage (ActiveX document projects). Hang on while you explore these and other enhancements. It's going to be a wild ride! Even the development environment has changed radically.

This chapter is intended to give you a taste of many of the exciting new features of Visual Basic 5. The chapter provides merely an overview; however,

it also tells you where you can turn in *Visual Basic 5 SECRETS* for more detailed information on the topics covered.

Visual Basic has changed in many ways from Version 4 to Version 5, and its capabilities have been greatly expanded. If it ever was, this programming environment is not now a toy. There are far more new features to the language and environment than can be covered in this brief summary. But here are some of my favorites

- Converting VB Applications from Version 4 to Version 5
- Native code compilation
- Changes to the IDE
- Creating ActiveX controls
- Firing events
- ActiveX document applications
- Add-ins

Porting Applications from Version 4 to Version 5

You should find the process of moving applications from Version 4 to Version 5 quite easy.

Bear in mind that it's smart not to overwrite source code in the old format. You should keep legacy projects intact, and the original source code separate, at least until you know the new versions work properly.

The easiest way to proceed is to simply open legacy projects in VB5. If you do this, you'll get a warning dialog like the one shown in Figure 5-1.

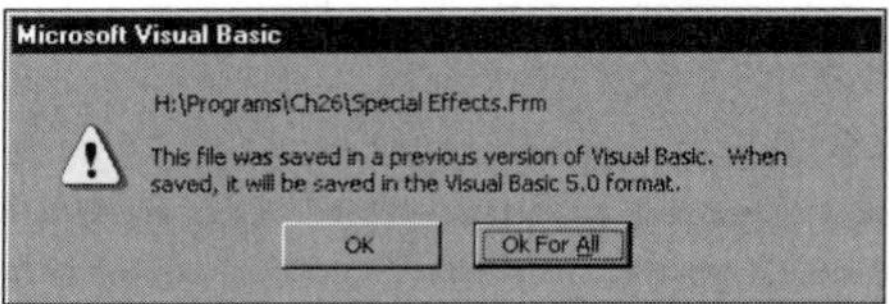

Figure 5-1: If you open legacy projects in VB5, Visual Basic will convert them for you automatically.

Click OK For All to convert all the modules in the old project.

Be careful not save the converted project yet. If you do, your legacy code will be overwritten. Instead, open the Project Explorer (found on the View menu). For each module, use the Save As item on the context menu, as shown in Figure 5-2, to save a new copy of the file without overwriting the old one. (Be sure to save the new file with a new name and/or in a new location.)

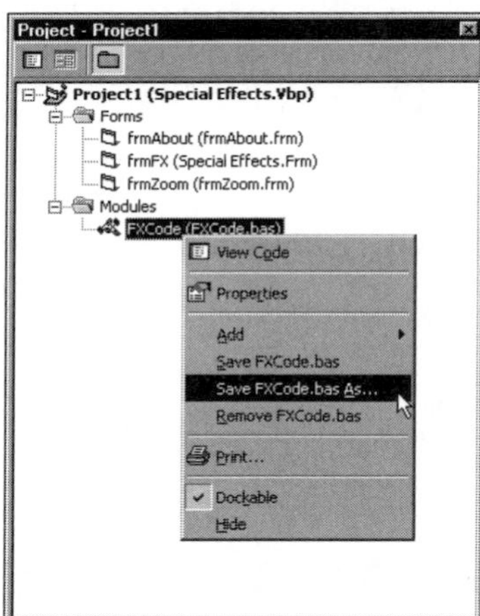

Figure 5-2: You can use the context menus in Project Explorer to save source modules without overwriting older versions of the files.

Once you have saved all the modules in the project under new names, choose Save Project As from the VB File menu to save the project's ***.Vbp*** file without overwriting the old project file (see Figure 5-3).

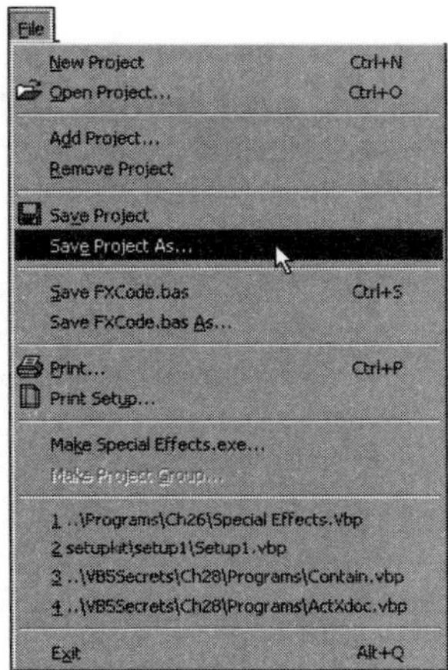

Figure 5-3: You can choose Save Project As to save a copy of the project file in the VB5 format without overwriting the VB4 project file.

Provided that the Upgrade ActiveX Controls option is enabled on the General tab of the Project Properties dialog (see Figure 5-4), Visual Basic will automatically convert control references in your project to upgraded versions of these controls, if they are present on your system. There is no good reason for disabling this option.

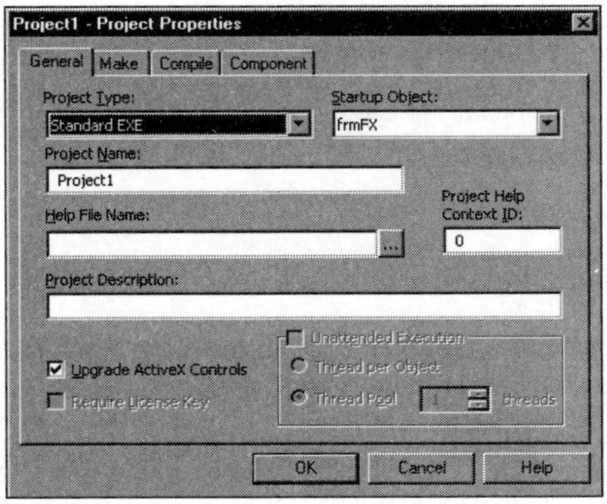

Figure 5-4: You should enable the Upgrade ActiveX Controls option on the General tab of the Project properties dialog so that upgraded versions of controls will be used in your projects.

Native Code Compilation

What may be the number one prayer of all Visual Basic fanatics has finally been answered! Visual Basic programs can now be compiled to native stand-alone code. If you wish, you can still compile to pseudocode (p-code). The fact is that p-code applications will be much smaller — and only a little slower — than native code compilations. In situations where program size is an important consideration — such as Web downloads — you may be wise to remain with p-code. This is particularly the case because the VB runtime library will already be present on many machines.

You use the Compile tab of the Project Properties dialog to select the compilation mode, as shown in Figure 5-5.

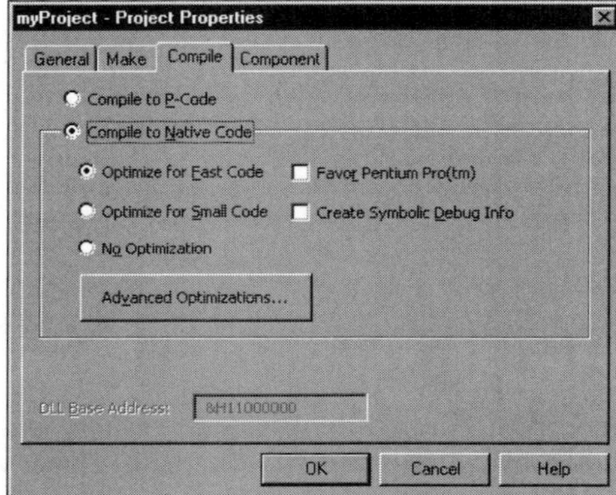

Figure 5-5: You can use the Compile tab of the Project Properties dialog to select the compilation mode for your projects.

For more information about compilation options and their consequences, see Chapter 16, "Optimizing Secrets."

Interface Enhancements

You'll find that even the appearance of the Visual Basic development environment has changed. You can now configure almost all aspects of your working VB environment to suit the way you like to work.

Figure 5-6 shows a project loaded in the VB5 environment. For detailed information on working with the VB5 IDE, see Chapter 2, "Exploring the Visual Basic IDE."

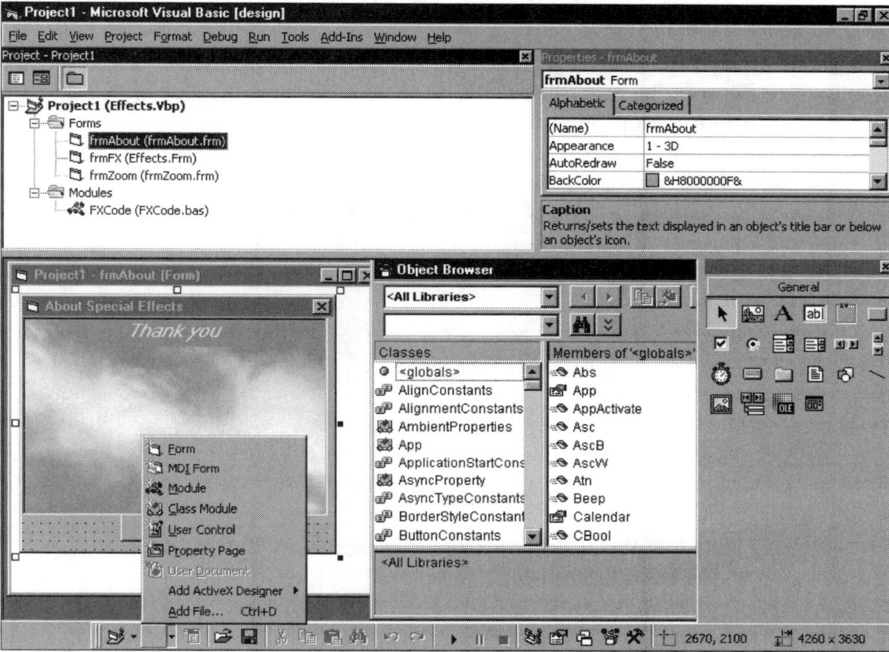

Figure 5-6: You can configure the new Visual Basic environment pretty much as you would like.

Docking

You use the Docking tab of the Options dialog, which you can open from the Tools menu, to set project docking options (see Figure 5-7). If a window is set as dockable on this tab, it can be attached to the main window (or to other windows attached to the main window).

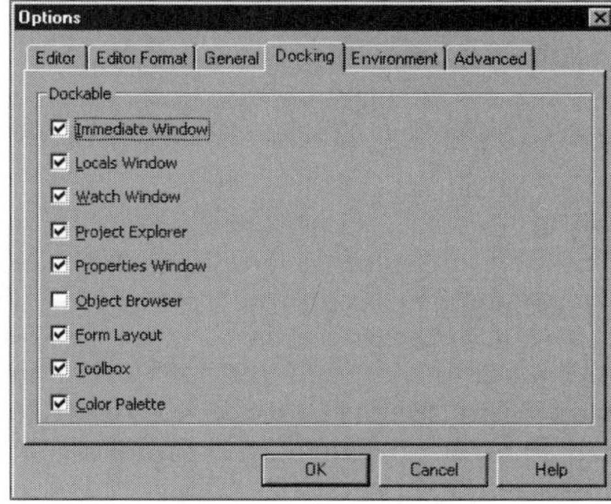

Figure 5-7: You can decide which windows will be dockable.

Templates

You can create new Visual Basic projects and forms based on templates (see Figures 5-8 and 5-9). Templates provide prebuilt projects and forms that already include substantial functionality.

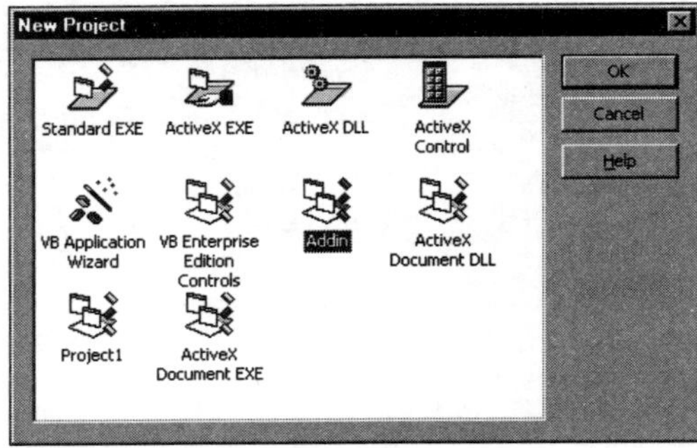

Figure 5-8: You can open a new VB project based on a preexisting template.

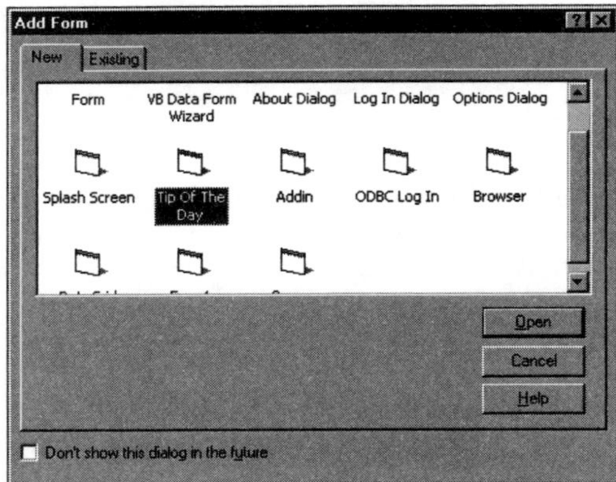

Figure 5-9: You can also base forms on templates.

The best part about using project and module templates in VB5 is that it is very easy to create your own templates. Any project — or module — that you create will appear as a template the next time the New Project or Add dialog is selected, provided that your template has been saved in the appropriate template directory. This means that it is very easy to create your own customized, reusable forms, modules, and projects.

Project Groups

A project group is a Visual Basic file group that combines several projects. Project group information is stored in a ***.Vbg*** file, while Visual Basic project file information is kept in a ***.Vbp*** file. Figure 5-10 shows a simple project group structure containing an ActiveX control project and a Standard Exe project.

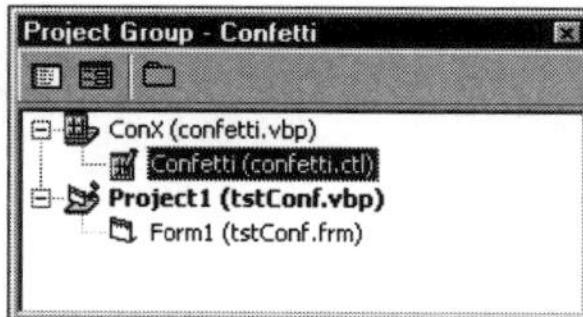

Figure 5-10: Project groups can contain several Visual Basic projects.

One of the main uses for Project Groups is to test in-process ActiveX controls and components in one instance of the Visual Basic IDE. This can make creating ActiveX controls much less tedious.

For more information on using Project Groups to work with ActiveX controls, see Chapter 24, "Understanding ActiveX Controls."

Form Layout

In the new, more object-oriented Visual Basic, you create the appearance of each object with a screen representation — including forms, UserControls, and UserDocuments — by manipulating each object's designer.

Figure 5-11 shows a UserDocument object, containing a Label control, on its designer.

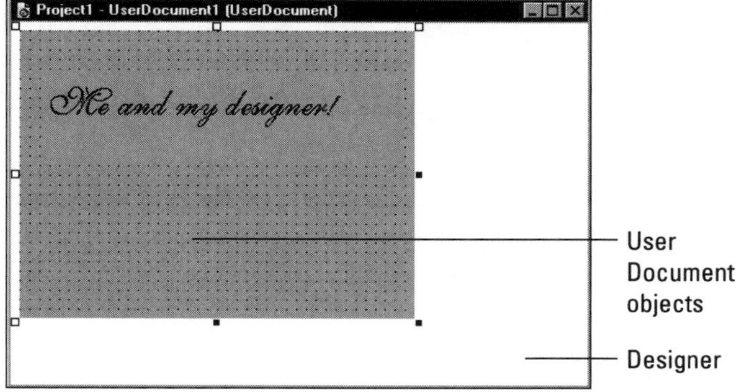

Figure 5-11: You manipulate objects such as forms, controls, and ActiveX documents at design time using the objects' designers.

Unlike VB4, objects are locked to the upper-left corner of their designers. To move the object away from the upper-left corner at runtime, you use a new window, the Form Layout. As shown in Figure 5-12, you can use the Form Layout to position forms on the screen.

Figure 5-12: You use the Form Layout to position forms and other objects on the screen.

You can use the Form Layout's context menu to configure and position the object. For example, as shown in Figure 5-13, you can use the Form Layout context menu to center a form on the screen. Choosing this item has the same effect as setting the form's StartUpPosition property to 2-CenterScreen. (By the way, StartUpPosition is a new form property.)

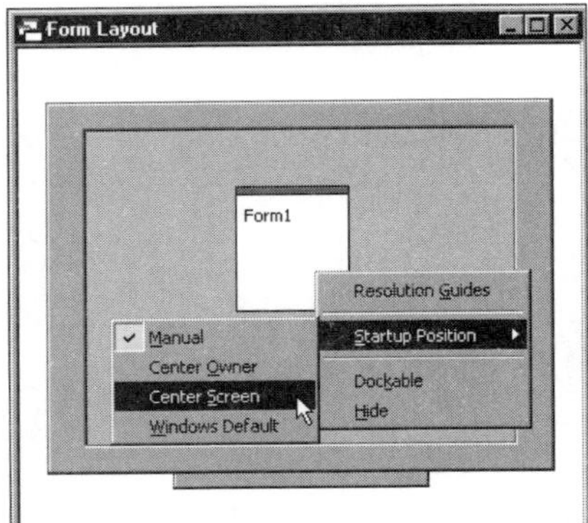

Figure 5-13: You can use the Form Layout context menu to position forms and other objects on the screen.

Code-Creation Aids

Visual Basic now comes with an impressive battery of tools that make writing code easier. These tools are available from the context menu in the Code Editor, as shown in Figure 5-14.

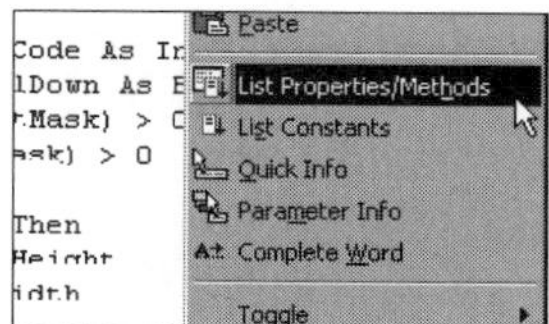

Figure 5-14: You'll find an impressive battery of code construction aids on the context menu in the Code Editor.

For a full explanation of how to use these tools, see "The Edit Menu" in Chapter 2.

Creating ActiveX Controls

My dream as a Visual Basic programmer was to create my own controls. It used to seem deeply unfair that the controls that I had to use to create great VB applications were written in Visual C++, and could not be written in VB. No more! Creating an ActiveX control in Visual Basic is now a simple matter of opening a new ActiveX Control project and implementing the control's interface.

VB5 even comes with a number of Wizards — including the ActiveX Control Interface Wizard, the Class Builder Wizard, and the Property Page Wizard — to simplify building controls. Figure 5-15 shows the Control Interface Wizard in action.

You can distribute ActiveX controls you create in VB on conventional media, or across the Web. Or, if you prefer to keep your controls a private affair, you can compile the control source code in the project that uses the control. This is a way to reap the benefits of true object-oriented programming.

Creating your own ActiveX controls in VB5 is explained in detail in Part VI, "Creating ActiveX Controls."

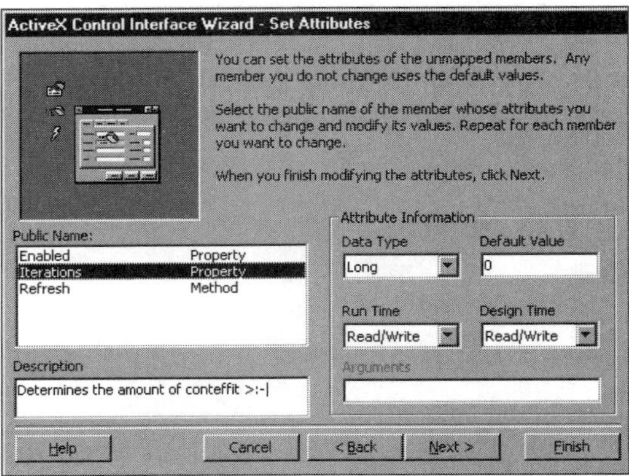

Figure 5-15: The ActiveX Control Interface Wizard helps you to create the interface for custom ActiveX controls.

Firing Events

I always wanted to fire a custom event. Really, I did. At least, it seemed like a better idea than having a custom event fire me! Seriously, folks, it felt like a real shame in VB4 that forms and classes could have custom properties and methods — but not events. In Version 5, you'll have no problem firing custom events that will be added to a module's event-handling framework. Events are fired using the RaiseEvent statement and received with the help of the WithEvents keyword.

For the basics, see "Creating, Firing, and Handling Custom Events" in Chapter 3, "Event-Driven Programming." For a discussion of some of the more sophisticated issues that come up — and an explanation of the differences between events that a control fires and ones it receives — see Chapter 25, "Creating the Control Interface."

ActiveX Document Applications

ActiveX document applications may just be the surprise hit of the new Visual Basic! An ActiveX document application consists of one or more "documents" and a related ActiveX component server. Actually, the "documents" in the ActiveX document application are structured OLE compound storage files whose persistent data can be accessed through standard OLE interfaces. And if that's not a mouthful, mate, I don't know what is.

The point is that ActiveX "documents" work in much the same way as, for example, a Word document. The Word document has persistent data that is entered by the user. When operations are performed, such as running a macro or opening a new file, the Word document invokes the exposed objects of ***Winword.Exe*** — its ActiveX server.

You, too, can create ActiveX document applications that behave in this sophisticated fashion. Best yet, you can deploy these document/server combos in containers such as Internet Explorer or the Office 97 Binder. From inside VB, an ActiveX "document" is just a UserDocument object with properties and controls. It behaves pretty much like a normal VB form.

To learn about ActiveX document applications, turn to Chapter 28, "Creating Internet Applications in VB."

Add-Ins

VB5 comes with a number of helpful add-ins and Wizards that you can activate using the Add-In Manager, as shown in Figure 5-16.

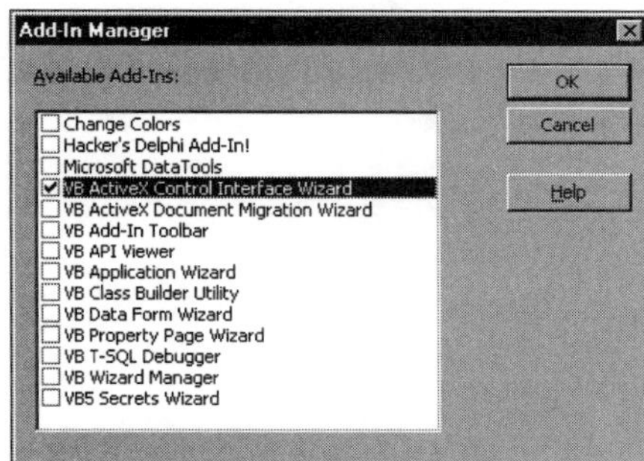

Figure 5-16: You use the Add-In Manager to enable add-ins and Wizards.

In addition to using the Add-In Manager to enable prebuilt add-ins, you can implement custom add-ins that you — or other users — can activate at will.

The WebBrowser Control

The Professional and Enterprise Editions of VB5 ship with the WebBrowser ActiveX control. This control allows you to easily add much of the functionality of Internet Explorer to any Visual Basic application. Read all about it in Chapter 28!

The new, much more robust, and fully object-oriented Visual Basic object hierarchy makes it easy to create your own add-ins (and Wizards) and seamlessly integrate them with the VB IDE. Learn the tricks of the add-in trade in Chapter 29, "Creating a VB Add-In," and Chapter 30, "Building a Wizard."

Summary

There is so much that is new in Version 5 of Visual Basic that this chapter has only touched on the tip of the iceberg. New features "featured" in this chapter are the ones that excite me most. I hope they excite you, too! There is no doubt that this is not your father's VB.

Topics discussed in this chapter included

- Porting legacy applications to VB5
- Native code compilation
- Docking
- Project and form templates
- Project groups
- Using the Form Layout
- Creating custom ActiveX controls
- Firing custom events
- ActiveX document applications
- The WebBrowser control
- Visual Basic add-ins

PART II

Programming 32-Bit Windows

Chapter 6

Windows 95: An Overview

This chapter provides an overview of Windows 95 — and its interface — from the viewpoint of the Visual Basic programmer. Windows 95 contains features that are important to end users of computers. With the release of NT 4.0, these interface features have been incorporated into Microsoft's heavy-duty operating system, as well. It's extremely exciting as developers to tap into that user enthusiasm and deliver programs that support the interface features of the Windows 95 shell.

Topics discussed in this chapter include:

- The Windows 95 shell
- Property sheets
- Wizards
- The use of OLE and ActiveX
- Multithreading
- Virtual machines and device drivers
- Changing expectations regarding user interface (UI)
- Setup programs
- Help files

The Windows 95 Shell

The Windows 95 operating system sports a new look and feel that is a marked improvement over previous versions of Windows in terms of graphic design, functionality, and ease of use. Windows NT 4.0 — both workstation and server versions — takes the power and performance of NT v3.51 and dramatically improves the user interface by adapting the Windows 95 look and feel. This interface is sometimes referred to as the Windows 95 *shell*. In this chapter, I'll talk about Windows 95 but most of the discussion applies to the user interface of NT4 as well.

Many elements that were used to implement the new functionality and appearance of the Windows shell are available to developers. For example, most of the controls used to build the Windows 95 user interface are available for your use in the Professional Edition of VB. In fact, professional developers *must* create applications with a Windows 95 look and feel and functionality. Simply put, users expect it — and require it — in contemporary programs.

The most important elements of the Windows 95 interface fall into the following categories:

- Custom controls.
- Common dialogs.
- Long filename support. (Although long filenames can help users to know the contents of a file in advance, developers should be cautious about releasing projects that use them because various kinds of compatibility issues can still cause problems.)
- Shortcut links.
- File viewers.
- Right mouse menus and property sheets.
- Ways to customize the Windows 95 interface.

Of these, we really don't need to think about long filename support, shortcuts, and file viewers. These are built into the Windows interface — and can be used for fun and profit — but you don't need to do anything special to implement them in your projects.

The Windows 95 custom controls (covered in detail in Chapter 8, "Windows User Interface Controls") fall into these groups:

- Status bars and toolbars
- Trackbars, progress indicators, up-down controls, and animation controls
- Image lists, list views, tree views, and column headers
- Tabs and property sheets
- Rich text controls

You undoubtedly are familiar with many of these controls from using Windows 95 and Windows 95 applications. For example, the Windows 95 Explorer uses a number of the controls; you can see an example of the column header, list view, status bar, and toolbar control in the view of the Explorer shown Figure 6-1. It's interesting that a number of these controls were specifically developed for the Explorer and later exported for the general use of Windows 95 developers.

You should integrate the Windows 95 controls and their functionality — discussed in detail in Chapter 8 — into your VB applications.

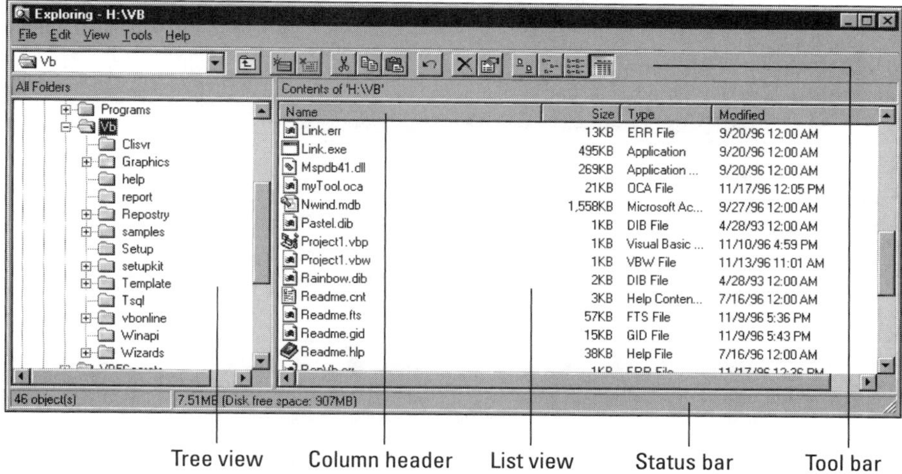

Figure 6-1: The Windows 95 Explorer includes a number of the controls that are used in Windows 95.

Property Sheets

Property sheets are important to Windows 95, because essentially all objects have them attached. An object's property sheet — which you open by choosing Properties from the object's context menu — is a tabbed dialog containing information about the object.

To see a simple example of a property sheet, you can embed information in an executable using VB's Project Properties dialog (which you access either by clicking the Options button in the Make dialog or by choosing Properties from the Project menu), as shown in Figure 6-2. (This figure shows the Project Properties dialog for the Flow program from Chapter 4.)

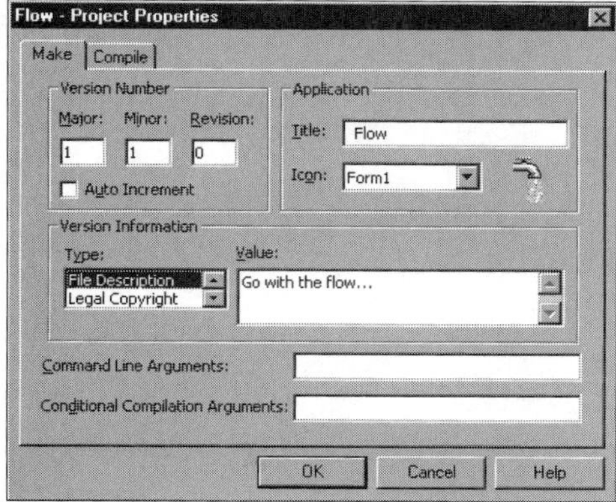

Figure 6-2: You can embed description and version information in a compiled executable.

After the program has been compiled, you can access its property sheet from its context menu, as shown in Figure 6-3.

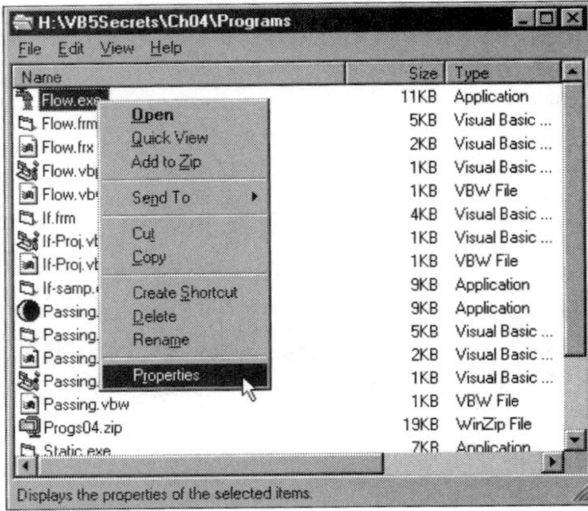

Figure 6-3: You can access the property sheet for an object such as an executable program by choosing Properties from the object's context menu.

If you select the Version tab on the property sheet for the executable, you'll find the descriptive information that you embedded in the program, as shown in Figure 6-4. For example, note that the value entered for File Description, the string "Go with the flow...," is now displayed as the file description.

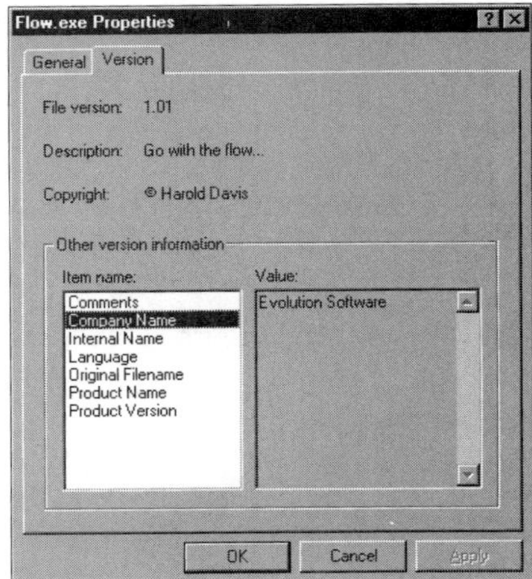

Figure 6-4: Version and descriptive information about an executable is available on the Version tab of its property sheet.

Chapter 8 explains how create "property sheets" in Visual Basic that your users can access by right-clicking objects in your program.

Wizards

Wizards are a standardized way to guide users through complex tasks. Wizards are a type of tabbed property sheet with a method that walks the user through a group of related dialog boxes.

Just as you can provide users of your programs with a Wizard to help with complex tasks, Visual Basic 5 provides you with a number of Wizards to help you with the chores involved in creating programs. The Wizards that ship with VB5 include

- VB Class Builder Wizard, which helps you implement classes and their members
- VB Data Form Wizard, which helps you build forms based upon local or remote data sources
- VB Application Wizard, which you can use to create the framework for an application (see the next section for an example)
- VB Property Page Wizard, which you can use to create ActiveX control custom property pages
- VB ActiveX Document Wizard, which translates project forms into ActiveX documents
- VB ActiveX Control Interface Wizard, which you use to design the interface for ActiveX controls

VB5 also includes a Wizard manager — sometimes called the *Wizard Wizard* — to help you create your own Wizards. Creating your own Wizards is covered in Chapter 8, "Windows User Interface Controls," and Chapter 30, "Building a Wizard."

These VB Wizards are actually Visual Basic add-ins — OLE server applications designed to interact with instances of the Visual Basic environment. (For more on add-ins, see Chapter 29, "Creating a VB Add-In.") You can see a list of available Wizards by choosing Add-In Manager from the Add-Ins menu.

The VB Application Wizard

The VB Application Wizard is a very useful way to jump-start application building. To start the Wizard, select VB Application Wizard from the New Project dialog, as shown in Figure 6-5.

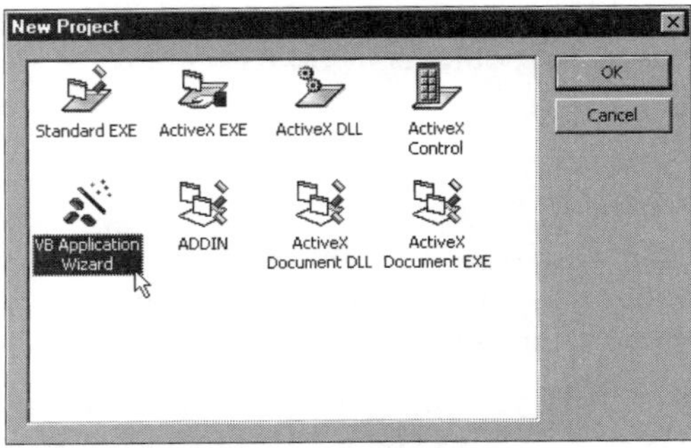

Figure 6-5: To start the VB Application Wizard, you select it from the New Project dialog.

The VB Application Wizard shows up in the New Project dialog because a file with a ***.Vbz*** extension, ***VB Application Wizard.Vbz,*** has been placed in the project's template directory. ***VB Application Wizard.Vbz*** is a text file containing, the class name — sometimes called the *programmatic ID*, or *ProgID* — of the OLE server program that is the Application Wizard.

You can use the Application Wizard to choose an interface type, as shown in Figure 6-6.

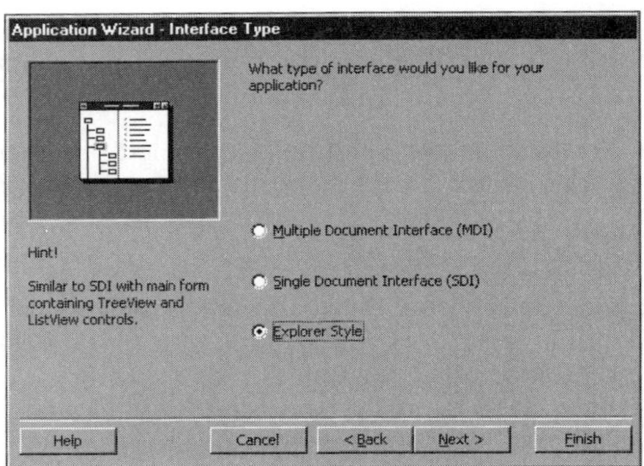

Figure 6-6: If you select Explorer Style for your interface type, the Application Wizard will add the appropriate controls to a form for you.

You can choose to have the Wizard add various facilities to your application, including Internet Connectivity (Figure 6-7); and additional forms including Splash, Login, and About screens (Figure 6-8).

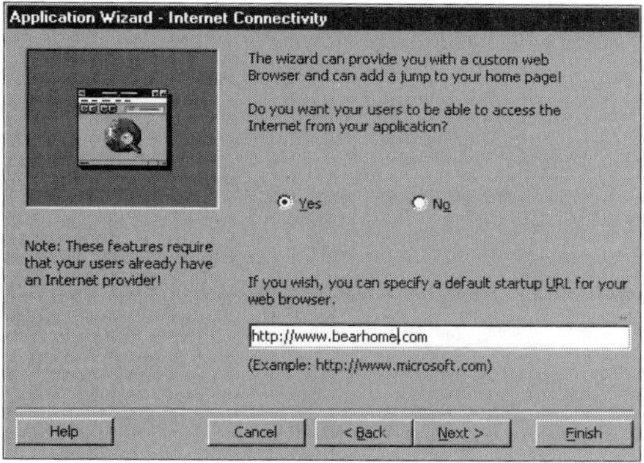

Figure 6-7: The Application Wizard can add Internet connectivity for you.

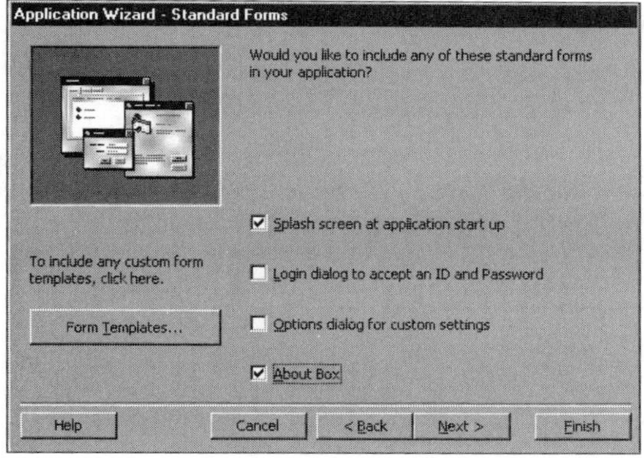

Figure 6-8: You can choose to have the Wizard add various screens to your application.

The final screen of the Application Wizard lets you name your application (see Figure 6-9). You can also use this screen to have a report generated with specific suggestions for further work on your application.

From here, it's hand over the wheel to the Wizard. Based on your input in the various screens of the Application Wizard, the underlying ActiveX server application generates appropriate forms and controls. This will take a while, and you can watch it happening. I think of it as watching a car go through the automatic washer — no human hands touch it. But, in the end, you'll have a relatively complete framework for an application, with much of the user interface already in place. If you specified the Explorer interface, with Internet capability, your application will look pretty much like the one shown in Figure 6-10.

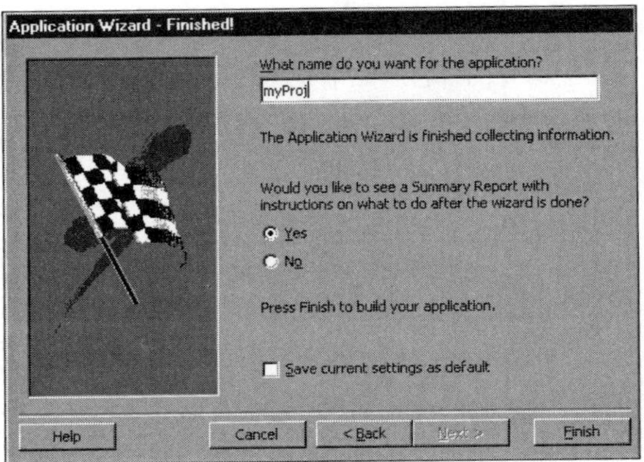

Figure 6-9: You can use the last screen of the Application Wizard to name your project and have a report generated.

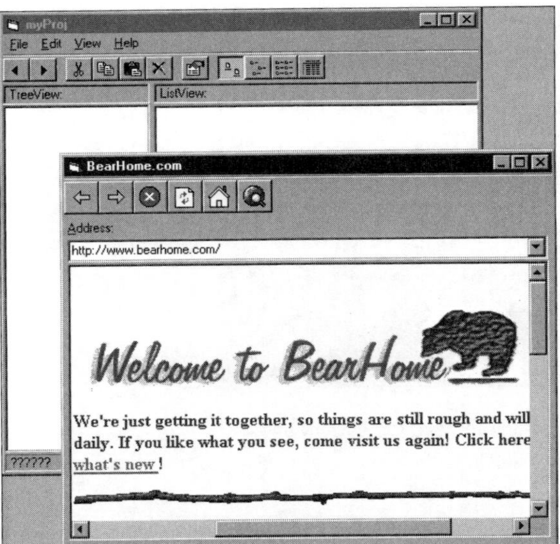

Figure 6-10: You can use the Application Wizard to generate a framework for an application that comes with most user interface elements "ready to go." (This figure shows a prebuilt Explorer interface, with attached Web browser.)

The "Easter Egg" in Windows 95

As you probably know, the term "Easter egg" refers to a graphic (often multimedia) embedded within a program. Usually, you need to perform some kind of trick — for example, a sequence of keystrokes — to start the Easter egg, which, typically, is used to credit the program's development team. In Chapter 19, "Runtime Display Secrets," I'll show you how to create your own Easter eggs (along with some triggering methods).

Here's how you can view the Windows 95 Easter egg, which shows the entire Windows 95 development team, as illustrated in Figure 6-11 (the names fly by in time to new age music).

1. Right-click an empty area of the desktop.
2. Choose New | Folder.
3. Name the folder as follows: **and now, the moment you've all been waiting for** (note that punctuation and capitalization count).
4. Press Enter to register the folder with that name.
5. Right-click the folder and rename it: **we proudly present for your viewing pleasure**. (Don't type a period after "pleasure"!) Once more, press Enter to register the folder with that name.
6. Finally, rename the folder a third time (again, be careful about capitalization and punctuation): **The Microsoft Windows 95 Product Team!**
7. Press Enter to register the folder name. Open the folder and the Easter egg will run. Enjoy!

By the way, this Easter egg will only run during the Windows session in which you create the folder. If you create it, following these instructions, and then turn your system off and on again, the egg will no longer play when you open the folder.

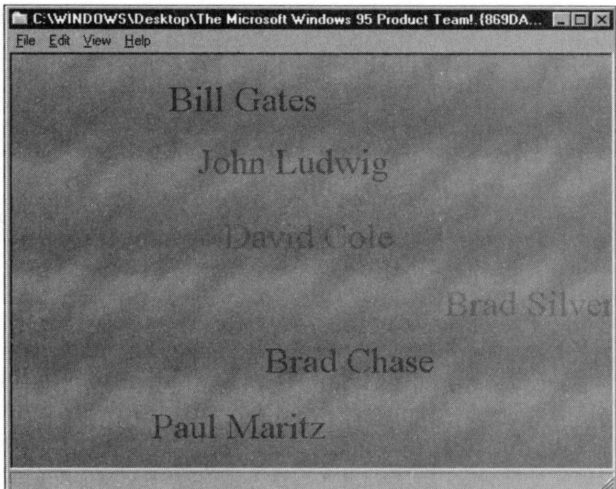

Figure 6-11: The Windows 95 Easter egg lets you watch the names of the developers of the operating system fly by to the strains of "new age" music.

OLE and Windows 95

OLE expert Kraig Brockschmidt has said that OLE as used in Windows 95 constitutes one third of the operating system. It's an important third. (For Brockschmidt's overview definition of OLE, see Chapter 1.)

My intention in Part V of *Visual Basic 5 SECRETS*, "Using ActiveX," is to provide you with the techniques, shortcuts, secrets, and tricks that you need to successfully use VB to create fully OLE-compliant programs about which your users will say, "¡Olé!" Of course, I'll discuss OLE further in that part of *Visual Basic 5 SECRETS,* but with a practical focus. In the meantime, it's a good idea to learn what the OLE technology is all about.

"ActiveX" is a new name for the technology that was formerly known as "OLE." I'll explain in detail the relationship between ActiveX and OLE in Part V. For now, you should know that ActiveX is an implementation of OLE. It's therefore important to get a feeling for what OLE is about.

OLE actually consists of four parts:

- A *compound document* model. OLE compound documents allow cross-platform structured storage for all kinds of information that is saved within a file.
- OLE automation, which permits OLE-compliant applications to expose methods and command sets that operate within and across applications.
- OLE drag and drop, which allows objects to be dragged from one application and dropped in another.
- General OLE services, including data transfer interfaces, memory management interfaces, and storage interfaces (these are only a few items from a truly extensive list of services).

Clearly, Windows 95 is largely built around component parts that make heavy use of these four aspects of OLE. OLE's integration into Windows 95 gives the user the "perspective that almost anything can be an object," in the words of Tony Williams, one of OLE's chief architects at Microsoft. It's a truism that applications that would truly have the look and feel of Windows 95 — as well as embrace the philosophy behind it — must implement OLE.

The ActiveX technology extends the object-oriented thinking behind OLE. Now, with Visual Basic 5, OLE controls — ActiveX controls — created in VB can be used by any other ActiveX container environment. The control container makes available, or exposes, ActiveX properties, events, and methods. For information on creating ActiveX controls in VB, see Part VI, "Creating ActiveX Controls."

More about Windows 95, the Operating System

Some other internal features of the Windows 95 operating system are important to programmers whose work must interact with the environment.

One of the most important features of Windows 95 is the central Registry, which is covered in detail in Chapter 9, "Using the Windows Registry," and Chapter 10, "Programming the Registry in VB." This section discusses other important new aspects of Windows 95: virtual device drivers, virtual machines, and multithreading.

Virtual Device Drivers

Windows 95 is built around a system of *virtual device drivers* (V*x*Ds) that handle program and operating system interaction with categories of devices. A V*x*D is a 32-bit protected-mode driver that manages a system resource, so that more than one program at a time can use the resource. The *x* stands for the type of driver. For example, a VPD is the virtual device driver that manages the printer device.

One of the great benefits of this way of doing things is that device vendors — for example, the manufacturer of a printer — need only provide limited additional information (termed a *mini-driver*) required by a specific device. A mini-driver in essence plugs into the V*x*D.

This contrasts extremely favorably with the situation in Windows 3.*x*. In general, Windows 3.*x* drivers were single-purpose and complex, leading to device driving code duplication on target systems, trouble and expense for device vendors, and greater probability of flaws in the device drivers.

Virtual Machines

A *virtual machine* (VM) is an environment in memory that to a running application looks like an entirely separate computer. The Windows 95 Virtual Machine Manager supplies each running application with a VM that has the system resources needed by that particular application.

One of the great benefits of running applications in their own VMs is that when an application crashes — for example, by causing a protection fault — most of the time only the application's own VM is brought down. This means an end to those dreadful Windows 3.1 "General Protection Fault" message boxes with an OK button, when it was really not OK at all.

Multithreading

Multithreading is a mechanism for running multiple applications simultaneously.

Under Windows 3.1, applications ran at the same time using a system known as *cooperative multitasking*. This system required the operating system to check the message queue from time to time and to relinquish control of the system to other running applications. You could easily write applications that were "hogs" because they did not frequently check the message queue. For reasons of backwards compatibility, Windows 95 cooperative multitasks 16-bit applications.

On the other hand, 32-bit applications running under Windows 95 are *preemptive multitasked*. This means that the operating system balances the needs of each running application and allocates resources appropriately. Because 32-bit applications do not need to be written to surrender control to other running tasks, they can take advantage of the multithreading facilities built into Windows 95.

Each concurrently running multithreading application is called a *process*. Each process contains one or more *threads*, units of code that get a *time slice* — an allocation of the available processing time — from the operating system and run concurrently with other threads. However, a 32-bit application can initiate more than one thread per process (in fact, it can initiate up to 255), enhancing the apparent speed of the application and enabling effective background processing of tasks.

The Window NT 4.0 Operating System

Because Windows NT version 4.0 ships with the Windows 95 shell (and interface controls), applications written for 95 will by and large run under NT. However, in a number of areas you'll have to test for which operating system is running and execute different code accordingly. (It's extremely important to thoroughly test applications in both environments.)

The best source for further information is the current release of the MSDN library. (For more information on MSDN, see the section "Quickly Finding Information in the Documentation" in Chapter 4.) I particularly recommend the article on the MSDN CD-ROM by Microsoft employee Nancy Winnick Cluts, "Tips to Ensure that your Windows 95 Application Runs under Windows NT."

Further Reading

If you want to learn more about Windows 95, I recommend two books out of the wealth of tomes that cover this operating system:

- Microsoft's *Windows 95 Resource Kit* (Microsoft Press, 1995) contains a wealth of information about Windows 95, oriented towards system administrators.
- In the "Secrets" series, Brian Livingston and Davis Straub have written a tremendously useful book: *Windows 95 SECRETS*, 3rd Edition (IDG Books Worldwide, 1995). *Windows 95 SECRETS* is aimed at power users who are interested in techniques for working effectively with Windows 95.

Setup Programs

Modern setup programs for 32-bit applications under Windows 95 and NT 4.0 have not changed that much from setup routines for 16-bit Windows 3.*x*, but there are some requirements for polished 32-bit installations you should know about. The Application Setup Wizard that ships with VB5 in many cases will automatically create an appropriate installation routine for you.

Requirements for 32-bit setup programs include

- Long filename support
- Application and extension registration
- Use of the Registry rather than initialization files for retaining information between sessions
- Links should be created for the Start menu (as opposed to Program Manager groups and icons)
- The creation of an automatic application removal utility
- The creation of a log file indicating exactly what the installation routine has done

In addition, 32-bit Windows users seem to be very impressed with the autorun feature for CD-ROM installs (autorun automatically starts a CD-ROM-based installation when the disk is placed in the drive).

You create an autorun setup by adding a text file named ***Autorun.Inf*** to the root directory of the CD-ROM. You set the Open line in this file to the name of the setup program that should be run automatically. For example:

```
[AutoRun]
OPEN=setup.exe
```

Setup programs are covered in Chapter 36, "Setup Programs."

Help Files

From the viewpoint of the user, Windows 95 help systems are enhanced in numerous ways, including

- A main menu that consists of a tabbed dialog rather than contents with a button bar
- Use of the tree view control to display books, subbooks, and individual pages of information
- Shortcut buttons
- A new context menu
- Improved copying and printing facilities

As you may know, it's not that hard to compile your own help files using the tools that Microsoft provides. In addition, there are a number of good third-party help authoring systems. Using the Help Compiler Workshop and third-party utilities are covered in Chapter 35, "Help Files."

In the world of software development, it is a truism that nothing stays the same. Help files, themselves, are in transition. It doesn't take a rocket scientist to realize that HTML Web pages share important characteristics with help files: both formats deal with structured text, and both allow hyperlinking. The result of this observation is that help files are undergoing a gradual — and not so gradual — change of format. There is no doubt that in a few years, most help systems will be written in HTML. Effectively dealing with this transition is covered in Chapter 35.

Summary

This chapter provided an overview of the Windows 95 shell. In addition I've

- Showed you how to embed file version information in a VB executable so that it will appear in the compiled program's property sheet
- Provided an overview of the Wizards available in VB5
- Showed you how to play the Windows 95 "Easter egg"
- Provided an overview of the functionality of OLE and ActiveX
- Discussed a number of important features of the Windows 95 operating system, including V*x*Ds, virtual machines, and multithreading
- Highlighted the most important new features of Windows 95 installation programs and help systems

Chapter 7

Windows Common Dialog Secrets

In this chapter I'll explain how to use Version 5 of the Common Dialog ActiveX control. (This control is listed in the Components dialog as Microsoft Common Dialog Control 5.0. It is usually familiarly referred to as the "common dialog control.")

The purpose of the common dialog control is to make it easy for developers to add dialogs with the standard Windows look, feel, and functionality to their own applications.

In this chapter, I'll also

- Go over the six kinds of common dialogs supported by the control in Windows 95
- Explain common dialog control constants and flags
- Show you the tabbed custom common dialog property
- Discuss entering flags and properties in code
- Tell you how to detect when the Cancel button has been pressed in a common dialog

Of course, the first step in using the common dialog control is to add it to your project. To do this, use the Components dialog to add the Microsoft Common Dialog Control 5.0 to your Toolbox, if it's not already there, as shown in Figure 7-1.

Once you've added the common dialog control to your Toolbox, double-click it to add the control to the currently active form in your project.

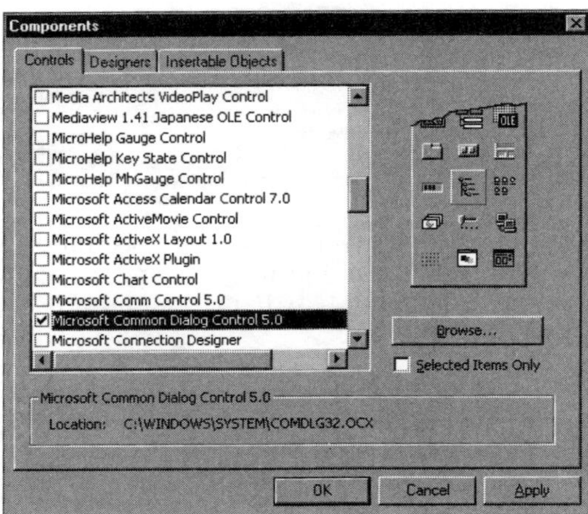

Figure 7-1: You must add the common dialog control to your Toolbox using the Components dialog before you can use it in your project.

The Purpose of the Common Dialog Control

The common dialog control functions as a *wrapper*, or intermediary, between Visual Basic and the library functions in the dynamic link library ***Comdlg32.Dll***. This file must be located in the ***Windows\System*** directory under Windows 95 and in the ***WinNT\System32*** directory under Windows NT 4. The filename for the control is ***Comdlg32.Ocx***.

The idea is to make it easy for Visual Basic (and other) programmers to access these functions using control properties set "visually" at design time in the Property Viewer, or with a nominal amount of code. One advantage of having the common dialogs easily available is standardization: When the user performs a familiar task, such as saving a file to disk, she will open a familiar dialog with which to do it.

You probably know this, but it's worth saying anyhow: In and of themselves, the common dialogs don't *do* anything other than bring up a display from which the user can make choices. If the user elects to save a particular file, choose a font, and so on, you still have to "wire" it — that is, add the code that performs the task in question.

By and large, ***Comdlg32.Ocx*** works quite well. There are six common dialogs that you can display in 32-bit Windows 95 applications using the ***Comdlg32.Ocx*** control (see Table 7-1) and the appropriate method.

Table 7-1 Common Dialogs

Common Dialog	*Method that Displays*	*Action Property Equivalence*
Color	.ShowColor	3
Font	.ShowFont	4
Opens WinHelp with the specified help file and topic	.ShowHelp	6
File Open	.ShowOpen	1
Print	.ShowPrinter	5
File Save As	.ShowSave	2

Comdlg32.Ocx is not a *windowing* control, meaning that, other than the Toolbox icon that it places on your form, in and of itself it does not paint anything on the screen either at design time or runtime. (An example of a simple control that is windowing is the command button. The design time appearance of a command button changes depending on the programmer's choices; at runtime its appearance can change depending on design, programming, and user choices.)

You should also know that you have absolutely no control — forgive the pun — over where on the screen ***Comdlg32.Ocx*** decides to place the dialog the user has opened.

The Action property is retained for the purpose of backwards compatibility with Visual Basic Version 3 (and earlier). There's really no reason to use it in code you write now. But, if you're curious about how it works, when you set the common dialog's action property, you invoke the appropriate dialog. Thus

```
CommonDialog1.Action = 3
```

is equivalent to

```
CommonDialog1.ShowColor
```

Control Constants and Flags

Whether you set up the common dialog control using the Properties window or in code (both ways are described later in this chapter), some of the most important aspects of the dialog that is to be opened are determined by the value of its .Flags property, for example,

```
CommonDialog1.Flags
```

The value of the .Flags property is made up of long integer values that can be added together for a combination of attributes. (This works the same way as the MsgBox function.)

Values can be expressed as integers, or, as is the usual modern practice, by their constant equivalents. The latter is the better practice because it makes it far more apparent what your code is expected to do.

The Object Browser can be used as a handy-dandy tool for determining available common dialog constants (and their numerical values), as shown in Figure 7-2.

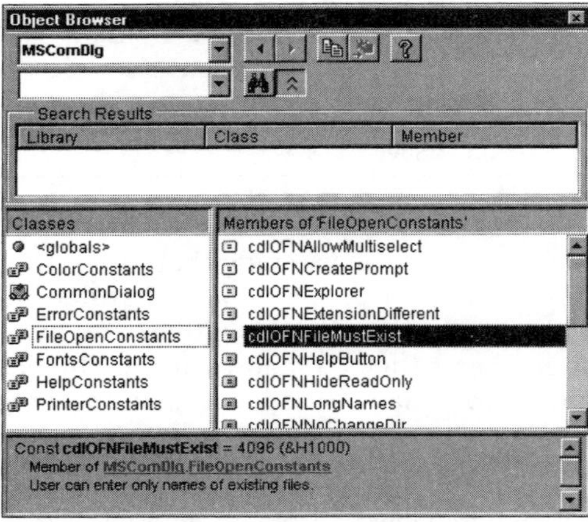

Figure 7-2: You can use the Object Browser to find common dialog constants.

For example,

```
CommonDialog1.Flags = cdlOFNOverWritePrompt + _
   cdlOFNHelpButton + cdlOFNPathMustExist
CommonDialog1.ShowSave
```

causes the File Save As dialog to open with a Help button on it. This dialog will generate a warning before letting the user select a file that already exists, and will not allow the user to enter a path that does not exist (see Figure 7-3).

You could, of course, use the numerical equivalent of the flag constants to the same effect:

```
CommonDialog1.Flags = 2066 '2066 = 2 + 16 + 2048
```

But I think you'll agree that the meaning of the first statement is a lot clearer.

Where do the constant values for the .Flags property come from? When the common dialog control is included in your project, you can automatically use the constant expressions in code without worrying about their values.

You can also use the Property Pages dialog (or Properties window) for the control at design time to set many control property values.

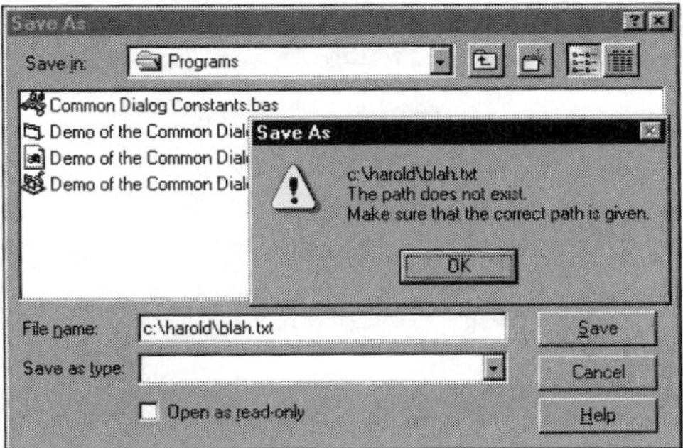

Figure 7-3: If the PathMustExist flag has been set, users will see this "path does not exist" warning if they attempt to save a file using a nonexistent path.

However, to set the value of the Flags property in the Properties window at design time, you'll need to know the numerical value for each constant (you can use either decimal or hexadecimal notation). There are three sources for the values and meanings of the flag constants:

- VB on-line help under CommonDialog Control Constants.
- VB on-line help under Flags Property, and then under each different dialog type.
- The Object Browser, under MSComDlg - Microsoft Common Dialog Control, lists constants with their correct integer decimal (and hexadecimal) values.

To get the Font dialog to display any fonts, you must first set the common dialog's .Flags property to include a constant value that tells it to show fonts. For instance,

```
CommonDialog1.Flags = cdlCFBoth
```

tells the common dialog to display both screen and printer fonts. If you don't send the control a font display flag first, you may spend some time tearing your hair out wondering why it keeps sending you back a cdlNoFonts error message, when you know perfectly well that you have oodles of fonts installed on your system (see Figure 7-4)!

You can use the flag cdlOFNExplorer (&H80000) to open an the Explorer-style Open File dialog box. Common dialogs that use this flag do not work under Windows NT 4. If you try to execute the ShowOpen method for a common dialog control that has been set with this flag value, you'll get an error message indicating that the "object doesn't support this method or property."

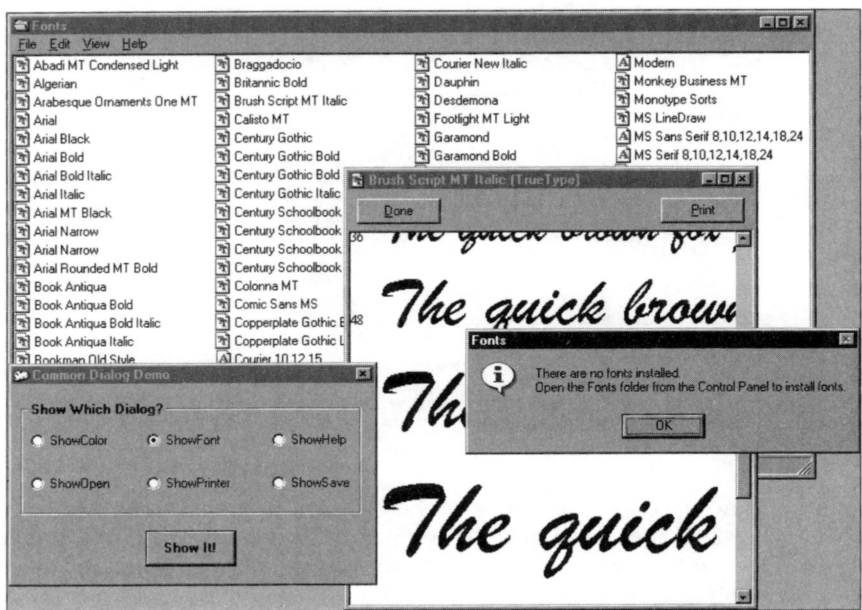

Figure 7-4: No fonts? No fonts? Huh? We don't think so....

Look Ma, No Code

It's easy to use the Properties window to set common dialog properties and flags without using any code. You simply set the properties — either in the Properties window or in the custom Property Pages dialog.

You access the custom Property Pages dialog for a control either by clicking the button in the value field for the Custom property in the Properties window (see Figure 7-5) or by choosing the Properties item from the context menu with the control selected.

You'll note that the values entered in one way are also automatically entered in the other. For example, if you change the .DialogTitle property to "Harold's File Save," when you open the custom dialog, the DialogTitle input box will also have the value "Harold's File Save."

Note that the .Flags property — which you must enter in the Property Page dialog as a numerical value — is, once again, 2066, meaning:

```
cdlOFNOverWritePrompt + cdlOFNHelpButton + cdlOFNPathMustExist
```

To open the dialog with the properties and flags you've entered takes one line of code:

```
CommonDialog1.ShowOpen
```

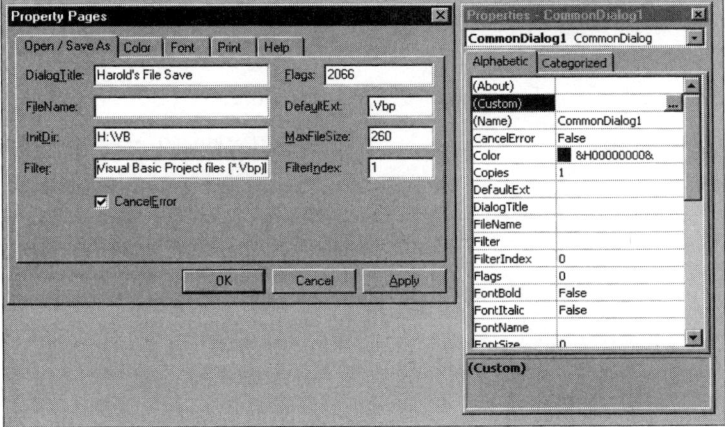

Figure 7-5: You can use the common dialog control's Property Pages dialog to change the property settings for the control.

A common dialog box will open, configured the way the properties and flags have been set (see Figure 7-6).

Figure 7-6: The title of Harold's File Save dialog was set at design time using the common dialog control's DialogTitle property.

The Filter Property

The Filter property governs the contents of the Files of Type list box that appears at the bottom of the File Save As and File Open dialogs. This is an important piece of this kind of common dialog's functionality, and the syntax of this property is quite fussy. Here's how it works.

As depicted in Figure 7-5, entering the following .Filter property in the viewer

```
Visual Basic project files (*.Vbp)|*.vbp|All Files (*.*)|*.*
```

yields the Files of Type list box shown in Figure 7-6.

Of course, you could enter this in code as a string literal and it would have the same effect:

```
Dim Fstring as string
...
Fstring = _
"Visual Basic project files (*.Vbp)|*.vbp|All Files (*.*)|*.*"
CommonDialog1.filter = Fstring
...
```

Suppose, as an experiment, you added a blank character at the end of Fstring:

```
Fstring = _
"Visual Basic project files (*.Vbp)|*.vbp|All Files (*.*)|*.* "
```

Although All Files (*.*) will appear in the Files of Type list box, when you select this option, no files will in fact appear. What's going on?

The syntax of the string literal that is equivalenced — one way or the other — to the .Filter property is

```
Desc1 |filter| Desc2 |filter|...DescN |filter
```

The descriptions can be anything you'd like; they don't have to include the conventional parentheses containing the file filter — for example, All Files (*.*) or Frodo's Files with No Extensions. The | is, of course, the pipe symbol, ASCII 124. The *filters* are wildcard file filters, entered in standard DOS syntax — for example, *.Txt, *.Doc, *.Frm, and so on.

Here's the important point: There can be no spaces between the filter and the pipe character, or after the last filter.

Flags and Properties in Code

As much fun as it is to do visual program design in VB, some of us are just not touchy-feely people and would prefer to program any chance we get. Died-in-the-wool codesters can easily enter all common dialog properties and flags in code rather than via the Properties window. The primary advantage of this approach is that you can dynamically program common dialogs so their appearance and features can change at runtime. If you set your common dialogs in code, one common dialog can take on many guises, bringing up one default filename one time, and another default filename at another. The same common dialog control can be opened as each of the six possible dialog flavors it contains.

An interesting possibility is to create your own wrapper functions, or even OLE servers that encapsulate your usual common dialog choices but allow you to pass changing variables, such as the default filename. (See Chapter 10, "Programming the Registry in VB," for a step-by-step example of how to do this.)

Another option — if you're up for working directly with the Windows APIs — is to bypass ***Comdlg32.Ocx*** and use the functions that are part of ***Comdlg32.Dll***. There are some advantages to doing this, including one less file to distribute at runtime (the common dialog control). However, the programming itself can be quite complex and involves working with the OPENFILENAME type. Although this is not impossible, I've included the type definition, so you can see what the common dialog control spares you from thinking about:

```
Type OPENFILENAME
   lStructSize As Long
   hwndOwner As Long
   hInstance As Long
   lpstrFilter As String
   lpstrCustomFilter As String
   nMaxCustFilter As Long
   nFilterIndex As Long
   lpstrFile As String
   nMaxFile As Long
   lpstrFileTitle As String
   nMaxFileTitle As Long
   lpstrInitialDir As String
   lpstrTitle As String
   flags As Long
   nFileOffset As Integer
   nFileExtension As Integer
   lpstrDefExt As String
   lCustData As Long
   lpfnHook As Long
   lpTemplateName As String
End Type
```

I've prepared a simple project — saved on the companion CD-ROM as ***Common.Vbp*** — that uses an array of option buttons (see Figure 7-7) to dynamically open all possible dialogs with one common dialog control.

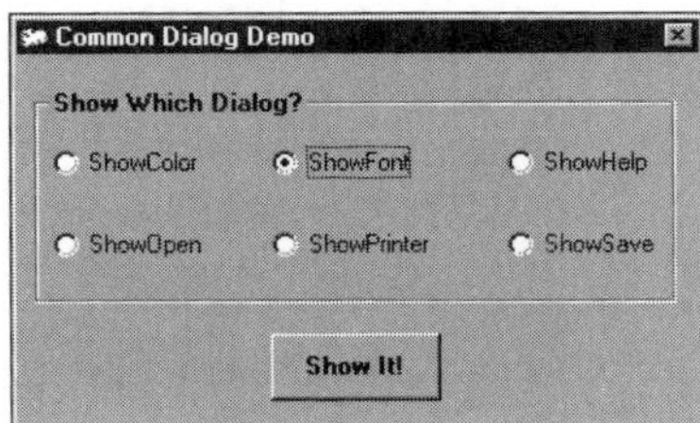

Figure 7-7: The demonstration program included on the CD-ROM dynamically demonstrates all the possible common dialogs.

The program code uses the fifth letter of the option button captions — ShowColor, ShowFont, and so on — to jump to the appropriate property value and Show statements. I've tried to add realistic flags and property values to the dialogs. Listing 7-1 shows the code:

Listing 7-1: Opening Common Dialogs

```
Private Sub cmdShow_Click()
   Dim x As Integer, Which As Integer
   Which = 0
   For x = 0 To 5
      If optWhich(x).Value = True Then Which = x
   Next x
   Select Case UCase(Mid(optWhich(Which).Caption, 5, 1))
      Case "C"
         CommonDialog1.Flags = cdlCCFullOpen
         CommonDialog1.ShowColor   'Action = 3
      Case "F"
         CommonDialog1.Flags = cdlCFBoth + cdlCFTTOnly
         CommonDialog1.FontName = "Times New Roman"
         CommonDialog1.FontSize = 20
         CommonDialog1.ShowFont    'Action = 4
      Case "H"
         CommonDialog1.HelpFile = "Vb5.Hlp"
         CommonDialog1.HelpCommand = cdlHelpContents
         CommonDialog1.ShowHelp   'Action = 6
      Case "O"
         CommonDialog1.DialogTitle = "Harold's File Open"
         CommonDialog1.Filter = _
      "Visual Basic project files (*.Vbp)|*.vbp|All Files (*.*)|*.*"
         CommonDialog1.Flags = cdlOFNAllowMultiselect + _
            cdlOFNExplorer + cdlOFNLongNames + cdlOFNFileMustExist
         CommonDialog1.ShowOpen  'Action = 1
      Case "P"
         CommonDialog1.Flags = cdlPDHidePrintToFile
         CommonDialog1.ShowPrinter 'Action = 5
      Case "S"
         CommonDialog1.DialogTitle = "Harold's File Save"
         CommonDialog1.Filter = _
            "Files will rule the world!|*.vbp|I don't think so!|*.*"
         CommonDialog1.Flags = cdlOFNOverwritePrompt + _
            cdlOFNHelpButton + cdlOFNPathMustExist
            'CommonDialog1.Flags = 2066
         CommonDialog1.ShowSave   'Action = 2
      Case Else
         MsgBox "Whoops!"
    End Select
End Sub
```

If you run the demonstration project, you can open all the dialogs. Figure 7-8 shows the Font dialog as this program has set it up.

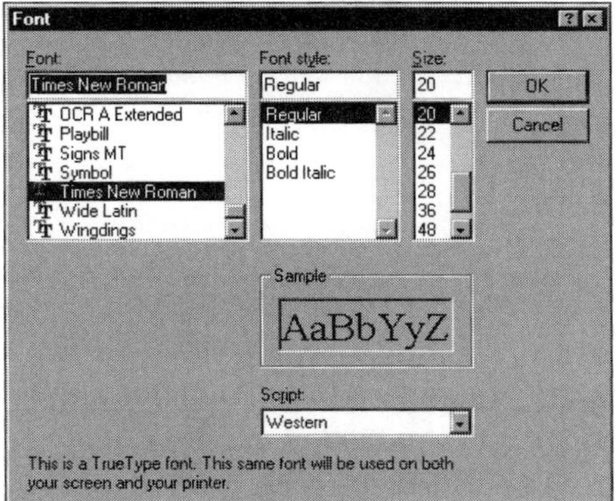

Figure 7-8: Here is the common Font dialog, with flags assigned so that it shows TrueType fonts available to both screen and printer.

Detecting Cancellation

When programming with the common dialogs, you will usually want to know if the user terminated the dialog by pressing the Cancel button. If so, the user decided not to go through with the action contemplated in the dialog, and any new values set in the dialog should be ignored. (By the way, for all the dialogs except ShowHelp, closing the dialog by clicking the Close button on the title bar of the dialog window is treated as the equivalent of pressing the Cancel button.)

Here's how to add trapping for cancellation to the example program. First, before any dialogs have been opened, set the common dialog's CancelError property to True. (You can do this either in the Properties window or in code.) If CancelError is set to True, the user's cancellation generates an error, cdlCancel (&H7FF3&).

Add an error-handling branch following the CancelError statement:

```
...
CommonDialog1.CancelError = True
On Error GoTo ErrHandler
...
```

Finally, add code to reset error handling and deal with ("handle") the cdlCancel error:

```
...
   End Select
   On Error GoTo 0 'Reset error handling
   'User didn't press Cancel.  Take an action with dialog value.
   Exit Sub
ErrHandler:
```

```
    If Err = cdlCancel Then
       MsgBox "User Pressed Cancel - ignore common dialog values!"
    End If
End Sub
```

The statement

```
On Error GoTo 0
```

reached after successful use of one of the common dialogs, disables any error handlers in the current procedure.

By the way, you could use the ErrHandler label to trap for other common dialog errors besides cdlCancel. For a full list of common dialog error constants, you can use the Object Browser (look at the members of the ErrorConstants class of the MSComDlg library), or check VB's on-line help under CommonDialog Error Constants.

Summary

This chapter covered Version 5 of the common dialog control, ***Comdlg32.Ocx***. ***Comdlg32.Ocx*** serves as an easy-to-use bridge between Visual Basic and many of the dynamic link library functions in ***Comdlg32.Dll***.

In this chapter, I've shown you

- How to open all the different kinds of dialogs available in ***Comdlg32.Ocx***
- How to obtain and use the correct values for common dialog flag constants
- How to set properties and flags in the Properties window
- How to set properties and flags in code
- How to detect cancellation of a dialog

In addition, I've covered some of the tricks for using the common dialogs, such as the Flag value required for the Font dialog to believe that your system has fonts, and the trick to correctly entering Filter properties.

Chapter 8

Windows User Interface Controls

The Professional and Enterprise Editions of VB5 ship with custom controls designed to help you give programs the look and feel of the Windows 95 shell. Programs that you build using these controls will operate the way that users have come to expect the Windows 95 user interface to work.

The controls covered in this chapter are

- SSTab
- TabStrip
- TreeView
- ListView
- ImageList
- Toolbar
- StatusBar
- RichTextBox
- Slider
- ProgressBar
- UpDown
- SysInfo
- FlexGrid

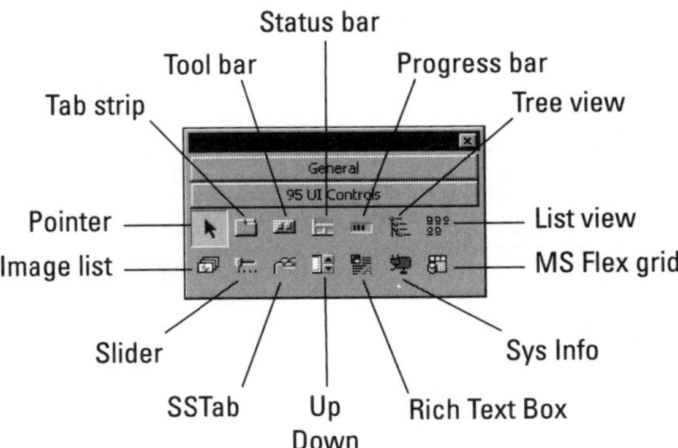

Figure 8-1: These are the Toolbox icons for the Windows 95 user interface controls.

This chapter shows you how to use these controls to create applications that not only follow the Windows 95 user interface conventions, but are Windows 95-like to the *n*th degree!

I believe in showing rather than telling. In my experience, the best way to learn a programming feature is to use it and see it in action. In that spirit, this chapter focuses on example projects that:

- Show you how to use the SSTab control to create a property sheet.
- Explain how to create a Wizard in VB, using a template generic Wizard. The code for the template Wizard is available on the *Visual Basic 5 SECRETS* companion CD-ROM as the ***Wizard.Vbp*** project in the directory associated with Chapter 8.
- Demonstrate the ProgressBar and Slider.
- Show just how much the RichTextBox can do.
- Demonstrate the use of the TreeView, ListView, and ImageList controls.
- Show you how to use the UpDown control — in combination with a "buddy" text box — to create a spinner.

Adding the User Interface Controls to Your Toolbox

Before you get going, you need make sure the controls you wish to use are in your Visual Basic Toolbox.

If the Windows 95 user interface controls are not already in your Toolbox, add them using the Components dialog (found on the Project menu). Table 8-1 shows the name of the control as it appears in the Components dialog, the related filename, and the Active controls contained in the Component dialog item. (A single ***.Ocx*** file can contain a number of separate controls.)

Table 8-1 Component Names and Controls

Name as it Appears in the Components Dialog	*Filename*	*ActiveX Controls Included*
Microsoft FlexGrid Control 5.0	***Msflxgrd.Ocx***	MSFlexGrid
Microsoft Rich Textbox Control 5.0	***Richtx32.Ocx***	RichTextBox
Microsoft SysInfo Control 5.0	***Sysinfo.Ocx***	SysInfo
Microsoft Tabbed Dialog Control 5.0	***Tabctl32.Ocx***	SSTab
Microsoft Windows Common Controls 5.0	***Comctl32.Ocx***	ImageList, ListView, ProgressBar, Slider, StatusBar, TabStrip, Toolbar, TreeView
Microsoft Windows Common Controls-2 5.0	***Comct232.Ocx***	Animation, UpDown

If you'd like to add all the Windows 95 user interface controls to one Toolbox tab, as shown in Figure 8-1, it's easy to do following these steps

1. First, right-click the Toolbox and choose Add Tab from the context menu that appears.
2. Give the Tab an appropriate name — for example, "95 UI Controls." Click OK.
3. Drag whatever controls you want to the new tab.

To keep the Toolbox set up this way between sessions, save a project with the desired configuration as a template (meaning, save the project in the ***Template\Projects*** directory).

Next time you want the Toolbox to have the custom configuration you've created, open the Template project.

Creating a Property Sheet

You can easily create property sheets using tab controls.

After starting a new project, I added an SSTab control to the form. In its default state, the tabbed dialog looks like the one in Figure 8-2. (This mini-application is available on the companion CD-ROM as ***Sheet.Vbp***.)

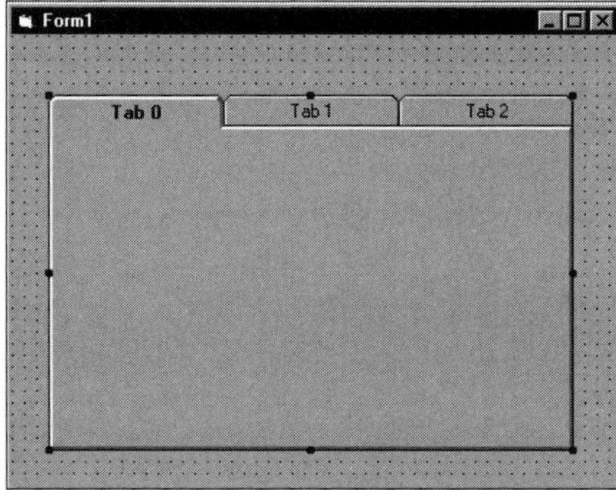

Figure 8-2: Here is an SSTab control dropped on a form.

When I compared it to a typical Windows 95 Properties dialog (see Figure 8-3), I saw that the control's tab shape was not the same as the one in the Properties dialog. To remedy this situation, I changed the default Style property for the SSTab control (the property page used for this is shown in Figure 8-3). The default Style property, 0-ssStyleTabbedDialog, needed to be changed to 1-ssStylePropertyPage.

A Tale of Two Tab Controls

You've probably noticed that the Professional and Enterprise Editions of VB5 ship with two tab controls: SSTab and TabStrip. Despite the initial letters in its name, the SSTab control is not a storm trooper tab — rather, it is based on a tab control originally created by Sheridan Software. Many developers prefer this control to the TabStrip, the Microsoft tab that ships as part of the Windows control set.

Both tab controls are very powerful and flexible; which you use is purely a matter of personal preference. (One argument for using the TabStrip as opposed to the SSTab is that if your project already uses components included in the ***Commctl32.Ocx***, you don't have to ship an additional file.)

The property sheet example uses the SSTab; I'll show you how to use the TabStrip control later in this chapter.

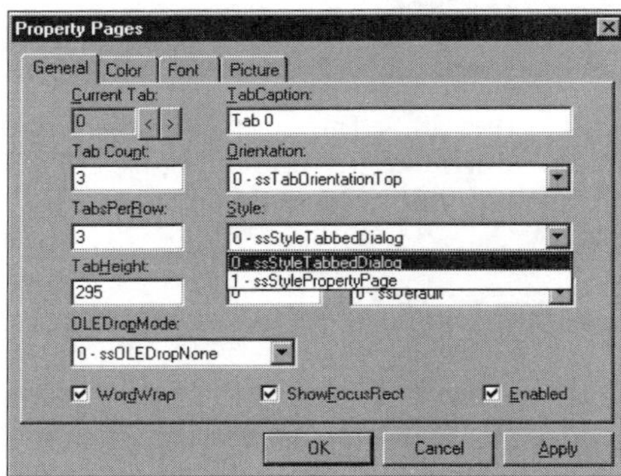

Figure 8-3: The SSTab Property Pages is a pretty typical Windows 95 Properties dialog (note that you can use this dialog to configure the runtime appearance of the SSTab control).

In previous versions, the constant names for these style settings were different. They used to be 0-Microsoft Office Tabbed Dialog and 1-Windows 95 Property Page, respectively.

For this mini-application, I only needed three tabs, so the default setting for the TabCount property was okay. Next, I entered the caption for the first tab in the TabCaption text box. Then I moved on to the next tab by clicking the right-pointing arrow to the right of the Current Tab list box.

After setting the captions for the other two tabs, I turned my attention to the placement of the command buttons at the bottom of my VB form. Looking again at the typical Windows 95-style Properties dialog (Figure 8-3), I saw that I needed three buttons: OK, Cancel, and Apply. Playing with the Windows 95 Properties dialog, I saw that the Apply button was enabled only when a change was selected by the user. My completed Properties dialog is shown in Figure 8-4.

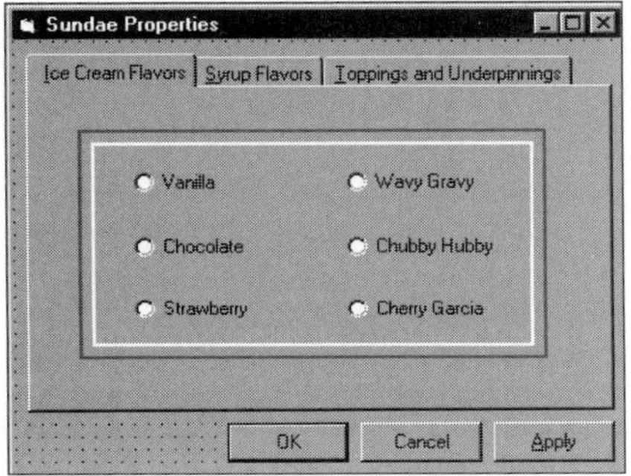

Figure 8-4: Here is the completed VB simulation of a Windows 95 Properties dialog.

Here's how this application works. When the program is launched, a form with a sundae bitmap in an image control appears on the screen. To change the properties of the sundae, the user can either choose the Properties item from the Sundae menu at the top of the form or right-click the sundae bitmap to open a pop-up menu.

The code that creates the pop-up menu uses the same menu that appears at the top of the form. Here's that code:

```
Private Sub imgSundae_MouseUp(Button As Integer, _
   Shift As Integer, X As Single, Y As Single)
   If Button = 2 Then
      PopupMenu mnuSundae
   End If
End Sub
```

Next, the Sundae Properties dialog appears on the screen. The user makes her sundae selections on each tab page. What gets a little tricky here is that the option button selected by the user on a particular tab page does not remain set in the control once the user moves on to the next tab page. So, in case the user moves either forward or backward through the tabs, I created a routine called SetPreviousTab and added code that restores the proper value to the tab control's click event. Listing 8-1 shows how to create a property sheet.

Listing 8-1: Creating a property sheet

```
Private Sub tabProperty_Click(PreviousTab As Integer)
    Dim X As Integer
    Select Case PreviousTab
        Case 0
            For X = 0 To 5
                If optIceCream(X) Then _
                    IceCream = optIceCream(X).Caption
            Next X
        Case 1
            For X = 0 To 5
                If optSyrup(X) Then _
                    Syrup = optSyrup(X).Caption
            Next X
        Case 2
            For X = 0 To 5
                If optToppings(X) Then _
                    Toppings = optToppings(X).Caption
            Next X
        Case Else
            MsgBox "Ain't got that many tabs, boss!"
    End Select
    SetThisTab
End Sub

Private Sub SetThisTab()
    Dim X As Integer
    Select Case tabProperty.Tab
        Case 0
            For X = 0 To 5
                If optIceCream(X).Caption = IceCream Then _
                    optIceCream(X).Value = True
            Next X
        Case 1
            For X = 0 To 5
                If optSyrup(X).Caption = Syrup Then _
                    optSyrup(X).Value = True
            Next X
        Case 2
            For X = 0 To 5
                If optToppings(X).Caption = Toppings Then _
                    optToppings(X).Value = True
            Next X
        Case Else
            MsgBox "Internal Error!"
    End Select
End Sub
```

The last thing that happens with a property sheet is when the user clicks either the Apply or OK button. If Apply is clicked, the changes the user has selected are registered and the Properties dialog remains on the screen. If OK is chosen, the changes are registered and the dialog closes.

To determine what the user has selected, I created a routine, GetUserChoices. For the sake of demonstration in this applet, I send up a message box that lists the "registered" selections.

```
Private Sub GetUserChoices()
    Dim X As Integer, Msg As String
    Select Case tabProperty.Tab
       Case 0
          For X = 0 To 5
             If optIceCream(X) Then IceCream = optIceCream(X).Caption
          Next X
       Case 1
          For X = 0 To 5
             If optSyrup(X) Then Syrup = optSyrup(X).Caption
          Next X
       Case 2
          For X = 0 To 5
             If optToppings(X) Then Toppings = optToppings(X).Caption
          Next X
       Case Else
          MsgBox "Ain't got that many tabs, boss!"
    End Select

    If IceCream = "" And Syrup = "" And Toppings = "" Then
       Msg = "You haven't chosen anything!"
    Else
       Msg = "Your Sundae consists of:" + vbCrLf + vbCrLf
       Msg = Msg + "IceCream Flavor:  " + IceCream + vbCrLf
       Msg = Msg + "Syrup Flavor:  " + Syrup + vbCrLf
       Msg = Msg + "Topping:  " + Toppings
    End If
       MsgBox Msg, vbInformation, "Have a good Sundae!"
End Sub
```

And that's it! When the application runs, the user can create quite a dish, as shown in Figure 8-5.

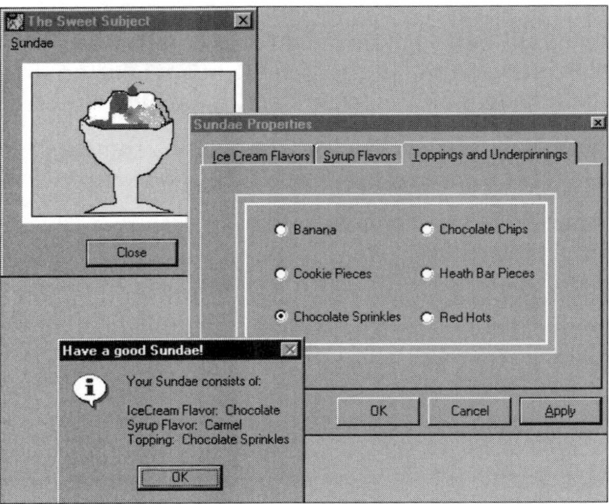

Figure 8-5: This Sundae should take care of that sweet tooth.

Using the TabStrip Control

Included with the Microsoft Windows common controls — meaning, part of the file ***Comctl32.Ocx*** — is a TabStrip control.

The Microsoft TabStrip control works differently from the SSTab control. In my opinion, it is not as user-friendly as the SSTab: Code is required to make it work. Instead of having access to individual tab pages at design time as with the SSTab control, you must manipulate the TabStrip pages with code at runtime. This means that you have to place all control containers on what appears to be the first tab page of the TabStrip control (see Figure 8-6). From there, using code, you can size the containers to fit the client area of the tab page and bring the correct container to the front using the ZOrder method.

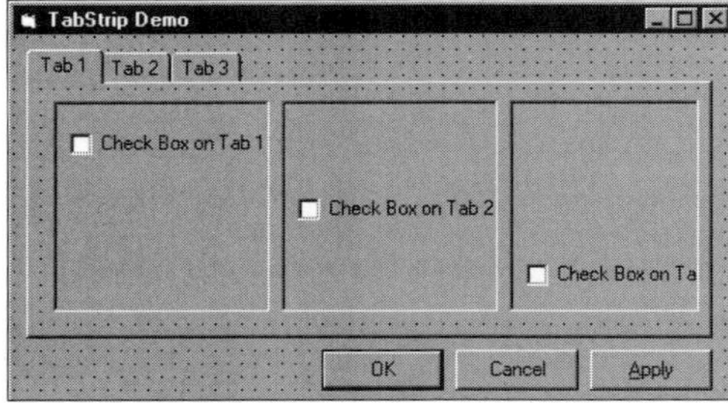

Figure 8-6: A TabStrip control has been placed on a form and three picture boxes are used as containers for other controls.

An example of a working TabStrip control with picture box containers is available on the companion CD-ROM as ***TabStrip.Vbp***.

Here's how to get the TabStrip control to work. Start a new project and add a TabStrip to a form, sizing it as you wish. Open the TabStrip Control Properties window found under the Custom property and move to the Tabs tab page to set up three tab pages. On the Tabs tab page enter a caption for the first tab page, and then press the Insert Tab button to create a second tab page. Enter a caption for this tab page, and then create a third tab page by again pressing the Insert Tab button. Add a caption for that tab page, and then click OK to close the Properties window.

Add an array of three picture box controls to act as containers to the TabStrip control, as shown in Figure 8-6. Add a different check box to each picture box, and then open the form's Code window.

Add the following code to the form's Load event to size the picture control array to cover the client area of the tab control and set the first picture control on top:

```
Private Sub Form_Load()
   Dim i As Integer
   For i = 0 To 2
      picContainer(i).Left = tabDemo.ClientLeft
      picContainer(i).Top = tabDemo.ClientTop
      picContainer(i).Height = tabDemo.ClientHeight
      picContainer(i).Width = tabDemo.ClientWidth
   Next
      picContainer(0).ZOrder 0
End Sub
```

Then, add a line of code to the TabStrip's Click event to bring the correct picture control to the front when the user changes tab pages:

```
Private Sub tabSundae_Click()
   picContainer(tabDemo.SelectedItem.Index - 1).ZOrder 0
End Sub
```

Run the demonstration application now and see how the picture boxes are resized and correctly brought to the front when a specific tab page is selected.

Using the Template Options Form

Visual Basic 5 contains various forms that you can use as templates for your own forms. These forms are located in the ***Template\Forms*** directory; you can access them every time you add a form to a project.

One template form is an Options dialog, frmOption. This form uses the TabStrip control and is pretty similar to the dialog displayed in Figure 8-6. Selecting the Options form as a template is a shortcut to getting the TabStrip to work for you. Not only have controls been added to the surface of the TabStrip, but some code — such as that allowing the user to tab from one panel of the dialog to the next — is already in place.

Creating a Wizard

As you probably know, Wizards are central to the metaphor of the Windows 95 user interface. Indeed, Wizards — or Experts and Coaches, other names for the same thing — are central to the way most major modern applications operate.

In Windows 95, Wizards are used to walk users through complex tasks. To the user, the Wizard appears to be a series of similar-sized panels, each including Back, Next, and Cancel buttons. (The Back button is disabled on the first panel.)

In addition, each panel contains whatever controls are necessary for the user to accomplish that panel's task. When the final panel is reached, the Next button's caption changes to Finish; when the user clicks this button, whatever code is needed to complete the Wizard's task is executed. An example of a Wizard that's part of the Windows 95 operating system is the Add New Hardware Wizard. (To see it, open the Control Panel and double-click Add New Hardware.)

Some Wizards — for example, Excel's ChartWizard — operate slightly differently in that a Finish button is always available, allowing the user to bypass subsequent panels at any time. If you'd like your Wizard to behave this way, you can easily modify the sample project.

You might think that a Wizard consists of a number of different forms. A Wizard put together this way could, for example, hide the first form when the second one was shown. All the forms would have the controls common to all — Back, Next, and Cancel — in exactly the same place.

Although there is nothing to stop you from putting together a Wizard in this way, it is easier, more efficient, and more elegant to use a single form with the common controls. You can manage the controls collection on the form to create the *illusion* of multiple panels by managing the visibility and invisibility of additional controls.

The *Visual Basic 5 SECRETS* companion CD-ROM provides template code that you can use to easily create a Wizard based upon a single form. The files you'll need from the CD-ROM are ***Wizard.Bas*** and ***Wizard.Frm***. In this section, I'll provide

- A step-by-step guide explaining how to use the generic Wizard template and code to create your own Wizards with ease
- A sample Wizard named ***SillyWiz.Vbp*** for you to play with
- An explanation of how the generic Wizard code works

The generic Wizard is actually not very exciting to look at (see Figure 8-7), but, as you'll see in a minute, it has plenty of built-in functionality.

The Wizard Wizard

Visual Basic 5 ships with the Wizard Wizard — more prosaically known as the Wizard manager — a tool designed to help you create Wizards that are add-ins. You can run the Wizard Wizard by selecting it from Visual Basic's Add-Ins menu, provided that it first has been enabled in the Add-In Manager.

The primary purpose of the Wizard Wizard is to manage the design time interface of Wizard panels, where the Wizard is intended to be used as an add-in that interacts with instances of the Visual Basic environment. I'll show you how to create this kind of Wizard — which can look like a seamless part of the VB environment to your users — in Chapter 30, "Building a Wizard."

Keep in mind that the Wizard Wizard produces no runtime implementation code other than that required to register Wizards created with it as add-ins. The primary purpose of the Wizard Wizard is to take care of design time panel display so that you can visually create the Add-In Wizard. However, there is nothing to stop you from using the panels that the Wizard Wizard creates as a starting place for your own Wizards — even if they are more the Sundae than add-in kind. (The "Sundae" Wizard is described later in this chapter; add-ins are explained in Chapter 29, "Creating a VB Add-In.") Just remember that you will be responsible for all runtime implementation of your Wizard, whether or not it is an add-in.

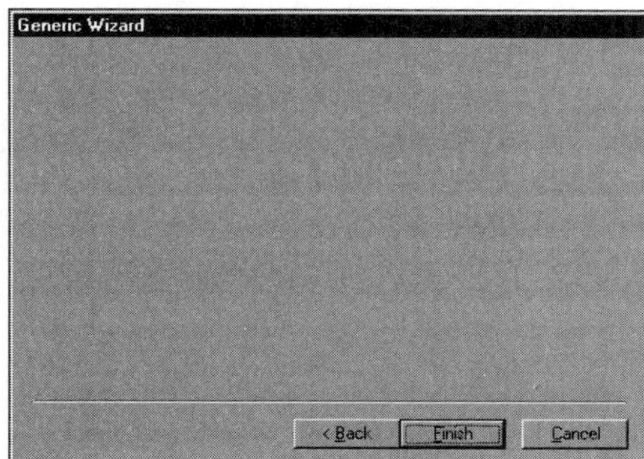

Figure 8-7: Here is the generic Wizard that you can use to easily build Wizards of your own.

Creating Your Own Wizards

Here's how you can use my generic Wizard to create your own Wizards:

1. Copy the Wizard files — ***Wizard.Bas***, ***Wizard.Frm***, and ***Wizard.Vbp*** — to your hard drive.
2. Open the ***Wizard.Vbp*** project. Save each file, and the project, under a new name.

3. Plan the number of panels you'd like and the number of controls that will be on each panel.

4. Open ***Wizard.Bas*** code module in the Code Editor. Find the SetUpWiz procedure. It will look like this:

```
Private Sub SetUpWiz()
    'Panel 1
    ItemsInPanel 0
    'Panel 2
    ItemsInPanel 0
    'Panel 3
    ItemsInPanel 0
End Sub
```

   The number of calls to ItemsInPanel represents the number of panels in the Wizard; the argument passed to ItemsInPanel tells the Wizard how many controls are on that panel. You need to change the code to reflect your particular Wizard. For example, if you wanted to create a four-panel Wizard with two controls on each panel, you would change SetUpWiz to read:

```
Private Sub SetUpWiz()
    'Panel 1
    ItemsInPanel 2
    'Panel 2
    ItemsInPanel 2
    'Panel 3
    ItemsInPanel 2
    'Panel 4
    ItemsInPanel 2
End Sub
```

5. Next, add the controls you'd like to the ***Wizard.Frm***. The Wizard manages the visibility and invisibility of these controls through their .Tag properties, so it's important that you set .Tag correctly. The first control you add should have its .Tag property set to 5. (This value is one more than the number of Wizard common controls. There are four controls on every panel: three buttons and a line.)

   The second control should have its .Tag property set to 6, and so on. You must set the .Tag properties so the panels are managed properly. In the example with two controls per panel, the controls should have .Tag properties as shown in Table 8-2.

Table 8-2 .Tag Properties for Controls on a Four-Panel Wizard with Two Controls per Panel

Panel	*Control .Tag Properties*
1	5,6
2	7,8
3	9,10
4	10,11

6. That's it for managing the appearance of the panels. You'll also want to add execution code that makes the Wizard actually do something. Usually, this code is called after the user clicks the Finish button. I've added a procedure for you to use in this fashion. It's called ShutDown and it has a message box as a placeholder that's called when the user clicks Finish:

```
Public Sub ShutDown()
  MsgBox "Doing what has to be done with values and stuff...ending!"
  Unload ThisWizard
  End
End Sub
```

Bear in mind that you still have at your disposal the values entered in all Wizard controls at this point; they have merely been hidden, not unloaded.

You might also need to place execution code, if the user presses Cancel, to clean up, restore, or whatever. This code should probably go in the cmdCancel click event of the template form.

You can easily add execution code to the events of any control on the panel (bearing in mind that controls that are not visible are also automatically disabled).

You can also add execution code when going forwards or backwards between panels — you'd probably have to check *which* panel you've just left — but this would be a little more tricky.

The Sundae Wizard

Figure 8-8 shows a Sundae Wizard that lets the user create an ice cream sundae with a choice of containers, ice creams, and toppings. This Wizard is saved on the CD-ROM as ***SillyWiz.Vbp***. It is much like the Tabbed Property Sheet sundae example earlier in this chapter.

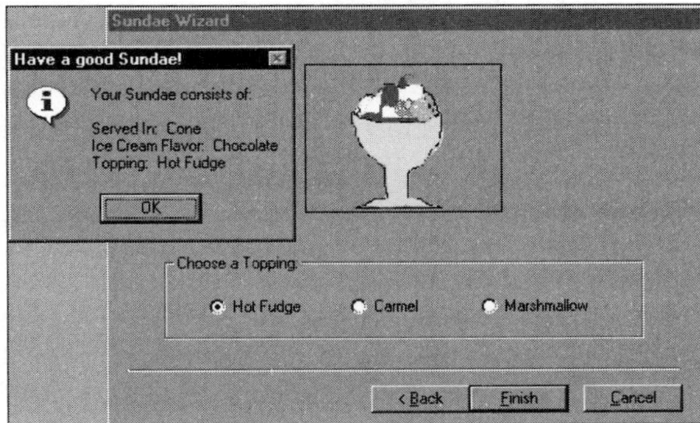

Figure 8-8: The Sundae Wizard employs the generic Wizard template project to guide users through the creation of a sundae.

The .Tag Property

You can use the .Tag property to store any information about controls you need for your program. All controls have a .Tag property, which isn't used by Visual Basic. It is intended for your use in identifying objects in your programs. The date type of a control's .Tag property is string and its default value is the empty string ("").

To create the Sundae Wizard, I started with the generic Wizard files and followed steps 1 through 4 for creating a Wizard based on the generic Wizard. At that point, my SetUpWiz procedure was as follows:

```
Private Sub SetUpWiz()
    'Panel 1
    ItemsInPanel 4
    'Panel 2
    ItemsInPanel 4
    'Panel 3
    ItemsInPanel 4
End Sub
```

In other words, the Sundae Wizard would have three panels, each containing four controls. While planning the Wizard, I also realized that I wanted an additional control to be common to all panels: the Image control containing a bitmap of a sundae. (You can see it in Figure 8-8.)

To modify the Wizard code to include another control on all panels, I changed the module level constant in ***SillyWiz.Bas*** from:

```
Const DesignTimeControls = 4 'num controls on all Wizards
```

to:

```
Const DesignTimeControls = 5 'num controls on all Wizards
```

Because I added a common control to all Wizard panels — the Sundae Wizard now has three buttons, a line, and an image control — the .Tag property for controls (explained in step 5) should start at 6 (not 5).

In addition to the common Wizard controls, the Sundae Wizard has a frame and an option button array with three buttons on each panel — adding up to four controls per panel.

The Sundae Wizard will now run and display all its panels as it should. To demonstrate how you might capture values from the Wizard's controls, I've added code to the ShutDown routine to display a message box showing the Sundae values selected by the user (see Figure 8-8):

```
Private Sub ShutDown()
    Dim X As Integer, Msg As String, Container As String, _
       IceCream As String, Toppings As String
    For X = 0 To 2
     With ThisWizard
```

```
            If .optContainer(X) Then Container = .optContainer(X).Caption
            If .optIceCream(X) Then IceCream = .optIceCream(X).Caption
            If .optToppings(X) Then Toppings = .optToppings(X).Caption
         End With
      Next X
      If Container = "" And IceCream = "" And Toppings = "" Then
         Msg = "You haven't chosen anything!"
      Else
         Msg = "Your Sundae consists of:" + vbCrLf + vbCrLf
         Msg = Msg + "Served In:  " + Container + vbCrLf
         Msg = Msg + "Ice Cream Flavor:  " + IceCream + vbCrLf
         Msg = Msg + "Topping:  " + Toppings
      End If
      MsgBox Msg, vbInformation, "Have a good Sundae!"
      Unload ThisWizard
      End
End Sub
```

The Wizard is now fully functional, although it can't serve up a real ice cream sundae, unfortunately!

The first time I ran the Sundae Wizard, I noticed one thing I wanted to change. When I clicked Finish, the Wizard disappeared before the message box with the sundae's contents was displayed. I decided I really wanted to have the final panel of the Wizard still on the screen while the message box was displayed (see Figure 8-8).

It was easy to make this modification. I simply commented out the line that invoked the .Hide methods for the Wizard, which was called just before the ShutDown procedure from ChangePanel, the routine that moves the user through the various panels of the Wizard.

Read on for an explanation of the Wizard's logic!

Understanding the Wizard Code

Here are the module-level declarations for ***Wizard.Bas***:

```
Option Explicit
Dim LastPanel As Integer, PanelItems() As Integer, _
    ThisPanel As Integer, ThisWizard As New frmWizard
Const DesignTimeControls = 4 'num controls on all Wizards
```

ThisPanel and LastPanel are variables that represent the number of the current panel and the last panel in the Wizard, respectively. PanelItems() is a dynamic integer array that will be used to track the controls on the current panel, with a twist: PanelItems(*x*), where *x* is the current panel, will be set to the number of controls on the current panel *plus* the value of PanelItems(*x*-1). For example, because the Sundae Wizard has three panels with four items each, PanelItems(3) = 12.

DesignTimeControls is the number of controls that are common to all the panels of the Wizard; it is one less than the first tag value for controls whose .Visible property the Wizard will manipulate.

The declaration of ThisWizard as New frmWizard means that ThisWizard is an instance of frmWizard. This is important to understand. All the code for the Wizard is in the ***.Bas*** module and applies to the ThisWizard instance, not to frmWizard. (The only code in frmWizard is a single line call to the code module when Back, Next, or Finish has been clicked.)

The generic Wizard project is set to start from Sub Main:

```
Public Sub Main()
   Dim I As Integer
   LastPanel = 0
   SetUpWiz
   'Show First Panel
   ThisPanel = 1
   ThisWizard.cmdBack.Enabled = False
   'Populate the form
   For I = 0 To ThisWizard.Controls.Count - 1
      If Val(ThisWizard.Controls(I).Tag) > DesignTimeControls And _
         Val(ThisWizard.Controls(I).Tag) <= DesignTimeControls + _
         PanelItems(1) Then
            ThisWizard.Controls(I).Visible = True
      End If
   Next I
   ThisWizard.Show
End Sub
```

Sub Main first calls the SetUpWiz procedure. SetUpWiz is where the number of panels and items per panel are set. In the case of the generic Wizard, there are three panels and no controls:

```
Private Sub SetUpWiz()
   'Panel 1
   ItemsInPanel 0
   'Panel 2
   ItemsInPanel 0
   'Panel 3
   ItemsInPanel 0
End Sub
```

The ItemsInPanel procedure that SetUpWiz calls reads values into the dynamic array ItemsInPanel, as described earlier:

```
Private Sub ItemsInPanel(HowMany As Integer)
   LastPanel = LastPanel + 1
   ReDim Preserve PanelItems(1 To LastPanel)
   If LastPanel > 1 Then
      PanelItems(LastPanel) = HowMany + PanelItems(LastPanel - 1)
   Else
      PanelItems(LastPanel) = HowMany 'only for first panel
   End If
End Sub
```

Returning to Sub Main, the rest of the procedure initializes the appearance of the first panel. It sets the .Enabled property of cmdBack to False because you can't go backwards from the first panel, and it uses the .Tag properties of all controls in the ThisWizard controls collection to set the .Visible property of all controls on the first panel to True:

```
For I = 0 To ThisWizard.Controls.Count - 1
   If Val(ThisWizard.Controls(I).Tag) > DesignTimeControls And _
      Val(ThisWizard.Controls(I).Tag) <= DesignTimeControls + _
      PanelItems(1) Then
         ThisWizard.Controls(I).Visible = True
      End If
Next I
```

Finally, the Wizard is displayed using its .Show method.

A procedure named ChangePanel is invoked whenever the user presses cmdBack (argument is 1) or cmdNext (argument is 2) in frmWizard (as mentioned, these are the only lines of code that are in frmWizard):

```
Private Sub cmdNext_Click()
   ChangePanel 1
End Sub

Private Sub cmdBack_Click()
   ChangePanel 2
End Sub
```

Here's the ChangePanel routine:

```
Public Sub ChangePanel(Which As Integer)
   Select Case Which
      Case 1  'Next or Finish
         If ThisPanel = 1 Then
            ThisWizard.cmdBack.Enabled = True
         End If
         ThisPanel = ThisPanel + 1
         If ThisPanel = LastPanel Then
            ThisWizard.cmdNext.Caption = "&Finish"
         ElseIf ThisPanel > LastPanel Then
            ThisWizard.Hide
            ShutDown
         End If
         SetNewPanel ThisPanel - 1, NextPanel(ThisPanel - 1)
      Case 2 'Back
         If ThisPanel = LastPanel Then
            ThisWizard.cmdNext.Caption = "&Next"
         End If
         SetNewPanel ThisPanel, PrevPanel(ThisPanel)
         ThisPanel = ThisPanel - 1
         If ThisPanel = 1 Then
            ThisWizard.cmdBack.Enabled = False
         End If
      Case Else 'shouldn't get here
         MsgBox "Internal Wizard Error!"
   End Select
End Sub
```

The procedure takes care of enabling the Back button if the Wizard is not displaying the first panel, changing the caption Next to Finish on the last panel, and calling the ShutDown procedure if Finish has been clicked. It also increments (or decrements) the contents of ThisPanel, as appropriate.

SetNewPanel does the actual work of managing the visibility of the new panel. It is called no matter which direction the Wizard is moving, but with different arguments if it is forwards or backwards. The NextPanel and PrevPanel functions, which are themselves called in the SetNewPanel procedure call, advance or decrement the next panel or previous panel argument, but in a way that avoids an out-of-range error (for example, going back from panel zero, or forward to panel four in a three-panel Wizard):

```
Private Function NextPanel(OldPanel As Integer) As Integer
   If OldPanel = LastPanel Then
      NextPanel = OldPanel
   Else
      NextPanel = OldPanel + 1
   End If
End Function
Private Function PrevPanel(OldPanel As Integer) As Integer
   If OldPanel = 1 Then
      PrevPanel = OldPanel
   Else
      PrevPanel = OldPanel - 1
   End If
End Function
```

Here's SetNewPanel:

```
Private Sub SetNewPanel(oldP As Integer, newP As Integer)
  Dim I As Integer
  If newP > oldP Then 'Forwards
    For I = 0 To ThisWizard.Controls.Count - 1
      If Val(ThisWizard.Controls(I).Tag) > PanelItems(oldP) _
        + DesignTimeControls And Val(ThisWizard.Controls(I).Tag) _
        <= PanelItems(newP) + DesignTimeControls Then
          ThisWizard.Controls(I).Visible = True
      Else
        If Val(ThisWizard.Controls(I).Tag) > DesignTimeControls Then
          ThisWizard.Controls(I).Visible = False
        End If
      End If
    Next I
  ElseIf newP > 1 Then 'Backwards
    For I = 0 To ThisWizard.Controls.Count - 1
      If Val(ThisWizard.Controls(I).Tag) <= PanelItems(newP) _
        + DesignTimeControls And Val(ThisWizard.Controls(I).Tag) _
        > PanelItems(PrevPanel(newP)) + DesignTimeControls Then
          ThisWizard.Controls(I).Visible = True
      Else
        If Val(ThisWizard.Controls(I).Tag) > DesignTimeControls Then
          ThisWizard.Controls(I).Visible = False
        End If
      End If
    Next I
Else 'special case for backwards to first panel
    For I = 0 To ThisWizard.Controls.Count - 1
      If Val(ThisWizard.Controls(I).Tag) <= PanelItems(newP) _
        + DesignTimeControls And Val(ThisWizard.Controls(I).Tag) _
        > DesignTimeControls Then
```

```
            ThisWizard.Controls(I).Visible = True
        Else
          If Val(ThisWizard.Controls(I).Tag) > DesignTimeControls Then
            ThisWizard.Controls(I).Visible = False
          End If
        End If
      Next I
    End If
End Sub
```

As with the code in Sub Main that sets up the first panel, this code uses the controls collection of ThisWizard to establish the visibility of controls, depending on the direction of movement, new panel, and .Tag property of each control. Although the logic is a touch complex, it will become easier to follow if you work it through with some actual examples. Once you've done so, you'll completely understand the Wizard logic and will be ready to modify it to create truly custom Wizards!

A ProgressBar and Slider Demo

It is rather straightforward which properties you need to set to make the ProgressBar and Slider controls functional. In this sample application, available on the companion CD-ROM as ***ProgSlid.Vbp***, the Slider is used to set the number of seconds that the ProgressBar will operate.

The Slider comes equipped with a handle (sometimes called a *thumb*) that the user slides to select a value. The properties that we are concerned with in this mini-app are Max and Min, which set the maximum and minimum values of the Slider, and Value, which is the value set by the user when she moves the Slider's handle.

Using the Slider control's properties, you can also set a range of values that the user can select. To configure a Slider in this way, make sure that the SelectRange property is set to True, and then set the SelLength and SelStart properties to set the length of the value selection and the value where the selection will start, respectively. For example, the Slider shown in Figure 8-9 has the following property settings: SelectRange = True, SelLength = 2, and SelStart = 0. As you can see in the figure, the range of the selection is two ticks and the default value of the Slider when the application is launched is a range between 0 and 2.

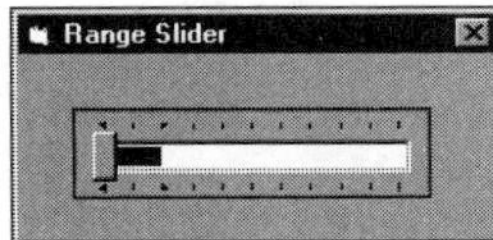

Figure 8-9: This Slider is set up to select from a range of values.

The ProgressBar control operates using blue "chunks" to graphically mark the passage of time. The demo application uses the properties Min and Max, which set the minimum and maximum values, and a property only available at runtime: Value.

After starting a new project, I dropped a Slider, ProgressBar, two command buttons — OK and Close — and a timer on a form.

The main action in this project occurs after the user has used the Slider to select the number of seconds the ProgressBar will operate and has clicked OK.

The OK button's click event is where the duration of the ProgressBar is set and Timer1 is enabled. Timer1's Timer event is fired the correct number of times as set in cmdOK_Click, based on the Timer1.Interval property and the Time variable (which stands for the total amount of time the ProgressBar should run).

```
Private Sub cmdOK_Click()
   Time = Slider1.Value * 1000
   Timer1.Interval = 100
   ProgressBar1.Max = Time
   Timer1.Enabled = True
End Sub

Private Sub Timer1_Timer()
   TimeElapsed = TimeElapsed + Timer1.Interval
   If TimeElapsed > Time Then
      Timer1.Enabled = False
       ProgressBar1.Value = 0
       TimeElapsed = 0
      Exit Sub
   End If
   ProgressBar1.Value = TimeElapsed
End Sub
```

When the application runs, it looks like the window shown in Figure 8-10.

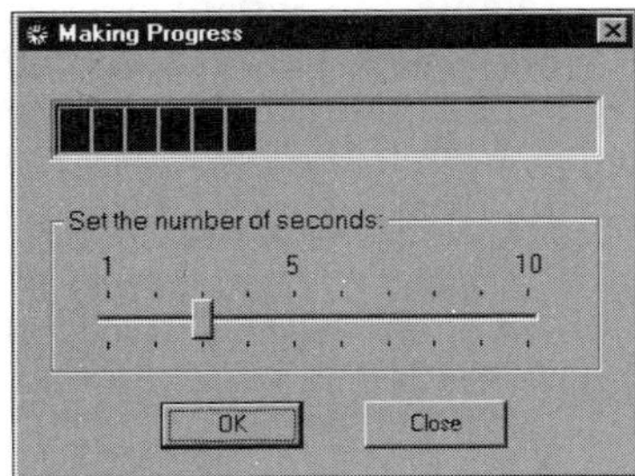

Figure 8-10: This application lets you watch the seconds go by.

A Text Editor Demo

This sample application uses the RichTextBox control as an integral part of a proto-text-editor application. It's not very full featured: It can only open, save, and print rich text files in addition to changing font attributes. However, it wouldn't be that hard to extend the application, word processing feature by word processing feature. The RichTextBox control is worth it. The font manipulation abilities of this control are quite snazzy, and leave ordinary multiline text boxes behind in the dust.

The RichTextBox application also includes the Toolbar, ImageList, and StatusBar controls. The application is on the companion CD-ROM in the Chapter 8 directory as ***RichText.Vbp***.

After starting a new project, I double-clicked the StatusBar control to add one to the form. By default, the status bar is aligned at the bottom of the form with one pane available (see Figure 8-11). To change the properties of the status bar, I selected Custom from the Properties window to access the Property Pages for the control, as shown in Figure 8-11.

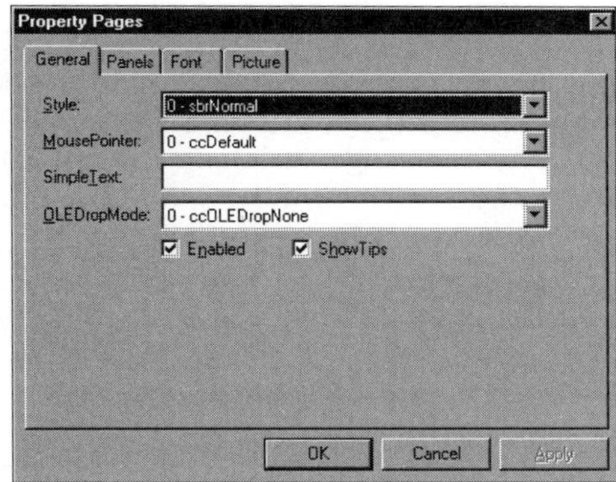

Figure 8-11: Here is the default StatusBar control and its Property Pages.

In the StatusBar Property Pages, I moved to the Panels tab, where I set the following properties for the first panel: Alignment to 1-Center, Style to 5-Time, and AutoSize to 1-Spring. Then I pressed the Insert Panel button to add a second panel, changed Alignment and AutoSize to the same settings that I used on the first panel, and set Style to 6-Date.

Next, I dropped a RichTextBox control onto the form, stretched it to the proper size, set the DisableNoScroll property to True, and changed the ScrollBars property to 3-Both.

After setting up a simple File menu containing Open, Save, Print, and Exit items, as well as a Style menu with a Font item, I added Toolbar, ImageList, and CommonDialog controls to the form.

I loaded four bitmap images representing Open, Save, Print, and Font into the ImageList using the Images tab of the control's Property Pages, as shown in Figure 8-12.

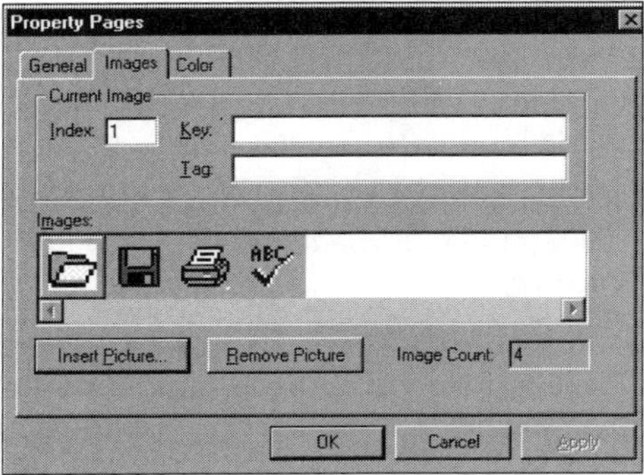

Figure 8-12: I used the Images tab page to load four images into the ImageList control.

Then I moved to the Colors tab page and set the BackColor property to light gray and the MaskColor property to white (see Figure 8-13). If these two properties are not set in this way, the images will look strange once they're loaded on the toolbar buttons; they'll look as if they are disabled.

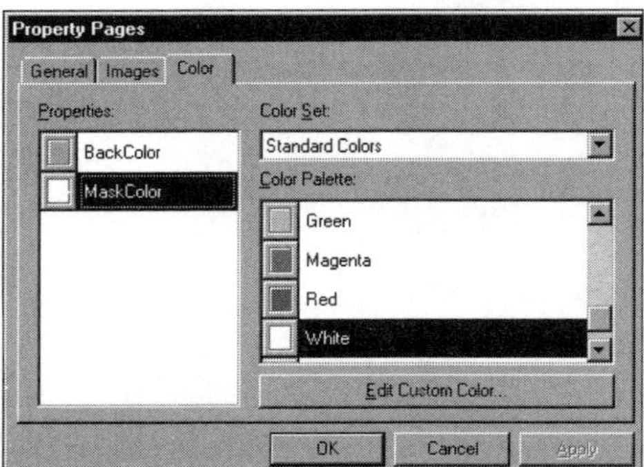

Figure 8-13: You use the Colors tab page to set the images' BackColor and MaskColor.

To load the images onto toolbar buttons, I opened the Toolbar control's custom Properties Pages (either select the Custom property or right-click the control). I linked the ImageList control to the Toolbar control using the drop-down list next to the ImageList property on the General tab. Then I moved to the Buttons tab page to create the toolbar buttons and assign their images (see Figure 8-14).

I pressed the Insert Button command button to create the first button. Next, I entered **Open** in the Key text box, entered **Open RTF File** in the ToolTipText text box, and assigned the ImageList control's first image to the button by typing **1** in the Image text box. I pressed Insert Button again to add the next button, assigning its properties as for the first button. I continued until all four buttons had been loaded.

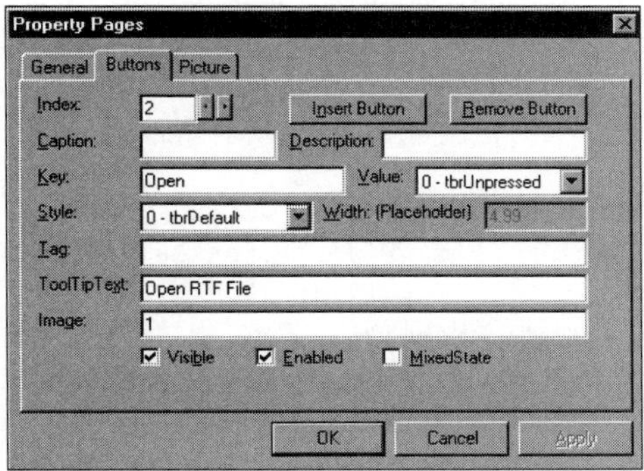

Figure 8-14: You use the Buttons tab page to insert toolbar buttons and assign images to them.

When this text editor application runs, the user can type whatever she wants into the RichTextBox; select sections of text for which to change the font, font size, and color; and so on. Also she can open ***.Rtf*** files, save the text in ***.Rtf*** format, and print what she has typed. The code for this project appeared rather straightforward until I started to wire it up. Then I discovered a few wrinkles that I'll tell you about next.

To make the toolbar buttons operational, I set calls to the corresponding menu items — using the Key values that I had set when I loaded the buttons — in a Select Case statement:

```
Private Sub Toolbar1_ButtonClick(ByVal Button As Button)
   Select Case Button.Key
      Case "Open"
         mnuOpen_Click
      Case "Save"
         mnuSave_Click
      Case "Print"
         mnuPrint_Click
      Case "Font"
         mnuFont_Click
   End Select
End Sub
```

The next job was to write the code that activated each menu item. The code that facilitates changing fonts and font attributes is shown in Listing 8-2:

Listing 8-2: Changing fonts and attributes

```
Private Sub mnuFont_Click()
   CommonDialog1.FontName = RichTextBox1.SelFontName
   CommonDialog1.FontSize = RichTextBox1.SelFontSize
   CommonDialog1.FontBold = RichTextBox1.SelBold
   CommonDialog1.FontItalic = RichTextBox1.SelItalic
   CommonDialog1.Color = RichTextBox1.SelColor
   CommonDialog1.FontStrikethru = RichTextBox1.SelStrikethru
   CommonDialog1.FontUnderline = RichTextBox1.SelUnderline
   CommonDialog1.CancelError = True
   On Error GoTo ErrHandle
   CommonDialog1.Flags = cdlCFBoth + cdlCFWYSIWYG + cdlCFEffects
   CommonDialog1.ShowFont
   On Error GoTo 0
   RichTextBox1.SelFontName = CommonDialog1.FontName
   RichTextBox1.SelFontSize = CommonDialog1.FontSize
   RichTextBox1.SelBold = CommonDialog1.FontBold
   RichTextBox1.SelItalic = CommonDialog1.FontItalic
   RichTextBox1.SelStrikethru = CommonDialog1.FontStrikethru
   RichTextBox1.SelUnderline = CommonDialog1.FontUnderline
   RichTextBox1.SelColor = CommonDialog1.Color
   Exit Sub
ErrHandle:
   If Not Err = cdlCancel Then Resume Next
End Sub
```

The Windows 95 common font dialog is used to process input regarding fonts. (I did mention that you need to add a common dialog control to the form, didn't I?) For more on how to work with the common dialogs, see Chapter 7, "Windows Common Dialog Secrets."

In the preceding code example, the common dialog control is first populated with the current RichTextBox information. Provided that the user makes a selection without canceling out, the settings in the font dialog are then assigned as values to the appropriate RichTextBox properties. By the way, if no text is selected before the common dialog is opened, font information is changed beginning at the insertion point.

Listing 8-3 shows how to print the contents of the control:

Listing 8-3: Printing the contents of a RichTextBox

```
Private Sub mnuPrint_Click()
   CommonDialog1.CancelError = True
   On Error GoTo ErrHandle
   CommonDialog1.Flags = cdlPDNoPageNums
   If RichTextBox1.SelLength = 0 Then
      CommonDialog1.Flags = CommonDialog1.Flags + cdlPDAllPages
   Else
      CommonDialog1.Flags = CommonDialog1.Flags + cdlPDSelection
   End If
   CommonDialog1.ShowPrinter
   Printer.Print
```

```
    RichTextBox1.SelPrint Printer.hDC 'Printer device context
    Printer.EndDoc
Exit Sub
ErrHandle:
    If Not Err = cdlCancel Then Resume Next
End Sub
```

This code uses the common dialog to set the current printer object, and then initializes the Printer object using its .Print method. The RichTextBox's .SelPrint method is called with the Printer's device context as an argument (not the device context returned by the common dialog, as in the sample code). Finally, the printer's .EndDoc method is called to terminate printing.

Here's the code behind the Open and Save items:

```
Private Sub mnuOpen_Click()
    CommonDialog1.CancelError = True
    On Error GoTo ErrHandle
    CommonDialog1.Filter = _
        "Rich Text File (*.Rtf)|*.rtf|All Files (*.*)|*.*"
    CommonDialog1.Flags = cdlOFNPathMustExist + cdlOFNHideReadOnly _
        + cdlOFNFileMustExist
    CommonDialog1.ShowOpen
    RichTextBox1.LoadFile (CommonDialog1.filename)
    On Error GoTo 0
    Exit Sub
ErrHandle:
    If Not Err = cdlCancel Then
        Resume Next
    End If
End Sub

Private Sub mnuSave_Click()
    CommonDialog1.CancelError = True
    On Error GoTo ErrHandle
    CommonDialog1.Filter = _
        "Rich Text File (*.Rtf)|*.rtf|All Files (*.*)|*.*"
    CommonDialog1.Flags = _
        cdlOFNCreatePrompt + cdlOFNOverwritePrompt + _
        cdlOFNPathMustExist + cdlOFNHideReadOnly
    CommonDialog1.ShowSave
    RichTextBox1.SaveFile (CommonDialog1.filename)
    On Error GoTo 0
    Exit Sub
ErrHandle:
    If Not Err = cdlCancel Then Resume Next
End Sub
```

Considering the power of its built-in methods, the RichTextBox control is extraordinarily powerful! Figure 8-15 shows some of what it can do.

Figure 8-15: Here is the RichTextBox strutting its stuff.

Displaying Hierarchies: The ListView and TreeView Controls

The TreeView control is used to display hierarchic information. The ListView control, often used in conjunction with TreeView, is used to show lists of information. The two controls should be quite familiar to users of Windows 95: The interface of the Explorer, the Windows 95 analog to the Windows 3.*x* File Manager, consists primarily of a TreeView control on the left and a ListView control on the right.

The sample project, saved on the CD-ROM as ***TLView.Vbp***, uses a TreeView control on the left-hand side of its form and a ListView on the right-hand side, just like Explorer. In addition, I added two ImageList controls and a four-member option button array to allow the user to select at runtime between the possible ListView modes (see Figures 8-16 and 8-17).

The demonstration application displays a range of years in hierarchic fashion. If each year is expanded, its months are displayed, and below that the days of the month. If nothing else, you can use the program to find out what day of the week your birthday falls on in 2005, and whether there is a February 29 in 2004! The ListView control is filled with the days of each expanded month.

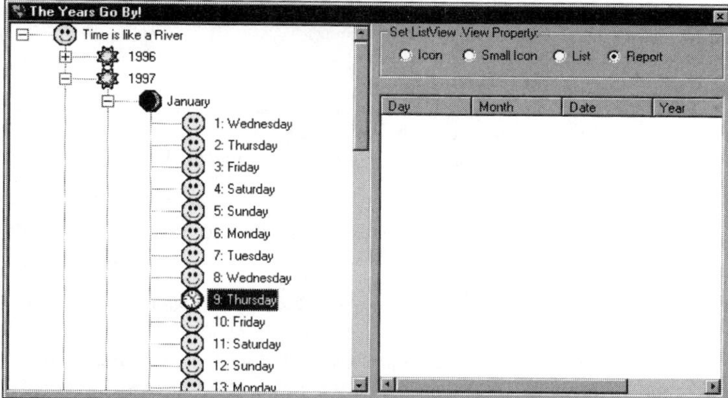

Figure 8-16: The TreeView control when expanded provides an excellent way to display hierarchic information.

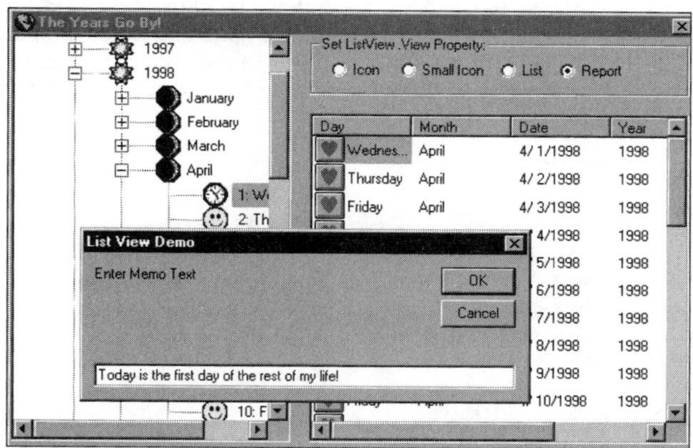

Figure 8-17: Here is the completed application that uses the TreeView and ListView controls.

If you use the ListView .View property, ListView controls can be toggled between four different states. Table 8-3 shows the possible values of .View and describes how a ListView control appears.

Table 8-3 ListView .View Settings

Constant	*Value*	*Consequence*
lvwIcon	0	Icon view is the default. Each ListItem object is represented by a full-sized (standard) icon and a text label, as shown in Figure 8-18.
lvwSmallIcon	1	In Small Icon view, each ListItem is represented by a small icon and a text label that appears to the right of the icon. The items are arranged horizontally, as shown in Figure 8-19.
lvwList	2	In List view, each ListItem is represented by a small icon and a text label that appears to the right of the icon. The items are arranged vertically, as shown in Figure 8-20. Small Icon view and List view are very similar except for the direction of the display.
lvwReport	3	In Report view, each ListItem is displayed with its small icons and text labels. You can provide additional information (SubItems) about each ListItem. The icons, text labels, and information appear in columns, with the leftmost column containing the small icon followed by the text label. Additional columns display the text for each of the item's SubItems. Figure 8-21 shows a ListView control set to Report view.

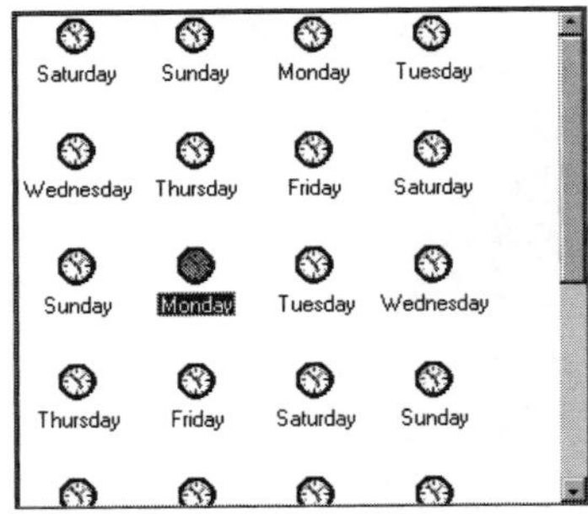

Figure 8-18: When the ListView control is set to Icon view, objects are represented by full-sized icons.

The important thing to realize about the .View property is that only when a ListView is in Report view will it display Column Headers and SubItems.

I'll be coming back to the subject, but you probably get the correct idea from Table 8-3 that ListView contains a collection of ListItems.

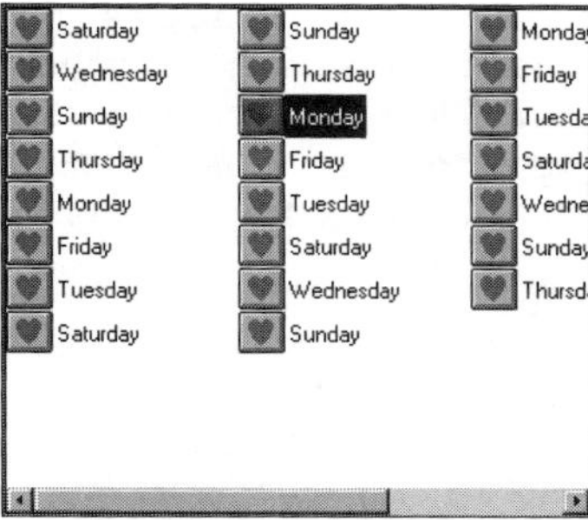

Figure 8-19: In Small Icon view, objects are represented by small icons arranged horizontally.

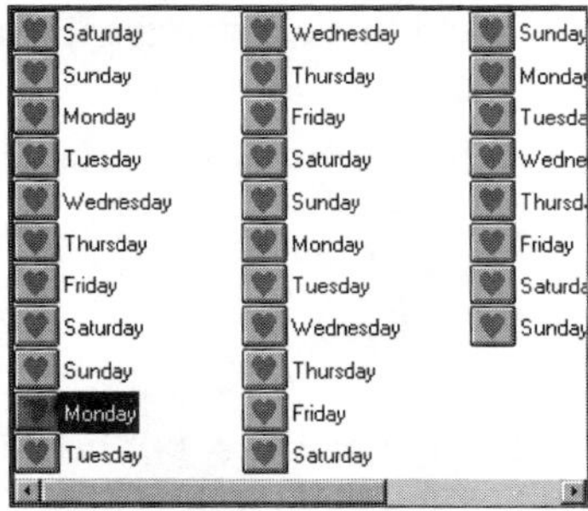

Figure 8-20: In List view, objects are represented by small icons arranged vertically.

Day	Month	Date	Year
Wednes...	April	4/ 1/1998	1998
Thursday	April	4/ 2/1998	1998
Friday	April	4/ 3/1998	1998
Saturday	April	4/ 4/1998	1998
Sunday	April	4/ 5/1998	1998
Monday	April	4/ 6/1998	1998
Tuesday	April	4/ 7/1998	1998
Wednes...	April	4/ 8/1998	1998
Thursday	April	4/ 9/1998	1998
Friday	April	4/ 10/1998	1998

Figure 8-21: Column Headers and SubItems are only displayed when a ListView control is set to Report view.

I added the two ImageList controls to the project to serve as "libraries" for the TreeView and ListView controls. I needed two ImageLists because I wanted the graphics representing the ListView ListItems to be smaller than those used in TreeView nodes. (Images stored in an ImageView control all have to be the same size.) You learned how to use the ImageList controls earlier in this chapter.

Although you can set many of the TreeView and ListView properties either in the Properties window or in code, with these controls I find it easiest to do as much as possible in code. The only property I set in the Properties window was TreeView1.Style, which I set to "Treelines, Plus/Minus, Picture, and Text" using a drop-down list. This setting means that the TreeView displays treelines, plus and minus signs to indicate whether a node is expanded or collapsed, a picture (if one is assigned to the node), and text. The constant and value equivalent, if this property were set in code, would be tvwTreelinesPlusMinusPictureText (or 7).

By the way, Chapter 10, "Programming the Registry in VB," contains another example that uses the TreeView control — in this case to display portions of the Registry.

To start with, I created form-level constants to provide the range of years the application would display:

```
Option Explicit
Const StartYear = 1997
Const StopYear = 2000
```

You can enter any values you'd like for these constants, but bear in mind that if you try to add several thousand years you'll probably be waiting until the next millennium for the program to load. (Actually, your system would probably run out of memory first.)

The Format Function

One more preliminary before I get started. I've used the Format function a great deal in the code that follows; you'll see a number of different ways to apply user-defined date expressions in calls to the Format function.

Format is truly one of the great little Visual Basic secrets. This powerful workhorse is so modest that you may not realize what it can do until you take it out for a spin or two. Format can take a variety of kinds of inputs and regurgitate the input based on either supplied formatting expressions or on user-defined formatting expressions. The trick, of course, is in the user-defined formatting expressions. For more information on them, see the topics User-Defined Date/Time Formats, User-Defined Numeric Formats, and User-Defined String Formats in VB's on-line help.

Here's the form load event and the routine it calls, PopulateTreeView. These procedures, which hook up the TreeView and ListView controls with their respective ImageList libraries, add a ColumnHeader object to ListView1, add a root node to TreeView1, and add first-level nodes to TreeView for each included year. (You can see in the code that PopulateTreeView calls another procedure, AddMonths, for each year that it creates.)

```
Private Sub Form_Load()
   ' Create an object variable for the ColumnHeader object.
   Dim clmX As ColumnHeader
   TreeView1.ImageList = ImageList1
   PopulateTreeView

   ' Add ColumnHeaders. The width of the columns is the width
   ' of the control divided by the number of ColumnHeader objects.
   Set clmX = ListView1.ColumnHeaders. _
      Add(, , "Day", ListView1.Width / 5)
   Set clmX = ListView1.ColumnHeaders. _
      Add(, , "Month", ListView1.Width / 5)
   Set clmX = ListView1.ColumnHeaders. _
      Add(, , "Date", ListView1.Width / 5)
   Set clmX = ListView1.ColumnHeaders. _
      Add(, , "Year", ListView1.Width / 5)
   Set clmX = ListView1.ColumnHeaders. _
      Add(, , "Memo", ListView1.Width / 5)
   ListView1.Icons = ImageList1
   ListView1.SmallIcons = ImageList2
End Sub

Private Sub PopulateTreeView()
   Dim X As Integer, YearToAdd As String, NodX As Node, _
      TopNode As Node
   Set TopNode = TreeView1.Nodes.Add(, , , _
      "Time is like a River", 5, 6)
   For X = StartYear To StopYear
      YearToAdd = Str(X)
      Set NodX = TreeView1.Nodes.Add(TopNode, tvwChild, , _
         YearToAdd, 1, 2)
      AddMonths NodX, X
   Next X
End Sub
```

It's important to understand that the .Add method operates on the TreeView's Nodes object, not directly on the TreeView control.

All arguments of the Nodes.Add method are optional; however, you'll generally want to include the fourth, which is the text that goes with the node. The first and second arguments represent the new node's "parent" and its relationship with that parent. The final two arguments are the index number of the node's graphic in the connected ImageList control — normally, and when selected.

AddMonths is passed the current node and the year that is having months added. The year will be used later to determine whether possible dates are valid dates — for example, 2/29/97 is not, because 1997 is not a leap year.

```
Private Sub AddMonths(NodX As Node, WhichYear As Integer)
   Dim X As Integer, MonthToAdd As String, _
      MonthNode As Node
   For X = 1 To 12
      MonthToAdd = ConvertMonth(X)
      Set MonthNode = TreeView1.Nodes.Add(NodX, _
         tvwChild, Str(X) & "/01/" & Str(WhichYear), _
         MonthToAdd, 3, 4)
      AddDays MonthNode, WhichYear, X
   Next X
End Sub
```

AddMonths starts a loop so that it can add a node for each month. Within the loop, converting the integer counter to the month string is done pretty slickly:

```
Private Function ConvertMonth(X As Integer) As String
   ConvertMonth = Format(Str(X) + "/01/1997", "mmmm")
End Function
```

Because the months are the same in every year, I could add the number representing the month to an arbitrary date string and use Format with "mmmm" as an expression to return only the string representation of the month.

A third argument is used in the Nodes.Add method (this was omitted from previous method calls). This is the *key* argument, which is a unique string that can later be used to identify the node. I've given the key argument — in standard date format — the value of the month that is being added, the first day of any month ("/01/"), and the value of the year. For example, "3/01/96" is the value for the March, 1996 node. You'll see why I've used this additional parameter shortly.

Each time a month node is created, the AddDays procedure is called with the month node, the year (passed downward from the higher level procedures), and the month as arguments. Here's AddDays:

```
Private Sub AddDays(MonthNode As Node, WhichYear As Integer, _
   WhichMonth As Integer)
   Dim X As Integer, ThisDay As String, DateStr As String
   X = 1
   Do While X <= 31
      DateStr = Str(WhichMonth) + "/" + Str(X) + "/" + _
         Str(WhichYear)
      If Not IsDate(DateStr) Then
            X = X + 1
      Else
         ThisDay = Format(DateStr, "dddd")
         ThisDay = Str(X) + ": " + ThisDay
         TreeView1.Nodes.Add MonthNode, tvwChild, , ThisDay, 5, 7
         X = X + 1
      End If
   Loop
End Sub
```

This procedure cycles through the *possible* days in a month. For each possible day, it creates the actual date string represented by the date (for example, 3/20/97 or 1/9/98).

The VB IsDate function is used to check whether this is a legal date. (For example, 2/30 of any year just would not do.) If the date is legitimate, a node is added for the day.

At this point, if you run the program, you have a perfectly charming — and accurate — expandable and collapsible date tree (see Figure 8-16). The next step is to add code so that the ListView gets populated. The usual place to do this is in a TreeView Expand event.

The demonstration program is designed so that it only fills ListView1 when a Month node is expanded. The code to do this uses the fact that I only added a Key parameter in the case of Month nodes; if the value of the .Key property of the node passed to the Expand event procedure is an empty string, the code simply exits the procedure. Otherwise, I have a Month node, and I can populate ListView with ListItems and SubItems. (The SubItems will only be displayed if ListView1.View is set to lvwReport.)

```
Private Sub TreeView1_Expand(ByVal Node As Node)
   Dim X As Integer, ThisDay As String, Month, Year As String, _
      ThisDate As String, itmX As ListItem, MonthStr As String
   If Node.Key = "" Then Exit Sub 'Do nothing
   Month = Format(Node.Key, "m")
   MonthStr = Format(Node.Key, "mmmm")
   Year = Format(Node.Key, "yyyy")

   X = 1
   Do While X <= 31
      ThisDate = Month + "/" + Str(X) + "/" + Year
      If Not IsDate(ThisDate) Then
         X = X + 1
      Else
         ThisDay = Format(ThisDate, "dddd")
         Set itmX = ListView1.ListItems.Add(, , ThisDay, 7, 4)
          itmX.SubItems(1) = MonthStr
          itmX.SubItems(2) = ThisDate
          itmX.SubItems(3) = Year
          itmX.SubItems(4) = ""
         X = X + 1
      End If
   Loop
End Sub
```

This works quite well in terms of adding items and SubItems to ListView1 (see Figure 8-17). Obviously, there is a great deal of flexibility in how you manipulate ListItems and their SubItems in your own code.

I've only added a few more features to this program (although you could make it into a pretty elaborate personal calendar program, if you were so inclined). First, here's the code to allow runtime choice of ListView1's .View property (placed in the click event of the option button array):

```
Private Sub optLV_Click(Index As Integer)
ListView1.View = Index
End Sub
```

Second, with ListView1 in report mode, there's a Memo field that contains nothing for each day of the month. Suppose I wanted to be able to enter and retrieve text from each day's Memo field?

I've entered rudimentary code to do this in the double-click event of ListView1. The procedure opens a text InputBox. If there is no existing text in the Memo field, it enters a string of its own as the default; otherwise, the default is the existing string. When the user clicks OK, the text in the InputBox is saved to the Memo field (see Figure 8-17).

```
Private Sub ListView1_DblClick()
Dim MemoValue, DfStr As String
   If ListView1.SelectedItem.SubItems(4) = "" Then
      DfStr = "Bulgy Bears Forever"
   Else
      DfStr = ListView1.SelectedItem.SubItems(4)
   End If
   MemoValue = InputBox("Enter Memo Text", "List View Demo", DfStr)
   ListView1.SelectedItem.SubItems(4) = MemoValue
End Sub
```

The information I needed in this procedure is accessed, of course, through the .SelectedItem property of ListView1.

Creating a Spinner

The UpDown control is represented by a pair of arrows, which the user clicks to increment or decrement a value in an associated control, known as a *buddy* control. When an UpDown control has been connected to its buddy, the two controls appear to the user to be one hybrid control.

You should use the UpDown control instead of the Spin Button control that shipped with Visual Basic 4.

Before using the UpDown control in a project, you have to add the Microsoft Windows Common Controls-2 library (***Cmctl232.Ocx***) to your Toolbox.

Most windowing controls that display data can be linked to the Buddy property of the UpDown control. It's common to use command buttons and text boxes for this purpose. Because the intrinsic label control is not windowing, you cannot use it as a buddy control.

The Buddy tab of the Property Pages of the UpDown control, as shown in Figure 8-22, can be used to assign a buddy control. You can also use this dialog tab to assign the buddy control's property that will be linked to the UpDown control.

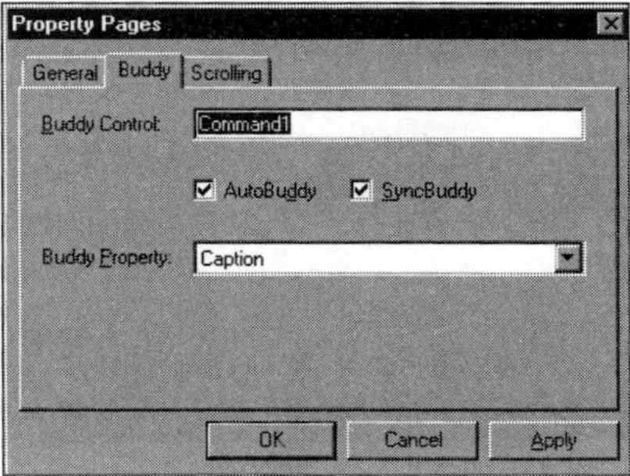

Figure 8-22: You can use an UpDown control's Property Pages to assign a buddy control and linked property.

If AutoBuddy is checked (or set to True in code), the UpDown control automatically uses the previous control in the tab order as its buddy control. If there is no previous control in the tab order, the UpDown control uses the next control in the tab order as its buddy control. Alternatively, you can use the UpDown's BuddyControl property to assign a buddy control.

At design time, when either the AutoBuddy property or the BuddyControl property is set, the buddy control automatically pairs up with the UpDown control by sizing and positioning next to it. (Buddies like to be close to one another.) You can use the Alignment property to position the UpDown control to the right or left of its buddy control.

The project saved on CD-ROM as ***Updown.Vbp*** combines an UpDown control with a buddy command button. The UpDown's SyncBuddy property was set to True and the linked Buddy property was set to the command button Caption property (see Figure 8-22).

I also made sure that the caption property of the command button was set to 40, the same as the Value property — or starting place — of the UpDown control.

When the user clicks the up arrow, the number displayed as the Command button's caption goes up; when the user clicks the down arrow, it goes down. I added the following code to the UpDown control's Change event:

```
Private Sub UpDown1_Change()
   If UpDown1.Value = 42 Then
      MsgBox "If 42 is the answer...", vbQuestion, _
         "what is the question?"
   End If
End Sub
```

When the user clicks the up arrow so that the value of the command button's caption — and the UpDown's Value property — is equal to 42, a message box is displayed, as shown in Figure 8-23.

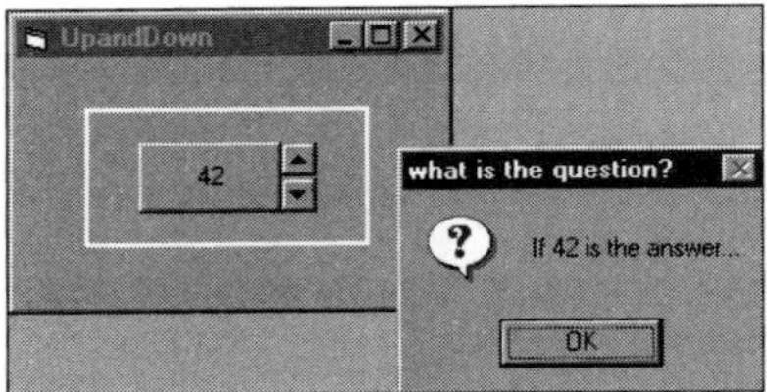

Figure 8-23: You can synch controls using the Buddy property.

SysInfo

You can use the SysInfo control to respond to changes in the system environment. For example, SysInfo fires an event when the display size changes or when a Plug and Play (PnP) device has been added to the system. The SysInfo control is invisible at runtime.

Possible uses for the SysInfo control include

- Determining operating system platform and version
- Detecting desktop and monitor size and resolution changes
- Detecting and managing plug-and-play devices
- Monitoring battery and power status

MSFlexGrid

The MSFlexGrid control displays and operates on tabular data. It allows complete flexibility to sort, merge, and format tables containing strings and pictures. For example, you can make an MSFlexGrid appear to be a spreadsheet. When bound to a Data control, MSFlexGrid displays read-only data.

You can put text, a picture, or both in any cell of a MSFlexGrid. The Row and Col properties specify the current cell in a MSFlexGrid. You can specify the current cell in code, or the user can change it at runtime using the mouse or the arrow keys. The Text property references the contents of the current cell.

If a cell's text is too long to be displayed in the cell, and the WordWrap property is set to True, the text wraps to the next line within the same cell. To display the wrapped text, you may need to increase the cell's ColWidth property or RowHeight property. You use the Cols and Rows properties to set the total number of columns and rows in a MSFlexGrid control.

Summary

This chapter covered the Professional Edition's ActiveX controls that are used to create Windows 95 user interface effects. Although a few of these controls are still a little rough around the edges, they are not difficult to work with, especially if you have some tricks up your sleeve (and that's what I'm here for). Creating applications that *look* like Windows 95 applications is easy.

These OCX controls are more than just pretty faces. Almost without exception, they possess powerful capabilities that will allow you to extend the functionality of your applications.

In this chapter, I showed you how to

- Create tabbed dialogs using Sheridan's Tabbed Dialog control
- Add context menus and property sheets to your applications
- Create your own Wizards
- Use the Slider and ProgressBar controls
- Use the RichTextBox control to change fonts within an edit control and to open, save, and print ***.Rtf*** files
- Use the TreeView and ListView controls to organize and display hierarchical information
- Use the UpDown control with a "buddy"

In addition, I provided overview information on the SysInfo and MSFlexGrid controls.

Chapter 9

Using the Windows Registry

This chapter explains the reasons for and functionality of the Windows Registry, which provides a central way of storing and retrieving system and application information. Topics covered include

- The philosophy and purpose of the Registry
- The persistence of Private Profile ***.Ini*** files
- The structure of the Registry
- Entering values in Registry keys
- Using ***Regedit.Exe***
- The contents of the Registry ***.Dat*** file
- Merging Registry ***.Reg*** files
- Registering OLE servers and OCXs using ***Regsvr32.Exe*** and ***Regocx32.Exe***

Changes made to the Registry are irrevocable in the sense that these changes take effect immediately when the Registry file is closed — with no further warning. Changing some Registry settings can have drastic effects, such as disabling important system functions. It's therefore prudent to make a backup Registry file — by choosing Export Registry File from Regedit's File menu — before experimenting with your Registry.

The Benefits of the Registry

Use of the central Registry is intended to provide the following benefits in Windows 95 for application software:

- A single location for application initialization data. In contrast, in Windows 3.*x*, Profile String files (***.Ini*** files) were used to store initialization data. Many ***.Ini*** files were thrown onto the target hard drive (usually in the Windows directory or the application's startup directory), and it wasn't necessarily obvious which ***.Ini*** file went with which application. (Also, some applications wrote and retrieved their data from the Public Profile files, ***Win.Ini*** and ***System.Ini***.)
- The ability to nest information, meaning that Registry keys can have subkeys.
- The ability to store and retrieve binary values in addition to simple strings.

In addition, there are a number of benefits to the operating system (OS) of using a central Registry. Obviously, the ultimate beneficiaries are the users of the OS. Those who write software to run under the OS will also find their life easier once they get used to the changes.

These benefits — as described in the *Microsoft Windows 95 Resource Kit* — include

- A single source of data for enumerating and configuring hardware, software, device drivers, and OS settings.
- An easy method for recovering this information in case of a system failure. The system automatically backs up the last good configuration (the last Registry settings that successfully started the computer and the Windows 95 OS).
- Increased ability of users and administrators to configure settings using the Control Panel tools, and other administrative tools, without direct editing of configuration files, thereby reducing the chance of syntactic errors in configuration information.
- The ability to use a set of network-independent functions to set and query configuration information remotely on a network, allowing greater ease of system administration.
- The ability to maintain multiple user preferences and access authorizations on a single machine.

The Persistence of Private Profile Strings (*.Ini* Files)

You should use the Registry for storing and retrieving initialization information. In fact, this is a requirement for official Windows 95 logo compliance. It also makes good programming sense, because Registry entries are easier to use, more flexible, and more secure than ***.Ini*** files ever were. (See Chapter 10, "Programming the Registry in VB," for full information on programming using the Registry.)

However, ***.Ini*** files have not disappeared (perhaps as in "the ***.Ini*** files, they shall always be with us!"). The Public ***.Ini*** files, ***Win.Ini*** and ***System.Ini***, have been retained for reasons of backwards compatibility. Some 16-bit applications simply insist on reading from and writing to these files. Also, the ***.Ini*** file format has been retained and, among the 32-bit API, you'll find new variants of the familiar ReadPrivateProfileString, WritePrivateProfileString, and so on.

This means that if you want to, you can perfectly well use ***.Ini*** files in your applications. However, except in certain special situations (which are described in a moment), you'd be out of your mind to do so. Using the Registry is just easier and better.

Peculiarly, some of Microsoft's own Windows 95 applications use ***.Ini*** files — either instead of or in addition to the Registry. (Ahem. "Do what we say, not what we do.")

For example, the Telephony API (TAPI) uses ***Telephon.Ini***. And, our own dearly beloved Visual Basic 5 makes some use of ***Vb.Ini***, for example, to register an add-in with VB (see Chapter 29, "Creating a VB Add-In" for details).

The Structure of the Registry

The Windows 95 Registry consists of a hierarchical structure divided into six subtrees. As I'll demonstrate later in the chapter, you can use the Registry Editor (***Regedit.Exe***), which is shown in Figure 9-1, to graphically display this structure.

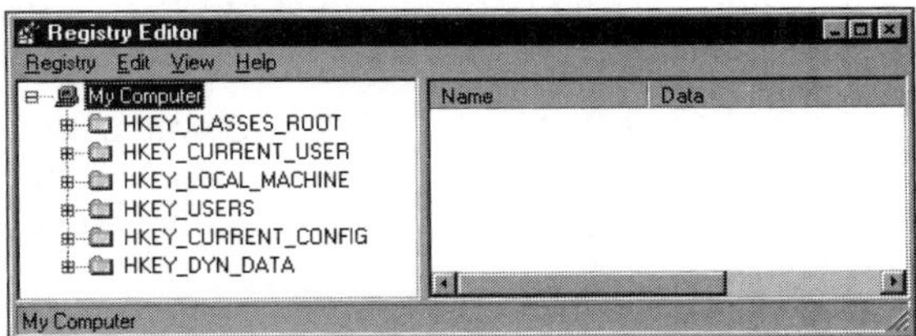

Figure 9-1: Here the Registry Editor — ***Regedit.Exe*** — is showing the six main branches of the Windows 95 Registry.

You most likely have a copy of ***Regedit.Exe*** already installed in your ***Windows\System*** directory. But, if you don't, you'll find a copy of this important program on the Visual Basic distribution CD-ROM in the ***Tools\RegistrationUtilities*** directory.

Formally, each branch heading starts with the keyword HKEY — for example, HKEY_CURRENT_USER. The keyword HKEY is used because each branch is a handle to a different set of key values.

Registry Hierarchy

Here are descriptions of the six subtrees — a subtree is a structure made up of keys and subkeys — and the kinds of information they contain

- **HKEY_CLASSES_ROOT** This branch contains file extension information, file/application associations to support drag and drop, OLE data, and information about Windows 95 shortcuts (which are, in fact OLE links). HKEY_CLASSES_ROOT is a simultaneously updated copy (an *alias*) of HKEY_LOCAL_MACHINE\Software\Classes.
- **HKEY_CURRENT_USER** The portion of HKEY_USERS applicable to the current user. If there is only one user, HKEY_USERS and HKEY_CURRENT_USER are the same.
- **HKEY_LOCAL_MACHINE** The computer and its installed hardware. Multiple configurations are possible and are dynamically updated.
- **HKEY_USERS** Desktop, network, and user specific information is kept here. (This information is stored in the file ***User.Dat***.)
- **HKEY_CURRENT_CONFIG** This branch contains display settings and the available printers.

- **HKEY_DYN_DATA** This branch stores information on Windows performance. (You can view this performance data using the System Monitor applications.)

From the point of view of initializing software, you will be working with the software subtree in HKEY_LOCAL_MACHINE (as noted, the classes subtree of this branch is aliased to HKEY_CLASSES_ROOT). User-specific information about the configuration of an application is stored in HKEY_USERS at the same relative subkey position as the information about that software in HKEY_LOCAL_MACHINE\Software\Description.

You may also need to use HKEY_LOCAL_MACHINE to obtain information about the target machine's hardware and HKEY_USERS to obtain user information such as user name, company name, telephone information, and so forth.

Differences between the Windows 95 and the Windows NT Registries

The Windows 95 and the Windows NT Registries are implemented in different ways. Some features included in the NT Registry are not included in the 95 Registry.

The primary difference between the two Registries that developers should know about is that the 95 Registry has no security attributes, and cannot be considered secure. The NT Registry, on the other hand, was designed with security considerations in mind.

You'll find some other significant differences, as well. The Windows 95 Registry does not replace ***Config.Sys***, ***Autoexec.Bat***, ***Win.Ini***, ***System.Ini***, or Program Manager groups. Older programs can still use these initialization files (and related configuration techniques).

Under NT, on the other hand, system configuration information that would have been placed in public ***.Ini*** files is mapped into the Registry. (***Win.Ini*** and ***System.Ini*** are retained so that 16-bit applications will run.)

Finally, you should know that some of the Registry API — for example, RegOpenKeyEx — do not behave identically under 95 and NT. Using the Registry APIs is covered in Chapter 10. The best source of knowledge about operating system compatibility problems for particular API functions is the *Win32 SDK Knowledge Base* in the MSDN library.

Keys

Entries in the Registry are of the form "key contains value." Keys, which can include subkeys, are typed depending on the data type of their values. Windows 95 and NT currently use three value data types for keys:

- **Binary** For example, hardware information is mostly stored as binary data and can be viewed in Regedit in binary or hex format.

- **Text** A string of text. For example, MyProgram's StartUp Greeting: "Frodo says Hi!"
- **DWord** A 32-bit unsigned integer or the address of a segment and its associated offset. DWord is a commonly used Windows SDK and Microsoft Foundation class (Visual C++) data type.

The data type of the key is indicated in Regedit by its icon (see Figure 9-2). (DWord values use the binary data type icon.)

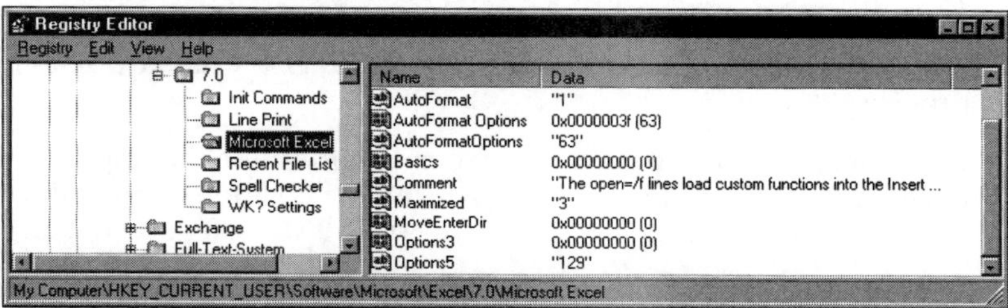

Figure 9-2: Here are key values displayed in Regedit (note the binary and text data type icons).

The size of a value cannot be larger than about 64K. (The limit to the total size of Registry entries depends on available hard disk space.)

The Software Subtree in HKEY_LOCAL_MACHINE

The HKEY_LOCAL_MACHINE subtree contains configuration and initialization information about all installed software that can write to the Windows 95 Registry. The entries in this branch apply to anyone using the physical computer. File association and OLE information is also included here.

Classes

The HKEY_LOCAL_MACHINE\Software\Classes subkey defines document types and provides information about OLE and filename extension associations that can be used by applications (for example, for drag and drop).

As noted, HKEY_CLASSES_ROOT is an alias for this subkey. In fact, HKEY_CLASSES_ROOT merely points to HKEY_LOCAL_MACHINE\Software\Classes for purposes of backwards compatibility with the Windows 3.*x* registration database.

The Classes subkey contains two types of subkeys:

- Filename extension subkeys, which specify the class definition associated with files of the given extension

- Class definition subkeys, which specify the shell and OLE properties of a class (type) of document

The CLSID subkey for an OLE server — such as an ActiveX control — listed in the Classes section contains an extremely important value — the server's Class ID, or CLSID. A CLSID is a hexadecimal number, generated when the OLE server was created, that uniquely identifies a server.

Description

The HKEY_LOCAL_MACHINE\Software\Description branch contains subkeys with the names and version numbers of installed software (assuming that the software wrote the information to the Registry as part of its installation process).

User-specific information about the configuration of an application is stored in HKEY_USERS at the same relative subkey position as the information about that software in HKEY_LOCAL_MACHINE\Software\Description.

During installation, applications should add information to the Software branch in the following form:

```
HKEY_LOCAL_MACHINE\Software\CompanyName\ProductName\Version
```

The subkey named

```
HKEY_LOCAL_MACHINE\Software\Microsoft\Windows\CurrentVersion
```

contains subkeys that include configuration information about software that is integrated with the Windows operating system.

Using Regedit

Running Regedit is the easiest way to examine the Registry tree and its keys and values (see Figures 9-1 and 9-2). You can also use Regedit to add or delete keys and manually edit values.

If you find yourself using Regedit a lot, you may wish to add a shortcut to it to your desktop or add it to your Windows Start menu. Under NT, ***Regedit.Exe*** is the 16-bit editor and ***Regedt32.Exe*** is for the 32-bit setting.

Watch out! ***Regedit.Exe*** comes with no safeguards to prevent you from editing it unwisely. Once you've made a change and closed Regedit, that's it! No "Do you want to save changes?" message; no nothing.

Therefore, if you don't know exactly what a key is for and what its valid values are, don't edit it manually. In addition, follow the procedures outlined in Regedit's on-line help and the *Microsoft Windows 95 Resource Kit* to make sure that your Registry is redundantly backed up before changing it.

You can edit the Registry from the DOS prompt. This may be useful if the Registry has become corrupt and you are having problems starting Windows 95.

To get to the DOS prompt without starting Windows 95, press F8 at the Starting Windows 95 notification. At the DOS prompt, type **Regedit /?** for instructions on using Regedit from DOS.

Repairing Corrupt Registries

You may not be aware that Windows 95 ships with an Emergency Recovery Utility (ERU). This program is on the Windows 95 CD-ROM in the ***Other\Misc\Eru*** directory. You can use it to create a backup of your system configuration. You can then place the backup on a bootable floppy disk. If you corrupt your Registry by mistake, you can use your backup in conjunction with the Emergency Restoration Utility (***Erd.Exe***) to restore your system.

There's another extremely useful utility, ***Regclean.Exe***, on your VB5 CD-ROM in the ***Tools\Regclean*** directory. You can use Regclean to fix Registry entries that no longer point to anything and to otherwise prune and care for the Registry.

Modifying Values in Registry Keys

You modify values by selecting Modify from the Regedit Edit menu or by right-clicking the key in question. Either action opens an Edit dialog — appropriate for the data type of the key — for the current key (see Figures 9-3 through 9-5). You can use the Edit dialog to change the value.

```
Edit Binary Value
Value name:
doc;dot;wiz;ppt;pot;mdb;xlt;xls;obd;obt;obz;
Value data:
0000  47 65 6E 65 72 61 6C 00  General.
0008  42 69 6E 64 65 72 73 00  Binders.
0010  50 72 65 73 65 6E 74 61  Presenta
0018  74 69 6F 6E 20 44 65 73  tion Des
0020  69 67 6E 73 00 4C 65 74  igns.Let
0028  74 65 72 73 20 26 20 46  ters & F
0030  61 78 65 73 00 4D 65 6D  axes.Mem
0038  6F 73 00 52 65 70 6F 72  os.Repor
0040  74 73 00 4F 74 68 65 72  ts.Other
0048  20 44 6F 63 75 6D 65 6E   Documen
0050  74 73 00 50 75 62 6C 69  ts.Publi
0058  63 61 74 69 6F 6E 73 00  cations.
0060  53 70 72 65 61 64 73 68  Spreadsh
OK  Cancel
```

Figure 9-3: The Edit Binary Value dialog is used by Regedit to change a binary value stored in the Registry.

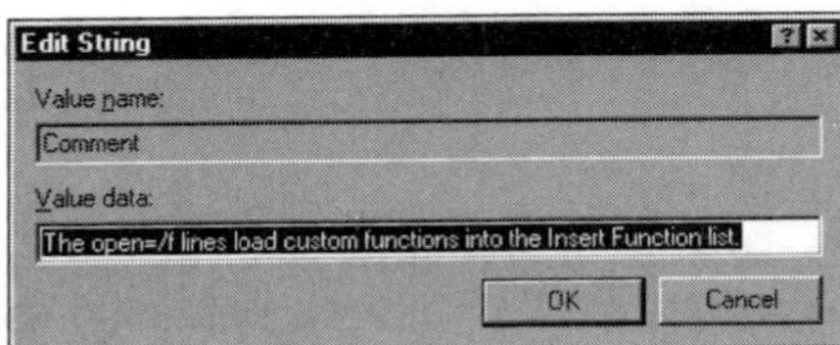

Figure 9-4: The Edit String dialog is used by Regedit to change a string value stored in the Registry.

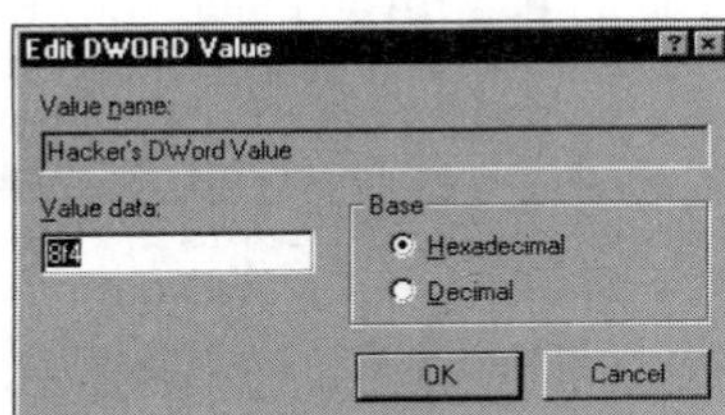

Figure 9-5: The Edit DWord Value dialog is used by Regedit to change a DWord value stored in the Registry.

Adding and Deleting Keys

To add a subkey, select the subkey's parent in the left pane of Regedit and choose New, either by right-clicking or by using the Edit menu. In either case, you'll then be able to select a key type, as shown in Figure 9-6.

Figure 9-6: You must choose the type of value that will be stored in it before you can add a new key.

To delete a key, select it in Regedit's right pane, right-click or use the Edit menu, and choose Delete. You'll see the warning shown in Figure 9-7. Choose Yes to go ahead with the deletion.

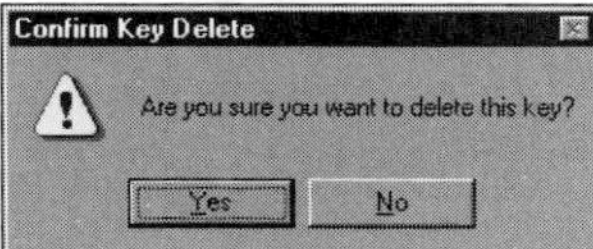

Figure 9-7: This is the only warning you'll get before the key is gone.

Editing the Registry as an ASCII File

Although the Windows 95 Registry is conceptually one data repository, physically it is stored as two files: ***User.Dat*** and ***System.Dat***. ***User.Dat*** includes information on user profiles and configuration choices; ***System.Dat*** contains hardware-specific and computer-specific settings. You can think of the Device Manager as the front end for changing much of the contents of ***System.Dat***.

User.Dat and ***System.Dat*** are binary files. Of course, you can view them or edit them in any editor capable of handling binary files. But you can also export the contents of the Registry as an ASCII file. The exported file will have a ***.Reg*** extension. You can export the entire contents of the Registry or a single branch.

You can then use any ASCII editor to modify the ***.Reg*** file. For example, Figure 9-8 shows a ***.Reg*** file in WordPad. After you are finished making changes, you can import the modified ***.Reg*** file back into the Registry. To export the Registry, choose Export Registry File from the Registry menu. To import it back, choose Import Registry File from the Registry menu.

Figure 9-8: Here is a portion of a ***.Reg*** file viewed in WordPad.

The Print selection on the Registry menu is probably something to avoid. Printing a Windows 95 Registry takes a long time and wastes a substantial amount of forestry products. Nor is the resulting printout terribly useful.

Merging Registry *.Reg* Files

Applications are often distributed with their own ASCII ***.Reg*** files. These ***.Reg*** files contain the keys and values required to correctly add the application to the Registry. Figure 9-9 shows entries from a typical Registry file.

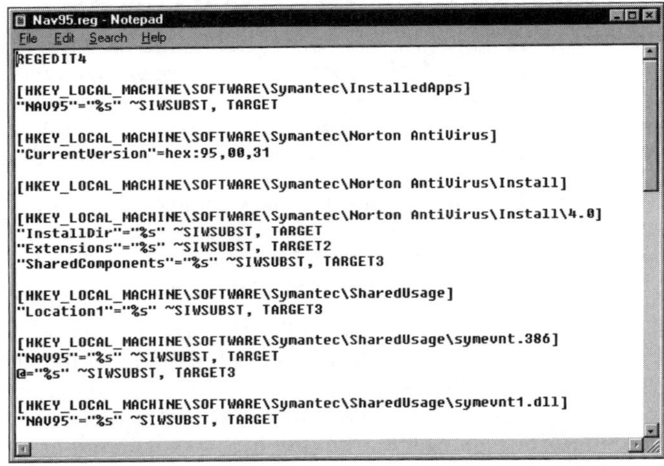

```
REGEDIT4

[HKEY_LOCAL_MACHINE\SOFTWARE\Symantec\InstalledApps]
"NAV95"="%s" ~SIWSUBST, TARGET

[HKEY_LOCAL_MACHINE\SOFTWARE\Symantec\Norton AntiVirus]
"CurrentVersion"=hex:95,00,31

[HKEY_LOCAL_MACHINE\SOFTWARE\Symantec\Norton AntiVirus\Install]

[HKEY_LOCAL_MACHINE\SOFTWARE\Symantec\Norton AntiVirus\Install\4.0]
"InstallDir"="%s" ~SIWSUBST, TARGET
"Extensions"="%s" ~SIWSUBST, TARGET2
"SharedComponents"="%s" ~SIWSUBST, TARGET3

[HKEY_LOCAL_MACHINE\SOFTWARE\Symantec\SharedUsage]
"Location1"="%s" ~SIWSUBST, TARGET3

[HKEY_LOCAL_MACHINE\SOFTWARE\Symantec\SharedUsage\symevnt.386]
"NAV95"="%s" ~SIWSUBST, TARGET
@="%s" ~SIWSUBST, TARGET3

[HKEY_LOCAL_MACHINE\SOFTWARE\Symantec\SharedUsage\symevnt1.dll]
"NAV95"="%s" ~SIWSUBST, TARGET
```

Figure 9-9: Here is ***Nav95.Reg***, a portion of the ASCII Registry file for Symantec's Norton AntiVirus for Windows 95 viewed in Notepad.

To merge one of these ***.Reg*** files into the Registry, double-click the file or right-click the file and choose Merge.

Registering OLE Servers and ActiveX Controls Using *Regsvr32.Exe*

You can register OLE servers and ActiveX controls with the Windows Registry in a number of ways. In particular, Visual Basic OLE server applications and controls are registered on your system when they are compiled. For more information about registering (and unregistering) OLE server applications that you write, see Chapter 20, "Understanding ActiveX and OLE," and Chapter 23, "Creating ActiveX Applications."

In a similar fashion, ActiveX controls are automatically registered on your system when you compile the control. (You don't have to worry about registering a control when you're debugging it in the VB environment; temporary registration is handled for you.) For more information on creating ActiveX controls, and the registration issues involved in distributing them, see Chapter 27, "Deploying VB ActiveX Controls on the Web."

However, what if you want to register an OLE server or control that someone else has compiled on your system? Or, what if you want to register a server (or control) of yours on someone else's system?

Two utilities that ship with VB5 handle these tasks for you. They are ***Regsvr32.Exe*** and ***Regocx32.Exe.*** Both programs are on the VB5 CD-ROM in the ***Tools\Registration Utilities*** directory.

You can use ***Regsvr32.Exe*** to manually register (and unregister) OLE Servers and OLE controls (OCXs). The program is passed a filename of an OLE object — a server or an ActiveX control — to register as a command-line parameter. If the filename is preceded with the /u switch, it unregisters, rather than registers, the OLE object. ***Regsvr32*** returns a message box stating whether it was successful. For example, if ***Regsvr32.Exe*** had been copied into the ***C:\Vb\Tools*** directory, running

```
C:\Vb\Tools\Regsvr32 C:\Windows\System\Keysta32.Ocx
```

would add the ***Keysta32*** OCX to the Registry. (***Regsvr32*** returns the message shown in Figure 9-10 if it successfully completes a registration.)

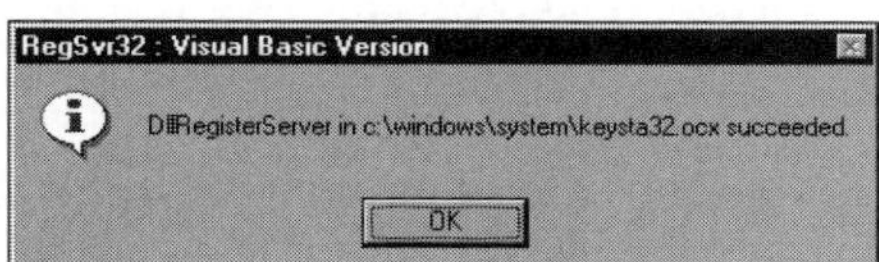

Figure 9-10: *Regsvr32.Exe* returns a message indicating that ***Keysta32.Ocx*** has been successfully registered.

You could unregister the same OCX (remove it from the Registry) by running ***Regsvr32*** with the /u switch:

```
C:\Vb\Tools\Regsvr32 /u C:\Windows\System\Keysta32.Ocx
```

What ***Regsrvr32*** actually does is call a function named DllRegisterServer. The message box shown in Figure 9-10 indicates that this function, which is responsible for asking an OLE object to register the classes it contains, has returned a success flag.

Registering OCXs Using *Regocx32.Exe*

Regocx32.Exe works just like ***Regsvr32.Exe***, except that it only applies to OCXs and does not return a message indicating the success or failure of the operation.

Regocx32 is designed for use in setup programs; it intentionally displays no dialogs when registering ActiveX controls.

Summary

This chapter covered what you need to know about the philosophy and structure of the Windows 95 Registry. After you've read it, manually editing Registry entries should be a piece of cake.

Topics I covered in this chapter included

- Knowing why ***.Ini*** files are still with us (and when to use them)
- Understanding the structure of the Registry
- Using ***Regedit.Exe***
- Exporting, importing, and merging ***.Reg*** files
- Adding, modifying, and deleting keys and values
- Manually registering OLE servers and ActiveX controls using ***Regsvr32.Exe*** and ***Regocx32.Exe***

You can consider this information as background material required for programming the Registry. You need to have it under your belt before you learn how to effectively program the Registry using VB5, which is the topic of the next chapter.

Chapter 10

Programming the Registry in VB

This chapter explains what you need to know to successfully use the Registry in your VB5 programs. Topics covered include:

- The Registry API
- Required declarations for the API and related structures
- The built-in VB Registry statements
- Retrieving keys, subkeys, branches, and values from the Registry
- Adding new keys and values
- Deleting keys
- Creating an OLE server application to encapsulate Registry functions
- Sample programs that you can use to interact with the Registry
- Registering a file extension

The Registry API

Here are the Registry-related APIs along with brief descriptions of what they do. (For more information on a specific API, look it up in the Win32 SDK online Reference; see Chapters 11, "The Win32 Software Development Kit (SDK), the Win32 API, and the Windows Messaging System." Also, you'll find quite a bit of information on how to use specific Registry APIs later in this chapter.)

RegCloseKey releases the handle of the specified key, thereby freeing resources.

RegConnectRegistry establishes a connection to a predefined Registry handle on another computer — for example, across a net. RegCloseKey is called when you are through with the connection.

RegCreateKey creates a key as specified in the function call. If the key already exists in the Registry, the function opens it. This function is provided for compatibility with Windows version 3.1. Win32-based applications can use RegCreateKeyEx instead.

RegCreateKeyEx creates the key as specified in the function. If the key already exists in the Registry, the function opens it. The key that the RegCreateKeyEx function creates has no values. You can use the RegSetValue or RegSetValueEx function to set key values.

RegDeleteKey deletes a key and all branches and subkeys below it. Note that RegDeleteKey only behaves this way under Windows 95; previously, you could not use it to delete a key with descendants.

RegDeleteValue removes a value from a Registry key.

RegEnumKey enumerates subkeys of an open Registry key. The function retrieves the name of one subkey each time it is called. This function is provided for compatibility with Windows version 3.1. Win32-based applications can use RegEnumKeyEx, which returns more information.

RegEnumKeyEx enumerates subkeys of an open Registry key. The function retrieves information about one subkey each time it is called. RegEnumKeyEx also retrieves the class name of the subkey and the time it was last modified.

RegEnumValue enumerates the values for an open Registry key. The function copies one indexed value name and data block for the key each time it is called.

RegFlushKey writes all the attributes of an open key into the hard drive data files of the Registry.

RegGetKeySecurity retrieves a copy of the security structure protecting an open Registry key (applies to Windows NT).

RegisterClass registers a window class for subsequent use (the class must next be created!). It's possible in theory to use the relevant APIs to register, create, and use a new window class from VB. Generally, however, C++ would be a more appropriate development language for doing this kind of thing. For more information about related APIs, see the Software Development Kit (SDK) (discussed in Chapter 11). Also, Desaware's Spyworks — a Help file containing links allowing you to download a demonstration of the current version is included on the companion CD-ROM — allows Visual Basic programmers easy access to much low-level Windows functionality.

RegisterClassEx is the version of RegisterClass intended for use with the Windows 95 shell. See RegisterClass.

RegisterClipboardFormat registers a new Clipboard format.

RegisterEventSource returns a handle that can be used with the ReportEvent function to log an event so that it can appear in the Event Viewer application. RegisterEventSource must be called with a source name that is a subkey of a log file entry under the EventLog key in the Registry.

RegisterHotKey defines a hot key.

RegisterWindowMessage defines a new Windows message that is unique throughout the system. The new message value can be used by calling the SendMessage or PostMessage functions and is intended to enable communication between cooperating applications. For more information, see Chapter 11.

RegLoadKey creates a subkey under HKEY_USER or HKEY_LOCAL_MACHINE and stores registration information from a *hive* file into that subkey.

RegNotifyChangeKeyValue indicates when a Registry key or any of its subkeys has changed.

RegOpenKey opens a Registry key for further action. This function is provided for backwards compatibility with Windows version 3.1. Win32-based applications should use RegOpenKeyEx instead.

RegOpenKeyEx opens the specified Registry key for further action.

RegQueryInfoKey retrieves information about a Registry key.

RegQueryValue is provided for backwards compatibility with Windows version 3.1. Win32-based applications should instead use RegQueryValueEx.

RegQueryValueEx retrieves the type and data for a value name associated with an open Registry key.

RegReplaceKey replaces the file backing a key and all its subkeys with another file, so that when the system is next started, the key and subkeys will have the values stored in the new file.

RegRestoreKey reads the Registry information in a ***.Reg*** ASCII file and copies it over the specified key. This Registry information may include a key and multiple levels of subkeys.

RegSaveKey saves the key and all of its subkeys and values to a file.

RegSetKeySecurity sets the security of an open Registry key using a supplied variable of type SECURITY_INFORMATION for the details of the security settings.

RegSetValue is provided for backwards compatibility with Windows version 3.1. Win32-based applications should instead use RegSetValueEx.

RegSetValueEx stores data in the value field of an open Registry key. It can also set additional value and type information for the open key.

RegUnLoadKey removes a key and subkeys (a hive) from the Registry. Although you can use RegUnLoadKey to remove a hive from the Registry, it does not modify the file containing the Registry information (see RegLoadKey for a definition of "hive").

A Hive Is...

A *hive* is a discrete body of keys, subkeys, and values that is rooted at the top of the Registry hierarchy and saved in the Registry's ***.Reg*** ASCII format.

API Declarations

The full declarations for Registry APIs and related types as required by Visual Basic can be found in the ***RegAPI.Bas*** module. (This module is on the *Visual Basic 5 SECRETS* companion CD-ROM in the directory for programs related to Chapter 10.) To use these declarations in your own project, simply copy the module to your project directory and add it to the project.

I won't reproduce all the related VB declarations and structures here; I'll include only enough to give you a feeling for what's involved. To view the correct syntax for the rest of the Registry API declarations, refer to the module that I just mentioned.

The general way to get the syntax for API declares is to use the API Text Viewer application and copy and paste the declarations you want into your project. (For more information about the API Text Viewer, see the section "Calling the Windows API" in Chapter 4, "The Visual Basic Language," and Chapter 11, "The Win32 Software Development Kit (SDK), the Win32 API, and the Windows Messaging System.")

Here are some Registry constants as defined in the Registry API module ***RegAPI.Bas***:

```
'Registry Constants
Public Const HKEY_CLASSES_ROOT = &H80000000
Public Const HKEY_CURRENT_USER = &H80000001
Public Const HKEY_LOCAL_MACHINE = &H80000002
Public Const HKEY_USERS = &H80000003
```

By the way, the module defines quite a few more constants covering topics such as access rights, error codes, and more. Here are the type definitions for the structures that contain information about the time of file creation and application security information:

```
Type FILETIME
    dwLowDateTime As Long
    dwHighDateTime As Long
End Type

Type SECURITY_DESCRIPTOR
    Revision As Byte
    Sbz1 As Byte
    Control As Long
    Owner As Long
    Group As Long
    Sacl As ACL
    Dacl As ACL
End Type
```

Note that SECURITY_DESCRIPTOR contains a reference, ACL, to a structure that is, itself, defined in the module. Here are some of the API declarations themselves (For readability, I've broken them up into multiple lines using line continuation characters):

```
Declare Function RegEnumKey Lib "advapi32.dll" Alias _
   "RegEnumKeyA" (ByVal hKey As Long, _
   ByVal dwIndex As Long, ByVal lpName As String, _
   ByVal cbName As Long) As Long

Declare Function RegEnumKeyEx Lib "advapi32.dll" Alias _
   "RegEnumKeyExA" (ByVal hKey As Long, _
   ByVal dwIndex As Long, ByVal lpName As String, _
   lpcbName As Long, lpReserved As Long, _
   ByVal lpClass As String, lpcbClass As Long, _
   lpftLastWriteTime As FILETIME) As Long

Declare Function RegGetKeySecurity Lib "advapi32.dll" _
   (ByVal hKey As Long, ByVal SecurityInformation As Long, _
   pSecurityDescriptor As SECURITY_DESCRIPTOR, _
   lpcbSecurityDescriptor As Long) As Long

Declare Function RegOpenKeyEx Lib "advapi32.dll" Alias _
   "RegOpenKeyExA" (ByVal hKey As Long, _
   ByVal lpSubKey As String, ByVal ulOptions As Long, _
   ByVal samDesired As Long, phkResult As Long) As Long
```

You can see that there is nothing particularly special here; these are run-of-the-mill external declarations that are easy to use provided you get the data types exactly right.

Note that 32-bit API functions do not use integer parameters; 16-bit values that were stored as integers are stored as longs. Also, you should bear in mind that that data type of a handle — for example, hKey typically represents a handle to a key — is long.

Finally, it is vital to understand that string variables referenced in the API are C strings, not VB strings, meaning that they are pointers to a memory location that stores null-terminated arrays of characters. (Null-terminated means that the final character in the array is an ASCII zero.)

To call a C function with a string parameter — this includes one of the APIs with a string parameter — from VB requires special handling. A number of techniques work for this — as discussed further in Chapter 11 — but here is one that is effective.

In your VB program, declare a string variable (in this example, szBuffer) and a length variable (lBuffSize):

```
Dim szBuffer As String, lBuffSize As Long
```

Next, use the Space function to give szBuffer a fixed length filled with spaces (make sure that the length parameter passed to the Space function is greater than the maximum string length you expect to retrieve with your API call):

```
szBuffer = Space(255)
```

As a last step before calling the API function, set lBuffSize to the length of szBuffer:

```
lBuffSize = Len(szBuffer)
```

Finally, you can use szBuffer and lBuffSize to call an API that requires a string argument. The value in szBuffer can than be accessed or assigned like a normal VB string. (The example code is a fragment from a project explained under "Using the API to Manipulate the Registry" later in this chapter):

```
Dim hKey As Long, KeyIndex As Long
...
hKey = HKEY_LOCAL_MACHINE
KeyIndex = 0
...
Do While RegEnumIndex <> ERROR_NO_MORE_ITEMS
   RegEnumIndex = RegEnumKey(hKey, KeyIndex, szBuffer, lBuffSize)
   ...
Loop
...
```

Here is the declaration for the RegEnumKey function:

```
Declare Function RegEnumKey Lib "advapi32.dll" Alias _
   "RegEnumKeyA" (ByVal hKey As Long, _
   ByVal dwIndex As Long, ByVal lpName As String, _
   ByVal cbName As Long) As Long
```

You'll see that the third and fourth parameters — ByVal lpName As String and ByVal cbName As Long — are declared as string and long, respectively. According to the documentation in the SDK, lpName contains the memory address of the buffer for the subkey name and cbName contains the size of the buffer (more on this in Chapter 11). However, if you set it up in VB as I've shown you, the translation from the API to VB works just fine.

The Built-in VB Registry Statements

There are four Registry-manipulation statements built into VB5. If this foursome suits your needs, you can easily use them — as I'll show you in a moment — with no fuss, no muss, no declarations, and no nothing.

One of the really nifty things about these statements is that they'll run intelligently under both 16-bit and 32-bit operating systems. Under Windows 95, they read and write to the Registry. Under Windows 3.*x*, these same statements read and write to ***Win.Ini***. If you're maintaining code for an application that runs both ways, what a convenience!

The VB Applications settings statements add and delete Registry keys and values below HKEY_CURRENT_USER\Software. Logically, these statements expect to read and write applications that are branches with sections that contain keys equal to values. In other words, these are virtual ***.Ini*** files that happen to be organized within the Registry. Here is a schematic representation:

```
MyApplication
   [Section Name # 1]
      Key1=Value
      Key2=Value
      ...
   [Section Name # 2]
      ...
```

The VB statements that manipulate these virtual ***.Ini*** files are as follows:

- **DeleteSetting** deletes a named key and its associated value from a named application and section. You can also use DeleteSetting to delete an entire section if no key is included as a parameter, and an entire application if no section or key parameters are included.
- **GetSetting** retrieves a single value from the named key in the named application and section.
- **GetAllSettings** retrieves all keys and values in a section.
- **SaveSetting** saves a value to a named key (in a named section and application).

To demonstrate how you can speedily and effectively use the built-in Registry statements, I've written a small application that demonstrates all possible uses of the four statements (see Figure 10-1). This project is available on the companion CD-ROM in the directory associated with Chapter 10's programs. It is saved as ***Settings.Vbp***.

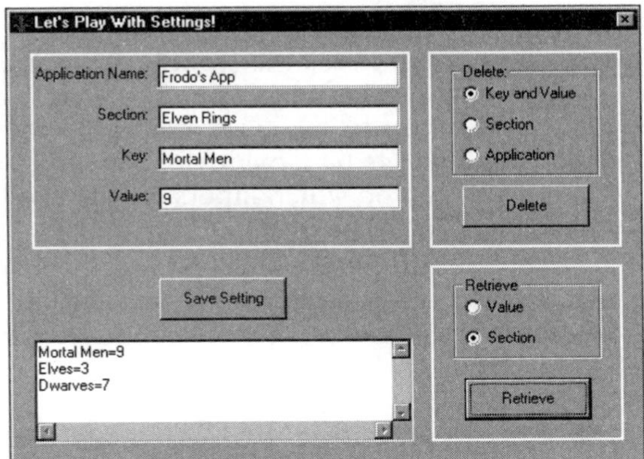

Figure 10-1: You can easily use the built-in VB Registry statements to save and retrieve initialization information (as in this sample application).

Here's how to use the SaveSetting statement (the code is in the cmdSave_Click event procedure):

```
SaveSetting txtAppName.Text, txtSection.Text, _
   txtKey.Text, txtValue.Text
```

This is pretty simple. But SaveSetting will not work unless it is passed an application name, section name, and key name. (The key value doesn't really matter; if txtValue.Text is left blank, the value added to the Registry will be 0.) For this reason, I've added code that does rudimentary validation testing on the input fields — in other words, that checks whether the user has entered something.

To simplify this code, I've written a function, TestContents, which is passed a control. TestContents returns False if the .Text property of the passed control is empty, and returns True otherwise. (Of course, you'd be in trouble, and would get a runtime error, if you tried to pass TestContents a control that had no .Text property.)

Passing a control to a routine as a parameter is a very useful technique when considerably more complex actions upon the passed control are required.

```
Private Function TestContents(c As Control) As Boolean
   If c.Text = "" Then
      TestContents = False
   Else
      TestContents = True
   End If
End Function
```

Here's the rest of the code needed to check the input text boxes and return appropriate messages. (I use essentially the same code to check that there actually is something in the input text boxes in several places in this program. I could have simplified things by moving the code to a subroutine, but, because there is some variation on which inputs are checked, I have not bothered to do this with such a simple program.)

```
If Not TestContents(txtAppName) Then
   MsgBox "You must enter an application name!",  _
      vbCritical, "Can't Go On Like This!"
   Exit Sub
End If

If Not TestContents(txtSection) Then
   MsgBox "You must enter a section!", vbCritical,  _
     "Can't Go On Like This!"
   Exit Sub
End If
If Not TestContents(txtKey) Then
   MsgBox "You must enter a key!", vbCritical, _
     "Can't Go On Like This!"
   Exit Sub
End If
```

If you click the Save Setting button and run the procedure, you can verify that it has added an application, section, key, and value to the Registry by running Regedit (see Figure 10-2).

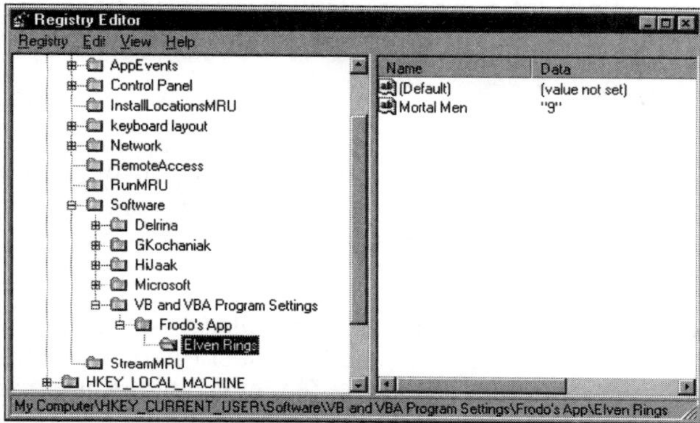

Figure 10-2: Running Regedit discloses that information has indeed been added to the Registry using VB's built-in statements.

The DeleteSetting statement comes in three flavors in one statement. Depending on the number of parameters passed to it, you can delete an individual setting (key and value), an entire section, or all settings for an application. Here's the code that implements all three modes of DeleteSetting (I've left out the code that checks for actual inputs):

```
Private Sub cmdDelete_Click()
   If optDelete(0).Value Then
      'Delete Key and Value
      ...
      DeleteSetting txtAppName.Text, txtSection.Text, txtKey.Text
   ElseIf optDelete(1) Then
      'Delete Section
      ...
      DeleteSetting txtAppName.Text, txtSection.Text
   Else
      'Delete All Settings for App
      ...
      DeleteSetting txtAppName.Text
   End If
End Sub
```

One problem with the DeleteSetting statement — and for the GetSetting statements as well — is that you will get a runtime error if you try to delete or retrieve applications, sections, or keys that don't exist.

A way to deal with this problem would be to only delete or retrieve settings that your application has made in its current session. That way you know that the settings are there. Settings might be created in a form load, used by the form, and deleted in the form's unload event.

However, this approach would place severe limitations on the utility of these statements. A better strategy would be to handle the error that results from trying to delete or get a nonexistent application, section, or key.

The buckshot approach is to add a statement that causes VB to ignore errors at the beginning of the procedures — cmdDelete_Click and cmdRetrieve_Click — that might cause the error:

```
Private Sub cmdDelete_Click()
    On Error Resume Next
```

If you try this, you'll see that it works fine. The only problem is that it effectively turns off error trapping in its scope, so if something else is wrong in your procedure you'll never get a specific error message identifying the problem.

The answer is to craft a response to the particular error caused when the user tries to delete a nonexistent application, section, or value from the Registry. This is called *trapping* the error. (Chapter 15 of this book is devoted to the topic of handling errors.)

First, you need to find the number of the error; it may not be what you expect. The way to do this is to cause the error and read the error message. Using DeleteSetting to try to delete Registry material that doesn't exist turns out to cause an error number 5: an invalid procedure call. (The cmdRetrieve_Click procedure with the code in it that I'll show you causes error number 13, type mismatch, when the user attempts to retrieve something that isn't there.)

The easiest way to find Visual Basic error numbers — and what they mean — is to search for the topic "Trappable Errors" in VB's on-line help.

The next step is to add a jump to error-handling code at the top of the procedure. (To be fancy, you can also give the error number a constant equivalent. This makes subsequent use of it clearer.)

```
Private Sub cmdDelete_Click()
   Const ErrInvalidProcCall = 5
   On Error GoTo ErrHandle
   ...
```

Finally, add the error handler itself at the bottom of the procedure. (Be sure to put an Exit Sub statement before the start of the error handler so that there's no chance of "falling through" by mistake.)

```
   ...
   Exit Sub
ErrHandle:
   If Err.Number = ErrInvalidProcCall Then
      MsgBox "You can't delete what ain't there!"
      Resume Next
   End If
End Sub
```

This code produces the error message shown in Figure 10-3 when a user attempts to delete nonexistent material from the Registry.

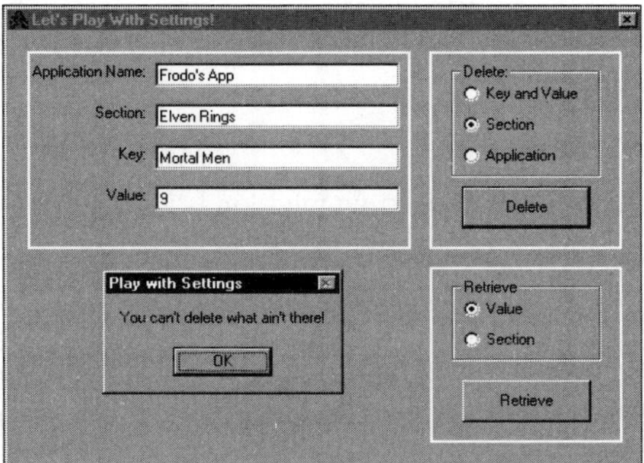

Figure 10-3: You can use error-trapping techniques to return an appropriate message when users try to delete nonexistent material from the Registry.

Okay! With that out of the way, here's the final bit of code in the project that calls the GetSetting function, which returns a value, or the GetAllSettings function, which returns all keys and values in a section. (Again, I've excerpted the code that tests for actual content in the input boxes.)

```
Private Sub cmdRetrieve_Click()
   Dim SectionSettings As Variant, IntX As Integer
   Const ErrTypeMismatch = 13
   On Error GoTo ErrHandle
   If optRetrieve(0).Value Then
      'Use GetSetting to return one value
      ...
      txtDisplay.Visible = True
      txtDisplay.Text = GetSetting(txtAppName.Text, _
      txtSection.Text, txtKey.Text, txtValue.Text)
      'txtValue functions as Default setting in syntax
   Else 'Use GetAllSettings to return entire section
      ...
      txtDisplay.Visible = True
      SectionSettings = GetAllSettings(txtAppName.Text, _
         txtSection.Text)
      For IntX = 0 To UBound(SectionSettings, 1)
         txtDisplay.Text = txtDisplay.Text & _
            SectionSettings(IntX, 0) & "=" & _
            SectionSettings(IntX, 1) & vbCrLf
      Next IntX
   End If
   Exit Sub
ErrHandle:
   If Err.Number = ErrTypeMismatch Then
      MsgBox "You can't retrieve what ain't there!"
      Resume Next
   End If
End Sub
```

We're pretty much through with this project — and now know all there is to know about the VB built-in Registry statements — but there are a few things to note in this last procedure.

First, GetSetting accepts an optional fourth parameter, which is the default value in case the setting doesn't exist or isn't set in the Registry — in which case the default passed to the GetSetting function is what it returns!

Second, note the way SectionSettings was declared as a variant. When SectionSettings is used as the return value for the GetAllSettings function, the information passed back to SectionSettings is in the form of a two-dimensional array (one of keys and one of values). You can pull the information out of SectionSettings by treating it as the array it has become. I thought I'd be extra cute and add an equal sign (=) between each key and value, and a line break between entries, when I read the array into txtDisplay:

```
For IntX = 0 To UBound(SectionSettings, 1)
   txtDisplay.Text = txtDisplay.Text & _
      SectionSettings(IntX, 0) & "=" & _
      SectionSettings(IntX, 1) & vbCrLf
Next IntX
```

Using the API to Manipulate the Registry

The Registry statements built-in to VB are all very well and good as far as they go — they are certainly delightfully easy to use — but often I find myself in situations where I want access to the full Registry. If you add the ***RegAPI.Bas*** module to your project, as described earlier in this chapter, and use the Registry API directly, you can manipulate the Registry effectively without the limitations of the statements built into VB.

It's easy to retrieve keys, subkeys, and values from the Registry. You can also, without much trouble, add new keys and values and delete keys. The extensive list of related API in the first section of this chapter should give you an idea of the extent of the possibilities. (Now, now, Igor! Down, Igor! I'm not suggesting using RegUnloadKey to cripple all your competitor's software. Forget it, Igor!)

Using VBA Constants for Common Nonprinting Character Codes

The VBA constant library includes predefined constants for common nonprinting character codes. For example, vbCrLf in the preceding example causes a carriage return / line feed, the equivalent in old versions of VB of adding Chr$(13)+Chr$(10) to your code. Other character code constants you should know about are:

```
Carriage return (vbCr = Chr$(13))
Line feed (vbLf = Chr$(10))
Backspace (vbBack = Chr$(8))
Tab (vbTab = Chr$(9))
```

You can easily use the Object Browser to find the predefined constants that are part of the VBA library.

Retrieving and Displaying Keys and Subkeys

Suppose I wanted to retrieve and display the branch of keys below HKEY_LOCAL_MACHINE and all the subkeys of each of the higher level keys. The idea here is only to retrieve two levels of keys, not the entire Registry structure.

I could use a TreeView control, one of the Windows custom controls discussed in Chapter 8, to display the two levels of keys. The result should look quite like the display in Regedit — although, of course, I can happily use different icons. I think the highest level of keys I display should be represented by a sun icon, and the branch under it by the earth.

Here's how to set up the TreeView control. Add a TreeView and an ImageList control to a new form (in the sample code the form is named frmDisplay). Make sure also to add the API declarations module to your project. (The project is on the companion CD-ROM as ***RegDisp.Vbp***.)

Add the following code to the frmDisplay_Resize procedure:

```
Private Sub Form_Resize()
   TreeView1.Height = frmDisplay.ScaleHeight
   TreeView1.Width = frmDisplay.ScaleWidth
End Sub
```

This causes the TreeView control to always be the size of the client area of frmDisplay; it is now resizable because it will change in dimensions when the user resizes frmDisplay.

Next, use ImageList1's Custom property in the Properties window to add the two icons — the sun and the earth — to the ImageList control (see Figure 10-4).

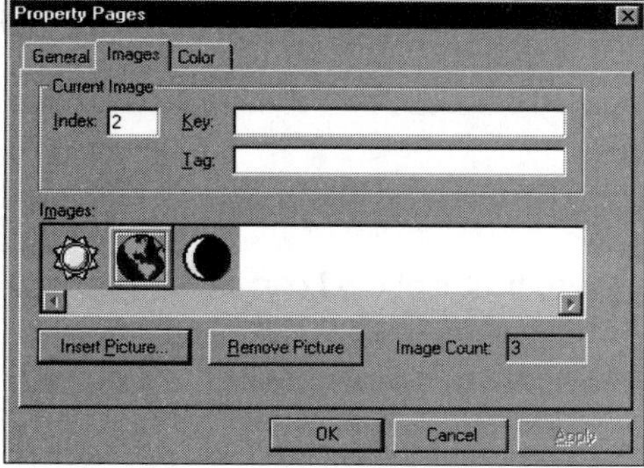

Figure 10-4: You can use the Images tab of the ImageList's Property Pages dialog to add images to the visual library stored in the control.

The images of the sun, earth, and moon that I added to the ImageList control's visual library in this project are icons that ship with Visual Basic. They're in the ***Elements*** directory under ***Vb\Graphics\Icons***.

A Very Good Thing — as Winnie-the-Pooh would say — about the Windows 95 shell is that the file common dialog displays the actual appearance of a file's icon, which, in the case of an ***.Ico*** file containing an icon, is all you need (see Figure 10-5)!

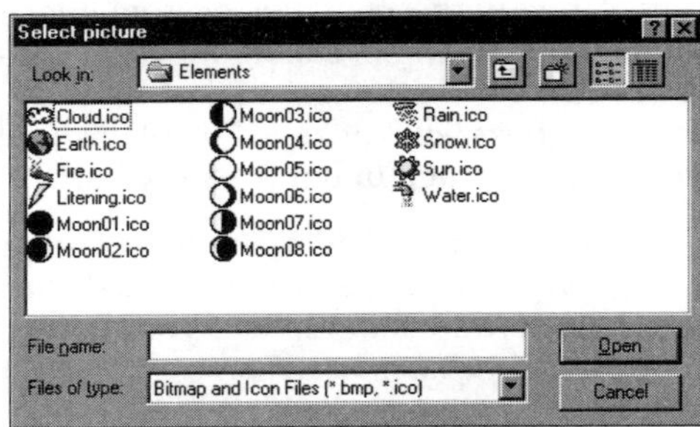

Figure 10-5: When you add a graphic — such as an icon — you see a preview of its appearance.

By the way, as long as the ImageList Property Pages dialog is open, select the General tab and set the size to 16×16 pixels. This is the smallest possible size, and about right for display in the TreeView control.

You must set the size in the ImageList Custom Properties dialog *before* you load pictures into the ImageList. Once the control contains imagery, it will not let you change the size (...ahem, Microsoft, are you listening?!). In other words, once image files have been loaded into the control, the size of the images is read only.

Getting back to displaying keys under HKEY_LOCAL_MACHINE, add a couple of declarations to frmDisplay's General Declarations section:

```
Option Explicit
'Global Variables
Public hKey As Long
Public NextLevel As Long
```

Next, place the following code to frmDisplay's Load event to set up the project:

```
Private Sub Form_Load()
   Dim KeyIndex As Long, RegEnumIndex As Long, _
      szBuffer As String, lBuffSize As Long, _
      Nodkey As Node, phkResult As Long, Indent As Long
   'Create Buffer for API calls
   szBuffer = Space(255)
   lBuffSize = Len(szBuffer)
   hKey = HKEY_LOCAL_MACHINE
   Indent = tvwChild
   KeyIndex = 0
   NextLevel = 0

   TreeView1.ImageList = ImageList1
   'Connect TreeView1 and ImageList1
```

The TreeView control's ImageList property is used to connect the control with an ImageList control (which serves as a picture library). The Indent variable holds the current state of the nodes being added to the ImageList. TvwChild is the default. It is a constant, defined as equivalent to 4, and means that the node being added to the TreeView control becomes a child of the relative mentioned in the Add method call of the Nodes collection. (Select "Add Method (Nodes Collection)" from VB's on-line help for a table that lists all relationship values.) Also note that the variable Nodkey has been declared of type Node.

KeyIndex is a counter variable used in RegEnumKey to cycle through all subkeys of the referenced key (in this case, HKEY_LOCAL_MACHINE). NextLevel keeps track of how many levels down the tree you are when adding pictures to the TreeView component. (You could use this variable if you wanted to extend the project one more level, or recursively to cover all nodes below the starting place.)

Here's the business end of the procedure:

```
    Do While RegEnumIndex <> ERROR_NO_MORE_ITEMS
        RegEnumIndex = RegEnumKey(hKey, KeyIndex, szBuffer, lBuffSize)
        If RegEnumIndex <> ERROR_SUCCESS And _
            RegEnumIndex <> ERROR_NO_MORE_ITEMS Then
            MsgBox "Reading Failure!"
            Exit Do
        End If
        If szBuffer <> Space(255) Then
            Set Nodkey = TreeView1.Nodes.Add(, Indent, , szBuffer, 1)
            RegOpenKeyEx hKey, szBuffer, 0, 1, phkResult
            NextLevel = NextLevel + 1
            DisplayKey phkResult, TreeView1.Nodes.Count, Indent
            NextLevel = NextLevel - 1
        End If
        szBuffer = Space(255)
        KeyIndex = KeyIndex + 1
    Loop
    Nodkey.EnsureVisible
End Sub
```

ERROR_SUCCESS and ERROR_NO_MORE_ITEMS are constants that are declared in the ***RegAPI.Bas*** module. They are two of the possible return codes for the RegEnumKey function.

The logic of this procedure is to loop until RegEnumKey returns ERROR_NO_MORE_ITEMS (meaning, "that's it for keys at this level, buddy"), adding 1 to the KeyIndex counter each time. There's basic error trapping; if RegEnumKey returns anything other than ERROR_SUCCESS ("I've got a key!") or ERROR_NO_MORE_ITEMS, the loop is aborted. It's a good idea to do this kind of checking of Registry API return codes to make sure the function was successful.

Assuming the function succeeded, szBuffer is checked for contents. If it has something in it, a first-level node is added to the TreeView control using the string contents of szBuffer. The final parameter in the Add method, 1, indicates the index value of the picture from the ImageList control that represents the node. (You can add another parameter consisting of an ImageList index number that will represent the node when it is selected.)

Next, the RegOpenKeyEx function is used to return a handle, phkResult, to the subkey named in szBuffer. With this information, DisplayKey, a routine to return the next level of keys and place them into the TreeView control, is called.

Here are the contents of DisplayKey:

```
Public Sub DisplayKey(ThisKey As Long, Level As Long, _
   Indent As Long)
   Dim KeyIndex As Long, RegEnumIndex As Long, _
      szBuffer As String, lBuffSize As Long, _
      Nodkey As Node, phkResult As Long, RetKey As Long

   szBuffer = Space(255)
   lBuffSize = Len(szBuffer)
   KeyIndex = 0
   Indent = tvwChild

   Do Until RegEnumIndex = ERROR_NO_MORE_ITEMS
      RegEnumIndex = RegEnumKey(ThisKey, KeyIndex, szBuffer, _
         lBuffSize)
      If RegEnumIndex <> ERROR_SUCCESS And _
         RegEnumIndex <> ERROR_NO_MORE_ITEMS Then
            MsgBox "Reading Failure!"
            Exit Do
      End If
      If szBuffer <> Space(255) Then
         If NextLevel < 2 Then
            Set Nodkey = TreeView1.Nodes.Add(Level, _
               Indent, , szBuffer, 2)
         Else
            Set Nodkey = TreeView1.Nodes.Add(Level, _
               Indent, , szBuffer, 3)
         End If
         RetKey = RegOpenKeyEx(ThisKey, szBuffer, 0, 1, phkResult)
         If RetKey = ERROR_SUCCESS Then
            Indent = tvwChild
            NextLevel = NextLevel + 1
            'Here's where you'd do a recursive call
            'or display the next level!
            'DisplayKey phkResult, NextLevel, Indent
            NextLevel = NextLevel - 1
         End If
      End If
      szBuffer = Space(255)
      KeyIndex = KeyIndex + 1
   Loop
End Sub
```

As you can see, this code is set up to display a third icon, a moon, for the next level down if the code is modified to go that far. It is also designed to be easily modified to recursively trace the entire HKEY_LOCAL_MACHINE branch of the Registry.

Should you change the program to operate recursively, a word of warning: You had better have plenty to do while it does its thing. This will take a while.

If you run the program, you'll get a nice Registry branch, with, shall we say, *different* icons (see Figure 10-6). Although this project is not very useful in and of itself, if you ever need to do an analysis of target registries, you can use its techniques to map them quickly.

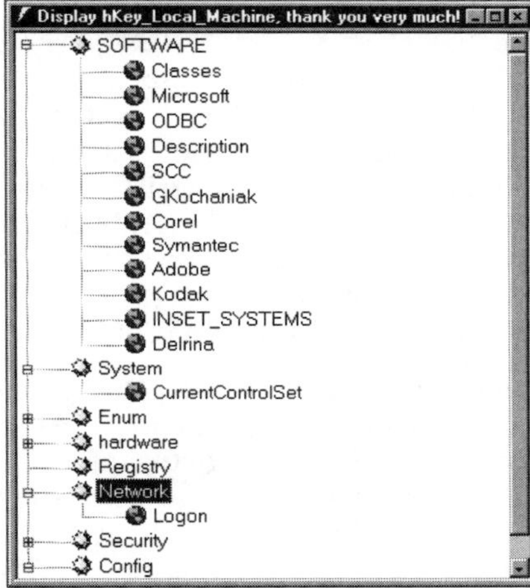

Figure 10-6: You can use the Registry API to access and display the contents of the Registry, in this case the top two levels of the HKEY_LOCAL_MACHINE branch.

Retrieving and Modifying Values

I often find myself wanting to retrieve the value that belongs to a particular key. Sometimes, I also want to modify the value and save it back in the Registry. Provided that I know the name of the key that stores the value and its location in the Registry tree, this is pretty easy to do using the RegOpenKeyEx, RegQueryValueEx, and RegSetValueEx functions.

I'll show you how to do this in an example project that reads the default user and company names into text boxes on a form (saved on the CD-ROM as ***Values.Vbp***). This is similar to the way many setup routines operate: The user is asked to change or verify the default name and company name when installing new software. A feature in the demonstration program not usually found in setup programs is that the user can save new default information back to the Registry by clicking the Apply button.

A word, and some caveats, about Registry locations. The default user information keys used in the sample program are the keys used by Microsoft and others to obtain information for their setup routines (see Figure 10-9). However, this information is stored in a number of places in the Registry (and becomes more complex when a machine is configured for multiple users).

To put this in another way, an application that I create can — and usually will — store user information in its own keys. Short of using Regedit to sleuth through your Registry, there's really no way to determine the location or names of these keys. Major vendors such as Microsoft are also perfectly capable of storing user information for different applications in different places.

The GetUserName function, discussed later in this chapter, is a simpler way to obtain user name information than the method used in this example. The example program follows the lead of many of Microsoft's setup programs and gets its default user name information from the DefName key of HKEY_USERS\.Default\Software\Microsoft\MS Setup (ACME)\User Info. (Note the period in front of Default; it's essential!) The GetUserName API, on the other hand, uses the Current User key of HKEY_LOCAL_MACHINE\System\Current\ControlSet\Control.

The choice is surely yours. (Obviously, you can set RegQueryValueEx to read from the GetUserName location if you so desire.) The point really is that you should never make the assumption that default Registry information is correct without giving the user a chance to override it. Once the user has altered or confirmed the default information, you should store it yourself in your own software's branch.

To set up the ***Values.Vbp*** demonstration program, add the Registry API declaration module (***RegAPI.Bas***) to your project and two text boxes to your startup form (see Figure 10-7). Here's the code in the form load event that places the default values in the form:

```
Private Sub Form_Load()
   Dim szBuffer As String, dataBuff As String, _
      ldataBuffSize As Long, hKey As Long, phkResult As Long, _
      RetVal As Long, Value As String, RegEnumIndex As Long

   'Create Buffer
   dataBuff = Space(255)
   ldataBuffSize = Len(dataBuff)

 szBuffer = ".Default\Software\Microsoft\MS Setup (ACME)\User Info"
   hKey = HKEY_USERS
   RetVal = RegOpenKeyEx(hKey, szBuffer, 0, KEY_ALL_ACCESS, _
      phkResult)
   If RetVal = ERROR_SUCCESS Then MsgBox "OKDokey"

   Value = "DefCompany"
   RetVal = RegQueryValueEx(phkResult, Value, 0, 0, dataBuff, _
      ldataBuffSize)
   If RetVal = ERROR_SUCCESS Then
```

```
      'Get rid of ze null terminator and read into text box
      txtCompany.Text = Left(dataBuff, ldataBuffSize - 1)
   Else
      MsgBox "Internal Error in RegQueryValueEx"
   End If

   Value = "DefName"
   RetVal = RegQueryValueEx(phkResult, Value, 0, 0, dataBuff, _
      ldataBuffSize)
   If RetVal = ERROR_SUCCESS Then
      txtName.Text = Left(dataBuff, ldataBuffSize - 1)
   Else
      MsgBox "Flubbed RegQueryValueEx on the second pass!"
   End If

   'Close the keys
   RegCloseKey hKey
   RegCloseKey phkResult
End Sub
```

If you run the program, you'll see that this code does, indeed, bring up the default user and organization name (see Figure 10-7) — at least, as set in the values of the keys it is hard-coded to read.

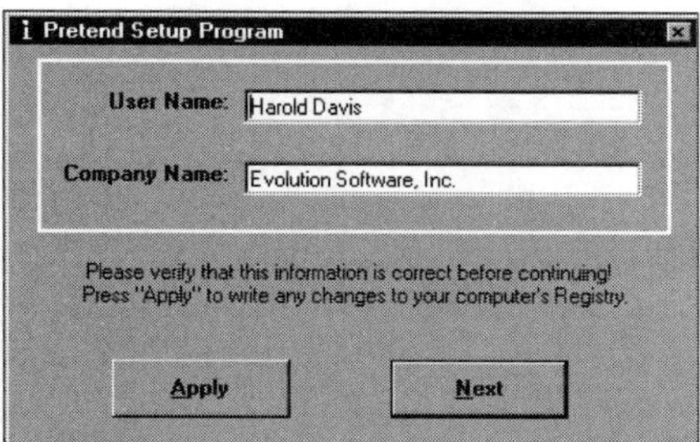

Figure 10-7: You can use the Registry API to retrieve the default user and company names.

RegQueryValueEx is definitely a little flaky about returning values. It's important to test for successful return of the function — which I do in the sample code using the ERROR_SUCCESS constant — before assuming you can do anything with the value. Also, I've found that it works best when you call the keys, whose values you want, in the order in which they appear in the Registry tree.

It's also helpful to test the RegOpenKeyEx function for success during the debugging process. Primarily, this is to make sure that the Registry path was entered precisely; any deviance will cause the function to fail. The code I used to test for the success of this function is commented out in the code sample:

```
'If RetVal = ERROR_SUCCESS Then MsgBox "OKDokey"
```

Here's the code that writes changes back to the Registry:

```
Private Sub cmdApply_Click()
  Dim NewName As String, NewCompany As String, phkResult As Long, _
     sSetValue As String, sValue As String, hKey As Long, _
     szBuffer As String, RetVal As Long

  NewName = txtName.Text
  NewCompany = txtCompany.Text
  szBuffer = ".Default\Software\Microsoft\MS Setup (ACME)\User Info"
  hKey = HKEY_USERS

  RetVal = RegOpenKeyEx(hKey, szBuffer, 0, KEY_ALL_ACCESS, _
     phkResult)
  'If RetVal = ERROR_SUCCESS Then MsgBox "OKDokey"
  sSetValue = "DefCompany"
  sValue = NewCompany
  RetVal = RegSetValueEx(phkResult, sSetValue, 0, REG_SZ, sValue, _
     CLng(Len(sValue) + 1))
  If RetVal <> ERROR_SUCCESS Then _
     MsgBox  "Failed to write to Registry!"

  sSetValue = "DefName"
  sValue = NewName
  RetVal = RegSetValueEx(phkResult, sSetValue, 0, REG_SZ, sValue, _
     CLng(Len(sValue) + 1))
  If RetVal <> ERROR_SUCCESS Then  _
     MsgBox "Failed to write to Registry!"
  'Close the keys
  RegCloseKey hKey
  RegCloseKey phkResult
End Sub
```

With all the code in place in the sample project, I can use it to change my default name and company in the Registry. If I change my name to "Captain Jean-Luc Picard" and my company name to "Federation Starship Enterprise," I can run ***Regedit.Exe*** to examine the correct keys and values and verify that they have been entered (see Figure 10-8).

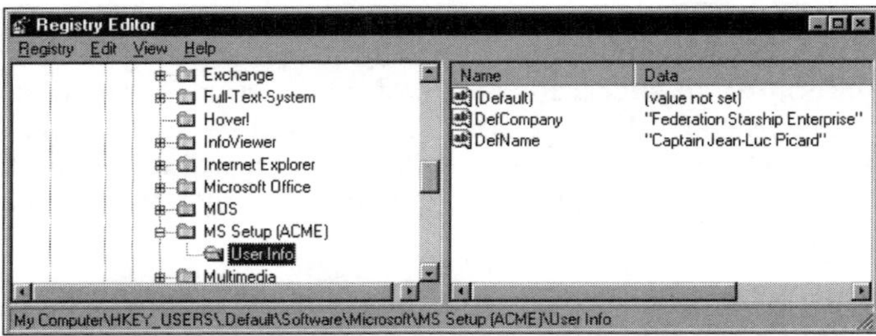

Figure 10-8: Using the RegSetValueEx API, you can write new default values to the Registry (but I'm not bald yet...).

Just to make sure that someone out there is really listening to the Registry, and the particular set of keys and values that is used by this demonstration program, it's fun to see that changes made using the ***Values.Vbp*** project are picked up by the setup program for the Library Edition of the Microsoft Developer Network CD-ROM (see Figure 10-9).

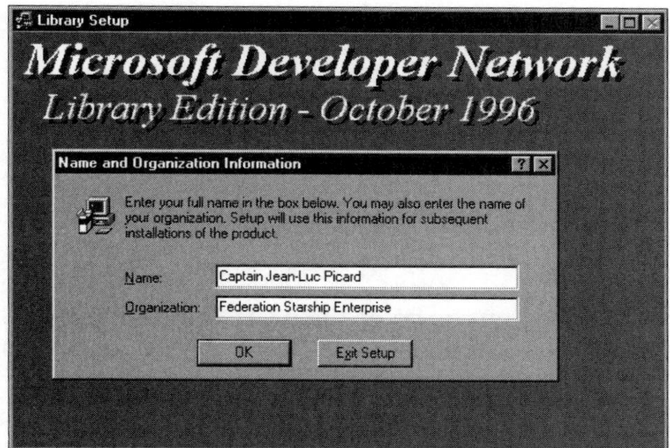

Figure 10-9: The setup program for the Library Edition of the Microsoft Developer Network CD-ROM retrieves the modified user information.

Reading and writing Registry values in your programs helps to give them that professional touch. Once again, as Pooh would say, Very Useful Stuff.

Getting Rid of the Null Terminator and Adding a Null Terminator

It's a good idea to get rid of the null terminator when returning C-style strings to VB. Otherwise, the null terminator (Chr(0)) may appear in your text display as a black box (literally). To get rid of the null terminator, clip off the last character using the Left function once the string has been returned:

```
txtCompany.Text = Left(dataBuff, ldataBuffSize - 1)
```

Likewise, when passing strings back you should add a character to the length variable to store the null terminator. You accomplish this by using the final parameter in the API function call, which indicates the string length. You can easily use the CStr function to return one character more (the null character) than the number of characters in the buffer:

```
RetVal = RegSetValueEx(phkResult, sSetValue, 0, REG_SZ, sValue, _
   CLng(Len(sValue) + 1))
```

NT 4.0 Versus 95

Windows 95 strings that are key values in the Registry always have a null terminator appended, but NT 4.0 key values are not always handled this way. Here's a function (from the ***RegAPI.Bas*** module) that will delete a final null terminator if it is there (and return the string intact if it is not):

```
Public Function ConvertString(tmpVal As String, _
   KeyValSize As Long) As String
   If (Asc(Mid(tmpVal, KeyValSize, 1)) = 0) Then
      'Win95 Null Terminated String, get rid of terminator
      ConvertString = Left(tmpVal, KeyValSize - 1)
   Else
      'WinNT Does NOT Null Terminate String
      ConvertString = Left(tmpVal, KeyValSize)
      'Null Not Found, Return String Only
   End If
End Function
```

You'll also find a module on the companion CD-ROM to this book, ***Convert.Bas***, containing a function, GetKeyValue, that encapsulates the process of converting and returning key values.

GetUserName

A quick way to retrieve the current user's name is to use the GetUserName API. Listing 10-1 displays the code that declares the API and uses it to retrieve the user name, placed in a project with no form modules. (This project is saved on the companion CD-ROM as ***UserName.Vbp***.)

Listing 10-1: Using GetUserName

```
Option Explicit
Declare Function GetUserName Lib "advapi32.dll" Alias _
   "GetUserNameA" (ByVal lpBuffer As String, _
   nSize As Long) As Long

Public Sub Main()
   Dim szBuffer As String, lBuffSize As Long, RetVal As Boolean
   'Create Buffer
   szBuffer = Space(255)
   lBuffSize = Len(szBuffer)
   RetVal = GetUserName(szBuffer, lBuffSize)
   If RetVal Then
      MsgBox "User name is " & UCase(Trim(szBuffer)), _
         vbInformation, "One User Over the Line..."
   Else
      MsgBox "GetUserName failed...sob!", vbInformation, _
         "One User Over the Line..."
   End If
End Sub
```

To set up this project, start a new project with the startup option set to Sub Main. Add a ***.Bas*** module to the project, and insert a procedure named Main in it. Add the code as indicated to the module. Remove the empty form from the project. When the project is run, a message box appears with the user name (see Figure 10-10).

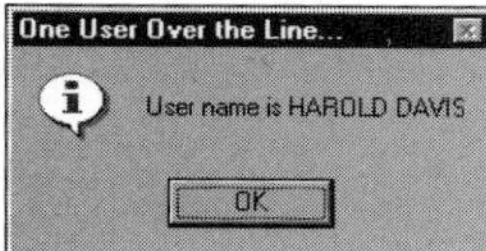

Figure 10-10: The GetUserName API returns the current user name.

Adding and Deleting Keys

The RegCreateKeyEx and RegSetValueEx functions make it easy to add keys, and then add newly named values to the keys. Listing 10-2 contains the code I wrote that adds a key for the Starship Enterprise, below that keys for some of its key officers (forgive the pun), and new values below each officer's key (name and race). (Figure 10-11 shows what the resulting structure looks like in Regedit.) The project is saved on the *Visual Basic 5 SECRETS* companion CD-ROM as ***Keys.Vbp***.

Listing 10-2: Adding keys and values to the Registry

```
Public Sub Main()
   Dim RetVal As Long, hKey As Long, subkey As String, _
      newkey As String, phkResult As Long, _
      SA As SECURITY_ATTRIBUTES, Create As Long, _
      NewValueName As String, Value As String
   hKey = HKEY_LOCAL_MACHINE
   subkey = "SOFTWARE\"
   newkey = "Starship_Enterprise"
   RetVal = RegCreateKeyEx(hKey, subkey & newkey, _
      0, "", REG_OPTION_NON_VOLATILE, KEY_ALL_ACCESS, _
      SA, phkResult, Create)
   subkey = AddASlash(subkey & newkey)
   newkey = "First_Officer"
   RetVal = RegCreateKeyEx(hKey, subkey & newkey, _
      0, "", REG_OPTION_NON_VOLATILE, KEY_ALL_ACCESS, _
      SA, phkResult, Create)
   NewValueName = "Name"
   Value = "Ryker, Will"
   RetVal = RegSetValueEx(phkResult, NewValueName, 0, REG_SZ, _
      Value, CLng(Len(Value) + 1))
   NewValueName = "Race"
   Value = "Human"
   RetVal = RegSetValueEx(phkResult, NewValueName, 0, REG_SZ, _
      Value, CLng(Len(Value) + 1))
   'Close the key
   RegCloseKey phkResult

   newkey = "Ships_Counselor"
   RetVal = RegCreateKeyEx(hKey, subkey & newkey, _
      0, "", REG_OPTION_NON_VOLATILE, KEY_ALL_ACCESS, _
      SA, phkResult, Create)
   NewValueName = "Name"
```

```
    Value = "Troy, Deana"
    RetVal = RegSetValueEx(phkResult, NewValueName, 0, REG_SZ, _
       Value, CLng(Len(Value) + 1))
    NewValueName = "Race"
    Value = "Betazoid"
    RetVal = RegSetValueEx(phkResult, NewValueName, 0, REG_SZ, _
       Value, CLng(Len(Value) + 1))
    'Close the key
    RegCloseKey phkResult

    newkey = "Science_Officer"
    RetVal = RegCreateKeyEx(hKey, subkey & newkey, _
       0, "", REG_OPTION_NON_VOLATILE, KEY_ALL_ACCESS, _
       SA, phkResult, Create)
    NewValueName = "Name"
    Value = "DATA"
    RetVal = RegSetValueEx(phkResult, NewValueName, 0, REG_SZ, _
       Value, CLng(Len(Value) + 1))
    NewValueName = "Race"
    Value = "He's an android, silly!"
    RetVal = RegSetValueEx(phkResult, NewValueName, 0, REG_SZ, _
       Value, CLng(Len(Value) + 1))
    'Close the key
    RegCloseKey phkResult
End Sub
```

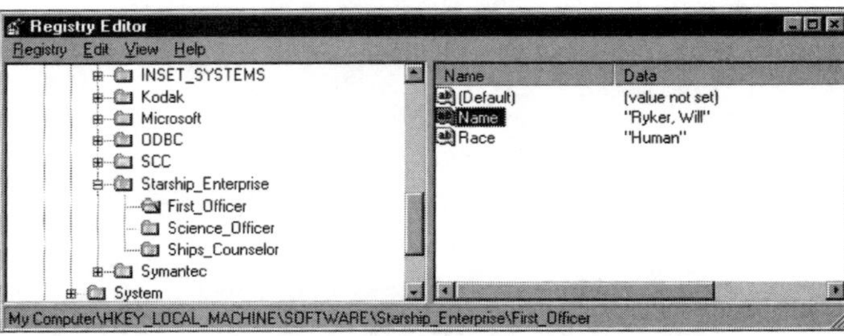

Figure 10-11: You can use the Registry API to create hierarchical Registry entries — for example, the Starship Enterprise in my Registry!

Each time I create the path for a new subkey in this code, I call a function named AddASlash. For example:

```
subkey = AddASlash(subkey & newkey)
```

AddASlash simply adds a backslash (\) at the end of the passed string if it doesn't already have one. This is important, because Registry subkeys must be invoked with backslashes separating concatenated subpaths. The situation in my example code is pretty simple, but things could get a lot more nested, in which case AddASlash could be seriously helpful. Listing 10-3 shows the AddASlash function:

Listing 10-3: Adding a slash at the end of a path

```
Public Function AddASlash(InString As String) As String
   'Add a "\" to end of InString if one was not given. This makes
   '  concatenation of subkeys easier later.
   If Mid(InString, Len(InString), 1) <> "\" Then
      AddASlash = InString & "\"
   Else
      AddASlash = InString
   End If
End Function
```

My next job is to get rid of the keys and values I've just added to the Registry. I'll use the RegDeleteKey function to do that.

First, I add a call to the show method of frmDelete at the end of the Sub Main procedure that creates the Starship_Enterprise structure:

```
...
frmDelete.Show
End Sub
```

frmDelete allows the user to delete the Enterprise structure completely, or only a subkey structure (see Figure 10-12).

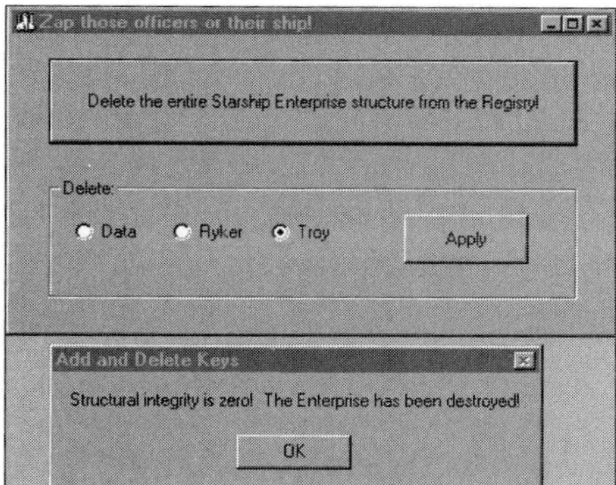

Figure 10-12: You can use RegDeleteKey to delete entire Registry structures. Who did it? Is it the Borg? The Dominion? The Klingons or the Romulans?

Be Careful with RegDeleteKey!

The Win32 version of RegDeleteKey will delete a key, all its subkeys, and all the values of the keys and subkeys. Obviously, you should use RegDeleteKey with care.

Listing 10-4 contains the code that deletes the entire Starship_Enterprise branch:

Listing 10-4: Deleting a branch from the Registry

```
Private Sub cmdDeleteShip_Click()
   Dim RetVal As Long, hKey As Long, szBuffer As String
   hKey = HKEY_LOCAL_MACHINE
   szBuffer = "SOFTWARE\Starship_Enterprise"
   RetVal = RegDeleteKey(hKey, szBuffer)
   If RetVal = ERROR_SUCCESS Then
      MsgBox "Structural integrity is zero!" & _
         "The Enterprise has been destroyed!"
   End If
End Sub
```

Deleting a single key and all its values works the same way, as shown in listing 10-5. (The message shown in Figure 10-13 indicates that the ERROR_SUCCESS flag was returned, and that the operation succeeded.)

Listing 10-5: Deleting a key and its values

```
Private Sub cmdApply_Click()
   Dim RetVal As Long, hKey As Long, SubKey As String, _
      SubsubKey As String
   hKey = HKEY_LOCAL_MACHINE
   SubKey = AddASlash("SOFTWARE\Starship_Enterprise")

   If optDelete(2).Value Then 'zap Troy
      SubsubKey = "Ships_Counselor"
   ElseIf optDelete(1).Value Then ' Ryker's turn to die
      SubsubKey = "First_Officer"
   Else 'By, by, Data
      SubsubKey = "Science_Officer"
   End If
   SubKey = SubKey & SubsubKey
   RetVal = RegDeleteKey(hKey, SubKey)
   If RetVal = ERROR_SUCCESS Then
   MsgBox "The Ship's " & SubsubKey & _
      " has been transported from the Registry!", , _
      "Be a Klingon today..."
   End If
End Sub
```

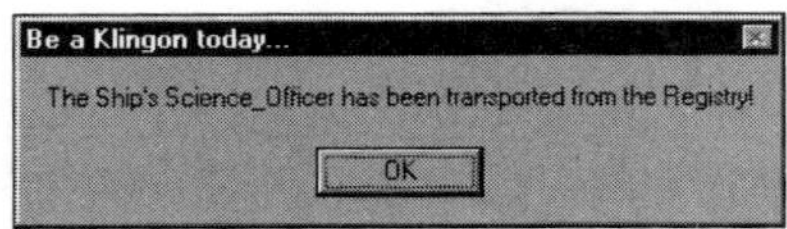

Figure 10-13: Here is a message from your friendly, neighborhood Klingons.

Using RegDeleteValue

If you just want to delete a value name and the value (but leave the key), use RegDeleteValue. For example, you might want to retain the Starship_Enterprise\First_Officer key, but delete the Race=Human value name and value.

RegDeleteValue works exactly like RegDeleteKey except that it's passed the value name rather than the name of the subkey to delete. The code to delete the value name and value Race=Human is in the frmDelete click event in the sample project. It's shown in Listing 10-6.

Listing 10-6: Deleting a value

```
Private Sub Form_Click()
    Dim RetVal As Long, hKey As Long, ValueName As String, _
        SubKey As String, phkResult As Long, _
        SA As SECURITY_ATTRIBUTES, Create As Long
    hKey = HKEY_LOCAL_MACHINE
    SubKey = "SOFTWARE\Starship_Enterprise\First_Officer"
    RetVal = RegCreateKeyEx(hKey, SubKey, _
        0, "", REG_OPTION_NON_VOLATILE, KEY_ALL_ACCESS, _
        SA, phkResult, Create)
    ValueName = "Race"
    RetVal = RegDeleteValue(phkResult, ValueName)
    If RetVal = ERROR_SUCCESS Then
        MsgBox "Let's use a more PC term than ""Race"" !"
    Else
        MsgBox "Error of some sort."
    End If
    RegCloseKey phkResult
End Sub
```

By the way, in the preceding routine, one of the MsgBox calls uses a string literal with embedded double quotes:

```
MsgBox "Let's use a more PC term than ""Race"" !"
```

As you perhaps know, this is one way to insert a quotation character within a string literal (see Figure 10-14).

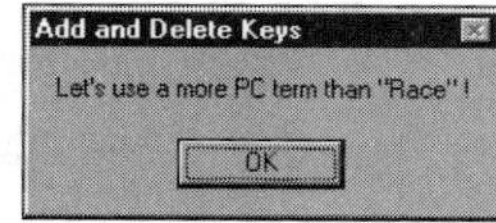

Figure 10-14: You need to use double quotes to display a single quote within a string literal.

Creating an ActiveX Server Application to Encapsulate the Registry APIs

That's a mouthful! And I'm getting a bit ahead of myself (yet again!): ActiveX component applications are covered in Chapter 23, "Creating ActiveX Applications." (For information on how to use class modules, see Chapter 14, "Visual Basic and OOP.")

Nonetheless, being able to create ActiveX component server applications easily is one of the most exciting aspects of 32-bit Visual Basic. An ActiveX component — also called an OLE server — is a natural for encapsulating some of the Registry calls I've demonstrated earlier in this chapter. Once the ActiveX component is complete, all you need to do to access its exposed methods is make sure that it is included in the References in your project and make a function call. You can use it over and over without having to recode the logic of calling the Registry API. Life couldn't be easier! If you encapsulate all of your code in an ActiveX component, it will all be modular and maintainable and usable from anywhere and you can spend more time at the beach!

This section describes step-by-step how to create an ActiveX server application that encapsulates the Registry API used to retrieve and save values in the ***Values.Vbp*** project. Because I've already worked through the logic involved earlier in this chapter, this is not as hard as it may sound. The project is saved on the *Visual Basic 5 SECRETS* companion CD-ROM as ***Server.Vbp***.

After I've explained the OLE server, I'll show you how to create a test project that calls it (saved on the CD-ROM as ***TestSer.Vbp***).

Creating the ActiveX Server

Follow these steps to create the ActiveX server:

1. In the Project Options dialog, select Sub Main as the startup form, enter a Project Name ("ReadandWriteRegVals") and enter an application description, as shown in Figure 10-15. Make sure that ActiveX Component is selected for the project's Start Mode (Figure 10-16).

   The application description you enter will appear in the References dialog when you reach the stage of testing the server (see step 9 and Figure 10-18).

2. Remove the default Form1 from the project. ActiveX components need no forms.

3. Add a code module to the project. Add a Sub Main procedure to this ***.Bas*** file. The Sub Main file will remain with no code. Make sure the project is set to start from Sub Main.

4. Add a class module to the project. Display the class module's Properties window (you can access this window from the class module's context menu). Set the class module's Name to RegData and set Instancing to 5-MultiUse (see Figure 10-17). Close the Properties window.

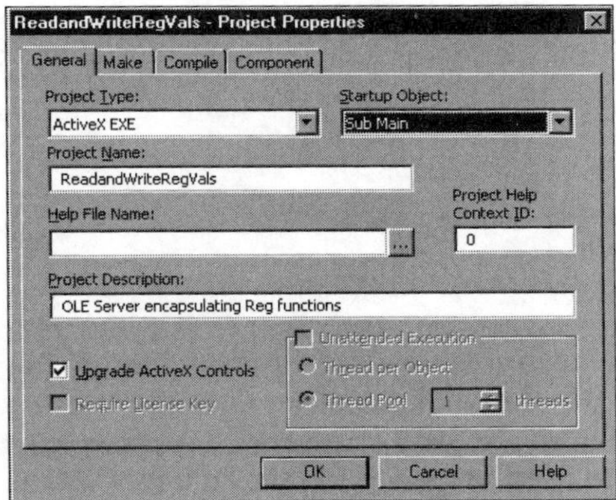

Figure 10-15: The Project Description you assign in the Project Properties dialog will be used to reference your ActiveX server later.

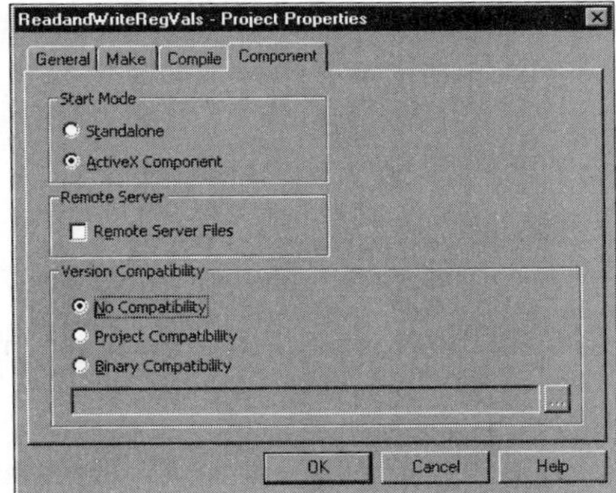

Figure 10-16: ActiveX servers should be set to start as an ActiveX component on the Component tab of the Project Properties dialog.

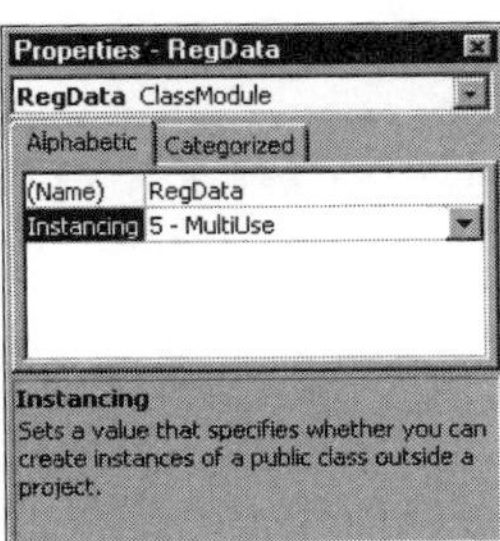

Figure 10-17: You use the Properties windows to set a Class module's Instancing properties.

5. Insert a new Property Procedure named Value in the class module. The property should be Public in scope. The following template code will be added to the class module:

```
Public Property Get Value()

End Property

Public Property Let Value(vNewValue)

End Property
```

The Get Property is used for pulling values out of the Registry and the Let for storing values to the Registry. The way it works is that the named Property, Value, can be used on either side of an equivalence. Property Get is called as though it were a normal function. However, the formal parameter list of a Property's Get and Let must match in name and type. The name vNewValue should not be changed; it matches the Property Get's function return. (If you do not follow these rules, you'll get a runtime syntax error.) For example:

```
Public Property Get Value(hKey As Long, SubKey As String, _
   ValueName As String) As String
   ...
End Property

Public Property Let Value(hKey As Long, SubKey As String, _
   ValueName As String, vNewValue As String)
   ...
End Property
```

In other words, vNewValue in the Property Let — the string input — is paired with the Property Get function-like string output.

6. Add needed declarations for the Registry API to the General section of the class module. (Note that Public constant, variable, and external function declarations are not allowed within a class module.) You could, alternatively, just add the declarations module to the project.

```
Option Explicit
'Registry Constants
Const HKEY_CLASSES_ROOT = &H80000000
Const HKEY_CURRENT_USER = &H80000001
Const HKEY_LOCAL_MACHINE = &H80000002
Const HKEY_USERS = &H80000003
Const REG_SZ = (1)          'Unicode null-terminated string
Const KEY_ALL_ACCESS = &H3F
Const ERROR_SUCCESS = 0&

Private Declare Function RegCloseKey Lib "advapi32.dll" _
  (ByVal hKey As Long) As Long

Private Declare Function RegOpenKeyEx Lib "advapi32.dll" Alias _
   "RegOpenKeyExA" (ByVal hKey As Long, _
   ByVal lpSubKey As String, ByVal ulOptions As Long, _
   ByVal samDesired As Long, phkResult As Long) As Long
```

```
Private Declare Function RegQueryValueEx Lib "advapi32" _
   Alias "RegQueryValueExA" (ByVal hKey As Long, _
   ByVal lpValueName As String, ByVal lpReserved As Long, _
   ByRef lpType As Long, ByVal szData As String, _
   ByRef lpcbData As Long) As Long

Private Declare Function RegSetValueEx Lib "advapi32" _
   Alias "RegSetValueExA" (ByVal hKey As Long, _
   ByVal lpValueName As String, ByVal Reserved As Long, _
   ByVal dwType As Long, ByVal szData As String, _
   ByVal cbData As Long) As Long
```

7. Add the Property Get Value and Property Let Value procedure code. Property Get must be passed as parameters the hKey, a Registry path, and the name of the value to be retrieved. It returns the value as a string. Property Let accepts the same parameters as Property Get, with the addition of the new value to be set (vNewValue).

   The logic of both procedures is taken from the ***Values.Vbp*** project, and is explained earlier in the chapter in my discussion of that project.

```
Public Property Get Value(hKey As Long, SubKey As String, _
   ValueName As String) As String
   Dim szBuffer As String, dataBuff As String, _
      ldataBuffSize As Long, phkResult As Long, RetVal As Long
   'Create Buffer
   dataBuff = Space(255)
   ldataBuffSize = Len(dataBuff)

   RetVal = RegOpenKeyEx(hKey, SubKey, 0, KEY_ALL_ACCESS, phkResult)
   RetVal = RegQueryValueEx(phkResult, ValueName, 0, 0, dataBuff, _
      ldataBuffSize)
   If RetVal = ERROR_SUCCESS Then
      Value = Left(dataBuff, ldataBuffSize - 1)
      'Get rid of ze terminator!
   Else
      MsgBox "Internal error in RegQueryValueEx!"
   End If
   'Close the keys
   RegCloseKey hKey
   RegCloseKey phkResult
End Property
```

   That's it for Property Get Value. Here's the Property Let Value procedure:

```
Public Property Let Value(hKey As Long, SubKey As String, _
   ValueName As String, vNewValue As String)
   Dim phkResult As Long, RetVal As Long
   RetVal = RegOpenKeyEx(hKey, SubKey, 0, KEY_ALL_ACCESS, phkResult)
   RetVal = RegSetValueEx(phkResult, ValueName, 0, _
   REG_SZ, vNewValue, CLng(Len(vNewValue) + 1))
   If RetVal <> ERROR_SUCCESS Then _
      MsgBox "Failed to write to Registry!"
   'Close the keys
   RegCloseKey hKey
   RegCloseKey phkResult
End Property
```

8. Run the server application. The application that tests this server will be running in another instance of VB. An alternative would be to compile the server, open a new project, and invoke the compiled server "for real."

Calling the Server

Here's how to call the server:

9. With the instance of VB that contains the server project running, open a new instance of Visual Basic. Start a new project. In the References dialog (select References from the Project menu), check OLE Server Encapsulating Reg Functions. (See Figure 10-18.) This was the Application Description entered in Step 1 (see Figure 10-15).

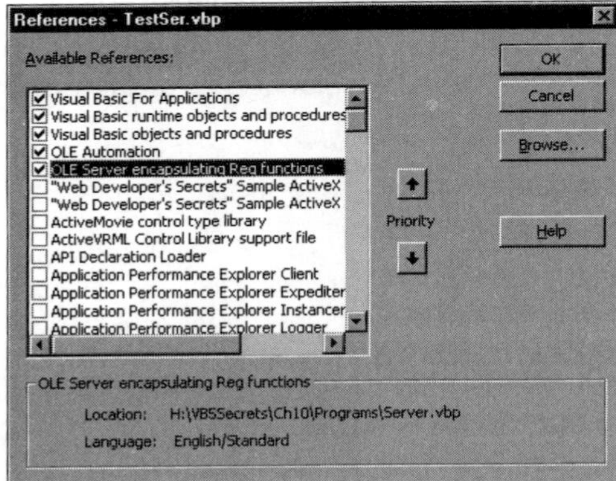

Figure 10-18: You can use the References dialog to include OLE server classes in the current project.

10. In a routine designed for retrieving values from the Registry, dimension a new copy of the ActiveX server's class module. The reference in the instancing statement is of the form: *application name.class module.*

    Call the Property Get procedure with the appropriate parameters. For example:

```
Private Sub cmdGet_Click()
   Dim X As New ReadandWriteRegVals.RegData
   txtReturn.Text = X.Value(GethKey, _
      txtSubKey.Text, txtValueName.Text)
End Sub
```

11. Similarly, create a routine to store values in the Registry with a variable representing a new instance of the ActiveX server's class module:

```
Private Sub cmdSet_Click()
    Dim X As New ReadandWriteRegVals.RegData
    X.Value(GethKey, txtSubKey.Text, _
       txtValueName.Text) = txtReturn.Text
End Sub
```

And that is *really* all there is to it. While creating and debugging OLE servers can be a touch tricky — more on this in Chapter 23 — obviously, there is nothing to calling exposed OLE methods other than a few lines of code.

Arguably, there are some limitations to the utility of this particular OLE server. For one thing, it only encapsulates two of the Registry APIs (as shown in Figure 10-19). More telling, to use Property Get Value and Property Let Value, you need to be able to pass them the correct hKey, the precise Registry path for the value you want to retrieve or change, as well as the correct name for the value.

Picky, picky, picky! It's still an awe-inspiring technology.

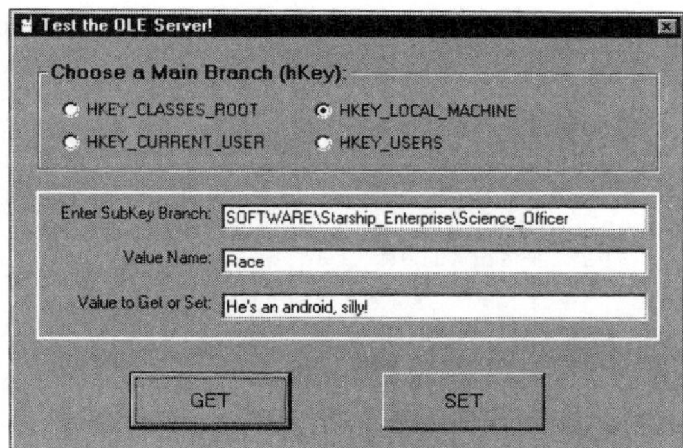

Figure 10-19: Here is how you would retrieve a value from the Registry by calling the OLE server.

Registering File Extensions

As a final topic in this chapter, I'll demonstrate how to register a file extension. Proper registration of a file extension causes the associated application to execute when a file with the extension is opened, usually with the opened file as a command-line argument. For example, provided that you have Word installed on your system, double-clicking a ***.Doc*** file in Windows Explorer should start Word and load the ***.Doc*** file.

In the example program I create here, a file extension of ***.Bad*** is associated with ***WeBe.Exe***. The project source code is saved on the CD-ROM as ***FileX.Vbp***, the executable as ***WeBe.Exe***, and a test file as ***Test.Bad***. (***Test.Bad*** is merely a renamed ***.Txt*** text file created in Notepad.)

For the final demonstration of the project to work (in other words, to be able to start ***WeBe.Exe*** by double-clicking ***Test.Bad***), you'll need to copy the file ***WeBe.Exe*** into your root C:\ directory. This is because the application's open command line has been entered in the Registry as "C:\WeBe.Exe %1". This has been hard-coded into the demo program. Of course, as another option, there is nothing to stop you from changing the open command line in the project source code and rerunning it.

In a new project, add the Registry API declarations module (***RegAPI.Bas***). Next, depending on the startup setting, place the code shown in Listing 10-7 in either the module containing Sub Main or in the default form's load event (and module):

Listing 10-7: Registering a file extension

```
Option Explicit
Public Const MAX_PATH = 256&

Public Sub Main()
  Dim sKeyName As String, sKeyValue As String, Retval As Long, _
     phkResult As Long
'Create a root entry for WeBe
sKeyName = "WeBe"
sKeyValue = "File Extension Demo"
Retval = RegCreateKey(HKEY_CLASSES_ROOT, sKeyName, phkResult)
Retval = RegSetValue(phkResult, "", REG_SZ, sKeyValue, 0&)
'Create a root entry that associates .Bad with "WeBe"
sKeyName = ".Bad"
sKeyValue = "WeBe"
Retval = RegCreateKey(HKEY_CLASSES_ROOT, sKeyName, phkResult)
Retval = RegSetValue(phkResult, "", REG_SZ, sKeyValue, 0&)

'Set the command line for WeBe
sKeyName = "WeBe"
sKeyValue = "C:\WeBe.Exe %1"
'Change sKeyValue to reflect actual location of executable!
Retval = RegCreateKey(HKEY_CLASSES_ROOT, sKeyName, phkResult)
Retval = RegSetValue(phkResult, "shell\open\command", _
   REG_SZ, sKeyValue, MAX_PATH)
MsgBox ".Bad" 'Run up something to show the test worked!
End Sub
```

If you run this program and then open ***Regedit***, you'll see that a file extension entry for ***.Bad*** has been created under HKEY_CLASSES_ROOT:

```
.Bad = WeBe
```

Also, a shell open command structure has been created for WeBe (see Figure 10-20).

To test that this really works, compile the program to create an executable file named ***WeBe.Exe***. Copy the file to your C:\ directory. In Windows Explorer, double-click any file with a ***.Bad*** extension. ***WeBe.Exe*** will execute (see Figure 10-21).

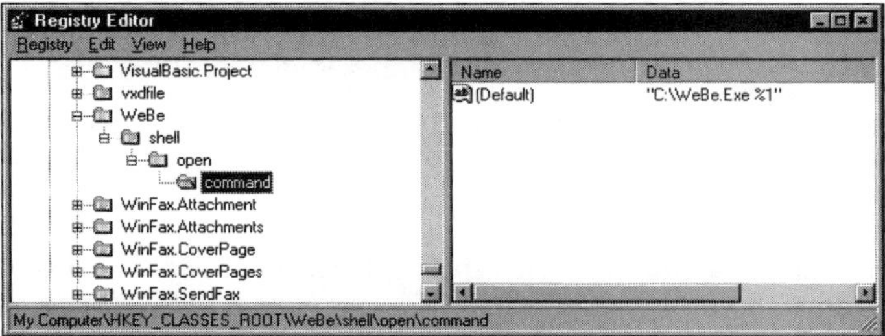

Figure 10-20: A Shell Open Command structure that invokes ***WeBe.Exe*** has been created for files with an extension of ***.Bad***.

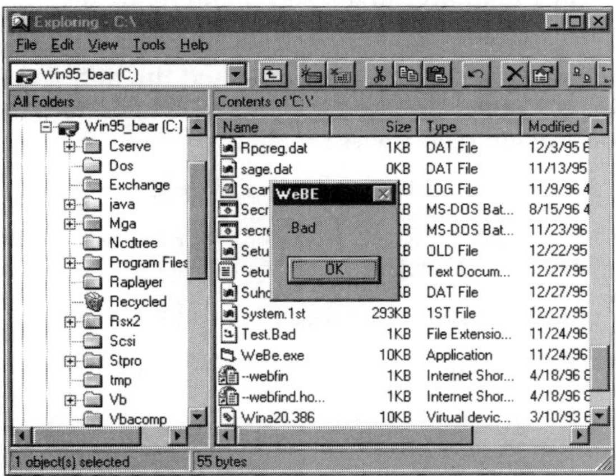

Figure 10-21: Double-clicking a filename with the ***.Bad*** extension in Explorer invokes the WeBe application.

In a word, once we're using the Registry to associate file extensions with executables — "we be Bad!"

Summary

If it's out there, it's in *Visual Basic 5 SECRETS*, at least in regards to programming the Registry. The information in this chapter should be sufficient to help you create polished applications that make full use of the Registry.

In this chapter, I

- Showed you the range of the available Registry API
- Provided an overview of what each API does
- Showed you how to declare Registry APIs, constants, and structures in your projects
- Provided a ***.Bas*** module with the declarations for you to use simply by adding it to your projects
- Explained how to convert back and forth between VB strings and C-style null-terminated strings
- Demonstrated how to use the four built-in VB Registry statements
- Showed how to retrieve and display keys and subkeys
- Demonstrated how to modify values and pointed out several ways to retrieve and save user information
- Described the GetUserName API, and explained the difference between where in the Registry this function reads its value and where Microsoft's setup routines normally read theirs
- Explained and demonstrated how to add and delete keys
- Provided step-by-step instructions for creating an OLE server application that encapsulates the Registry API
- Told you how to call the OLE server application from your own projects
- Demonstrated how to associate a file extension with an executable file

Chapter 11

The Win32 Software Development Kit (SDK), the Win32 API, and the Windows Messaging System

This chapter discusses the Win32 Software Development Kit (SDK), the Win32 API, the Windows messaging system and some related topics. In the chapter I'll

- Describe the tools included in the SDK and explain some of those that are most useful to VB programmers
- Tell you how to get the most out of the SDK documentation
- Demonstrate some of the Win32 APIs most commonly used by VB programmers
- Show how to write code that gracefully handles the differences between Windows 95 and Windows NT
- Discuss writing 32-bit programs that run under Windows 3.*x* using the Win32s APIs
- Explain the Windows messaging system
- Demonstrate how to intercept Windows messages to place your application's icons on the Windows 95 "tray"

The SDK

The Software Development Kit (SDK) is available from Microsoft; for example, you'll receive it if you join MSDN with a Level 2 membership. Microsoft makes a concerted effort to keep the SDK up to date on a subscription basis to MSDN members; recent releases of the SDK cover Windows 95, NT 4, and 32-bit development extensively.

The SDK is a copious collection of tools whose utility and design range from the sublime to the ridiculous. It also includes a truly mind-boggling quantity of on-line documentation, particularly focusing on the Windows APIs. Although C development is the primary thrust of the SDK, no serious Windows developer can afford to be without it — for the Windows API documentation, if nothing else.

From the viewpoint of the Visual Basic developer, the SDK is important and something one should know about. However, the primary importance to a VB programmer is for its documentation of the Windows API, not for the tools included with it, which are serviceable, but not top of the line.

The Win32 SDK provides many tools to help you develop stable and powerful applications. Some of these are specific to platforms — for example, Win32s, Windows 95, or Windows NT. These tools include support for developing applications that include:

- Remote Procedure Call Support (RPC)
- OLE
- Multimedia
- Win32s
- Shell extensions
- Pen windows
- Telephony API (TAPI)
- Messaging API (MAPI)

In addition, the SDK includes help compiler tools and two setup toolkits — from InstallShield and Microsoft.

The InstallShield setup toolkit included in the SDK is more along the lines of a working demonstration than a complete product. Although InstallShield is the leading professional installer, you'll need to obtain a copy of the full version of the program to create real-world, customized setup programs.

Unfortunately, nowhere in the copious documentation is there a comprehensive list of what all the programs shipped as part of the SDK do. (There is an OLE Tools help file that documents four of the OLE tools included in the SDK.)

Some of these utilities run under DOS and some under Windows. Some — such as ***Spy.Exe*** — are thoroughly documented and well designed. (I'll be discussing the Spy utility, which lets you view Windows messages being received by a window, later in this chapter.) The purpose of some of the other SDK programs is not so clear, which is why I've put together these descriptions.

The SDK Tools

So that you can take greater advantage of the power of the SDK tools, this chapter describes some of the more important ones. For further information on these applications, try the application's help system (if it comes with one), or open the application and play with it.

Abview32.Exe

Abview32.Exe functions as a simple MAPI client in order to test MAPI applications.

Apfcvt.Exe

Apfcvt.Exe is, essentially, a search-and-replace utility that operates on binary files such as executables.

Aviedit.Exe

Aviedit.Exe is a multimedia file (***.Avi***) playback and edit utility. You could use it to prepare and test multimedia screen captures used in an on-line tutorial.

CapScrn.Exe

CapScrn.Exe captures video images from a computer screen and turns them into ***.Avi*** files. You can capture sound along with the video, for example, by speaking into a microphone to explain what is happening on the computer screen.

Cl32Test.Exe

Cl32Test.Exe tests OLE client programs.

Cmccli32.Exe

Cmccli32.Exe is a sample mail client, used for testing mail applications.

Compress.Exe (and *Expand.Exe*)

Compress.Exe is a DOS application for compressing files. It is Microsoft's analog to PKZip; it is used in the setup application that ships with VB. ***Compress.Exe*** (and its reverse number, ***Expand.Exe***, which expands files that have been compressed using ***Compress.Exe***) are useful utilities to have on your system. You can use them to manually prepare files for inclusion in an installation, and to decompress programs without running a setup program.

Dbwin.Exe

You can use ***Dbwin.Exe*** to set a system log for debugging purposes.

Ddespy.Exe

You use ***Ddespy.Exe*** to track and display DDE messages and callbacks.

DDTest32.Exe

You can use ***DDTest32.Exe*** to test load time and other characteristics of Device Independent Bitmap (DIB) imagery.

Dfview.Exe

Dfview.Exe displays the contents and organization of a compound OLE document. Once a compound document file has been loaded, DFView displays its contents using two types of windows: one for displaying the storage hierarchy and another for displaying a stream's contents. (If you are interested in tools for working with compound OLE documents, you may be interested in the explanation of ActiveX Document applications in Chapter 28, "Creating Internet Applications in VB.")

Dlgedit.Exe

Dlgedit.Exe is used to create, and edit, dialogs that can be compiled into an external resource (***.Res***) file. Using dialogs and string literals compiled into an external resource file can be a good way to approach issues of internationalization. You can create a separate ***.Res*** file for each target language, using standardized dialog names for all versions of the resource file. Which ***.Res*** file is distributed with the executable would depend on the language to be used.

The tools in ***Dlgedit*** are generic visual design tools (see Figure 11-1). Although they are crude by VB5 standards, they work (and compared to what was available ten years ago...).

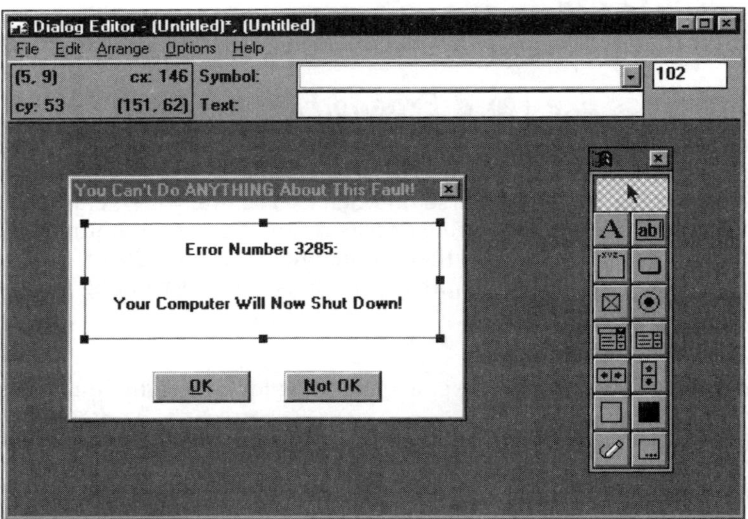

Figure 11-1: The Dialog Editor provides some basic design tools for creating and editing dialogs.

You'll find more information on using external resource files in Chapter 16, "Optimizing Secrets," and Chapter 18, "Managing MDI Applications and Menus."

Dobjview.Exe

Dobjview.Exe is a tool for viewing objects placed on the Clipboard and objects that can be transferred via drag and drop.

Espexe.Exe

Espexe.Exe is a tool used to develop telephony applications under 32-bit Windows. ***Espexe*** is a TAPI service provider that appears as a multiline telephony system. In other words, your TAPI application can use ***Espexe*** for testing purposes with no actual telephony hardware attached.

Fontedit.Exe

Fontedit.Exe is a character-by-character font editor (see Figure 11-2).

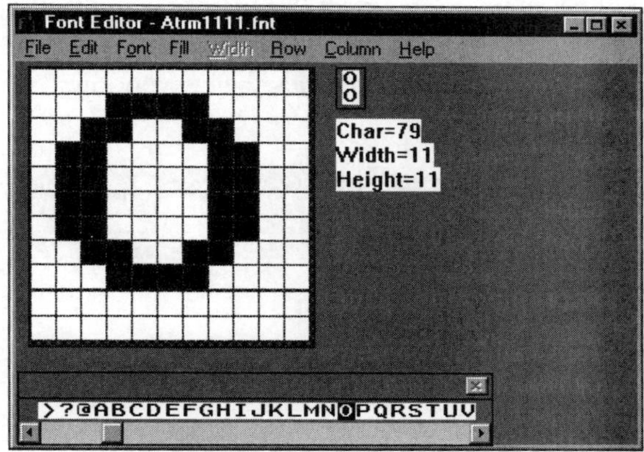

Figure 11-2: You can use the SDK Font Editor application to create customized fonts.

Hcw.Exe

Hcw.Exe is the Help Workshop program, which provides a comprehensive tool set in a visual workshop environment for creating and editing help systems. Notably, Help Workshop provides convenient access to all the WinHelp APIs.

In addition, you can use Help Workshop to easily determine a topic's ID and source file. If the Help Author command on the File menu is checked, and you right-click any topic (including pop-ups), you can click Topic Information to view information about that topic. If the Include .Rtf Filename And Topic ID box in the Compile A Help File dialog box was checked when the help file was compiled, you'll see information about the ***.Rtf*** file that includes the topic, and its topic ID.

For more on creating help systems, see Chapter 35, "Help Files."

Hw32.Exe

You use ***Hw32.Exe***, or HeapWatch32, to view Win32 application heaps and monitor them for memory leaks. The interface has three levels, depending on the information you want to view:

- The Summary view window shows a list of the heaps for all of the Win32 applications currently running in the system.
- The Details view window shows all of the memory objects in the selected heap.
- The Object view window shows the allocated memory block for the given object. Memory leaks are searched for by taking snapshots from the Details view window, before and after a given operation is performed. Memory objects that exist after the post-operation snapshot are potential memory leaks and can be further investigated.

Figure 11-3 shows the HeapWatch32's Summary view window.

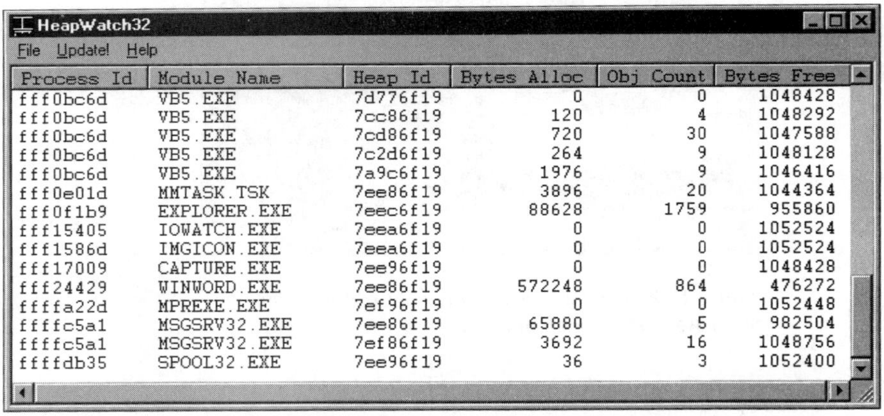

HeapWatch32

File Update! Help

Process Id	Module Name	Heap Id	Bytes Alloc	Obj Count	Bytes Free
fff0bc6d	VB5.EXE	7d776f19	0	0	1048428
fff0bc6d	VB5.EXE	7cc86f19	120	4	1048292
fff0bc6d	VB5.EXE	7cd86f19	720	30	1047588
fff0bc6d	VB5.EXE	7c2d6f19	264	9	1048128
fff0bc6d	VB5.EXE	7a9c6f19	1976	9	1046416
fff0e01d	MMTASK.TSK	7ee86f19	3896	20	1044364
fff0f1b9	EXPLORER.EXE	7eec6f19	88628	1759	955860
fff15405	IOWATCH.EXE	7eea6f19	0	0	1052524
fff1586d	IMGICON.EXE	7eea6f19	0	0	1052524
fff17009	CAPTURE.EXE	7ee96f19	0	0	1048428
fff24429	WINWORD.EXE	7ee86f19	572248	864	476272
fffa22d	MPREXE.EXE	7ef96f19	0	0	1052448
ffffc5a1	MSGSRV32.EXE	7ee86f19	65880	5	982504
ffffc5a1	MSGSRV32.EXE	7ef86f19	3692	16	1048756
ffffdb35	SPOOL32.EXE	7ee96f19	36	3	1052400

Figure 11-3: You can use HeapWatch32 to watch heaps assigned to 32-bit applications and monitor them for leaks.

Imagedit.Exe

Imagedit.Exe, or Image Editor, is a full-fledged professional tool that you can use to create and edit bitmaps, icons, and cursors for your applications on a pixel-by-pixel basis (see Figure 11-4).

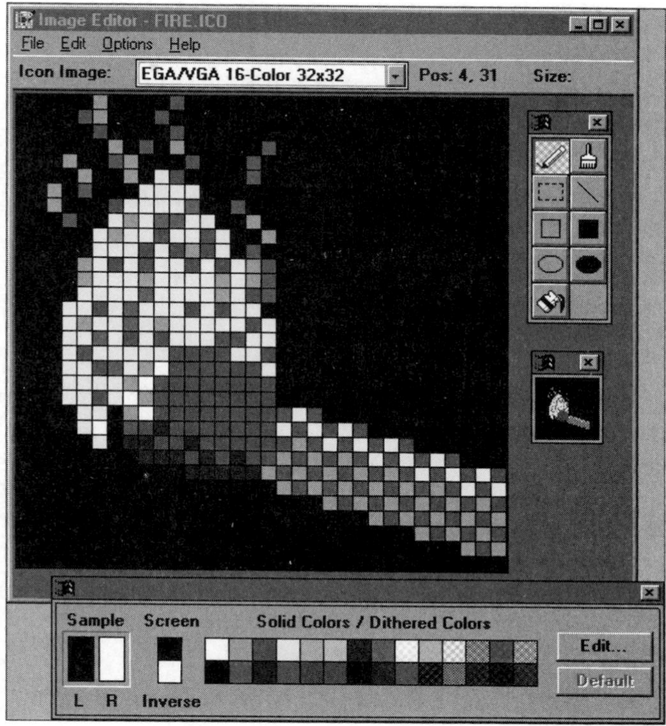

Figure 11-4: An iconized image of a match being manipulated (it's a hot time tonight at Image Editor!).

The Image Editor includes several neat features that you should know about. The IDE is very straightforward, containing three design tools: a Toolbox that includes a pointer, brush, marquis tool, and so on; a color palette that lets you set two colors, one for the left mouse button and one for the right; and a View window that shows the image you are working on at true size. Using the Edit menu, you can set the brush size and whether grid lines are visible.

If you resize the application window while working on an image, the image dynamically resizes itself, zooming larger or smaller as you adjust the window.

Irotview.Exe

Irotview.Exe dynamically displays the contents of an OLE object's table as it is running.

Mdbvu32.Exe

Mdbvu32.Exe is a tool for viewing MAPI message stores and interactively testing MAPI applications.

Ole2vw32.Exe

The OLE 2.0 Object Viewer, ***Ole2vw32.Exe***, helps creators of OLE-compliant applications better understand what is happening in their programs. It is also a powerful testing tool that lets you verify that your objects and interfaces are behaving as expected. Because the primary source of information for this tool is the Registry, you could also use the Object Viewer to check the accuracy of the OLE registration information.

The OLE Object Viewer is intended to help developers find the answers to the following questions, among others:

- What OLE 2.0 objects are installed on my system? (This information appears in the Object List pane.)
- What interfaces does a given object support? (This information appears in the Interface List pane.)
- Is an object an in-process server or handler, or is it local? What are its registration database entries? (This information appears in the Object Information pane.)
- Does this object support this interface correctly? (Check the Interface Viewer for this information.)

However, because ***Ole2View.Exe*** is itself extensible (see the topic Ole2View Interface Viewer DLLs in Ole2View's on-line help), it can answer many more of your questions about OLE objects!

Porttool.Exe

You can use ***Porttool.Exe*** to help identify the portions of legacy 16-bit source code that might need to be changed to make your applications Win32-compatible. The tool provides a brief description of the problem and a possible solution.

Porttool.Exe performs a string search of the source code input. Although it is aimed at C source code, it is completely configurable. You can use profile files to determine how you'd like it to behave and what substitutions you want it to make. (For that matter, changes in calls to the APIs would need to be flagged in any language.)

PviewWindows 95.Exe

Pview.Exe is a process and thread viewer.

Send32.Exe

You can use ***Send32.Exe*** to test initiation of the MAPI process.

Spy.Exe

Spy.Exe is an excellent tool for snooping on the contents of the Windows message stream. There is more information about the Windows messaging system later in this chapter. With Version 5, VB programmers can use subclassing (and related techniques) to intercept Windows messages being sent to a form or control. Exactly what messages are sent following specific user actions thus becomes important to VB programmers; you can easily use Spy to find this out.

Spy lets you select the window whose messages you want to view. (You can select all windows, if you like.) You can send output to a screen window — which will, itself, affect the Window messages displayed — or to a file or a serial port.

For example, if you start a VB project with a default startup Form1 and add a command button to it using Spy's Select window, you can select Form1 as Spy's current selection (see Figure 11-5). By the way, note that the class name for a VB form remains ThunderForm; ain't history grand?

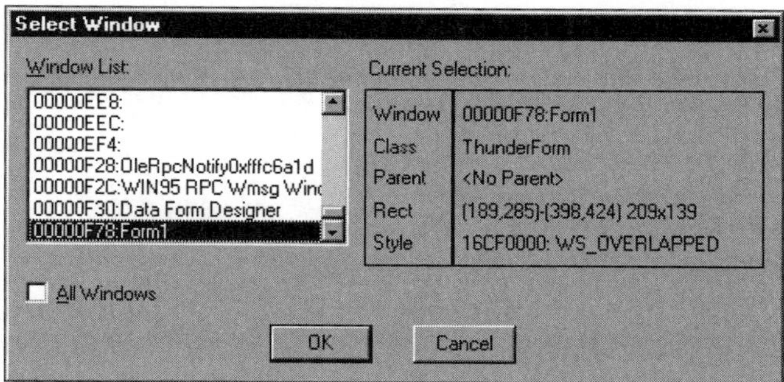

Figure 11-5: You can use the Spy utility to observe the Windows message stream in relationship to a Visual Basic form.

If you then start Spy (by clicking the Start! menu) and double-click the command button, you'll get a message stream something like the one shown in Figure 11-6.

Stress.Exe

The ***Stress.Exe*** application provides a way to munch up selected system resources to stress test applications in a low resources situation. Stress can be set to munch these resources: the global heap, user heap, GDI heap, disk space, and file handles. Appropriately, this utility has an elephant for its icon (the icon is depicted later in this chapter in Figure 11-7).

Tb14.Exe

Tb14.Exe is a TAPI 32-bit browser that allows a developer to interactively call into the Windows telephony interface and examine all returned information.

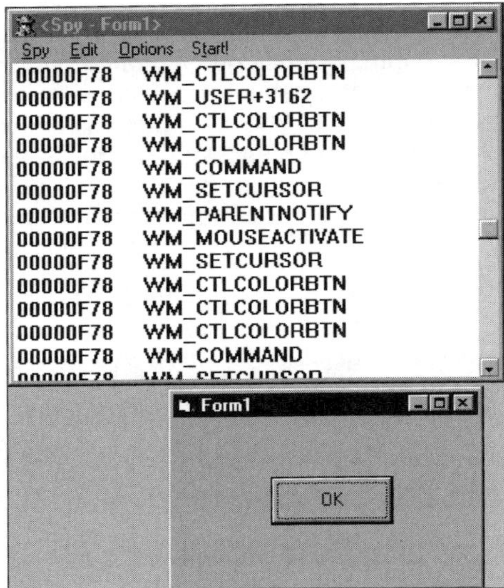

Figure 11-6: Here is the Spy utility showing the Windows message stream after a VB form has been selected.

Vidcap.Exe

Vidcap.Exe is a data-capture application that lets you capture video sequences onto your computer. With Vidcap — part of the Video for Windows system — you can capture individual images or entire video sequences from a VCR, a videodisc player, or a video camera and microphone.

Wcheck.Exe

Wcheck.Exe is a pretty groovy game of checkers! Go figure.

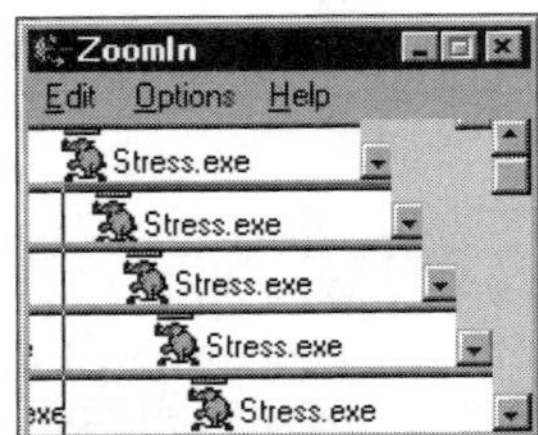

Figure 11-7: You can use ***Zoomin.Exe*** to capture a portion of the screen — for example, a stressed elephant.

Windiff.Exe

Windiff.Exe is a directory and file comparison utility, useful in those version control situations that seem to come up so often in team development situations.

Zoomin.Exe

The ZoomIn utility captures a portion of the screen (see Figure 11-7). This is useful because you can copy the contents of ***Zoomin*** to the Clipboard and paste it into an image editing utility — such as ***Imagedit.Exe*** — where you can use it as part of an icon or bitmap.

Navigating the SDK Documentation

Although there is — as I've said earlier — a ton of SDK documentation, unfortunately very little of it covers the SDK tools (see the earlier description of these tools). Also unfortunate, from the viewpoint of the VB programmer, is the fact that the SDK and its documentation are almost entirely intended for C programmers. This means that the detailed API descriptions tend to be the most useful thing in the documentation for VBers.

My suggestion is that you go straight to the Win SDK Help file (and bypass all others). This file is located on the Start menu under Windows SDK Online References. Open the file by double-clicking it and select Query from the Tools menu. Make sure that Win32 is selected as the subset for searching (see Figure 11-8). Enter the topic, or name of the API, you want to find out about.

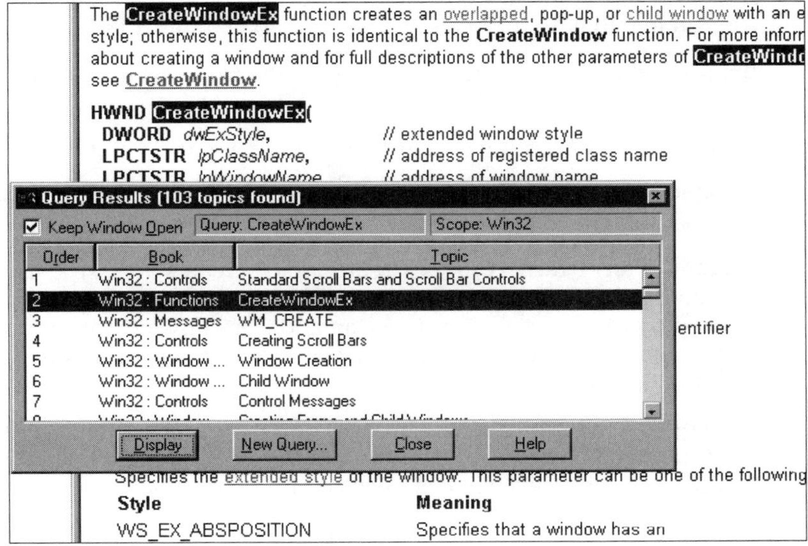

Figure 11-8: You can use the Win SDK help Query utility to quickly locate the information you need.

The keyword Index, also located under help, is also useful for quickly retrieving the information you need.

Windows API Functions Commonly Used in VB

VB5 is such a feature-rich environment that you certainly can use it to write complex applications that never call the Windows APIs. However, if you want to unleash the full power of Windows — and extend VB almost infinitely — sometimes API calls are necessary (or advisable). Usually, these calls fall into one of four categories:

- Registry functions, when you require Registry querying and manipulation beyond the power of VB's built-in statements (see Chapter 10, "Programming the Registry in VB")
- System information functions
- Graphics and display functions
- Functions, such as Message functions, for retrieving information unavailable from VB

Here are some of the APIs that are most commonly used by VB programmers — except the Registry API, which was covered extensively in Chapter 10 — along with brief descriptions of what they do.

My experience is that it is always easier to understand the operations of the API with an actual example. That's why I've included numerous examples in the next section of this chapter; they use many of the APIs described here.

BitBlt Moves a bitmap from a source device context to a destination; often used to manipulate the scaling, size, and appearance of bitmap graphics.

BringWindowToTop Brings a window to the front (to the top of the ZOrder) and activates it; see SetActiveWindow.

ClipCursor Confines the cursor to a rectangular area on the screen.

CreateCompatibleDC Prepares an image in memory, such as before copying the image to the compatible device.

CreateCursor, DestroyCursor CreateCursor creates a cursor with the specified size, bit patterns, and hot spot. DestroyCursor destroys a cursor created by the CreateCursor function and frees any memory it occupied. (You should not use this function to destroy a cursor that was not created with the CreateCursor function.)

CreateProcess Creates a new process and its primary thread. The new process executes the specified executable file. (This function supersedes WinExec, which, however, has been retained for backwards compatibility.)

DeleteObject Deletes an object from memory. Also see ReleaseDC.

DiskSpaceFree Gets free space on specified disk. The Declare statement is found in ***Common.Bas*** in the ***Setupkit*** subdirectory of Visual Basic:

```
Declare Function DiskSpaceFree Lib "VB5STKIT.DLL" _
   Alias "DISKSPACEFREE" () As Long
```

DragAcceptFiles, DragFinish DragAcceptFiles registers a window as accepting dragged files; DragFinish releases memory that Windows allocated for use in transferring dragged file.

EnumChildWindows Gets a list of child windows that belong to the specified parent window.

ExtFloodFill Fills an area of the display surface with the current brush.

ExtractIcon, DrawIcon, LoadIcon These functions manipulate icons.

FillRect Fills a rectangle using the specified brush.

FindExecutable Finds and retrieves the name and handle of the executable that is associated with a specified filename.

GetActiveWindow Retrieves the handle of the active window associated with the thread that calls the function.

GetCursorPos Gets the cursor's position, in screen coordinates.

GetDesktopWindow Retrieves a handle to the Windows desktop window, which covers the entire screen and is the area on top of which all icons and other windows are painted.

GetDiskFreeSpace Returns information about a disk, including the amount of free space on the disk.

GetModuleFileName Returns the full path and filename of the executable file containing a specified module. (When run under 32-bit Windows, the function returns long filenames when the application's version number is greater than or equal to 4.00 and the long filename is available. If these conditions are not met, it returns only 8.3 format filenames.)

GetPaletteEntries, CreatePen, SelectObject These functions manipulate color palettes.

GetParent Gets the handle of a window's parent.

GetSystemDirectory Gets the path of the Windows system directory. Applications should not create files in the system directory. If the user is running a shared version of Windows, the application does not have write access to the system directory. Applications should create files only in the directory returned by the GetWindowsDirectory function.

GetSystemInfo Returns information about the current system. This function replaces GetWinFlags, which is obsolete and is not used in the Win32 API.

GetSystemMenu Allows access to the Window menu for copying and modifying system menu items. (You open this menu by clicking the form icon in Windows 95; in Windows 3.*x* it was known as the System menu or Control menu.)

GetSystemMetrics Gets system metrics, which are the dimensions (widths and heights) of Windows display elements. All dimensions retrieved by GetSystemMetrics are in pixels.

GetVersionEx Returns information about the version of the operating system that is currently running (supersedes GetVersion).

GetWindowLong, SetWindowLong Gets or sets window style information.

GetWindowPlacement, **SetWindowPlacement** Gets or sets the show state and the normal (restored), minimized, and maximized positions of a window.

GetWindowRect Retrieves the dimensions of the specified window in screen coordinates.

GetWindowsDirectory Gets the path of the Windows directory. See GetSystemDirectory.

GetWindowText Gets the caption of a window or the text in a control. GetWindowText cannot retrieve the text of an edit control located in another application.

GetWindowTextLength Retrieves the length, in characters, of a window's title bar text (if the window has a title bar). If the window is a control, the function retrieves the length of the text within the control.

GlobalMemoryStatus Retrieves information about current available memory. The function returns information about both physical and virtual memory.

IsIconic, IsWindowVisible, IsZoomed Finds the state of a window, determining whether it is minimized, visible, or maximized.

LoadCursor Loads the specified cursor resource from the application's executable.

PlaySound Plays a sound specified by the given filename, resource, or system event.

ReleaseDC Deletes a device context from memory. Also see DeleteObject.

RemoveMenu Deletes a menu item from a menu.

RoundRect Draws a rectangle with rounded corners. The rectangle is outlined with the current pen and filled with the current brush.

SendMessage Sends a message to a window. For example, the message WM_PAINT tells a window procedure that the window's client area has changed and must be repainted. In another example, there is no built-in VB property that tells you how many lines there are in multiline text box. However, if you use SendMessage to send an EM_GETLINECOUNT message to the text box, it will return the number of lines the text box contains.

There are numerous other messages you can use, or you can create your own. For more information, see "The Windows Messaging System" later in this chapter and the "Messages Overview" topic in Win32 SDK's on-line help.

SetActiveWindow Activates a window. See BringWindowToTop.

SetCapture Sends all mouse input to the specified window belonging to the current thread, regardless of whether the cursor is within that window. Only one window at a time can capture the mouse. If the mouse cursor is over a window created by another thread, the system will direct mouse input to the specified window only if a mouse button is down.

SetCursorPos Moves the cursor to the specified location.

SetWindowPos Changes the size, position, and ZOrder (the three-dimensional order in which objects are placed) of a child, pop-up, or top-level window.

WinHelp Starts ***Winhelp.Exe***, the Windows Help application. You can pass a specific help file and topic for it to open.

Using the APIs in the Real World

In this section, I'll show you some real-world uses for the APIs in Visual Basic applications. These uses of the APIs are fairly straightforward; I've set up each one in its own procedure.

The applications are saved on the *Visual Basic 5 SECRETS* companion CD-ROM in the directory for programs related to Chapter 11. My thought is that you can easily incorporate these routines into your own projects. To make this easier, I've included on the CD-ROM two code modules:

- ***APIDec.Bas*** includes the declarations for many of the API functions, structures, and constants used in the examples in this chapter.
- ***APICode.Bas*** includes generalized code that uses these API functions, developed in the examples in this chapter.

Making a Form Stay on Top

To get a form to stay on top — that is, always appear above all other windows, even if it is not active — as if the form's ZOrder were always set to 0, call the SetWindowsPos API. SetWindowsPos needs to be passed the handle of the form, the constant HWND_TOPMOST, and the proper flags. Listing 11-1 contains the declarations — from the ***APIDec.Bas*** file — for SetWindowsPos and the related constants:

Listing 11-1: SetWindowPos declaration and constants

```
Option Explicit
Declare Function SetWindowPos Lib "user32" _
   (ByVal hwnd As Long, ByVal hWndInsertAfter As Long, _
   ByVal x As Long, ByVal y As Long, ByVal cx As Long, _
```

```
    ByVal cy As Long, ByVal wFlags As Long) As Long
Public Const SWP_NOMOVE = &H2
Public Const SWP_NOSIZE = &H1
Public Const SWP_SHOWWINDOW = &H40
Public Const SWP_NOACTIVATE = &H10
Public Const HWND_TOPMOST = -1
Public Const HWND_NOTOPMOST = -2
```

The code that follows, Sub FormOnTop — from the ***APICode.Bas*** file — is a generalized routine that sets the form whose handle has been passed to the procedure to always be on top (or not), depending on the value of the Boolean also passed. For example, you could call FormOnTop from a form's paint event to make sure the form was always on top:

```
FormOnTop Me.hWnd, TRUE
```

You could also call FormOnTop with another form's handle as the argument:

```
FormOnTop frmOnTop.hWnd, FALSE
```

Listing 11-2 shows the FormOnTop procedure:

Listing 11-2: Setting a window on top

```
Public Sub FormOnTop(Handle As Integer, OnTop As Boolean)
   Dim wFlags As Long, PosFlag As Long
   wFlags = SWP_NOMOVE Or SWP_NOSIZE Or _
      SWP_SHOWWINDOW Or SWP_NOACTIVATE
   Select Case OnTop
      Case True
         PosFlag = HWND_TOPMOST
      Case False
         PosFlag = HWND_NOTOPMOST
   End Select
   SetWindowPos Handle, PosFlag, 0, 0, 0, 0, wFlags
End Sub
```

In the demonstration program on the CD-ROM, FormOnTop is called from two different menu items. One sets the current form to always on top, using Me.hWnd. The other sets frmOnTop, which, of course, is not the form the menu is on. The menu item that represents each form is checked when the form is always on top, unchecked otherwise.

If you use a menu click event to allow the user to toggle a state, it's easy to test for the current state using the menu's .Checked property.

Here's the code that sets this up for frmOnTop:

```
Private Sub mnuOnTopOtherForm_Click()
   If Not mnuOnTopOtherForm.Checked Then
   'turn ontop on
      FormOnTop frmOnTop.hwnd, True
      mnuOnTopOtherForm.Checked = True
   Else 'turn it off
      FormOnTop frmOnTop.hwnd, False
      mnuOnTopOtherForm.Checked = False
   End If
End Sub
```

This is easy and kind of fun (see Figure 11-9)!

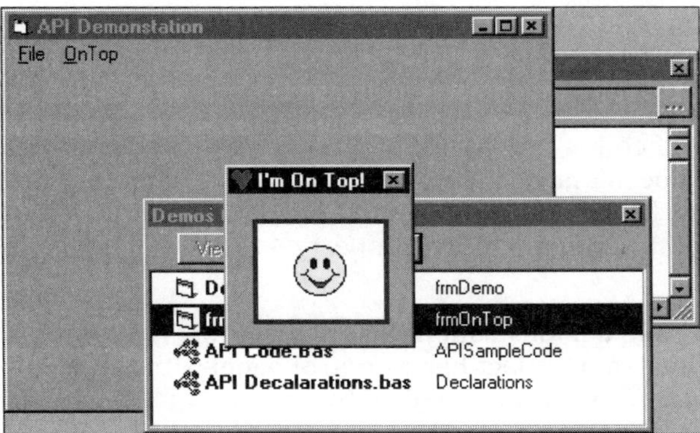

Figure 11-9: The smiling form is always on top, even when it's not active!

What happens if you set more than one window to always be on top using SetWindowsPos? Good question. I thought you'd never ask. The windows set on top are above all other windows, but can be repositioned above and below each other. In other words, always on top windows behave like normal windows, but only with respect to one another.

Moving Controls Between Forms

You can use the SetParent function to move a control from one form to another. This can save both time and resources. In a program that uses a large list box in six different dialogs, you can have one list box that you move to the right dialog when needed instead of having six large list box controls. This way you don't have to fill the list box each time you need it.

Here's how it works. The declaration for SetParent — from ***APIDec.Bas*** — is

```
Declare Function SetParent Lib "user32" _
   (ByVal hWndChild As Long, ByVal hWndNewParent As Long) _
   As Long
```

Simply pass SetParent the handle of the child control and the handle of the form you want to make its new parent (adoption by API!). By the way, if you need the handle of the old parent, SetParent will return it.

I've generalized this a little for the ***APICode.Bas*** module. My MoveControl procedure is passed a control (to move) and a form (to be the new parent). MoveControl then calls the SetParent API using the .hWnd property of each, as in Listing 11-3:

Listing 11-3: Moving a control to a new parent

```
Public Sub MoveControl(Child As Control, NParent As Form)
   Dim RetVal As Long
   RetVal = SetParent(Child.hWnd, NParent.hWnd)
   'Could pass back previous parent handle (RetVal) if needed!
End Sub
```

A danger here, of course, is passing MoveControl a child control as an argument that doesn't have a handle property. For example, labels have no .hWnd property. If you pass MoveControl a label as its first argument — or another control that has no .hWnd property — you'll generate a runtime error.

I've set up a sample demonstration that involves moving a list box around three forms. The demo project has a control panel with three option buttons and a command button. It has been set to stay on top, using the routine in the last section. The project also has three forms: Form1, Form2, and Form3. Form1 loads with a list box, lstBearsLike, that I've populated with a few items. (See Figure 11-10.) The demonstration moves lstBearsLike from form to form. (We may be switching this child to a new foster form a little too frequently!)

Setting up the control panel (which is the project's startup form) and loading the other three forms is simple:

```
Option Explicit
Dim CurrentParent As Integer

Private Sub Form_Load()
   Form3.Show
   Form2.Show
   Form1.Show
   CurrentParent = 0 'Form1
   FormOnTop Me.hWnd, True
   Me.SetFocus
End Sub
```

Without calling the SetFocus method, Me.SetFocus, for the control panel form, the control panel form would not have the *focus* — that is, be the active form — when its load procedure had concluded. Because all user interaction with this project is supposed to take place on the control panel form, I certainly want it to have the focus.

Here's the Form1 load event, populating lstBearsLike:

```
Private Sub Form_Load()
   lstBearsLike.AddItem "Honey"
   lstBearsLike.AddItem "Salmon Berries"
   lstBearsLike.AddItem "Salmon (the fish)"
   lstBearsLike.AddItem "Chocolate Covered Nuts"
End Sub
```

lstBearsLike's .Sorted property is set to True at design time, so the list box is automatically alphabetized.

Here's the code for the cmdMove click procedure:

```
Private Sub cmdMove_Click()
   Dim Newform As Integer, I As Integer
   For I = 0 To 2
      If optForm(I) Then Newform = I
   Next I
   If Newform <> CurrentParent Then
      Select Case Newform
         Case 0 'Move to Form1
            MoveControl Form1.lstBearsLike, Form1
         Case 1 'Move to Form2
            MoveControl Form1.lstBearsLike, Form2
         Case 2  'Move to Form3
            MoveControl Form1.lstBearsLike, Form3
         Case Else
            MsgBox "Internal Error!"
         End Select
         CurrentParent = Newform
   End If
```

This routine actually calls MoveControl, with the appropriate form as a parameter. Our demonstration program is up and running (see Figure 11-10)!

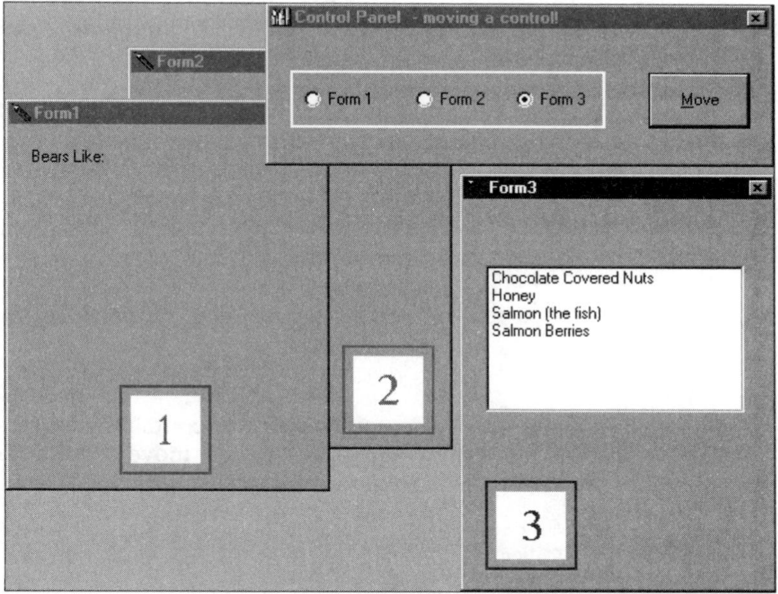

Figure 11-10: You can use the SetParent API to move a control from one form to another.

Of course, the single line:

```
If optForm(I) Then Newform = I
```

is VB shorthand for:

```
If optForm(I).Value = True Then
   Newform = I
End If
```

Locking Users Onto a Control

Suppose you'd like to make sure that users of your application do something in a control before they can move on. For example, a frame might contain an array of option buttons. The user might have to choose an option (click an option button) before she can do anything else. This is logically sort of equivalent to a modal dialog, in which the user must click OK or Cancel before she can proceed. It's easy to enforce virtual modality of a control by restricting the cursor using the APIs. If the cursor is restricted and there is no available keyboard access, the user will be limited to choices that can be made using the cursor (that is, the mouse) in the restricted area. The demonstration project — on the CD-ROM as ***LockUsrs.Vpb*** — locks users onto a frame. A user can take no further action until she has clicked a control on the frame.

Of course, you might want to use the ClipCursor function for some other purpose besides making a "modal" control.

The declarations you'll need — from ***APIDec.Bas*** — are

```
Declare Function GetDesktopWindow Lib "user32" () As Long
Declare Function GetWindowRect Lib "user32" _
   (ByVal hwnd As Long, lpRect As RECT) As Long
Declare Function ClipCursor Lib "user32" (lpRect As Any) As Long
Type RECT
   Left   As Long
   Top    As Long
   Right  As Long
   Bottom As Long
End Type
```

If you add a frame, in the demo named fraLock, containing an array of option buttons to the startup form, you can lock cursor movements onto the frame by adding the following code to the form load event:

```
Private Sub Form_Load()
   GetWindowRect fraLock.hwnd, ControlRect
   ClipCursor ControlRect
End Sub
```

I've placed the code that unlocks the cursor in the option button array — which is named optLock — click event (see Listing 11-4). This way, the cursor is freed no matter which option button is clicked (see Figure 11-11).

Listing 11-4: Using ClipCursor to restore cursor movement

```
Private Sub optLock_Click(Index As Integer)
   Dim ScreenRect As RECT, ScreenHandle As Long
   ScreenHandle = GetDesktopWindow 'Get Screen's Handle
   GetWindowRect ScreenHandle, ScreenRect
   ClipCursor ScreenRect 'Restore Cursor
End Sub
```

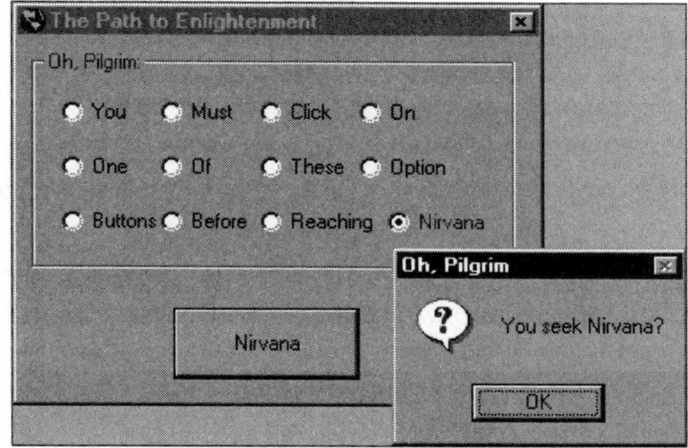

Figure 11-11: You use ClipCursor to ensure that the mouse cursor cannot be moved outside the frame containing an array of option buttons until one of them has been clicked.

You can use the GetDesktopWindow function to return a handle to the entire screen, as in the example. You might wish, instead, to only free access to the entire form. You can do this by passing GetWindowRect the handle to the form. In this case, you must be sure to restore access to the screen at some point — possibly in the form's unload event.

Changing Your Application's Window Menu

The Window menu in Windows 95 appears when you click once on the small icon in the upper-left corner of a form. (In Windows 3.*x*, the Window menu was known as the System menu or Control menu; it appeared when the user clicked on the Control box on the upper-left corner of a form.) You might want to modify the system-provided Window menu, for example, by removing the Close item to make sure that the user cannot close the form.

It's easy to modify a form this way. Here are the API declarations you'll need, again from ***APIDec.Bas***:

```
Declare Function GetSystemMenu Lib "user32" _
   (ByVal hwnd As Long, ByVal bRevert As Long) As Long
Declare Function RemoveMenu Lib "user32" _
   (ByVal hMenu As Long, ByVal nPosition As Long, _
   ByVal wFlags As Long) As Long
```

Listing 11-5 shows the generalized procedure — located in ***APICode.Bas*** — that deletes the Close item (and the separator bar above Close) from the Window menu of the form whose handle is passed to it:

Listing 11-5: Modifying the system menu to prevent closing

```
Public Sub TakeCloseOff(Handle As Long)
   Dim SysMenHandle As Long, RetVal As Long
   SysMenHandle = GetSystemMenu(Handle, 0)
   'Get the handle of Form1's Window menu
   RetVal = RemoveMenu(SysMenHandle, 6, MF_BYPOSITION)
   'Take out Close item
   RetVal = RemoveMenu(SysMenHandle, 5, MF_BYPOSITION)
   'Take out separator that is now on bottom
End Sub
```

The call to this procedure from the demonstration project — ***SysMenu.Vbp*** — is located in command button cmdRemove's click event:

```
TakeCloseOff cmdRemove.Parent.hwnd
```

The result is a Window menu that is missing the bottom separator and the Close item, as shown in Figure 11-12.

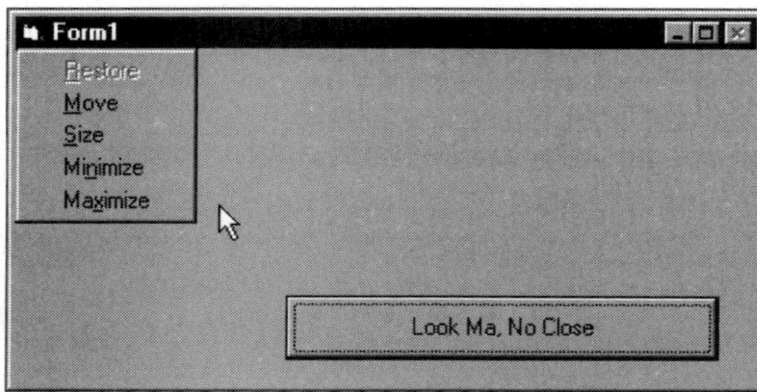

Figure 11-12: You can use the APIs to modify a form's Window menu.

This really couldn't be much simpler! It's worth noting that the RemoveMenu function, when passed the MF_BYPOSITION flag, deletes the menu item whose number is passed in the second-to-last parameter, counting down from zero at the top.

By the way, if you run this program (or use the generalized procedure), you'll see that Windows not only removes the Close item from the Window menu, it also disables the form's Close button (the "X" in the upper-right corner of the form).

Checking for Low System Resources

You can use the GlobalMemoryStatus API to determine amounts of various kinds of memory that are available on a 32-bit Windows system.

You can also use the SysInfo ActiveX control — which ships with the Professional Edition of VB5 — to determine available resources.

GlobalMemoryStatus takes one argument, a structure of type MEMORYSTATUS. This structure contains eight long variables. The first is a value that should be passed to GlobalMemoryStatus indicating the amount of memory to be allocated in bytes for the instance of the MEMORYSTATUS structure. Because each of the eight variables is declared in VB as long integer, and longs are each allocated 4 bytes of storage, calculate 4*8=32, and pass 32 as the first element of the structure. Here are the other elements, those returned by the GlobalMemoryStatusCall, and their meanings:

- **dwMemoryLoad** A number between 0 and 100 that gives a general idea of current memory utilization, in which 0 indicates no memory use and 100 indicates full memory use.
- **dwTotalPhys** The total number of bytes of physical memory.
- **dwAvailPhys** The number of bytes of physical memory available.
- **dwTotalPageFile** The total number of bytes that can be stored in the paging file. (This number does not represent the actual physical size of the paging file on disk.)
- **dwAvailPageFile** The number of bytes actually available in the paging file.
- **dwTotalVirtual** The total number of bytes in the user mode portion of the virtual address space of the calling process.
- **dwAvailVirtual** The number of bytes of available memory in the user mode portion of the virtual address space of the calling process.

Here is the declaration for the GlobalMemoryStatus function and the MEMORYSTATUS type from ***APIDec.Bas***:

```
Declare Sub GlobalMemoryStatus Lib "kernel32" _
   (lpBuffer As MEMORYSTATUS)
Type MEMORYSTATUS
   dwLength As Long
   dwMemoryLoad As Long
   dwTotalPhys As Long
   dwAvailPhys As Long
   dwTotalPageFile As Long
   dwAvailPageFile As Long
   dwTotalVirtual As Long
   dwAvailVirtual As Long
End Type
```

The generalized procedure I've written to call GlobalMemoryStatus is located in the ***APICode.Bas*** module and is named CheckResources. The CheckResources function passes back as parameters the various values of the elements of the MEMORYSTATUS structure. In addition, it accepts an argument, BlowAlarm, that sets a percentage below which a system alarm should be fired. BlowAlarm is compared with the 100 minus the .dwMemoryLoad element; if BlowAlarm is less than the value, CheckResources returns True. Otherwise, it returns False.

This gives you a chance to take appropriate action depending on the situation, such as sending out a warning message or not loading additional libraries.

Listing 11-6 contains the CheckResources function:

Listing 11-6: Checking system resources

```
Public Function CheckResources(Percent As Long, _
   Optional BytesPhys As Variant, Optional FreePhys As Variant, _
   Optional BytePage As Variant, Optional FreePage As Variant, _
   Optional UserBytes As Variant, Optional FreeUser As Variant, _
   Optional BlowAlarm As Variant) As Boolean
   Dim HowMuchMemory As MEMORYSTATUS
   HowMuchMemory.dwLength = 32
   GlobalMemoryStatus HowMuchMemory
   Percent = HowMuchMemory.dwMemoryLoad
   BytesPhys = HowMuchMemory.dwTotalPhys
   FreePhys = HowMuchMemory.dwAvailPhys
   BytePage = HowMuchMemory.dwTotalPageFile
   FreePage = HowMuchMemory.dwAvailPageFile
   UserBytes = HowMuchMemory.dwTotalVirtual
   FreeUser = HowMuchMemory.dwAvailVirtual
   If Not IsMissing(BlowAlarm) Then
      If BlowAlarm >= 100 - Percent Then
         CheckResources = False 'Blow Alarm
      Else
         CheckResources = True
      End If
   Else
      CheckResources = True
   End If
End Function
```

I've declared the CheckResources function using the Optional keyword for all parameters except Percent, the first. This enables the function to be called with just the one or two arguments you care about — for example, see the About Box project in the next section — without having to call it using dummy arguments for the remaining parameters. (You can only use the Optional keyword with variant arguments.)

To make sure that I don't get a Type Mismatch error when calling CheckResources without passing it a BlowAlarm parameter — as in the upcoming example, in which I am only interested in Percent — I've used the IsMissing function to test for BlowAlarm's presence. If BlowAlarm is missing, I skip the comparison that would have generated a syntax error.

In the ***LowRes.Vbp*** project, which demonstrates the use of this function, I've added two status bars at the bottom of the form (see Figure 11-13). The status bars are continually updated with system information by a Timer control that is set to fire every three seconds. The Timer's Timer event code calls the CheckResources function and updates the status bar; if general memory is less than 25 percent, it displays a message box.

```
Private Sub Timer1_Timer()
   Dim x As Boolean, Percent As Long, BytesPhys As Long, _
      FreePhys As Long, BytePage As Long, FreePage As Long, _
      UserBytes As Long, FreeUser As Long, BlowAlarm As Integer

   BlowAlarm = 25 'Blow alarm if general memory less than!
   x = CheckResources(Percent, BytesPhys, FreePhys, BytePage, _
      FreePage, UserBytes, FreeUser, BlowAlarm)
   sbSystem1.Visible = True
   sbSystem2.Visible = True
   sbSystem1.Panels(1).Text = "Memory utilization: " + _
      Str(Percent) + "%"
   sbSystem1.Panels(2).Text = "Physical Memory: " + Str(BytesPhys)
   sbSystem1.Panels(3).Text = "Free Physical Memory: " _
      + Str(FreePhys)
   sbSystem2.Panels(1).Text = "Paging File: " + Str(BytePage)
   sbSystem2.Panels(2).Text = "Free Paging File: " + Str(FreePage)
   sbSystem2.Panels(3).Text = "User Address Space: " _
      + Str(UserBytes)
   sbSystem2.Panels(4).Text = "Free User Space: " + Str(FreeUser)
   If Not x Then
      MsgBox "Available System Wide Memory Resources are" + _
         Str(100 - Percent) + _
         "%", vbExclamation, "Hull Integrity Warning"
   End If
End Sub
```

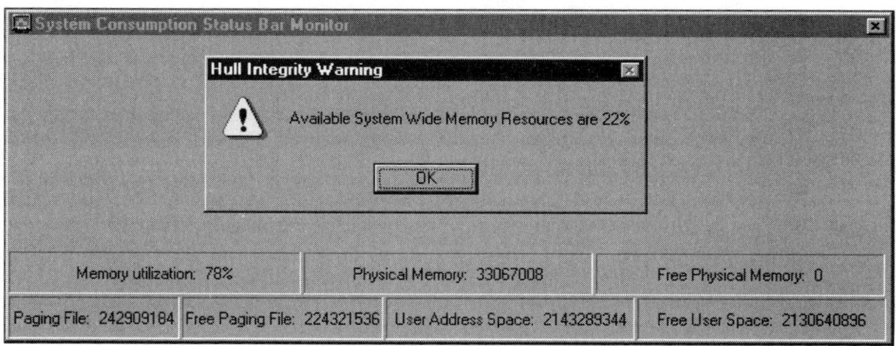

Figure 11-13: You can use GlobalMemoryStatus to monitor resource information and fire an alarm if resources have fallen below a specified percentage.

By the way, if you compile this program, it makes a kind of handy-dandy rough-and-ready resource checker. (If you're going to bother to do this, you might want to format the display strings so they are more readable.) You could use it to check the incremental resource consumption of applications as you open them.

An About Box that Displays System Information

In this section, I'll show you how to create a generic, reusable About box. (The project is on the *Visual Basic 5 SECRETS* companion CD-ROM as ***About.Vbp***.)

The lower portion of the About box displays system information (see Figure 11-14); of course, I'll tell you how to get and display this information. (I'll also tell you how to invoke the Microsoft System Information Utility, if you'd like.) The upper part of the About box displays application and software vendor information. What's very neat is that — with the exception of the icon — all of this information is loaded automatically from the App object's properties. You can set these properties on the Make tab of the Project Properties dialog, as shown in Figure 11-14.

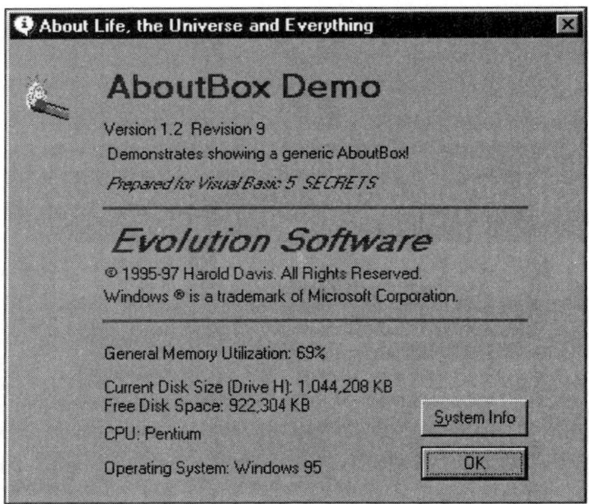

Figure 11-14: Using the App object and the Windows APIs, you can easily create a generic, reusable, automatically customizing About box that includes system information.

You can access the Make options settings either from Make on the File menu, or through Properties on the Project menu. You need never change this About box form by hand. Simply add it and the modules containing the supporting declarations and procedures to your project, and — in the blink of an eye — a customized About box!

First things first. The About box form, named AboutBox, is loaded from mnuAbout on the Help menu (see Figure 11-15). This menu is arranged in the Windows default standard, with a single Help Topics item, followed by a separator, followed by the About menu item.

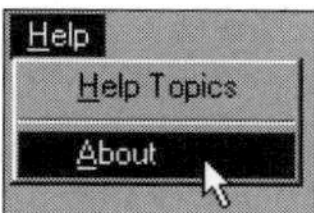

Figure 11-15: It's customary to show an About box from the Help menu.

To load the About box, as usual, use its Show method. (Most often, About boxes are shown modally.)

```
Private Sub mnuAbout_Click()
    AboutBox.Show vbModal
End Sub
```

I've used AboutBox's Show method with the vbModal constant as an argument. This makes AboutBox *modal;* it has to be closed before the user can take any action outside the form. VbModal (or 1) and vbModeless (or 0) are VB5 constants; the default, if no constant is used with the Show method, is modeless.

The controls on AboutBox (many labels and one image) are actually populated in the AboutBox load procedure. The first part of this population uses as values some of the properties of the App object. (For a full list of the App object's properties, look it up in VB's on-line help.)

To set the App object properties for a particular project, use the Make tab page of the Project Properties dialog (see Figure 11-16), and then compile the project.

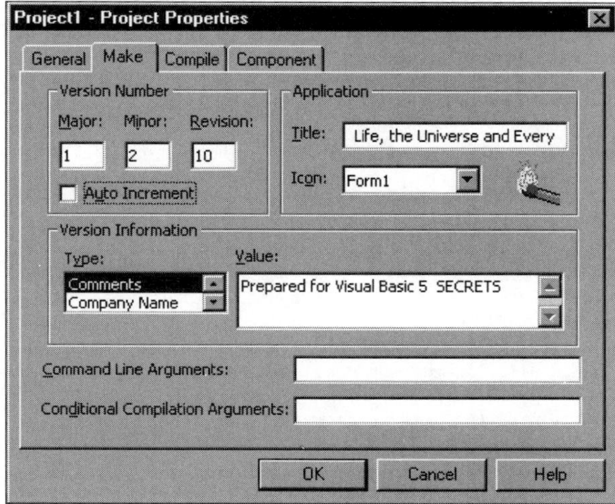

Figure 11-16: The Make tab page of the Project Properties dialog lets you change the properties of the project's App object.

Listing 11-7 shows the first part of the AboutBox load event code. All the application-related labels are automatically filled based on the App property values. The only thing you would need to change if you used this code for your own applications would be the location of the icon to be loaded into imgAppIcon (assuming that this location wasn't Form1).

Listing 11-7: Displaying application information

```
Private Sub Form_Load()
   Dim Percent As Long, x As Boolean, DiskSize, FreeKB, _
   Drive As String, dw As Long, ThisOs As String, CPU As String, _
   ThisSys As SYSTEM_INFO
   Me.Caption = "About " + App.Title
   'Center the AboutBox on the screen
   CenterForm Me
   'Next line is the only line you need to change
   imgAppIcon.Picture = Form1.Icon
   '
   lblAppName.Caption = App.ProductName
   lblVersion.Caption = "Version " & App.Major & "." & App.Minor & _
      "  Revision " & App.Revision
   lblDescription.Caption = App.FileDescription
   lblComments.Caption = App.Comments
   lblCompany.Caption = App.CompanyName
   lblCopyright.Caption = Chr(169) + " " + App.LegalCopyright & _
      " All Rights Reserved."
   lblTrademark.Caption = App.LegalTrademarks
   ...
```

You can use Chr(169) to get a true copyright symbol rather than using (C). (The ASCII code for the copyright symbol is 169.)

The remainder of the load procedure places information in the labels about memory utilization, drive space, the CPU, and the operating system, as shown in Listing 11-8.

Listing 11-8: Displaying system information

```
   ...
   ' Get current Windows configuration and system info
   ' Handles 32 bit OS only;
   ' Use conditional compilation to handle 16-bit
   x = CheckResources(Percent)
   lblResources.Caption = "General Memory Utilization: " &  _
      Percent & "%"
   GetDisk DiskSize, FreeKB, Drive
   lblDiskSpace.Caption = "Current Disk Size (Drive " +  _
      Left(Drive, 1)+ "): " + Format(DiskSize, "###,###") + _
      " KB" + vbCrLf + " Free Disk Space: " + _
      Format(FreeKB, "###,###") + " KB"
   dw = GetVersion()
   If dw And &H80000000 Then
      ThisOs = "Windows 95"
   Else
      ThisOs = "Windows NT"
   End If
```

```
    lblOS.Caption = "Operating System: " + ThisOs
    GetSystemInfo ThisSys
    Select Case ThisSys.dwProcessorType
        Case 386
            CPU = "386"
        Case 486
            CPU = "486"
        Case 586
            CPU = "Pentium"
        Case 2000
            CPU = "R2000"
        Case 3000
            CPU = "R3000"
        Case 4000
            CPU = "R4000"
        Case 21064
            CPU = "A21064"
        Case Else
            CPU = "Unknown Processor!"
    End Select
    lblCPU.Caption = "CPU: " + CPU
End Sub
```

First of all, general memory utilization is obtained using the first argument returned from the CheckResources function, located in the ***APICode.Bas*** module. (Earlier in this chapter, I showed you how CheckResources works, and explained how to set it up using the Optional keyword and the IsMissing function so that it could be called with only its first parameter.)

Next, the GetDisk procedure is called. GetDisk finds the name of the current disk drive and passes back as parameters the total space on the drive, the available space on the drive, and the name of the drive. Listing 11-9 shows the GetDisk code, from ***APICode.Bas***:

Listing 11-9: Finding available drive space

```
Public Sub GetDisk(DiskSize, FreeKB, Drive As String)
    Dim x As Boolean, SectorsPerCluster As Long, _
        BytesPerSector As Long, FreeClusters As Long, _
            TotalClusters As Long,Buffer As String
    Buffer = Space(255)
    x = GetCurrentDirectory(Len(Buffer), Buffer)
    Drive = Left(ConvertCToVBString(Buffer), 3)
    x = GetDiskFreeSpace(Drive, SectorsPerCluster, _
        BytesPerSector, FreeClusters, TotalClusters)
    If x Then
        DiskSize = (SectorsPerCluster * BytesPerSector * _
            TotalClusters) \ 1024 'Convert to KB
        FreeKB = (SectorsPerCluster * BytesPerSector *  _
            FreeClusters) \ 1024 'Convert to
    Else
        MsgBox "Internal GetDisk error!"
    End If
End Sub
```

The next step is to convert the C-style string returned by GetCurrentDirectory to a VB string, by lopping off the last character (the null terminator). I figure that I'll be doing this a lot, so why not make it into the function in Listing 11-10 (also in ***APICode.Bas***):

Listing 11-10: Converting a C-style string to a VB string

```
Public Function ConvertCToVBString(InString As String) As String
   ConvertCToVBString = Left(InString, Len(InString) - 1)
End Function
```

To actually find the drive designation (all I'm really interested in), I only need the first three characters of the current directory:

```
Drive = Left(ConvertCToVBString(Buffer), 3)
```

Finally, I can call GetFreeDiskSpace, passing it Drive as its first parameter. (GetFreeDiskSpace's declaration is about what you'd expect; it is in the ***APIDec.Bas***.) The next step is to read the return values from the function, convert them to kilobytes, and pass them back.

Returning to the AboutBox load event, I next format the drive space information and add it to the form's labels.

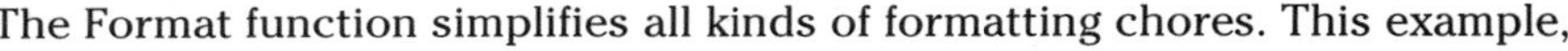

The Format function simplifies all kinds of formatting chores. This example,

```
Format(DiskSize, "###,###")
```

causes commas to appear every three digits in a six- (or fewer) digit number.

For the final step, filling in the CPU and Operating System and labels on the About box form, I used two APIs: GetVersion and GetSystemInfo.

You may have noticed that VB5 comes with an About dialog that you can use as a template. (Simply add a form to your project, and select About Dialog from the New tab of the Add Form dialog.) This prebuilt About dialog uses the properties of the App object, as does the custom About Box developed in this section. The appearance of the two About dialogs is somewhat different, however.

Invoking the Microsoft System Information Utility

Both the VB5 template About dialog and the custom About box developed in this section allow the user to invoke the Microsoft System Information utility (see Figure 11-17) when a command button is clicked.

The declarations for API functions, constants, and all required code are on the companion CD-ROM in the ***SysInfo.Bas*** module. The main procedure, StartSysInfo, tries to determine and validate the location and existence of the System Information executable (***Msinfo32.Exe***). If it can be found, it is launched using the Shell function.

The module defines a number of constants, including those required to locate ***Msinfo32.Exe*** in the Registry:

```
Const gREGKEYSYSINFOLOC = "SOFTWARE\Microsoft\Shared Tools Location"
Const gREGVALSYSINFOLOC = "MSINFO"
Const gREGKEYSYSINFO = "SOFTWARE\Microsoft\Shared Tools\MSINFO"
Const gREGVALSYSINFO = "PATH"
```

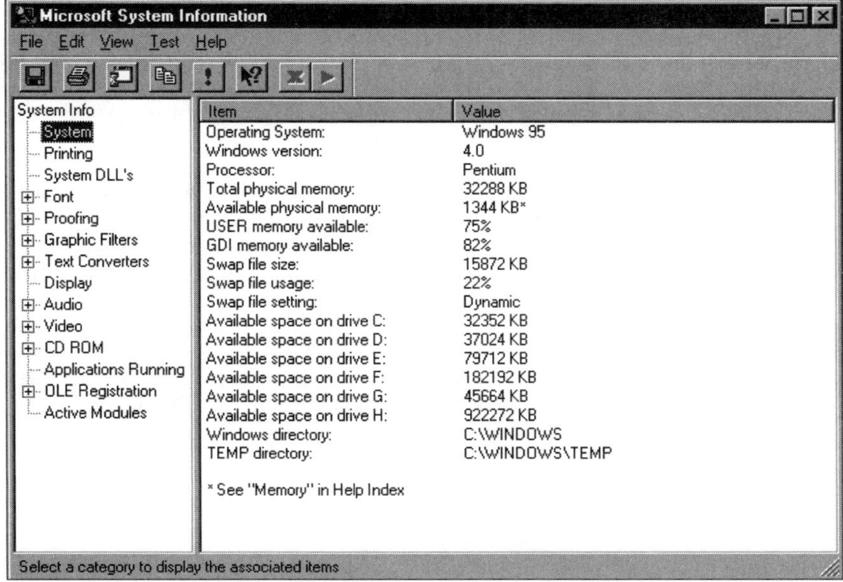

Figure 11-17: Your applications can allow the user to invoke the Microsoft System Information utility, which displays a great deal of information about the user's system.

Listing 11-11 shows the code:

Listing 11-11: Launching the Microsoft System Information utility

```
Public Sub StartSysInfo()
   On Error GoTo SysInfoErr
   Dim rc As Long
   Dim SysInfoPath As String
   If GetKeyValue(HKEY_LOCAL_MACHINE, _
      gREGKEYSYSINFO, gREGVALSYSINFO, SysInfoPath) Then
   ElseIf GetKeyValue(HKEY_LOCAL_MACHINE, _
      gREGKEYSYSINFOLOC, gREGVALSYSINFOLOC, _
      SysInfoPath) Then
      If (Dir(SysInfoPath & "\Msinfo32.Exe") <> "") Then
         SysInfoPath = SysInfoPath & "\Msinfo32.Exe
      Else
         GoTo SysInfoErr
      End If
   Else
      'Oops! File cannot be found!
      GoTo SysInfoErr
   End If
   Call Shell(SysInfoPath, vbNormalFocus)
   Exit Sub
SysInfoErr:
   MsgBox "System Information Utility not found!", vbOKOnly
End Sub
```

Getting the Windows Directory

Developers often need to know the user's Windows directory or System directory. To track down this information, you need to use the GetWindowsDirectory and GetSystemDirectory functions (they work in the same way).

A side note here is that under 32-bit Windows it is bad practice to copy files to the ***Windows\System*** directory because if the user is running a shared version of Windows your application may not have write access to the System directory. The directory returned by GetWindowsDirectory should be used for this purpose.

In general, it's a good idea to add as few files as possible to any "public" locations. If you can keep all files for your program in the directory and file structure your installation specifically creates for it, so much the better.

Here's the declaration for GetWindowsDirectory:

```
Declare Function GetWindowsDirectory Lib "kernel32" Alias _
   "GetWindowsDirectoryA" (ByVal lpBuffer As String, _
   ByVal nSize As Long) As Long
```

You could use the following code to display the location of the Windows directory in a message box, as shown in Figure 11-18:

```
Private Sub Form_Click()
   Dim Buffer As String, x As Long
   Buffer = Space(255)
   x = GetWindowsDirectory(Buffer, Len(Buffer))
   MsgBox "Windows Directory is: " + _
      ConvertCToVBString(Buffer), vbInformation, "Where is Windows?"
End Sub
```

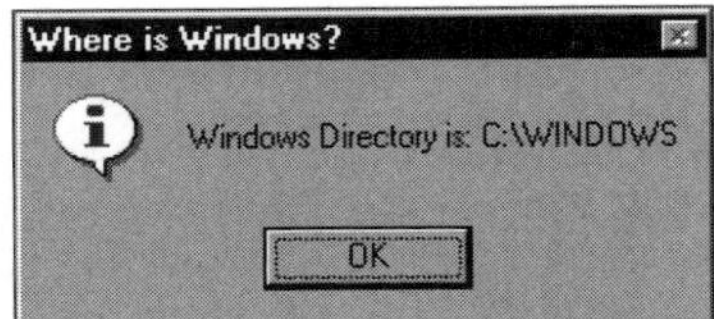

Figure 11-18: You can use the GetWindowsDirectory function to return the location of the Windows directory.

Monitoring Active Windows

Using the GetWindowText and GetActiveWindow functions, it's easy to set up a no-frills monitor of active windows, bearing the mind that, under 32-bit Windows, these functions will only return information about the current thread. (In this context, "active window" actually means "active window in the current thread.")

Here are the declarations for GetWindowText and GetActiveWindow:

```
Declare Function GetWindowText Lib "user32" Alias _
   "GetWindowTextA" (ByVal hwnd As Long, _
   ByVal lpString As String, ByVal cch As Long) As Long
Declare Function GetActiveWindow Lib "user32" () As Long
```

Here's the code — placed in a Timer event — that calls these functions and places the results in a multiline text box control every time the Timer is fired (see Figure 11-19):

```
Private Sub Timer1_Timer()
   Dim hCurrent As Long, Buffer As String, nChars As Integer
   Buffer = Space(255)
   hCurrent = GetActiveWindow()
   nChars = GetWindowText(hCurrent, Buffer, 255)
   txtMonitor.Text = txtMonitor.Text & vbCrLf & _
      ConvertCToVBString(Buffer)
End Sub
```

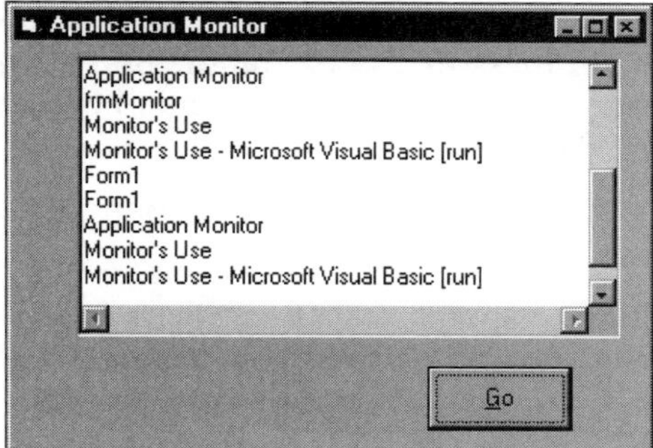

Figure 11-19: You can use GetActiveWindow and GetActiveText to retrieve the contents of the caption of a window as it is activated.

You can use the Print method of the Debug object to display values when a VB program is running in the design time environment. For example:

```
Debug.Print ConvertCToVBString(Buffer)
```

added in addition — or instead of — the text box display used in this example causes the active window text to be displayed in VB's Immediate pane.

Onward and Upward

The demonstration projects in this section have shown some ways of using the APIs to extend Visual Basic. (Also have a look at the section "The Windows Messaging System" later in this chapter.)

Of course, there is much more! These examples only scratch the surface. Although figuring out how to use the API functions from VB is not always easy, the reward is that there are lots and lots of API functions.

Additionally, there are functions that do the same thing as related custom controls. For example, I could use the GetOpenFileName in ***Comdlg32.Dll*** to open an Open common file dialog without bothering with the common dialog control. (See Chapter 7, "Windows Common Dialog Secrets," for information on ***Comdlg32.Ocx***).

Altogether, there is no limit to what you can do once you've gotten the basics of API calls under your belt.

Writing Code for Windows NT 4 and Windows 95

Windows 95 and Windows NT 4 (Server and Workstation) are both based on the Win32 APIs, and both use the Windows 95 shell as their user interface. This means that by and large — with the exceptions outlined later in this section — programs written for one will also run on the other without modification as long as you're not attempting some kind of trickery with the hardware layer like Windows 95 does.

The only way to find out for sure is to thoroughly test your applications on both operating systems.

Current information on writing programs that run on both operating systems can be found at *http://www.microsoft.com/win32dev/guidelns/Windows 95vsNT.htm*.

Determining the Operating System

You can obtain information about which operating system is running by using the GetVersionEx API function. The declarations, constants, and code required to easily tell which operating system your program is running on are saved on the companion CD-ROM in the ***WhichOS.Bas*** module in the ***WhichOS.Vbp*** project. Listing 11-12 contains the constant, type, and API declarations from the module:

Listing 11-12: Declarations for using GetVersionEx

```
Public Const VER_PLATFORM_WIN32_NT = 2
Public Const VER_PLATFORM_WIN32_WINDOWS = 1
Public Const VER_PLATFORM_WIN32s = 0

Type OSVERSIONINFO
   dwOSVersionInfoSize As Long
   dwMajorVersion As Long
   dwMinorVersion As Long
   dwBuildNumber As Long
   dwPlatformId As Long
```

```
    szCSDVersion As String * 128        '  Maintenance string
End Type
Declare Function GetVersionEx Lib "kernel32" _
    Alias "GetVersionExA" (lpVersionInformation As _
    OSVERSIONINFO) As Long
```

Listing 11-13 shows code, in a Sub Main procedure, that will end the program if it is not running under Windows NT 4 or Windows 95, and display operating system information if it is:

Listing 11-13: Determining the operating system

```
Public Sub Main()
    Dim OS As OSVERSIONINFO
    OS.dwOSVersionInfoSize = Len(OS)
    GetVersionEx OS
    If OS.dwMajorVersion < 4 Then
        MsgBox "Sorry, Windows 95 or NT4 or later required!", _
            vbInformation, "This program is gone!"
        End 'Terminate execution
    Else
        Debug.Print "OK. We're in! Windows 95 or NT4..."
        Select Case OS.dwPlatformId
            Case VER_PLATFORM_WIN32_WINDOWS
                MsgBox "Win 32 and Windows 95 running!", _
                    vbInformation, "Visual Basic 5 SECRETS"
            Case VER_PLATFORM_WIN32_NT
                MsgBox "Windows NT Version" & Str(OS.dwMajorVersion) & _
                    " Build " & Str(OS.dwBuildNumber) & " running!", _
                    vbInformation, "Visual Basic 5 SECRETS"
            Case Else
                MsgBox "Clueless!", _
                    vbInformation, "Visual Basic 5 SECRETS"
        End Select
    End If
End Sub
```

If you run this project under Windows NT 4 or Windows 95, you'll get a message box like the one shown in Figure 11-20.

Figure 11-20: You can use the GetVersionEx API to provide your program with information about which platform it is running on.

Common Problems

As a generalization, Windows 95 is more forgiving then NT. Common problems encountered include:

- Different treatment of null-terminated strings
- Hard-coding of Registry locations that are not the same on the two operating systems
- Hard-coding of file locations that are not the same on the two operating systems
- More complete implementation of security and access rights scheme under NT
- Different treatment of legacy 16-bit handle invocations
- Different treatment of access to hardware components between Windows 95 and NT

NullTerminated Strings

A null-terminated, or C-style, string uses a null (an ASCII character 0) to mark the end of the string. To use a string in VB that is null terminated, you must first strip the Chr(0) off the end of the string.

Some Registry values are stored as null terminated strings under Windows 95 and without the null terminator under NT 4 (see "Retrieving and Modifying Values" in Chapter 10 for more information). It's pretty easy to use a function that will strip the null terminator if it is there, and leave the string intact if it is not, as in Listing 11-14:

Listing 11-14: Strip the null terminator, if it is there

```
Public Function ConvertString(tmpVal As String, _
   KeyValSize As Long) As String
   If (Asc(Mid(tmpVal, KeyValSize, 1)) = 0) Then
      'Win95 Null Terminated String, get rid of terminator
      ConvertString = Left(tmpVal, KeyValSize - 1)
   Else
      'WinNT Does NOT Null Terminate String
      ConvertString = Left(tmpVal, KeyValSize)
      Null Not Found, Return String Only
   End If
End Function
```

Hard Coding

The answer to problems that arise when a programmer has assumed that a Registry structure or a file will be present in a specific location, and hard-coded accordingly, is simple: just don't.

Bear in mind that the structure of the Registry is different under Windows 95 and NT, as are the locations of important system files. Test for the presence of the Registry structure or key, and for the location of a particular file (unless you've placed the entry or file yourself — and even then, it's not a bad idea to test for it).

Chapter 13, "Secrets of Good Programming Practice," provides techniques for locating a file on a system, in case it's not where you expect it to be.

Hard coded calls to ***Winhelp.Exe*** presents a particular problem. WinHelp, invoked with a version 2.0 help file as its argument, will run under Windows 95 and fail (with an error message) under Windows NT 4. The correct procedure is to create a process using the help file, whose ***.Hlp*** extension will automatically start the correct help engine on both systems.

Security and Access

Windows NT was designed with security in mind. An application you create inherits the rights, permissions, and limitations of the user running the program under NT. This means that your application may not be able to save files or write to the Registry (unless the user running it has Administrator privileges).

16-bit Handles

A *handle* represents a way to access a Windows resource, such as a window. Windows 3.*x* used 16-bit handles; the Win32 API uses 32-bit handles. (In 32-bit versions of VB, handles are stored as Long variables; in 16-bit VB, they were stored as Integers.)

When Windows 95 hits a 16-bit handle, it will pack it with zeros and convert it to a 32-bit handle for you. Windows NT does no such thing. Therefore, old code that uses 16-bit handles may run successfully on Windows 95, and will certainly fail on NT 4. The answer to this one, of course, is to make sure that your legacy code is completely rewritten and does not contain 16-bit handles before trying to run it under either 32-bit operating system.

ANSI Versus Unicode

Unicode is a character encoding system that includes almost all the world's written languages — including character sets for the Cyrillic, Greek, Roman, Thai, Turkish, Arabic, Hebrew, and Japanese Kana languages, among others. ANSI is a much more limited character encoding system, requiring correspondingly less storage, based on the Roman character set. ANSI is the native character set for strings under Windows 95, while Windows NT uses Unicode exclusively for internal handling of strings.

The Win32 API are designed so that each function included in the APIs comes in two flavors: one Unicode and one ANSI. These two functions have one name. It's the compiler's job to determine which flavor should be invoked.

Although Windows NT does all its work in Unicode, it does not necessarily expect you to speak to it in Unicode. An API function invoked under NT with an ANSI string in turn invokes another API, MultiByteToWideChar, which converts the ANSI string to Unicode. The Unicode version of the API is then run. Strings passed back are converted from Unicode to ANSI by another API, WideChartoMultiByte.

Unicode strings are processed more efficiently internally — as well as encompassing more of the world's characters. Although you don't have to prepare code differently in VB now based on the two encoding schemes, at some point in the future, ANSI support will most likely be dropped. It's time to start thinking Unicode.

Using the Win32s API

The Win32s APIs are a subset of the full Win32 API set. Their purpose is to let you create 16-bit applications for Windows 3.1 that have binary equivalence across the 32-bit platforms (Windows 95 and NT).

This goal is accomplished provided that you:

- Stick to the functions included in the Win32s subset
- Include conditional code so that runtime code varies depending on the operating system
- Ship your 16-bit programs with the DLLs that allow Win32s programs to run on Windows 3.*x*
- Make sure that the Win32s files are installed on any target 16-bit systems

The Win32s SDK comes with a setup program that automates the process of installing platform extensions on 16-bit systems. Win32s applications can only be created on 32-bit (Windows 95 or NT) platforms.

The feature set supported by Win32s is surprisingly rich. Future releases even expect to support the Windows 95 user interface controls. But, of course, some features of Windows 95 — such as multithreading — simply cannot be simulated in Windows 3.*x*. For full details on what is available in Win32s, consult the Win32s SDK.

Because the entire Win32 API is exported by Win32s, any Win32-based application can be loaded into Windows 3.*x*. This, however, does not mean that every Win32 API will return successfully. Although all Win32 API functions will be loaded by Win32s, Win32 functions that cannot be implemented in Windows 3.1 — such as paths, threads, transformations, or asynchronous file I/O — will fail and return error codes.

The error codes returned by 32-bit APIs unsupported under Win32s depend on the API function. Usually, Win32s will set the last-error code to ERROR_CALL_NOT_IMPLEMENTED, which you can retrieve by using the (Win32s implemented) API GetLastError. However, Win32-based applications do not need to rely exclusively on error return codes, but can determine which Windows platform they are running on in advance by calling the GetVersionEx function.

An application should selectively, using conditional compilation, as a runtime feature implement different functionality when it is run with Windows 3.1 using Win32s or when it is run on Windows 95.

The Windows Messaging System

The idea behind the Windows messaging system is that Windows notifies applications of events by sending them messages. Imagine a steady stream of messages — for example, each time the mouse moves. Some, perhaps many, of these messages are relevant to your application. As your application processes its messages, you find some messages that are relevant to (meaning, need to be processed by) a particular "window" (meaning form or windowed control) within your application.

Here are some common kinds of messages:

- WM_messages are windows messages. For example, WM_COMMAND is sent when a menu item is clicked (or accelerator keys are used to the same effect) or a control event is fired (actually, when the control passes a notification back to its parent window). The message's parameters specify the identity of the menu or control that sent the message and, if it is a control, the handle of the control.
- EM_messages are used by applications to communicate with edit controls. For example, an application sends an EM_GETLINE message to copy a line of text from an edit control and place it in a buffer.
- LB_messages are used by applications to interact with list boxes. For example, an application sends an LB_GETITEMRECT message to retrieve the dimensions of the rectangle that bounds a list box item as it is currently displayed in the list box.

Of course, there are many more message types. The Spy application, discussed in the section "The SDK Tools" earlier in this chapter, provides a good way to get a feeling for the varieties of messages that Windows and Windows applications are constantly getting and sending. The ***SubClass.Vbp*** and ***Tray.Vbp*** examples that I explain later in this section should also help you understand what the different kinds of messages mean, and how to use them.

In the early days of GUI, before the emergence of Windows visual development environments, an important part of any Windows program was a series of gigantic case statements that directed each incoming Windows message properly. This code naturally had to have mechanisms for responding to the messages (a process termed *message dispatching*). The routine attached to a window that takes care of message dispatching for a given window is that window's *window procedure*.

For example, if the incoming message said that the mouse had dragged the outer edge of a resizable form, the code that redimensioned and repainted the newly sized form would have to be invoked.

You can access the message stream being sent to a particular window using the CallWindowProc API function. Using a technique called *subclassing* — which I'll explain later in this chapter — once you've intercepted the messages being sent to a form or control, you can write your own code to extend or change the behavior of the object.

As I'll show you in the examples later in this section, CallWindowProc returns two important arguments, wParam and lParam. In a nutshell, wParam tells you what windowing object is receiving the message, and lParam tells you what the message is. For example, wParam could tell you that Form1 is receiving a message, which from lParam you could tell is a WM_MOUSEMOVE, or mouse movement.

Visual Basic certainly allows programmers to create sophisticated applications without ever knowing a thing about Windows messaging. But if you take the time to learn a little about Windows messaging, you can easily create callback functions in VB5 that subclass the message stream to an object, enabling some great new features that were previously unavailable in VB. (For an example, see the ***Tray.Vbp*** application later in this section.)

Adding Context Menus to List Boxes

In this demonstration — the project is saved on the *Visual Basic 5 SECRETS* companion CD-ROM as ***Context.Vbp*** — I'll show you how to use the SendMessage API to add a context menu to the contents of a list box (see Figure 11-21). In addition to SendMessage, the project uses three other API functions that you haven't encountered yet: GetMenu, GetSubMenu, and TrackPopUpMenu. Here are the function declarations from ***APIDec.Bas*** (for the constant declarations needed by these functions, refer to the module itself):

```
Declare Function SendMessage Lib "user32" Alias _
   "SendMessageA" (ByVal hwnd As Long, _
   ByVal wMsg As Long, ByVal wParam As Long, _
   lParam As Any) As Long
Declare Function GetMenu Lib "user32" (ByVal hwnd As Long) As Long
Declare Function GetSubMenu Lib "user32" _
   (ByVal hMenu As Long, ByVal nPos As Long) As Long
Declare Function TrackPopupMenu Lib "user32" _
   (ByVal hMenu As Long, ByVal wFlags As Long, _
   ByVal x As Long, ByVal Y As Long, ByVal nReserved As Long, _
   ByVal hwnd As Long, lprect As Any) As Long
```

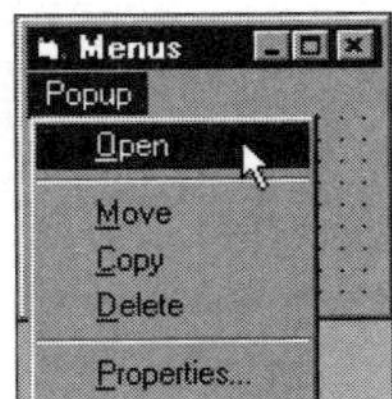

Figure 11-21: This application demonstrates how you can add context menus to items in a list box.

- SendMessage sends a message to a window, calls the window procedure for the destination window, and does not return until the window procedure has processed the message.
- GetMenu retrieves the handle of the menu belonging to the specified window.
- GetSubMenu retrieves the handle of the pop-up menu activated by the specified menu item.
- TrackPopupMenu displays a floating pop-up menu at a specified location and keeps track of the selection of items on the pop-up menu. The floating pop-up menu can appear anywhere on the screen.

To set up this project, I added a FileListBox control to the startup form (frmMain) and, using the Menu Editor, added a menu structure (PopUpMenu) to frmMenu (see Figure 11-22). Next, I added the ***API Declarations*** and ***API Code*** modules to the project. While I was at it, since I felt like getting fancy, I added the AboutBox I showed you earlier in this chapter.

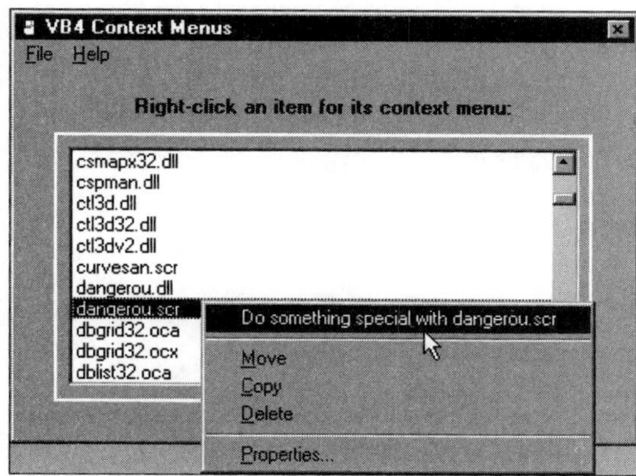

Figure 11-22: A separate form is used to create the pop-up menu structure.

In frmMain's load event, I set the .Path property of the FileList control to the ***System*** directory, using the technique that I showed you earlier in this chapter for getting its location. (Setting a FileList control's .Path property causes it to be loaded with the items in the specified directory.)

```
Private Sub Form_Load()
    Dim Buffer As String, x As Long
    Buffer = Space(255)
    x = GetSystemDirectory(Buffer, Len(Buffer))
    lstFiles.Path = ConvertCToVBString(Buffer)
    CenterForm Me
End Sub
```

The context menu should be opened (popped up) by a mouse click, which is initiated by a MouseDown event. Hence, the procedure that invokes the pop-up menu is placed in the lstFiles_MouseDown procedure. To start with, everything that is not a right-click can be ignored.

```
Private Sub lstFiles_MouseDown(Button As Integer, _
   Shift As Integer,  x As Single, Y As Single)
   Dim hMenu As Long, hSubMenu As Long, ResultVal As Long, _
   MenuHeight As Long, MenuWidth As Long, MenuString As String, _
   IndexLst As Long, ItemRect As RECT
   If Button = vbRightButton Then
   ...
```

Next, using the height coordinate passed by the MouseDown procedure and a function named GetIndex (discussed later), the list item that was clicked needs to be selected (since a right-click doesn't normally do this) and assigned as the current value of the list's .ListIndex property.

```
      IndexLst = GetIndex(Y)
      'a right-click on a list doesn't normally select it...
      lstFiles.ListIndex = IndexLst
```

Next, construct a menu string based on the name of the item that has been right-clicked. Using the GetMenu and GetSubMenu functions, get the handle of the first menu item under PopUpMenu (see Figure 11-21):

```
      If lstFiles.List(lstFiles.ListIndex) <> "" Then
         MenuString = lstFiles.List(lstFiles.ListIndex)
         hMenu = GetMenu(frmMenu.hwnd)
         hSubMenu = GetSubMenu(hMenu, 0)
```

Find the end of the list box text (for use placing the context menu):

```
         MenuWidth = (Me.Left + lstFiles.Left + _
            Me.TextWidth(MenuString)) \ Screen.TwipsPerPixelX + 20
```

Next, use SendMessage — yes, we're finally getting to the SendMessage API — to send a LB_GETITEMRECT message to lstFiles. (There is, of course, no reason a control's event code can't send messages to the control.)

```
         ResultVal = SendMessage(lstFiles.hwnd, LB_GETITEMRECT, _
            IndexLst, ItemRect)
```

LB_GETITEMRECT is used to retrieve the dimensions of the rectangle that bounds a displayed list box item. Actually, only the top of the rectangle will be needed:

```
         MenuHeight = (Me.Top + (Me.Height - Me.ScaleHeight) + _
            lstFiles.Top) \ Screen.TwipsPerPixelY + ItemRect.Top
```

Next, I've modified the text of the menu item caption, and, using the height and width parameters already developed, called the TrackPopUp API to pop it up!

```
...
         frmMenu!mnuPopOpen.Caption = "Do something special with " _
            & MenuString
         'pop it up!
         ResultVal = TrackPopupMenu(hSubMenu, TPM_LEFTALIGN, _
```

```
            MenuWidth, MenuHeight, 0&, frmMenu.hwnd, ByVal 0&)
         'execution waits for user action
         MsgBox "Place code for each menu item in the Menu Form", _
            vbInformation, "Context"
      End If
   End If
End Sub
```

The only thing that remains to explain is the GetIndex function. Here's the code:

```
Private Function GetIndex(Y As Single) As Long
   'Function returns the ListIndex for the list when the user
   'just pressed the mouse at Y vertical coordinate
   Dim OurRect As RECT, ResultVal As Long, Index As Long
   'Set the default  return value
   GetIndex = -1
   If lstFiles.ListCount < 1 Then Exit Function
   Index = SendMessage(lstFiles.hwnd, LB_GETTOPINDEX, 0, 0&)
   ResultVal = SendMessage(lstFiles.hwnd, LB_GETITEMRECT, Index, _
      OurRect)
   If ResultVal <> 0 Then
      GetIndex = Index + (Y \ (Screen.TwipsPerPixelY * _
         OurRect.Bottom))
   End If
End Function
```

GetIndex is passed the height coordinate for the current mouse position as given by the MouseDown event procedure. It returns the .ListIndex of the item in the list box. If you look at the code, you'll see that it does this by using the SendMessage Function twice: once to retrieve the .ListIndex of the topmost visible item in the list with a LB_GETTOPINDEX message, and once to get the height of a list item with the LB_GETITEMRECT message.

Intercepting the Message Stream

You can intercept the messages being sent to a form by subclassing the class that was used to create the form.

Figure 11-23 shows the interception Windows messages being sent to a form displayed in the VB Immediate pane. Debug.Print commands are used to generate the display in the Immediate pane. (The demonstration project is saved on the companion CD-ROM as ***Subclass.Vbp***.)

Of course, the numerical messages don't do you much good. To make use of them, you have to know what the values mean. For example, the value that means that a message has been sent saying that the mouse moved over a window or control is &H200. You define a constant:

```
Public Const WM_MOUSEMOVE = &H200
```

and then tests for equivalence to the constant, taking appropriate action when the message equals the constant. I'll show you how to do this in the next example, adding an icon to the Windows 95 tray.

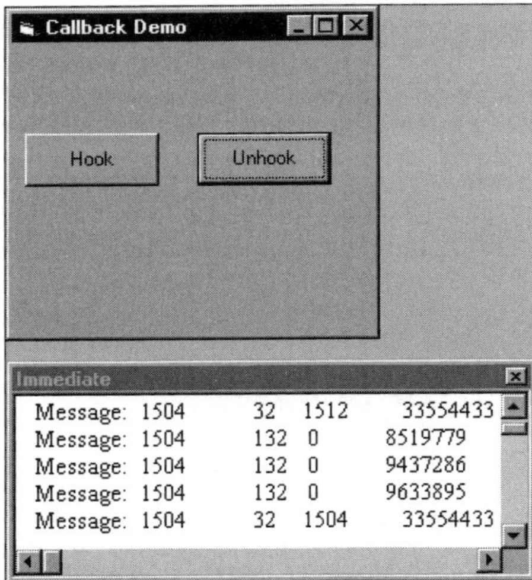

Figure 11-23: You can intercept the Windows message stream being sent to a particular window by subclassing the window.

You can find the Windows message constants and their values by using the API Text Viewer application that ships with VB5.

You'll need to understand some preliminary matters before you can understand how the subclassing example works. First, a *callback function* — or *callback* — is a user-defined function designed to handle a series of values generated by an API function. You can use the AddressOf keyword, which is new to Version 5 of VB, to reference the address of a function used as a callback. (The callback function must have the argument set required by the original API function.)

For example, the statement

```
lpPrevWndProc = SetWindowLong(gHW, GWL_WNDPROC, _
   AddressOf WindowProc)
```

tells VB that the user-defined function WindowProc has been passed to the SetWindowLong API as an argument. AddressOf is serving as a pointer to a function, which is why this relationship is sometimes called a *function pointer*.

Use of callbacks and the AddressOf keyword are subject to a number of limitations. All function pointers must be within a ***.Bas*** module — they cannot be in a form or class module. You cannot use AddressOf to reference a function that is external to the current project.

You should also know that once you start referring to user-defined functions with a pointer — for example, using their memory address — you have left the protection of the Visual Basic development environment behind. The slightest error in syntax will probably cause VB to crash. Take precautions accordingly if you are going to be working with function pointers — save your work often, and make backups.

Here are the declarations from the ***Subclass.Bas*** module:

```
Declare Function CallWindowProc Lib "user32" Alias _
   "CallWindowProcA" (ByVal lpPrevWndFunc As Long, _
   ByVal hwnd As Long, ByVal Msg As Long, _
   ByVal wParam As Long, ByVal lParam As Long) As Long
Declare Function SetWindowLong Lib "user32" Alias _
   "SetWindowLongA" (ByVal hwnd As Long, _
   ByVal nIndex As Long, ByVal dwNewLong As Long) As Long
Public Const GWL_WNDPROC = (-4)

Global lpPrevWndProc As Long
Global gHW As Long
```

WindowProc is the callback function that is used to hook into the message stream using the AddressOf keyword:

```
Function WindowProc(ByVal hw As Long, ByVal uMsg As Long, _
   ByVal wParam As Long, ByVal lParam As Long) As Long
   Debug.Print "Message: "; hw, uMsg, wParam, lParam
   WindowProc = CallWindowProc(lpPrevWndProc, hw, _
      uMsg, wParam, lParam)
End Function

Public Sub Hook()
   lpPrevWndProc = SetWindowLong(gHW, GWL_WNDPROC, _
      AddressOf WindowProc)
End Sub

Public Sub Unhook()
   Dim tmp As Long
   tmp = SetWindowLong(gHW, GWL_WNDPROC, _
      lpPrevWndProc)
End Sub
```

To try this out, initialize the variable holding the handle of the form that will be subclassed in the form's load event:

```
Private Sub Form_Load()
   gHW = Me.hwnd
End Sub
```

Call Hook to start the subclassing, and Unhook to stop it:

```
Private Sub cmdHook_Click()
   Hook
End Sub

Private Sub cmdUnHook_Click()
   Unhook
End Sub
```

Adding an Icon to the Windows 95 Tray

Figure 11-24 shows the Windows 95 Taskbar. The area on the right-hand of the Taskbar, where the clock is shown in Figure 11-24, is known as the *tray*.

Figure 11-24: Here's the Windows 95 Taskbar; the Start button is on the left, and the tray, with clock displayed, is on the right.

In this section, I'll show you how to place your application's icon on the tray. (The sample code is saved on the CD-ROM in the ***Tray.Vbp*** project.) Next, I'll demonstrate how to respond to Windows messages received by the icon. By responding to these messages, you can display a form when the user double-clicks the tray icon, display a context menu, and more.

Just because you can place your application's icon in the tray does not mean you should. It's probably most suitable for applications such as resident antivirus protection, which is running all the time, or utilities, such as a sound card volume control.

The first step is to check — using the declarations and techniques explained earlier in this chapter in the section on Windows 95 and Windows NT — that Windows 95 or Windows NT 4 is running. (If not, there's no tray....)

The project starts up from Sub Main in the ***Tray.Bas*** module because a tray application will not normally display a form until the user activates it. Here's the Sub Main code:

```
Public Sub Main()
   Dim OS As OSVERSIONINFO
   OS.dwOSVersionInfoSize = Len(OS)
   GetVersionEx OS
   If OS.dwMajorVersion < 4 Then
        MsgBox "Sorry, Windows 95 or NT4 or later required!", _
         vbInformation, "This program is gone!"
      End
   Else
      Debug.Print "OK. We're in! 95 or NT4..."
   End If
   Load frmTray
End Sub
```

The tray application's form — frmTray — has its Visible property set to False at design time, so that it will not display until we're ready for it to do so.

Backing up for a second, here are the declarations in the ***Tray.Bas*** module (other than those related to determining the version of the operating system):

```
Type NOTIFYICONDATA
   cbSize As Long
   hwnd As Long
```

```
    uID As Long
    uFlags As Long
    uCallbackMessage As Long
    hIcon As Long
    szTip As String * 64
End Type

Public Const WM_USER = &H400
Public Const cbNotify& = WM_USER + 42
Public Const uID& = 61860
Public myNID As NOTIFYICONDATA

Declare Function ShellNotifyIcon Lib "shell32.dll" _
    Alias "Shell_NotifyIconA" (ByVal dwMessage As Long, _
    lpData As NOTIFYICONDATA) As Long
Public Const NIM_ADD = &H0
Public Const NIM_DELETE = &H2
Public Const NIM_MODIFY = &H1
Public Const NIF_MESSAGE = &H1
Public Const NIF_ICON = &H2
Public Const NIF_TIP = &H4
Public Const WM_MOUSEMOVE = &H200
Public Const WM_LBUTTONDOWN = &H201
Public Const WM_LBUTTONUP = &H202
Public Const WM_LBUTTONDBLCLK = &H203
Public Const WM_RBUTTONDOWN = &H204
Public Const WM_RBUTTONUP = &H205
Public Const WM_RBUTTONDBLCLK = &H206
Public Const WM_MBUTTONDOWN = &H207
Public Const WM_MBUTTONUP = &H208
Public Const WM_MBUTTONDBLCLK = &H209

Declare Function CallWindowProc Lib "user32" Alias _
    "CallWindowProcA" (ByVal lpPrevWndFunc As Long, _
    ByVal hwnd As Long, ByVal Msg As Long, _
    ByVal wParam As Long, ByVal lParam As Long) As Long
Declare Function SetWindowLong Lib "user32" Alias _
    "SetWindowLongA" (ByVal hwnd As Long, _
    ByVal nIndex As Long, ByVal dwNewLong As Long) As Long
Public Const GWL_WNDPROC = (-4)

Global lpPrevWndProc As Long
Global gHW As Long
```

The NOTIFYICONDATA type, ShellNotifyIcon API, and constants beginning with NIF_ are used to manipulate the Windows tray. As I discussed earlier in this section, constants starting with WM_ represent specific Windows messages. The constant cbNotify& is user-defined, and used to identify this application in the callback function. You should make sure that it is greater than WM_USER, the largest of the predefined Windows messages. I've defined it as equal to WM_USER + 42. Similarly, uID& is used as an identifier in the structure that places the icon on the tray. In addition, the module contains the Hook and Unhook procedures, familiar from the previous subclassing example. (WindowProc, which I'll explain in a minute, is a little different this time because it contains the code that actually responds to messages generated by the user.)

```
Public Sub Hook()
   lpPrevWndProc = SetWindowLong(gHW, GWL_WNDPROC, _
      AddressOf WindowProc)
End Sub

Public Sub Unhook()
   Dim tmp As Long
   tmp = SetWindowLong(gHW, GWL_WNDPROC, _
      lpPrevWndProc)
End Sub
```

When Sub Main loads the form, it executes the code in its Load event (while remaining invisible):

```
Private Sub Form_Load()
   gHW = Me.hwnd
   myNID.cbSize = Len(myNID)
   myNID.hwnd = gHW
   myNID.uID = uID
   myNID.uFlags = NIF_MESSAGE Or NIF_TIP Or NIF_ICON
   myNID.uCallbackMessage = cbNotify
   myNID.hIcon = Me.Icon
   myNID.szTip = Me.Caption & Chr(0)
   ShellNotifyIcon NIM_ADD, myNID
   Me.Move (Screen.Width - Me.Width) \ 2, _
      (Screen.Height - Me.Height) \ 2
   Hook
End Sub
```

This code populates the instance of the NOTIFYICONDATA structure and calls the ShellNotifyIcon API, placing the form's icon — in this case, a snowflake — in the tray, as shown in Figure 11-25. (The ToolTip text shown in Figure 11-25 is set to be the caption of the form in this code, but you could set it to anything you want.)

Figure 11-25: You can use an instance of the NOTIFYICONDATA structure and the ShellNotifyIcon API to add an application's icon to the tray.

Before concluding, the form load code centers the (still invisible) form on the screen, and invokes the Windows message callback function. Here's the contents of WindowProc:

```
Function WindowProc(ByVal hw As Long, ByVal uMsg As Long, _
   ByVal wParam As Long, ByVal lParam As Long) As Long
   If wParam = uID Then
      Select Case lParam
         Case WM_MOUSEMOVE
            Debug.Print "MouseMove"
         Case WM_LBUTTONDOWN
            Debug.Print "Left Button Down"
         Case WM_LBUTTONUP
            Debug.Print "Left Button Up"
         Case WM_LBUTTONDBLCLK
            Debug.Print "Left Button Doubleclick"
            'show form
            frmTray.Visible = True
            AppActivate frmTray.Caption
         Case WM_RBUTTONDOWN
            Debug.Print "Right Button Down"
            'show pop-up menu
            frmTray.PopupMenu frmTray.mnuThing, _
               vbPopupMenuRightAlign, , , frmTray.mnuHer
         Case WM_RBUTTONUP
            Debug.Print "Right Button Up"
         Case WM_RBUTTONDBLCLK
            Debug.Print "Right Button Double Click"
            ChangeTray
         Case WM_MBUTTONDOWN
         Case WM_MBUTTONUP
         Case WM_MBUTTONDBLCLK
         Case Else
            Debug.Print "Unknown message: " & lParam
      End Select
   End If
   WindowProc = CallWindowProc(lpPrevWndProc, hw, _
      uMsg, wParam, lParam)
End Function
```

Here's how this works. For example, when the user double-clicks the tray icon with the left mouse button, the callback function knows that the message is being sent to our application because wParam = uID. If LParam = WM_LBUTTONDBLCLK, the procedure knows "our" icon has been double-clicked with the left mouse button. The code that's executed then makes the hidden form visible and activates it (see Figure 11-26):

```
frmTray.Visible = True
AppActivate frmTray.Caption
```

Figure 11-26: The user makes the form visible by double-clicking the icon in the tray.

Other possible user events are intercepted in the same fashion and can be used to add code to modify the tray application. For example, you could change the icon on the tray and the ToolTip when the user double-clicks with the right mouse button, as shown in Figure 11-27:

```
Case WM_RBUTTONDBLCLK
   ChangeTray
...
Public Sub ChangeTray()
   frmTray.Icon = frmTray.Label1.DragIcon
   myNID.hIcon = frmTray.Icon
   myNID.szTip = Trim(frmTray.Text1.Text)
   ShellNotifyIcon NIM_MODIFY, myNID
End Sub
```

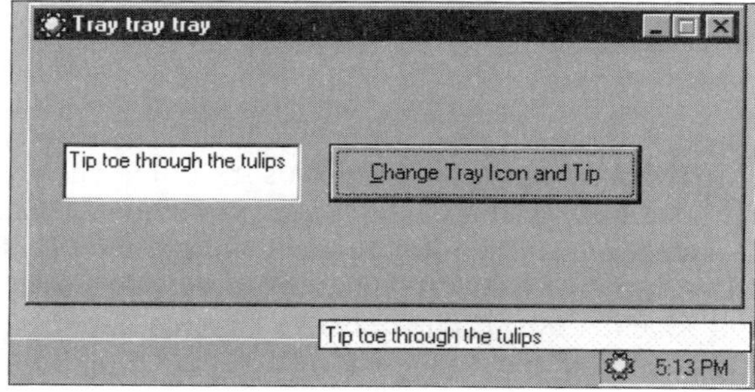

Figure 11-27: You can use the ShellNotifyIcon API to change the icon and ToolTip on the tray.

The ChangeTray procedure is invoked both when the user double-clicks the tray icon and from the command button on the tray form itself.

The new icon (the sun as opposed to the snowflake) is stored in the DragIcon property of an invisible label control, which is an extremely low-resource way to add additional icons to your forms.

It's pretty typical to add a context menu to applications that are iconized on the tray, as shown in Figure 11-28.

Figure 11-28: You can easily add context menus to your applications that are iconized on the tray.

The menu, named mnuThing, has been added to the form. It's invoked like this:

```
Case WM_RBUTTONDOWN
frmTray.PopupMenu frmTray.mnuThing, _
   vbPopupMenuRightAlign, , , frmTray.mnuHer
```

Working with menus is explained in detail in Chapter 18.

It's extremely important to release the callback function and delete the tray icon when unloading your tray application:

```
Private Sub Form_Unload(Cancel As Integer)
   Unhook
   ShellNotifyIcon NIM_DELETE, myNID
End Sub
```

One other point: You probably won't want to let users minimize your tray applications. A minimized tray application should only display its icon on the tray; it shouldn't display a minimized window as well. To implement this, when the user minimizes the form, you would want to restore it to its normal size, and make it invisible. The following code, placed in the form resize event, will take care of this:

```
Private Sub Form_Resize()
   If Me.WindowState = vbMinimized Then
      Me.Hide
      Me.WindowState = vbNormal
   End If
End Sub
```

Summary

The coverage in this chapter has ranged from extremely practical to sublimely theoretical.

I started by telling you about the tools included in the Win32 Software Development Kit (SDK), including:

- Dialog Editor
- Help Workshop
- Heap Walker
- Image Editor
- OLE Object Viewer
- Spy

I went on to discuss navigating the SDK documentation.

The next part of this chapter gave a capsule summary of some of the APIs most commonly used by VB programmers. Turning from theory to practice, example projects in "Using the APIs in the Real World" showed you how to use these functions to:

- Make a form stay on top
- Move controls between forms
- Lock users onto a control
- Change an application's Window menu
- Check system resources
- Create a generic About form
- Get the ***Windows*** and ***System*** directories
- Monitor windows use in the current thread

The chapter continued with a discussion of developing for Windows NT 4 (as well as Windows 95) and the Win32s API subset. Finally, I explained the operation of the Windows messaging system and provided some detailed examples:

- Using the SendMessage API function to create a context menu within a list box control
- Intercepting the Windows message stream
- Placing a program icon on the Windows tray, and responding to the messages created by user interaction with that icon

Chapter 12

Using Visual SourceSafe (Enterprise Edition)

The Enterprise Edition of Visual Basic Version 5 ships with an independent versioning software application, Microsoft Visual SourceSafe (VSS). There are two Visual SourceSafe programs, the VSS Administrator and the VSS Explorer.

When installing VSS, use the Custom installation and make sure the Enable SourceSafe Integration option is checked. This automatically connects VSS to the Visual Basic IDE, adding a VSS menu item to the bottom of the VB5 Tools menu. You can also do a separate installation of SourceSafe after the initial install of VB5 is completed.

Visual SourceSafe is a version control system primarily created for software development by programming teams. At the same time, it can be very useful to the solo programmer. Essentially, VSS is a virtual lending library with a librarian — the VSS Administrator — and files that can be "borrowed" by programmers with project access rights using the VSS Explorer. This chapter provides an overview of both sides of the Visual SourceSafe coin: administering VSS and using VSS as a programmer.

The Visual SourceSafe Administrator topics discussed include

- Adding users and setting passwords
- Changing user access rights by project
- Setting administration options

On the user side of VSS, I will discuss

- Creating a Visual SourceSafe project
- Adding files to a project
- Visual SourceSafe integration into the Visual Basic IDE
- Checking files out of the VSS library
- Returning files to the VSS library
- Diffing a file

Visual SourceSafe Administrator

Visual SourceSafe Administrator is used to add users (programmers) and define their access rights to various VSS projects. You don't need to use a password to launch VSS Administrator, but a message box wisely suggests that you create a password for the administrator. After you add a password for the administrator, you must remember it or you are out of luck. As the Visual SourceSafe manual states, "If you forget the password assigned to the administrator, you cannot run Visual SourceSafe Administrator to change it.... If the administrator's password is lost, contact Microsoft Technical Support Services for assistance." In case you need it, the VSS support line number is (206) 635-7014; have your product ID number handy.

When launched, the Visual SourceSafe Administrator application looks similar to the window shown in Figure 12-1 (although there wouldn't be any added users except for the administrator, yet).

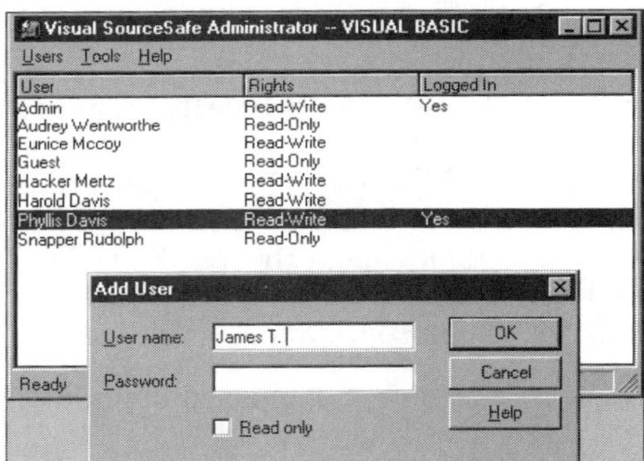

Figure 12-1: The Visual SourceSafe Administrator application window showing eight users (including the Administrator). At this point we're getting ready to add a new user.

Adding Users

You select the first item on the menu bar shown in Figure 12-1, Users, to add users, delete users, or edit passwords. To add a new user, choose Add User from the Users menu. The Add User dialog shown in Figure 12-1 opens. Here you can add new users' names, enter passwords, and, if you desire, restrict users immediately to read-only access. If you select Read Only here, the user will only have read access to any VSS project. This option sets a permanent read-only access across the board. If instead you want to restrict access rights to certain projects and grant full rights to others for the new user, you should set these rights using the Project Rights dialog discussed in the next section.

Changing Access Rights by Project

You need to take a few steps to set access rights for each user:

1. You have to create a Visual SourceSafe project before you can set user rights for that project. You create VSS projects (not to be confused with Visual Basic projects — they are two different animals) by using the Visual SourceSafe Explorer or in Visual Basic itself. Creating a VSS project using either of these methods is discussed later in this chapter.
2. Next, you have to open the SourceSafe Options dialog shown in Figure 12-2 (choose Options from the Tools menu), and select the Enable Project Security option on the Project Security tab page.

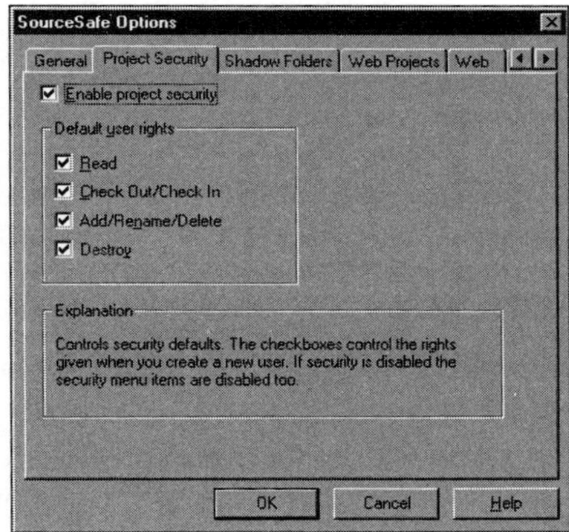

Figure 12-2: To be able to set user rights, you need to select the Enable Project Security option on the Project Security tab in the SourceSafe Options dialog.

From there, choose the Rights by Project item on the Tools menu. The Project Rights dialog shown in Figure 12-3 will open. As you can see in the figure, some users have full access while others are restricted to read-only rights for the selected Scuba project. To add or deny user rights, select the user's name and change her or his rights using the check boxes at the bottom of the dialog.

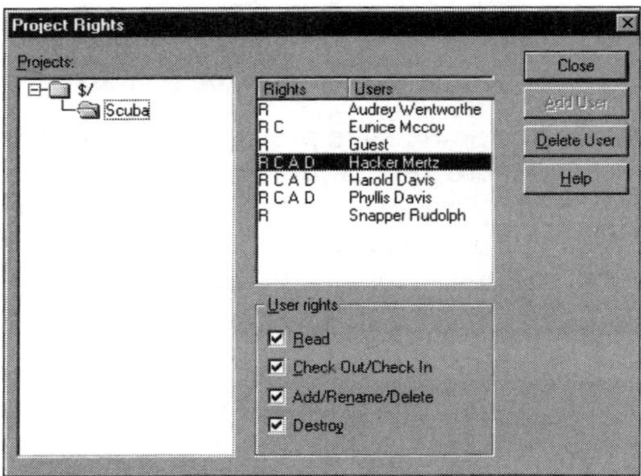

Figure 12-3: The project administrator uses the Project Rights dialog to set user rights for specific projects. In this case, some users only have read-only rights while others have full access.

Administration Options

You can set other administration options using the SourceSafe Options dialog. Some of the available options are

- **General** Use this tab page to allow multiple checkouts of files (by default, VSS allows a file to be checked out by only one person at a time); to allow automatic logon for network users; to set the default VSS database; to set the system log (this will record every action taken by VSS users and provide an audit trail for version tracking).
- **Project Security** This tab page lets the administrator enable project security and set default user rights.
- **Shadow Directories** The administrator can use this tab page to set up a "shadow directory" — a centralized directory, usually located on a server, that contains the latest versions of all project files.
- **Web Projects** The administrator can use this tab page to set options for an individual Web project, including assigning a VB project as a Web site, assigning a URL, specifying a virtual root, and specifying a deployment path.
- **Web** Use this tab page to set options for all Web projects you work on. Here you can specify a proxy for remote deployment through a firewall and set the default filename for Web pages.
- **File Types** Use this tab page to set default file types for file lists that appear in VSS users' dialog boxes. For example, you could create a file group for Visual Basic that included the following file types: ***.Bas**, ***.Frm**, ***.Frx**, ***.Vbp**, and ***.Res**.

To summarize, you use the Visual SourceSafe Administrator application to set up users and their passwords, define user rights, and create a centralized project directory. VSS Administrator also functions as a background project safety net by storing each file version in a dedicated VSS database.

You use the Visual SourceSafe Explorer, discussed in the next section, to coordinate project version control.

Using Visual SourceSafe Explorer

Visual SourceSafe Explorer was created with a team of programmers in mind, but it can also be valuable for those flying solo because it will keep track of versioning even if you are working alone. When you launch Visual SourceSafe Explorer, the VSS Explorer window opens, as shown in Figure 12-4.

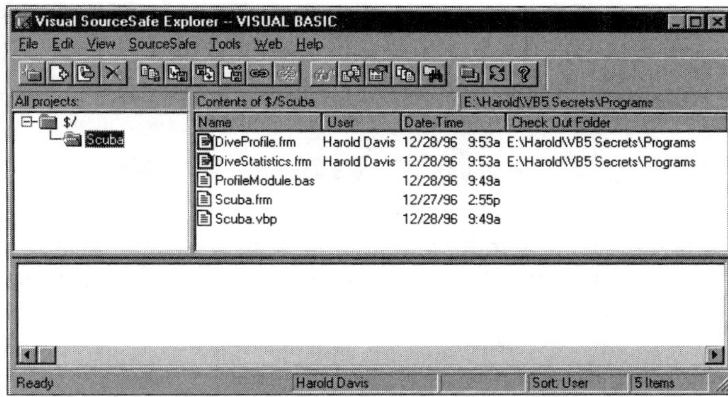

Figure 12-4: Here's the Visual SourceSafe Explorer with the Scuba project selected. VSS helps to keep project files coordinated.

VSS keeps track of project files and their changes so you don't have to. Using Visual SourceSafe, you can check out a file's history, revert to an earlier version of a file, and compare the differences between file versions.

VSS creates a virtual folder named **$/** as the root directory where VSS projects are stored.

Creating a VSS Project Using VSS Explorer

The first step on the road to version control is creating a Visual SourceSafe project. As mentioned, a VSS project is not the same as a Visual Basic project; they certainly are two different, albeit related, kinds of animals.

The VSS project is a collection of files, any type of files, even ones that Visual Basic does not recognize. Consequently, a VSS project could contain a file that is not in a VB project (for example, a Word template or C++ file). In addition, a Visual Basic project could be part of a Visual SourceSafe subproject. One VSS project could contain many Visual Basic projects.

To create a new Visual SourceSafe project, highlight the folder in the left pane of the VSS Explorer where you want the project to be placed. Then choose Create Project from the File menu at the top of VSS Explorer window. In the dialog that opens, type the project name and any comments about the project — reasons for creation, a project description, and so forth. When you are finished, click OK and the new project appears in the VSS Explorer window. (For this chapter I created a demonstration project named Scuba, which appears under the VSS root directory **$/** in Figure 12-4.)

From there, you can add files to the project using the Add Files item on the File menu. In addition, you can open Windows Explorer and drag and drop files into a project. If you have not yet created the Visual Basic files that will go into the VSS project, you can add them later from Visual Basic because Visual SourceSafe is fully integrated into Visual Basic.

VSS Integration into Visual Basic

If you are a designated Visual SourceSafe user (that is, Visual SourceSafe Explorer is installed on your system and a system administrator has added you as a VSS user with the Visual SourceSafe Administrator application), the inclusion of Visual SourceSafe in Visual Basic should be automatic.

To see if VSS is correctly hooked into Visual Basic, launch VB and check out the Tools menu. If a SourceSafe item has been appended to the menu, as in Figure 12-5, you're in. (The submenu you see on your screen may be different than the one shown in Figure 12-5, depending on whether you are logged on to a VSS project.)

If there is no SourceSafe item at the bottom of the Tools menu, SourceSafe is not working correctly. Chances are that Visual SourceSafe has not been registered to work with Visual Basic. Here's how to fix the problem.

To register VSS with VB, close any programs that are running, and then run the Add/Remove Programs applet found in the Windows Control Panel. On the Install/Uninstall tab page, select Microsoft Visual SourceSafe V5.0 from the list of installed applications. Next, click the Add/Remove button. The Visual SourceSafe 5.0 maintenance program will launch, displaying a window with the three buttons: Add/Remove, Reinstall, and Remove All. Click the Add/Remove button. The next window will show exactly what portions of Visual SourceSafe are installed on your system. Select the Enable SourceSafe Integration item and click Continue. The maintenance program will add the VB integration and finish up. Launch VB again. Visual SourceSafe should now be available on the Tools menu.

Note that the default — "Typical" — VSS installation *does not* select the Enable SourceSafe Integration item.

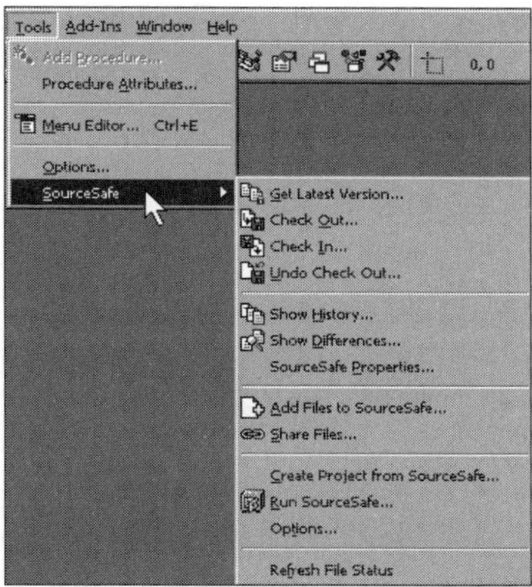

Figure 12-5: Visual SourceSafe attaches a SourceSafe item to the bottom of the Visual Basic Tools menu.

Creating a VSS Project Using Visual Basic

You can also quickly create a VSS project when working in Visual Basic. Just choose Create Project from the SourceSafe menu found on the VB Tools menu. In the dialog that appears, enter the name of the new project and click OK.

Checking Files Out and Back In

There are two ways to proceed from here. You can open a Visual Basic project that contains files included in a VSS project. Or, you can create a new VB project and add any of these new Visual Basic files to a Visual SourceSafe project.

To add the new Visual Basic files to a Visual SourceSafe project, save the VB project. When you do, a message box will ask whether you want to "Add this project to SourceSafe?" Click Yes. From there, you can specify what VSS project the files will be added to or create a new project, and select exactly which VB files will be added to the Visual SourceSafe database.

To use a VB project that has already been added to the Visual SourceSafe database, just launch VB and open that project.

In VB projects containing files that are part of a Visual SourceSafe project, the icons in the VB Project Explorer change. The icons for any files attached to a VSS project — a form, for example — acquire a small blue padlock in their lower-left corner. Also, if you are a user with read-write access, a small page icon appears to the left of the regular VB form or module icons. Once you use the Check Out item on the Tools menu to check a file out of the VSS database, the small blue padlock disappears from the file's icon and a red check mark appears in the page icon. (In Figure 12-6, for instance, the first file on the list in the Project window, ***DiveProfile.frm***, has been checked out.)

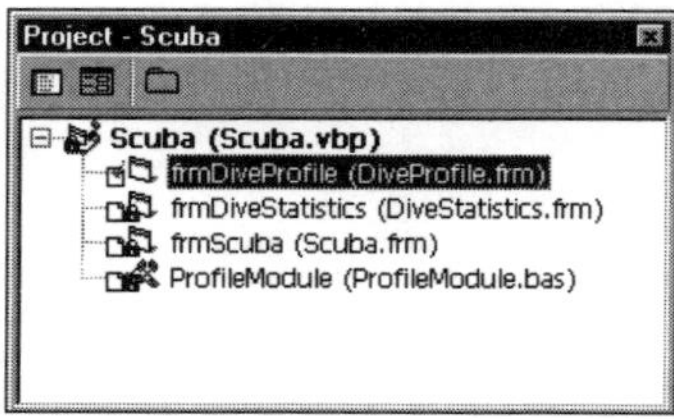

Figure 12-6: To check out a file, choose Check Out from the SourceSafe menu. In the Project Explorer shown here, the DiveProfile form has been checked out.

Check Out retrieves the file in read-write form so it can be altered and later returned to the VSS database for diffing. (More on diffing in a moment.) Any item in a VSS project that is not checked out tells you so in VB. The words "read only" appear in the form or module's title bar.

To return a file to the VSS database, select it in the VB Project Explorer and then choose Check In from the Tools menu, or check it back in using VSS Explorer.

Finding Changes Made to a File: Diffing

To *diff* a files means to determine how it is different from another file. Normally a file is diffed against another version of itself.

Once files are checked back into Visual SourceSafe, the versioning power of VSS comes into play. Open the Visual SourceSafe Explorer and select the project whose files were changed. Highlight a file that was checked back in and then choose Tools | Show History. You'll see a version history window similar to the window at the back of Figure 12-7.

Figure 12-7 shows the history of a VB file, ***Scuba.Frm***. As you can see in the history window in the figure, the file was created on 12/27/96 at 2:55 PM and it is version 1. The second entry for this file shows that it was checked back in on 12/28/96 at 11:11 AM and that it is version 2. The third entry, version 3, shows that it was checked back in on the same day as version 2 at 11:19 AM.

To see the differences between the second and third versions of this file, select the two versions and then click the Diff button. The window at the front of Figure 12-7 will open, listing the differences between the versions in a gray box. From here, you can accept the changes in version 2 of the file by leaving it as it is, or you can use the Rollback button in the History window to return to a previous version of the file.

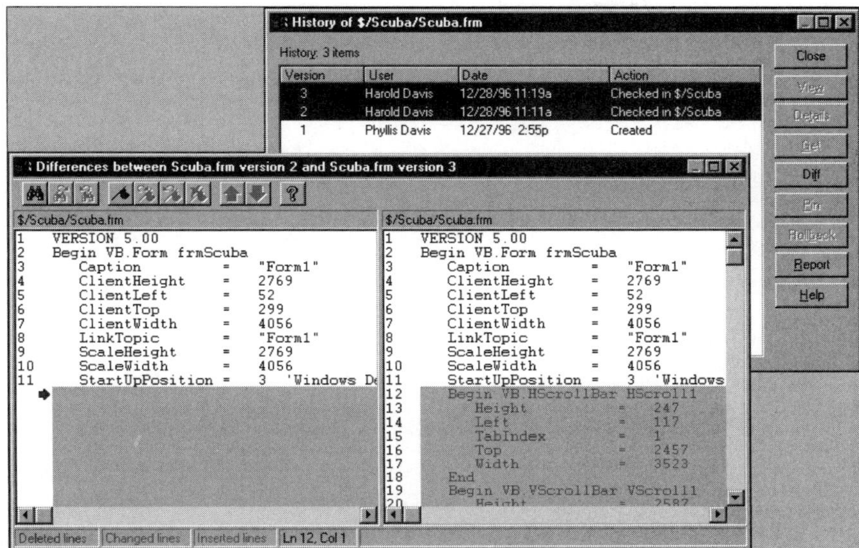

Figure 12-7: You use the Diff button to find the differences between two versions of a file.

Summary

Microsoft Visual SourceSafe is a versioning system designed to protect complex projects by creating a database containing all changes that a file has been through. Created with teams of programmers in mind, VSS actually consists of two applications: Visual SourceSafe Administrator, which sets up users and their access rights, and Visual SourceSafe Explorer, which keeps track of the many versions a project's files go through during project creation.

In this chapter, I discussed using the Visual SourceSafe Administrator to

- Add users and set passwords
- Change user access rights by project
- Set administration options

On the user side of VSS — VSS Explorer — I showed you how to

- Make sure that the VSS is properly integrated with Visual Basic
- Create a Visual SourceSafe project and add files to it
- Check files out of and return files to the VSS library
- Look at a file's version history and determine how it differs from other versions

PART III

Coding Secrets

Chapter 13

Secrets of Good Programming Practice

I start out in this chapter by going over those characteristics that make for good programming: clarity, elegance, sound design, and common sense. As I've said before in *Visual Basic 5 SECRETS*, I'm a firm believer in showing, not just telling. Therefore, I'll continue with specific programming techniques and tricks for solving common VB conundrums easily and sensibly.

This chapter covers quite a few topics, including:

- Good architectural design of VB applications
- Naming clarity and conventions
- Adding custom properties and methods to forms
- Creating and firing custom form events
- Creating a stack within VB
- Interrupting Do loops
- Handling list boxes with finesse and clarity
- Parsing and manipulating strings (including VB code)
- A neat way to automatically round numbers
- Enumerating fonts

Good Programming Practice

Developing software is an extremely complex process. Successfully mastering this process involves attention both to detail and to the overall picture.

Software development can be broken down into the following distinct activities:

- Defining a problem
- Architectural design
- Detailed design
- Coding
- Debugging
- Testing
- Maintenance

The key point about this list is that *planning* — of one sort or another — should take up a great percentage of the software developer's time. (At least four of the seven items on this activities list involve planning rather than actual code construction.)

As a practical matter, it is typical for organizations, and programmers, to plunge into a project without having fully understood what is involved. Due to this haste, creative — and possibly better — solutions to problems are overlooked. All too often, one approach after another is tried and abandoned, leaving hulking forgotten bodies of code that are tactfully called "prototypes." In the worst cases, there is a wake-up call: "We need that application by the end of the week" (or month, or year). There's no time at this point to plan it out from scratch. The most recent of the "prototypes" becomes the basis for the final version. No one should be surprised if a project developed in this way contains bloat and bugs, and is not easy to maintain.

My message is that whatever the size of your project — be it a one-routine Lilliputian or a hundred-form-and-module Brobdingnagian — from the start allocate at least as much time for planning as for coding. It's a good idea to plan things to the level where you can articulate each routine's logic in pseudocode before you even start programming.

Pseudocode and PDL

Pseudocode is a loosely defined term meaning any way of precisely defining the operations of a routine in English. Sometimes routines are first written in pseudocode; the pseudocode is eventually replaced with actual code and becomes the comments for the code.

PDL (Program Design Language) is a formalized version of pseudocode that was created by the company Caine, Farber & Gordon in the 1970s.

You should use pseudocode, or PDL, to describe the idea behind a routine, rather than to describe how any specific programming language will implement the idea. One effective technique is to write pseudocode of greater and greater specificity until the final translation into program code is nearly automatic.

Unfortunately, in the real world, you may not feel that you have the luxury to spend time planning and designing projects. (My advice is still to find the time.) Everything involves trade-offs. Indeed, one truism about software is that you can design a program for one out of these three things: speed, resource consumption, and maintainability.

The logic behind this old saying is that code that is truly optimized for either speed or resource consumption follows some truly twisted turns.

With modern program design — particularly in an environment such as VB's, which is never going to win speed or resource consumption contests in any case — the balance has shifted to maintainability.

There are armies of maintenance programmers still keeping legacy mainframe programs going. Successful Visual Basic 5 programs written today may well need maintaining for years to come. (Arguably, the maintenance issues with VB programs are much greater than with mainframe applications due to a far richer, more flexible, and extensible language.) If maintenance is not considered as a very important aspect of any substantial project, it is going to mean very big trouble in the years to come.

The maintainable program has been crafted for clarity. It's easy to read. (Easy to read, of course, means easy for someone who understands programming and the language it was written in.) It almost doesn't need comments because it is self-commenting: Routines tell what they're doing and why with just a glance.

Creative programmers often work very hard to find an easier way to do something. In general, as Pooh would say, this is a Very Good Thing. In fact, it's almost always a waste of time to try to bull your way through a problem by brute force. However, if the easier way results in loss of clarity, then maybe it's not such a good thing. In other words, by all means go for a clever or tricky way to do something, but only if you truly understand it and someone who has never discussed it with you (read, a maintenance programmer) will understand it once they've seen it (and looked a few things up).

Architectural Design of Applications

The upper level organization of a project — its architecture — should be well planned. Each routine should have a clearly defined and distinct purpose. Because a module is a grouping of routines, each module should present a coherent rationale for its grouping.

In addition, it often makes sense to structurally divide applications: One part might be used to encapsulate "business rule" verification, another to access a database, and a final part for interaction with the users and their input.

The architectural approach that Microsoft's Information Technology Group (ITG) has adopted for Visual Basic development internal to Microsoft uses four architectural layers:

- User interface (UI)
- Data
- Transaction
- External access

In this model, the user interface layer contains all code necessary for response to user interaction, and nothing else. This layer is the only layer that should reference forms, controls, and so on. It includes all event-handling code and handles display, responding to changed window states, and initiating user requests.

The data layer supplies all data to the UI layer for display, and all data to the transaction layer. The data layer is responsible for local initialization operations as well as organizing, formatting, and sorting incoming and outgoing data. In addition, business rules enforcement should be located in the data layer.

The transaction layer uses the data layer as a kind of information buffer. The transaction layer is responsible for overseeing the operation of the external access layer, which actually communicates with an external data source. Although this model is aimed at relatively large client/server applications, the general principles are applicable to programs of almost any size. Try to group like code with like code, separate by intended functionality, and generalize to promote reusability.

Naming Clarity and Conventions

Naming clarity is extremely important. The easiest way to tell what a variable contains is by reading its name, if it has been named well. Similarly, the first pass at deciphering what a routine does is its name.

In other words, good variable names tell readers what might be assigned to the variable. It's better to think conceptually and name the variable after what it represents rather than after a programming process: Counter is not a particularly good variable name.

It's pretty standard to use single letters for integer variables (for example, I, X) and to use capitalization to make variable, and procedure, names easier to understand. For example, Sub ComputesTheBiggest() is easier to read than Sub Computesthebiggest().

Microsoft Consulting Services has produced a white paper — "Visual Basic Programming Conventions," available on the MSDN CD-ROM — that proposes naming conventions loosely based on Hungarian naming (see the preceding sidebar). The primary thrust of the Microsoft proposals are to prefix control and form references with three-letter indications of the nature of the referenced object (for example, txtManifest for a text box, and frmShowInventory for a form) and to prefix variable names with letters indicating their type and scope (for example, gbStretch for a global Boolean).

The Hungarian Naming Convention

Charles Simonyi, a Hungarian, invented a variable naming convention that is pretty generally applied to C programming. Hungarian names are made up of a base type (in lowercase) followed by a prefix and a qualifier. Maybe they do look like Hungarian, at that!

As you may have noticed, my own practice in *Visual Basic 5 SECRETS* has not been entirely consistent. I stand by my statement that clarity is all that really matters, although, when working with a team, keeping to a consistent naming convention becomes more important. My practice tends to be to follow the Microsoft-modified Hungarian suggestions for object names, but not for variables. In really simple projects, I'll sometimes not even bother with it for objects and accept the default names — for example, List1, List2 — when these seem clear enough.

Custom Form Properties and Methods

Custom — meaning user-defined — form properties and methods are easy to implement. If the property or method is created using the Public keyword, it is available to other modules in a project. The advantage of adding your own properties and methods to a form is that it helps to encapsulate forms; all the code the form needs is in one place — namely, part of the form module.

Adding a Custom Method

As an example, suppose you wanted to add to a form a .Center method that would center the form on the screen. You could add a Public Sub to a form that is a variation of the generalized CenterForm procedure I've used previously (see the ***APICode.Bas*** module in Chapter 11, "The Win32 Software Development Kit (SDK), the Win32 API, and the Windows Messaging System."):

```
Public Sub Center()
   Me.Move (Screen.Width - Me.Width) \ 2, _
      (Screen.Height - Me.Height) \ 2
End Sub
```

This method procedure can now be called using the dot operator (.), like any other method. To demonstrate, if the form is named Form1 and the project is set to start from Sub Main, the following code first loads and displays the form and then calls the custom method that centers the form on the screen:

```
Public Sub Main()
   Form1.Show
   Form1.Center
End Sub
```

(The sample code is saved on the companion CD-ROM as ***Custom.Vbp***.)

Adding a Custom Property

You can add a new property to a form simply by declaring a public variable in the form module. For example:

```
Public MyProperty As String
```

This custom property can then be assigned values (and return values) externally to the form module. In Sub Main, MyProperty could be set:

```
Form1.MyProperty = "Elbereth Gilthoniel!"
```

The value in MyProperty can now be accessed from anywhere consistent with the normal rules of scoping. From within Form1, no module identifier is required:

```
Private Sub Form_Load()
   Me.Caption = MyProperty
End Sub
```

By the way, form variables — and custom methods — can be used without loading a form into memory.

Another way to add custom properties to a form is with matched Property Get and Property Let procedures. Property Get is used to return the value, and Property Let is used to assign the value. Doing things in this way allows you to execute code within Property Get and Property Let procedures. In keeping with good coding practice, you can use Property Get and Property Let to hide portions (or all) of an object's data and only expose selective access to the object.

It's easy to create read-only properties this way by providing a Property Get procedure without a Property Let and changing the protected private variable that is referenced by the procedure from within the code. As an example, suppose you had a variable called MyWealth that kept track of how much money you had. You could declare MyWealth as a private variable at the form module level:

```
Private MyWealth As Double
```

Read-only access to the value of MyWealth could be implemented through a Property Get procedure:

```
Property Get Wealth() As Double
   Wealth = MyWealth
End Property
```

Property Wealth could now be used to display the current value of MyWealth:

```
Private Sub Command1_Click()
   Label1 = Format(Wealth, "Currency")
End Sub
```

In the meantime, internal protected code could increment and decrement the value of MyWealth itself. In this rather trivial example, a timer control adds $100.00 to MyWealth every time it is fired:

```
Private Sub Timer1_Timer()
   MyWealth = MyWealth + 100#
End Sub
```

As a formal matter, if you use paired Property Get and Property Let procedures, Get operates like a function; the last parameter of Let is meant to be the analog to the return value of the matched Get.

For example, if you declared a module-level private variable

```
Private EntityName As String
```

you could create Property Get and Property Let procedures that include execution code:

```
Public Property Get Elvishness() As String
   If EntityName = "Frodo" Then
      Elvishness = "Hobbit"
   Else
      Elvishness = "Elf"
   End If
End Property

Public Property Let Elvishness(vNewValue As String)
   If vNewValue = "Saruman" Then
      MsgBox "Not a valid Elf value!"
   Else
      EntityName = vNewValue
   End If
End Property
```

In the sample project, the Elvishness property is accessed in a command button's click event:

```
Private Sub Command2_Click()
   Command2.Caption = Form1.Elvishness
End Sub
```

If you assign the value Saruman to the Elvishness property in Sub Main:

```
Form1.Elvishness = "Saruman"
```

the message "Not a valid Elf value!" appears, and EntityName's value is not changed. If you assign the value "Frodo" to Elvishness,

```
    Form1.Elvishness = "Frodo"
```

the return value of the Property Get Elvishness procedure is Hobbit. When any other value is assigned to Elvishness, for example,

```
Form1.Elvishness = "Legolas"
```

its return value is Elf.

Creating your own properties and methods can be very powerful and can help you properly craft access to form-level variables. In the "life isn't perfect" department, however, it is not possible to add a custom property to a VB form that will then show up in the Properties window at design time.

Setting the Default Property

As you probably know, objects — such as forms and controls — can have a default property that is implied when the object is invoked without a property. For example, Text is the default property of a text box. This means that

```
Text1.Text = "Federation Starship Enterprise"
```

has exactly the same effect as

```
Text1 = "Federation Starship Enterprise"
```

Because VB knows that Text is the default property, it is implied in the second statement.

In Visual Basic 5, you can decide for yourself what object property or method should be the default. This means that you can change defaults for objects that already have them, and add default properties to objects — such as forms — that do not. You can even have a custom property that you created be the default.

For example, earlier in this section, I showed you how to create a custom form property — MyProperty. This property was then set from a code module:

```
Form1.MyProperty = "Elbereth Gilthoniel!"
```

After MyProperty has been set as the default property for Form1, you can accomplish the same results without mentioning it explicitly:

```
Form1 = "Elbereth Gilthoniel!"
```

Here's how to set MyProperty as the default property for Form1:

1. With a VB object open in Code view, choose Procedure Attributes from the Tools menu. Click the Advanced button to expand the dialog, as shown in Figure 13-1.
2. In the Name drop-down list, select the member that is the current default, if there is one. Select None in the Procedure ID drop-down list to remove the default status of the member.
3. In the Name drop-down list, select the member you want to make the default (for example, My Property).
4. Select Default in the Procedure ID drop-down list.

You can use the Object Browser to determine the default member for an object and to access the Procedure Attributes dialog.

To use the Object Browser to find the default member of an object, select the class of the object in the Classes list. The default member will have a little blue ball displayed above and to its left in the Members list. (You'll see this ball above the listing for MyProperty in Figure 13-2, although, of course, it doesn't appear blue.)

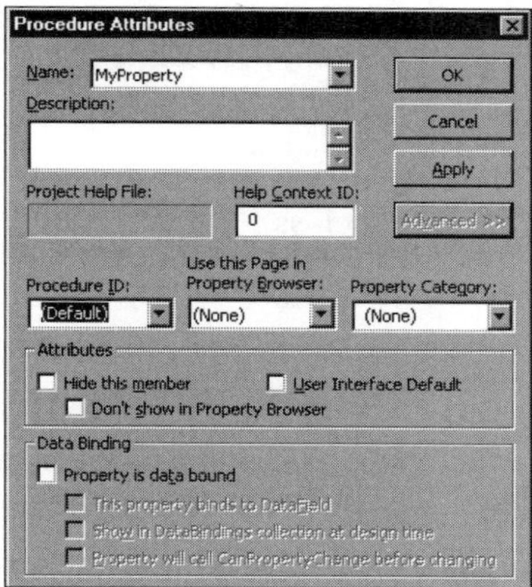

Figure 13-1: You can use the Procedure Attributes dialog to make a property the default.

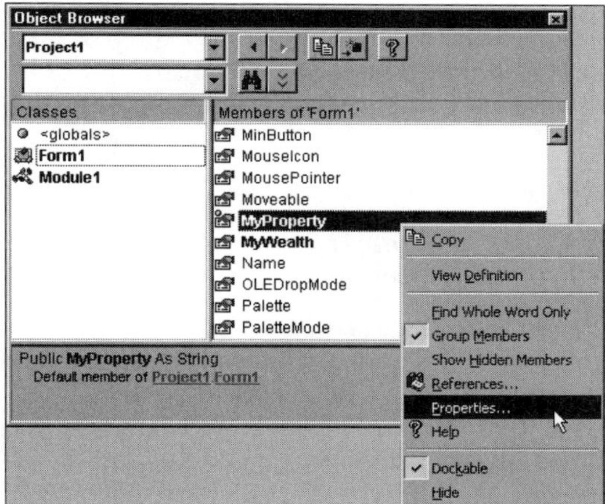

Figure 13-2: You can tell the default member of a class using Object Browser by the little blue ball appearing above and to the left of the member.

Once you've found the default member, if you'd like to change it, you can access the Procedure Attributes dialog by selecting Properties from the member's context menu, as shown in Figure 13-2.

Firing Custom Events

Custom events must be fired from within a class module. (Working with class modules is covered in depth in Chapter 14, "Visual Basic and OOP.")

The way it works is pretty straightforward. Within the class module, you declare your event (the event used in the example is named "Fired"):

```
Public Event Fired()
```

The event is triggered (synonymous with *raised*, and *fired*) using the RaiseEvent statement, shown here within a class function named "beenFired":

```
Public Function beenFired()
   RaiseEvent Fired
End Function
```

You must be very clear that you are completely responsible for firing any custom events. No *deus ex machina* will take care of this for you.

In the example, I call the class module's beenFired method (which triggers the Fired event) from Form1's Timer event, which adds to MyWealth. Every time MyWealth increases, beenFired is called and Fired is triggered:

```
Private Sub Timer1_Timer()
   MyWealth = MyWealth + 100#
   tellMe.beenFired
End Sub
```

To have VB add an event-handling framework to Form1, at the beginning of the form you need to declare a private instance of the class using the WithEvents keyword:

```
Private WithEvents tellMe As Class1
```

If you click on the Objects list for Form1, you'll now find a tellMe object. A corresponding Fired event will appear in the Procedures list, as shown in Figure 13-3.

Before you can use a class method such as beenFired, you need to create an instance of the class (in addition to declaring the class). If the class fires custom events, the Set statement must be used. For example, you could create the tellMe instance of Class1 in Form1's Load event:

```
Private Sub Form_Load()
   ...
   Set tellMe = New Class1
End Sub
```

If you add a message box statement to the Fired event of the tellMe class

```
Private Sub tellMe_Fired()
   MsgBox "This event has been way fired!", _
      vbExclamation, Me.Caption
End Sub
```

every time the event is fired — when the Timer event increments MyWealth — the event handler code is invoked and the message box displayed, as shown in Figure 13-4.

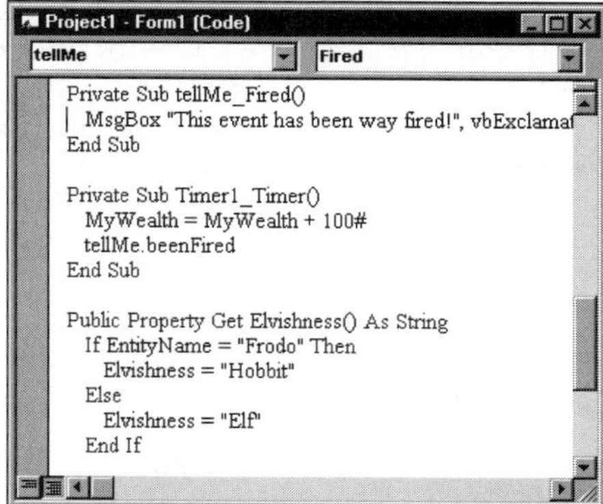

Figure 13-3: You can add an event fired in a class module to a form's event handlers by declaring an instance of the class module using the WithEvents keyword.

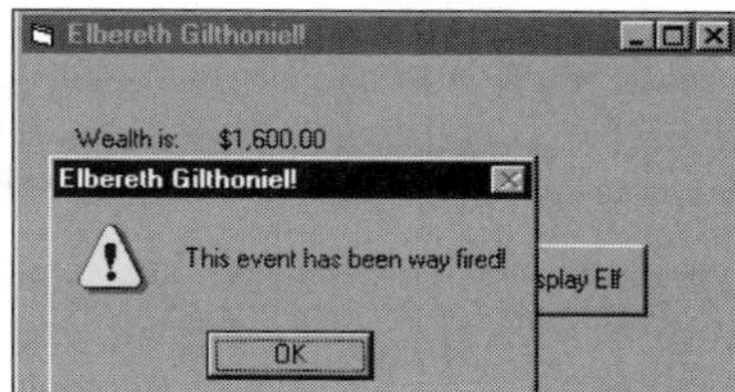

Figure 13-4: Code placed in the custom event handler is executed every time the custom event is fired.

Implementing a Stack As an Array

Visual Basic includes some very flexible and unusually powerful features, such as the ability to dynamically redimension arrays on the fly while preserving values. This example, saved on the CD-ROM as ***Mouse.Vbp***, illustrates how to use a dynamic array to implement a stack.

A *stack* is a data structure with the property that each new item added to it becomes the next item that is accessed from it. (By its very nature, a stack is not a random-access structure. Only the top item in the stack is available to the program at any one time.)

Mouse changes the cursor — also called the "mouse pointer" — to a new cursor selected at random. It uses a stack to store the value of the current cursor, enabling the user to go backwards through the stack to the previous cursor. There is no limit to the size of this stack — and to the number of cursors that can be kept track of — except that the stack is implemented in an integer array. (I suppose that if 32,676 cursors are not enough, you could always redeclare MStack as an array of longs!) Here are the module declarations for MStack, the stack array, and StackTop, the variable that tracks the current element in the array (the top of the stack):

```
Option Explicit
Dim MStack() As Integer 'Mouse Stack
Dim StackTop As Integer 'Top of the Stack
```

The procedure PushStack adds the current cursor to the top of the stack, and redimensions the stack array if necessary, as shown in Listing 13-1.

Listing 13-1: "Pushing" an array implemented as a stack

```
Private Sub PushStack(NewMouseValue As Integer)
   If StackTop = UBound(MStack) Then
      ReDim Preserve MStack(UBound(MStack) + 1)
   End If
   StackTop = StackTop + 1
   MStack(StackTop) = Screen.MousePointer
   Screen.MousePointer = NewMouseValue
End Sub
```

PopStack moves in the opposite direction, replacing the current cursor with the value at the top of the stack (the previous cursor) and then decrementing the size of the stack array by one, as shown in Listing 13-2.

Listing 13-2: "Popping" an array implemented as a stack

```
Private Sub PopStack()
   If StackTop >= 0 Then
      Screen.MousePointer = MStack(StackTop)
      StackTop = StackTop - 1
      If StackTop > 0 Then
         ReDim Preserve MStack(UBound(MStack) - 1)
      End If
   End If
End Sub
```

The stack should be initialized with a dimension:

```
Private Sub InitializeMouse()
   ReDim MStack(10)
   StackTop = -1
End Sub
```

You can place a call to InitializeMouse in the Form load event, or elsewhere as appropriate. To choose a new cursor at random and place the current cursor value on top of the stack, call PushStack with a random cursor generator:

```
Private Sub cmdPush_Click()
   PushStack Rnd * 15
End Sub
```

(The values 0-15 in 32-bit Visual Basic are valid MousePointer constants. See the topics "MousePointer Property" and "MousePointer Constants" in VB's online help. The use of the Rnd function returns a random MousePointer value.)

To return to the previous cursor, simply call PopStack:

```
Private Sub cmdPop_Click()
   PopStack
End Sub
```

The example program is now complete and, on the whole, fun to play with (see Figure 13-5).

Figure 13-5: The Mouse Stack program demonstrates how to use stacks to store cursor values.

Implementing stacks with dynamic arrays can be a very good approach to structuring your data access in VB in situations where last-in-first-out (LIFO) — rather than random — access is appropriate.

Interrupting a Do Loop

A common problem involves allowing the user to interrupt time-consuming loop operations. It's very frustrating for users to have the computer churning and churning away at something that there is no way to halt short of pressing Ctrl+Alt+Delete. This is particularly true when the user has realized that asking the computer to perform the operation in the first place was a mistake. (At least, in 32-bit Windows, you can end the current task with Ctrl+Alt+Delete. In earlier versions of Windows, this kind of situation often led to user reboots.)

As a part of user-friendly interface design, it makes sense to allow the interruption of time-consuming loops when the user presses a key or clicks a mouse button — perhaps the Escape key or the left mouse button. (Of course, you'll have to take appropriate action in this situation to make sure that data is not corrupted because a calculation has been interrupted.)

A fairly common way to do this is to call the DoEvents function within the time-consuming loop, which yields execution so the operating system can process other events. Some other part of your program can then trap specific keys being pressed, and take appropriate action to shut down the loop. However, this is a very messy way to do things and can lead to all sorts of problems with respect to reentry into the loop.

A better approach is to use the GetAsyncKeyState API and check within the loop to see if specific keys have been pressed. The code in Listing 13-3 interrupts an (otherwise infinite) loop when the user presses the Escape key or left mouse button:

Listing 13-3: Interrupting a Do loop

```
Option Explicit
Private Declare Function GetAsyncKeyState Lib "user32" _
   (ByVal vKey As Long) As Integer
Const VK_ESCAPE = &H1B
Const VK_LBUTTON = &H1
Private Sub Command1_Click()
   Do
      If GetAsyncKeyState(VK_ESCAPE) < 0 Or _
         GetAsyncKeyState(VK_LBUTTON) < 0 Then
         Debug.Print "Exiting"
         Exit Do
      End If
   Loop
   Debug.Print "Looping"
End Sub
```

Note that you can find GetAsyncKeyState's possible constant arguments (the "VK" is short for "Virtual Key") in the API Text Viewer application under "Constants."

Managing List Boxes

A common problem in VB applications is managing list box controls. Here are some techniques that you can use in most applications that have to program these controls.

Tracking Multiple List Boxes

Often you'll want to have two or more list boxes acting in concert. For example, suppose one list box tracked inventory item numbers and another the name of the item. When an item was selected by number in this situation, you'd need a mechanism that also selected that item's name.

The sample program, saved on the CD-ROM as ***ListDemo.Vbp***, demonstrates two techniques for handling this common VB programming problem. Each technique results in slightly different display characteristics. In the demonstration, I've added three list boxes to a form, as shown in Figure 13-6.

The first two list boxes are populated with the letters of the alphabet, the third with the numbers 1 through 26:

```
Private Sub Form_Load()
   Dim X As Integer
   For X = 1 To 26
      List1.AddItem Chr(X + 64)
      List2.AddItem Chr(X + 64)
```

```
        List3.AddItem Str(X)
    Next X
End Sub
```

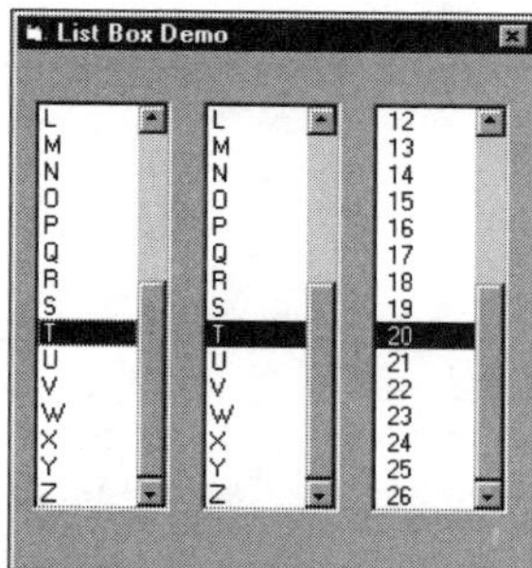

Figure 13-6: The click events of the three list boxes are connected.

The first technique uses the TopIndex property of the first list box, List1. TopIndex — which is only available at runtime — sets or returns the index value of the topmost element in the list box. (You may be more familiar with the ListIndex property, which sets or returns the currently selected item.) You can use the TopIndex property so that when the user scrolls through the first list box, the others scroll correspondingly.

To set up this scenario, add a timer control to the form with its .Enabled property set to True and its .Interval set to a small number (such as 10).

The Timer's Interval Property

The unit of measurement used by the timer's Interval property is milliseconds. If the Interval is set to 1000, the timer is fired — meaning, its Timer event is activated — once every second. If the Interval is set to 10, the timer is fired one hundred times a second. When the timer is being used to update a display — such as the demonstration program — it really doesn't much matter what number you select for the Interval property, as long as it is small enough not to cause noticeable "bumps" in the program's operation.

Next, add the code shown in Listing 13-4 to the timer's Timer event:

Listing 13-4: Synchronizing list boxes

```
Private Sub Timer1_Timer()
    Static PrevList1 As Integer
    Dim TopList1 As Integer
    TopList1 = List1.TopIndex
    If TopList1 <> PrevList1 Then
```

```
      List2.TopIndex = TopList1
      List3.TopIndex = TopList1
      PrevList1 = TopList1
   End If
   If List1.ListIndex <> List2.ListIndex Or _
      List1.ListIndex <> List3.ListIndex Then
      List2.ListIndex = List1.ListIndex
      List3.ListIndex = List1.ListIndex
   End If
End Sub
```

This code uses a static variable, PrevList1, to track the TopIndex value of List1. If it has changed, the TopIndex properties of List2 and List3 are updated accordingly, and the new TopIndex value is assigned to PrevList1. The final bit of code ensures that if an item is selected in List1, it is also selected in List2 and List3.

If you try out this example, you'll see that when you scroll through List1, List2 and List3 behave exactly as List1 does. This may be the behavior you want in your application. It does have the potential drawback that users cannot take actions on list boxes other than List1.

To see another approach, set the Enabled property of Timer1 to False (that way we won't have Timer1's Timer event coming back to haunt us). Then add the following procedure to the form:

```
Private Sub SetList(c As Control)
   Static PrevList As Integer
   Dim TopList As Integer
   TopList = c.TopIndex
   If TopList <> PrevList Then
      List1.TopIndex = TopList
      List2.TopIndex = TopList
      List3.TopIndex = TopList
      PrevList = TopList
   End If
   List1.ListIndex = c.ListIndex
   List2.ListIndex = c.ListIndex
   List3.ListIndex = c.ListIndex
End Sub
```

The logic of this procedure is the same as that of the timer's event handler. The only difference is that it is called from the click event handlers of each list box:

```
Private Sub List1_Click()
   SetList List1
End Sub

Private Sub List2_Click()
   SetList List2
End Sub

Private Sub List3_Click()
   SetList List3
End Sub
```

This effectively connects the three list boxes whenever any of their click events are fired.

A consideration with the second technique is that — although the list boxes are synchronized whenever any one of them fires a click event, such as selecting an item — scrolling by itself does not fire a click event. List boxes connected in this way will appear unbalanced until the user moves the cursor into the client area of one of the boxes.

Avoiding List Box Deletion Errors

The way you would intuitively think to delete multiple items from a list box leads to a runtime error. To see what I mean, add a list box to a form and set its MultiSelect property to 1-Simple. (This allows the user to select multiple items at one time.) Next, populate the list box. (Sample code is saved on the CD-ROM as ***Removing.Vbp***.)

You would think that the natural way to remove selected items from a list box would be to cycle through all the items and delete selected ones, for example:

```
Private Sub cmdRemove_Click()
    Dim x As Integer
    For x = 0 To List1.ListCount - 1
        If List1.Selected(x) Then
            List1.RemoveItem x
        End If
    Next x
End Sub
```

However, if you run this code with multiple items selected, you will get runtime error 381, "Invalid property array index" (see Figure 13-7).

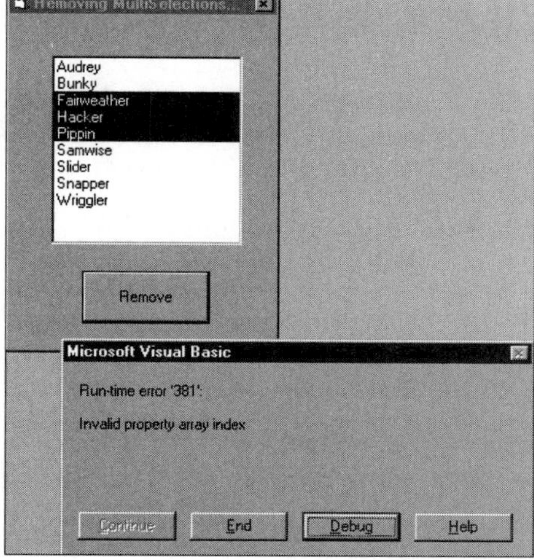

Figure 13-7: The intuitive way of removing multiple selections from a list box leads to this runtime error.

This error occurs because x, the counting variable, ranges to the top number of items that were in the box even though some of those items have been deleted during the procedure. In other words, although ListCount is decremented when an item is removed from the list box, x is not. At some point, therefore, x will be a number greater than the number of items in the list box.

The fix is to convert the For...Next loop to a Do While loop with an internal counter, as shown in Listing 13-5:

Listing 13-5: Deleting multiple items from a list box

```
Private Sub cmdRemove_Click()
   Dim x As Integer
   x = 0
   Do While x < List1.ListCount
      If List1.Selected(x) Then
         List1.RemoveItem x
      Else
         x = x + 1
      End If
   Loop
End Sub
```

Copying Selected List Box Items to the Clipboard

As a final list box demonstration, I'll show you how to copy selected list box items to the Clipboard (and paste them into a RichTextBox control). This demonstration is saved on the CD-ROM as ***Clip.Vbp***. The simple Clipboard operations it demonstrates are, of course, control independent — meaning that you could use the same techniques to copy and paste to and from any control.

For more information on the Clipboard object and its methods, look it up in VB's on-line help. You can find the Clipboard constants under the topic "Clipboard Object Constants"; you can also find them by using the Object Browser.

To copy multiple objects from a list box to the Clipboard, use the Clipboard object's SetText method, as shown in Listing 13-6:

Listing 13-6: Copying multiple items to the Clipboard

```
Private Sub cmdCopy_Click()
   Dim ClipStr As String, I As Integer
   Clipboard.Clear
   ClipStr = ""
   For I = 0 To List1.ListCount - 1
      If List1.Selected(I) Then
         ClipStr = ClipStr & List1.List(I) + vbCrLf
      End If
   Next I
   Clipboard.SetText ClipStr
End Sub
```

To paste the contents of the Clipboard back to a RichTextBox, use the Clipboard's GetText method (with an appropriate constant argument):

```
Private Sub cmdPaste_Click()
    RichTextBox1.Text = ""
    RichTextBox1.Text = Clipboard.GetText(vbCFText)
End Sub
```

Figure 13-8 shows copying multiple selected items from a list box into the Clipboard, and from the Clipboard into a Rich Text box.

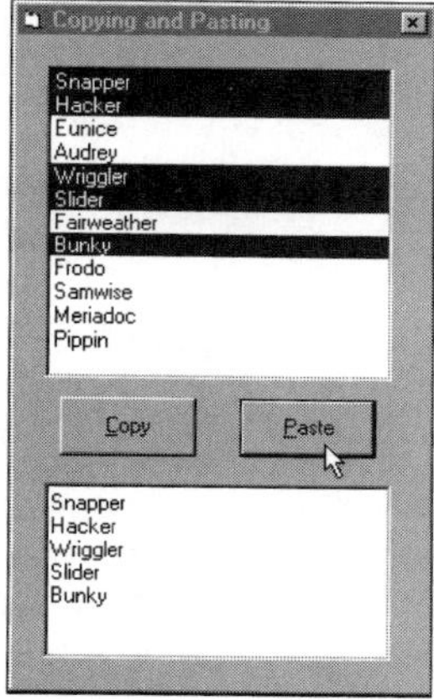

Figure 13-8: You use the Clipboard object's SetText and GetText methods to copy and paste.

String Manipulation

As experienced developers have come to learn, successfully manipulating strings is an extremely important part of the art — or craft, or science, if you prefer — of programming. Indeed, as one wizened fellow said to me, glancing up from his monitor festooned with dancing code windows, "In one sense, all of programming can be reduced to string manipulation."

Visual Basic gives us an incredibly rich string manipulation environment, replete with numerous built-in string manipulation functions. Also, the native VB string data type is very easy to work with as compared, for example, to Delphi, in which strings of greater than 255 characters must be stored in arrays of single characters (leading to all kinds of nasty string conversion chores).

I cannot, of course, demonstrate all of VB's string manipulation facilities in this section, but I will show you a few tricks and techniques that you can easily transpose to many real-world programming situations.

Capitalizing Words in a String

Listing 13-7 contains a function that capitalizes the first letter of each word in a string:

Listing 13-7: Capitalizing the first letter in a string

```
Private Function CapFirstLetter(InString As String, _
   DeLim As String)As String
   Dim PosDel As Integer
   Mid(InString, 1, 1) = UCase(Mid(InString, 1, 1))
   PosDel = InStr(InString, DeLim)
   While PosDel <> 0
      Mid(InString, PosDel + 1, 1) = UCase(Mid(InString, _
         PosDel + 1, 1))
      PosDel = InStr(PosDel + 1, InString, DeLim)
   Wend
   CapFirstLetter = InString
End Function
```

I've generalized the function, but normally the second parameter passed ("DeLim") would be a string consisting of a single space (" "), because that's what usually separates, or *delimits,* words.

CapFirstLetter first capitalizes the first letter in the input string. It then uses the InStr function to find the first occurrence of the delimiter (a space). When it finds the delimiter, it capitalizes the letter following it and goes on to find the next occurrence of the delimiter.

I've hooked up the CapFirstLetter function to two text boxes as follows:

```
Private Sub cmdCap_Click()
   Text2.Text = ""
   Text2.Text = CapFirstLetter(Text1.Text, " ")
End Sub
```

This project is saved on the companion CD-ROM as ***Cap1rst.Vbp***. As you can see from Figure 13-9, it does a pretty good job.

Three things to note: You could use this function on any control that holds text — for example, a RichTextBox. Also, because words are delimited with a space character, a word on a new line that has been created with word wrapping will not be capitalized unless you enter a space before the word. In addition, because the delimiter is a space, the second of two hyphenated words will not be capitalized.

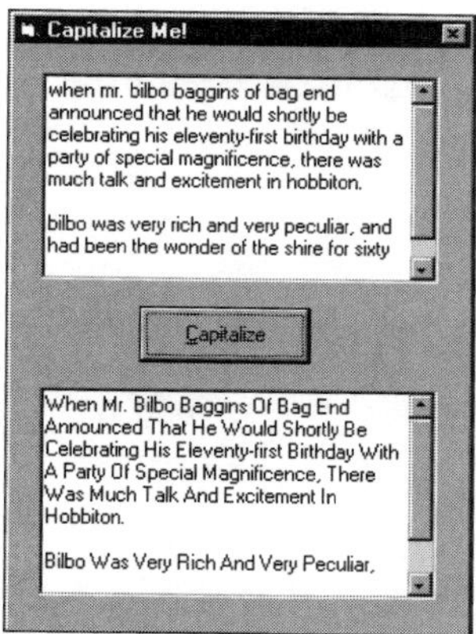

Figure 13-9: You can use the UCase, Mid, and InStr functions to capitalize the first letter in every word.

Parsing VB Code and Checking Line Lengths

Length.Vbp is a small program that demonstrates how to use the Len and Trim functions to check line lengths (it also uses Val and Str for type conversions). Perhaps more importantly, it shows that you can treat a Visual Basic code file as just another text file to be opened, parsed, and manipulated to your heart's content.

The initial part of the code uses the Common Dialog control to select a ***.Bas*** file to check. (For an explanation of the common dialogs, see Chapter 7, "Windows Common Dialog Secrets.")

```
Private Sub Command1_Click()
    Dim Ourfile As String
    CommonDialog1.CancelError = True
    On Error GoTo ErrHandler
    CommonDialog1.DialogTitle = "Select BAS Module"
    CommonDialog1.Filter = "VB Code Modules (*.Bas)|*.Bas"
    CommonDialog1.Flags = cdlOFNFileMustExist
    CommonDialog1.ShowOpen
    On Error GoTo 0
    Ourfile = CommonDialog1.filename
    CheckLen Ourfile, Val(txtLen.Text)
    Exit Sub
ErrHandler:
'User Cancelled
End Sub
```

Once a file has been selected, the CheckLen procedure is called with the file and a value to check line lengths against, as shown in Listing 13-8:

Listing 13-8: Checking line lengths

```
Private Sub CheckLen(FN As String, CL As Integer)
   Dim Lin As String, Lcount As Integer
   Lcount = 1
   Open FN For Input As #1
   Do While Not EOF(1)
      Line Input #1, Lin
      If Len(Trim(Lin)) > CL Then
         MsgBox "Line " + Str(Lcount) + " is too long. It is " + _
            Str(Len(Trim(Lin))) + " characters long.", _
            vbCritical, FN
      End If
      Lcount = Lcount + 1
   Loop
   Close
End Sub
```

The selected file is opened and assigned, line by line, to a variable, whose length is compared to the passed parameter. As shown in Figure 13-10, if the length is greater than the parameter, a message box that includes the long line's number and character length is displayed.

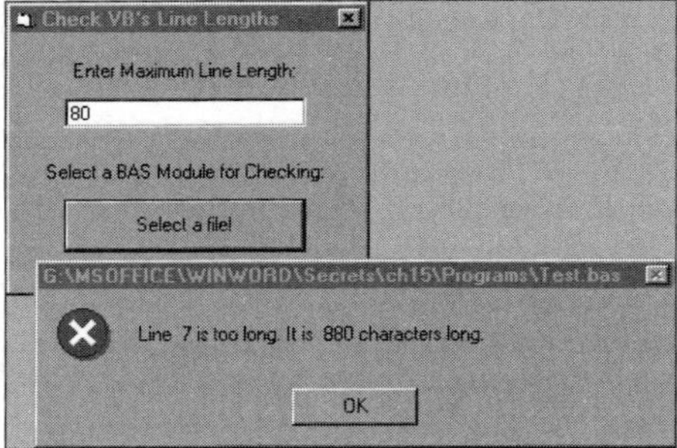

Figure 13-10: Visual Basic code modules can be parsed like any other text file (the demonstration tests ***.Bas*** files for overly long lines).

With the idea that parsing and manipulating VB code itself is possible, this application could go much further. It's not too big a step from here to using string manipulation functions to add (or subtract) line continuation characters as appropriate, indent code, or perform other automated code processing tasks.

Rounding Numbers

Listing 13-9 contains a generalized function that rounds off numbers to an arbitrary number of decimal places (use DecimalPlaces = 0 to round off to an integer):

Listing 13-9: Rounding numbers

```
Public Function RoundNumber(InNum As Variant, _
   DecimalPlaces As Integer) As Variant
   Dim Tmp As Double, DecShift As Long
   Tmp = CDbl(InNum)
   DecShift = 10 ^ DecimalPlaces
   RoundNumber = (Fix((Tmp + 0.5 / DecShift) * DecShift)) / DecShift
End Function
```

I've called the function from a form with three text boxes (see Figure 13-11) as follows:

```
Private Sub cmdRound_Click()
   txtResult.Text = RoundNumber(Val(txtNumber.Text), _
      Val(txtPlaces.Text))
End Sub
```

The project is saved on the companion CD-ROM as ***RoundNum.Vbp.***

Note the use of the Fix function within RoundNumber. Like the Int function, Fix returns the integer portion of a number, except that if the number is negative, Fix returns the first negative integer greater than or equal to the number (and Int returns the first negative integer less than or equal to the number).

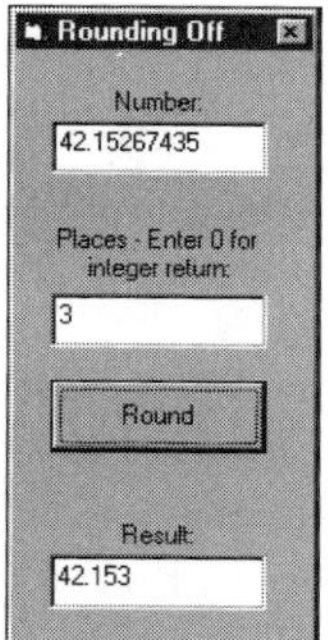

Figure 13-11: You can easily use Visual Basic's built-in functions to round off numbers.

Enumerating Fonts

It's often necessary to determine what fonts are available for display and printing on a given system. The code in the ***Fonts.Vbp*** project uses the Fonts and FontCount properties of the Printer and Screen objects to display fonts available to each object (see Figure 13-12), as you can see in Listing 13-10:

Listing 13-10: Displaying fonts

```
Private Sub Form_Load()
   DisplayFonts
End Sub

Private Sub DisplayFonts()
   Dim X As Integer
   For X = 0 To Printer.FontCount - 1
      lstPrinter.AddItem Printer.Fonts(X)
   Next X
   For X = 0 To Screen.FontCount - 1
      lstScreen.AddItem Screen.Fonts(X)
   Next X
End Sub
```

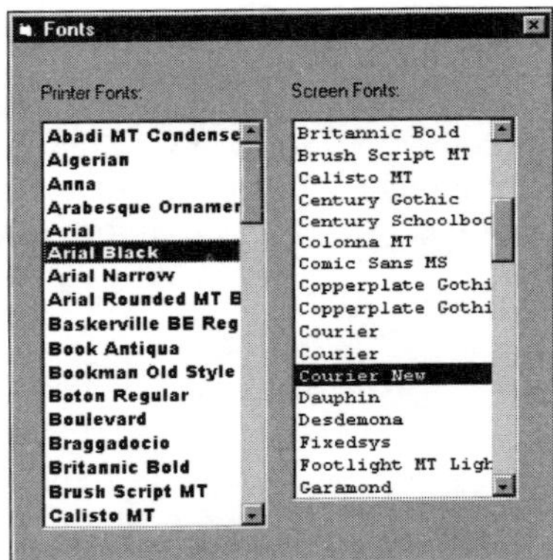

Figure 13-12: You can use the Printer and Screen objects to display available fonts.

If you needed to determine which fonts were available to both objects, you could loop through both lists and add only those fonts common to both.

To add a *soupçon* of interest to the resulting display (see Figure 13-12), I've placed code in each list box's click event that sets the list box font to the value of the current item:

```
Private Sub lstPrinter_Click()
   lstPrinter.Font = lstPrinter.List(lstPrinter.ListIndex)
End Sub

Private Sub lstScreen_Click()
   lstScreen.Font = lstScreen.List(lstScreen.ListIndex)
End Sub
```

Since *lstBox*.List(*lstBox*.ListIndex) always returns the current lstBox item, this code causes each list box — when its click event is fired — to use the current item as its display font.

Summary

This chapter proceeded from the general to the specific. I started with a general discussion of good programming practice, architectural project design, and good identifier naming. From there, I moved to the specific. Demonstrations in this chapter showed you how to:

- Add (and use) custom form properties and methods
- Set a custom property as the default property of an object such as a form
- Fire a user-defined event in a class module
- Respond to user-defined events in form event handlers
- Simulate a stack, thereby keeping track of a changing mouse cursor
- Respond to user input to interrupt a continuous loop
- Manipulate and control list boxes
- Capitalize the first letter of all words in a text string
- Edit Visual Basic source code stored in a file on disk
- Check text stored in a file for line lengths
- Round numbers
- Enumerate all fonts available to the Screen and Printer objects

Chapter 14

Visual Basic and OOP

In this chapter, I will demystify the important concepts of OOP (object-oriented programming) and explain how Visual Basic Version 5 fits into the OOP scheme of the programming universe. I'll also demonstrate how to harness the power of OOP in your VB5 programs.

Topics covered in this chapter include

- An Overview of OOP
- Visual Basic Version 5 and OOP
- Classes and class modules
- Objects and collection objects
- The Application object
- The Class Builder utility
- Extending an existing control

OOP: An Overview

Object-oriented programming theory was originally formulated as part of the process of creating languages intended to simulate real life. For example, Simula, one of the first OOP languages and an ancestor of Smalltalk, was designed by Norwegians Ole-Johan Dahl and Krysten Nygaard in 1967 as a tool for creating simulations. (By the way, Bjarn Stoustroup, the creator of C++, has acknowledged Simula as the source for the notion of classes as implemented in C++.)

Simulation seems to naturally involve groups of things: people, molecules, stocks, and so on. It's a small step from "thing" to "object." Objects, like people, have internal characteristics (private properties). They also have characteristics they present to the world (public properties). You can tell objects what to do — and they do it, in their own way (methods and events, respectively). In addition, many objects share some of the same common characteristics (inheritance).

As this metaphor suggests, intensive OOP programming — as opposed to programming that borrows a few OOP concepts, such as object encapsulation — tends to work best with systems that are easily expressed using organic models. These systems are, almost by definition, too complex to fully comprehend in a conventional, procedural fashion and are subject to ongoing change. In the introduction to *The Tao of Objects,* Bruce Eckel wrote, "...I practiced procedural programming, the structured techniques, and all that, but it never really made sense to me — it never seemed *whole*.... Because I can now think in more powerful terms, I can solve much more complex problems."

Most programming languages in commercial use today — including C++, Delphi, and Visual Basic — are *hybrid* OOP languages, meaning that they implement some (but not necessarily all) OOP concepts and also allow conventional procedural program construction. At a minimum, to construct OOP programs, a language needs to provide facilities for object and code reuse, and some capability to create new, extended objects within the language based on existing objects.

Of the languages just mentioned, Visual Basic has historically had the least consistent OOP implementation, although Version 5 contains far more OOP capabilities than earlier versions. Key enhancements to Version 5 — particularly the addition of facilities for firing custom events, creating ActiveX controls, and subclassing an object's message stream — mean that you can now create VB programs that are truly object oriented.

Of course, as you probably know, VB has a flavor all its own. Those who regard "object-oriented" as a phrase for fetish worship will have to learn how to speak Visual Basic as well as the language of objects.

Encapsulation

You can think of *encapsulation* as bringing objects to life by bundling implementation details. In this way, objects can interact by calling each other's methods, setting each other's properties, and sending each other messages. The use of encapsulated objects creates appropriate levels of "coupling," or connection, between parts of a program. This leads naturally to the *hiding* of implementation details.

An object hides its implementation details by only allowing access through controlled routines ("access procedures"). All internal procedures and variables ("properties") are protected in scope and cannot be accessed or manipulated from outside the object. Hiding implementation details helps in the creation of modular, maintainable, and reusable code.

VB5 makes it easy to create complex encapsulated objects. As I've noted before, VB forms are objects with an interface that is visible on the screen. Class modules make it easy to create objects that do not have visible components, and Property procedures make it easy to create access routines to objects.

Inheritance

Inheritance means being able to create a new object that is based on an existing object. The new object's events, properties, and methods are derived from those of the original object.

Inheritance allows you to construct classes in a hierarchical fashion. For example, *programmer* is a subclass of *thinking person* is a subclass of *person* — in general, most objects of the class programmer have inherited many characteristics of the object person, such as eyes, ears, kidneys, and so on. Or, a text box is a descendant of a generalized class that you can think of as a windowing control.

Unfortunately, VB only allows one level of inheritance within a project: Dim X As New *object*. After that, you can't really inherit further from X, meaning that it's not really possible to create user-defined classes of descendant objects. However, you can obtain some of the advantages of inheritance by adding a wrapper to existing objects, and creating a new object that is an extended version of the original. This process — which is sometimes called *delegation* — will be explained later in the chapter in the section "Extending an Existing Control."

You can create your own ActiveX controls in Visual Basic 5 (see Part VI, "Creating ActiveX Controls"). There is nothing to stop you from creating a control based on an existing control — meaning that the new control inherits from the old one. You can iterate this process as many times as you'd like.

It's particularly important to understand the concepts and implementation of objects and classes when you start rolling your own controls.

Polymorphism

Polymorphism means that objects know what appropriate actions to take, provided they are sent a message they can understand. The point is that different objects may take different actions when sent the same message because they implement inherited methods differently.

If you tell ten different programmer objects to create a procedure that does X — the Programmer.GoCodeX method — you will most likely get ten different implementations of X. If you have Boat, Truck, and Airplane objects, they should all know what to do with a SteerRight method call. SteerRight produces a different action for each of the objects depending on the implementation of the method: Boats steer by moving the rudder, trucks by moving the wheels, and so on.

In most OOP languages, polymorphism is implemented using inheritance. For example, the hypothetical Boat, Truck, and Airplane classes inherit the SteerRight method from their common hypothetical ancestor, the Vehicle class. Each class overrides the template SteerRight method that is inherited from the ancestor Vehicle class and adds its own implementation details.

Visual Basic, on the other hand, does not implement polymorphism via inheritance. Instead, polymorphism is implemented through multiple exposed ActiveX control *interfaces*. (A control's interface is its exposed properties and methods.)

To take full advantage of OOP in Visual Basic, expect to create and use hierarchies of ActiveX controls.

Early and Late Binding

Early binding means that the VB compiler knows what object is being called, and can check the object's type library to see if members that are invoked are present in that object. You can early bind objects by declaring them using a specific class:

```
Dim X As Vehicle  'Early Binding
```

Late binding means that the VB compiler will not be able to determine until runtime what the object is. This requires the inclusion of more code, to check that the invoked members actually exist, and is slower, because the actual checking must be done at runtime. You can late bind objects by declaring them As Object:

```
Dim X As Object   'Late Binding
```

Messaging Systems

In a conventional procedural program, logic is controlled with flow control statements: If, Do While, and so forth. The implication is that the entire logic of the program can be conceptualized and put into concrete statements at the time of program design, something that may not always be true. In particular, it will often be false in applications designed to model the dynamics of change in the real world.

In object-oriented programming, messages sent to the objects determine flow control. This is a more flexible way to simulate real-world conditions. Objects respond to messages sent to them and can initiate messages to other objects. In VB, to send a message to an object, you call a method of the object.

In Version 5, you can now subclass the messages being sent to a form or control.

Subclassing is a technique that allows you to intercept the message stream and write your own code to extend or modify the behavior of the object receiving the messages. (The term subclassing is also sometimes used to describe the process of deriving one class from another.)

To subclass a message stream, you must use a pointer to a function, called a *function pointer*, which is implemented using the AddressOf keyword. The user-defined function that is specified when using the AddressOf keyword is termed a *callback*, or *callback function*.

For some examples of implementing callback functions and windows subclassing, see Chapter 11, "The Win32 Software Development Kit (SDK), the Win32 API, and the Windows Messaging System."

Visual Basic Version 5 and OOP

Visual Basic — like most languages in commercial use — can be used in a more or less objected-oriented fashion, depending on application design and development style. In what ways, exactly, can VB best be used as an OOP programming language?

Visual Basic fully supports object encapsulation. Forms are encapsulated objects with windowing capabilities; class modules are encapsulated objects that don't support windowing. You can easily use Property procedures to appropriately hide property implementations from external objects.

Forms As Classes

As you've probably surmised, the default form — Form1 — created by a Visual Basic project is actually an instance of a class. To verify this, open a Standard Exe project, and add the following code to the click event of Form1:

```
Private Sub Form_Click()
   Dim newForm As New Form1
   newForm.Show
End Sub
```

When you run the project, if you click on the instance of Form1 that VB created for you by default, another — identical — instance of Form1 will be displayed. An object variable declared As New contains Nothing until the variable is used, at which point VB creates an instance of the object, based on the declared class. In the example

```
Dim newForm As New Form1
```

the class is Form1.

What's happening here is that Visual Basic creates a hidden global object variable for each form class. You can think of it as if VB had added the following invisible line of code to your project:

```
Public Form1 As New Form1
```

When you implicitly create an instance of Form1, either by designating Form1 as the startup object, or by invoking Form1's Show method, you're in fact referring to this hidden global object variable.

The Forms collection — explained later in this chapter in the section "Collection Objects" — keeps track of each hidden form class in a project. You can use this collection to track and control the forms in your project.

Referencing Objects

VB lets you derive a new object from an existing object using the New keyword. This constitutes one level of inheritance, but is insufficient to let the programmer truly benefit from working with extended class hierarchies. However, you can create ActiveX controls with as many levels of inheritance as you'd like.

The keyword As lets you declare a variable as an object (very vague) or as a specific (more precise). (For the implications of the difference, see "Early and Late Binding" earlier in this chapter.) The keyword As has a very special meaning when combined with the keyword New: Declare a variable of the type indicated, and create an instance of it in memory the first time it is referenced.

Thus,

```
Dim MyForm As Form1
```

is quite different from

```
Dim MyForm As New Form1
```

In the first case, a reference to the object is created, but no new object is actually being instanced. More than one object variable can refer to the same object. Because these variables are references to (rather than copies of) the object, any change in the underlying object is reflected in all variables that refer to it.

In the second case, when you use the New keyword in the Dim statement (or in a Set statement), an instance of the object is created. The new instance is not loaded into memory until the first reference is made to it, or to one of its object's members.

I use the term "instance" many times in this chapter, and it can be confusing. Think of "instance" as a verb synonymous with "create."

This confusion primarily arises because classes must be explicitly instanced before they can be referenced:

```
Dim x As New clsShips
```

whereas forms can be either explicitly or implicitly instanced ("created"). Explicit form instancing works exactly like class instancing:

```
Dim X As New Form1
```

Implicit form instancing occurs when you load a form using its Show method or when VB starts a new project with Form1. In this case, what is being instanced is still a copy of an internal form object; it's just that some of the mechanics are hidden from you. (See the discussion in the previous section, "Forms As Classes.")

With a default project set to StartUp from Sub Main, if you try to assign a value to an object reference:

```
Option Explicit
Dim x As Form1

Public Sub Main()
   x.Caption = "Long live OOP!"
   x.Show
End Sub
```

you'll get runtime error 91, "Object variable or With block variable not set," even if there is a Form1 in your project. On the other hand, if x is used as a new instance of Form1:

```
Option Explicit
Dim x As New Form1

Public Sub Main()
   x.Caption = "Long live OOP!"
   x.Show
End Sub
```

a copy of Form1, complete with the "Long live OOP!" caption, happily loads without error.

You can use the Set statement to create variables that refer to objects. For example,

```
Set X = Form1
```

assigns the Form1 object to the variable X. On the other hand,

```
Set X = New Form1
```

assigns a new instance of Form1 to X, and implicitly creates it.

Generally, the Dim keyword is used with objects that can be early bound, and the Set statement with objects that have to be late bound.

One feature that makes VB "feel" object-oriented is the possibility of using built-in objects from within VB. You can access properties and methods of these built-in objects. Examples of built-in objects include the App (Application) object, the Screen object, the Printer object, and the VBIDE object (the current instance of the VB IDE). These objects are used in what can only be described as a very OOP style.

Although it can be very handy to access properties of, for example, the App object (see the examples later in this chapter), the importance of this pales next to the OOP significance of OLE and ActiveX.

You can use VB to create OLE objects that expose methods to any application capable of using external OLE server methods. You can also use exposed OLE methods of server applications from within VB. And, finally, with Version 5 of VB, you can create ActiveX controls.

The implication of the integration of OLE into Windows (and VB's ability to easily create server applications and ActiveX controls) is that Windows — and, in some cases, a network — itself has become a kind of super-object environment. In effect, ActiveX is an overall implementation of object-orientation that is not language dependent, and runs across applications.

VB server applications can expose methods and properties to OLE clients and VB can use the exposed methods of any OLE server application.

ActiveX controls can be used privately within a project. They can be registered on a system, and used in other VB5 projects — or in any development environment capable of providing a container for ActiveX controls. ActiveX controls created in VB can even be deployed on the Web; you can use tools such as the ActiveX Control Pad to manipulate their interface and create HTML pages using them.

As I've hinted already, you can manipulate VB to exhibit more OOP behavior than it contains naturally, particularly in the areas of inheritance and polymorphism. Doing this is a matter of performing a few tricks, and, more importantly, establishing and keeping to programming standards. I'll show you how to do so later in this chapter in the sections entitled "Class and Class Modules" and "Extending an Existing Control."

The techniques you learn in this chapter will prove particularly relevant to the process of create ActiveX controls.

Classes and Class Modules

A *class* is the template from which an object is made. In other words, a class is an idea or construct, while the related object is an implementation, or instance, of the idea.

For example, a form is an object that is windowing. You can give each form its own class name — for example, Form1, or, perhaps more intelligibly, frmClassDemo, by setting the .Name property of the form object. Each form, be it of the class Form1 or frmClassDemo, is based on a generic form class that Visual Basic implements for you. The generic form class has all kinds of familiar properties (for instance, Caption and BackColor) and methods (for example, Show and Line). As you know, you can expand tremendously on the generic form class when you create your own form classes (and form objects based on those classes).

Similarly, a class module is a nonwindowing construct that is used as a template for objects that are instances of the class. The properties and methods of a class (including a form-based class) are collectively referred to as *members*. You get to invent the idea behind the class. This means that you can have any properties and methods you'd like as implementations of the class concept in your class module. Forms, and controls, come with a number of predefined events — for example, the form Load and Click events.

In contrast, all class modules have only two events: Initialize and Terminate. You can fire events in class modules using the RaiseEvents statement. These events can be added to the event-handling framework of an object by using the WithEvents keyword. For an example of firing a custom event in a class module, and responding to it in a form module, see "Firing Custom Events" in Chapter 13, "Secrets of Good Programming Practice."

Class Module Events

A class module's Initialize event is fired when an application creates an instance of a class. (For that matter, a form's Initialize event is fired in the same way.) You do this *indirectly* by referring to a property of an instance of a class (or a form) in your code. For example, if you name a class module MyClass and give it a Public property by declaring a public variable Prop (as explained in Chapter 13), you could add code to the class Initialize event to test when it was fired:

```
Option Explicit
Public Prop As String

Private Sub Class_Initialize()
   MsgBox "I've been fired!"
End Sub
```

To display the "I've been fired!" message box, reference an instance of MyClass elsewhere in your project, for example, from Form1's click event:

```
Private Sub Form_Click()
   Dim X As New MyClass
   X.Prop = "Howdy-doody!"
End Sub
```

A class module's (or a form's) Terminate event is fired when all references to an instance of the class are removed from memory when all the variables that refer to the object are set to Nothing, or when the last reference to the object falls out of scope. As an example, take the MyClass class, and add code to show a message box in its terminate event:

The CreateObject Function

If you are creating an instance of an OLE automation object, you can use an indirect reference, provided that the object's interface has been added to your project using the References dialog. The other option is to directly use the CreateObject function:

```
Dim X As Object
Set X =
CreateObject("MyClass")
```

To create a class that can be instanced as an OLE automation object, you need to set the class module's Instancing property so that it is creatable. See the discussion that follows and Part V of this book, "Using ActiveX," for additional details.

```
Option Explicit
Public Prop As String

Private Sub Class_Initialize()
   MsgBox "I've been fired!"
End Sub

Private Sub Class_Terminate()
   MsgBox Prop, vbInformation, "Dylan Thomas: 1952"
End Sub
```

If you add a form-level variable of type MyClass to Form1, and indirectly instance the new class in Form1's load event, you'll still get the "I've been fired!" message box as the instance is initialized and before Form1 is displayed (as shown in Figure 14-1):

```
Option Explicit
Dim X As New MyClass

Private Sub Form_Load()
   X.Prop = "Do not go gentle into that good night!"
End Sub
```

Figure 14-1: The instanced class's Initialize event is fired by an indirect reference from Form1's load event.

To fire the instance of the class's Terminate event, set the variable referring to the instance equal to Nothing. For example, in a command button's click event,

```
Private Sub Command1_Click()
   Set X = Nothing
End Sub
```

setting the instance of the class variable to Nothing fires the class's Terminate event, as shown in Figure 14-2.

Class Module Properties

Class modules have either one or two intrinsic properties, depending on the kind of project the class module is in, as I'll explain in a moment. That makes only two events and one or two ready-made properties. Any methods? Nope. You can give a class as many custom methods as you like, but there are none that come prebuilt. You can think of prebuilt properties, methods, and events as belonging to the class's parent; in this sense all forms have a Show method because the root form class, cloaked deep within VB, has a Show method.

Falling Out of Scope

You can explicitly trigger a class variable's terminate event by assigning Nothing to the variable. In addition, the terminate event is triggered when the last reference to the instance of the class falls out of scope. This sounds like a line from some kind of OOP lonely hearts Country & Western song — "I'll be a cowboy until the last reference falls out of scope" — but, what does it mean? If you instance X as class of type MyClass at the global (project) level, X stays in scope as long as the project runs; if X is declared at the form level, it stays in scope as long as the form is loaded in memory (and is triggered by the form being unloaded); if X is declared local to a procedure, the terminate event is triggered when the procedure is done. Dare I say "for instance," in the preceding example, if X is declared in the form load event procedure rather than at the form level, like so

```
Option Explicit

Private Sub Form_Load()
    Dim X As New MyClass
    X.Prop = "Do not go gentle into that good night!"
End Sub
```

the class's initialize and terminate events are fired one right after the other, both before Form1 loads.

Figure 14-2: You can trigger the instance of the class's Terminate event by setting its variable reference to Nothing.

The one property that all class modules have is Name, which means the name of the class. Class modules have — or do not have — an Instancing property depending on the kind of project that they are in, as shown in Table 14-1. The Instancing property is used to specify whether instances of a class can be created outside a project, as I'll explain further in a moment.

Table 14-1 Project Types and Class Module Instancing Property Values

Project Type	*Does a class module in this type of project have an Instancing property?*	*Possible values for the class module's Instancing property*
Standard EXE	No	N/A
ActiveX EXE	Yes	1 - Private
		2 - PublicNotCreatable
		3 - SingleUse
		4 - GlobalSingleUse
		5 - MultiUse
		6 - GlobalMultiUse
ActiveX DLL	Yes	1 - Private
		2 - PublicNotCreatable
		5 - MultiUse
		6 - GlobalMultiUse
AddIn	Yes	1 - Private
		2 - PublicNotCreatable
		3 - SingleUse
		4 - GlobalSingleUse
		5 - MultiUse
		6 - GlobalMultiUse
ActiveX Control	Yes	1 - Private
		2 - PublicNotCreatable
ActiveX Document DLL	Yes	1 - Private
		2 - PublicNotCreatable
		5 - MultiUse
		6 - GlobalMultiUse
ActiveX Document EXE	Yes	1 - Private
		2 - PublicNotCreatable
		3 - SingleUse
		4 - GlobalSingleUse
		5 - MultiUse
		6 - GlobalMultiUse

You can set the Name and Instancing properties at design time in the Properties window, as shown in Figure 14-3 (provided that the project types support class module instancing).

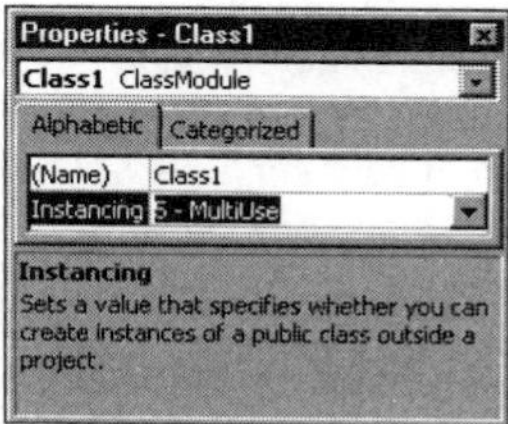

Figure 14-3: You can use the Properties window to set intrinsic class module properties at design time.

The Instancing Property determines whether a class can be instanced from outside the current project.

Class modules that are not externally creatable — such as those in ActiveX control projects, which do not allow external creation — must be created using mechanisms explicitly provided within the project.

Table 14-2 shows the meanings of the six possible settings for a class module's Instancing property.

Table 14-2 Settings for the Instancing Property of a Class Module

Setting	*Meaning*
1 - Private	The class module is private (local in scope) to the project. It cannot be externally created. Other applications aren't allowed access to type library information about the class, and cannot create instances of it. Private objects are only for use within your application or component.
2 - PublicNotCreatable	Not externally creatable, but can be used externally once it has been created by the application or component.
3 - SingleUse	Allows other applications to create objects based on the class, but every object of this class that a client creates starts a new instance of your server.
4 - GlobalSingleUse	Similar to SingleUse, except that properties and methods of the class can be invoked as if they were simply global functions.

(continued)

Table 14-2 (Continued)

Setting	*Meaning*
5 - MultiUse	Allows other applications to create objects based on the class. One instance of your application can provide any number of objects created in this fashion, regardless of how many applications request them. If your server is not running when the class object is created, the server is started.
6 - GlobalMultiUse	Similar to MultiUse, with one addition: Properties and methods of the class can be invoked as if they were simply global functions. It's not necessary to explicitly create an instance of the class first, because one will automatically be created.

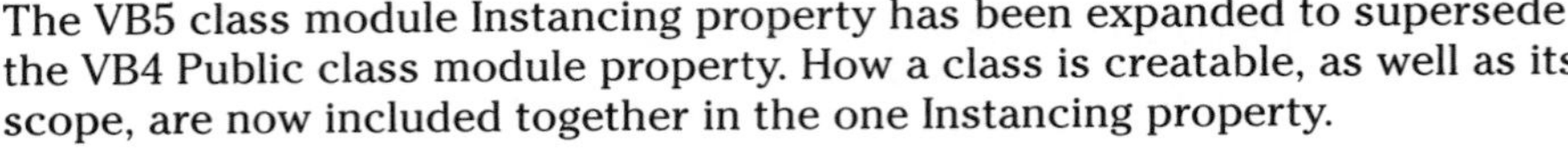

The VB5 class module Instancing property has been expanded to supersede the VB4 Public class module property. How a class is creatable, as well as its scope, are now included together in the one Instancing property.

When a class is creatable, you can use the techniques discussed earlier in this chapter to create instances of the class from other applications. This means creating the instance *explicitly*, by using the CreateObject function. For example:

```
Set MyInstance = CreateObject("MyProject.MyClass")
```

Alternatively, you can *implicitly* use the Dim statement with the As New keywords:

```
Dim MyInstance As New MyClass
```

OLE class module properties are, of course, covered further in Part V of this book.

Chapter 13 demonstrated how to add properties to forms. You add properties to class modules in the same ways:

- Properties that can be accessed from outside the module can be declared as public variables at the module level.
- Properties that are intended to be used only within a module are declared as private variables at the module level.
- You can write Property Get and Property Let procedures to provide external access to properties in which further code is executed, perhaps for validation. You can use property procedures to protect internal variables, and to implement read-only properties.

Of course, once a property has been added to a class module it is read to, or written from, in the normal fashion using an instance variable for the class, for example:

```
X.MyProperty = "Rattlesnake"
EmployeeList(I) = X.MyProperty
```

Property Set Procedures

Property Set procedures behave exactly like Property Let procedures, except that Property Set is used to set a reference to an object (Property Let is used to set a value).

As with Property Let, if you want to be able to read the property as well as write it, Property Set must be paired with a Property Get procedure.

Property Let procedures execute procedure code whenever a value is assigned to the property, whereas Property Set procedures execute procedure code whenever a user sets an object reference.

As an example, the following Property Set procedure changes the caption of the form that is passed as an argument to the procedure:

```
Public Property Set ChangeForm(frm As Object)
   frm.Caption = "Bulgy Bears are marshals of the Lists!"
End Property
```

Here's how you might invoke the Property Set procedure (with results as shown in Figure 14-4):

```
Option Explicit
Public X As New MyClass

Public Sub Main()
   Dim Z As New Form1
   Set X.ChangeForm = Z
   Z.Show
End Sub
```

Figure 14-4: You can use Property Set procedures to change the properties, such as Form.Caption, of referenced objects.

Note that Set X.ChangeForm = Z both instances X, the class, and invokes the ChangeForm Property Set procedure with Z (an instance of Form1) as the argument.

Class Modules and User-Defined Types

There is a natural correspondence between VB class modules and user-defined types (UDTs). Both are used to group user-defined, structured data.

It's hard to imagine any kind of complex procedurally oriented structured code that doesn't make extensive use of UDTs. (Indeed, another term for "user-defined type" is "user-defined structure.") However, UDTs don't work very well with VB5's OOP features. For example, you can't make a collection out of variables of a user-defined type. (Collections of objects are discussed later in this chapter.) Of course, you *can* do lots of things with UDTs — including manipulate them in arrays and include function pointers as UDT values — and I wouldn't expect them to vanish from VB any time soon. However, to better practice the VB OOP model, you should get in the habit of using class modules rather than UDTs. (The allergic reaction of classes to user-defined types is sufficiently strong that if you try to define a public UDT within a form, or class, module, you'll get a runtime error.)

The correspondence is one to one: The variables that make up the parts of a user-defined type become the public properties of a class module. For example, the UDT:

```
Public Type TNarnianShip
   Captain As String
   CrewNum As Integer
   Destination As Variant
   WaterBarrels As Long
End Type
```

could be accessed:

```
Dim DawnTreader As TNarnianShip
DawnTreader.Captain = "Prince Caspian"
```

Using a class module (named clsNarnianShip) rather than a structure, public properties are defined:

```
Option Explicit
Public Captain As String
Public CrewNum As Integer
Public Destination As Variant
Public WaterBarrels As Long
```

The properties of an instance of the class are accessed normally:

```
Dim DawnTreader As New clsNarnianShip
DawnTreader.Captain = "Prince Caspian"
```

An important difference between UDTs and instances of classes is that you can assign a class instance to a variant variable, which you can then use to reference the class:

```
Dim Q As Variant
...
Set Q = DawnTreader
Form1.Caption = Q.Captain
...
```

Collection Objects

A *collection object* provides a way to refer to, and manipulate, related objects. Some collections are built into VB. In addition, you can define your own collections of class instances. Metaphorically, user-defined collections are to class instances as arrays are to UDTs.

VB's predefined collections include

- Controls: all the controls on a form
- Forms: all the forms in a project
- Printers: all available printers

In addition, certain other objects contain predefined collections. For example, the VBE object is the root object that contains all other objects and collections included in Visual Basic for Applications. You can use the collections of the VBE object to access

- Projects, using the VBProjects collection
- Windows, using the Windows collection
- Code editing windows, using the CodePanes collection
- Command bars, using the CommandBars collection

Another important example is the VBIDE object — representing an instance of the Visual Basic IDE — which includes various collections that are useful for creating add-ins (see Chapter 29, "Creating a VB Add-In"). An additional example is the ImageList control, which contains a ListImage collection (see Chapter 8, "Windows User Interface Controls").

You can iterate collections by using the For Each...Next statement. Alternatively, you can use the collection's .Count property to cycle through the items in a collection by using the item's index, but this can be slightly confusing because many predefined collections are zero-based (for example, For x = 0 to Collection.Count - 1) for reasons of backwards compatibility, while user-defined collections are one-based (For x = 1 to Collection.Count). Also, if you add or delete items while iterating, the index and count will be changed, most likely causing a loop error. In a word, it's often better to use For Each...Next.

A collection expands and contracts automatically; you can think of it as an array that takes care of its own redimensioning. You can access items in a collection by index, as mentioned, but this can take some care because indices can change when you remove or add items. You can also locate items by a string key, if one was assigned when the item was added. Although you can control where an item is added to a collection — and, for that matter, sort a collection — by default an item is added at the end of a collection, and collections are unsorted.

Collections have three methods: Add, Item, and Remove. (See Table 14-3.)

Table 14-3 Collection Object Methods

Method	*Syntax*
Add	Collection.Add(*item*,*key*,*before*,*after*)
Item	Collection.Item(*index*)
Remove	Collection.Remove *index*

The Add and Remove methods are used to — you guessed it — add and remove members from the collection. *Key*, *before,* and *after* are optional arguments. *Key* specifies a unique string that you can use instead of the member's index to access a specific member.

You can specify *before* or *after*, but not both. The *before* or *after* argument indicates the placement of the member by index number or key identifying string of the succeeding, or preceding, member, respectively.

You use the Item method to return a specific member, either by index number or unique key value. If the value provided for the index doesn't match an existing collection member, a runtime error is triggered.

Because Item is the default method for a collection object, the following two lines of code are equivalent:

```
MsgBox Forms(1).Caption
MsgBox Forms.Item(1).Caption
```

As mentioned, it's better to use For Each...Next than the Count property to gain access to all members in a collection. Many of the predefined collections run from 0 to Count-1; Forms(0) is actually the first item in the forms collection.

Using the forms and controls collections, you can display the names of all loaded forms, and all controls on each form, in a list box, as shown in Figure 14-5. (The sample code is from a project saved on the CD-ROM as ***Collect.Vbp***.)

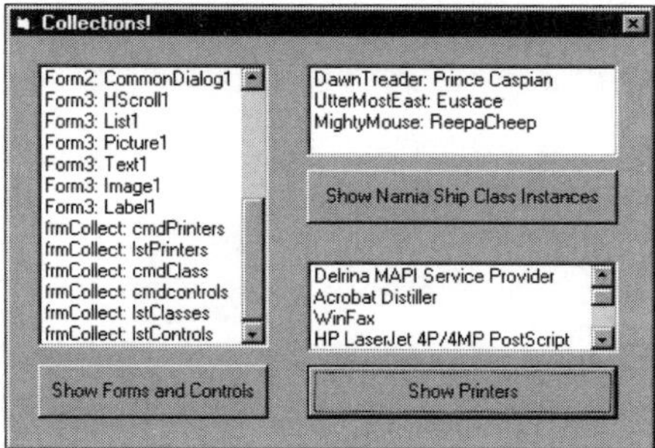

Figure 14-5: You can use the forms collection to cycle through loaded forms, the controls collection to cycle through controls on a form, the printers collection to cycle through available printer devices, and a user-defined collection to cycle through its members.

```
Private Sub cmdcontrols_Click()
   Dim obj As Object, ctl As Control
   lstControls.Clear
   For Each obj In Forms
      For Each ctl In obj.Controls
         lstControls.AddItem obj.Name & ": " & ctl.Name
      Next ctl
   Next obj
End Sub
```

In pretty much the same way, you can display all available printer devices (see Figure 14-5):

```
Private Sub cmdPrinters_Click()
   Dim prt As Printer
   For Each prt In Printers
      lstPrinters.AddItem prt.DeviceName
   Next prt
End Sub
```

To cycle through (and display) a user-defined collection, you first need to define the collection. Using the clsNarniaShip class module, Listing 14-1 shows the code — in the sample project's Sub Main — that defines three classes based on it, and creates a collection of the classes:

Listing 14-1: Creating a collection of classes

```
Option Explicit
Public DawnTreader As New clsNarniaShip
Public UtterMostEast As New clsNarniaShip
Public MightyMouse As New clsNarniaShip
Public Ship As New Collection
```

```
Public Sub Main()
   'Create a collection
   With Ship
      .Add DawnTreader
      .Add UtterMostEast
      .Add MightyMouse
   End With
   'Add Class property values and instance classes
   DawnTreader.Name = "DawnTreader"
   UtterMostEast.Name = "UtterMostEast"
   MightyMouse.Name = "MightyMouse"
   DawnTreader.Captain = "Prince Caspian"
   UtterMostEast.Captain = "Eustace"
   MightyMouse.Captain = "ReepaCheep"
```

You'd display the members of the Ship collection in a list box (see Figure 14-5) like so:

```
Private Sub cmdClass_Click()
   Dim Member As Variant
   lstClasses.Clear
   For Each Member In Ship
      lstClasses.AddItem Member.Name + ": " + Member.Captain
   Next Member
End Sub
```

This demonstration shows how you can use the forms collection to cycle through loaded forms, the controls collection to cycle through controls on a form, and the printers collection to cycle through available printer devices. Finally, you can cycle through the members of a user-defined collection.

Is It a Collection?

Here's another collection, based around a class named clsShip with a .CaptainName property (the project is saved on the companion CD-ROM as ***IsItCol.Vbp***):

```
Option Explicit
Public Enterprise As New clsShip
Public Voyager As New clsShip
Public OldEnterprise As New clsShip
Public Endurance As New clsShip
Public Surprise As New clsShip
Public Peaquod As New clsShip
Public Submarine As New clsShip
Public Bounty As New clsShip
Public Ships As New Collection

Public Sub Main()
   Dim Member As Variant
   Enterprise.CaptainName = "Picard"
   Voyager.CaptainName = "Janeway"
```

```
    OldEnterprise.CaptainName = "Kirk, James T."
    Endurance.CaptainName = "Shackleton"
    Surprise.CaptainName = "Aubrey"
    Peaquod.CaptainName = "Ahab"
    Submarine.CaptainName = "Little Nemo"
    Bounty.CaptainName = "Bligh"
    With Ships
       .Add Enterprise
       .Add Voyager
       .Add OldEnterprise
       .Add Endurance
       .Add Surprise
       .Add Peaquod
       .Add Submarine
       .Add Bounty
    End With

    For Each Member In Ships
       Form1.lstCaps.AddItem Member.CaptainName
    Next Member
    Form1.Show
End Sub
```

The code loads the .CaptainName property into a list box that has its Sorted property set to True (see Figure 14-6). Using a sorted list box is often a very convenient way to sort collection items. Of course, it's perfectly possible to write code that uses conventional sorting algorithms to sort collections based on their indices.

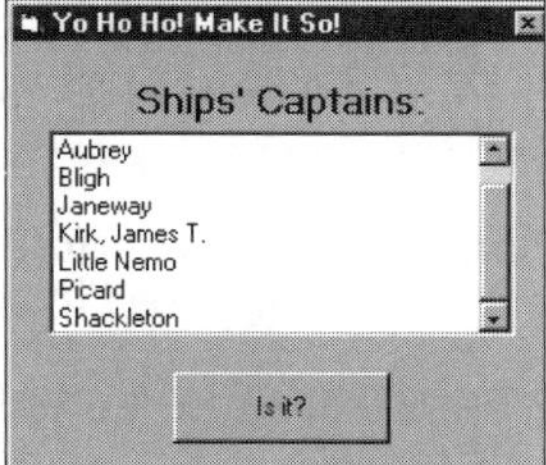

Figure 14-6: A sorted list box displays the CaptainName properties of the items in the Ships collection.

How can you verify that an object is a user-defined collection as opposed to some other sort of object with collection-like characteristics, such as a list box? The following function, called from the "Is it?" button in the ***IsItCol.Vbp*** project, does the trick by checking whether any of the collection properties or methods generate an error:

```
Private Function IsItACollection(obj As Object) As Boolean
   Dim Var As Variant
   IsItACollection = True
   With obj
      On Error GoTo Fail
      .Add .Count
      Var = .Item(.Count)
      For Each Var In obj
      Next
      .Remove .Count
   End With
Exit Function
Fail:
IsItACollection = False
End Function
```

If you pass the Ships collection to this function as an argument, it is a collection, all right; a list box is not. It's of interest as an illustration of what, exactly, constitutes a user-defined collection.

A Stack Using Class Instances and a Collection

In the preceding chapter, I showed you how to implement a stack using a dynamic array to keep track of the cursor state. (See the section "Implementing a Stack as an Array.") In this example, I'll demonstrate how to implement a stack using a class instance and a collection. Although I could, once again, keep track of cursor states with the stack, for the sake of variety, I'll use a stack to track a form's .BackColor property. You could use the Push and Pop methods of the generic stack class module used in this project — the class module is ***Stack.Cls*** and the project ***ColorStk.Vbp*** — in any situation calling for a stack.

To set up this project, I used a ShowColor common dialog control to allow the user to set a new .BackColor property value for the form (see Figure 14-7).

After setting the BackColor property, the procedure calls the clsStack Push method to add the old color to the end of the stack:

```
Private Sub cmdChange_Click()
   Dim TmpColor As Long
   CommonDialog1.Flags = cdlCCRGBInit + _
      cdlCCPreventFullOpen
   CommonDialog1.CancelError = True
   On Error GoTo ErrHandle
   TmpColor = frmColorStack.BackColor
   CommonDialog1.Color = TmpColor
   CommonDialog1.ShowColor
   frmColorStack.BackColor = CommonDialog1.Color
   On Error GoTo 0
   x.Push TmpColor
   Exit Sub
ErrHandle:
   'Canceled - do nothing
End Sub
```

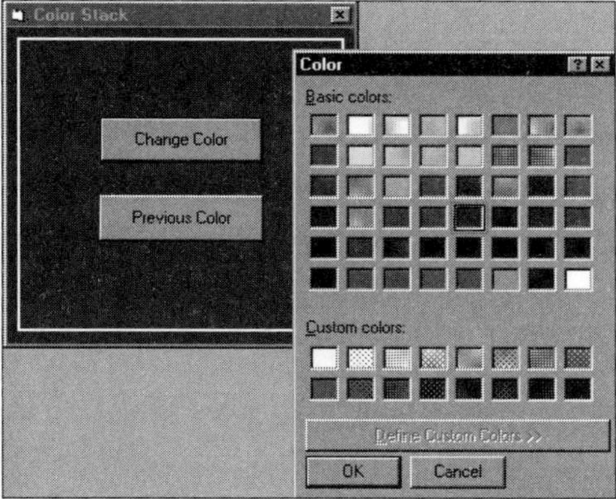

Figure 14-7: The ColorStack application shows how to implement a stack using a collection and an instance of a class.

Make sure to instance a class variable based on the class module so that you can call the class methods and properties:

```
Dim x As New clsStack
```

The procedure that sets the form's .BackColor property back to its last value "pops" the stack:

```
Private Sub cmdPrev_Click()
   If x.Count >= 1 Then
      frmColorStack.BackColor = x.Pop
   Else
      MsgBox "I'm back at the beginning!"
   End If
End Sub
```

It also uses the class instance .Count property so as not to go back past the beginning of the stack. Listing 14-2 shows the contents of the clsStack class module:

Listing 14-2: "Pushing" and "popping" a class collection stack

```
Option Explicit
Private ColorStack As New Collection

Public Sub Push(Var As Variant)
   ColorStack.Add Var
End Sub

Public Function Pop() As Variant
   With ColorStack
      If .Count Then
         Pop = ColorStack(.Count)
         .Remove .Count
      End If
```

```
   End With
End Function

Property Get Count() As Variant
   Count = ColorStack.Count
End Property
```

You can see that this implementation is exceedingly simple. Push merely adds the passed argument to the ColorStack collection. Pop returns the current top (last added) item in the ColorStack collection, and then removes it from the collection. The Count property returns the current collection, or stack, size.

The Application Object

You access the Application object — termed the App object — by using the App keyword. Although the App object has no events or methods, it has quite a few properties that are useful for finding out, or specifying, information about the currently running application.

Chapter 11 explained how to use the App object's descriptive properties — such as FileDescription and LegalCopyright — to automatically fill in the labels on a project About box (see the section "An About Box that Displays System Information"). Here, I'll cover the App object's Path and PrevInstance properties.

App.Path

App.Path returns the current application path (the directory path from which the current instance of the application was launched). For example, the compiled sample program ***AppPath.Exe*** copies all the files in the directory where it is located into a FileListBox control (see Figure 14-8). It takes only two lines of code to copy the files from the application's path to the FileListBox control and copy the current path to the form's caption:

```
File1.Path = App.Path
Form1.Caption = App.Path
```

App.PrevInstance

You can easily use App.PrevInstance to see whether a previous instance of an application is running, and to prevent multiple copies of an application from running simultaneously, if desired:

```
Private Sub Form_Load()
   If App.PrevInstance Then
      MsgBox "One copy at a time, greedy!"
      End
   Else
      MsgBox "No previous instance running!"
   End If
End Sub
```

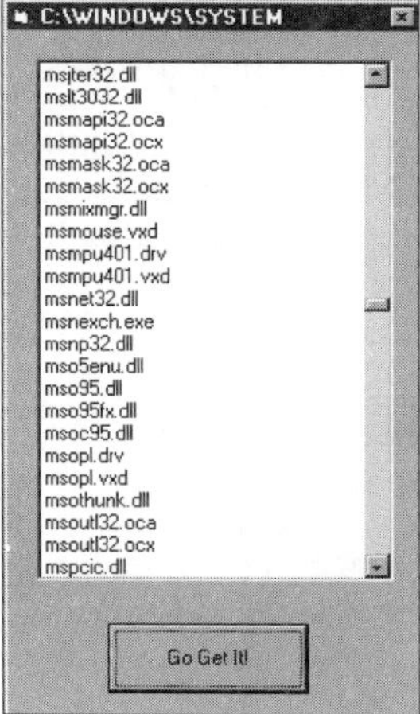

Figure 14-8: You can use the App object's .Path property to display all files on the application path.

To test this, you should compile the program; otherwise, the PrevInstance property won't count design time copies running in multiple VBIDE instances as previous instances. Once it has been compiled, the AppPath application will use the PrevInstance property of the App object to detect if other instances of itself are running, as shown in Figure 14-9.

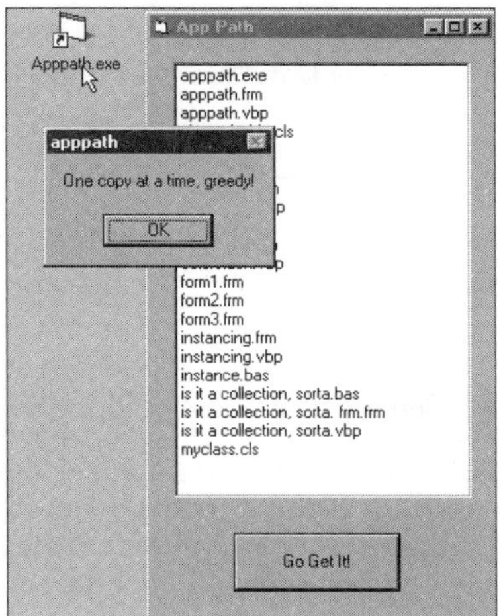

Figure 14-9: The App object's PrevInstance property can detect whether a previous instance of your application is running!

The Class Builder Utility

The Class Builder Utility is a Visual Basic add-in that helps you create and manage collections and classes. If you enabled the Class Builder add-in by checking the appropriate box in the Add-In Manager, a Class Builder Utility item will appear on the Add-Ins menu. When you choose this item, you'll see a dialog like the one shown in Figure 14-10.

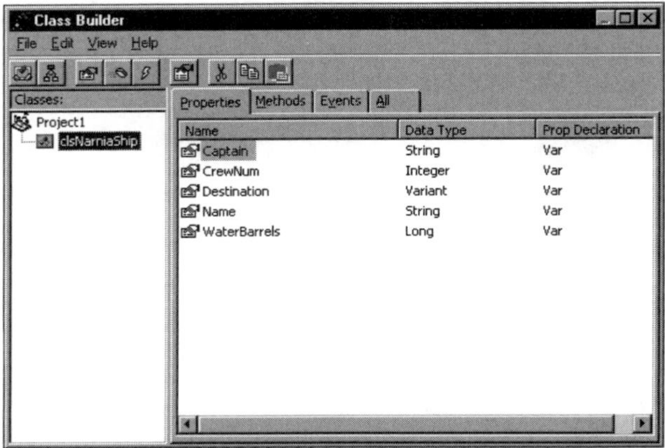

Figure 14-10: The Class Builder Utility is a VB add-in that you can use to create and manage project classes and collections.

Using the Class Builder Utility, you can generate program code that will:

- Create a new class
- Set class module properties (see the section "Class Module Properties" earlier in this chapter)
- Add properties, methods, and events to a class
- Create a new collection
- Define class and collection creation attributes

Extending an Existing Control

One of the great pleasures of working in a truly OOP language is that you can derive a new control from an existing control. This means that the new control inherits properties, events, and methods from an existing control. You can then, in a process sometimes called *subclassing*, add your own user-defined properties, events, and methods to the new control. A benefit of doing things this way is that you don't have to reinvent the wheel (or the text box, or whatever); your new control already has the functionality of its parent ready to roll. In Part VI, I'll show you how to derive a new control from an existing control.

In the meantime, it's easy to include the functionality of an existing control in a class module that you can then extend with user-defined properties and methods, without creating a whole new control. This process has been called *delegation*, although I think *wrapping* would be a more descriptive term, because the old control is wrapped along with new functionality in the class module. You should understand, however, that the wrapping cannot take place unless the class is passed an instance of the control it extends.

As with most class modules, the code a wrapping class encapsulates is completely reusable. To use the extended "control" more than once in your project, simply instance multiple copies of the class (and pass each instance a different frame control).

You will probably find this easier to understand with an example. ***Delegate.Vbp*** wraps a Frame control that has two extended methods: Stick and UnStick. These methods use the techniques introduced in Chapter 11, in the section "Locking Users Onto a Control," to lock the cursor to the frame and unlock the cursor. There are four methods in the StickyPanel class module: Create, which initializes the extended frame; Destroy, which makes it go away; Stick; and UnStick.

The StickyPanel class module has several private — and, therefore, internal — variables:

```
Option Explicit
Private rPanel As Frame, fExist As Boolean, _
   FrameRect As RECT
```

rPanel serves as a reference to the copy of the frame control that StickyPanel uses. fExist checks whether the class has already been instanced. FrameRect uses the windows RECT type to track the cursor boundaries in the .Stick method. (I've added the ***APIDec.Bas*** module from Chapter 11 to this project so that I don't have to reenter the API and type definitions.)

Before you can use the StickyFrame, you must create it. The controls built into VB automatically handle their own creation and destruction; we'll have to do this manually.

The Create function returns a Boolean indicating its success. Create must be passed a Frame — although you could easily generalize this class definition to work with all windowing controls. The function sets the internal frame reference to the passed frame control, and sets the fExist flag to True.

```
Public Function Create(ptoPanel As Frame) As Boolean
   If fExist Then Destroy 'clean old instances before making new one
   On Error GoTo CreateError
   Set rPanel = ptoPanel
   fExist = True
   Create = True
   Exit Function
CreateError:
  MsgBox Error(Err)
  Create = False
End Function
```

At the other end of the extended control's life cycle, Destroy sets the fExist flag to False and removes the internal frame reference from memory:

```
Public Sub Destroy()
   Set rPanel = Nothing
   fExist = False
End Sub
```

Stick and UnStick check whether the StickyFrame has been created and then use the logic explained in Chapter 11:

```
Public Sub Stick()
   If fExist Then
      GetWindowRect rPanel.hwnd, FrameRect
      ClipCursor FrameRect
   Else
      MsgBox "StickyPanel has not been created!"
   End If
End Sub

Public Sub UnStick()
   Dim ScreenRect As RECT, ScreenHandle As Long
   If fExist Then
      ScreenHandle = GetDesktopWindow 'Get Screen's Handle
      GetWindowRect ScreenHandle, ScreenRect
      ClipCursor ScreenRect 'Restore Cursor
   Else
      MsgBox "StickyPanel has not been created!"
   End If
End Sub
```

To use a StickyFrame control, first instance a class based on the StickyPanel class module:

```
Dim X As New StickyPanel
```

If you're going to need multiple StickyFrames, just create other class instances, for example:

```
Dim X As New StickyPanel, Dim Y As New StickyPanel, _
  Dim Z As New StickyPanel
```

Next, call the class Create method with the actual frame control that is to be extended as an argument:

```
Private Sub cmdCreat_Click()
   Dim Retval As Boolean
   Retval = X.Create(Frame1)
   If Not Retval Then
      MsgBox "Unable to create StickyPanel control!"
   End If
End Sub
```

Calling the Destroy, Stick, and UnStick methods is, well, a matter of calling them:

```
Private Sub cmdDestroy_Click()
   X.Destroy
End Sub

Private Sub cmdStick_Click()
   X.Stick
End Sub

Private Sub cmdUnStick_Click()
   X.UnStick
End Sub
```

As the demonstration application shows (see Figure 14-11), we have successfully extended a frame control in a reusable fashion.

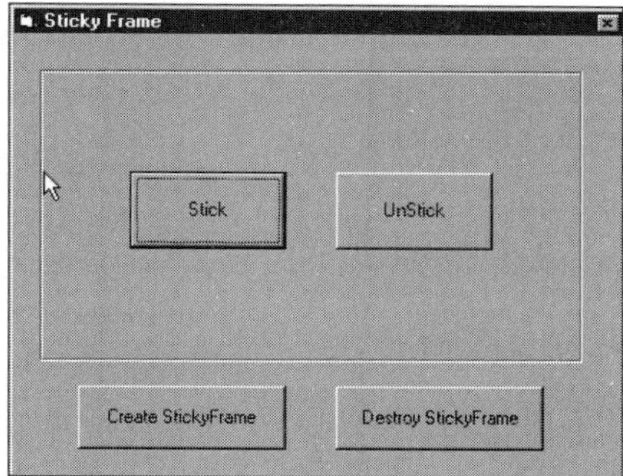

Figure 14-11: The Delegation project shows how to extend an existing control by instancing a class with Create and Destroy methods.

Summary

There are those who view life as a glass half empty and those who view it as a glass half full. Although Visual Basic Version 5 does not feature a class system that allows for easy inheritance from existing classes except in the context of ActiveX controls, it does include some very powerful features. It's really up to the developer to start thinking in a OOP fashion and make good use of the OOP facilities that do exist in VB5. This chapter showed you how to use a number of these features to create object-oriented code, including

- Writing code in reusable class modules that can be instanced repeatedly
- Creating user-defined collections of objects
- Extending existing controls with a wrapper class module

In addition, I've covered quite a few related topics, such as:

- Basic OOP concepts, including inheritance, encapsulation, polymorphism and messaging
- Instancing and creating classes and forms
- Collection objects, including the Forms collection, the Controls collection, and the Printers collection
- The App object
- Class events, properties, and methods
- The Class Builder Utility

The demonstrations developed in this chapter showed you how to

- Manipulate a user-defined collection of class objects
- Use a generic class module as a stack
- Create a class module that extends the capabilities of a control

Chapter 15

Handling Errors

This chapter covers three related topics: avoiding bugs in your programs, including error-handling code in your VB code, and debugging programs that do, unfortunately, include bugs.

In this chapter, I'll delineate the different kinds of errors. In addition, I'll show you how to:

- Use the VB error statements
- Program with the Err object
- Raise an error
- Create a user-defined error
- Use the VB debugging tools
- Use the Immediate pane
- Work with assertions

Kinds of Errors

You may encounter three kinds of errors in Visual Basic projects:

- Syntax and compile time errors
- Runtime errors
- Errors of logic and design

Where Do "Bugs" Come from?

The term "bug" was first used in the 1950s by Rear Admiral Grace Hopper, one of the authors of COBOL, to refer to a literal bug — a moth of some kind — that was causing a vacuum-tubed behemoth to malfunction. These days, of course, "bug" means any error or problem that causes a program to malfunction.

Syntax and compile time errors result from code that has been improperly constructed. In other words, syntax and compile time errors occur when program statements have failed to meet the requirements of the formal language definition (meaning that the statement cannot be processed by the compiler). Such errors are easy to spot due to the finite number of statements (and, therefore, finite number of possible errors) and the excellent syntax error checking included in the Visual Basic design time environment (see the section "Syntax and Compile Time Errors" later in this chapter).

Errors of logic and design fall off the scale on the other end. Logical errors — the classical mysterious "bugs in the machine" — can be very hard to pin down, even with the extensive debugging aids built into Visual Basic. The best cure for design flaws is prevention, meaning taking enough time to rigorously plan program architecture and user interfaces (see Chapter 13, "Secrets of Good Programming Practice").

Obviously, short of not including bugs in the first place, the best debugging tool in the universe is an analytic and sharp mind that can eliminate possibilities one by one. (In the worst case scenario, debugging comes back to the Sherlock Holmes dictum: "When you have eliminated the impossible, whatever remains, *however improbable*, must be the truth.") But modern tools can help. A section towards the end of this chapter tells you how to use VB's extensive debugging features.

It's a safe assumption that anyone who has worked with VB for a while can — with the help of automatic syntax checking — produce code that will compile properly. Similarly, most programmers have their own approach to debugging programs involving logical problems.

By the way, running a project in the VB IDE by choosing Start With Full Compile (rather than just Start) from the Run menu will serve to test all of the code in a project. Starting without full compilation may just test code that is invoked.

For example, code within a command button's click event may contain an error. If you start the program without full compilation, you won't find this out unless the button is clicked.

Runtime errors are a potentially more embarrassing issue: These are errors that tend not to show up on your machine when you test your programs. This can happen when a customer uses a function of your program that is very deep into the logic of your program and is seldom used. Eccentric operating system and hardware configurations can also cause idiosyncratic errors.

Examples of runtime errors include

- A statement that attempts to divide by zero.
- A statement that tries to load a missing file.
- A statement that tries to access an OLE server that is not present on the system.
- The infamous runtime error number 91: "Object variable or With block variable not set." This one's often caused by referencing rather than instancing an object, for example,

```
Dim x As Form1
x.Caption = "blah"
```

rather than

```
Dim x As New Form1
x.Caption = "blah"
```

- Many, many others!

Of course, some runtime errors are so severe that your program won't compile; it will give you an error message instead. These errors are usually syntax-like in nature but are a bit too subtle for the Auto Syntax Check to detect. An example would be the error number 91, caused when you attempted to assign a value to a referenced object (rather than to an object that has been instanced, and, therefore, exists). A mismatch between the number of parameters in a routine call and the routine's number of formal arguments is another example (you'll probably get the error "Argument not optional"). These runtime "errors of syntax" must, of course, be fixed before you can continue with your program. Fortunately, they're usually pretty easy to clean up.

The first appearance of a serious runtime error — meaning one that passes the compiler — is likely to occur when your most important client loads the program the first time. These errors are often caused by real-world vagaries that you simply haven't previously encountered.

Visual Basic provides some good tools for working with — or *trapping* — runtime errors. The runtime library recognizes that there is an error and allows you to trap it and take some corrective action. The bulk of this chapter concentrates on using these tools to gracefully work with, and handle, runtime errors in compiled programs — the topic of most concern to the serious developer.

Syntax and Compile Time Errors

Syntax and compile time errors (*syntax* errors for short) result from improperly constructed code, meaning code that fails to meet the formal requirements of the language's definition. The *Language Reference* that ships with the Professional Edition of Visual Basic Version 5 includes formal definitions of all VB functions, keywords, and statements. Chapter 4 of this book, "The Visual Basic Language," provides a concise overview of VB language elements and how you can put them together.

Examples of syntax errors include sending the wrong number of parameters to a procedure, entering keywords incorrectly, omitting punctuation from a Visual Basic statement, mismatching If and End Ifs, mismatching loops in general, and spelling variables incorrectly. One common cause of these errors is omitting the line continuation character at the end of a line.

This kind of error is easy to deal with if you follow some simple practices. To quickly catch and fix syntax errors, you should require variable declarations in projects and turn on the Auto Syntax Check option (found on the Editor tab of the Options dialog).

You require variable declaration in projects by adding the Option Explicit statement at the beginning of every module in a project. Alternatively, choose Tools | Editor and make sure the Require Variable Declaration box is checked. This automatically inserts an Option Explicit statement at the beginning of every new form or module in a project. (Note that it does not add the Option Explicit statement retroactively. Selecting Require Variable Declaration will not have an impact on existing modules.)

Requiring variable declarations disallows implicit variable declarations. (For more information on this topic, see Chapter 4.) This means that a program containing undeclared variables cannot be run. Typographic errors in variable names will be pinpointed immediately.

The Auto Syntax Errors option works similarly. You set this option by choosing Tools | Editor Options and making sure the Auto Syntax Errors box is checked. You should routinely work with this setting enabled. If this setting is enabled, Visual Basic displays an error message and highlights the offending code as soon as you enter a syntax error in the Code window. Here are two examples of how this works.

I have my Syntax Error Text set to display in bright red. This way, any statements that don't pass syntactic muster are unmistakably brought to my attention right away. You set colors for the various kinds of editor text in the Options dialog shown in Figure 15-1. (Choose Tools | Options and click the Editor Format tab page.) By the way, in VB5, an optional error indicator will also appear in the margin if Margin Indicator Bar is selected on the Editor Format tab page.

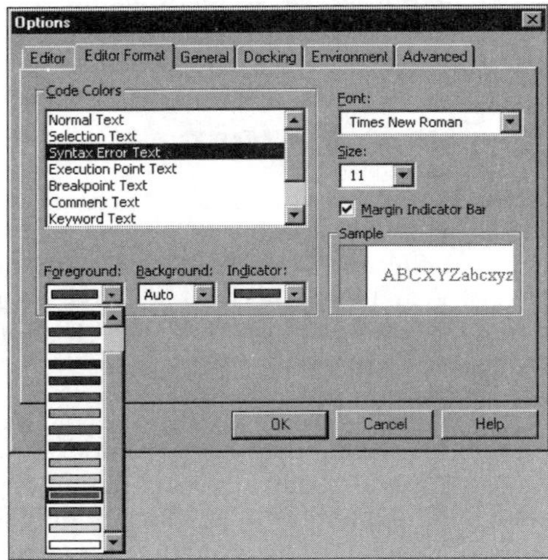

Figure 15-1: You set the foreground color of the Syntax Error Text in the Editor tab page of the Options dialog.

For example, if you start an If statement and leave the line without completing it, you'll get an Auto Syntax Check compile error message saying "Expected: Then or GoTo" (see Figure 15-2).

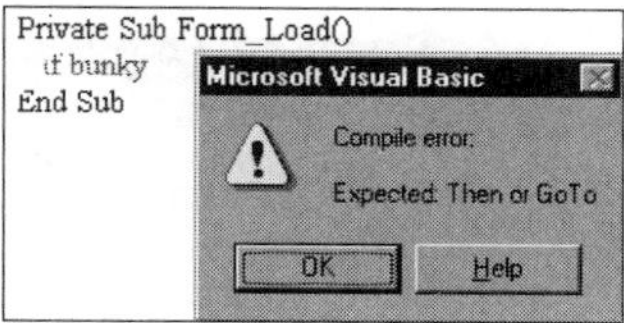

Figure 15-2: Here the Auto Syntax Check has caught an If with no Then.

For another example, let's say you create a subroutine, Bunky, with two string parameters, and attempt to call it as follows:

```
Bunky ("Baby Elephant", "Small Pig")
```

When the cursor leaves the line of code that attempts to call the Bunky procedure, you'll get the syntax error message shown in Figure 15-3.

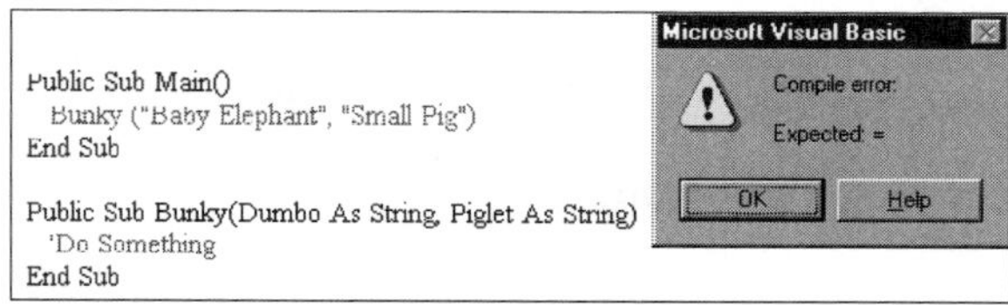

Figure 15-3: A syntactically incorrect procedure call leads to an obscure syntax error.

The error message depicted in Figure 15-3 is Visual Basic's not terribly clear way of saying that subroutines — as opposed to functions — should be invoked either with the Call keyword or without parentheses around the arguments. The two correct ways to rewrite the offending statement — neither includes an equal sign — are:

```
Call Bunky("Baby Elephant", "Small Pig")
```

or

```
Bunky "Baby Elephant", "Small Pig"
```

As the last example shows, although you've clearly done something wrong if you get a syntax error message, the error message does not always accurately reflect the nature of your sin. Rather than getting into a lather about this, the best way to pinpoint the problem — if simply looking at the code (or reading the error message) doesn't do it — is to look up the statement in question in on-line help (or the *Language Reference* manual) and carefully compare its formal definition with the actual statement as you've written it.

Turning on the options Require Variable Declaration and Auto Syntax Check makes dealing with these kinds of things — the programmer's equivalent of typos — no sweat.

Some Guidelines for Testing Programs

Programs usually operate on ranges of data. For example, a program may read the value of an integer input by the user. Integers in VB can range from -32,768 to 32,767. (Obviously, if the value could not vary, there would be no point in reading it. You could use a constant.)

The limits of that value, -32,768 and 32,767, are called its *bounds*. When trying to check your programs for potential problems, it's smart to consider the range of such values. This means checking values at the bounds of the possible range for the variable, as well as some mid-range values and any other values that you have reason to suspect may cause problems.

A great many logical errors are caused by *one-off* conditions. A one-off error occurs when a counter or loop is off by one. You should suspect one-off errors whenever there is a logical error with a loop or counter involved. A usual symptom that one-off errors "present" — to use the language of physicians — is an index of an array (or list box) going out of bounds under apparently random conditions. A common mistake like this is starting a loop counter at zero in one place and at one in another place. Using constants for boundary arguments helps to avoid this mistake. Mixed up values in an array, particularly when the values are off by only a few positions, are another sign of the dreaded one-off flu.

As an example of a common, but deadly, range error, suppose a program reads a value that represents the number of items in an inventory. After adding all the inventory items' costs, the program finds the average item cost by dividing by the inventory number. This is no problem for 1, or 1500, or 2000 items, but what if the user enters 0? Even though it is in the allowed range for unsigned integers, dividing by this value will result in an error.

Checking a program's bounding values is vitally important. In general, there will be bounds for every crucial variable, and you should check every combination of these values when running a program to see how they interact. This is particularly important when it comes to array indices. You should check mid-range values as well. It may turn out that some combination of such values will also generate unexpected errors.

The longer you test a program under usual and unusual operating circumstances, the more confidence you should have in it. As programs get more complex, the testing period normally grows longer and longer. This is why major software companies often send out thousands of preliminary versions of their software for beta testing and use automated error-testing software that runs through all possible inputs.

You should also attempt to duplicate every runtime problem that might occur to see how a program will react. A problem with this is that in real life, considering the immense variety of systems out there and the different ways that software gets used, this is difficult. Certainly, time spent trying to "break" your applications is time well spent.

Operations on files are one of the great generators of real-life runtime errors. For example, what if the disk is full and the user tries to write to it? What if the specified input file doesn't exist? What if the specified file to write is read-only? What if the disk has been removed? What if the user asks the application to write record -15 in a file? It is hard to generate every conceivable set of problematic circumstances, of course, but the closer you come, the more polished and professional your applications will be.

On Error, Resume, and Resume Next

At a procedural level, the On Error statement is used to enable error handling and specify the location of an error-handling routine within a procedure.

- **On Error GoTo *line*** Turns on error handling within the current procedure. When a runtime error occurs within the procedure, control branches to the location specified by *line,* a line label or number. (Modern VB practice is generally to use descriptive line labels rather than line numbers.)
- **On Error Resume Next** Use of this statement means that when a runtime error occurs, execution is transferred to the statement immediately following the one that causes the error.
- **On Error GoTo 0** Disables any error handler that has been activated in the current procedure.

Without an On Error statement, any runtime error is *fatal*. Fatal errors cause a message to be displayed and terminate program execution.

On Error Resume Next is the statement to use if you want program execution to continue no matter what. It's a bit like saying, "Ignore the hiccups; just keep on going." The danger of this approach can be that it does not give you information about potential problems. Microsoft recommends using On Error Resume Next when accessing objects; however, you can create an error handler that selectively resumes operation at the next statement only for certain kinds of errors:

```
Private Sub GetThatRemoteThing()
   On Error GoTo ErrHandle
   ...
   Exit Sub
ErrHandle:
   If Err >= 429 And Err <= 451 Then 'OLE Automation Error
      Resume Next
   Else
      Resume
   End If
End Sub
```

Error-handling routines use the Err object's properties and methods (more on the Err object later in this chapter). The Err object's default property is Number, so the references to Err in the preceding code are implicit references to Err.Number. (To find errors and their numbers, look up "Trappable Errors" in VB's on-line help. Some common errors and their numbers are listed later in this chapter in Table 15-3.)

Be sure to place an Exit Sub or Exit Function statement before the error-handling label in your procedures so code that executes normally won't inadvertently "drop down" into the error-handling code.

```
Public Sub Main()
    On Error GoTo ErrHandler
    Call Bunky("Baby Elephant", "Small Pig")
    ...
    Exit Sub 'Normal termination if no error
ErrHandler:
    'Deal with those pesky errors
End Sub
```

The Resume statement — which will itself cause an error if invoked anywhere other than in an error handler — has three possible forms:

- **Resume** Resumes execution with the statement that caused the error. If no intervening action has been taken to fix the error, this causes a fatal error because — as explained in a moment — an error handler can only process one error at a time.
- **Resume Next** Resumes execution with the statement following the statement that caused the error.
- **Resume *line*** Resumes execution at a line label or number (which must be within the same procedure as the error handler).

If an error handler has been turned on with an On Error statement, it is termed *enabled*. An enabled error handler that is actually invoked because of an error is said to be *active*. An error handler can only handle one error at a time. Suppose an error occurs while an error handler is active (think of it as error number two). The current error handler can't handle the second error. Execution passes back through the program's chain of procedures until an enabled, but inactive, error handler is found to deal with error number two. The procedure containing the enabled but inactive handler becomes the active procedure. If no such handler is found, the error becomes fatal.

For developing and testing programs, error-handling code that uses the Err object's Name and Description to display a message and then resumes execution at the next statement is generally sufficient. Error handling of this sort warns the developer that there is a potential problem and yet allows the program to execute as much code as possible. Error handling designed for a program in general release should be more sophisticated and should allow the user to fix errors if possible. For example, if there is no disk in the A drive, the user should be able to put one in and then resume program execution.

In the following routine, if the user enters zero in Text1 (or leaves the control empty), a divide by zero error is generated. (By the way, the error-handling routines in this chapter are part of a project saved on the CD-ROM as ***Error.Vbp***.) The error handler passes up an appropriate message (see Figure 15-4) and continues execution with the statement following the one generating the error (MsgBox "I'm Next!"):

```
Private Sub Command1_Click()
   On Error GoTo ErrHandle
   Dim x, y, z
   x = Val(Text1)
   z = 1: y = 1
   z = y / x
   MsgBox "I'm Next!"
   Exit Sub
ErrHandle:
   MsgBox "Error Number:" + Str(Err.Number) + "; Description: " + _
      Err.Description + ".", vbInformation, _
      "The Friendly Error Handler"
   Resume Next
End Sub
```

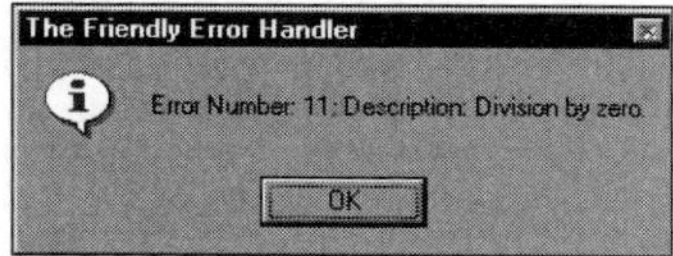

Figure 15-4: The simple error handler uses the properties of the Err object to display a message describing the error.

If Err's Number property equals zero (implicitly, Err = 0), it means that no error has been generated in the current procedure. Error generation is an event, so thinking of an error being fired makes sense. As I'll discuss later, to *raise* an error means to fire that error, just as raising an event using the RaiseEvent statement fires the event.

You can find out if there were errors in the current procedure by testing the truth or falsity of the proposition Err = 0, as shown in Listing 15-1.

Listing 15-1: Testing for an error condition

```
Private Sub Command2_Click()
   On Error Resume Next
   Dim x, y, z
   Dim GoodNews As Boolean
   x = Val(Text1)
   z = 1: y = 1
   z = y / x
   GoodNews = (Err = 0) 'Assign proposition value to GoodNews
   If Not GoodNews Then
```

```
      MsgBox "Something went wrong; probably divided by zero!"
   Else
      MsgBox "All's well!"
   End If
End Sub
```

The Err Object

The Err object contains information about runtime errors. It has the properties and methods listed in Tables 15-1 and 15-2.

Table 15-1 The Err Object's Properties

Property	*Purpose*
Number	Returns or sets the error number. The valid range of values is from 0 to 65,535.
Source	Sets or returns the name of the object or application that generated the error — for example, the name of the current VB project.
Description	Contains a description of the error based on the error number. If this string doesn't exist, Description contains the string "Application-defined or object-defined error."
HelpFile	Project's help file.
HelpContext	Help file context ID.
LastDLLError	Returns a system error code produced by a call to a DLL that returned a failure flag (32-bit only).

Table 15-2 The Err Object's Methods

Method	*Purpose*
Clear	Clears all properties of the Err object. (This method is equivalent to the Err = 0 statement in previous versions of Visual Basic.) You should use the Err.Clear method to explicitly clear the Err object after you have handled an error. VB calls the clear method automatically whenever a Resume, Exit Sub, Exit Function, Exit Property, or On Error statement is executed.
Raise	Generates a runtime error. It can also be used to set the Err object's properties, as described in Table 15-1.

The Raise Method

The Raise method takes the following arguments: *Number*, *Source*, *Description*, *HelpFile*, and *HelpContext*. All except *Number* are optional.

The Error Function

The syntax used in Versions 1 through 3 of VB, in which the Err function returned the current error number and Error(Err) returned the description of the error, has been retained for purposes of backwards compatibility. Because Number is the default property of the Err object, Err by itself returns the error number. This means that the Error function still returns a description of the current error when it is called with Err as an argument.

Number is a long integer that identifies the error. Internal and user-defined Visual Basic errors are between 1 and 65,535. (User-defined errors are discussed in greater detail in a moment.)

Common Trappable Errors

Table 15-3 lists some common trappable errors in Visual Basic. This is an abbreviated list; you can find more errors by searching the subcategories under "Trappable Errors" in VB's on-line help. In addition, custom controls and other objects can have their own error values.

Table 15-3 Some Common Trappable Errors

Error Number	*Description*
3	Return without GoSub
5	Invalid procedure call
6	Overflow
7	Out of memory
9	Subscript out of range
10	Array is fixed or temporarily locked
11	Division by zero
13	Type mismatch
14	Out of string space
16	Expression too complex
17	Cannot perform requested operation
20	Resume without error
28	Out of stack space
51	Internal error
52	Bad file name or number

(continued)

Table 15-3 *(Continued)*

Error Number	*Description*
53	File not found
54	Bad file mode
55	File already open
57	Device I/O error
58	File already exists
59	Bad record length
61	Disk full
62	Input past end of file
63	Bad record number
67	Too many files
68	Device unavailable
70	Permission denied
71	Disk not ready
74	Cannot rename with different drive
75	Path/file access error
76	Path not found
91	Object variable or With block variable not set
298	System DLL *[dll name]* could not be loaded
321	Invalid file format
335	Could not access system registry
336	Object server not correctly registered
337	Object server not found
340	Control array element does not exist
341	Invalid control array index
342	Not enough room to allocate control array item
343	Object is not an array
344	Must specify index when using object array
360	Object is already loaded
361	Can't load or unload this object
362	Controls created at design time cannot be unloaded
380	Illegal property value
381	Illegal property array index

Error Number	Description
384	A form cannot be moved when minimized or maximized
401	Can't show nonmodal form when modal form is displayed
419	Permission to use object denied
421	Method not applicable for this object
423	Property or method not found
424	Object required
426	Only one MDI form allowed
427	Invalid object type; Menu control required
428	Pop-up menu must have at least one submenu
429	OLE automation server cannot create object
430	Class does not support OLE automation
432	Filename or class name not found during OLE automation operation
438	Object doesn't support this property or method
440	OLE automation error
445	OLE does not support this action
449	Argument not optional
450	Wrong number of arguments
451	Object not a collection
24574	No fonts exist (common dialog error)
28664	No printer device drivers were found (common dialog error)
28670	Load of required resources failed (common dialog error)

The LastDLLError Property

The LastDLLError Property, a read-only property, returns a system error code produced by a dynamic link library (DLL) call. The DLL function sets an error code when it returns a Failure flag that can be retrieved. For example, the following code calls the GetDiskFreeSpace function (discussed in Chapter 11):

```
Private Sub Form_Click()
Dim RetVal As Boolean
   RetVal = GetDiskFreeSpace("Hacker", 2, 3, 4, 5)
   If RetVal Then
      MsgBox "Function Call Succeeded"
   Else
      MsgBox "LastDLLError code = " + Str(Err.LastDllError)
   End If
End Sub
```

Obviously, this call will fail because the function is expecting an expression that evaluates to a root drive as its first argument (see Figure 15-5).

Figure 15-5: When a call to a DLL fails, the LastDLLError property of the Err object returns an error code supplied by the DLL.

You should refer to the DLL's documentation to determine what the error code means.

Raising an Error

To test error-handling routines, you must be able to create errors. Some errors, such as the division by zero example earlier in this chapter, are easy to create. Others — such as 28, "Out of stack space," or 61, "Disk full" — may be time consuming and cumbersome to create (if you can do it at all).

Fortunately, the Err object's Raise method makes it easy to simulate the occurrence of any error. (Actually, "simulating" may be the wrong word. From the program's point of view, once you have raised an error, that error has occurred.)

It's easy to raise an error, as shown in Listing 15-2.

Listing 15-2: Raising an error

```
Private Sub cmdRaise_Click()
   On Error GoTo ErrMessage
   Err.Raise Val(Text1)
   Exit Sub
ErrMessage:
   MsgBox "You have generated error number " & _
      Str(Err.Number) & " ; Description: " & Err.Description & _
      " error.", vbInformation, "Error Demo"
   Resume Next
End Sub
```

If you enter a number — for example, 13 — and run the procedure, the error you input is created ("raised"), as shown in Figure 15-6.

By the way, if you call the Err object's Raise method with 0 as an argument, Err.Number will be not be 0. Because Err.Number = 0 by definition means that no errors have been raised, passing 0 as a parameter to the Raise method causes an error. Err.Raise 0 generates an Err.Number equal to 5 ("Invalid procedure call").

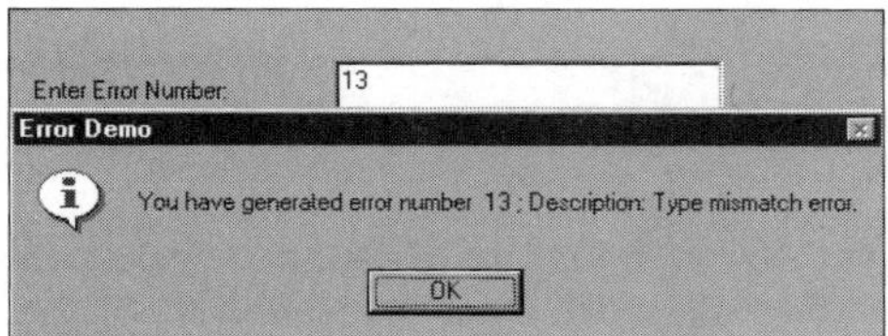

Figure 15-6: Using the Err object's methods, it's easy to "raise" (fire) an error.

Raising a User-Defined Error

A user-defined error is a custom error whose number and description you invent yourself. You employ user-defined errors when you need to trap errors that aren't built into VB and the Err object. In other words, your code itself will raise the error under certain conditions. Using custom errors is important in any complex program; when creating an ActiveX application or control, it becomes particularly vital to create errors that give significant information about what caused them.

You use the Err.Raise method to assign user-defined error numbers and descriptions. In theory, you can use any unoccupied error number between 1 and 65,535, inclusive. (This is the valid range of values for the Err.Number property.) For example, there are no predefined error numbers 1, 2, or 21 through 27. But, to avoid any possibility of conflicting with predefined error numbers, it's a good idea to start your user-defined error numbers at the highest possible one — 65,535 — and work your way down from there:

```
Const MyBigBadError = 65535
Const MyNextError = MyBigBadError - 1
...
```

For fun and games, you could use the Raise method to change the description of an existing error number, but that sounds like a really bad idea — except for scaring friends (see the frightening message in Figure 15-7). As shown in Listing 15-3, this code changes the description of error 91 ("Object variable or With block variable not set") and then fires the error:

Listing 15-3: Changing the description of a predefined error

```
Private Sub Form_Click()
   Dim Silly As String
   Debug.Print txtDesc ' Show the value of txtDesc.text in the
                       ' lower pane of the Debug Window
   Silly = "You've referenced an object rather than instancing it,"
   Silly = Silly + " and now you, and your computer,"
   Silly = Silly + " are going to die!!!!"
   Err.Raise 91, , Silly
   Dim x As Form1
   x.Caption = "blah"
End Sub
```

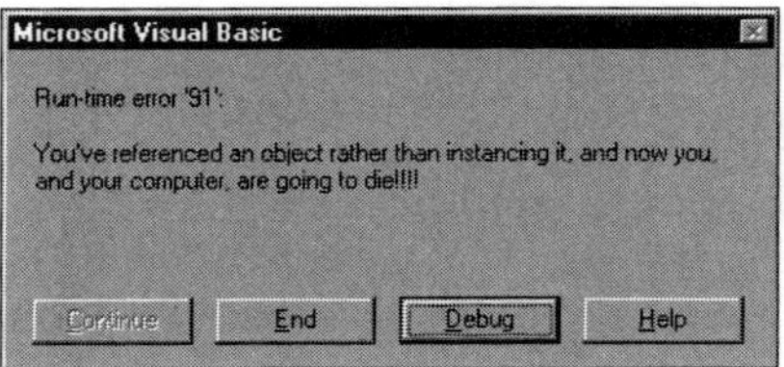

Figure 15-7: It's possible to scare your friends and co-workers by changing common error descriptions.

Changing the text of error messages is good for more than fun and games. It's sometimes desirable to change the error message text to something that may be more informative — or less frightening — than the original text.

The original concept was that the Number property for a user-defined error in an OLE automation object would go up from vbObjectError (-2147221504). Since that conception, Visual Basic has used error numbers up to vbObjectError + 512. You should start your error numbers for an OLE automation server (for example, ActiveX applications and controls) higher than that:

```
Const MyFirstError = 1 + vbObjectError + 512
Const MyNextError = MyFirstError + 1
...
```

The procedure shown in Listing 15-4 raises an error based on user input of a number and description — Text1 and txtDesc are text boxes — and then displays the error:

Listing 15-4: Raising a user-defined error

```
Private Sub cmdRUDE_Click()
   Dim S As String
   Err.Raise Text1, , txtDesc
   S = "The following Error occurred:" + vbCrLf + vbCrLf
   'add the error string
   S = S + Err.Description + vbCrLf
   'add the error number
   S = S + "Number: " + CStr(Err.Number)
   'beep and show the error
   Beep
   MsgBox S, vbExclamation, "User-Defined Error Demonstration"
   Resume Next
End Sub
```

Now, this is the kind of thing you could go to town with. There are limitless possibilities for creating your own errors (see Figure 15-8)!

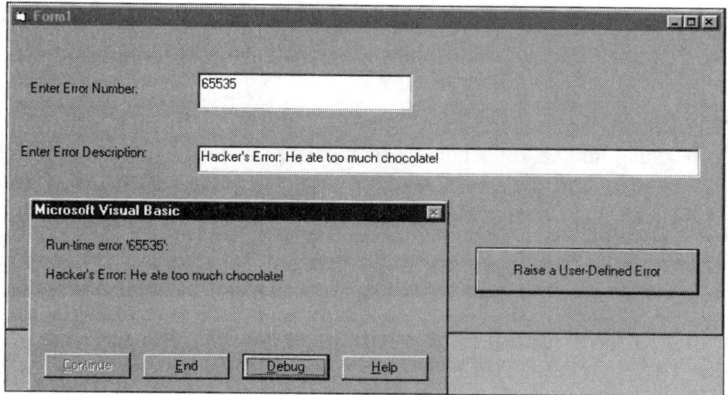

Figure 15-8: You can use the Err object's Raise method to define and file a custom error, in this case error number 65535: "Hacker's Error: He ate too much chocolate!"

Debugging Tools

Logical errors in a program are usually harder to find than compile or runtime errors. A logical error may be buried deep in a long chain of complex procedure calls, object relationships, and statements. Those misbegotten assumptions we hold onto the longest — the classical *idée fixe* — tend to be behind stubborn logical errors. A flexible mind, and the willingness to understand cause and effect one step at a time, is a prerequisite for successful debugging.

Fortunately, Visual Basic provides some debugging tools that you can use to help locate errors in logic.

The Lowly Message Box Versus Debug.Print

You can use the MsgBox function to display variable values during program execution. It is very easy to insert at strategic points temporary message boxes that output the contents of any variables you are unsure of. You can thus use the lowly message box as an important debugging tool.

You can use the Print method of the Debug object in a very similar fashion. Expressions that are the argument of Debug.Print are displayed in the Immediate pane as the Debug statements are executed. The advantages of using Debug.Print are twofold: Program execution is not interrupted (as with message boxes), and you can leave the Debug statements in — without compromising performance — when you compile.

Quick Access to Debugging Commands

You can use the Debug menu for easy access to debugging tools, including Toggle Breakpoint, Instant Watch, Calls, Step In, and Step Over. In addition, you can display the Debug toolbar, which provides buttons for easy access to most debugging functions. To display the Debug toolbar, choose Toolbars from the View menu, and make sure Debug Toolbar is checked.

One aid in fixing program logic is that you can edit some code without stopping the program. You can select Break from Visual Basic's Debug menu to temporarily stop the program. Now you can change the code and then continue with program execution. In Break mode, Visual Basic usually allows programming changes up to the level of declaring new variables.

To determine the contents of variables, you can set a *breakpoint.* When a breakpoint is reached, program execution halts. You can set (or remove) a breakpoint in the Code window in three ways. With your cursor positioned at the statement where you want to break, either:

- Press F9
- Choose Debug|Toggle|Breakpoint
- Choose Toggle|Breakpoint from the context menu in the Code window

The selected statement becomes bold to indicate that a breakpoint has been set. (By the way, execution actually breaks at the end of the line preceding the breakpoint.)

To view the contents of variables at the breakpoint, set a watch by choosing Add Watch from the Debug menu. When the breakpoint is reached, the contents of variables included in the Watch List are displayed in the Debug window. The Debug window lets you check the values of a program while it's in a *break state*. A break state occurs when you choose Break from the Run menu or when the program reaches a breakpoint.

The *Watch window* — or, as it is sometimes called, *Watch pane* — shows the value of the expressions you have added to the Watch List. For example, in Figure 15-9, the Watch pane shows the value of the variable Silly that has been added to the Watch List. The *Immediate window* — sometimes called the *Immediate pane* — is used to monitor debug statements you have added to your code using the Debug.Print method. (See the sidebar "The Lowly Message Box Versus Debug.Print" earlier in this section.)

For example, the following Debug statement:

```
Debug.Print Silly
```

causes the contents of the variable Silly to be displayed in the Immediate pane, as shown in Figure 15-10 (see "Raising a User-Defined Error," earlier in this section). You can also use the Immediate pane to enter code for immediate execution when your program is in Break mode.

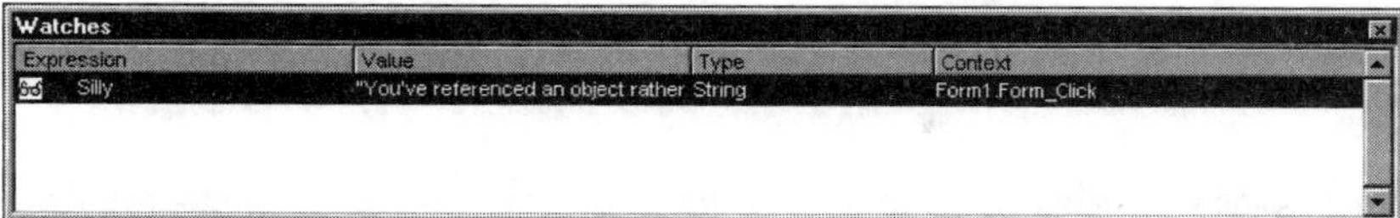

Figure 15-9: You can view the contents of a variable in the Debug window when a breakpoint has been set and the variable added to the Watch List.

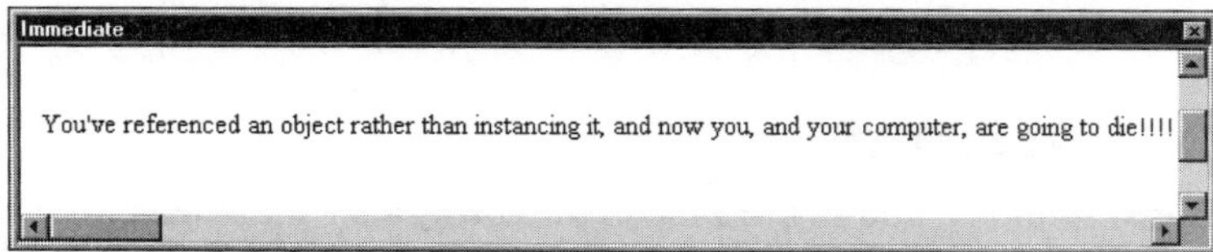

Figure 15-10: The Immediate pane displays output generated by the Print method of the Debug object.

The Locals window automatically displays all of the declared variables in the current procedure and their values. You can display the Locals window by choosing it on VB's View menu.

The Calls box, which you display by pressing the button containing an ellipses to the right of the procedure list box in the Locals window, shows a list of all procedures activated but not finished in the project. In other words, this is a list of nested procedure calls that tell you how you got to the breakpoint.

Other VB debugging tools include line-by-line program execution (stepping) and the ability to change variable values while a program is running.

Single stepping is a powerful debugging tool that can give you a precise picture of what a program is doing.

A number of related debugging commands — all on the Debug menu — are available in VB5 in break mode:

- Step Over (Shift+F8): Similar to stepping except that when the current statement contains a call to a procedure, Step Over executes the called procedure as a unit and then returns to the next statement in the current module.
- Run To Cursor (Ctrl+F8): Selects a statement further down the code where you want execution to stop. Run To Cursor helps you leap over large blocks of code that you do not wish to view.
- Set Next Statement (Ctrl+F9): Sets a different line of code to execute next (must be within the current procedure). Set Next Statement allows you to back up in the debugging process.
- Show Next Statement: Places the cursor on the line that will execute next.

Debugging and Mouse and Keyboard Input

Before finishing with debugging, you should know about one problem. Because VB programs are event driven, if you place a breakpoint in a MouseDown or KeyPress event procedure and you release the mouse button or key while the program is in a break state, you may never get a MouseUp or KeyUp event when the code continues. In other words, keep in mind that Visual Basic programs respond to the Windows environment, and if you change that environment while debugging, you may get unexpected results.

Using Assertions

An *assertion* is a statement placed in a program that allows the program to check its own code as it runs. Assertions should be used to double-check underlying assumptions about program logic.

You can use the Assert method of the Debug object to create assertions that will never appear in a compiled application.

The argument for the Debug.Assert method is a Boolean statement. If the statement evaluates to False when the Debug.Assert expression is processed, the application enters break mode with the statement highlighted. For example, suppose you had a routine in your program that assumed that the user had entered a specific name from a list. You could test that assumption using an assertion:

```
Private Sub procHobbit_Click()
   Dim isHobbit As Boolean
   isHobbit = False
   isHobbit = (Text1 = "Frodo" Or Text1 = "Bilbo" Or _
      Text1 = "Samwise")
   Debug.Assert isHobbit
   'continue processing
End Sub
```

When the program is run in the VB environment, processing continues without interruption, unless an invalid name has been entered. In that case, when VB evaluates the Debug.Assert statement, it will find that the argument is False, enter break mode, and highlight the assertion, as shown in Figure 15-11.

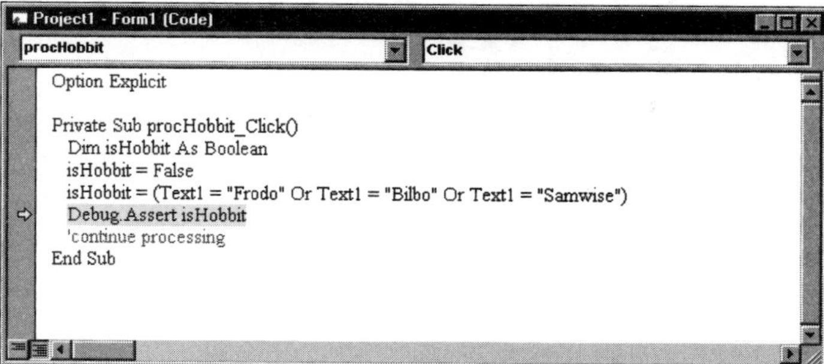

Figure 15-11: You should use the Debug.Assert method so that programs test the underlying logical assumptions in their code as they run.

Handling Errors in Objects

When applications use a number of objects — such as ActiveX controls — it can become quite difficult to determine the nature of an error, and which object is generating it. It's therefore important to include proper error handling in ActiveX servers and controls, particularly if your objects will be distributed to other developers.

For more information, see the discussion of Handling Errors in ActiveX controls in Chapter 26, "Implementing Control Functionality."

Summary

This chapter covered debugging and the debugging tools available in Visual Basic. First, I discussed the three kinds of errors that you can encounter: syntax and compile time errors, runtime errors, and logical (or design) errors. Then, I moved on to handling runtime errors, debugging techniques, and how to efficiently use the tools that Visual Basic provides.

The topics I covered included

- Using On Error GoTo, On Error Resume Next, and On Error GoTo 0 statements in your procedures
- Resume and Resume Next Statements
- Error numbering
- The Err object and its properties and methods
- Use of the Err object's LastDLLError method

- Raising errors
- Raising user-defined errors
- Toggling breakpoints and using the Immediate, Watch, and Local windows
- Using stepping tools
- Using assertions

Chapter 16

Optimizing Secrets

This chapter shows you how to optimize your programs for actual, and apparent, performance. By “apparent performance” I mean how slow or fast the application appears to the user. Often, this is more important than the actual speed of code execution. Provided that you let the user know that something important is going on — for example, loading, initializing, validating, or connecting — she is more likely to forgive delays.

I'll also cover the consequences of native code compilation — and the meaning of the native code compilation switches.

When you distribute an application, it's reasonable for the users to assume that your application will behave in a civilized fashion. In other words, your programs shall not trash hard drives, spread viruses, or needlessly waste the user's time. The relationship between your application and the user, like all relationships, will work much better if the application communicates — for example, by displaying the message “Please wait...loading.” — when it needs to perform time-consuming tasks.

In addition to techniques for optimizing actual and apparent performance, this chapter discusses other important programming techniques that are optimization related, including:

- Splash screens
- Shelling
- Conditional compilation
- Using external resource files
- Measuring speed
- Using the Code Profiler
- Optimizing for speed
- Optimizing apparent speed
- Minimizing memory consumption
- Finding files on disk
- Recursion

Splash Screens

You use splash screens to keep the user informed — and entertained — during the initial program load. While a splash screen is displayed, project forms can be loaded, databases accessed, local databases initialized, and information validated. You can perform any time-consuming operations you'd like and get them out of the way under the cover of a splash screen. In addition, displaying an initial splash screen gives you the opportunity to provide author, publisher, and copyright information in the context of a polished and professional program load (see Figure 16-1).

Figure 16-1: It's easy to create attractive splash screens that make time-consuming initialization code more palatable to users.

A splash screen usually is a borderless form with labels for displaying information and image controls for displaying graphics. You can use timer controls to provide animations or update display information.

The simplest way to load a splash screen from Sub Main is to call the splash screen's Show method modally and then unload the splash screen using a timer control. Set the Interval property of the timer control to something reasonable, such as 5000 (five seconds), and make sure its Enabled property is set to True. For example:

```
Sub Main ()
   frmSplash.Show vbModal
   'load program forms after frmSplash has unloaded
   frmStartProject.Show
End Sub

Sub tmrSplash_Timer()
   'Interval expired - unload frmSplash
   Unload Me
End Sub
```

Setting up a splash screen in this fashion, however, makes it more difficult to implement the functional point of having a splash screen: executing code while the splash screen is showing. Ideally — because it is the simplest way to do things — the entry point to this code would be frmStartProject's Load event. But, the way the example is set up, frmStartProject isn't loaded until frmSplash is unloaded. You could work with this by placing calls to start up code from frmSplash, but this is a bit of a kludge. At best, the user would still have to wait for subsequent form loads. It's a far better idea to have frmStartProject (and any other forms the project needs) load while frmSplash is showing.

The way I set this up in the sample project — saved on the companion CD-ROM as ***Splash.Vbp*** — is to show frmSplash as a modeless form. Initialization, and loading of the frmStartProject form, continues immediately.

Then I needed to use the SetWindowPos API function (see the section "Making a Form Stay on Top" in Chapter 11) to make sure that frmSplash stays on top of other forms that are loaded. I also set frmStartProject's Enabled property to False in Sub Main so that the user can't access any form controls or events until initialization is complete (other forms that appear behind the splash screen should also be set this way).

The sample also sets the cursor (Screen.MousePointer) to the hourglass and only changes it back to the default when the splash screen is unloaded. To keep updating the splash screen, I've added secondary timers (tmrThis, tmrThat), which expand the lblThis and lblThat labels. You could animate the image control in the same way.

Here's the API declaration and Sub Main code:

```
Option Explicit
' Constants for SetWindowPos API parameters
Public Const HWND_TOPMOST = -1
Public Const SWP_NOSIZE = &H1
Declare Function SetWindowPos Lib "User32" _
   (ByVal hWnd As Long, ByVal hWndInsertAfter As Long, _
   ByVal x As Long, ByVal Y As Long, _
   ByVal cx As Long, ByVal cy As Long, ByVal wFlags As Long) As Long

Sub Main()
   'Project is set to StartUp from Sub Main()
   frmStartProject.Enabled = False
   Screen.MousePointer = vbHourglass
   frmSplash.Show
   ' Shows frmSplash while the main form is loading
   frmStartProject.Show
End Sub
```

Here's the code in frmSplash:

```
Option Explicit
Private Sub Form_Load()
   Dim lTop As Long, lLeft As Long, RetVal as Long
   'Center splash screen and retrieve position in pixels
   lTop = (Screen.Height \ 2 - Me.Height \ 2) \ _
      Screen.TwipsPerPixelY
   lLeft = (Screen.Width \ 2 - Me.Width \ 2) \ Screen.TwipsPerPixelX
   RetVal = SetWindowPos(Me.hWnd, HWND_TOPMOST, lLeft, lTop, 0&, _
      0&, SWP_NOSIZE)
End Sub
```

```
Private Sub tmrSplash_Timer()
    ' Unloads this form when the interval is reached.
    'Enable project form
    frmStartProject.Enabled = True
    'Restore cursor
    Screen.MousePointer = vbDefault
    'Unload splash screen
    Unload Me
End Sub

Private Sub tmrThat_Timer()
    'Update lblThat
    lblThat = lblThat + "and that "
End Sub

Private Sub tmrThis_Timer()
    'Update lblThis
    lblThis = lblThis + "and this "
End Sub
```

That's it!

Starting a Large Application

You can also use a splash screen to load an entirely separate executable using the Shell statement. The idea here is that you could divide your program in two: a small executable the loads the VB runtime libraries and the splash screen, and a larger executable. Doing this cuts down the apparent total loading time, which is the amount of time it seems to take before the application's form becomes active.

You could implement shelling in a timer with its .Interval property set appropriately. For example, the following timer event code — from ***ShellSpl.Vbp*** on the companion CD-ROM — loads Notepad after VB's Form1 has been on the screen for 2 seconds:

```
Private Sub tmrShell_Timer()
    Dim Retval As Long, FileName As String
    FileName = "Notepad.Exe"
    Retval = Shell(FileName, vbNormalFocus)
    Unload Me
End Sub
```

TwipsPerPixel Methods

TwipsPerPixelX returns the number of twips per pixel for an object measured horizontally and TwipsPerPixelY returns the twips per pixel of an object measured vertically. It's common to use these methods to convert measurements to pixels, as required by most API display functions.

Substitute your own large VB executable for ***Notepad.Exe***, and you have a launching program in which each part takes about half the time it normally would to just load the large program. Since you can use the first part to display a message ("Stand By: Loading Application"), this is a technique well worth considering.

The Shell Function

You're probably somewhat familiar with the Shell function (see the preceding example), which is used to run an external executable program. The big issue when using Shell within your applications — if you need to return to the shelling application — is keeping control of execution flow once you've handed it off to an external application. When, precisely, if ever, will execution control return to the shelling code?

Generally, you'll want to return execution to the shelling program when the external program closes. Achieving this in Win32 is somewhat different than used to be under 16-bit operating systems. I'll show you how it works in a moment.

The Shell function return data type is a long. Despite some documentation that states otherwise, Shell will not open applications based on associated document files (for example, you cannot pass Shell a ***.Doc*** file and expect Word to be launched).

The programs demonstrating the Shell Function are saved on the companion CD-ROM as ***ShellTer.Vbp***.

Launching an Application Using a File Association

To launch an application using an associated file, you can use the ShellExecute API function. For example, to launch Notepad with a file named ***Poo.Txt*** loaded — provided that ***Poo.Txt*** is located in the root C:\ directory — you could use the following code (see Figure 16-2):

```
Option Explicit
'Declare ShellExecute and Constants
Private Declare Function ShellExecute Lib _
   "shell32.dll" Alias "ShellExecuteA" _
   (ByVal hwnd As Long, _
   ByVal lpOperation As String, _
   ByVal lpFile As String, _
   ByVal lpParameters As String, _
   ByVal lpDirectory As String, _
   ByVal nShowCmd As Long) As Long
Private Const SW_SHOWNORMAL = 1

Private Sub cmdAssociate_Click()
Dim RetVal As Long
   RetVal = ShellExecute(Me.hwnd, _
      vbNullString, _
```

```
        "Poo.Txt", _
        vbNullString, _
        "c:\", _
        SW_SHOWNORMAL)
End Sub
```

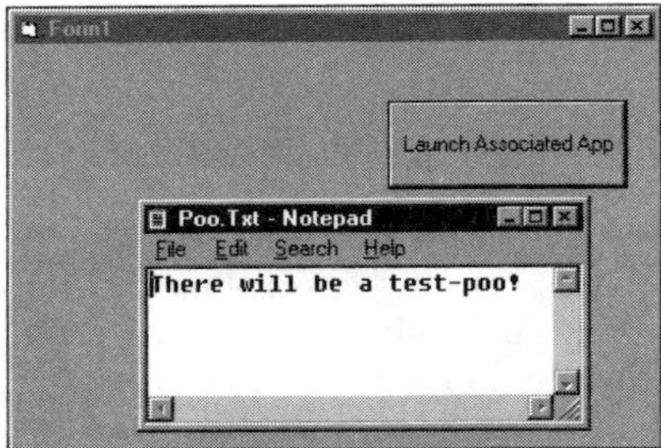

Figure 16-2: You can start an application by association using the ShellExecute API function.

To find constants and their values for API functions, use the API Viewer with Constants rather than Declares selected.

If API Viewer has been enabled in the Add-Ins Manager, you can use the API Viewer directly from the VB environment.

Waiting for a Shelled Program to Terminate

The Shell function executes an external program. The first argument to the function is a string representation of the executable; the second is a constant flag indicating the style of window in which the program is to run (see Table 16-1).

Table 16-1 Shell Function WindowStyle Constants

Constant	*Value*	*Description*
vbHide	0	Window is hidden and focus is passed to the hidden window.
vbNormalFocus	1	Window has focus and is restored to its original size and position.
vbMinimizedFocus	2	Window is displayed as an icon with focus.
vbMaximizedFocus	3	Window is maximized with focus.
vbNormalNoFocus	4	Window is restored to its most recent size and position. The currently active window remains active.
vbMinimizedNoFocus	6	Window is displayed as an icon. The currently active window remains active.

16-Bit Shell Function

Because you get an instance handle back from the 16-bit version of Shell, you could shell and test whether a program had terminated by using the GetModuleUsage function (not included in the Win32 API), which returns the number of programs using a module:

```
Dim Handle as Integer
Handle = Shell ("NotePad.Exe", vbNormalFocus)
Do While GetModuleUsage (Handle) > 0
   DoEvents
Loop
```

If you have to write an application that runs under Windows 3.*x* as well as 32-bit Windows, you should know that the Shell function works differently under 32-bit and 16-bit Windows. 16-bit Shell returns the handle of the running instance of the shelled program, whereas 32-bit Shell returns a process ID. A process ID uniquely identifies the shelled program, but knowing the process ID is not sufficient to access the program. Every program that needs access to the shelled process must pass the process ID to the Win32 OpenProcess API and obtain a handle to the shelled process.

Here are the declarations you'll need to shell and wait for the termination of the shelled program under Win32:

```
Private Declare Function OpenProcess Lib "kernel32" _
   (ByVal dwDesiredAccess As Long, ByVal bInheritHandle As Long, _
   ByVal dwProcessId As Long) As Long
Private Declare Function WaitForSingleObject Lib "kernel32" _
   (ByVal hHandle As Long, ByVal dwMilliseconds As Long) As Long
Private Declare Function CloseHandle Lib "kernel32" _
   (ByVal hObject As Long) As Long
Private Const INFINITE = &HFFFF
```

The following code uses the 32-bit Shell return of a process ID. The OpenProcess function uses it to return a handle that is unique — that is, specific to this procedure — for the shelled process. Finally, WaitForSingleObject is called with the unique handle. WaitForSingleObject enters an efficient wait state that is on the harsh side: It may not use any resources, but your program is dead. The screen does not even get repainted. Shelling from the VB design environment using this procedure will cause the VB IDE to shut down until the shelled program closes because VB is the real program waiting for the shelled operation to complete (see Figure 16-3).

If you try this code, you'll see that it works fine. The "I'm Back!!!" message box won't appear until you close Notepad. If you drag the shelled application (Notepad) around, you'll observe that, as I mentioned, screen redraw within the VB environment has been suspended!

Figure 16-3: Calling WaitForSingleObject with a process handle causes execution to resume only after the process has terminated; the suspension of activity is so complete in the calling application that the screen is not even redrawn.

```
Private Sub cmdShandTer_Click()
   Dim hProg, hProc, RetVal As Long
   Const PROCESS_ALL_ACCESS = 0
   hProg = Shell("Notepad.Exe", vbNormalFocus) 'returns taskID
   'Get process handle
   hProc = OpenProcess(PROCESS_ALL_ACCESS, False, hProg)
   'wait until the process terminates
   If hProc <> 0 Then
      RetVal = WaitForSingleObject(hProc, INFINITE)
      CloseHandle hProc
   End If
   MsgBox "I'm Back!!!"
End Sub
```

As far as I'm concerned, this complete suspension of CPU cycles to the calling process is not really acceptable. (In some situations, I could imagine using it as a special effect.)

To rectify the situation, I've first written a function that returns a value based on whether the called process is still active:

```
Private Declare Function GetExitCodeProcess Lib "kernel32" _
   (ByVal hProcess As Long, lpExitCode As Long) As Long
Private Const INFINITE = &HFFFF

Private Function IsActive(hprog) As Long
   Dim hProc, RetVal As Long
   Const PROCESS_QUERY_INFORMATION = 0
   Const STILL_ACTIVE = 259
   hProc = OpenProcess(PROCESS_QUERY_INFORMATION, False, hprog)
   If hProc <> 0 Then
      GetExitCodeProcess hProc, RetVal
   End If
   IsActive = (RetVal = STILL_ACTIVE)
   CloseHandle hProc
End Function
```

GetExitCodeProcess returns a value of STILL_ACTIVE (which is defined equal to 259) in its second argument if the process passed by handle is still active.

To test this function, I've added a StatusBar, a Timer control, and a command button to the example project. The command button opens the external application, sets a module-level process identifier variable, and enables the timer. The timer calls the IsActive function, and based on its return value, updates the StatusBar, as shown in Figure 16-4:

```
Dim IsProg As Long 'Module level declare
...
Private Sub cmdActive_Click()
  IsProg = Shell("Notepad.exe", vbNormalFocus)
  Timer1.Enabled = True
End Sub

Private Sub Timer1_Timer()
   If IsActive(IsProg) Then
      StatusBar1.SimpleText = "ACTIVE"
   Else
      StatusBar1.SimpleText = "NOT ACTIVE"
   End If
End Sub
```

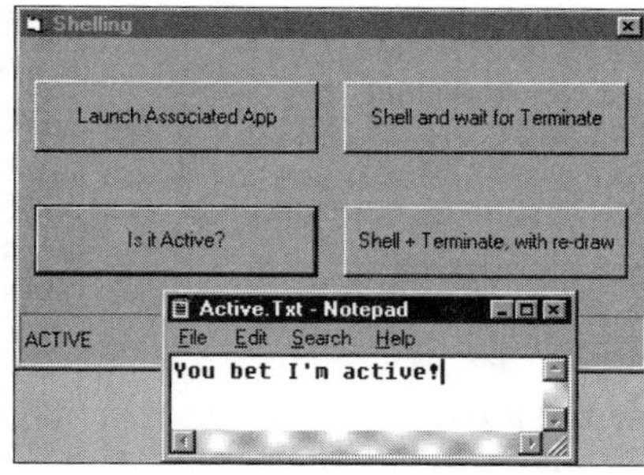

Figure 16-4: The IsActive function determines whether an external process is active.

I can now put the two halves — the Shell and Terminate code, and the IsActive function — together in a way that allows screen redrawing of the original application using our old friend, the DoEvents statement. The original application idles in a Do While loop that calls DoEvents, which allows screen redraw, until the shelled application is no longer active. Once it's no longer active, execution returns to the original application, as verified by a message box (see Figure 16-5).

```
Private Sub cmdRedraw_Click()
   Dim hprog, hProc, RetVal As Long
   Const PROCESS_ALL_ACCESS = 0
   hprog = Shell("NotePad.Exe", vbNormalFocus) 'returns taskID
   'Get process handle
```

```
   Do While IsActive(hprog)
      DoEvents
   Loop
   hProc = OpenProcess(PROCESS_ALL_ACCESS, False, hprog)
   'wait until the process terminates
   If hProc <> 0 Then
      RetVal = WaitForSingleObject(hProc, INFINITE)
      CloseHandle hProc
  End If
  MsgBox "I'm Back!!!"
End Sub
```

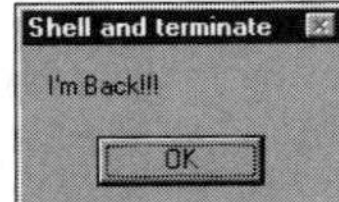

Figure 16-5: This message box tells you that execution has returned to the original application.

Pseudocode Compilation Versus Native Code Compilation

An exciting new feature in Visual Basic 5 — and one that Visual Basic developers have long requested — is the ability to compile executables to native code. This is an either, or: You can compile a given program to native code or pseudocode. (Pseudocode is the compiler default.)

In this section, I'll briefly discuss the advantages and disadvantages of each. Then I'll explain the meaning of native code compiler switches.

What Is Pseudocode?

Pseudocode — or p-code, as it is sometimes called — executables are fully compiled into a tokenized language. This tokenized compiled pseudocode is then translated on the fly — interpreted — by the Visual Basic runtime module into machine code.

You can think of Visual Basic p-code as an intermediate step between high-level Visual Basic and low-level machine codes.

As my Grandmother used to say, "The advantages of the one are not the disadvantages of the other."

In a nutshell:

- Programs that are compiled to pseudocode are smaller in size.
- Generally, native code compiled programs, while larger, execute more quickly.
- A negative to pseudocode compilation is that you have to distribute the Visual Basic runtime library (*.Dll*) in addition to the executable. However, partly offsetting this is the fact that many target systems already have Visual Basic runtimes installed.

According to Microsoft, "in real-world tests, client applications typically ... [spend] about 5% of their total execution time executing the p-code. Hence, if native code was instantaneous, using native code for these programs would provide at most a 5% performance improvement."

The implication is that, in most situations, there is very little performance boost to be gained from native code compilation. Of course, it's difficult to benchmark performance, particularly because applications do not always perform in the same way on different hardware. I'd suggest testing any applications in which execution speed is critical both ways, using some of the benchmarking techniques explained later in this chapter.

Microsoft notes the following specific kinds of programs that will benefit from native code compilation (again, if your project is not on this list, the implication is that native code compilation is unlikely to benefit you much):

- Programs that do a lot of primitive operations on hard-typed, nonstring variables (such as complex financial calculations or fractal generators)
- Computationally intensive programs
- Programs that move bits and bytes around frequently within local data structures

Conversely, programs that spend much time calling the Windows API, invoking ActiveX objects, manipulating strings, or using functions in the VBA library are not likely to see much improvement from native code compilation.

Native Code Switches

You use the Compile tab page of the Project Properties dialog to select native code compilation rather than the default, pseudocode compilation. You reach the Compile tab, shown in Figure 16-6, by choosing Project Properties from the View menu or by choosing Options from the Make Exe dialog.

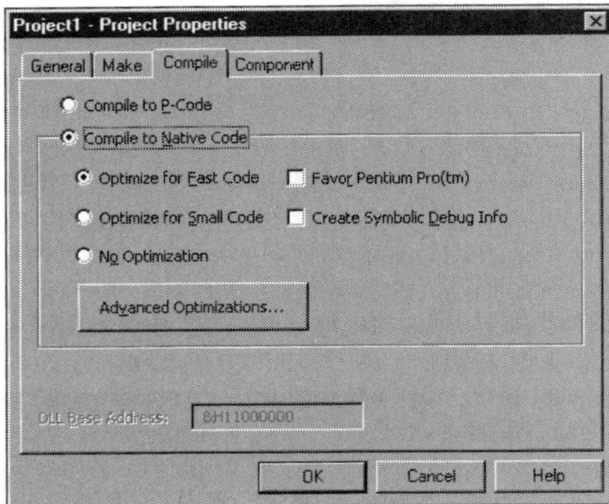

Figure 16-6: You use the Compile tab page of the Project Properties dialog to select compilation options.

The Compile tab provides a number of options (see Figure 16-6). You can choose to have your native code executable optimized for speed, size, or not at all. If Favor Pentium Pro is selected, code is generated that runs faster on Pentium Pro processors (but slower on other CPUs). Selecting Create Symbolic Debug Info causes debug information to be generated that can be viewed in the Visual C++ environment.

There are more options in the Advanced Optimizations dialog, shown in Figure 16-7. These optimizations constitute unsafe computing: If you know what you are doing, selecting these options may speed your executables. But you risk creating code that may be unstable.

Most of these options involve removing internal checks on your code. Personally, I like being protected from my own carelessness, particularly when I've been up for 48 hours straight, alone with my Jolt, finishing a project.

Aliasing refers to calling the same variable by more than one name. This happens, for example, when a global variable is passed to a routine and then used by the routine both as a global variable and a parameter.

If you're sure there is no aliasing present in your project, selecting Assume No Aliasing allows the compiler to apply optimizations that it could not otherwise use — for example, storing variables in registers and performing loop optimizations.

Selecting Remove Array Bound Checks turns off array bounds error checking and removes checks for the correct number of dimensions of the array.

Microsoft warns that selecting this option "may speed up array manipulation but invalid memory locations may be accessed and result in unexpected behavior or program crashes."

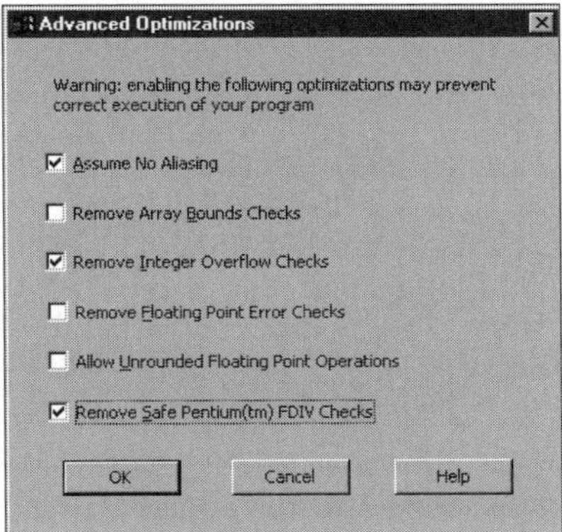

Figure 16-7: The Advanced Optimizations dialog allows you to select native code compilation options that may speed your code, but are potentially unsafe.

By default in Visual Basic, a range check is made on every integer value. Selecting Remove Integer Overflow Checks turns off this error checking, which can speed up integer calculations. However, if integer variables are overflowed, you won't get an error message — and you probably will get weird results.

Similarly, a check is made on every calculation of a floating-point data type — Single and Double — to be sure that the value is within range and that there are no divide by zero or other invalid operations involved. If you select Remove Floating Point Error Checks, this error checking is turned off. Once again, this can speed things up, but if something goes wrong, you won't receive an error message, you'll just get anomalous results.

Allow Unrounded Floating Point Operations, when selected, allows VB to handle floating-point calculations more efficiently. In line with the theme of the Advanced Optimizations dialog, a possible negative consequence is that the comparison of two floating-point values you expect to be equal may be evaluated as unequal.

Remove Safe Pentium FDIV Checks removes checking so that the code for floating-point division is faster and smaller. Selecting this option may produce slightly incorrect results on Pentium processors with the FDIV flaw. (You could use this switch, together with an appropriate calculation, to test for the presence of the FDIV Pentium flaw.)

Conditional Compilation

You can control which part of your project is compiled using #If...#ElseIf... #Else...#End If statements. Conditional compilation blocks use the value of *conditional compiler constants* (discussed in a moment) to determine which code blocks are included in the final executable program that is compiled.

Code that is ignored due to conditional compilation adds no size to the finished executable and consumes no resources. A good way to think of this is that conditional compilation lets you easily and selectively comment out blocks of code. A common use is to include code with conditional constants for debugging purposes.

An important use of conditional compilation is to handle differences between operating platforms. For example, as I discussed in Chapter 11, there are some differences between Windows 95 and Windows NT 4 that need to be handled conditionally if these features are included in your code and you wish it to run on both 32-bit platforms.

Another use for conditional compilation is to include an external resource file — containing string literals, bitmaps, and so forth — based on a conditional constant. This is an excellent technique for internationalizing an application; see the section "External Resource Files" later in this chapter for details.

You could also use conditional compilation to include, or exclude, code used for debugging or measuring the speed of parts of an application. See the section "Measuring Speed" later in this chapter.

Conditional Constants

You cannot mix and match conditional compiler constants with other code. In other words, you can only use them for conditional compilation. (For example, you cannot set a conditional constant based on the evaluation of a normal If statement).

Conditional constants are True when the expression assigned to them evaluates to -1, and False otherwise. You can assign other conditional constants and arithmetic and logical operators (excluding Is) to a conditional constant. For example:

```
#Const Final = 0 'False
#Const TestCode = -1 'True
#Const Elvish = -1 'True
#Const English = Not #Elvish 'False
```

You can create your own constants in three ways. First, you can use the #Const compiler directive within a module. No matter where this directive appears in the module, the conditional constant has a module-level scope; but note that conditional constants declared in this way are *always* local to the module in which their declaration appears.

You can declare a conditional constant that is global to the project on the command line using the /d switch or on the Advanced tab of the Options dialog.

For example, you could use the /make switch to compile a VB project with conditional constants from the command line:

```
C:\Vb\Vb5.Exe /make Project1.Vbp /d TestCode=-1 : Elvish=-1
```

The most common way to enter project-wide conditional constants is on the Make tab of the Project Properties dialog (see Figure 16-8).

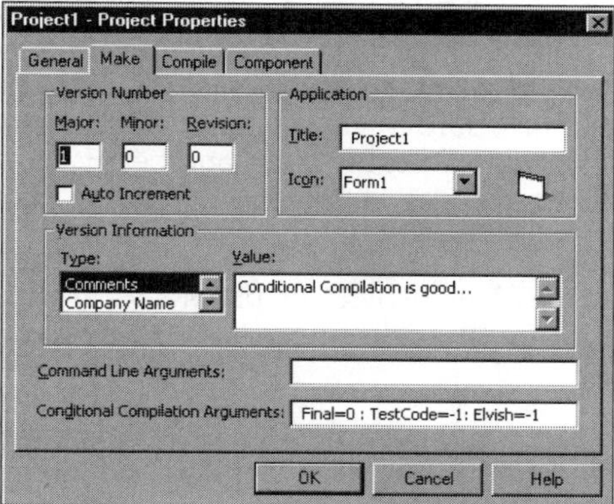

Figure 16-8: You can set global conditional compiler constants using the Make tab of the Project Properties dialog.

External Resource Files

Suppose that you needed to prepare versions of your software for many different races and languages — for instance, English, Elvish, and Klingon. (As members of the Federation, we do have to consider the Cardasians, Ferengi, Klingons, Romulans, Vulcans and all those others out there.) Wouldn't it be neat if you could concentrate on the program logic itself, and give out a list of string literals (and graphics) needed to translate your program display into the various different languages, which assistants could compile for you? For example, you could have 1 = "My Test Program" (Main form caption), 2 = "OK," and so on, translated into all those languages.

You can do exactly this using conditional compilation and external resource files. By the way, external resource files are also helpful when you simply need to prepare numerous versions of a program with slightly different displays, even if all the versions are in English.

One benefit of this scheme — that is, separating screen elements such as text and pictures from the program itself — is that the resource files can be outsourced without compromising the security of the actual project files.

To add a compiled external resource file (***.Res*** file) to your project, choose Add File from the Project menu. You can only load one ***.Res*** file at a time in a project (if you try to load a second, you'll get an error message). This means that there are two ways you can deal with external resources:

- You can have one resource file for each language. Internal identification numbers for elements should be identical. For example, in ***English.Res***, the string "OK" might have an ID of 101 and in ***German.Res***, "Ja" would also have an ID of 101. Only one of these files would be loaded into the project at a time.

- You can provide one large resource file with resources sorted by language and offset from one another by a specific number. Then use conditional compilation to only compile the resources needed into your program. If you take this approach, make sure to allow enough space between language groups when assigning identification numbers to your resources; that way, you'll have room to add elements as your needs expand.

To make this a little less abstract, I've prepared a sample program, saved on the CD-ROM as ***External.Vbp***. This project displays a form with language elements in either English or Elvish, depending on the way the conditional compilation flag is set.

I have prepared three ***.Res*** files, on the companion CD-ROM as ***English.Res***, ***Elvish.Res***, and ***Both.Res***. I created them using Sheridan Software's Resource Assistant (part of the VBAssist program), which is shown in Figure 16-9. Alternatively, I could have used Visual C++'s Developer Studio, or any Windows-based resource editor capable of handling 32-bit ***.Res*** or ***.Rc*** files.

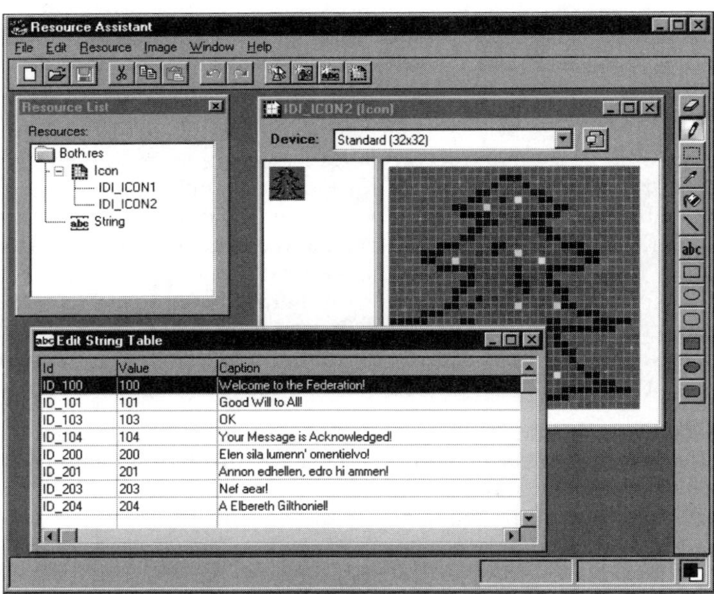

Figure 16-9: You can use VBAssist's Resource Assistant — or other resource editing tool — to prepare an external resource file.

The sample application has ***Both.Res*** loaded and uses conditional compilation with an offset to correctly add the proper resources to the project. I prepared ***Both.Res*** based on the information in Table 16-2 with English values from 100 on and Elvish values from 200 on.

Table 16-2 Information to be Included in the Compiled Resource (*.Res*) File

Value (ID)	*Function*	*String Literal Contents*
100	Form.Caption	Welcome to the Federation!
101	Label1.Caption	Good Will to All
102	Image1.Picture	Firecracker icon
103	Command1.Caption	OK
104	Message Box text	Your Message is Acknowledged!
200	Form.Caption	Elen sila lumenn' omentielvo!
201	Label1.Caption	Annon edhellen, edro hi ammen!
202	Image1.Picture	Christmas tree icon
203	Comman1.Caption	Nef aear!
204	Message Box text	A Elbereth Gilthoniel!

Here's the code required to load the Elvish version of the project:

```
Option Explicit
Public Offset As Integer

Private Sub Form_Load()
   #Const Elvish = -1 'True
   #If English Then
      Offset = 100
   #ElseIf Elvish Then
      Offset = 200
   #Else
      MsgBox "Attempting to Load Unknown Language!"
   #End If
   Me.Caption = LoadResString(Offset)
   Label1 = LoadResString(Offset + 1)
   Image1 = LoadResPicture(Offset + 2, vbResIcon)
   Command1.Caption = LoadResString(Offset + 3)
End Sub

Private Sub Command1_Click()
   MsgBox LoadResString(Offset + 4), _
      vbInformation, _
      LoadResString(Offset)
End Sub
```

To change to the English version, simply change the #Const statement:

```
#Const English = -1 'True
```

Alternatively, you could set the constant value on the Make tab of the Project Properties dialog.

This being 32-bit Windows, I can run both the English and Elvish versions at the same time in different copies of the VB development environment, with the results shown in Figure 16-10. I think they both look great!

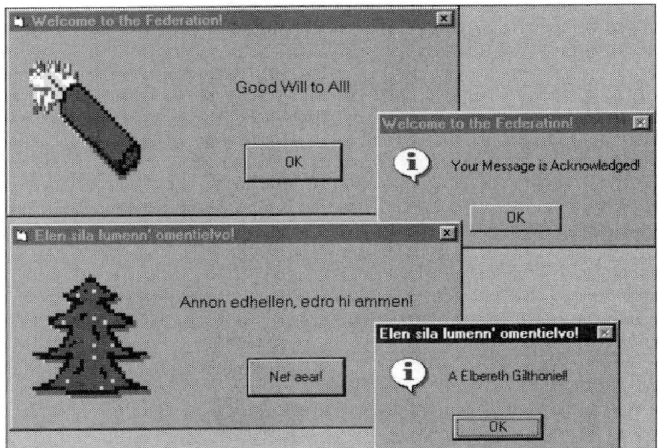

Figure 16-10: Conditionally compiled external resource files are a great way to localize applications.

Optimizing

When programmers speak of "optimizing," they usually mean "optimizing for speed." In fact, you can seek to optimize program speed, apparent speed, display, apparent display, or memory consumption. To attempt to optimize all of these is not inherently contradictory, although sometimes it seems that way. You'll have to decide what's most important and set your optimizing priorities accordingly.

I'll start with speed, because in one respect it's the easiest: You can, without too much difficulty, reliably quantify the time program code consumes.

Before you can really optimize for speed, you need to be able to measure how fast the different parts of your program are. Without identifying bottlenecks, it's impossible to determine which parts of your code could use fine-tuning. There is little point in working to optimize procedures that are not taking time as it is: If it ain't broke, don't fix it. Actual time spent computing can be deceptive, meaning that without analytic measuring tools, you can't really be sure how long anything is taking.

Measuring Speed

My time measuring procedures are saved on the companion CD-ROM in a module named ***Time.Bas***. There are two procedures, StartTimer and StopTimer, which you should use like bookmarks around any code you want to measure.

These simple procedures use the GetTickCount API from the Kernel32 library. GetTickCount provides a more accurate count of elapsed time than the VB time functions. It measures elapsed time in milliseconds since Windows was started.

Trivia buffs may wish to know that the internal Windows timer returns to 0 after it has been on continuously for approximately 49.7 days.

Here's the ***Time.Bas*** module:

```
Option Explicit
Declare Function GetTickCount Lib "kernel32" () As Long
Public BeginTime As Long

Public Sub StartTimer()
   BeginTime = GetTickCount()
End Sub

Public Sub StopTimer()
   Dim EndTime As Long
   EndTime = GetTickCount()
   MsgBox "Total time used: " + vbCrLf + _
      Format((EndTime - BeginTime) / 1000#, "###0.0000") + _
      " Seconds", _
      vbInformation, "Elapsed Time"
End Sub
```

If you wish, you can modify the code in the StopTimer procedure to display in the Immediate pane using the Debug object's Print method.

The sample application — saved on the CD-ROM as ***Timer.Vbp*** — uses the Timer Code procedures to measure how long various computations take. These operations are:

- Iterating 100,000 times using a For...Next loop. Elapsed time: 0.032 seconds.
- Iterating 100,000 times using a Do While loop. Elapsed time: 0.137 seconds.
- Adding 10,000 strings (the example string is: "Hacker") to an array using For...Next. Elapsed time: 0.177 seconds.
- Adding 10,000 strings (again, the example uses "Hacker" as the sample string) to an array that is dynamically redimensioned each time. Elapsed time: 0.284 seconds.
- Adding 10,000 strings of one randomly generated alphabetical character each to a dynamically redimensioned array. Elapsed time: 1.469 seconds.

These times are based on a compiled version of the program (obviously, operations take longer from within the VB environment). Also, of course, they are system dependent (although relative relationships should remain more or less the same across systems). A final caveat is that, particularly under multithreaded operating systems, absolute numbers depend on the computer's state and what else it is doing simultaneously.

You could certainly draw the conclusion from these sample tests that dynamically redimensioning arrays makes performance suffer and that using the VB random generator (the Rnd function) really causes performance hits.

Listing 16-1 contains the code for the test procedures:

Listing 16-1: Measuring elapsed time

```
Option Explicit
Private Sub cmdForNext_Click()
Dim i As Long
   StartTimer
   For i = 1 To 100000
   Next i
   StopTimer
End Sub

Private Sub cmddowhile_Click()
   Dim x As Long
   StartTimer
      Do While x < 100000
         x = x + 1
      Loop
   StopTimer
End Sub

Private Sub cmdBigStringArray_Click()
   Dim i As Integer
   Dim Contains(10000) As String
      StartTimer
         For i = 0 To 9999
            Contains(i) = "Hacker"
         Next i
      StopTimer
End Sub

Private Sub cmdDyna_Click()
   Dim i As Integer
   Dim Contains() As String
   StartTimer
   For i = 0 To 9999
      ReDim Preserve Contains(i)
      Contains(i) = "Hacker"
   Next i
   StopTimer
End Sub

Private Sub cmdRandom_Click()
   Dim i As Integer
   Dim Contains() As String
   StartTimer
```

```
    For i = 0 To 9999
        ReDim Preserve Contains(i)
        Contains(i) = Asc(Rnd * 26)
    Next i
    StopTimer
End Sub
```

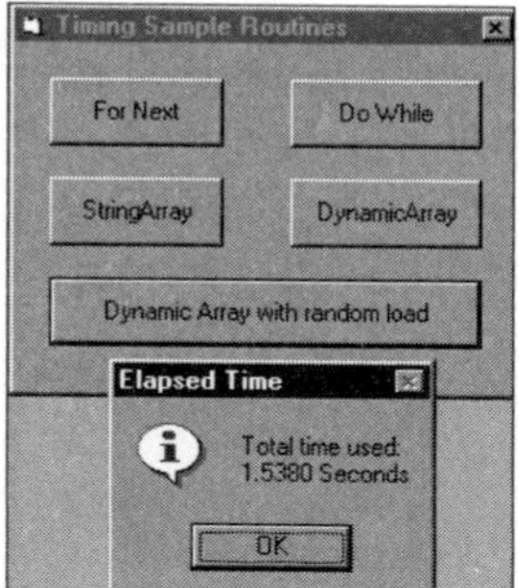

Figure 16-11: It's easy to measure elapsed time consumed by program code.

Optimizing for Speed

You can use the techniques and rules of thumb in this section to increase the actual speed of your applications.

Avoid variant variables. Use explicit variable typing as enforced by the Option Explicit statement, and beware of any implicit variable conversions.

For example, the statement

```
Dim I,J,K As Integer
```

creates an integer variable (K) and two variants (I and J). The syntax is deceptive, making it easy for you to think you've explicitly typed all your variables, when, in fact, some are variant. Watch out for this one!

Whenever possible, use integer variables and integer mathematics. Byte, Integer, and Long are the Intel family of processor's native data types, and operations that use them are surprisingly fast. You can do a tremendous amount using integer math.

Consider separating large applications into a number of separate OLE servers to take advantage of 32-bit Window's preemptive multitasking. You can use remote OLE automation to hand off some processing tasks to the remote CPU.

Avoid copying strings when it's not necessary.

For file I/O operations, use binary (rather than text or random) access.

Replace arrays with collections when this is faster, and use For Each on the collection rather than indexing. If you can associate a unique key with each collection item, collections are the faster choice. However, arrays are better for sequential access when you must traverse all the items in the collection or array. If possible, avoid using the Before or After parameter when adding collection items. It takes more time to add an item to the collection if it has to be positioned.

If you'll be using a property more than once, read it into a variable and use the variable. For example,

```
For I = 1 to 5
   optWhich.Caption = Command1.Caption
Next I
```

is slower then

```
Saying = Command1.Caption
For I = 1 to 5
   optWhich.Caption = Saying
Next I
```

Optimizing Apparent Speed

Optimizing apparent speed covers two related topics: speeding up the screen display and rearranging aspects of your program so it appears to display faster. Here are some suggestions that cover both.

Don't perform time-consuming operations — such as initializing a database — in your form load event. Because the operation will delay the appearance of the form on your screen, the user will perceive the applications as slow.

Do start your application using a splash screen such as the one described earlier in this chapter to hide time-consuming initial operations.

Use Image controls instead of Picture controls. Picture controls use a lot more resources — they are "windowing," whereas Image controls are not. If you have to display a picture that can be clicked on and possibly dragged and dropped, an Image control is all you need.

Label controls are extremely easy on resource consumption (they are not "windowing").

You can use a hidden label to store text you'll need.

You can also use the DragIcon property of a Label control to store icons your project may require.

Use the Line method instead of the PSet method to draw on objects.

Set ClipControls to False in the Properties window for forms and controls in your project to speed up redraw times. If you set ClipControls to True, graphics methods in Paint events repaint the entire object. If you set it to False, only newly exposed areas are repainted, which is probably all you need.

Make sure a control is hidden (by setting its Visible property to False) when making multiple changes involving control properties. This will ensure that the control is only repainted once — when its Visible property is set to True — rather than one time for each property change.

Experiment with the setting for the AutoRedraw property, which enables automatic repainting of a Form or PictureBox control. Sometimes turning AutoRedraw off can free a goodly hunk of memory.

To minimize apparent load time, keep forms hidden but loaded until you need them. (Of course, this consumes more memory than loading forms only as they are needed. Life is filled with such trade-offs!)

Communicate with your users. Use progress indicators such as the Windows 95 ProgressBar control. Display messages indicating what is happening. Allow users to cancel out of lengthy processes.

Access data stored on disk as infrequently as possible. If your program has to read some information, why not read as much as possible? The incremental additional time will not be noticeable and the additional data will be instantly available when it is needed. Of course, you must implement this strategy intelligently so that you don't end up wasting time reading extra data that is never used.

Minimizing Memory Consumption

There a number of ways of reducing the space your application takes up in memory. Often, however, you have to decide what goal to prioritize. Hiding forms consumes memory but reduces the load time for those forms. You'll have to decide. Certainly, under 32-bit Windows, memory consumption seems to be a less crucial issue than it was previously. The suggestions in this section will help you avoid needlessly wasting memory.

Completely unload forms. When variables contain instances of forms that are no longer needed, set them to Nothing. For example:

```
Dim X As New Form1
'Do Things With X
...
Unload X
Set X = Nothing
```

It's a good idea to assign Nothing to an instanced object variable even when that variable represents a form that has been unloaded using the Unload statement.

Reclaim space assigned to string variables that are no longer needed by assigning an empty string to the variable:

```
MyString = "" 'Reclaim the space
```

Although the space taken up by local string, and other, variables will be reclaimed automatically as the variable goes out of scope, global variables will never go out of scope while the project runs. If you must have global strings in your project, assign empty strings to them when you don't need them any more to reduce conspicuous memory consumption.

If your program no longer needs a dynamic array, reclaim space used by the array by using the Erase statement to safely delete the array:

```
Erase MyArray
```

Erase completely deallocates dynamic array storage space. Use ReDim Preserve with smaller upper bounds on arrays in which you need to keep some elements but can shrink the array size to take up less room in memory. Avoid variant variables, which are memory hogs and take up more space in memory than a fixed variable type containing the same information. Of course, in some circumstances variant use is appropriate — for example, to avoid possible overflow errors. Once again, trade-offs!

Delete dead code. Remove all code that is not referenced in the course of execution flow in your project, including unused variables.

Reclaim memory used by graphics in Image and Picture controls. If you're not going to use the control again, don't merely hide it; delete the graphic from memory. Here are three ways to do so:

```
Image1.Picture = LoadPicture()
```

or

```
Set Image1.Picture = Nothing
```

or, for forms and picture controls, because they have an AutoRedraw property,

```
Form1.AutoRedraw = True
Form1.Clear
Form1.AutoRedraw = False
```

Pictures (graphics) can be shared between picture controls and image controls, so there is no reason to load a graphic more than once. For example:

```
MyPic = LoadPicture("C:\Windows\Arches.Bmp")
Image1 = MyPic
Picture1 = MyPic
```

If you load a picture into multiple controls or forms at design time, a copy of the picture is saved with each control or form. Instead, load it once and save on memory, and the time required for multiple disk reads.

It's even better yet to completely avoid storing pictures at design time. Instead, store the pictures as resources (see the section "External Resource Files" earlier in this chapter) and load them as needed at runtime with the LoadResPicture function. If not all the pictures used in a form and its controls are used simultaneously, this saves on memory. It can also speed up form loading because not all the pictures need to be loaded before the form can be shown.

Finding Files on Disk

The demonstration program in this section shows you how to see whether a file is located in the application's directory or on the path. The idea goes back to the splash screen project at the beginning of this chapter: Take care of the dirty work quickly and up front. You can cover it with a splash screen or animation.

The dirty work in question concerns files necessary to your application, such as database files, encryption key files, and so forth. In a full-fledged application, you would store the names and locations of these files in the Registry (see Chapter 10, "Programming the Registry in VB"). You would then use routines similar to the one in this chapter to check that the files were actually present in the location. You could even use an expandable structure — a collection or dynamic array — in case you didn't know the number of files whose location you'd eventually have to verify. Once you verified the location of the files, you could assign their location to global variables (or to elements in a global structure).

The real point of doing this is what happens when the file *is not* found. The demonstration first, automatically, tries to locate the file in the application directory or in any directory on the path. If the file can't be located, the user is given a chance to point to the file location (see Figure 16-12). If necessary, for example, the user could copy the file to her hard drive.

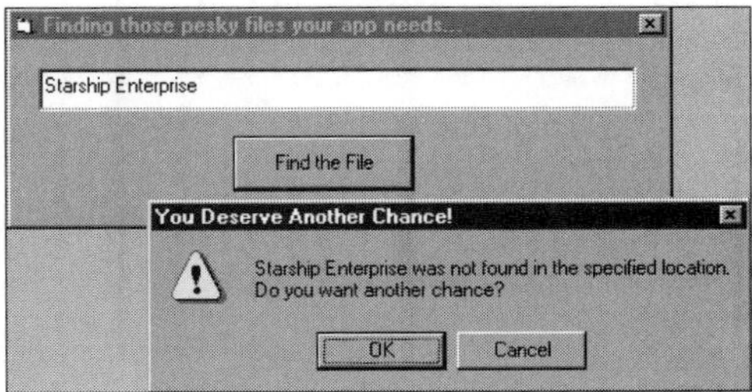

Figure 16-12: The demonstration program gives the user another chance to locate crucial files.

The project — saved on the CD-ROM as ***FindFile.Vbp*** — makes extensive use of file routines in a module I've named ***Files.Bas***.

As shown in Listing 16-2, the Exists function uses the VB FileLen function to determine whether a file exists:

Listing 16-2: Testing for the existence of a file

```
Public Function Exists(F As String) As Boolean
'    Tests for the existence of a file
Dim X As Long
   On Error Resume Next
   X = FileLen(F)
   If X Then
```

```
      Exists = True
   Else
      Exists = False
   End If
End Function
```

StripPath strips the path and returns the raw filename, as shown in Listing 16-3.

Listing 16-3: Returning a filename with the path stripped

```
Public Function StripPath(T As String) As String
   ' Strips path, returns filename
   On Error Resume Next
   Dim X As Integer
   Dim ct As Integer
   StripPath = T
   X = InStr(T, "\")
   Do While X
      ct = X
      X = InStr(ct + 1, T, "\")
   Loop
   If ct > 0 Then StripPath = Mid(T, ct + 1)
End Function
```

FindFile searches for the filename it has been passed first in the application's directory and next along the path. If the file is found, the function returns the fully qualified location of the first occurrence. If the file cannot be found, FindFile returns an empty string, as you can see in Listing 16-4.

Listing 16-4: Finding a file

```
Public Function FindFile(SearchFile As String) As String
   Dim Path As String, CurrentDir As String
   Dim found As Integer, semicolon As Integer
   On Error GoTo ErrHandle
   CurrentDir = App.Path
   If Right(CurrentDir, 1) <> "\" Then CurrentDir = CurrentDir + "\"
   found = Dir(CurrentDir & SearchFile) <> ""
   If Not found Then
      Path = Environ("PATH")
      If Path <> "" Then
         If Right(Path, 1) <> ";" Then Path = Path + ";"
            semicolon = InStr(Path, ";")
            Do
               CurrentDir = Left(Path, semicolon - 1)
               If Right(CurrentDir, 1) <> "\" Then _
                  CurrentDir = CurrentDir + "\"
               found = Dir(CurrentDir & SearchFile) <> ""
               Path = Right(Path, Len(Path) - semicolon)
               semicolon = InStr(Path, ";")
            Loop While ((semicolon <> 0) And Not found)
         End If
   End If
   If found Then
      FindFile = CurrentDir & SearchFile
```

```
    Else
       FindFile = ""
    End If
    Exit Function
ErrHandle:
    MsgBox "Error Number: " + Str(Err.Number) + _
       ";Description: " + Err.Description
    Resume Next
End Function
```

This relatively complex little function uses the VB Environ function to return the current path string and then "walks along" the path, stripping it apart into directories using the path statement's semicolon delimiters.

The Find File demonstration code itself first calls the Exists function to see whether the text entered in txtFile is an existing file:

```
Private Sub cmdFind_Click()
   Dim FileOut As String, FileIn As String, RetVal As Long
   FileIn = Trim(txtFile.Text)
   If Not Exists(FileIn) Then
   ...
```

If the file was found as specified, all is well and execution exits via the Else clause at the bottom of the procedure. If, however, the file can't be found:

```
      ...
      FileOut = FindFile(StripPath(FileIn))
      If FileOut = "" Then
         RetVal = MsgBox(FileIn + " was not found in" _
            + "the specified location." + _
            vbCrLf + "Do you want another chance?", _
            vbExclamation + vbOKCancel, _
            "You Deserve Another Chance!")
         If RetVal = vbOK Then RepairIt FileIn
         Exit Sub
      End If
      ...
```

FindFile is called with the stripped path version of the input file as its argument. If FindFile returns an empty string, meaning that a file with the right name cannot be found in either the application directory or along the path, the user is given the chance to rectify the situation in the ReachIt procedure (described in a moment).

Here's the end of the cmdFind subroutine:

```
   ...
   Else
      FileOut = FileIn
   End If
   MsgBox "File Found: " + fileout, vbInformation, _
      "Global File Variable assignment!"
   txtFile.Text = fileout
End Sub
```

Selecting the Text in a TextBox Control

To select the text in a TextBox control when the control gets the focus, as in the File Find demonstration, add the following code to the control's GotFocus event:

```
Private Sub txtFile_GotFocus()
    txtFile.SelStart = 0
    txtFile.SelLength = Len(txtFile.Text)
End Sub
```

The primary reason for doing this is if you think the user will usually wish to discard the text.

The RepairIt code in the demonstration program is quite bare bones, but it could be made elaborate and could include all kinds of conditional instructions.

```
Private Sub RepairIt(FileIn As String)
    CommonDialog1.filename = FileIn
    CommonDialog1.InitDir = App.Path
    CommonDialog1.ShowOpen
    txtFile.Text = CommonDialog1.filename
    cmdFind_Click
End Sub
```

The end of the procedure calls cmdFind_Click again. I added a Cancel button to cmdFind's message box function to avoid creating an endless circle if the file is never found and the user can't rectify the situation. (The file named "Starship Enterprise" — with no extension — shown in Figure 16-13 is unlikely to ever be added to the user's system.)

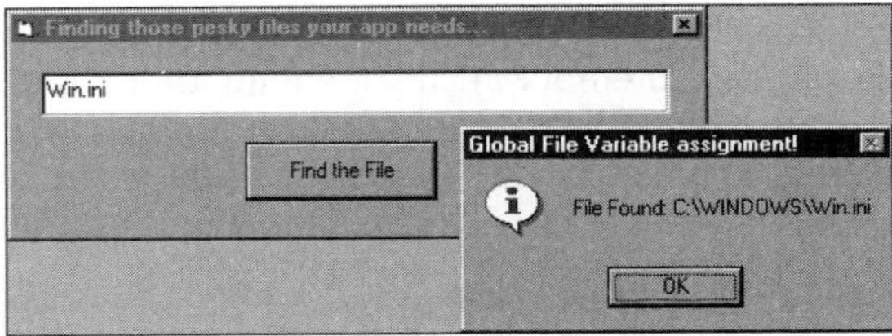

Figure 16-13: The FindFile routine can be used to locate files that are needed by your application.

Obviously, you don't need this application to tell you the location of ***Win.Ini*** (see Figure 16-13). But if your application relies on the presence of certain crucial files, adding a file location procedure similar to this one helps make your code more bulletproof. If nothing else, you could use it to make sure your application has access to its own help file, and copy the help file into an appropriate location if need be.

Recursion

The topic of this section — recursion — bears a kind of inverse relationship to the topic of this chapter, which is optimizing code. Although recursive methods for solving programming problems are often elegant, may take very little code, and can reflect the underlying nature of the algorithm involved with clarity, VB programs that use recursion will almost certainly take longer to execute than similar projects that are nonrecursive. This chapter has covered optimizing for different things: speed, apparent speed, memory consumption, and so on. You might want to think of recursion as optimizing for algorithmic clarity.

A recursive procedure is one that calls itself. If you can formulate a problem so that at each step there is either an obvious solution or the same formal parameters that you started out with, you have a good candidate for a recursive solution. *Deep recursion* is when you have many nested recursive procedures calls. The deeper the recursion, the more likely your program is to run out of memory or generate stack errors.

Direct recursion occurs when a procedure calls itself, as in the example that follows. *Indirect recursion* occurs when a procedure calls another procedure that in turn calls the first one (there can, of course, be intermediate steps in this process). A rather trivial example of indirect recursion occurs in the sample program in the last section, ***FindFile.Vbp***: Under certain conditions — when the subject file isn't found — cmdFind_Click calls the sub RepairIt. RepairIt concludes with an indirect recursive call to cmdFind_Click.

Recursion is often used in attempts to program artificial intelligence. It is related to OOP in the sense that both techniques involve winding something up and letting it run.

Any recursive program can be recoded in an iterative fashion, generally resulting in faster but less clear code.

In VB, when a procedure calls itself using direct or indirect recursion, it must keep track of the recursively called procedure's information as if it were a new procedure call. Therefore, one recursive procedure that is nested a hundred calls deep generates as much overhead as one hundred different procedures. (Languages such as Prolog that are optimized for recursion eliminate much of this overhead.)

To minimize stack overhead if you design a procedure that is deeply recursive, use as few formal parameters as possible in the procedure. If possible, declare variables that are local to the procedure as Static to avoid having to make redundant local variable declarations. But watch out for *side effects* — a term for unintended consequences — of the Static declarations.

Example: The Fibonacci Series

The Fibonacci series is named after the 13th century mathematician, Leonard Pisano, who used the pseudonym Fibonacci. This series of numbers is obtained by beginning with 0 and 1, adding them, and then adding the two previous numbers to obtain the next number. This series is an obvious candidate for recursive generation; the Nth number in the Fibonacci series equals the Nth - 1 number plus the Nth - 2 number.

This series of numbers occurs in many kinds of patterns in nature — for example, the spiraling behavior of petals in a flower. Pisano first "discovered" these famous numbers when working out the number of rabbits to be eventually expected when starting with one mating pair. The demonstration Fibonacci program is on the CD-ROM as ***Fib.Vbp***.

Listing 16-5 contains the recursive function that generates the Fibonacci series:

Listing 16-5: Generating the Fibonacci series

```
Private Function Fib(N As Long) As Long
   DoEvents
   If N = 0 Then
      Fib = 0
   ElseIf N = 1 Then
      Fib = 1
   Else 'Recursive call
      Fib = Fib(N - 1) + Fib(N - 2)
   End If
End Function
```

More than about 25 Fibonacci numbers and this recursion gets pretty deep. I've added a DoEvents call to the function so that at least the screen is redrawn (and it's easier for you to bail out if you decide to).

You can call the Fib function and add it to the list box in one fell swoop (see Figure 16-14):

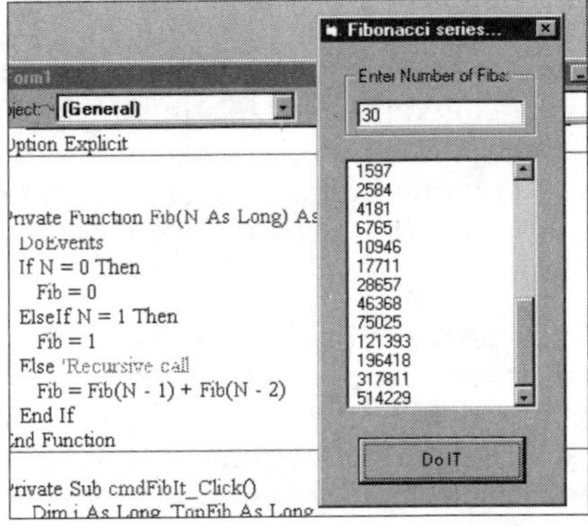

Figure 16-14: You can use a recursive function call to generate the Fibonacci series.

```
Private Sub cmdFibIt_Click()
    Dim i As Long, TopFib As Long
    Screen.MousePointer = vbHourglass
    lstFib.Clear
    TopFib = Val(txtHowMany)
    For i = 0 To TopFib
        lstFib.AddItem Str(Fib(i)) 'Call Fib function
    Next i
    Screen.MousePointer = vbDefault
End Sub
```

Example: Greatest Common Divisor

The Greatest Common Divisor example, saved on the CD-ROM as ***Divisor.Vbp***, uses a recursive function to calculate the greatest common divisor of two numbers. (By the way, the technique used for the calculation is known as the *Euclidean algorithm*, which should give you some idea about how old it is.)

Listing 16-6 shows the recursive function:

Listing 16-6: Calculating the greatest common divisor of two numbers

```
Private Function GreatestCommonDiv(N1 As Double, N2 As Double) _
    As Double
    If N2 = 0 Then
        GreatestCommonDiv = N1
    Else
        GreatestCommonDiv = GreatestCommonDiv(N2, N1 Mod N2)
    End If
End Function
```

Here is the module code that calls the function and displays the result (as shown in Figure 16-15):

```
Private Sub Command1_Click()
    Dim GCD As Double
    Label2 = ""
    GCD = GreatestCommonDiv(Val(Num1), Val(Num2))
    Label2 = Str(GCD)
End Sub
```

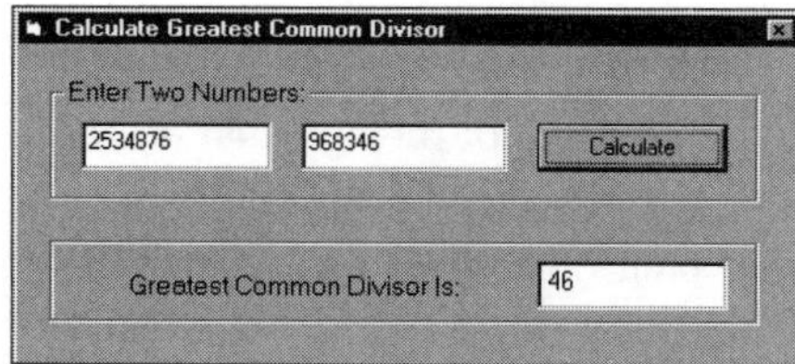

Figure 16-15: You can use recursion to calculate the greatest common divisor of two numbers.

Summary

This chapter covered important material on how to optimize the speed of your programs. In addition, it discussed issues of "apparent speed": even if your program takes a long time to do something, how to best placate users while it is doing that something.

These topics are thematically related to creating programs that make a good initial impression. A number of the topics in this chapter show you how to make sure that your program does just that.

This chapter also explained how to optimize for things other than speed. I showed how to optimize code for memory consumption. In addition, I introduced several techniques that make sense for other "optimization" reasons: conditional compilation for optimizing the number of platforms your code can be compiled for, external resource files for optimizing the number of different languages your program can display, and recursion for optimizing algorithmic elegance.

In this chapter, I provided extensive tips on how to optimize a program's:

- Apparent speed
- Actual speed
- Display speed
- Memory consumption

In addition, specific examples and discussions in this chapter showed you how to

- Use an initial splash screen to hide time-consuming initialization routines
- Control shelling to external applications under 32-bit Windows
- Decide between pseudocode and native code compilation
- Use the native code compiler switches
- Speed up the loading of a massive application by breaking it up and shelling
- Use an external resource file and conditional compilation to display different language versions — in this example program, English and Elvish — of an application
- Insert your own code to measure execution speed
- Check for the existence, and location, of files crucial to your application and give the user the chance to correct any problems
- Use recursion to calculate the Fibonacci series and the greatest common divisor of two numbers

PART IV

Display Secrets

Chapter 17: Secrets of Good Interface Design

Chapter 18: Managing MDI Applications and Menus

Chapter 19: Runtime Display Secrets

Chapter 17

Secrets of Good Interface Design

Good interface design starts at the drawing board when an entire software project is still in the earliest of development phases. A good user interface dances hand-in-hand with well-designed code architecture; they complement each other and work together — they are *user-friendly*.

Unfortunately, that's not the way an interface is normally designed. What usually happens is that the interface emerges from the program design after the programmer has dropped all the controls needed onto a form and has added the code that makes the controls work — in other words, the interface is often a haphazard afterthought.

In a perfect software design world, the programming team developing the code would work in tandem with an interface design team who would make what the user sees good to look at, easy to use, and fun, too. Unfortunately, this is not the case in the real world. Most software is designed by programmers who, while they are excellent thinkers and coders, have not been trained as designers.

This chapter covers the following topics:

- Handling a user's interface expectations and meeting her goals
- Letting the user have fun
- Controlling the user's actions in an event-driven environment
- Setting defaults and tab order
- Making controls unavailable
- The user interface aspect of error handling

As I move through the chapter, I will first discuss general design principles that you should consider at the earliest development stages. For example, you should gauge your user's expectations and thoroughly consider your application's user interface and how the user will approach it.

Then I will progress to more design-specific topics, including controlling the user's actions and handling application errors in a way that does not mystify or make a possibly bad situation worse.

Interface Design and the Back Seat

Most software on the market today is like a car with two people in it: one driving and one in the back seat. The car's driver is the code that makes the application run — it is in total control of the car and usually does not take much notice of the passenger in the back seat. The passenger is the interface design, sitting back there with a road map, trying to make suggestions about a better route that the driver gleefully ignores.

Software is not created for the programmer but for the *user*. And it is the user's goals and expectations that you must keep in mind when developing a project. If users can be quickly productive with a software product, they will buy it — and that's money (hopefully) in the developer's pocket.

"All right," you say, "just what do I have to do to keep the user happy?" Many software users today tend to be in the "Jane Six-Pack" class of computer users. There are those who do not want to know what is going on inside the computer, those who are like elephants stomping around an application and will not read or follow instructions, and others who tiptoe like timid mice, literally frightened of the computer itself. (Hey, I'm not kidding; I've seen people who are afraid to turn a computer on!) As use of computer technology continues to spread, there will be more and more of these technologically illiterate "dummy" users.

Generally, this kind of user has several hidden goals:

- "I don't want to look stupid and feel intimidated."
- "I don't need a lot of gadgets; I just want to get my work done as quickly as possible."
- "I don't want to lose everything I've been working on for the last nine hours."
- "I don't want to be bored; I want to have fun."

Unfortunately, most software in the marketplace does everything it can to foil users, almost helping them to make mistakes, feel bad and panicky, work slowly, and become bored and frustrated. This happens because the software developers get so caught up in code design and implementation that they forget what they started doing it for in the first place: creating a package for the user.

For instance, take a look at Figure 17-1. This figure displays the HiJaak Capture settings dialog. (HiJaak Capture is a screen capture program that is part of HiJaak95 from Inset Systems, Inc. I don't mean to single out this program. It does its job very well and its interface is no worse than many others.)

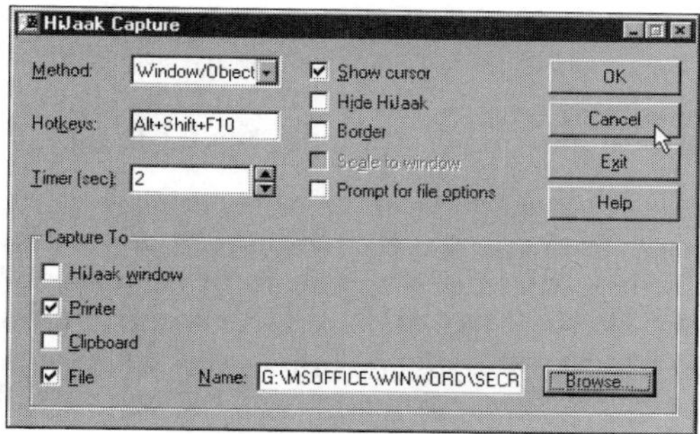

Figure 17-1: Although the HiJaak Capture application works reasonably well for taking screen shots, its interface and design concept could use some tweaking.

The settings dialog displayed in Figure 17-1 and the HiJaak application conception itself has several problems. In the dialog pictured in Figure 17-1, the Cancel button does not cancel the settings that the user has made (as one would expect); it shuts down the application. Also, the settings that you select in this dialog are not saved when you shut down the application. Consequently, you have to select the settings you want each time you launch the application. Finally, when you're capturing screens, no message box warns you if a new capture is going to overwrite an existing file.

Here are some general principles to keep in mind when beginning the design of a software project:

- Good interface design helps the user accomplish more. Be as clear, consistent, and concise with your window design as you are with your code architecture.
- Create an environment that works the way a user expects it will. For example, if you create a Windows 95-style Properties window, the Apply button should register the changes the user has made, but not close the window; in contrast, the Close button should both register the changes and close the window.
- Try not to nest important functions too deeply; in other words, don't make the user go digging through dialog after dialog (or menu after menu) to find a certain property or setting. Besides having to waste time looking for the specific property, the poor user will eventually have to close down all those dialogs.
- Organize window space by grouping related items visually, using frames, panels, and rectangles. Most people tend to look at things from left to right and top to bottom. Try to figure out people's habits and use them to your advantage.

- Be creative and playful with the available design tools but don't confuse the user with too many colors or fonts. This approach will make your applications look unorganized, and the user won't know where to start or will be too dazzled to know where to look. Keep the old adage, "less is more," in mind.

Up to now, interface design seems to have been largely ignored by the software community. However, that does appear to be changing with the advent of Windows 95 and the vast expansion of the home computer market. An interesting book with provocative ideas about interface design is *About Face: The Essentials of User Interface Design* by Alan Cooper (IDG Books Worldwide, 1995).

A Kinder, Gentler Interface

The computer world is constantly changing, metamorphosing into something new, different, and better. The user interface of ten years ago is a far cry from the interface of today. Thankfully, developers have more flexibility with interface design. Much more is possible than it used to be. Take, for example, the DOS environment — its commands (which were hardly decipherable to Jane Six-Pack), its two-tone color scheme, and its inability to handle more one thing at a time. Now, consider the Windows 95 shell — its flexible, multitasking work environment; the many possible color configurations; and the way a novice can quickly learn her way around and become productive. Windows 95 makes the computer work for the user, whereas DOS made the user work hard at computing. Today, developers and interface designers are busy figuring out how to integrate Web functionality in useful and exciting ways into their programs. Tomorrow, who knows?

Consider this comparison when you develop a user interface and the underlying code structure for an application, and try to figure out what you can add to make your application work for the user. Simplicity is truly the key. Your program will be much more effective and easy to use if you can boil your interface elements down to basic sets that are logically grouped.

When designing an interface:

- Think about the purpose of the form and the fewest controls you can incorporate to make it easy to use.
- Plan out how the code interacts with the controls and vice versa. For example, suppose that you are creating a virtual sundae (like the one in Chapter 8, "Windows User Interface Controls"). The interface could offer a check box that the user would select to include a topping on the sundae. Underneath the topping check box could be an array of option buttons that the user would employ to select a topping flavor. In a good interface, the option buttons would be disabled until the user selected the check box.
- Think about things that you *don't* want the user to be able to do with the form and restrict the user's actions through code and control properties.

- Don't set up repetitive tasks. For example, don't add any confirmation windows if you can help it. If you have an Add Client button that opens an Add Client dialog, the user will click Cancel if she doesn't want to add a client. If she does want to add a client, she will enter the information and click OK. From there, in many applications, a message box will appear saying "Adding Client to Records" or some such nonsense. The user knows that she is adding a client when she clicks OK; she doesn't need confirmation or the extra work of shutting down a message box. (Suppose that she had to enter 300 new clients; she'd have to click the OK button in that confirmation message box 300 times. Ugh!)

And with all of this in mind, don't forget that users just want to have fun! People learn faster and perform better when they are interested in what they are doing. After all, a task only becomes work when you don't want to be there. Adding color, special fonts, and custom features to an interface can make it more eye-catching. Also, try to add something quirky that makes the user chuckle.

User Interface Design As Fashion

Trends come and go in user interface design, just as they do in other design-driven arenas, such as the world of fashion.

Sometimes these trends are the result of an important programming paradigm change. For example, the rise of single document interface (SDI) compared to multiple document interface (MDI) applications can be traced to the ability to run multiple applications under 32-bit Windows. (It's not as important to be able to open multiple copies of a "document" in an application if you can achieve the same effect by opening multiple copies of the application.) Another example is the rise in popularity of applications that mimic Web browsers for their interface, which can undoubtedly be traced to the emergence of the Web as a powerful force in computing. On the other hand, some user interface trends can be just plain inappropriate. For instance, there are applications that just should not run from a browser interface.

It's important to distinguish valid trends, which are the result of technological advances, from the silly trends. Incorporating valid trends in your interfaces makes your applications look contemporary. In addition, incorporating interface trends that are familiar to your users probably improves the usability of your applications.

Controlling the User's Actions in an Event-Driven Environment

"Wait a minute," you say, "the title of this section is an oxymoron. How can you control the user in an environment where she can activate any control at any time?" As with crowd control at a theater or stadium, there are ways to direct an application's users in the correct direction without coming right out and scaring them by displaying a message box like the one shown in Figure 17-2.

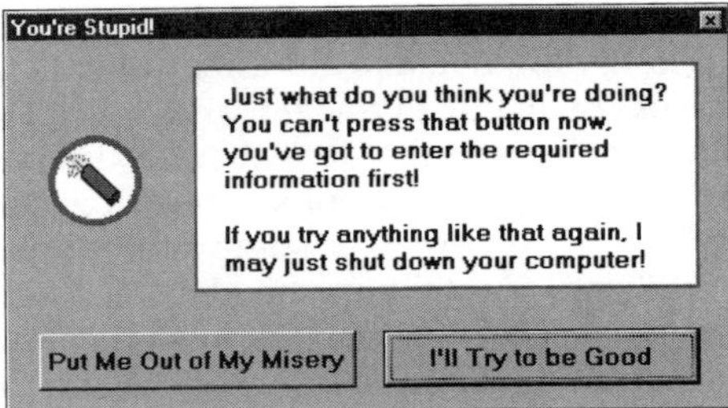

Figure 17-2: You should coddle users and nudge them in the right direction, not scare them away with a message like this one.

If you can think of a way to do it, direct the user, telling her what to do — only giving her a limited set of options, if necessary. This way she won't have to constantly figure out what to do and break her train of thought in the process.

There are several ways to guide the user: by disabling controls, setting defaults, and setting the tab order for a form.

Setting Defaults and Making Options Unavailable

When you are creating a program, after deciding which controls will collect and display the information that the program will handle, you should come up with default values for each of these controls. Defaults are hints to the user about what string or setting is expected for a control. In a text box that collects information about a person — her name and address, for example — you could set default values for each text box. To make it easy for the user to enter information (and so she does not have to delete the default text in each box to enter new information), using code you could make sure the dummy text in each box is selected when the user tabs through the text boxes (see Figure 17-3).

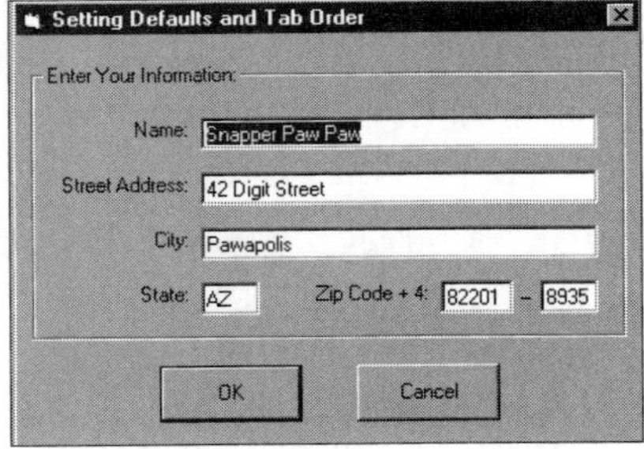

Figure 17-3: Adding default text to text boxes is a good way to provide clues about exactly what should be entered. Preselecting the default text makes it easy to delete the dummy text and enter new information.

In the dialog shown in Figure 17-3, you could also limit the number of characters that the user could enter in the State and Zip Code text boxes. If the user tried to enter too many characters, you could give an aural indication, such as a chime or ding, that she had reached the limit of the text field. I wouldn't, however, send up a message box saying, for example, that she can only enter two letters in the state text field — that would be rather annoying. (Of course, too much in the way of sound effects can also drive users crazy!)

Another way to guide the user is to make controls unavailable to her until she has performed some action, such as entering information into a text box or making a certain selection. The Properties window displayed in Figure 17-4 makes good use of this approach. The user cannot click the Edit Pattern button until she has selected a pattern that can be edited.

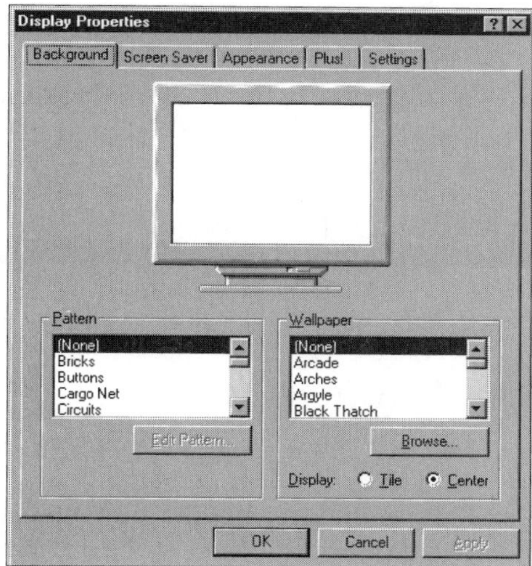

Figure 17-4: The Windows 95 Display Properties dialog contains an Edit Pattern command button that is disabled until the user selects a pattern.

All of this information may be obvious to you, but take a look at the software on the market. Many programs don't even take care of the simplest user issues.

Setting Tab Order

An application's windows have to "flow" just as a house does. If you walk into a house with bad flow, the progression from room to room is choppy, with a room here and a room there. Moving through the house seems odd and often you feel lost because there is no sense to the layout. A form with flow should have a cursor that moves in an ordered progression when the user presses the Tab key. This is an order that you, the programmer, determine using the controls' TabIndex property.

Besides setting the tab order to let the user move easily around a form, you can use tab order to set which control will have the focus when the form opens. You can also exclude controls from the tab order entirely by setting their TabStop property to False.

To set up the tab order of a form, select the control with a TabIndex property that you want to have the focus first; this can be a text box, a combo box, or a command button, for instance. Then move to the Properties window and set the selected control's TabIndex property to 0. Select the next control that you want in to appear in the tab order and change its TabIndex property to 1, and so on.

As you set the controls' TabIndex properties, be sure that you create a logical order. Don't skip around. Move across from left to right or top to bottom, setting up the form's flow. As mentioned, make the user's habits work to your advantage.

Even if you set an OK button's Default property to True, the button will not automatically appear as the default if the tab stops are not set correctly. For example, suppose you have two command buttons — one captioned OK and the other Cancel — on a form where the OK button's Default property is set to True and the Cancel button's TabIndex property is set to 0. When the form opens, the Cancel button will have the focus, and the OK button won't have the dark outline indicating that it is the default button. To correct this problem, make sure that the tab stop for the OK button comes before the tab stop for the Cancel button.

Dealing with Error Conditions

It is a truism that any program, no matter how well crafted, will sometimes behave improperly, a situation known as an *error condition*. Error conditions can be subtle, affecting the validity of the data the program displays, or they can be gross, crashing the entire system. The cause of the error condition can be faulty programming — a very common example involves accessing improper memory addresses — or it can be caused by the operating system or the hardware. The only thing that can be said with any certainty is that at some point your program is likely to encounter an error condition.

Truly, the first thought on any developer's mind when dealing with the user interface aspect of errors in an application should be: "I don't want to scare the user." I'm sure you've encountered the message box shown in Figure 17-5. This message box is actually confusing and threatening to the beginning user. (A novice user of my acquaintance said that the first time she saw this message box, she freaked out and didn't know how to proceed.)

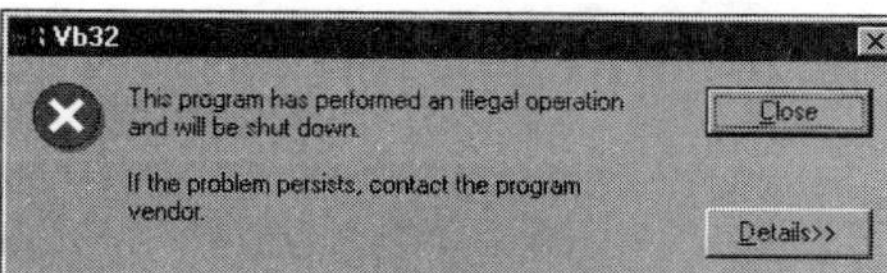

Figure 17-5: The message that the program has caused an error and is shutting itself down is not very user-friendly. The big red encircled "X" scares the user, and the information displayed when the user clicks the Details>> button is hardly illuminating or helpful.

Any application should deal with errors and these errors can, of course, be trapped. (For details on error handling, see Chapter 15, "Handling Errors.") Instead of displaying a dire message with a big "X" and threatening words such as "illegal," you could send up a message box for a particular error that accurately describes the problem and tells the user in simple language what action she should take. Or you could display no message for a particular problem and the program could take care of it all by itself, continuing without the user ever knowing that anything happened. Figure 17-6 shows a better message box than the one shown in Figure 17-5. Besides not giving the user confusing information that she cannot use, such as the data displayed when the Details>> button is pressed, the message box in Figure 17-6 reassures the user and tells her what to do and what her options are.

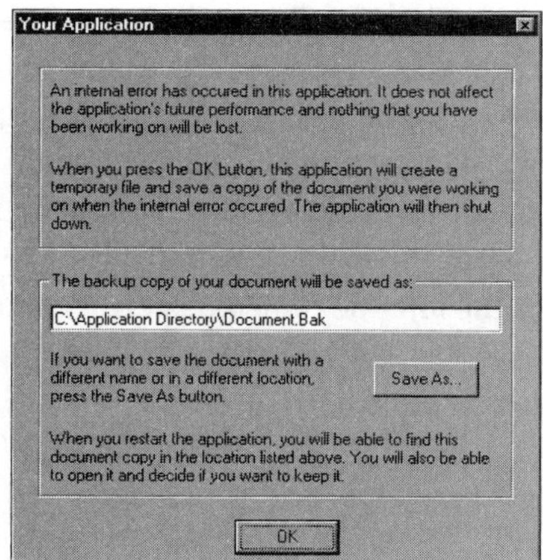

Figure 17-6: This message box supplies the same information as the one shown in Figure 17-5, but without the scare tactics. It informs the user that there is a problem and reassures her that she does not have to worry. It also gives her information she can use about opening the saved document copy after she relaunches the application.

So, instead of adding error messages to an application that point fingers and are imprecise — "You did this wrong!" or "Illegal procedure, shutting down program!" — you should keep error messages to a minimum and display them only if there is some action that the user absolutely has to take, such as saving a file that will otherwise be lost.

Summary

Designing an interesting, concise user interface is just as difficult as designing the code architecture for an application. Unfortunately, an application's interface usually gets swept under the rug and left until the very end (or not considered at all).

Programs are created by developers for the user. Many times this important point is lost in the hectic atmosphere that generally accompanies project development. If you take a look at the software available in the marketplace, you'll discover interfaces that are frustrating to users, that make them feel inadequate and panicky, and that actually slow them down.

In the normal course of project development, user interfaces are often given less attention than any other aspect of the program. Some major applications are even written without the involvement of a professional designer. Paradoxically, it seems to be the user interface that determines the commercial success or failure of most applications.

When creating an application and its user interface, you should consider the following:

- Handling a user's interface expectations and meeting her goals
- Letting the user have fun and making the work go faster
- Going along with user interface design trends that are based on changed technologies (but not those that are just plain silly)
- Controlling the user's actions in an event-driven environment by setting defaults, making controls unavailable, and setting their tab order
- Keeping scare tactics out of the interface when dealing with problems

Chapter 18

Managing MDI Applications and Menus

MDI (*multiple document interface*) project design is important because many applications should allow users to open similar documents simultaneously. Menus are discussed in the same chapter as MDI applications because proper menu functionality is crucial to MDI.

This chapter covers the following topics:

- Managing MDI projects
- Creating wallpaper for MDI applications
- Sizing MDI child forms in the form load event
- Menu contention
- Menu control arrays
- Adding and deleting menu items at runtime
- Loading menus from external resource files

Creating MDI Applications

MDI, or *multiple document interface,* applications maintain multiple *child* forms within a single container form (the *parent*). In contrast, SDI, or *single document interface,* applications are based upon a single window that is used for all user interactions. Notepad and WordPad are SDI applications; Word for Windows and Excel are classical MDI applications. MDI applications let a user easily work on a number of different sets of data at once, perhaps dragging information between child windows, and possibly using a Window menu to navigate between child windows.

The VB Application Wizard offers a third project style, in addition to MDI and SDI: Explorer style. Explorer style projects are SDI applications with a hierarchical tree-view pane that looks, in style, like Microsoft's Internet or Windows Explorer.

With the advent of 32-bit true multitasking versions of Windows, MDI application design has become slightly less fashionable than it once was. As an example of this shift in application design, Windows 3.*x*'s File Manager is a true MDI application. But Explorer, File Manager's analog under Windows 95, is not. It's expected that users will open multiple instances of the Explorer application to perform operations that would have been accomplished using multiple child windows in one instance of File Manager.

Nevertheless, MDI application design is very appropriate for many situations, particularly those that are document-centric or based around repetitive multiple instances of a single financial form.

In Visual Basic, an MDI application contains one — and only one — parent form, called an *MDI form*. You add the MDI form to an application using the Project menu (or the context menus in the Project Explorer).

Child forms are contained within the parent form at runtime (although this is not true at design time). To create an MDI child form, set a normal form's MDIChild property to True.

MDI parents and children are represented at design time by icons that are different than the icon for normal forms in the Project window, as shown in Figure 18-1.

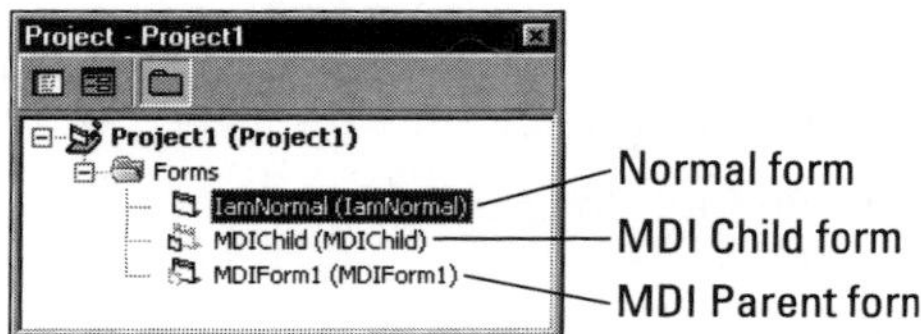

Figure 18-1: Icons in the Project window identify MDI child forms, MDI parent forms, and normal forms.

The forms within an MDI application take on these special characteristics at runtime:

- All child forms are restricted to the MDI parent form's *client* (internal) area.
- A minimized child form's icon appears on the MDI form rather than the user's desktop. Minimizing the MDI form not only minimizes the parent but also all its children; the family grouping is represented by one icon. Restoring the MDI form restores it and all its children to the state they were in before being minimized.
- A maximized child form's caption is combined with the caption of the MDI form and displayed in the MDI form's title bar.
- By default, an active child's menus (if it has any) take over the MDI parent's menu bar (see the section "Menu Contention" later in this chapter). The menus are not displayed on the active child form; in other words, MDI children do many things, but they don't display menus within their own borders.

Managing Children

To show you a good way to manage MDI children, I'll first set up the framework for an MDI application (saved on the CD-ROM as ***MyMDI.Vbp***). The initial stages of this demonstration point out the problems with what — at first blush — appears to be the easiest way to handle tracking children.

The ***MyMDI*** project contains two forms, an MDI parent and an MDI child, logically named MDIParent and MDIChild. The project's startup form is MDIParent.

As a first step, I've used the Menu Editor to add a menu to the parent form. This provides a mechanism for adding child forms and displaying a Window menu, as shown in Figure 18-2. A *Window menu* is a special menu that displays the captions of all open child forms below a separator bar (which you can see in Figures 18-4 and 18-5). It's traditional (but not, of course, required) to include items that arrange child forms — such as Cascade, Tile, and Arrange Icons — at the top of a Window menu. To make a top-level menu item a Window menu, simply select the item in the Menu Editor and check the WindowList check box, as shown in Figure 18-2.

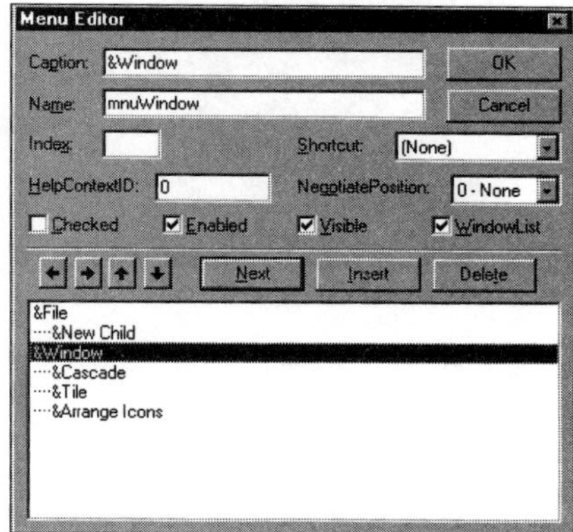

Figure 18-2: To make a top-level menu an MDI Window menu, make sure that, with the menu selected, the WindowList box is checked.

I've added a public variable, ChildCount, to MDIParent to keep track of the number of open child forms. ChildCount is set to 0 in the MDIParent load event. A new instance of the MDIChild form is created and shown in the click event associated with mnuNew:

```
Option Explicit
Public ChildCount As Integer

Private Sub MDIForm_Load()
   ChildCount = 0
End Sub

Private Sub mnuNew_Click()
   Dim X As New MDIChild
   ChildCount = ChildCount + 1
   X.Show
End Sub
```

The form load event of MDIChild is used to make each instance of the child display a caption that includes the ChildCount variable:

```
Private Sub Form_Load()
   Me.Caption = "Child # " + CStr(MDIParent.ChildCount)
End Sub
```

So far, sort of so good! You can add new child forms to MDIParent, as shown in Figure 18-3. If you never deleted a child form — by closing it — ChildCount would work fine as a way to track children.

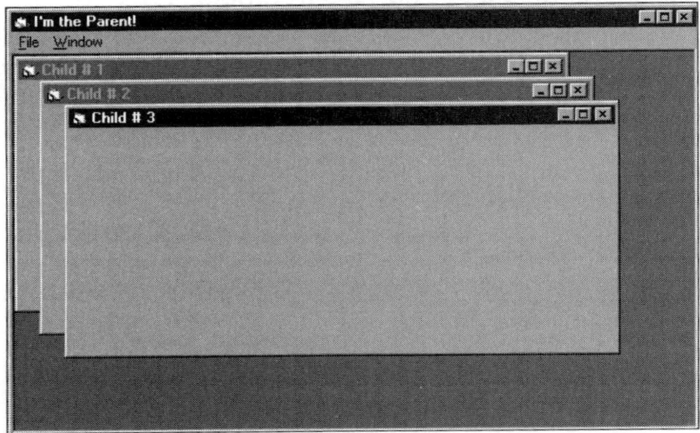

Figure 18-3: You can add as many new instances of a child form as you like to a MDI parent.

Let's take a slight tangent at this point, and add the code necessary to make the upper part of the Window menu functional. The Arrange method of MDIParent is called with an appropriate intrinsic constant as an argument in each case:

```
Private Sub mnuCascade_Click()
   Me.Arrange vbCascade
End Sub

Private Sub mnuTile_Click()
   Me.Arrange vbTileHorizontal
End Sub

Private Sub mnuArrange_Click()
   Me.Arrange vbArrangeIcons
End Sub
```

Figure 18-3 shows cascading forms, Figure 18-4 shows the results of "arranging the icons" (all minimized child forms are aligned along the lower portion of MDIParent), and Figure 18-5 shows horizontally tiled child forms.

If you look closely at Figures 18-4 and 18-5, you'll see a digital time display on the menu bar. To add this clock to the menu, I added a menu item named mnuTime in the position on the menu bar where I wanted the time to show. I unchecked the visible property of mnuTime. The design time caption of mnuTime doesn't matter because it will never display, but you'll have to enter something or the Menu Editor won't accept the mnuTime item. Next, I added a timer control to the MDIParent form. I set the timer's enabled property to True, and its interval to 1000 (meaning, one second).

The code in the timer event sets mnuTime to visible if it is not already, and then adds a nice little clock in its position on the menu bar:

```
Private Sub Timer1_Timer()
   If Not mnuTime.Visible Then mnuTime.Visible = True
   mnuTime.Caption = Format(Now, "h:nn:ss AM/PM")
End Sub
```

I've also added a RichTextBox control to MDIChild. With the control originally positioned in the upper-left corner of MDIChild's client area, the following code placed in the MDIChild resize event guarantees that the RichTextBox control expands and contracts to fill the entire form client area, no matter how it is sized:

```
Private Sub Form_Resize()
   RichTextBox1.Height = Me.ScaleHeight
   RichTextBox1.Width = Me.ScaleWidth
End Sub
```

Moving back to the MDI framework, it's clear that a problem arises when child forms are closed. As shown in Figure 18-4, gaps appear in the child identification numbers.

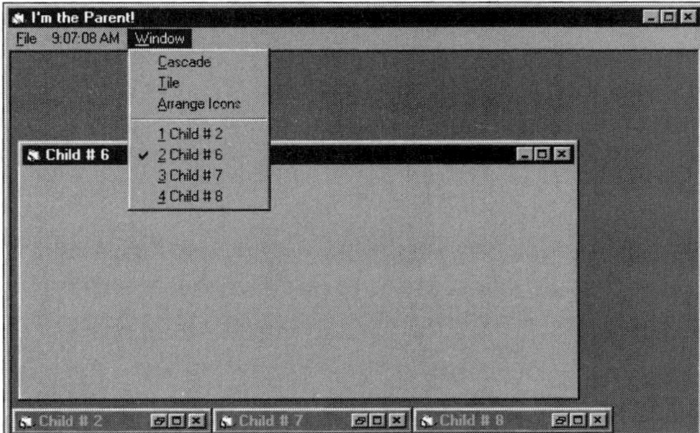

Figure 18-4: Gaps have begun to appear in the numbers assigned for tracking MDI children.

You can "improve" the situation slightly by adding code to MDIChild that decrements the ChildCount each time an instance is unloaded:

```
Private Sub Form_Unload(Cancel As Integer)
   MDIParent.ChildCount = MDIParent.ChildCount - 1
End Sub
```

However, this still isn't so great! It's perfectly possible to get into the situation shown in Figure 18-5, where there are multiple child instances with the same identification number. (You could "achieve" this result by added child forms, deleting them, and then adding new child forms.) Fortunately, we'll soon be able to take care of this!

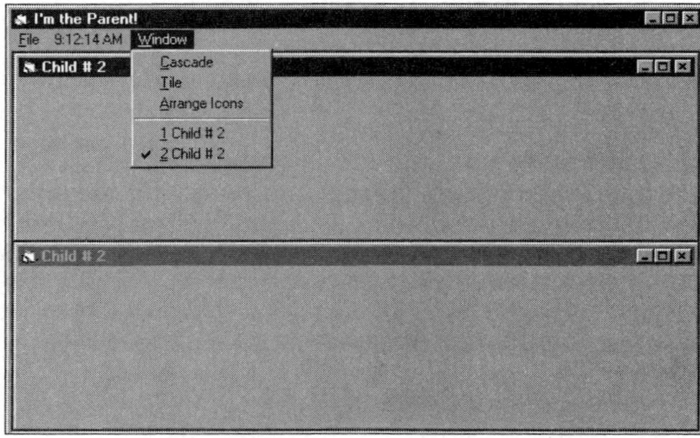

Figure 18-5: Without an adequate child tracking scheme, two children can easily be assigned the same identification number.

Loading Modeless Child Forms

Error number 401, "Can't show non-modal form when modal form is displayed," can seem quite puzzling in the context of MDI applications until you remember that, by definition, all child forms are nonmodal. You can't load a modeless form, such as a child, from a modal form. To avoid this error, place the code that opens the modal form and the child form in a procedure. When the user has completed actions in the modal form, the code hides it, retrieves values, unloads it, and loads the child:

```
Private Sub mnuModal_Click()
   frmModal.Show vbModal
   'Retrieve values from frmModal
   Unload frmModal
   mnuNew_Click 'show MDI child, e.g., modeless form
End Sub

'Close/Show Child Button on Modal form
Private Sub cmdShow_Click()
   Me.Hide 'Hide modal form - don't load child here!
End Sub
```

A Framework for Tracking Children

The problem with the scheme for tracking children as it has been developed so far is that when a child is deleted, its siblings with higher identification numbers don't have their numbers decremented. We can fix that! Let's alter the procedure that adds a new child instance to store the identifier the instance is given in the identifier's Tag property:

```
Private Sub mnuNew_Click()
   Dim X As New MDIChild
   ChildCount = ChildCount + 1
   X.Tag = CStr(ChildCount)
   X.Show
End Sub
```

Captions can now be generated in each MDIChild based on the instance's Tag property. But note that the caption must be set in the form Activate event, not the form Load event. (Referencing a form's property loads the form. The statement X.Tag = causes X to load, but its Tag hasn't yet been set.)

Here's the MDIChild Activate code:

```
Private Sub Form_Activate()
   Me.Caption = "Child # " + Me.Tag
End Sub
```

Each MDIChild instance when it unloads calls a Public procedure that's part of the MDIParent module, passing the value of its own tag as an argument:

```
Private Sub Form_Unload(Cancel As Integer)
   MDIParent.SetChildNumbers Val(Me.Tag)
End Sub
```

The SetChildNumbers procedure uses the forms collection to walk through all MDIChild instances, adjusting those with a higher valued tag than the form that is closing before finally decrementing ChildCount by one.

```
Public Sub SetChildNumbers(ClosingForm As Integer)
   Dim I As Integer
   For I = 0 To Forms.Count - 1
      If TypeOf Forms(I) Is MDIChild Then
         If Val(Forms(I).Tag) > ClosingForm Then
            Forms(I).Tag = CStr(Forms(I).Tag - 1)
            Forms(I).Caption = "Child # " & CStr(Forms(I).Tag)
         End If
      End If
   Next I
   ChildCount = ChildCount - 1
End Sub
```

Another useful way to track instances of children is to establish a dynamic array based upon a user-defined structure that contains information regarding the child. For example:

```
Type FormState
   FileName As String
   Dirty As Boolean
   Deleted As Boolean
End Type
```

You may have to use this technique when you need to store file-specific information (such as a filename) with each child form instance.

Minimizing All Children

You can use the forms collection for another purpose: to minimize all open MDIChild forms (as shown in Figure 18-6). Here's the code for doing so:

```
Private Sub mnuMin_Click()
   Dim I As Integer
   For I = 0 To Forms.Count - 1
      If TypeOf Forms(I) Is MDIChild Then
         Forms(I).WindowState = vbMinimized
      End If
   Next I
End Sub
```

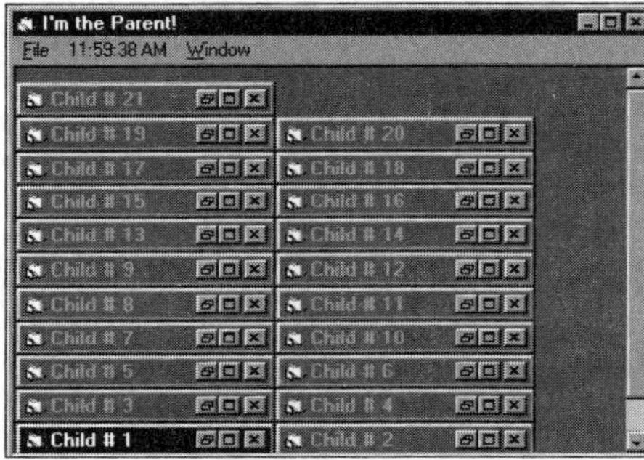

Figure 18-6: You can iterate through the forms collection to perform an action — such as minimizing — on all forms of a specific type.

Closing All Children

You can close all the open MDIChild instances in a similar fashion, but there is a twist. If you unload forms going from 0 to the collection count property minus one, you'll generate an error because the variable that tracks the iterations is not adjusted as the collection count gets smaller because forms are closed. You can solve this problem by going from the top down:

```
Private Sub mnuClose_Click()
   Dim I As Integer
   For I = Forms.Count - 1 To 0 Step -1
      If TypeOf Forms(I) Is MDIChild Then
         Unload Forms(I)
      End If
   Next I
End Sub
```

Creating Wallpaper for an MDI Application

You can easily add "wallpaper" — meaning something other than the default solid background of the parent MDI form — to the background of an MDI application, as shown in Figure 18-7. The trick is to add a child form to serve as a holder for the wallpaper. In the example program, this form is named, logically, Wallpaper. (You make Wallpaper a child form by setting its MDIChild property to True.)

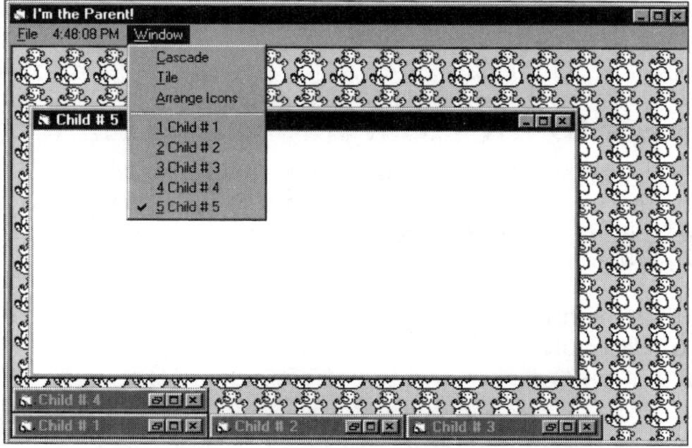

Figure 18-7: It's easy to add a tiled "wallpaper" effect to your MDI applications.

Load whatever picture file you'd like (for example, a ***.Bmp*** or ***.Wmf*** file) into Wallpaper by setting its Picture property. Next, add code to Wallpaper's activate event that manipulates the form's ZOrder (*ZOrder* is the property that governs the back-to-front order of windows) to make sure that it stays "behind" other child forms:

```
Private Sub Form_Activate()
   Me.ZOrder 1
End Sub
```

Now add code to Wallpaper and MDIParent (using the Move method) to make sure that the size of the MDI parent form and its wallpaper stay in tandem when either is resized:

```
' in Wallpaper
Private Sub Form_Resize()
   If Me.WindowState = vbNormal Then
      Me.Move 0, 0, MDIParent.ScaleWidth, _
         MDIParent.ScaleHeight
   End If
End Sub
```

```
' in MDI Parent
Private Sub MDIForm_Resize()
   WallPaper.Move 0, 0, Me.ScaleWidth, _
      Me.ScaleHeight
End Sub
```

That pretty much does the trick. To make sure that child forms stay on top when iconized (as in Figure 18-7), you should add a line of code to the resize event of MDIChild:

```
Private Sub Form_Resize()
   ...
   If WindowState = vbMinimized Then ZOrder 0
End Sub
```

Using BitBlt to Create a Repeating Wallpaper

If you want, you can set the Wallpaper form so that it shows a repeating image, in an effect similar to setting Windows wallpaper to Tiled using the Control Panel. Figure 18-7 shows repeating tiled wallpaper, created using the technique explained here.

The BitBlt API is used in the paint event of the wallpaper form to create the tiled effect. BitBlt copies a bitmap from a source to a target. Here are the declarations that you need to add to the Wallpaper form:

```
Private Declare Function BitBlt Lib "gdi32" _
   (ByVal hDestDC As Long, ByVal X As Long, _
   ByVal Y As Long, ByVal nWidth As Long, _
   ByVal nHeight As Long, ByVal hSrcDC As Long, _
   ByVal xSrc As Long, ByVal ySrc As Long, _
   ByVal dwRop As Long) As Long

Const SRCCOPY = &HCC0020
```

You'll need to add a bitmap as Wallpaper's picture. It should be at least 32 × 32 pixels. (To test this, you can use the bitmap I've supplied, ***Bear.Bmp***, or one of the bitmaps — such as ***Argyle.Bmp*** — installed on your system by Windows.)

Make sure that Wallpaper's AutoRedraw property is set to False. If AutoRedraw is set to True, Visual Basic updates the form's appearance automatically, and bypasses the form Paint event. When AutoRedraw is set to False, the form is repainted using the code that has been placed in the Paint event.

Listing 18-1 contains the code that tiles the bitmap. You should place it in Wallpaper's paint event:

Listing 18-1: Creating repeating wallpaper

```
Private Sub Form_Paint()
   Dim X As Integer, Y As Integer, D As Long
   Dim PatternHeight As Integer, PatternWidth As Integer
   Dim SM As Integer
   ScaleMode = vbPixels
   PatternHeight = 32
   PatternWidth = 32
```

```
    For X = 0 To ScaleWidth Step PatternWidth
       For Y = 0 To ScaleHeight Step PatternHeight
          D = BitBlt(hDC, X, Y, PatternWidth, _
             PatternHeight, hDC, 0, 0, SRCCOPY)
       Next Y
    Next X
    ScaleMode = SM 'probably twips
End Sub
```

Sizing Child Forms in the Form Load Event

When you show a new MDI child form, it is automatically sized and placed at the next *cascade* location, meaning to the right and below the last child window. This is the default behavior even if all child windows are closed. (In other words, if you open three child windows and close them all, a fourth child window will be opened in the position it would have occupied had the original three children still been open.)

You can alter this sometimes inappropriate default placement by placing a Move method call in the load event of child forms. For example:

```
' in MDIChild
Private Sub Form_Load()
    Move MDIParent.Width \ 4, MDIParent.Height \ 4, _
       MDIParent.Width \ 2, MDIParent.Height \ 2
End Sub
```

You could alter this code to fit new child form placement to the positioning of other child forms, or in any way that meets the requirements of your application.

Setting a Custom Cursor

If you like, you can set a custom cursor — also called a *mouse pointer* — for your MDI application. One example is the hand, shown as the cursor in Figure 18-8. (The hand cursor file ***Paw.Cur*** is in the ***MyMDI*** project directory on the companion CD-ROM.) You can create custom cursors in most applications that can create and edit resources, such as Sheridan Software's Resource Assistant (described in Chapter 32, "Using VBAssist and VBA Companion"). Cursor design includes a *hot spot* that sets the area that responds to activation of the cursor (for example, the hot spot for the default arrow pointer is just in front of the tip of the arrow).

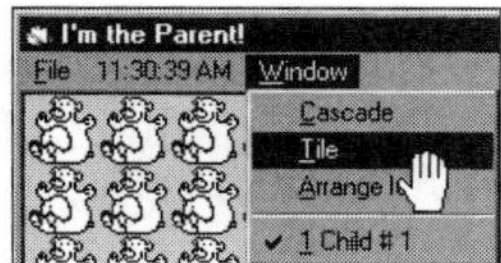

Figure 18-8: A custom cursor can be loaded into the MouseIcon property; the MousePointer property is then used to activate the custom cursor.

A custom cursor can be loaded into the MouseIcon property of a form (and many other objects) at design time in the Properties window.

The MouseIcon property of a Label control is a good place to store custom cursors because additional Labels do not consume much in the way of resources.

The custom cursor is then activated when the MousePointer property is set to vbCustom (equal to 99). For example, if a custom cursor has been loaded into MDIParent's MouseIcon property, you can switch back and forth between the custom cursor and built-in cursors:

```
...
MDIParent.MousePointer = vbCustom ' switch to custom cursor (99)
...
MDIParent.MousePointer = vbHourGlass ' switch to Hourglass (11)
...
MDIParent.MousePointer = vbDefault ' (0)
...
```

However, there is a limitation to setting a cursor this way: The custom cursor only appears in the client areas of the MDI parent form and the child forms. In other words, when the cursor passes over the menu bar area of the forms, it turns back into the default arrow pointer.

To globalize the use of the custom cursor across the MDI application, you can use the MouseIcon and MousePointer properties of the screen object. Because there's no way to change Screen object properties settings at design time, the custom cursor resource must be loaded in code. Here's how you'd do it in MDIParent's load event:

```
Private Sub MDIForm_Load()
   On Error Resume Next
   ...
   Screen.MouseIcon = LoadPicture("Paw.Cur")
   Screen.MousePointer = vbCustom
End Sub
```

By the way, when you add a custom cursor using the LoadPicture statement as I just explained, you have to be a bit careful about the relative location of the cursor file when running the project in design mode. One possibility is to hard-code the fully qualified location of the cursor file. A better bet is to place the cursor file in a directory accessed by your Path variable or in the directory that is active when the project is activated. Note, however, that different directories are active depending on how you start the project. If you start the project by double-clicking the ***.Vbp*** file, the directory containing the ***.Vbp*** will be active (and should contain the cursor file). If, on the other hand, you first start Visual Basic and then use the File menu to open the ***.Vbp*** file, the default Visual Basic directory will be active (and should contain the cursor file).

If you enter the cursor location without qualification, as in the example,

```
Screen.MouseIcon = LoadPicture("Paw.Cur")
```

you have to make sure that the file is appropriately located, or the changed cursor will not load.

It's also a good idea to add an error-handling statement — such as On Error Resume Next — to the procedure loading the cursor. That way, just in case the cursor isn't found, your project will run anyway without displaying an error message.

You can easily add a toolbar to an MDI application using any container control that supports an Align property. (For example, you could use a Picture control or the VSElastic control described in Chapter 33, "VideoSoft's VS-Ocx, VSFlex, and VSView.") The Windows 95 Toolbar control demonstrated in Chapter 8, "Windows User Interface Controls," lets you quickly and easily add Windows 95-style toolbars that automatically support ToolTips (information displayed about each toolbar button when the mouse passes across the button).

Managing Menus

Menus are a crucial part of any application. Visual Basic comes with the Menu Editor (which was shown in Figure 18-2), a powerful design time menu creation tool explained in Chapter 2, "Exploring the Visual Basic IDE," and used in many of the demonstrations in *Visual Basic 5 SECRETS*. This section focuses on runtime menu manipulation — meaning manipulating menus in code.

Menu Contention

As you probably know, if a child form in an MDI application contains a menu, it takes over the menu bar of the parent form in the MDI application when the child is activated. This is true, although an OLE object has, itself, taken over the child form's menu bar. As an example, return to the ***MyMDI.Vbp*** project for a moment, remove the RichTextBox control from the MDIChild form, and add an OLE container control. Insert a new embedded object — such as a Word for Windows document — in the container. (For more information on using the OLE control, see Chapter 21, "Creating Applications that Support OLE.") Add a menu item to MDIChild — for example, a single menu item captioned Hello and named mnuHello. When the child form with the embedded OLE object becomes active, its menus take over the parent menu bar. When the OLE object is activated, the menus of the OLE object — in this case, Word for Windows — take over MDIChild's menu bar, which, in turn, takes over the MDIParent menu bar.

Suppose you want the embedded OLE object to leave MDIChild's menus (and, further along the process, MDIParent's menus) alone. You can easily accomplish this objective by setting MDIChild's NegotiateMenus property to False. You can think of setting this property to False as sending a message to the OLE object along the lines of, "Would-be imperialist conqueror, go home!" (The default value for this property, which must be set at design time, is True.)

You can also integrate MDIChild's menu with the OLE object's menu, as shown in Figure 18-9. Provided that MDIChild's NegotiateMenus property is set to True, you can use a top-level menu item's NegotiatePosition at design time to integrate the menu item with the OLE object's menu. NegotiatePosition has four possible settings, as shown in Table 18-1.

Table 18-1 Settings for the NegotiatePosition Property of a Top-Level Menu Item

Setting	*Consequences*
0 - None	This is the default value for the property. The menu item isn't displayed on the menu bar when the OLE object is active.
1 - Left	The menu is displayed at the left end of the menu bar when the OLE object is active (to the left of the object's menus).
2 - Middle	The menu is displayed somewhere in the middle of the menu bar when the OLE object is active, as shown in Figure 18-9.
3 - Right	The menu is displayed at the right end of the menu bar when the object is active (to the right of the object's menus).

In the example shown in Figure 18-9, I've set the NegotiatePosition property for mnuHello to 2-Middle, and as a result, Hello is sandwiched between Table and Help in Word's normal OLE menu.

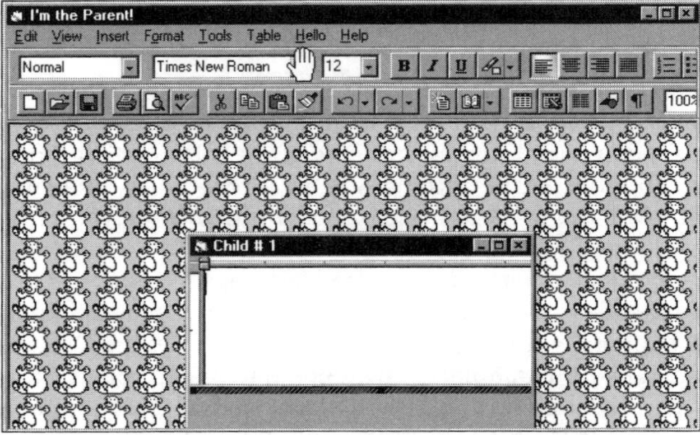

Figure 18-9: The Hello menu item's NegotiatePosition property has been set to 2-Middle, placing Hello in the midst of the normal Word for Windows OLE menu.

Menu Naming

You can look at menu names from two viewpoints: the end user's and the developer's. The name the end user is concerned with is actually the *caption* property of a menu item, not the menu item's *name*, which will be the primary concern of developers.

Captions

Menu captions should make the purpose of the menu item clear to the user. Generally, menu captions should be unique (although menu items attached to different top-level menus can have the same name).

Each menu item should have a (unique to its level) *access key*. Access keys let you have keyboard access to the click events of menu items by pressing the Alt key simultaneously with the access key.

You assign access keys by placing an ampersand (&) in front of the character in the menu item's caption that will become the access key. Conventionally, the first letter in a menu's caption is set as the access key, unless some other letter offers a stronger mnemonic (or is already in use).

Menu Terminology

A *menu* is a top-level menu item whose caption will appear on the menu bar. Confusingly, the word *menu* is also used to refer to any or all of the items or subitems contained in a menu structure. *Menu item* is sometimes used in this general and rather vague fashion as well.

Strictly speaking, a *menu item* is a menu beneath a top-level menu. A *submenu* is a menu item with menu items below it, which are called *submenu items*. A *menu control array* is a set of menu items on the same menu (or submenu) that share the same name and event procedures, with different menu items in the menu array distinguished by their assigned index value.

Figures 18-10 and 18-11 show how these parts of a menu structure fit together in practice.

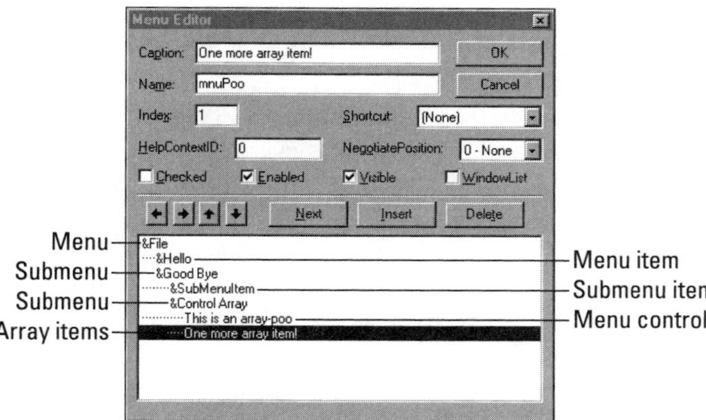

Figure 18-10: You use the Menu Editor to add menus, menu items, submenus, submenu items, and menu control arrays to windows.

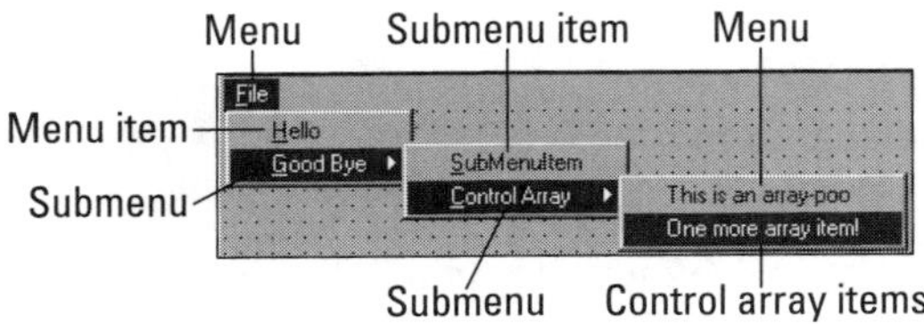

Figure 18-11: Menus can contain menu items, submenus, and menu control arrays.

Internal Menu Names

Internal menu names — the value of the menu's Name property — is what you'll use internally to refer to the menu in code. As always, it's important to name with care. A number of "primitive" cultures believe that if you know the name of something, you have power over it. This is certainly true of menu items! If you can't find them, you can't make them do tricks. Particularly with large projects, it becomes very hard to determine in the Code Editor or Properties window where a menu item is in the menu hierarchy.

Microsoft suggests prefixing menu names with "mnu," suffixing menu items and submenu items with the word "item," and suffixing menu control array items with the word "array," as shown in Table 18-2.

Table 18-2 Microsoft-Suggested Internal Naming Conventions for Menus

Element	*Example*
Menu	mnuFile
Menu item	mnuFileHelloItem
Menu array item	mnuFileGoodControlPooArray
Submenu item	mnuFileGoodSubItem

The prefix "mnu" is certainly a good idea, because it makes the object instantly recognizable as a menu, although the suffixes are optional.

What may be more important than the suffixes is naming menu items to include their entire hierarchy. The example in Figure 18-2 follows this convention, in which items in the File menu include "File" as part of their name. For example: mnuFileOpen, mnuFileSave, mnuFileExit. If "File Open" had submenus, the submenu items would include their genealogy in their name: mnuFileOpenRtf, mnuFileOpenDoc, and so on. The surprising advantage of this is that — because the Code Editor and the Properties window group objects alphabetically — all the items on a given menu will be located contiguously.

Menu Control Arrays

You can use menu control arrays to simplify code when you can use a common code block for all items in an array. For example, the same click event code could handle all the menu items in a control array — perhaps using the menu control array index number to control execution.

You can also use menu control arrays to create a new menu item dynamically at runtime (see the section "Dynamic Menu Handling" that follows).

You create menu control arrays in the Menu Editor. Control array items must be contiguous in the menu structure and at the same level. You create a menu control array by giving items the same name and assigning them a zero-based index identifier, as shown in Figure 18-10. Code can easily be assigned to the click event of the two-element menu control array created in Figure 18-10 and shown in Figure 18-11. For example, to display a message box with the caption of the menu control array item that has been clicked, you'd add the following code to the event:

```
Private Sub mnuPoo_Click(Index As Integer)
   MsgBox mnuPoo(Index).Caption
End Sub
```

This accurately determines which array element has been clicked (as shown in Figure 18-12). Obviously, you could use the index value for more sophisticated processing.

Figure 18-12: You can use the index value in a menu control array click event handler to determine which element of the array was clicked.

Submenu Nesting

Each top-level menu in a window can have up to five nested layers of submenus. Just because you can doesn't mean you should! Don't create mazes of submenus that make it impossible for the user to find items she is looking for. Do organize menus intelligently. Try to make every possible menu item needed in a given context visible in that context. You can use enabling and disabling to only provide access to relevant menus. Where appropriate, you can go further and hide menus that are not relevant to particular users or tasks.

Pop-Up Menus

Pop-up menus, sometimes called *context* menus, are menus displayed in floating locations when the right or left mouse button is clicked.

To create a pop-up menu, you must use the Menu Editor to create a series of submenu items. The parent menu of the submenu items should have its Visible property set to False.

Figure 18-13 shows two pop-up menus, and their menu items, with the parent menu's Visible property unchecked. (The project that shows how to invoke these pop-up menus is saved on the companion CD-ROM as ***PopDemo.Vbp***.)

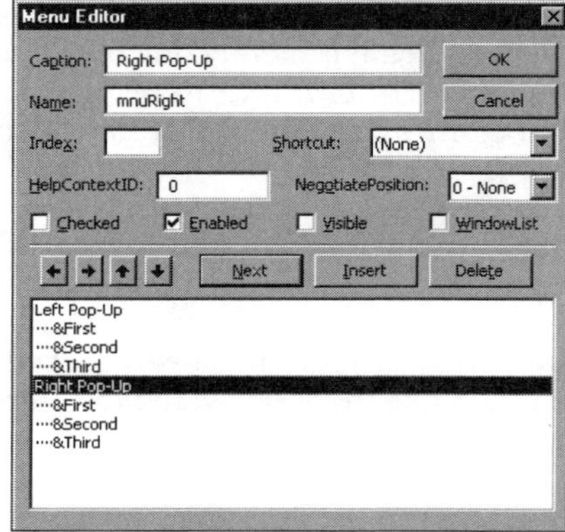

Figure 18-13: To set up a pop-up menu, you must first set the Visible property of the parent of the pop-up menu items to False.

Once you have created a pop-up menu, with its invisible parent, in the Menu Editor, the PopupMenu method of a form is invoked when the pop-up menu needs to be displayed. If no form is specified in the PopupMenu method call, the method assumes that the currently active form is intended. The syntax of the PopupMenu method is

```
form.PopupMenu MenuName, Flags, X, Y, BoldCommand
```

All parameters except the menu name, which is the name of the invisible parent of the pop-up submenu items, are optional. *Flags* specifies constant values selected from those shown in Tables 18-3 and 18-4. The *Flags* setting controls the location and behavior of the pop-up menu. *X* and *Y* are the coordinates where the pop-up menu is displayed. If the coordinates are omitted, the current mouse location is used. *BoldCommand* specifies a name of the pop-up submenu item to display in bold in the pop-up menu.

There are two kinds of constants available for use in the Flags parameter: Location, shown in Table 18-3, and Behavior, shown in Table 18-4. You can use one constant of each type by joining them with the Or operator.

Only one pop-up menu can be displayed at a time. If you want to change the pop-up menu displayed — for example, display left and right mouse button context menus — you'll have to wait until the first one is no longer displayed to show the second one.

Table 18-3 Pop-Up Menu Flags Constant (Location Settings)

Constant Name	*Value*	*Description*
vbPopupMenuLeftAlign	0	The left side of the pop-up menu is located at the X position of the PopupMenu method. This is the default.
vbPopupMenuCenterAlign	4	The pop-up menu is centered at X.
vbPopupMenuRightAlign	8	The right side of the pop-up menu is located at X.

Table 18-4 Pop-Up Menu Flags Constant (Behavior Settings)

Constant Name	*Value*	*Description*
vbPopupMenuLeftButton	0	An item on the pop-up menu reacts to a mouse click only when you use the left mouse button. This is the default.
vbPopupMenuRightButton	2	An item on the pop-up menu reacts to a mouse click when you use either the right or the left mouse button.

Here's an example, from the ***PopDemo.Vbp*** project, of invoking the pop-up menu parent captioned Left Pop-Up (and named mnuLeft):

```
PopupMenu mnuLeft, vbPopupMenuLeftButton Or vbPopupMenuLeftAlign, _
    , , mnuLeftFirst
```

The project is set up to let the user decide whether mnuLeft or mnuRight should be displayed when the Form's click event is fired:

```
Private Sub mnuContext_Click()
   If mnuContext.Caption = "&Left" Then
      mnuContext.Caption = "&Right"
   Else
      mnuContext.Caption = "&Left"
   End If
End Sub
```

Here's the complete code for the Form click handler, which displays the pop-up menu selected by the user, as shown in Figure 18-14.

```
Private Sub Form_Click()
   If mnuContext.Caption = "&Left" Then
      PopupMenu mnuLeft, vbPopupMenuLeftButton Or _
         vbPopupMenuLeftAlign,,, mnuLeftFirst
   Else
      PopupMenu mnuRight, vbPopupMenuRightButton Or _
         vbPopupMenuRightAlign,,, mnuRightSecond
   End If
End Sub
```

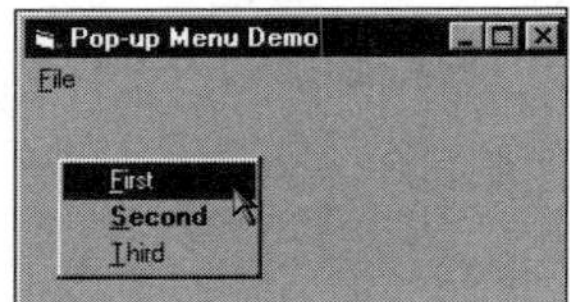

Figure 18-14: You can let user input guide which pop-up menu will be displayed.

Dynamic Menu Handling

Dynamic menu handling means changing the way menus look at runtime (dynamically), usually in response to user actions. The Window List capability of MDI parents (see the section "Creating MDI Applications" earlier in this chapter) is an example of dynamic menu handling built into Visual Basic: A menu item is added for each child form in the MDI project as it is shown. An example of dynamic menu handling you might want to add to an application of your own is a menu item for each new document opened in an application.

Every menu item has Checked, Enabled, and Visible properties that you can easily set dynamically in code.

Note that menu items whose Visible property is set to False are not only rendered invisible, they are also automatically disabled. This means that you don't have to worry about users triggering events belonging to invisible menu items.

Using VB's native capacity — extended judiciously with the use of the Windows APIs — you can do quite a bit more dynamic menu handling fairly easily.

Down and Dirty

You can control the visibility of all menu items and submenus beneath a top-level menu with the Visible property of the top-level menu. This means that you can easily toggle the visibility of entire menu structures at runtime.

As an example, I've added a menu bar to a demonstration project (saved as ***DownDirt.Vbp***) with top-level menu items named Peter, Paul, and Mary. Each menu also includes a number of subitems. The idea is that the user can decide at runtime which menu structure should be visible (and active), as shown in Figure 18-15.

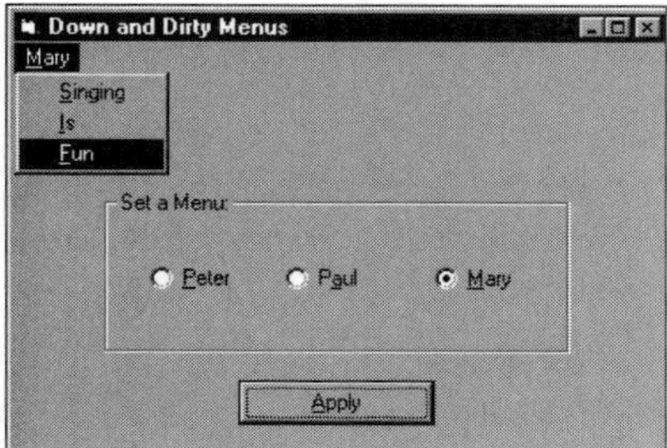

Figure 18-15: You can use the top-level menu's Visible property to toggle the visibility of entire menu structures.

To set this up, I've included code in the form load event that sets the Visible property of all three top-level menus to False:

```
Private Sub Form_Load()
   mnuPeter.Visible = False
   mnuPaul.Visible = False
   mnuMary.Visible = False
End Sub
```

The menu structure that is made visible is determined by the user selection in an array of option buttons once the Apply button is clicked:

```
Private Sub cmdApply_Click()
   If optPPM(0) Then              'show Peter's menu
      mnuPeter.Visible = True
      mnuPaul.Visible = False
      mnuMary.Visible = False
   ElseIf optPPM(1) Then          'show Paul's menu
      mnuPeter.Visible = False
      mnuPaul.Visible = True
      mnuMary.Visible = False
   Else                                  'show Mary's menu
      mnuPeter.Visible = False
      mnuPaul.Visible = False
      mnuMary.Visible = True
   End If
End Sub
```

Removing Menu Items

The project saved as ***RemoveM.Vbp*** demonstrates how to dynamically remove menus using the GetMenu, GetSubMenus, and RemoveMenu APIs. Note that you should manipulate the Visual Basic visibility properties of menus and menu items in preference to using this technique which can, in some cases, result in unexpected runtime errors.

Here are the API declarations:

```
Private Declare Function GetMenu Lib "user32" _
   (ByVal hwnd As Long) As Long
Private Declare Function RemoveMenu Lib "user32" _
   (ByVal hMenu As Long, ByVal nPosition As Long, _
   ByVal wFlags As Long) As Long
Private Declare Function GetSubMenu Lib "user32" _
   (ByVal hMenu As Long, ByVal nPos As Long) As Long
```

The RemMenu function accepts the handle of the window containing the menu bar as its first parameter, and the position of the top-level menu and submenu to be removed as its remaining arguments. Position is specified in a zero-based fashion, meaning the leftmost top-level menu is located at position 0, its first menu item is located at 0,0, and so on. GetMenu is use to retrieve a handle to the entire menu attached to the window. GetSubMenu is used to retrieve a handle to the specific top-level menu. RemoveMenu is used to remove the indicated menu item. The return value of the RemoveMenu API is assigned to the RemMenu function (see Listing 18-2).

Listing 18-2: Removing a menu item

```
Public Function RemMenu(ByVal Handle As Long, _
   ByVal TopPos As Long, ByVal SubPos As Long) As Boolean
   RemMenu = False
   Const MF_BYPOSITION = &H400&
   Dim hMenu As Long, hSubMenu As Long, retval As Boolean
   hMenu = GetMenu(Handle)
   hSubMenu = GetSubMenu(hMenu, TopPos)
   retval = RemoveMenu(hSubMenu, SubPos, MF_BYPOSITION)
   RemMenu = retval
End Function
```

Here's the code that calls the RemMenu function when the Remove button has been clicked:

```
Private Sub cmdRemove_Click()
   If Not RemMenu(Me.hwnd, Val(txtTop), Val(txtSub)) Then
      MsgBox "Remove Menu Function Failed!", vbCritical, "Sorry!"
   End If
End Sub
```

If you compare the menu shown in Figure 18-15 with the menu shown in Figure 18-16, you'll see that the values entered in Figure 18-16 have indeed removed the specified menu. (The top-level menu Mary is at position 2; its menu item Is is at position 1.)

Adding Menu Items

Here's a well-kept secret: You can dynamically add menu items at runtime without going outside VB to use the APIs. This technique uses the Load statement to add new elements to a dynamic control array of menu items. The normal use of Load is to load a form into memory without showing it (that is, making it visible).

To see how this works, let's turn to the sample project I've set up, saved as ***NewMenus.Vbp***.

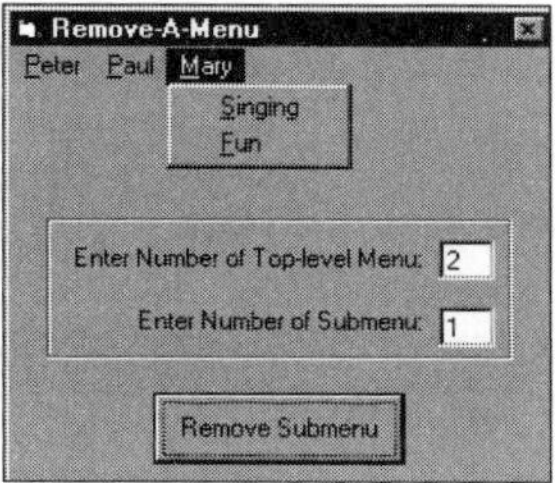

Figure 18-16: You can use the RemoveMenu API to remove menu items.

The first step involves a little hanky-panky with the Menu Editor, as shown in Figure 18-17. File and Exit are perfectly normal Menu Editor entries. The next menu editor field is a top-level menu — captioned Test &Menu Structure and named mnuTest — whose Visible property has been set to False. Below mnuTest is the first element of the control array structure, mnuDummy (with an index value of 0). The important thing to note is that the caption value of mnuDummy has been intentionally omitted.

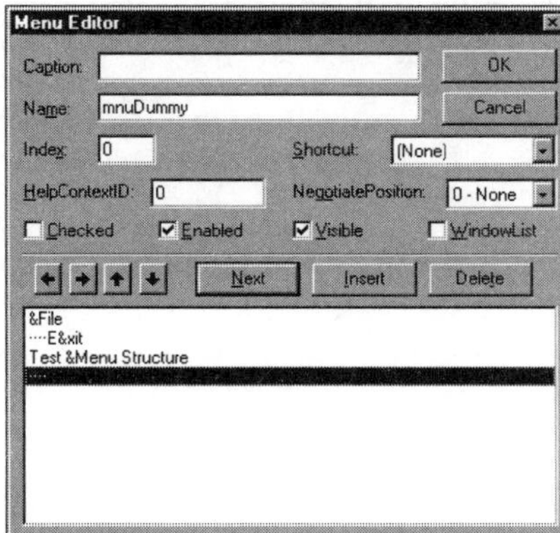

Figure 18-17: Entering a zero-index menu control array element is the first step towards dynamically adding submenu items.

The actual code required to add new submenus to the mnuTest structure is quite simple, as shown in Listing 18-3.

Listing 18-3: Adding a submenu

```
Private Sub cmdApply_Click()
   Static ItemCount As Integer
   If txtNew = "" Then
      MsgBox "You haven't entered a caption for the menu!", _
         vbInformation, ProgTitle
      Exit Sub
   Else
      If ItemCount > 0 Then
         Load mnuDummy(ItemCount)
      Else
         mnuTest.Visible = True
      End If
      'Set properties of new menu
      mnuDummy(ItemCount).Caption = txtNew
      mnuDummy(ItemCount).Checked = chkChecked
      mnuDummy(ItemCount).Enabled = chkEnabled
      ItemCount = ItemCount + 1
      'Reset txtNew
      txtNew = ""
   End If
End Sub
```

ItemCount tracks the number of mnuDummy arrays elements that have been added to mnuTest. For the first one (element 0), there is no need to do a dynamic load because the submenu already exists (albeit without a caption). However, the first time the procedure is run, you need to set the visibility of the mnuTest structure to True.

Once a new element has been added to the menu array, its properties — the caption and whether it should be checked and/or enabled — are set based on user input, as shown in Figure 18-18. Note that if the user enters an ampersand (&) as part of the caption for a new menu item, the character following the ampersand will dynamically become an access key.

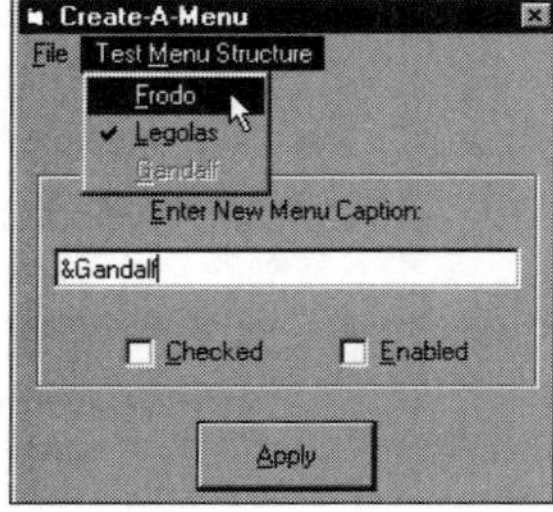

Figure 18-18: The Load statement is used to dynamically add menu items, which can include dynamically generated access keys.

It's a good idea to provide a mechanism for displaying which dynamically created menu item has been activated. The way to do this (as I explained earlier under "Menu Control Arrays") is to use the Index value passed to the click event of a menu control array structure. In many programs, this might involve a Select Case statement applied to the Index variable; in this case, because all you need is the value of the array member's caption string, you can use the index value directly with results, as shown in Figure 18-19.

```
Private Sub mnuDummy_Click(Index As Integer)
   Const Quote = 34
   MsgBox "You've clicked on the menu captioned: " & Chr(Quote) & _
      mnuDummy(Index).Caption & Chr(Quote), vbInformation, ProgTitle
End Sub
```

Figure 18-19: Programmers can use the Index variable, which is automatically passed to menu control array event procedures, to determine which menu item has been activated.

To include a quote within a string literal, as in Figure 18-19, refer to the quote by its ASCII equivalent (chr(34)).

Loading Menu Strings from External Resource Files

Chapter 16, "Optimizing Secrets," demonstrated how to load captions and icons from an external resource file. The specific text and images loaded in the sample application, ***External.Vbp***, depended on which language the application was in as set by a conditionally compiled project offset number (100 represented English, and 200 represented "Elvish").

Loading external menu strings works in pretty much the same way. Unless you are going to dynamically load menu items as described in the previous section, you'll need to use the Menu Editor to set up a menu structure. Although you should assign names to all menus, you don't have to give them captions because these will be replaced with external strings anyhow.

I've made a copy of the ***External.Vbp*** project so I can show you how this works. The resource file, ***Both.Res***, that is part of the project has been expanded to include some new strings to accommodate the menus, as shown in Table 18-5.

Table 18-5 Menu String Resources

ID	*English String*	*Elvish String*
105	&File	&Laita
106	&New	&Cuio
107	E&xit	&Pheriain
108	&Window	&Aglar
109	&Help	&Eglerio!

The code that sets the menu captions is placed in the form load event based on which conditional constant is set to True, as you can see in Listing 18-4.

Listing 18-4: Loading menu strings from external resource files

```
Private Sub Form_Load()
   #Const Elvish = True
   #If English Then
      Offset = 100
   #ElseIf Elvish Then
      Offset = 200
   #Else
      MsgBox "Attempting to Load Unknown Language!"
   #End If
   ...
   mnuFile.Caption = LoadResString(Offset + 5)
   mnuNew.Caption = LoadResString(Offset + 6)
   mnuExit.Caption = LoadResString(Offset + 7)
   mnuWindow.Caption = LoadResString(Offset + 8)
   mnuHelp.Caption = LoadResString(Offset + 9)
End Sub
```

This results in the menu display shown in Figure 18-20.

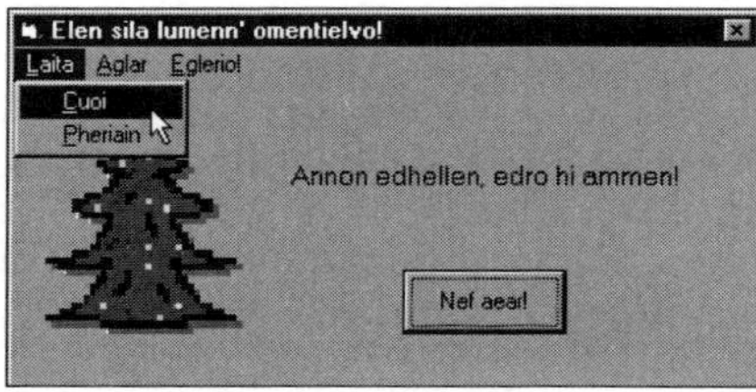

Figure 18-20: It's easy to internationalize menus by loading caption strings from external resource files.

To flip the application into English, simply substitute

```
#Const English = True
```

for

```
#Const Elvish = True
```

Response to menu event activation is handled in the usual fashion, although all string literals should be loaded externally using the offset. For example:

```
Private Sub mnuHelp_Click()
   MsgBox LoadResString(Offset + 4), _
      vbInformation, _
      LoadResString(Offset)
End Sub
```

Summary

Creating a framework for managing MDI applications is easy if you use the techniques explained in this chapter. Topics covered included

- Tracking MDI child forms
- Showing MDI child forms from a modal form
- Using the forms collection to minimize or close all child forms
- Adding "wallpaper" to an MDI application
- Creating "tiled" wallpaper
- Sizing child forms in the form load event
- Setting a custom cursor

This chapter also demonstrated how to push the envelope of the powerful Menu Editor. I covered

- Menu naming
- Using the NegotiatePosition property
- Menu control arrays
- Creating pop-up menus
- Controlling the visibility of menus at runtime
- Removing menu items at runtime
- Adding menu items at runtime
- Loading menu strings from an external resource file

Chapter 19

Runtime Display Secrets

The appearance of your application makes a big difference in the way users feel about it. (See Chapter 17, "Secrets of Good Interface Design," for more information about visually literate software development.)

This chapter covers various techniques for customizing the look and feel of Visual Basic applications, including

- Generating confetti
- Shading forms
- Exploding a form (this effect is sometimes called a "zoom")
- Creating a "marquee" effect

Easter eggs are secret displays embedded in an application. Usually, they show information about the program's creators. An example is the Windows 95 Easter egg (you'll find information on triggering the Windows 95 Easter egg in Chapter 6, "Windows 95: An Overview.")

In this chapter, I will show you how to create your own Easter eggs.

The chapter concludes by letting you in on the "secret" life of VB forms: I'll demonstrate how to manipulate VB forms and project files as ASCII text!

Special Effects

From the user's viewpoint, *Visual* Basic is about visual effects. Provided that you don't overdo it, nothing will make your applications more successful than snappy special effects. As I'll show you, it's easy to create world-class visuals without using third-party tools. (At the same time, you can use third-party tools to easily add a distinctive look to applications; see Chapter 31, "Overview of Third-Party Tools," for the specifics).

The spectacular graphics that you learn how to create in this chapter are all contained in one application, saved on the CD-ROM as ***Effects.Vbp***. (You can access the effects that the application generates through the Special Effects menu.)

All the procedures used are contained in one code module, ***FXCode.Bas***. You can simply add this module to your projects and call the routines it contains, passing them your project's forms as arguments.

The code for several of the special effects procedures is too lengthy to reproduce entirely in the text of *Visual Basic 5 SECRETS*. I will, of course, explain, how the procedures work. And the full code is available on the CD-ROM.

Confetti

The confetti effect consists of multicolored squares flashing on the screen in random fashion (like a many-hued digital virtual ticker parade), as shown in Figure 19-1.

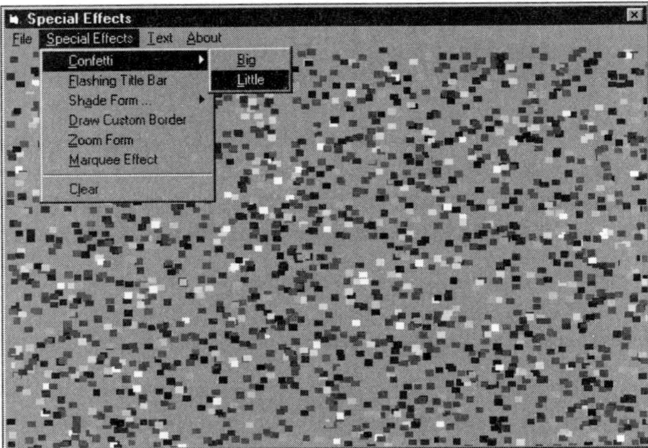

Figure 19-1: You can easily add a randomly generated colorful "confetti" effect to your applications.

The Confetti routine uses the QBColor function to return random RGB color values. RGB color values (as returned by the RGB function used by Visual Basic) are a single number (typed as a long integer) that represents red, green, and blue components of specific colors to be displayed. The values of each intensity of the three components range from 0 to 255. The RGB values returned by QBColor represent a small subset of possible RGB values because there are only 15 possible QBColor return values — something like saying, "Get me the primary colors, please!" The form's Line method is used to actually draw the confetti boxes at random locations on the form. (The optional B directive at the end of the Line method call causes a box to be drawn; the optional F directive specifies that it should be filled in.)

The size of the boxes depends on the ScaleMode passed to the procedure. (Figure 19-1 shows small confetti with the Size parameter set to vbTwips; you can generate larger confetti by setting the Size parameter to vbPixels.) The form's ScaleMode property, you will note, is restored to its original setting at the end of the procedure, as shown in Listing 19-1:

Listing 19-1: Generating "confetti"

```
Public Sub Confetti(Frm As Form, Size As Integer)
   Dim I As Integer, X1 As Integer, Y1 As Integer, _
      Color As Long, OldScaleMode As Integer
   OldScaleMode = Frm.ScaleMode
   Frm.ScaleMode = Size
   Randomize
```

```
    For I = 1 To 100
        X1 = Rnd * Frm.ScaleWidth
        Y1 = Rnd * Frm.ScaleHeight
        Color = QBColor(Rnd * 15)
        Frm.Line (X1, Y1)-(X1 + 85, Y1 + 65), Color, BF
    Next I
Frm.ScaleMode = OldScaleMode
End Sub
```

Confetti should be called from a Timer control. (In the demonstration program, the Timer's interval property is set to 1.) Enable the Timer when you want confetti to fall; disable it when you want the confetti to stop.

Flashing the Title Bar

It's simple to get the title bar of a window to flash as often as you want using the FlashWindow API function. This effect can be like having your application wink at the user. It's certainly attention getting!

As with all special effects, its a good idea not to overuse this one. An application containing multiple blinking title bars is almost guaranteed to drive your users crazy.

Here's the declaration for the API:

```
'API Declaration for FlashWindow
Declare Function FlashWindow Lib "user32" (ByVal hwnd As Long, _
    ByVal bInvert As Long) As Long
```

To use this function to flash the title bar, set the second parameter to True.

The return value of the FlashWindow function is not — as you might expect — the success or failure of the flashing operation. Rather, the value is whether the passed window was active before the function call.

As you'll see if you try out the demonstration, the flashing continues on the Windows 95 Taskbar even when the window is minimized. You could add title bar flashing to an iconized tray application (see Chapter 11 for information on constructing tray applications) to get attention — for example, when an emergency condition occurs.

If you want the flashing to keep on going, you should call the API from an enabled timer control, as shown in Listing 19-2.

Listing 19-2: Flashing the title bar

```
Private Sub tmrFlash_Timer()
    Call FXCode.FlashTitle(Me.hwnd, True)
End Sub
...
'API Call
Public Sub FlashTitle(Handle As Long, ReturnOrig As Boolean)
    Call FlashWindow(Handle, ReturnOrig)
End Sub
```

Shading a Form

Shading a form is a common but striking effect where the background of a form goes from light to dark. Typically, this means that the background is lighter at the top and darker at the bottom, but you can certainly alter the sample code to suit yourself.

One application that you've surely seen that uses a shaded form is the Microsoft setup program, which uses a form that progresses from light blue at the top to dark blue at the bottom.

Listing 19-3 contains the code in the ShadeForm procedure that draws a shaded red, green, or blue background on the passed form:

Listing 19-3: Shading a form

```
...
'Save current form/mode settings
DS = frm.DrawStyle
DW = frm.DrawWidth
SM = frm.ScaleMode
SH = frm.ScaleHeight
'settings for shading
frm.DrawStyle = vbInsideSolid
frm.DrawWidth = 2
frm.ScaleMode = vbPixels
frm.ScaleHeight = 256
For I = 0 To 255
   Select Case TheColor 'Shade Form Based on passed color
      Case 0
         frm.Line (0, I)-(frm.Width, I + 1), _
            RGB(255 - I, 0, 0), B 'red
      Case 1
         frm.Line (0, I)-(frm.Width, I + 1), _
            RGB(0, 255 - I, 0), B 'green
      Case 2
         frm.Line (0, I)-(frm.Width, I + 1), _
            RGB(0, 0, 255 - I), B 'blue
      Case Else
         MsgBox "Internal Error in Color Selection!"
   End Select
Next I
'Restore original form/mode settings
frm.DrawStyle = DS
frm.DrawWidth = DW
frm.ScaleHeight = SH         'must be restored before ScaleMode
frm.ScaleMode = SM
...
```

The form's DrawStyle property controls the line style output from graphics methods (such as the Line method called later in the procedure). DrawWidth sets the width of the Line method's output to 2 pixels. ScaleMode sets the units of measurement of the form's coordinate system, as shown in Table 19-1.

Table 19-1 Values of the ScaleMode Property

Setting	*Constant*	*Comments*
0	vbUser	This is the custom setting, meaning that one or more of the ScaleHeight, ScaleLeft, ScaleTop, or ScaleWidth properties have been set to a custom value.
1	vbTwips	The default (one inch = 1440 twips).
2	vbPoints	Points are a unit of typographic measure (one vertical inch = 72 points).
3	vbPixels	Represents the smallest unit of monitor or printer resolution.
4	vbCharacter	Horizontal = 120 twips and vertical = 240 twips per "character."
4	vbInches	
5	vbMillimeters	
6	vbCentimeters	

You're probably used to reading a form's ScaleHeight and ScaleWidth properties to access the units of measurement of a form — and to find the client area of a form. You can also use ScaleHeight and ScaleWidth to set a form's internal coordinate dimensions; here ScaleHeight is used to set the number of vertical lines in the form background to 256. A For...Next loop calls the Line method once for each of those lines.

The Line method draws a one ScaleHeight-high box (the B directive is specified) on each form "line." The width of the box is the form's client width. The color gradient is achieved by incrementing the specified primary value of the RGB function using the loop index. For example, Blue is the third argument of RGB, and the variable I is stepping from 0 to 255 (and drawing 1/256th of the form background each time):

```
RGB(0, 0, 255 - I), B 'blue
```

Table 19-2 shows the RGB function equivalents of some common colors.

Table 19-2 RGB Function Color Equivalents

Color	*Red*	*Green*	*Blue*
Black	0	0	0
Blue	0	0	255
Green	0	255	0
Cyan	0	255	255

(continued)

Table 19-2 *(Continued)*

Color	*Red*	*Green*	*Blue*
Red	255	0	0
Magenta	255	0	255
Yellow	255	255	0
White	255	255	255

Drawing Borders on a Form

You can use the Line method to draw as many lines as you want around the borders of a form. The effect, which is shown in Figure 19-2, appears like a beveled picture frame. Listing 19-4 shows the code that does it:

Listing 19-4: Drawing borders on a form

```
Public Sub DrawBorder(frm As Form, NumLines)
   Dim I As Integer, Restore As Boolean, OldScaleMode As Integer
   Const DrawWidth = 2
   OldScaleMode = frm.ScaleMode
   frm.ScaleMode = vbPixels
   Restore = frm.AutoRedraw
   frm.AutoRedraw = True
   For I = DrawWidth - 1 To NumLines * 3 Step 3
      frm.Line (I, I)-(frm.ScaleWidth - 1 - I, _
         frm.ScaleHeight - 1 - I), , B
   Next I
   frm.ScaleMode = OldScaleMode
   frm.AutoRedraw = Restore
End Sub
```

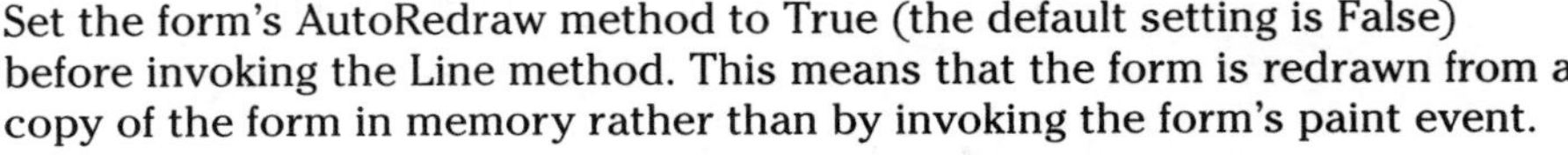

Set the form's AutoRedraw method to True (the default setting is False) before invoking the Line method. This means that the form is redrawn from a copy of the form in memory rather than by invoking the form's paint event.

If you'd like to draw the borders in a color other than black, simply set the form's ForeColor property before applying the Line method. For example:

```
frm.ForeColor = vbYellow
```

Figure 19-2: You can use the Line method to customize the look of your forms.

Exploding a Form

Exploding a form — sometimes referred to as a form *zoom* — means making the form appear in an explosion from a point at the center of the form. You produce the effect by hiding the form in code and then drawing successively larger rectangles in the color of the form on the screen. When the rectangles are the same size as the form, the form is displayed and the zooming halted.

The apparent speed of the explosion is controlled by the number of rectangles that are drawn. (A word to the wise: Exploding a form is a great way to get attention and users love it, but don't make the process too drawn out.) If you like, you can zoom from an origination point other than the form center, although this requires playing with the code I've provided.

Drawing directly on the screen (rather than on a form) requires the use of some API functions. Listing 19-5 contains are the declarations:

Listing 19-5: Exploding form API declarations

```
Type RECT
        Left As Long
        Top As Long
        Right As Long
        Bottom As Long
End Type
Declare Function CreateSolidBrush Lib "gdi32" _
  (ByVal crColor As Long) As Long
Declare Function DeleteObject Lib "gdi32" _
  (ByVal hObject As Long) As Long
Declare Function GetDC Lib "user32" (ByVal hwnd As Long) As Long
```

```
Declare Function GetWindowRect Lib "user32" (ByVal hwnd As Long, _
   lpRect As RECT) As Long
Declare Function ReleaseDC Lib "user32" (ByVal hwnd As Long, _
   ByVal hdc As Long) As Long
Declare Function SelectObject Lib "gdi32" (ByVal hdc As Long, _
   ByVal hObject As Long) As Long
Declare Function Rectangle Lib "gdi32" (ByVal hdc As Long, _
   ByVal X1 As Long, ByVal Y1 As Long, _
   ByVal X2 As Long, ByVal Y2 As Long) As Long
```

The ExplodeForm procedure works by getting the current form dimensions and location by calling the GetWindowRect API with the forms handle as an argument:

```
...
GetWindowRect frm.hwnd, ThisRect
RectWidth = (ThisRect.Right - ThisRect.Left)
RectHeight = ThisRect.Bottom - ThisRect.Top
```

Next, it obtains a device handle for — that is, a way to reference — the screen, creates a Windows brush based on the form color, and saves a copy of the old brush:

```
ScreenDevice = GetDC(0)
NewBrush = CreateSolidBrush(Color)
OldBrush = SelectObject(ScreenDevice, NewBrush)
```

Finally, the rectangles are actually drawn on the screen using the screen device context handle and the Rectangle API:

```
For I = 1 To Steps
   XRect = RectWidth * (I / Steps)
   YRect = RectHeight * (I / Steps)
   X = ThisRect.Left + (RectWidth - XRect) / 2
   Y = ThisRect.Top + (RectHeight - YRect) / 2
   'Incrementally draw the rectangle
   Rectangle ScreenDevice, X, Y, X + XRect, Y + YRect
Next I
```

It's important to restore the old brush, delete the screen device handle, and destroy the brush that was used to draw the rectangles:

```
Call SelectObject(ScreenDevice, OldBrush)
Call ReleaseDC(0, ScreenDevice)
DeleteObject (NewBrush)
...
```

Creating a Marquee Effect

A "marquee" effect — moving shapes that appear to be lit on the edge of a form — is quite an attention grabber (as you can see from Figure 19-3).

The Marquee procedure is called from a timer control (for best results, set the interval property between 50 and 250). This causes the procedure to be successively invoked, giving the appearance of motion.

Figure 19-3: You can use the code in the ***FXCode.Bas*** module to add moving "marquee" effects to your applications.

The heart of the effect is drawing shapes in the appropriate locations on the form. This is handled in a procedure DrawShape, which uses the Circle and Line methods to create a total of eight different kinds of shapes on the form. Two of the shapes are created using the following code:

```
...
'Circle
frm.Circle (HorizontalSpread, VerticalSpread), Size, FillColor
...
'Square
frm.Line (HorizontalSpread - (Size \ 2), _
   VerticalSpread - (Size \ 2))-(HorizontalSpread + (Size \ 2), _
      VerticalSpread + (Size \ 2)), FillColor, BF
...
```

DrawShape is called repeatedly from the Marquee procedure to draw the required shapes on the top, bottom, left, and right border of the form. For example, here is the code that does this for the top and right sides of the form:

```
...
' Do the top
For I = 1 To Across
   ...
   DrawShape frm, WhichShape, FillColor, BackColor, _
      HorizontalSpread, VerticalSpread, FormScaleHeight, _
      FormScaleWidth
   ...
Next I

' Do the right side
For I = 1 To Down - 1
   DrawShape frm, WhichShape, FillColor, BackColor, _
      HorizontalSpread, VerticalSpread, FormScaleHeight, _
      FormScaleWidth
...
```

To view the full source code, refer to the ***FXCode.Bas*** module on the companion CD-ROM.

Printing 3D Text on a Form

It's easy to use a form's Print method and the properties of the form's Font object to display text directly on a form. For example:

```
frm.Font.Name = "Arial"       ' select a font
frm.Font.Italic = True        ' set font properties
frm.Font.Size = 48            '
frm.CurrentX = 200            ' position the cursor
frm.CurrentY = 100
frm.Print "from IDG Books"   ' display text
```

The color of the text depends upon the current setting of the form's ForeColor property, which you can set in code at runtime.

To jazz up the text display a bit, you can make it appear three dimensional by added subsequent calls to the Print method with the text's position moved slightly. For example, the PrintName procedure displays text in yellow with an over the left shoulder highlight and an under the right foot shadow, as shown in Figure 19-4.

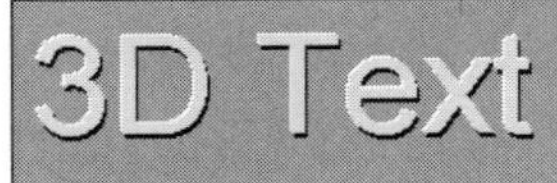

Figure 19-4: You can make text appear three dimensional by using successive calls to a form's Print method.

As you can see in Listing 19-6, PrintName places the passed text on the passed form at the passed starting location.

Listing 19-6: Displaying three-dimensional text on a form

```
Sub PrintName(frm As Form, TheName As String, _
   X As Integer, Y As Integer)
   'X,Y are the starting print locations
   Dim OldScaleMode As Integer, OldForeColor As Long
   OldScaleMode = frm.ScaleMode
   OldForeColor = frm.ForeColor
   If frm.ScaleMode <> vbTwips Then frm.ScaleMode = vbTwips
   frm.ZOrder 0                    'needed to print over drawn colors
   frm.ForeColor = RGB(32, 32, 32) 'very dark gray for shadow
   frm.Font.Name = "Arial"
   frm.Font.Size = 48
   frm.CurrentX = X                'position the cursor
   frm.CurrentY = Y
```

```
    frm.Print TheName           'display the text
    frm.ForeColor = RGB(255, 255, 255)  'white for highlight
    frm.CurrentX = X - 35     'position highlight (to the upper left)
    frm.CurrentY = Y - 45
    frm.Print TheName           'print white highlight
    frm.ForeColor = vbYellow    'set to standard yellow
    frm.CurrentX = X - 25       'display between highlight and shadow
    frm.CurrentY = Y - 35
    frm.Print TheName           'print yellow
    frm.ScaleMode = OldScaleMode 'restore ScaleMode!
    frm.ForeColor = OldForeColor 'restore ForeColor
End Sub
```

Placing Easter Eggs in Your Programs

An *Easter egg* is an embedded display in an application that is triggered by some secret — or not so secret — user action. Often, the names of a program's creators are displayed in an Easter egg. Generally, Easter eggs are the software equivalent of vanity license plates. That is, they serve no useful purpose other than tickling their owner's fancy. (I have to admit, my car has a vanity plate!)

Easter eggs can constitute a statement of pride in software authorship. As such, they can serve as a morale booster in tough and complex team programming situations. Although Easter eggs don't serve much practical purpose, they are fun to think about and do demonstrate some useful programming techniques.

Triggering an Egg

Generally, eggs are triggered by some sequence of mouse movements and keyboard inputs. The project that demonstrates adding special visual effects to forms (***Effects.Vbp***) has an About box (shown in Figure 19-5) that contains an embedded Easter egg.

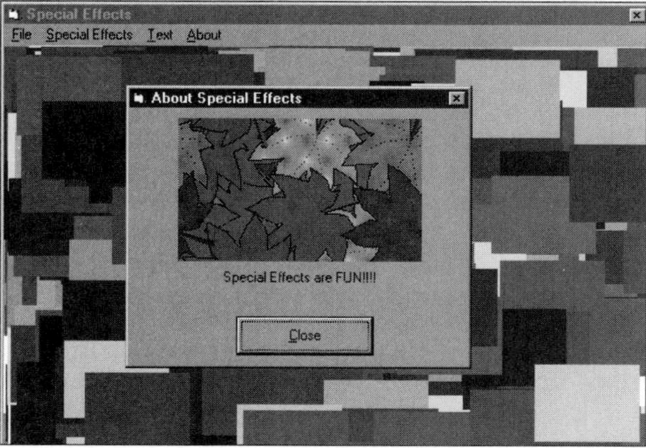

Figure 19-5: This About box contains an Easter egg.

To trigger the egg, click the autumn leaves bitmap in the About box. Next, simultaneously hold down the Ctrl, Shift, and F10 keys. The egg will start to operate, meaning that an invisible Picture control — containing a bitmap of clouds — is resized to occupy the entire About box form and becomes visible. Scrolling banners — actually labels — next start to work their way down the Picture control.

This all appears quite seamless.

The code that activates this egg is located in the KeyDown event of the Picture control that holds the bitmap of autumn leaves. (For the Picture control to receive keyboard input for processing, it must have the focus, which is why it must be clicked.) Listing 19-7 contains the code:

Listing 19-7: Activating an egg in response to keyboard input

```
Private Sub Picture1_KeyDown(KeyCode As Integer, Shift As Integer)
   Dim ShiftDown As Boolean, CtrlDown As Boolean
   ShiftDown = (Shift And vbShiftMask) > 0
   CtrlDown = (Shift And vbCtrlMask) > 0
   If KeyCode = vbKeyF10 Then
      If ShiftDown And CtrlDown Then        ' Trigger that egg!
         pctEgg.Height = Me.ScaleHeight
         pctEgg.Width = Me.ScaleWidth
         pctEgg.Visible = True
         Timer1.Enabled = True
      End If
   End If
End Sub
```

Of course, you can add complexity in a number of ways to egg-triggering events. It's perfectly possible to monitor the KeyDown events of a number of different controls, and require that the right sequence of controls have the focus before the keyboard input to that control is registered. Another possibility is to use a dynamic array, a string, or a stack structure (such as the ones developed in Chapter 13, "Secrets of Good Programming Practice," and Chapter 14, "Visual Basic and OOP") to "record" keyboard input; the triggering event could be made up of many separate inputs. (As an example, the user might have to hold down the Ctrl and Shift keys, enter **CAPTAIN**, release the Ctrl and Shift keys, hold down the Alt key, and enter **PICARD**.)

If you want to be a real sadist, you can require that each user action occur in a specific amount of time (under penalty of having to start over). To do this, use the GetTickCount API function, which was explained under "Measuring Speed" in Chapter 16, "Optimizing Secrets."

Making the Egg Move

You'll have noticed that a successful trigger of the egg in the preceding code causes a Picture control to become visible and enables a timer:

```
' I am triggered!
pctEgg.Height = Me.ScaleHeight
```

```
pctEgg.Width = Me.ScaleWidth
pctEgg.Visible = True
Timer1.Enabled = True
```

Note that the code sizing pctEgg to the client area of the form could be placed elsewhere (for example, when the form loads) because pctEgg is invisible anyhow. The important lines of code are the ones enabling the timer and making pctEgg visible.

To set this up, you'll need to add a Picture control (such as pctEgg) to the form at design time with its Visible property set to False. The visibility of all controls placed on top of pctEgg is controlled by pctEgg's Visible property.

When placing layered controls on a form, it can be difficult to get to the bottom ones at design time. To do so, select the control (using the Properties window if necessary). Then choose Bring to Front (Ctrl+J) from the Order item on the VB Format menu (or from the context menu).

In the demonstration, there is one label, named MoveMe, placed on pctEgg. The code in the timer control moves the label down pctEgg and changes its caption information. The effect is an animated, moving text display that progresses down the window. Figure 19-6 shows one of the labels from this animated sequence. (I added a cloud bitmap to pctEgg's Picture property to make this egg look somewhat like the Windows 95 Easter egg.)

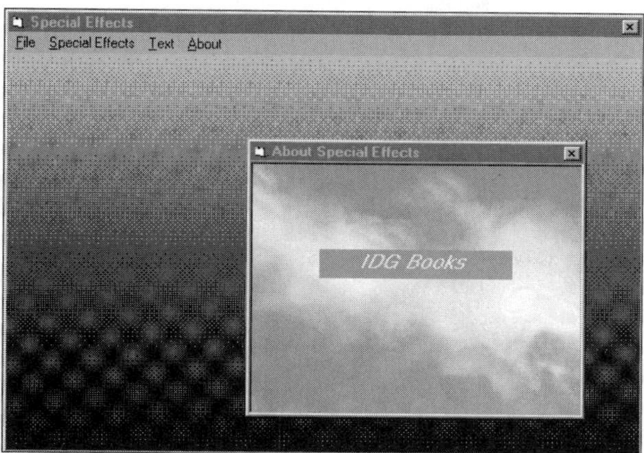

Figure 19-6: This Easter egg displays text moving down the sky....

The timer Interval property is set to 300 to give each label caption a chance to be read as it moves along. Listing 19-8 shows the timer event code:

Listing 19-8: Moving an egg display

```
Private Sub Timer1_Timer()
    Static Flag As Integer
    Dim MoveBy As Integer
    'scalemode is twips!
```

```
   If MoveMe.Top > Me.ScaleHeight Then
      MoveMe.Top = 0
   Else
      MoveBy = -100
   End If
   MoveMe.Move MoveMe.Left, MoveMe.Top - MoveBy
   'Debug.Print MoveMe.Top
   Select Case Flag
      Case 0
         MoveMe.Caption = "Thank you"
      Case 1
         MoveMe.Caption = "for"
      Case 2
         MoveMe.Caption = "reading"
      Case 3
         MoveMe.Caption = "Visual Basic 5"
      Case 4
         MoveMe.Caption = "SECRETS"
      Case 5
         MoveMe.Caption = "by Harold Davis"
      Case 6
         MoveMe.Caption = "from"
      Case 7
         MoveMe.Caption = "IDG Books"
   End Select
   Flag = Flag + 1
   'resets flag variable to 0 on 8th cycle
   If Flag = 8 Then
      Flag = 0
   End If
End Sub
```

This code moves the label (MoveMe), which starts at the top of pctEgg, down to the bottom of pctEgg, 100 twips lower each time the event is fired:

```
MoveBy = -100
...
MoveMe.Move MoveMe.Left, MoveMe.Top - MoveBy
```

Remember that as MoveMe moves down, the number represented by MoveMe.Top increases. When MoveMe reaches the bottom of the form, it is placed back up at the top:

```
If MoveMe.Top > Me.ScaleHeight Then
      MoveMe.Top = 0
```

It can be difficult to determine what changes to make in code that moves controls. Using Debug.Print can help you to easily track control location coordinates by viewing the contents of the Debug window. For example:

```
Debug.Print MoveMe.Top
```

continuously displays the value of MoveMe.Top as the egg runs.

The static Flag variable is used to loop continuously through the eight possible values for MoveMe's caption. Each time the timer code is fired, Flag increments by one; after it hits seven, it goes back to 0.

This demonstration Easter egg, simple as it is, works quite well and is really rather elegant. Obviously, the beauty and complexity of your own Easter eggs are limited only by your time, ingenuity, and imagination. Many of the techniques described earlier in this chapter — for example, confetti — are perfect for eggs.

The Secret Life of Forms

It's a helpful fact that many kinds of Visual Basic source files — including form (*.Frm*), module (*.Bas* and *.Cls*), project (*.Vbp*), and group (*.Vbg*) files — are just plain vanilla ASCII. Table 19-3 shows the Visual Basic 5 source files that are formatted as plain text, and the function of the files. (Many ASCII source files are associated with a binary file that contains resources related to the source file. For example, *.Frx* files contain binary information — such as graphics — related to a form (*.Frm*) module.)

Table 19-3 VB5 ASCII Source Files

Filename Extension	*Purpose*
.Bas	Code source module
.Cls	Class source module
.Ctl	User Control file
.Dob	User Document form file
.Dsr	Active Designer file
.Frm	Form file
.Pag	Property Page file
.Vbg	Visual Basic group project
.Vbp	Visual Basic project

The fact that the source code for VB modules and projects is ASCII makes it possible to easily automate project and form parsing: A program — such as an add-in — can open a form, parse its text, alter the ASCII text that represents the form to suit, and save the changed version.

It also means that you can manually edit form and project files using any handy ASCII editor (such as Notepad). There are times — for example, if you're adding the same menu structure to a number of forms — when it is easier to work with forms in their straight ASCII aspect.

Inside Forms

Information inside forms is organized hierarchically. You can tell that an object is a child of another object because the subobject is indented to the right (the text selected in Figure 19-7 represents a label placed on a form). Logical groups are bracketed with Begin and End statements.

The text of a form file starts with a Visual Basic version statement ("VERSION 5.00") as shown in Figure 19-7.

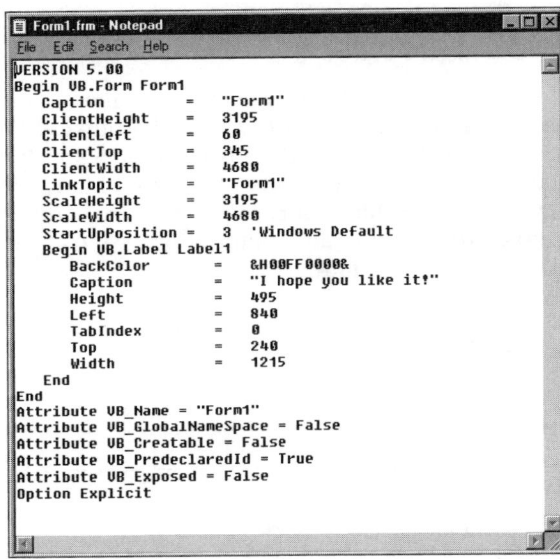

```
VERSION 5.00
Begin VB.Form Form1
   Caption         =   "Form1"
   ClientHeight    =   3195
   ClientLeft      =   60
   ClientTop       =   345
   ClientWidth     =   4680
   LinkTopic       =   "Form1"
   ScaleHeight     =   3195
   ScaleWidth      =   4680
   StartUpPosition =   3  'Windows Default
   Begin VB.Label Label1
      BackColor       =   &H00FF0000&
      Caption         =   "I hope you like it!"
      Height          =   495
      Left            =   840
      TabIndex        =   0
      Top             =   240
      Width           =   1215
   End
End
Attribute VB_Name = "Form1"
Attribute VB_GlobalNameSpace = False
Attribute VB_Creatable = False
Attribute VB_PredeclaredId = True
Attribute VB_Exposed = False
Option Explicit
```

Figure 19-7: The secret of VB forms is that they are really ASCII files; the text shown includes a Label control captioned "I hope you like it!"

Next, objects and code are placed in the following order:

- Form properties
- Control properties
- Menu structure
- General declarations
- Procedures

Control properties and menu structures can contain nested Begin...End blocks. For example, a submenu would be nested within a menu block; a label placed on a Picture control would be nested within the picture control.

For example, the text displayed in Figure 19-7 is the ASCII representation of a form with a single skinny Label control captioned "I hope you like it!" The Label's BackColor property is set to Blue (I happen to know that &H00FF0000& is blue, because I set the label at design time).

You can easily edit the Label's properties, maybe changing BackColor to 65535 (yellow), the caption to "Yes!," and the Height to 695. Next time the project containing the form is opened, the form will reflect the changes you've made.

It's not unusual to want to copy a menu structure from one form to another. This is easy to do using copy and paste on forms in ASCII mode, but time consuming to do using VB's Menu Editor.

For example, suppose I wanted to copy the Special Effects menu from ***Effects.Frm*** (frmFX) to another form. The beginning of the menu structure is shown in Figure 19-8.

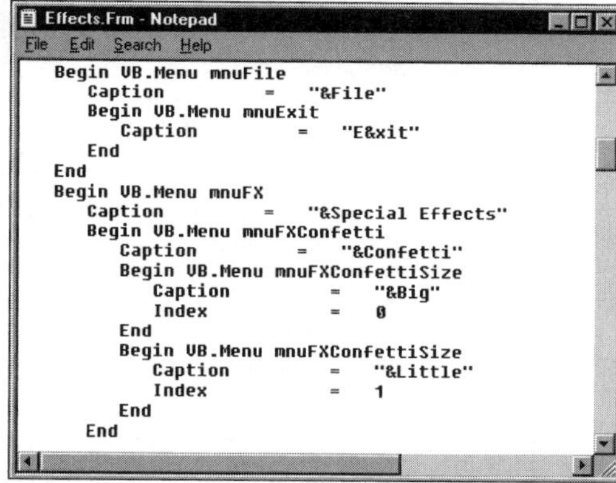

Figure 19-8: Menus are organized hierarchically when you look at the ASCII representation of forms.

If I copy this structure to the Clipboard (careful to get everything between matched Begin and End keywords) and then paste it to a new form, the new form displays the copied menu structure in its entirety when it is loaded, as shown in Figure 19-9.

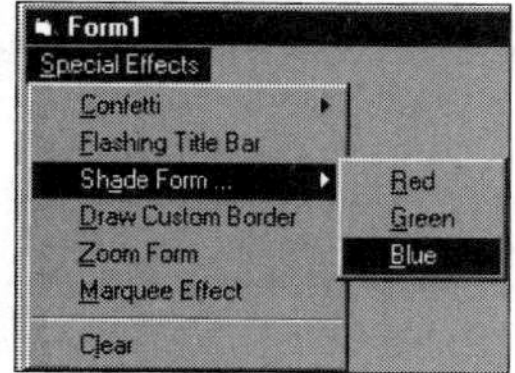

Figure 19-9: It can save time to copy and paste ASCII menu structures.

Inside Project Files

Visual Basic project (*.Vbp*) files are also saved in an ASCII text format. Project files list the filenames of included forms and modules, objects, and references.

If a project has trouble loading due to missing references (or references that point to an incorrect location for a file), manually editing the ***.Vbp*** file as ASCII text may be the easiest way to troubleshoot and repair the situation.

Table 19-4 shows the possible keywords and values that you can include in a ***.Vbp*** project file. Note that there is no requirement that project file entries be in the order presented in Table 19-4 (or in any particular order, for that matter).

Table 19-4 Project (*.Vbp*) Files and Their Contents

Keywords and Values	***Meaning***
Type = "Project Type"	Type of project, for example, Exe or Control.
Object = *"object.path"*	An ActiveX control or insertable object. There's a separate entry for each such control or object.
References = (*reference-stringlist*)	Reflects your settings in the References dialog box. Lists any references in addition to the default VB settings.
ProjWinSize = *top*[, *left*[, *width*[, *height*]]]	Initial position and size of the Project window.
ProjWinShow = *show*	Value indicating the display condition of the Project window. If *show* is 0, the Project window is hidden; if it is 1, the window is minimized; and, if it is 2, the window is normal.
Name = *"stringexpression"*	Project name.
Command32 = *"stringexpression"*	Initial setting for Command.
IconForm = *"stringexpression"*	Specifies the application icon.
HelpFile = *"path"*	File name of the WinHelp file containing Help for the application.
HelpContextID = *"stringexpression"*	The context ID for the Help topic called when the user clicks the ? button in the Object Browser after selecting the application's Object Library.
ResFile32 = *"filename"*	The resource file associated with the project.
Title = *"stringexpression"*	The application title used in the Make tab page of the Project Properties dialog. This name appears on the Properties dialog of the executable compiled using the project file.
CondComp = *expression*[; *expression*]...	Conditional compilation arguments, separated by semicolons.

Keywords and Values	***Meaning***
EXEName32 = *"stringexpression"*	Filename used as the application's ***.Exe*** filename in the Make tab page of the Project Properties dialog.
Path32 = *"stringexpression"*	Path setting listed in the Make tab page of the Project Properties dialog. Specifies where the executable is placed after it is made.
StartMode = *switch*	Reflects the StartMode setting made on the Component tab page of the Project Properties dialog.
Description = *"stringexpression"*	Description of the project. Appears in the Object Browser when the project is selected.
CompatibleEXE = *path*	Used only with ActiveX components. This is a path to an earlier version of the executable and is the reference used to determine whether changes made to this project break compatibility for controlling applications using the older executable version of this project.
VersionCompatible = *switch*	Set by Visual Basic (should not be edited by hand). Indicates whether the project is currently compatible with the ***.Exe*** identified by CompatibleEXE.
MajorVer = *digits*	Major release number of the project; 0 - 9999.
MinorVer = *digits*	Minor release number of the project; 0 - 9999.
RevisionVer = *digits*	Revision level of the project; 0 - 9999.
AutoIncrementVer = *switch*	Indicates whether the RevisionVer setting will increment automatically each time the project is modified and saved.
VersionComments = *"stringexpression"*	Version-specific comments. Version information is set using the Make tab of the Project Properties dialog.
VersionCompanyName = *"stringexpression"*	Name of the company that developed this version. Version information is set using the Make tab page of the Project Properties dialog.
VersionFileDescription = *"stringexpression"*	Version-specific file information. Version information is set using the Make tab of the Project Properties dialog.
VersionLegalCopyright = *"stringexpression"*	Copyright notices applicable to this version. You set version information using the Make tab page of the Project Properties dialog.
VersionLegalTrademarks = *"stringexpression"*	Trademark notices for trademarks used with this version. You set version information using the Make tab page of the Project Properties dialog.
VersionProductName = *"stringexpression"*	Product name used on this version. You set version information using the Make tab of the Project Properties dialog.

The *.Vbp* file also includes native code compilation switch settings for each project, as described in Chapter 16. If p-code rather than native code compilation is selected, you'll still find the native code switches included, along with the following line (meaning compile to pseudocode):

```
CompilationType=-1
```

For example, take a pretty normal project with a project file named ***HackerProject.Vbp***. This project has some modules, objects and references. It is shown in Project Explorer in Figure 19-10.

Figure 19-10: The HackerProject contains various different files types.

Listing 19-9 shows the contents of the project file that corresponds to the hierarchy shown in Project Explorer:

Listing 19-9: A sample ***.Vbp*** file

```
Type=Exe
Reference=*\G{00020430-0000-0000-C000-
   000000000046}#2.0#0#C:\WINDOWS\SYSTEM\STDOLE2.TLB#OLE Automation
Object={6B7E6392-850A-101B-AFC0-4210102A8DA7}#1.1#0; COMCTL32.OCX
Object={F6125AB1-8AB1-11CE-A77F-08002B2F4E98}#2.0#0; MSRDC20.OCX
Reference=*\G{56A868B0-0AD4-11CE-B03A-
   0020AF0BA770}#1.0#0#C:\WINDOWS\SYSTEM\quartz.dll#ActiveMovie
   control type library
Reference=*\G{8A41BBBC-ABF3-11CF-B8E7-0080C6026268}#1.0#0#C:\PROGRAM
   FILES\PLUS!\MICROSOFT INTERNET\A-VRML\AVVIEW.oca#ActiveVRML
   Control Library
Reference=*\G{24807AE2-1BC8-11D0-B49B-
   00A0C911E8B6}#1.0#0#..\..\VB\WINAPI\APILOAD.EXE#API Declaration
   Loader
Form=Form1.frm
Module=Module1; Module1.bas
Class=Class1; Class1.cls
ResFile32="..\Ch18\Programs\Both.res"
IconForm="Form1"
Startup="Form1"
HelpFile="HackerHelp"
```

```
Title="HackerProject"
Command32=""
Name="HackerProject"
HelpContextID="0"
Description="Hacker needs caffeine badly..."
CompatibleMode="0"
MajorVer=1
MinorVer=42
RevisionVer=0
AutoIncrementVer=1
ServerSupportFiles=0
VersionComments="This is just a demo"
VersionCompanyName="Evolution Software, Inc."
VersionFileDescription="Hacker's Text"
VersionLegalCopyright="None"
VersionLegalTrademarks="None"
VersionProductName="VB5 Secrets"
CompilationType=-1
OptimizationType=0
FavorPentiumPro(tm)=0
CodeViewDebugInfo=0
NoAliasing=0
BoundsCheck=0
OverflowCheck=0
FlPointCheck=0
FDIVCheck=0
UnroundedFP=0
StartMode=0
Unattended=0
ThreadPerObject=0
MaxNumberOfThreads=1
```

You could add a UserControl project named ***OurGroup.Vbp*** to the HackerProject, forming a project group named ***OurGroup.Vbg***. The combined project hierarchy is shown in Project Explorer in Figure 19-11.

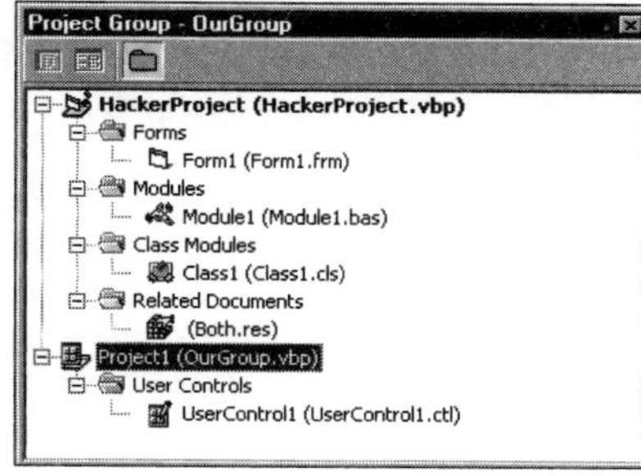

Figure 19-11: Project groups consist of multiple project files.

In this case, the new project group file — ***OurGroup.Vbg*** — simply lists the project files that it includes:

```
VBGROUP 5.0
StartupProject=HackerProject.vbp
Project=OurGroup.vbp
```

Summary

You can use special effects to make an application something special. Users appreciate visual effects that are out of the ordinary. Special effects can break up what would be a tedious task with something humorous, get the user's attention, or just make a form more appealing to the eye.

Easter eggs are the hidden "vanity plates" that many programmers add to their applications. Even though most eggs are accessed with simple mouse clicks and keystrokes, they can be extremely difficult to find.

Topics covered in this chapter included

- Special display effects
- Creating confetti
- Using the QBColor function
- Using the RGB function
- The Line method
- The FlashWindow function
- The Scale properties
- Shading a form
- Drawing borders on a form
- Exploding a form
- Getting a device context handle to the screen
- Using the Rectangle function to draw directly on the screen
- Creating a marquee
- Using the Print method
- Creating 3D text
- Triggering an Easter egg
- Making the egg move
- Form (***.Frm***) , Project (***.Vbp***), and Project Group (***.Vbg***) files as ASCII text

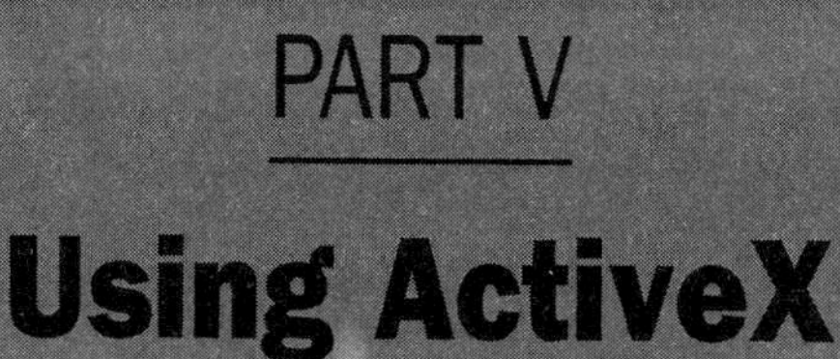

PART V

Using ActiveX

Chapter 20

Understanding ActiveX and OLE

In the time between the release of Version 4 and Version 5 of Visual Basic, OLE has assumed even greater importance to developers who are interested in creating programs that use the functionality of other programs, or in creating objects that can be used by other applications. In addition, the entire OLE technology has been given a brand new name: ActiveX.

VB5 applications can include ActiveX (read, OLE) features such as drag and drop. (Drag me, drop me — treat me like an object!) Taking Visual Basic and ActiveX one step further, ActiveX Executables (ActiveX Exe projects) and ActiveX DLLs (ActiveX DLL projects) are OLE server applications that can be controlled by OLE clients. ActiveX document projects (both Exe and DLL) are forms with properties, events, and methods that you can view using Internet Explorer. And ActiveX controls are compiled components (with an ***.Ocx*** extension) that can be used by any application capable of hosting OLE controls.

To summarize, using Visual Basic you can create

- Standard executables that "speak" OLE through implementation of such features as drag and drop
- Applications that are OLE clients of ActiveX OLE server applications
- ActiveX servers that can be controlled by other applications
- ActiveX document applications that are forms that you can view using Internet Explorer browser (and using the Office 97 Binder)
- ActiveX controls that are full-fledged, cross-application components

As explained in Chapter 14, "Visual Basic and OOP," Visual Basic Version 5 is object oriented in many important ways. There is no doubt that Version 5 is the most significantly OOP release yet.

Chapter 14 focused on VB5's internal facilities for creating object-oriented programs (such as collections and class modules). But Visual Basic has an important place in a wider sea of objects than merely those available internally to VB programs. The real point of OOP is to take advantage of existing programs, yours and those written by others. Why reinvent the wheel? In this sense, the true object model that VB embraces is closer to that of Windows than that of academically derived object-oriented programming languages.

This is also the point of ActiveX (and OLE), which operates in the universe of much of the Windows operating system and most current Windows applications. ActiveX is an ongoing attempt to craft an object-oriented future independent of programming language (and platform).

The ability to create ActiveX servers in VB — and now, with Version 5, the ability to create ActiveX controls — is immensely powerful and important.

Part V of *Visual Basic 5 SECRETS*, "Using ActiveX," begins the exploration of VB's participation in this universe of objects. This participation covered in Part V is fourfold:

- You can easily embed OLE objects in your VB programs by using the OLE container control.
- Your VB programs, acting as clients, can manipulate the exposed object methods of ActiveX server applications such as those included in Office 97.
- You can create Visual Basic applications that are themselves ActiveX servers — which can then be used by your own, or others', client applications.
- Using the tools provided in the Enterprise Edition of VB, you can manage, and create, remote ActiveX servers.

Creating ActiveX controls using Visual Basic 5 is so exciting that it has a part to itself — Part VI, "Creating ActiveX Controls." In addition, you'll find information on ActiveX Document applications in Chapter 28, "Creating Internet Applications in VB."

This chapter provides the material you'll need to fully understand the ActiveX and OLE technology. Chapters 21 through 23 explain how to apply that understanding practically.

Topics covered in this chapter include:

- The OLE object model and definition
- The relationship between OLE and ActiveX
- Communication modes
- Visual Basic Version 5 and ActiveX objects
- MAPI (Messaging API)
- Compound files and structured storage
- ActiveX components and the Registry

What Is an OLE Object?

OLE, as referred to in *Visual Basic 5 SECRETS*, means the object linking and embedded standard, version 2.*x*. However, the phrase "object linking and embedding" has become misleading. Object linking and embedding are only part of the story. Although the initial version of the OLE standard, OLE 1, was primarily intended to enable object linking and embedding in compound documents, OLE 2 lives to enable and facilitate component integration and software.

You may recall OLE expert Kraig Brockschmidt's definition of OLE that I quoted in Chapter 1 of *Visual Basic 5 SECRETS*:

OLE is a unified environment of object-based services with the capability of both customizing those services and arbitrarily extending the architecture through custom services, with the overall purpose of enabling rich integration between components.

Less abstractly, OLE provides a consistent standard that enables objects — ActiveX applications and components — to *communicate* with one another for the purpose of using each other's code. The objects do not need to know in advance what object they will be communicating with, nor does their code need to be written in the same language.

ActiveX applications are conceptually divided into *servers* — objects that make their methods and properties available to others — and *clients* — applications that use exposed server objects, methods, and properties. (Note that there is certainly nothing to stop an application from being both a client and server.) Some kinds of servers — for example, ActiveX controls — can fire events that can then be responded to by code in a client.

You may find that an alternate terminology makes more intuitive sense. Another word sometimes used for OLE clients is *controller*. It's appropriate to think of OLE clients controlling OLE servers, which make themselves available to be controlled.

Asynchronous Versus Synchronous Communication

Not only is OLE about communication between objects (as just discussed), the communication is *synchronous*. Synchronous communication involves a two-way conversation (see Figure 20-1). The calling application (the client) makes a call and waits for a response. The receiving application (the server) waits for the call. Upon receiving the call, the receiving application makes a response while the calling application is still on the line.

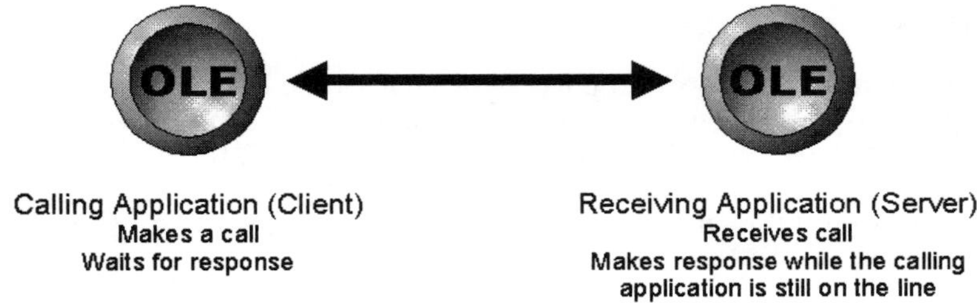

Figure 20-1: OLE 2 conversations are synchronous.

Older inter-object communications standards — such as OLE 1 and DDE — communicated *asynchronously*. In an asynchronous conversation, the calling application makes a call without waiting for a response (see Figure 20-2). Asynchronous communication is like sending a ham radio message, or a piece of Internet e-mail. Until you receive an explicit acknowledgment, you don't really know that the intended recipient got the message.

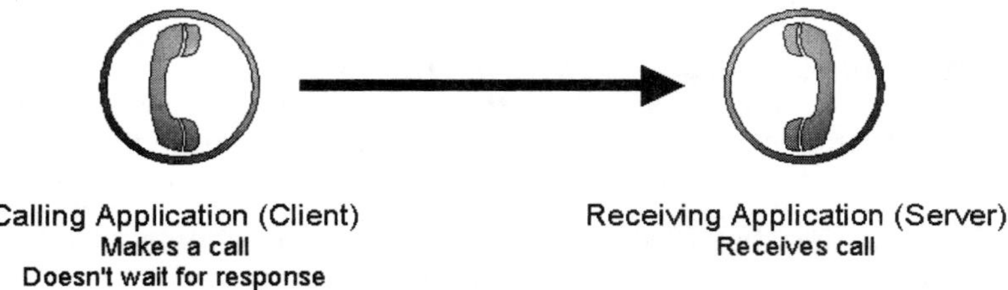

Figure 20-2: Asynchronous communication is a one-way street.

As those of you who've programmed with DDE will agree, asynchronous communication between object applications can be problematic. Without explicit acknowledgment from the server application, you simply don't know whether the client's request was executed. Communication can time out. The list of what can go wrong with asynchronous communication is a long one. For many reasons, it's less reliable and harder to program than synchronous communication between objects.

With OLE 2's synchronous communications protocol, you don't have to worry whether your call connected: Communication functions called do not return until the called function in the server program completes its task. Therefore, these communication functions can return values that indicate whether the requested action was successfully performed, and, if not, why.

The OLE Interface

Given that an important part of the OLE model is that server objects neither have to be written in the same language as clients nor have any advance knowledge of what kind of client object might call them, how do OLE servers and clients communicate when that virtual "phone" rings? Objects that conform to the OLE standard must implement a standardized *interface*.

OLE objects can have has many interfaces as their designer would like, generally grouped by functionality. A given interface will display a "table of contents" of the functions it contains and provide a means for executing those functions.

The Object Browser uses the exposed interface of ActiveX objects to show you the members — properties, methods, and events — of the component or application. Visual Basic clients can use these properties and methods — and respond to the events — even though the implementation details of the interface are hidden. (That is, unless you have access to the source code, in VB or some other language.) Your client programs only need to use the familiar *Object.Method* and *Object.Property* syntax to access ActiveX server members. Events that can be fired by an object — such as an ActiveX control — are displayed in the event handler framework in the client's code window. You can add code to respond to events fired by the ActiveX component as appropriate.

The ActiveX Object Definition

An ActiveX object is defined as one that adheres to the Component Object Model (COM) originally defined by Microsoft. Microsoft has turned the definition of the specification over to a public industry group, the Active Group.

You can find more information about the Active Group on their Web site. The URL is *http://www.activex.org*.

A compliant object has the following characteristics:

- An OLE object is implemented as binary code. Therefore, it can be written in any source language.
- The object is encapsulated (lives in) an executable file (usually **.Exe** for applications and **.Ocx** for controls) or in a dynamic link library (**.Dll** file).
- The object contains data of two types: *presentation data,* which is required for screen display or printing, and *internal data*. You can think of both kinds of data as properties that are private to the object.
- The object also contains functions for manipulating its data.
- The object provides a standardized interface for other objects to communicate with it (described earlier).
- The object participates in *marshaling* — the process of passing function arguments and return values among processes and machines. Routines in the system file **Compobj.Dll** manage marshaling.

Figure 20-3 is a generalized diagram showing the structure of an OLE 2 object.

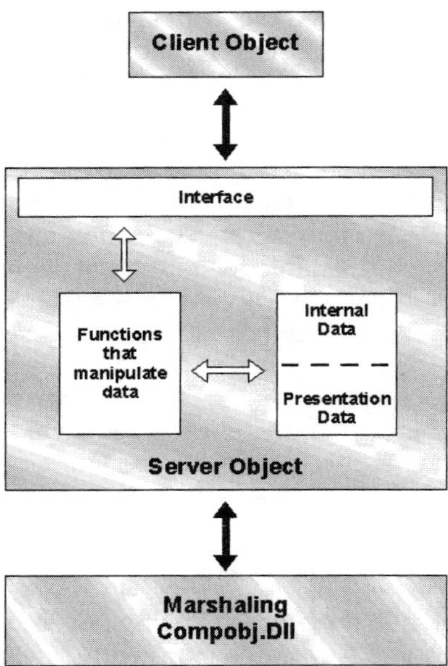

Figure 20-3: The internal structure of an OLE server object includes an interface as well as functions that manipulate data.

What an ActiveX Object Does

Actually, what ActiveX applications in their OLE server role mostly do is wait. In 1652, Milton wrote, "Those also serve who only stand and wait." He could have been describing OLE servers, which often do nothing until they are called. Of course, there are quite a few objects that go both ways: They wait to be called as servers, but in the meantime they're quite busy, perhaps as clients calling other server objects. For example, Word can be called as a server by an external client object; it can sure keep busy in the meantime by updating an embedded spreadsheet, for example.

In general, OLE objects are expected to support a number of protocols and provide a number of services:

- Objects are expected to provide an interface to their internal commands — "automate" — so that other objects can make the server object perform the specified operations on its data. Hence the phrase "OLE automation server." For example, an Excel object has a method that allows an external client to cause it to load a spreadsheet.
- OLE objects are expected to support drag and drop. If the object windows, it should respond appropriately to data or objects dropped on it using the mouse.

- OLE objects support Uniform Data Transfer (UDT), which is a mechanism for handling the exchange of formatted data structures between applications. UDT transfers are made by conveying pointer information rather than the data itself, so that large amounts of data don't have to be read into memory.
- OLE objects are expected to participate in an OLE-defined architecture called structured storage, using an OLE service, *compound* files. Compound files define a way to share the contents of a file among components, using a mechanism that can be thought of as "a file system within a file system" (as described in a moment).

In the context of compound documents, OLE objects are supposed to:

- Embed themselves appropriately within a container document, and render their data appropriately on the screen or printer. For example, a Word document could contain an embedded Excel spreadsheet object.
- Maintain links between embedded objects — comparable to the DDE automatic link — so that data can be updated automatically.
- Support in-place activation and editing in response to user actions. This means providing an appropriate visual editing interface in the context of the container. For example, an embedded CorelDraw object in a Word document can be edited using Corel's tools.

OLE objects provide an internal object known as a *moniker,* which encapsulates a pointer to an object and the mechanism for re-creating the pointer if necessary. In DDE terms, the pointer is a path to the linked object along with a method for locating the linked object, should the absolute path become inaccurate.

How Visual Basic Version 5 Works with ActiveX

In general, VB5 works with ActiveX objects in a number of different ways:

- You can install ActiveX controls in the VB Toolbox. You can then embed these tools into a form. You can set the control's properties in the Properties window or in code, you can invoke its methods in code, and you can place VB code in its published event handlers.
- You can work with exposed members of ActiveX servers within code after you instance the ActiveX object by using the Dim statement with the New keyword or the Set statement. Once you have instanced the object, you can invoke its properties and methods by using the object variable and the dot operator. You can use these techniques to include and manipulate, for example, Excel spreadsheets and Word for Windows documents within your VB applications.

- You can use the OLE control — its Toolbox icon is shown in Figure 20-4 — as a container for embedding objects on your form. You can think of the control and its properties and methods as an interface to embedded and linked objects. I'll discuss the OLE control further in Chapter 21, "Creating Applications that Support OLE."

Figure 20-4: The OLE control's Toolbox icon looks like this.

- You can use VB to create ActiveX OLE server objects with properties and methods. Your VB client objects can then invoke the exposed properties and methods of your servers. For more information, see Chapter 23, "Creating ActiveX Applications."
- With Version 5, you now have the exciting ability to easily create ActiveX controls that can be used by any application capable of hosting OLE controls. (See Part VI, "Creating ActiveX Controls.")
- You can create ActiveX Document applications, which are applications that support OLE compound storage. By creating an ActiveX Document application, you can essentially turn VB forms into full-fledged Web applications. (See Chapter 28.)

VB and Drag and Drop

OLE implements drag and drop to allow the transfer of data and other information from one object (the "source") to another (the "target"). What happens is that the source application constructs a data object that corresponds to the subject of the drag operation. When an application is notified that it is the drop target, it takes any actions necessary to receive the data.

Controls that you can drag — most controls except the Line, Menu, Shape, Timer, and CommonDialog controls — have two properties that you can set:

- DragMode determines whether dragging is *automatic* or *manual*.
- DragIcon sets the icon to be used during a dragging operation.

In an automatic drag, VB handles the operation by recognizing the start of the drag, changing the cursor appropriately, and notifying the target of a drop. By contrast, you are responsible for managing a manual drag operation. Your application must initiate the drag using the .Drag method, respond to the drag with its own event code, change the cursor appropriately, and notify the target. Chapter 21 contains examples of both automatic and manual dragging.

The Drag method begins, ends, or cancels a drag operation of any control that supports drag and drop. The syntax for the drag method is

```
object.drag action
```

Table 20-1 shows the possible values for the action argument.

Table 20-1 Possible Values for the Drag Method's Action Parameter

Constant Equivalent	*Value*	*Description*
vbCancel	0	Cancels drag operation
vbBeginDrag	1	Begins dragging object
vbEndDrag	2	Ends dragging and drops object

You don't need to use the Drag method to begin an automatic drag; that's one of the points of putting drag on automatic pilot by setting DragMode to automatic. In some circumstances, you may wish to start a drag operation using the Drag method even though dragging is automatic.

Prior to Version 4 of Visual Basic, Drag was an asynchronous method, meaning that subsequent statements were executed even though the Drag action wasn't finished. In Visual Basic Version 5, Drag is a synchronous method in which subsequent statements aren't executed until the drag action is finished.

Two event handlers respond to dragging operations:

- DragDrop is fired when a drag-and-drop operation is completed as a result of dragging a control over a form or control and releasing the mouse button or using the Drag method with its action argument set to vbEndDrag. Code is placed in the DragDrop event to control what happens after a drag operation is completed.
- DragOver is fired, multiple times, when a drag-and-drop operation is in progress. You can use this event to monitor the mouse pointer as it enters, leaves, or rests directly over a valid target using the *state* parameter of the method. The mouse pointer position determines the target object that receives this event.

You can use DragOver to set what happens after dragging is initiated but before a control drops onto a target. For example, you can verify to the user that a target is a valid drop by highlighting the target (set the BackColor or ForeColor property of the target) or by displaying a special drag pointer (set the DragIcon or MousePointer property from code).

State is an integer parameter that corresponds to the transition state of the control being dragged in relation to a target. It has three possible values, as described in Table 20-2.

Table 20-2 Possible Values of the DragOver Event's State Parameter

Value	*Meaning*
0	Enter (source control is being dragged within the range of a target)
1	Leave (source control is being dragged out of the range of a target)
2	Over (source control has moved from one position in the target to another)

The simplest paradigm for setting up a drag-and-drop operation involves only two steps:

1. Set to automatic the DragMode properties for the controls that will be sources and targets for the drag-and-drop operation.
2. Add code to appropriately handle DragOver and DragDrop events to the targets.

The mechanics of programming drag and drop will be covered further in Chapter 21.

VB and Containers

To add an embedded container object to a VB form, draw an OLE container on your form using the OLE control. Set its OLETypeAllowed property to 1-Embedded. The OLE control is now set up to be an embedded container. You can select the object that will be the contents of the container using the Insert Object item on the OLE control's pop-up menu (see Figure 20-5).

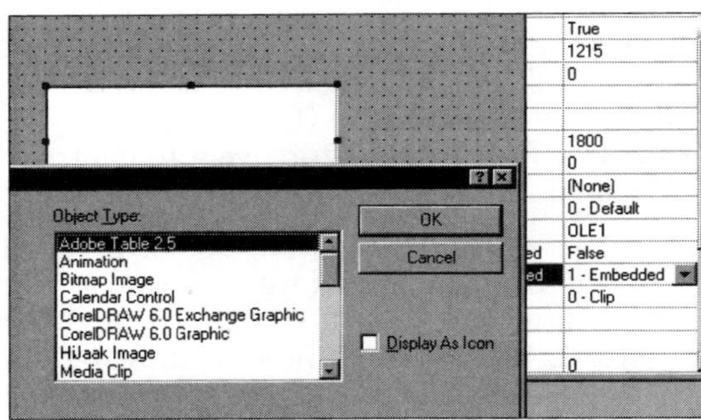

Figure 20-5: You can embed objects in a VB form using the container control.

Linked objects are like embedded objects except that the linked container has a moniker that allows the object inside the container to locate the source it is linked to. You configure an OLE control to hold a linked object by setting its OLETypeAllowed property to 0-Linked. You can then link objects to the container by using the Paste Special item on the OLE control's pop-up menu.

An *embedded server* is a server that can build an object in a container. For example, if you place a generic Word document in an OLE container control, when you double-click the control at runtime, Word starts, letting you create the specific object you want embedded, as shown in Figure 20-6. This is *in-place activation*. An activation is considered "in-place" when you do not have to leave the containing application to perform the action the object takes on activation.

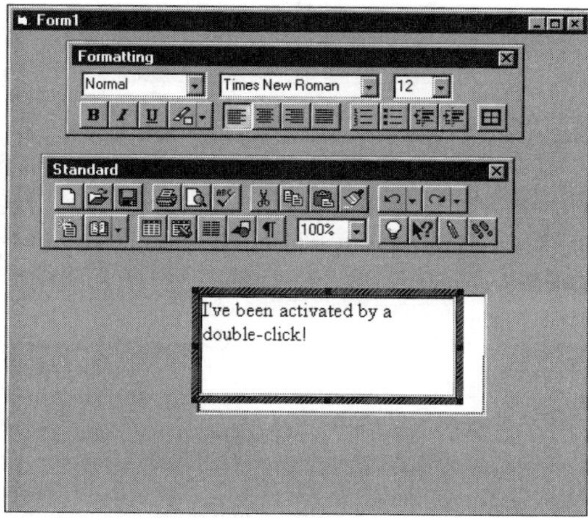

Figure 20-6: Double-clicking a generic Word document placed in an OLE control activates a miniature Word editing environment.

Each object has a default action that is invoked by double-clicking the control if its AutoActivate property is set to vbOLEActivateDoubleclick (a constant equal to 2). Often this is all you need to bring up the editing environment for the object and open it for editing; however, this is not the only action possible. For example, a linked object might simply update when activated.

You can customize the response to double-clicking by writing your own event handler if you first set the control's AutoActivate property to vbOLEActivateManual (a constant equal to 0). You use the DoVerb method to open an object for an operation, such as editing. The operation is indicated by the verb parameter passed with the method call. Although each object can support its own set of verbs, Table 20-3 shows standard verbs every object should support.

Table 20-3 Standard Arguments for the DoVerb Method

Constant	*Value*	*Description*
vbOLEPrimary	0	The default action for the object.
vbOLEShow	-1	Activates the object for editing. If the application that created the object supports in-place activation, the object is activated within the OLE container control.
vbOLEOpen	-2	Opens the object in a separate application window. If the application that created the object supports in-place activation, the object is activated in its own window.

(continued)

Table 20-3 (Continued)

Constant	Value	Description
vbOLEHide	-3	For embedded objects, hides the application that created the object.
vbOLEUIActivate	-4	If the object supports in-place activation, activates the object for in-place activation and shows any user interface tools. If the object doesn't support in-place activation, the object doesn't activate, and an error occurs.
vbOLEInPlaceActivate	-5	If the user moves the focus to the OLE container control, creates a window for the object and prepares the object to be edited. An error occurs if the object doesn't support activation on a single mouse click.
vbOLEDiscardUndoState	-6	Used when the object is activated for editing to discard all record of changes that the object's application can undo.

MAPI

MAPI, the Messaging APIs, may seem like a digression at this point. What it has in common with OLE is communication between objects — standardized communication. MAPI is Microsoft's messaging architecture for connecting applications to a wide range of messaging services.

For one thing, simple mail functionality — for instance, a Send Mail item on the File menu — is required for Microsoft certification of Windows 95 compliance. For another, depending on the kind of application you are writing, users may both expect and require sophisticated message handling.

You can achieve MAPI functionality by using the MAPI OLE controls (***Msmapi.Ocx***) or by calling the Messaging APIs directly.

Using the MAPI Controls

If the MAPI controls (see Figure 20-7) are not already in your Toolbox, add them by selecting the Components dialog from the VB Project menu and checking Microsoft MAPI Controls 5.0 (***Msmapi32.Ocx***).

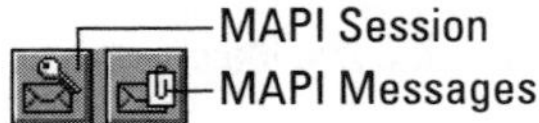

Figure 20-7: Here are the two MAPI custom control icons as they appear in the Toolbox or on a form.

You use the MAPI session control to establish a messaging session based on the properties supplied either in the Properties window or in code. Two methods apply to the control: SignOn and SignOff.

The SignOn method starts the Logon dialog for the user into the account specified by the UserName and Password properties, and provides a session handle to the underlying message subsystem. The session handle is stored in the SessionID property.

For example, the following code starts the Logon dialog for the user profiled as "MS Exchange Settings 1" (on my system this is established as Jean-Luc Picard, with "MakeItSo" as his password):

```
MAPISession1.UserName = "MS Exchange Settings 1"
MAPISession1.SignOn
```

The simple sample mail application is saved on the CD-ROM as ***Mapi.Vbp***.

Next, configure the MAPI messages control with the session handle from the MAPI session control:

```
MAPIMessages1.SessionID = MAPISession1.SessionID
```

Set the MsgIndex property of the control to -1 to indicate that an outgoing message is being composed:

```
MAPIMessages1.MsgIndex = -1
```

Presumably, in real life, you'd pick the text for the subject of a message out of a user-supplied text box rather than, as here, entering it in code:

```
MAPIMessages1.MsgSubject = "Welcome to the Federation!"
```

The message text, itself, is supplied by text that the user enters into a RichTextBox control (see Figure 20-8):

```
MAPIMessages1.MsgNoteText = RichTextBox1.Text
```

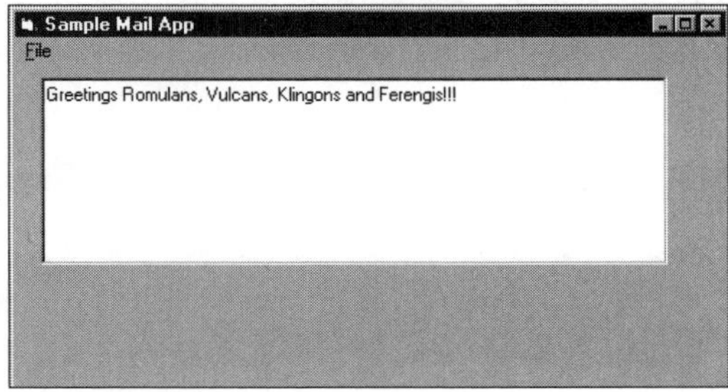

Figure 20-8: You can use the RichTextBox control to allow users to compose mail messages.

Finally, show the user's address book, call the ResolveName method to make sure there is a match on the recipient's name (you can trap the error if the name doesn't resolve), send the message, and log out of the MAPI system:

```
MAPIMessages1.Show
MAPIMessages1.ResolveName
MAPIMessages1.Send
MAPISession1.SignOff
```

Here's the entire procedure for a very simple MAPI send:

```
Private Sub mnuMail_Click()
   MAPISession1.UserName = "MS Exchange Settings 1"
   MAPISession1.SignOn
   MAPIMessages1.SessionID = MAPISession1.SessionID
   MAPIMessages1.MsgIndex = -1
   MAPIMessages1.MsgSubject = "Welcome to the Federation!"
   MAPIMessages1.MsgNoteText = RichTextBox1.Text
   MAPIMessages1.Show
   MAPIMessages1.ResolveName
   MAPIMessages1.Send
   MAPISession1.SignOff
End Sub
```

As you can see from Figures 20-8 and 20-9, as far as it goes, this works just fine.

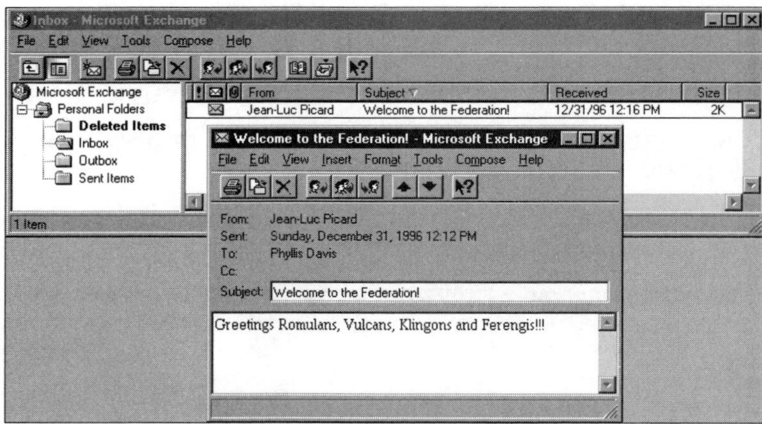

Figure 20-9: When the recipient opens mail that was generated in a VB app, it looks just like any other mail.

Receiving mail using the MAPI controls works pretty much like sending it. Here's the code required for reading a message into the RichTextBox control, with the sender's name and subject matter placed in the Form1's caption:

```
Private Sub mnuGet_Click()
   MAPISession1.UserName = "MS Exchange Settings 1"
   MAPISession1.SignOn
   MAPIMessages1.SessionID = MAPISession1.SessionID
   MAPIMessages1.FetchUnreadOnly = True
   MAPIMessages1.FetchMsgType = ""
   MAPIMessages1.Fetch
   Form1.Caption = "FROM " + MAPIMessages1.MsgOrigDisplayName + _
      ": " + MAPIMessages1.MsgSubject
   RichTextBox1.Text = MAPIMessages1.MsgNoteText
   MAPISession1.SignOff
End Sub
```

You can set various options by using the properties of the MAPIMessages control. Only unread mail will be "fetched." The FetchMsgType property specifies the type of messages that are fetched; the empty string, the — default — means an interpersonal message type.

Once the Fetch method has been executed, the MsgOrigDisplayName property holds the name of the sender, the MsgSubject property holds the subject of the message, and MsgNoteText contains the text of the message.

As this code demonstrates (see Figure 20-10), it's just as easy to wire your applications to receive messages as to send them. You should be aware that the samples are fairly crude — for example, they do not include even the simplest error handling to deal with a user pressing the Cancel button in one of the Exchange dialogs that the controls open.

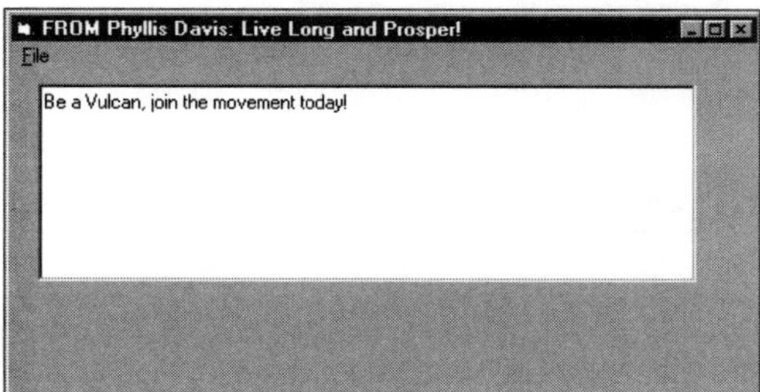

Figure 20-10: It's easy to receive mail using the MAPI controls.

Messaging API Functions

If you prefer, you don't really need the MAPI controls. It's pretty easy to call the MAPI functions (they are located in the file ***Mapi32.Dll***). Table 20-4 shows the simple MAPI functions available to VB and Table 20-5 shows the related types.

Table 20-4 Simple MAPI Functions

Function	*Description*
MAPILogon	Begins a session with the messaging system
MAPIFindNext	Returns the ID of the next (or first) message of a specified type
MAPIReadMail	Reads a mail message
MAPISaveMail	Saves a mail message
MAPIDeleteMail	Deletes a mail message
MAPISendMail	Sends a mail message, allowing greater flexibility than MAPISendDocuments in message generation
MAPISendDocuments	Sends a standard mail message using a dialog box
MAPIAddress	Addresses a mail message
MAPIResolveName	Displays a dialog box to resolve an ambiguous recipient name
MAPIDetails	Displays a recipient details dialog box
MAPILogoff	Ends a session with the messaging system

Table 20-5 MAPI Types

Type	*Description*
MapiFile	File attachment information
MapiMessage	MAPI message information
MapiRecip	Recipient information

The best source of further information on declaring and using these functions and types is the section of the Office Developer's Kit entitled "Simple MAPI for Visual Basic" (available on the MSDN CD-ROM).

Compound Files and Structured Storage

When you embed objects of one type within containing objects of another type — as in OLE — you need a storage mechanism that keeps track of the different kinds of things being stored and their locations.

Compound files, an implementation of the concept of *structured storage*, internally organize information into *storages* — which act like directory structures — and *streams* — which act like files.

You can save objects using an embedded application's ability to work with compound files.

In addition, ActiveX Document applications provide a way to use OLE-structured storage techniques in your applications (see Chapter 28 for more information).

ActiveX Applications and the Registry

Information about OLE objects in the Registry branches from HKEY_CLASSES_ROOT. The entries under HKEY_CLASSES_ROOT identify object applications, the location of their data, and a unique numerical identifier for each object class used in your application (CLSID).

However, these entries, although vital to the successful operation of OLE applications, are pretty much opaque (see Figure 20-11). You probably won't get very far editing them by hand.

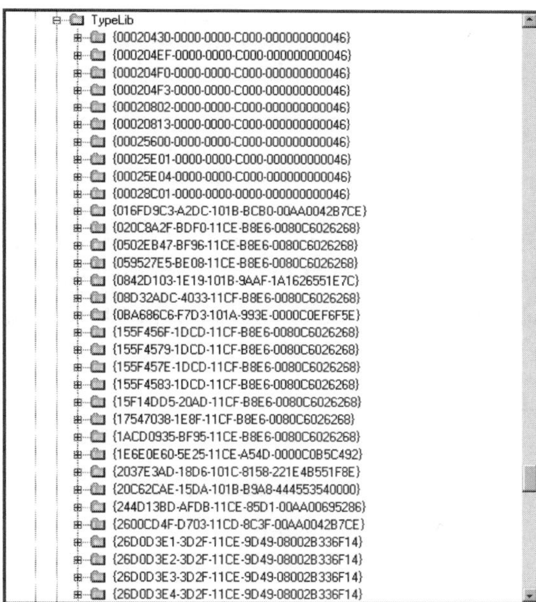

Figure 20-11: Class ID (CLSID) entries in the Registry are hard to fathom.

Fortunately, registration of VB OLE applications is mostly handled for you. VB automatically takes care of temporary registration of server applications that are running in the IDE. In addition, ActiveX applications and controls are generally referred to in code using their names, not their CLSID.

The first time a compiled ActiveX application is run, it is registered with the system. In addition, if you create a setup program using the Setup Wizard (see Chapter 36, "Setup Programs"), the resulting program will automatically register the OLE server application on the target system.

You can use the Regsvr32 utility — located on the VB5 CD-ROM in the ***Tools\REGISTRATIONUTILITIES*** directory — to manually register and unregister servers. The /u command-line flag indicates that the server is to be unregistered. For example, you could register a server ***MyInProcessServer.Dll***:

```
C:\Vb\RegSvr32 MyInProcessServer.Dll
```

You could unregister the same in-process OLE DLL:

```
C:\Vb\RegSvr32 /u MyInProcessServer.Dll
```

Although you'll normally use an ActiveX object's name to program it, you'll need to understand CLSIDs for some purposes — such as deploying ActiveX controls on the Web.

For more information on CLSIDs and the Registry, see Chapter 9, "Using the Windows Registry." Deploying Visual Basic ActiveX controls on the Web is explained in Chapter 28.

Summary

This chapter covered the basic information you need to know to start exploring ActiveX and OLE programming in greater detail. In this chapter, I explained

- How VB development fits into the greater ocean of ActiveX objects
- What, exactly, is an ActiveX object
- ActiveX and OLE
- OLE clients and servers
- Synchronous and asynchronous communication
- How two ActiveX objects communicate
- The concept of structured storage
- ActiveX applications and the Registry

In addition, I showed you how to

- Insert embedded or linked objects using the OLE control
- Integrate simple MAPI into your applications using the MAPI controls

Chapter 21

Creating Applications that Support OLE

The preceding chapter, "Understanding ActiveX and OLE," provided an overview of OLE theory and how it is implemented in Visual Basic Version 5. This chapter continues where Chapter 20 left off with an in-depth look at the OLE Container control.

I'll start with a few examples of basic drag-and-drop programming. It's important to understand two points:

- The programmer is responsible for coding much of the implementation of a drag-and-drop operation.
- The mechanics of this implementation is essentially the same whether or not OLE is involved — at least up to the final action that the drag-and-drop operation precipitates.

Topics covered in this chapter include

- Programming drag and drop
- Linking and embedding objects at design time
- Creating objects at runtime
- In-place activation and negotiation
- Drag and drop and OLE

Drag-and-Drop Warm-Up Exercises

As a first pass at drag-and-drop programming — saved on the CD-ROM as ***Drag1.Vbp*** — I'll show you how to drag and drop a label control placed on a form.

In the Properties window, I've set the label — named lblDrag — to have an initial caption value of Drag me! LblDrag's .BackColor property is, for the time being, left at the default value, vbButtonFace (this constant's value is -2147483633). If you set lblDrag's .DragMode property to 1-Automatic, when you run the project you can now drag it around the form, although it doesn't do much yet.

Taking this a small step further, you can set the DragIcon property of lblDrag — either in code or using the Properties window — so that the cursor changes when the label is dragged. In the example project, I've set the drag cursor to the cloud and rain icon (***Rain.Ico***) available in the ***Elements*** subdirectory of the VB icon samples directory — very appropriate, I think, for drag and drop.

Let's get down to business! If you add a menu structure to the project form, it's easy to add code that lets the user enable and disable dragging (see Figure 21-1).

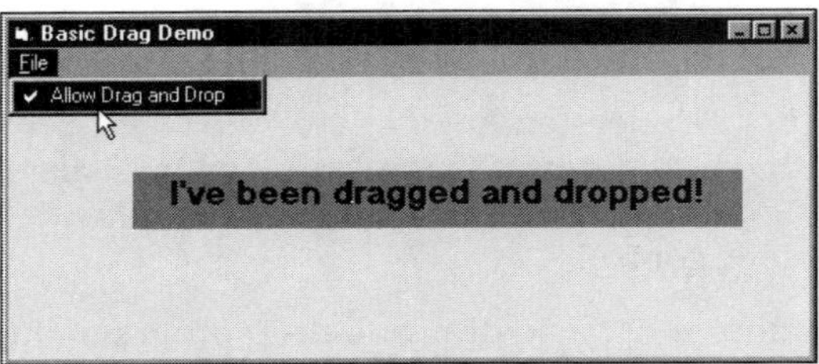

Figure 21-1: You can use the DragOver and DragDrop events to easily implement drag-and-drop programming.

For this to work, the lblDrag's DragMode property should load with the default value 0-Manual, which really means, don't drag unless a specific Drag method is invoked. Here's the menu click procedure code:

```
Private Sub mnuDD_Click()
   If Not mnuDD.Checked Then
      lblDrag.DragMode = 1 'Automatic
   Else
      lblDrag.DragMode = 0 'Manual
   End If
   mnuDD.Checked = Not mnuDD.Checked
End Sub
```

You can also have the label actually do something when it's dragged: changing caption, color, and location. This code goes in the DragOver event of the *target* — in this case, the form:

```
Private Sub Form_DragOver(Source As Control, X As Single, _
   Y As Single, State As Integer)
   Source.Caption = "I'm being dragged!"
   Source.BackColor = vbRed
   Source.Left = X
   Source.Top = Y
End Sub
```

As basic code, this works fine, as you'll see when you try it out: *Source* in the code refers to the label control. Its caption changes, its color becomes red, and its location is set by the passed mouse location parameters.

But it can be refined, because, as this is written, the label can be dragged until it is most of the way out of the form on either the right or bottom side. You can add code to check for and correct this. Listing 21-1 contains the revised procedure:

Listing 21-1: Using the form DragOver event to move a control on a form

```
Private Sub Form_DragOver(Source As Control, X As Single, _
   Y As Single, State As Integer)
   Source.Caption = "I'm being dragged!"
   Source.BackColor = vbRed
   If X > Me.ScaleWidth - Source.Width Then
       X = Me.ScaleWidth - Source.Width
   End If
   Source.Left = X
   If Y > Me.ScaleHeight - Source.Height Then
      Y = Me.ScaleHeight - Source.Height
   End If
   Source.Top = Y
End Sub
```

All that remains is to add code to complete a drop. This will just change the caption and color of the label control for a final time because the label control's location parameters are as they were in the final DragOver event call. The drop code goes in lblDrag's DragDrop event (not the form's DragDrop event):

```
Private Sub lblDrag_DragDrop(Source As Control, X As Single, _
   Y As Single)
   Source.Caption = "I've been dragged and dropped!"
   Source.BackColor = vbBlue
End Sub
```

This little application is fun to play with! As you can see, once you get the hang of it, drag-and-drop programming is pretty easy.

Let's go on to another example.

More Dragging and Dropping

The next example — saved on the CD-ROM as ***Drag2.Vbp*** — shows how to add code to DragDrop events that discriminates between different drag sources and takes actions based on the drag source. The actions this code takes are somewhat comparable to the actions you might take with an OLE object.

Picture Controls

The form contains four Picture controls, two that can be drop targets — pctTarget1 and pctTarget2 — and two that cannot — pctHarold and Picture1. PctTarget1, pctTarget2, and pctHarold contain a picture (a photograph converted to a ***.Bmp*** file); their Autosize property has been set to True so that the Picture control is the exact size of the contained picture (see Figure 21-2).

Watch Out for Whose DragDrop Event it Is!

The code in this example in the form's DragOver event causes lblDrag to move as it's dragged. This makes for a nice screen display as you move the label around the screen but contains the seed of a problem: When you finally let go of that mouse and cause a DragDrop event, that DragDrop event belongs to the label, not the form, because the label has been following the mouse. The code in this example handles this problem by responding to the drop in the label's DragDrop event. By going this route, you lose some flexibility: If the code could be placed in the form's DragDrop event, you'd be able to deal with information about the source and the target in one procedure. This is the more usual way to do things, but, of course, it does not let you move the control around in the DragOver event. Here's a form DragDrop procedure revised accordingly:

```
Private Sub Form_DragDrop(Source As Control, X As Single, _
    Y As Single)
    Source.Caption = "I've been dragged and dropped!"
    Source.BackColor = vbBlue
        If X > Me.ScaleWidth - Source.Width Then
            X = Me.ScaleWidth - Source.Width
        End If
        Source.Left = X
        If Y > Me.ScaleHeight - Source.Height Then
            Y = Me.ScaleHeight - Source.Height
        End If
    Source.Top = Y
End Sub
```

By using a "ghost" control and manipulating its visibility properties, you could also create the appearance of moving the control around.

Here's code to enforce the rules about which kind of picture box control can be dropped on another and to copy the contents of the source to the target when dropping is allowed:

```
'pctTarget1's DragDrop event
pctTarget1.Picture = Source.Picture
pctTarget1.BackColor = vbRed
```

This sets up pctTarget1 so that it will copy the contents of any Picture control's Picture property to its own Picture property. Picture1 has no picture, and its BackColor property is set to vbRed. When Picture1 is dropped on pctTarget1, the picture is emptied out of pctTarget1 and its BackColor property is set to vbRed, becoming a red, square shape on the screen (like Picture1). On the other hand, pctTarget2 discriminates between Picture1 and the other Picture controls; it won't accept Picture1 at all:

```
'pctTarget2's DragDrop event
If Source.Name = "pctHarold" Then
   pctTarget2.Picture = Source.Picture
Else
   MsgBox "Your kind of picture box is not accepted!"
End If
```

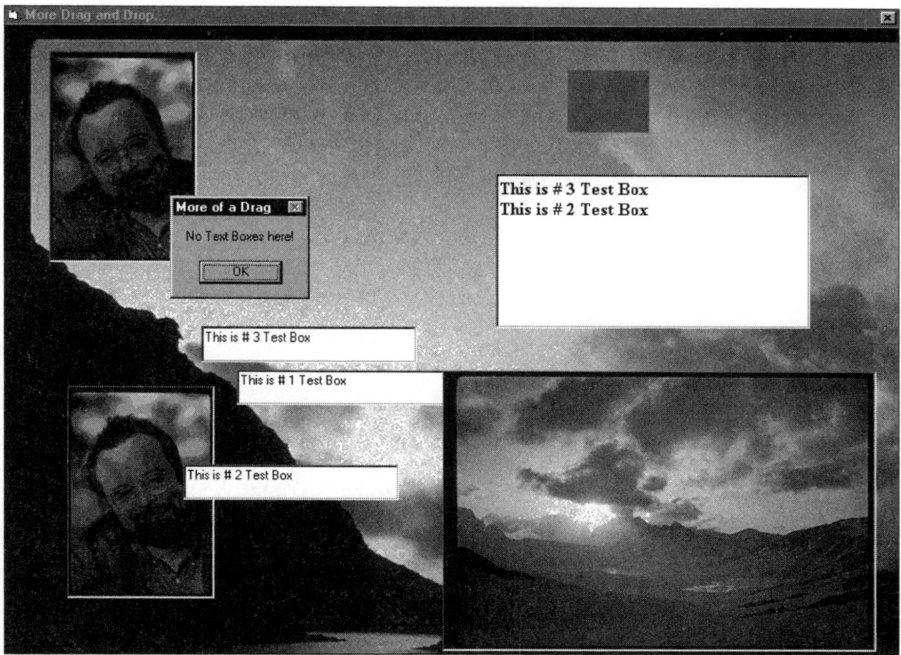

Figure 21-2: You can change the content of Picture controls and Text controls using drag and drop.

I've also placed an array of text boxes and a RichTextBox control on the form. When the text boxes are dropped on the RichTextBox, their contents get added to the existing contents of the RichTextBox control (see Figure 21-2). Here's the RichTextBox control's DragDrop event:

```
Private Sub RichTextBox1_DragDrop(Source As Control, x As Single, _
   y As Single)
   If TypeOf Source Is TextBox Then
      RichTextBox1.Text = RichTextBox1.Text + Source.Text + vbCrLf
   Else
      MsgBox "I only take text boxes!"
   End If
End Sub
```

The If TypeOf...Is construction is used to check that the source is a text box control before the drop is accepted.

You can also write the DragDrop events for pctTarget1 and pctTarget2 to take care of the possibility that something other than a picture control might be dropped on these targets, as shown in Listing 21-2.

Listing 21-2: Replacing control contents using drag and drop

```
Private Sub pctTarget1_DragDrop(Source As Control, x As Single, _
   y As Single)
   If TypeOf Source Is PictureBox Then
      pctTarget1.Picture = Source.Picture
      pctTarget1.BackColor = vbRed
   ElseIf TypeOf Source Is TextBox Then
      MsgBox "No text boxes here!"
   End If
End Sub

Private Sub pctTarget2_DragDrop(Source As Control, x As Single, _
   y As Single)
   If TypeOf Source Is PictureBox Then
      If Source.Name = "pctHarold" Then
         pctTarget2.Picture = Source.Picture
      Else
         MsgBox "Your kind of picture box is not accepted!"
      End If
   ElseIf TypeOf Source Is TextBox Then
      MsgBox "No text boxes here!"
   End If
End Sub
```

Using the OLE Control

I've already shown you how to automatically create an OLE container by dropping the OLE control on your form. In fact, it's best to think of the OLE control as a custom control that provides OLE containers for OLE objects. In other words, the OLE container control enables you to add insertable objects to the forms in your Visual Basic applications. You can do this in a number of ways.

With the OLE control, you can create a placeholder in your application for an insertable object. The object itself is created either at design time using OLE dialog boxes (Insert Object and Paste Special are discussed later in this chapter) or at runtime by setting the appropriate properties. The object can either be embedded or linked. You can also bind the OLE container control to a database using the Data control.

Tables 21-1 and 21-2 list the key OLE control properties and methods.

Table 21-1 OLE Container Control Key Methods

Method	***Comments***
Close	Closes an embedded object and terminates the connection to the application that provided the object.
Copy	Copies an object within an OLE control to the system Clipboard. All embedded and linked information is copied.
CreateEmbed	Creates an embedded object based on a file or class. See "Embedding Versus Linking" later in this chapter.
CreateLink	Creates a linked object from the contents of a file. The arguments of this method are equivalent to, and override, the SourceDoc and SourceItem properties.
Delete	Deletes an OLE object from memory.
DoVerb	Opens an OLE object for an operation. See the discussion of the DoVerb method in Chapter 20, "Understanding ActiveX and OLE."
FetchVerbs	Updates the list of verbs an object supports.
InsertObjDlg	Lets you display the Insert Object dialog box at runtime so that the user can select an object (or object type) for insertion in the OLE container.
Paste	Copies data from the Clipboard to an OLE control. See "Creating Objects at Design Time" later in this chapter.
PasteSpecialDlg	Displays the Paste Special dialog box at runtime, allowing the user to select from its options, including linking or embedding the object in the Clipboard. See "The Paste Special Dialog" later in this chapter.
ReadFromFile	Loads an object from a file created using the SaveToFile method.
SaveToFile	Saves an OLE object to a binary file. If the object is linked, only the link information and an image of the data is saved to the specified file. The object's data is maintained by the application that created the object. If the object is embedded, the object's data is maintained by the OLE container control and can be saved by your Visual Basic application.
Update	Updates an object in the OLE control based on the object's native application.

If you create an embedded object at design time, the SourceDoc and Class properties (see Table 21-2) work the same way as those specified using the CreateEmbed method's arguments. To find possible values for the *class* argument on your system, you can select the Class property in the Properties window. The button next to the class property displays the available class names.

To use the Paste method, set the OLETypeAllowed property, and then check the value of the PasteOK property. You can't paste successfully unless PasteOK returns a value of True.

If the Paste method was carried out, the OLEType property is set to vbOLELinked (value = 0) or vbOLEEmbedded (value = 1), depending on whether the object is linked or embedded. If the Paste method wasn't carried out, the OLEType property is set to vbOLENone (value = 3).

Table 21-2 OLE Container Control Key Properties

Property	*Comments*
AppIsRunning	Returns or sets a value that indicates whether the application that created the OLE object is running.
AutoActivate	Depending on the setting of the AutoActivate property, an OLE object is activated manually (AutoActivate is set to vbOLEActivateManual (0)), by double-clicking (AutoActivate is set to vbOLEActivateDoubleclick (2)), when it gets the focus (AutoActivate is set to vbOLEActivateGetFocus (1)), or automatically (vbOLEActivateAuto (3)) — which means using the object's normal activation method.
AutoVerbMenu	If AutoVerbMenu is True, the default, right-clicking the object at runtime displays a list of the verbs that can be applied to the object.
Class	Returns or sets the class name of an OLE object (the OLE object's program ID).
Data	Sends data to an application that created an object.
DataText	Sends or retrieves straight text from an OLE object.
FileNumber	The file number to be used when reading or saving a file.
Format	Returns or sets the format when sending data to or receiving data from an application that created an object.
lpOleObject	Returns the address of the object for use in API calls.
MiscFlags	Sets or returns a flag value that allows you to force the OLE control to use memory to store the object while it's loaded and/or to override the control's default behavior of allowing in-place activation for objects that support it.
Object	Lets you specify an object whose properties and methods you want to use in an OLE automation task.
ObjectAccept Formats	An array of strings, each element of which describes a valid format that can be used in the Format property when exchanging data with an object using the Data and DataText properties.
ObjectAccept FormatsCount	The number of elements in the ObjectAcceptFormats array. Because ObjectAcceptFormats starts at element 0, if you needed to iterate through the array, you'd terminate at ObjectAcceptFormatsCount - 1.

Property	***Comments***
ObjectGetFormats	An array of strings, each element of which is a format of data that can be provided by the object.
ObjectGet FormatsCount	The number of elements in the ObjectGetFormats array. Because ObjectGetFormats starts at element 0, if you needed to iterate through the array, you'd terminate at ObjectGetFormatsCount - 1.
ObjectVerbFlags	Returns the menu state for a verb in the ObjectVerbs array.
ObjectVerbs	A string array with each element containing a verb — an action that can be performed on the object. Note that there are six standard verbs available for every object that may not be listed by name in the ObjectVerbs array. See "ObjectVerbs Property" in VB's on-line help for further information.
ObjectVerbsCount	The number of elements in the ObjectVerbs array. Because ObjectVerbs starts at element 0, if you needed to iterate through the array, you'd terminate at ObjectVerbsCount - 1.
OLEDropAllowed	Determines whether an OLE control can be an OLE drop target.
OLEType	Returns whether an OLE control contains a linked object, an embedded object, or no object.
OLETypeAllowed	Sets whether an OLE control can contain a linked object, an embedded object, or no object.
PasteOK	Returns a value indicating whether the contents of the Clipboard can be pasted to an OLE control.
SizeMode	Controls the display of an object within the container.
SourceDoc	Returns or sets the filename to use when you create an object.
SourceItem	Returns or sets the data within the file to be linked when you create a linked object.
UpdateOptions	Returns or sets a value specifying how an object is updated when linked data is modified. The possibilities are: vbOLEAutomatic (the default, 0). The object is updated each time the linked data changes. VbOLEFrozen (value = 1). The object is updated whenever the user saves the linked data from within the application in which it was created. VbOLEManual (value = 2). The object is updated only by using the Update method.

Let's have a look at some of these properties and methods in action.

This example — saved on the CD-ROM as ***Verbs.Vbp*** — displays the contents of the ObjectVerbs, ObjectAcceptFormats, and ObjectGetFormat arrays of an OLE object selected by the user (see Figure 21-3).

The class name of the object is placed in the example form's caption. (Note that the default verb appears twice in the ObjectVerb array, the first time as element 0.)

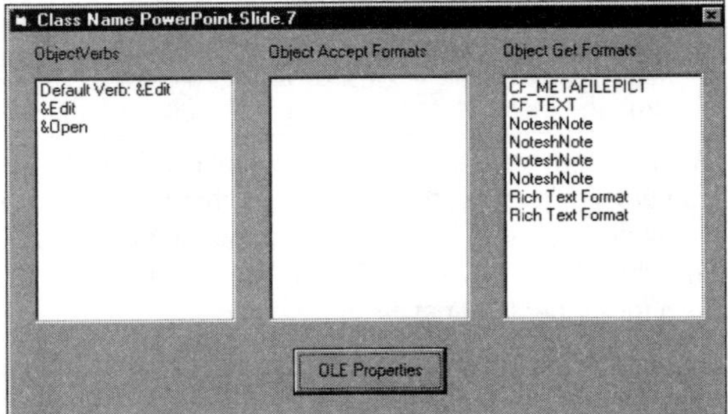

Figure 21-3: OLE Object information (in the Figure, the object is a PowerPoint slide) can easily be retrieved using the methods of the OLE container control.

Listing 21-3 shows how object Verbs and Formats of an OLE object.

Listing 21-3: Displaying object Verbs and Formats

```
Private Sub cmdInsert_Click()
   Dim I  As Integer
   ' Display the Insert Object dialog box.
   Ole1.InsertObjDlg
   Form1.Caption = "Class Name " + Ole1.Class
   Ole1.FetchVerbs    ' Fetch verbs.

   lstVerb.Clear
   lstAccept.Clear
   lstGet.Clear

   ' Fill the verbs list box.
   lstVerb.AddItem "Default Verb: " + Ole1.ObjectVerbs(0)
   For I = 1 To Ole1.ObjectVerbsCount - 1
      lstVerb.AddItem Ole1.ObjectVerbs(I)
   Next I

   'Fill the Accept Formats list box.
   For I = 0 To Ole1.ObjectAcceptFormatsCount - 1
      lstAccept.AddItem Ole1.ObjectAcceptFormats(I)
   Next I

   ' Fill the Get Formats list box.
   For I = 0 To Ole1.ObjectGetFormatsCount - 1
      lstGet.AddItem Ole1.ObjectGetFormats(I)
   Next I
End Sub
```

The next example — saved on the CD-ROM as ***Link1.Vbp*** — involves operations performed on a Word for Windows document that has been linked into an OLE container control. Embedding and linking (and the differences between the two) are discussed further in the section "Embedding Versus Linking," later in this chapter.

The document to be linked is on the CD-ROM as ***Source.Doc***. To follow the example, you need to copy this file to your hard drive. (Of course, you'll also need a copy of Word for Windows on your system.) To link the document, add an OLE container control to your form. When you add the control to your form, the Insert Object dialog opens (see Figure 21-4). Select the Create From File option button. The Link check box appears along with a Browse button that you can use to locate the file you wish to link. Once you have selected the file, you should check the Link box.

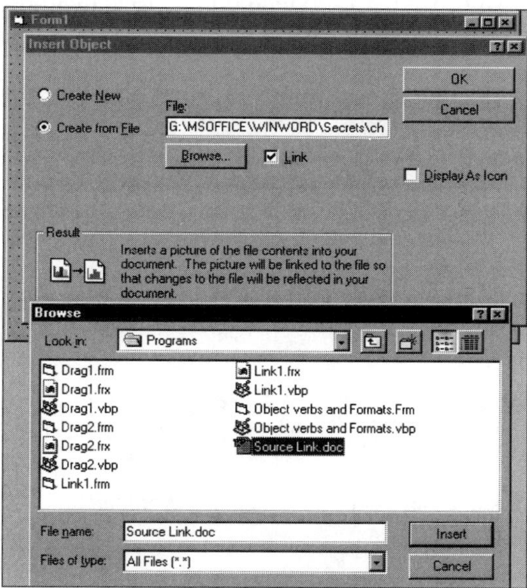

Figure 21-4: You can use the Insert Object dialog to link a document to a Visual Basic OLE container control.

Make sure to set the SizeMode property of the OLE control to 1-Stretch so that the entire Word document appears as a thumbnail in the OLE control (see Figure 21-5). The default would only show a small portion of the document.

The Source document contains a letterhead and a bookmark for positioning where our VB application will insert the contents of a text box control. (Because this is a letterhead for animals, the bookmark is named animal.) See Figure 21-5.

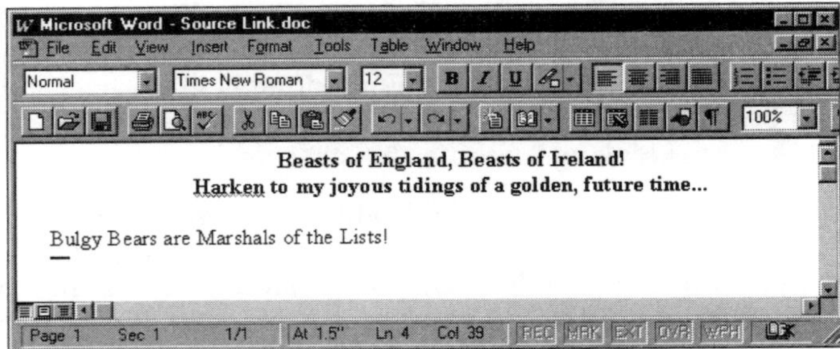

Figure 21-5: Here is the Source Link document in Word for Windows.

The sample program has four command buttons (see Figure 21-6). Start Word starts Word for Windows with the linked file and sets an object variable that holds an instance of the Word Basic object.

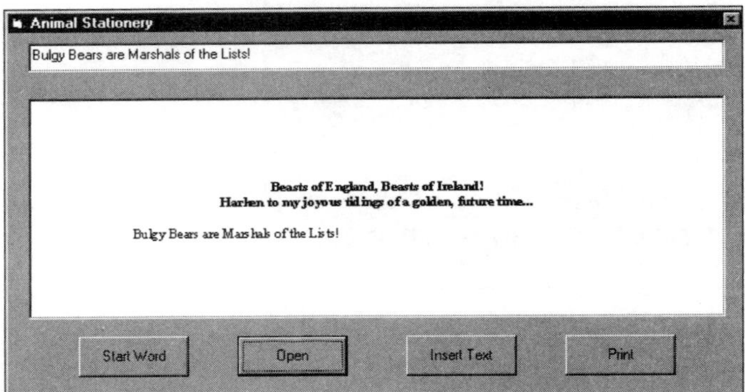

Figure 21-6: It's easy to link a Visual Basic application to a Word for Windows document using the OLE control.

The Open command button opens the linked Word document for editing in its native environment. This step would not be required if you just wanted to apply OLE automation methods to the WordBasic object. For example, you could use a statement such as

```
objWord.FileOpen OLE1.SourceDoc 'objWord is WordBasic object
```

to open the linked file for further OLE automation actions without displaying the Word environment.

The Insert Text command button places the text in the Text control of the VB application at the animal bookmark's position in the linked document.

The Print command button prints the Word for Windows document.

Using the DoVerb method, you can only manipulate an object in the OLE container control on the basis of the verbs it provides. Word for Windows provides neither a verb to insert text nor one to print documents. (If you run the Object Verbs and Formats application from the last section on Word, you'll find two verbs: Edit and Open.) There is certainly no verb that causes a macro command to be executed. To do this, you'll need to reference the WordBasic object.

The best source of information on programming the Word 7 OLE object is the topic "Using OLE Automation with Word" in Word's on-line help. It's a subtopic of "More Word Basic Information," which is a subtopic of "Word Basic Reference."

Word 8 — included in the Office 97 suite — uses a new and improved model for the OLE objects it exposes. For example, the object usually invoked at the top of its hierarchy is Word.Application, rather then Word.Basic. For detailed coverage of programming the exposed Office 97 objects, see Chapter 22, "Controlling 'Foreign' Application Objects."

You will probably be pleased to know that the Word 7 object structure has been retained for purposes of backwards compatibility. In other words, VB code that references objects belonging to Word.Basic will still function properly.

To start with, declare a form-level variable to hold the WordBasic object:

```
Option Explicit
Dim objWord As Object
```

The code in the Start Word procedure instances objWord so that the WordBasic methods can be referenced:

```
Private Sub cmdStart_Click()
    Set objWord = CreateObject("Word.Basic")
End Sub
```

The following Set statement is functionally equivalent to the one in the procedure:

```
Set objWord = OLE1.object.Application.WordBasic
```

To open the Word for Windows editing environment, use the OLE control's DoVerbs method with an argument of 0 (Edit):

```
Private Sub cmdOpen_Click()
    OLE1.DoVerb (0)
    Me.SetFocus
End Sub
```

The procedure returns focus to the VB application after Word comes up.

Going to the bookmark and inserting the text from Text1 is easy:

```
Private Sub cmdInsert_Click()
    objWord.EditGoto "Animal"
    objWord.Insert Text1.Text
End Sub
```

By the way, here's the DDE equivalent to this procedure:

```
Text1.LinkMode = vbLinkNone
Text1.LinkTopic = "WinWord|" + OLE1.SourceDoc
Text1.LinkItem = "Animal"
Text1.LinkMode = vbLinkManual
Text1.LinkPoke
Text1.LinkMode = vbLinkNone
```

Similarly, calling up WordBasic's print command on the linked document is a breeze:

```
Private Sub cmdPrint_Click()
   objWord.FilePrint
End Sub
```

When the VB application shuts down, it's important that it takes care of freeing the object variable and closing Word for Windows:

```
Private Sub Form_Unload(Cancel As Integer)
   OLE1.Close 'Close Word
   Set objWord = Nothing
End Sub
```

There are a caveat and a warning regarding the OLE Close method. The caveat is that if the OLE control didn't start Word — perhaps it was running before the DoVerbs method was invoked — the OLE control's Close method won't shut it down.

The warning is that changes to the linked document will not automatically be saved; you'll have to handle this yourself, perhaps by calling WordBasic's FileClose or FileSave methods before the OLE control's Close method is invoked. Here's the complete code for the sample application:

```
Option Explicit
Dim objWord As Object

Private Sub cmdStart_Click()
   Set objWord = CreateObject("Word.Basic")
End Sub

Private Sub cmdOpen_Click()
   OLE1.DoVerb (0)
   Me.SetFocus
End Sub

Private Sub cmdInsert_Click()
   objWord.EditGoto "Animal"
   objWord.Insert Text1.Text
End Sub

Private Sub cmdPrint_Click()
   objWord.FilePrint
End Sub

Private Sub Form_Unload(Cancel As Integer)
   OLE1.Close 'Close Word
   Set objWord = Nothing
End Sub
```

Embedding Versus Linking

Embedded objects are entirely contained on your form and within your VB application. This approach has the following advantages:

- The object's data is totally under the control of your application and cannot be renamed, moved, or deleted by another application.
- The embedded object is automatically installed wherever your executable is installed.

Some disadvantages of embedding are

- The size of your executable is increased to reflect the inclusion of the object's data.
- Your application is managing its own copy of the embedded object, meaning that changes are only made to it and not other copies. Embedded objects cannot be centrally managed so that changes made to one copy are reflected in all copies.
- Once an embedded object is placed within the OLE control, it can only be acted on using the OLE verbs provided by the object. For example, a link between the contents of a text box and the embedded object can only be achieved if the embedded object provides a verb to make the link. This is why, in the example in the previous section, a Word for Windows document was linked rather than embedded.
- When the application that created the embedded object is activated, it can only work on the embedded object.

From the point of view of the linked object, the advantages of being linked rather than embedded are

- Changes that are made to the linked data are updated among all linked copies. Central administration of linked objects is possible.
- Your executable doesn't increase as much in size, because only the link information and not the complete data is stored with the executable.
- There can be a greater vocabulary for working with a linked object because you are not limited to the OLE verbs provided by the object.

The disadvantages of being linked rather than embedded are that:

- Your application can fail with a cryptic error message ("Unable to activate object") if the underlying data file has been moved, renamed, or deleted (see Figure 21-7).
- Activating a linked object opens the application's own work space as opposed to starting in-place editing. This may consume more resources and give the user too much control over the application's native controls.

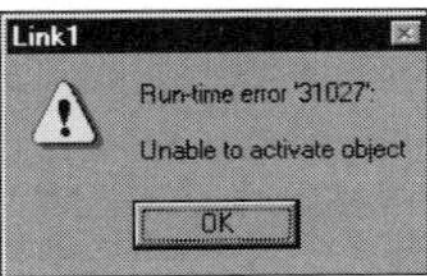

Figure 21-7: Playing games with a linked application; the underlying file has been moved!

Using the OLE Container's Pop-Up Menu

When you draw a new OLE container control on a form, the Insert Object dialog box is displayed. You use this dialog to create a linked or embedded object (as explained further in a moment). If you choose Cancel, no object is created.

At design time, right-click the OLE container control to display a pop-up menu, as shown in Figure 21-8. The commands displayed on this pop-up menu depend on the state of the OLE container control, as shown Table 21-3.

Table 21-3 Availability of OLE Control's Pop-Up Menu Commands

Command	*When the Command is Available*
Insert Object	Always enabled
Paste Special	Enabled when the Clipboard object contains a valid object
Delete Embedded Object	Enabled when the OLE container control contains an embedded object
Delete Linked Object	Enabled when the OLE container control contains a linked object
Create Link	Enabled when the control's SourceDoc property is set
Create Embedded Object	Enabled when the control's Class (described in a moment) or SourceDoc property is set

Finding Class Names

You can get a list of the class names available from the OLE control by selecting the Class property of the OLE container control in the Properties window and clicking the Properties button (see Figure 21-9).

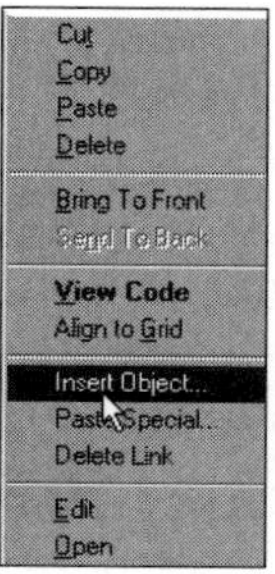

Figure 21-8: You can use the OLE control's pop-up menu to insert objects and create or delete links.

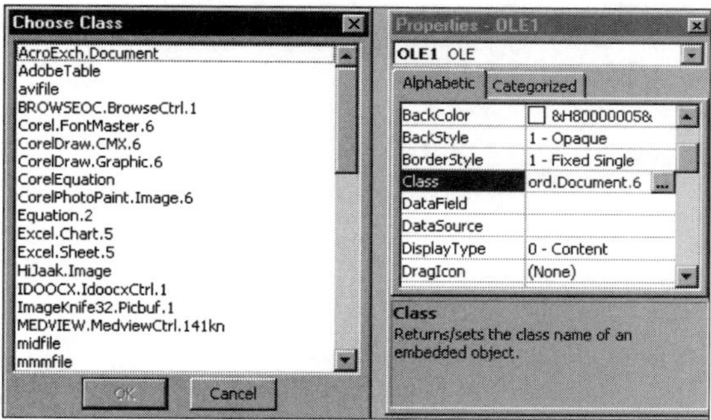

Figure 21-9: The Class property of the OLE control displays a list of available class names.

Creating Objects at Design Time

One OLE container control can contain only one object at a time. This object — be it linked or embedded — can be created in a number of ways:

- By using the Insert Object or Paste Special dialog boxes (runtime or design time)
- By setting the Class property in the Properties window and then using the OLE control's pop-up menu (design time only)
- By using the methods of the OLE control at runtime

This boils down to three ways to create objects at design time: by using the Insert Object dialog, by using the Paste Special dialog, or by setting a class.

The Insert Object Dialog

The Insert Object dialog presents two important choices:

- Should an object be linked or embedded? The differences between the two were just discussed. Note that a new object cannot be linked. Only objects created from a file can be linked. (You could, however, subsequently create a link.) Figure 21-4 showed the Insert Object dialog with a linked object; Figure 21-10 shows the Insert Object dialog with an embedded object.
- Should an object be new or created from a file? There's another consideration besides the fact that you cannot link a new file. If you want the object to include default data — such as the letterhead and bookmark in the preceding example — you should create it based on an existing file.

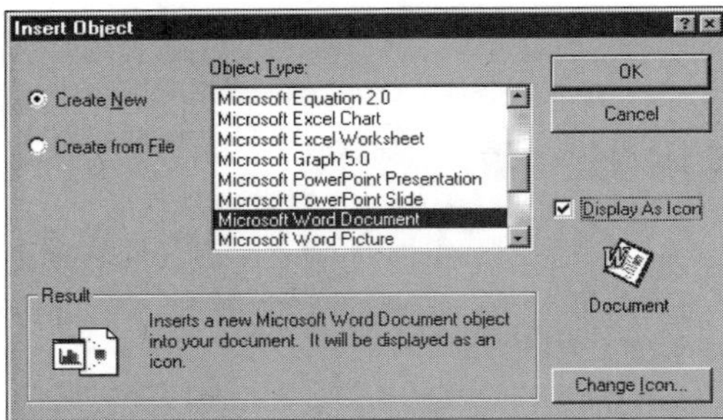

Figure 21-10: You can use the Insert Object dialog to create a new embedded document.

Additionally, you can choose (as in Figure 21-10) to have your object displayed as an icon (see Figure 21-11). Although in-place activation still brings up the object's application, you see the object as an icon rather than seeing the application's work space.

Figure 21-11: Objects displayed as icons can still be edited using in-place activation.

The Paste Special Dialog

Provided that you have copied material from an OLE server application to the Clipboard, you can use the Paste Special dialog to embed or link the material to an OLE container control (see Figure 21-12). The Paste Special dialog is particularly useful when you want to link or embed a portion of a file — for example, a paragraph from a Word for Windows document. At design time, the Paste Special dialog is available from the OLE control's right mouse pop-up menu.

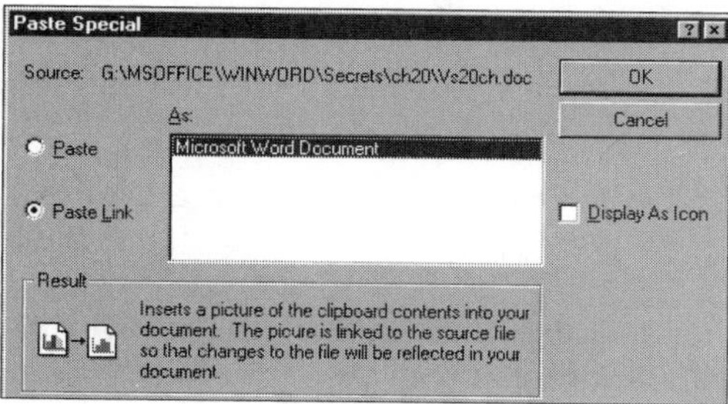

Figure 21-12: You use the Paste Special dialog to paste an OLE object from the Clipboard to an OLE container control.

Setting the Object's Class

The final design time mechanism for filling an OLE container is to set the OLE container's class property and then choose Create Embedded Object from the OLE control's pop-up menu.

Creating Objects at Runtime

To display the Insert Object dialog to allow the user to choose from the dialog's options, use the OLE control's InsertObjDlg method:

```
Private Sub cmdInsert_Click()
   OLE1.InsertObjDlg
   If OLE1.OLEType = vbOLENone Then
      MsgBox "You didn't really create an object!"
   End If
End Sub
```

The Paste Special dialog works in the same way, with the PasteSpecialDlg method:

```
Private Sub cmdPaste_Click()
   If OLE1.PasteOK Then
      OLE1.PasteSpecialDlg
      If OLE1.OLEType = vbOLENone Then
         MsgBox "You didn't really paste an object!"
      End If
   Else
      MsgBox "Data contained in Clipboard can't be" + _
         " pasted into OLE control"
   End If
```

```
End Sub
```

Using the Methods of the OLE Control

You can create a linked object at runtime using the OLE control's CreateLink method:

```
OLE1.CreateLink "C:\Secrets\ch21\programs\Source.doc"
```

You can use the .SourceItem property to specify the data you want to link from within the file.

To create an embedded object at runtime, use the .CreateEmbed method:

```
OLE1.CreateEmbed "C:\Secrets\ch21\programs\Source.doc"
```

To create an empty embedded object at runtime, use the CreateEmbed method without specifying a source document. For example:

```
Private Sub cmdCreate_Click()
   OLE1.CreateEmbed "", "Word.Document"
   OLE1.DoVerb 0
End Sub
```

In-Place Activation and Menu Negotiation

If you'd like the object's menu to appear on your form following in-place activation (see Figure 21-13), you must add at least one menu item to the form. This menu item need not be invisible.

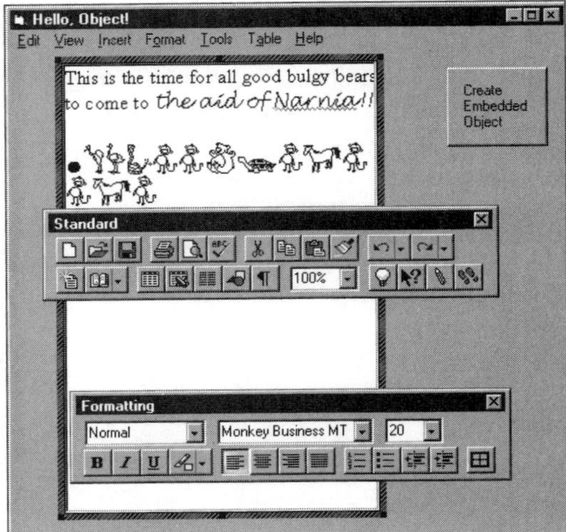

Figure 21-13: To make an in-place activated menu appear on the form of an OLE control, make sure the form has at least one menu item.

Menu negotiation determines what menus appear when there are competing claims to menu display space. This subject was discussed in greater detail in Chapter 18, "Managing MDI Applications and Menus."

As I explained in Chapter 18, you can set a menu item's NegotiatePosition property in the Menu Editor (see Figure 21-14).

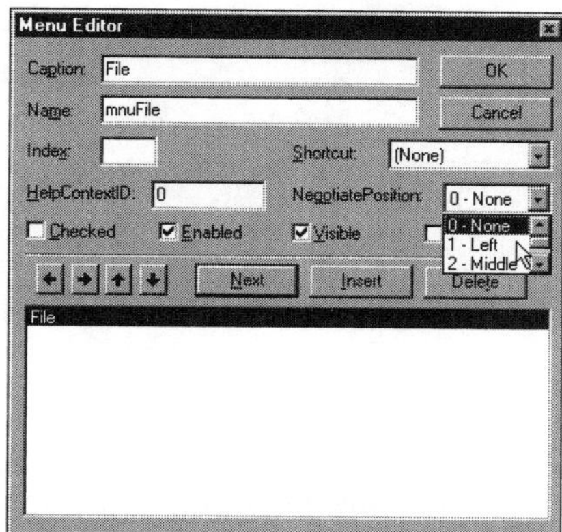

Figure 21-14: You can use the Menu Editor to set menu negotiation.

If NegotiatePosition is set to 0-None, the form's native menu item will disappear once the OLE object's application has been activated. Otherwise, the NegotiatePosition property determines where the native menu item appears.

Dropping in on the OLE Control

This chapter started with drag-and-drop programming and will conclude with a demonstration of dragging and dropping in the context of the OLE control: May the circle be unbroken!

The demonstration — on the companion CD-ROM as ***Embed.Vbp*** — allows the user to drag and drop text box controls on an OLE control that contains an empty, embedded Word for Windows object (see Figure 21-15). (Creating an empty, embedded Word object was described earlier in the section on runtime use of the OLE control methods.)

Here's how this project works. First, a variable is declared to hold the instance of the WordBasic object:

```
Option Explicit
Dim objWord As Object
```

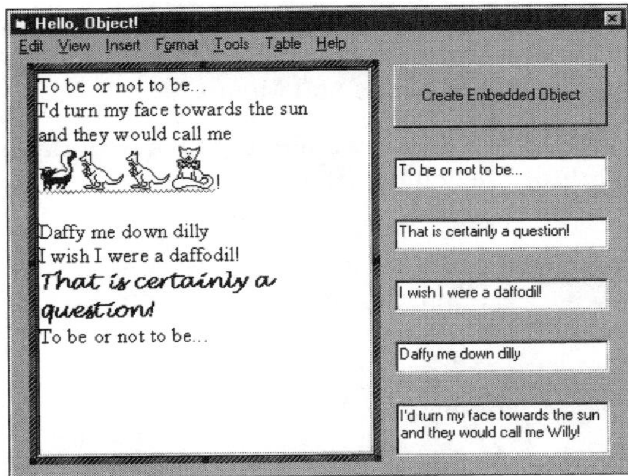

Figure 21-15: Drag-and-drop programming techniques work great with OLE!

The user can click the Create Embedded Object command button to create an empty embedded Word document and instance the objWord variable:

```
Private Sub cmdCreate_Click()
   OLE1.CreateEmbed "", "Word.Document"
   OLE1.DoVerb 0
   Set objWord = CreateObject("Word.Basic")
   Me.SetFocus
End Sub
```

Each of the text box controls has its DragMode property set to 1-Automatic. A DragIcon from the VB icon library — a lightening bolt — has also been set.

When a text box is dropped on the OLE control, the code in its DragDrop event checks whether the control contains an embedded object. If not, one is created and the objWord variable is instanced. In either case, the text property of a dropped control is inserted in the embedded Word for Windows object:

```
Private Sub OLE1_DragDrop(Source As Control, X As Single, _
   Y As Single)
   On Error Resume Next
   If Not OLE1.OLEType = vbOLEEmbedded Then
      OLE1.CreateEmbed "", "Word.Document"
      OLE1.DoVerb 0
      Set objWord = CreateObject("Word.Basic")
      Me.SetFocus
   End If
   objWord.Insert Source.Text + vbCrLf
End Sub
```

If you play with dragging the text boxes onto the OLE control, you'll see that once their contents have been inserted in the embedded object, you can use all of Word's formatting tools (see Figure 21-15).

It's important to dereference the objWord variable when it's no longer needed:

```
Private Sub Form_Unload(Cancel As Integer)
    OLE1.Close
    Set objWord = Nothing
End Sub
```

The SaveToFile Method

To be or not to be.... That's often a question with objects. Because an embedded OLE object does not persist beyond the life of its container, suppose you'd like to save the contents of your embedded OLE object?

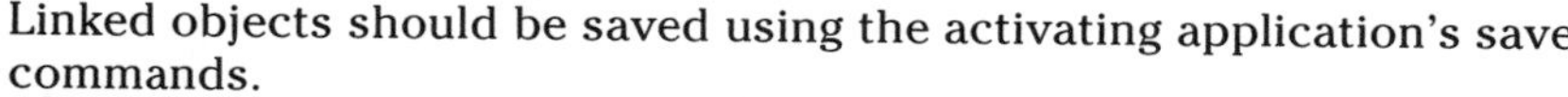

Linked objects should be saved using the activating application's save commands.

The OLE control comes with two methods — SaveToFile and ReadFromFile — that allow you to save and retrieve embedded OLE objects as binary files.

The process of saving an embedded OLE object is pretty simple: Open a file for binary access and call the OLE control's SaveToFile method. Once the object has been saved, it can be opened and displayed in an OLE container. To do this, open the file for binary access and use the OLE control's ReadFromFile method.

I've added two menu items to the ***Embed.Vbp*** project's Form1 File menu: mnuSave and mnuOpen. Note that the NegotiatePosition setting for the File menu has been changed to 1-Left so that the Save and Open menus will appear even after in-place activation and menu negotiation.

Here's the basic code for saving the embedded OLE object:

```
Dim FileNumber As Long
FileNumber = FreeFile
Open "MyOLE.Hld" For Binary As #FileNumber
OLE1.SaveToFile FileNumber
Close #FileNumber
```

A bit of checking should be added to this, as shown in Listing 21-4: Is there really anything to save?

Listing 21-4: Using the SaveToFile method

```
Private Sub mnuSave_Click()
    Dim FileNumber As Long
    If OLE1.OLEType = vbOLEEmbedded Then
        FileNumber = FreeFile
        Open "MyOLE.Hld" For Binary As #FileNumber
        OLE1.SaveToFile FileNumber
        Close #FileNumber
    Else
        MsgBox "No embedded object to Save!"
    End If
End Sub
```

Here's the code for opening the embedded OLE object. (It borrows the Exist procedure that tests for the existence of a file from the File Utilities module developed in Chapter 16, "Optimizing Secrets.")

```
Private Sub mnuOpen_Click()
   Dim FileNumber As Long
   If Exists("MyOLE.Hld") Then 'file exists
FileNumber = FreeFile
      Open "MyOLE.Hld" For Binary As #FileNumber
      OLE1.ReadFromFile FileNumber
      Close #FileNumber
   Else
      MsgBox "There's nothing to open!"
   End If
End Sub
```

Both the Open and Save procedures work nicely. You could, however, improve them with common dialog access for setting the name of the file being opened or saved.

I've provided a sample file, ***MyOLE.Hld***, created with this demonstration using the OLE control with an embedded object. You can open this file using the demonstration program (see Figure 21-16).

Figure 21-16: It's easy to save the contents of embedded OLE objects in binary files.

Summary

This chapter had two themes: how to program drag and drop, and the mechanics of the OLE container control.

Demonstration projects showed you coding techniques to handle drag and drop. Topics covered in these projects included

- Enabling and disabling dragging at runtime
- Visibly moving objects
- Using drag and drop to replace control contents
- Dropping controls on an embedded OLE object

The OLE container control was explained in detail. Topics discussed included

- OLE control methods
- OLE control properties
- The OLE control's pop-up menu
- Object verbs and formats
- In-place activation
- Linking and embedding
- Creating objects at design time
- Creating objects at runtime
- The basics of OLE menu negotiation
- Saving the contents of embedded OLE objects

Chapter 22

Controlling "Foreign" Application Objects

Chapter 21, "Creating Applications that Support OLE," showed you how to use the OLE container control to link or embed objects from other applications into your Visual Basic projects. This chapter continues that theme, but with a twist: the subject matter is using OLE automation and the ActiveX interface to manipulate another application's exposed objects from VB without using the OLE control.

Topics covered in this chapter include

- Navigating object hierarchies
- Instancing an ActiveX object
- Using an ActiveX component application as a custom control
- ActiveX component object libraries
- Visual Basic for Applications (VBA)

In the real world, the biggest programming headaches involving the use of OLE from Visual Basic to control foreign ActiveX components lie in understanding the objects that the application exposes and getting adequate information about how to manipulate these objects' methods and properties. Applications — such as Office 97 — are becoming more rigorously object-oriented, which makes this easier. You can use VB's Object Browser to explore the structure of ActiveX applications once you've added a reference to the application's library to your project. It may also help to have access to the developer's documentation — such as a Software Development Kit (SDK) or Resource Kit — for the specific ActiveX application.

Sample projects in this chapter demonstrate how to use Access, Excel, and Word as foreign ActiveX components from within Visual Basic. (The old way of putting this is that these applications are functioning as OLE servers.)

In this chapter, I'll show you how to write Visual Basic programs that:

- Use Excel to create a handy-dandy Visual Basic program for calculating loan payments in just a few lines of code
- Use Excel to "spell check" the contents of a RichTextBox control (or text box control) in a VB program
- Create a customized Word document header from within VB (and generally play with Word documents)
- Display the names of all "Reports" associated with an Access database and print a copy of the report

The demonstration programs in this chapter were prepared and tested using Office 97 Professional (which includes Version 8 of Access, Excel, and Word). Some of the techniques used may work with earlier OLE versions of these applications, but you may have to make some adjustments in syntax and object names.

Working with ActiveX Components

As the examples later in this chapter show, to successfully control a foreign ActiveX component you must:

- Understand how to create and start an instance of the desired object exposed by the ActiveX component. You do this using the New keyword, the CreateObject function, or the GetObject function. (See the sidebar for the distinction between CreateObject and GetObject.)
- Understand the scope of the object within your application. For example, an object that is instanced (created) within a procedure will generally be destroyed when that procedure goes out of scope. You should explicitly release an object variable (by setting it to Nothing) if it is still in scope but you don't need it any more.
- Know the object's hierarchy. What are the exposed members within the object available to ActiveX automation clients? Objects within objects — termed "subobjects" or "dependent objects" — generally must be started using a method of the object above them in the hierarchy.
- Know the methods that the ActiveX object, and subobjects, expose and the syntax for those methods. The best way to find this information is to use the Object Browser (see "Referencing an Object That Supplies an Object Library" later in this chapter) or to obtain the ActiveX server application's documentation.

GetObject Versus CreateObject

You should use the GetObject function when there is a current instance of the object already created, or if you want to create the object with a file already loaded (for example, a Word object with a loaded document). If there is no current instance of the object created, and you don't want the object started with a file loaded, use the CreateObject function instead.

Note that if an object has registered itself as a single-instance object, only one instance of the object is created, no matter how many times CreateObject is called. With a single-instance object, GetObject always returns the same instance when called with the zero-length string (""), and an error is caused if the object's path name is left off. You can't use GetObject to obtain a reference to a class created with Visual Basic.

Referencing an Object that Supplies an Object Library

An *object library* supplies a definition of an ActiveX component application by listing all the objects the application contains and their members. (The members of an object are its interface, meaning properties, events, and methods.)

If an object supplies a library, it will be listed in the References dialog (which you open via the Visual Basic Project menu). To include an object library in the current project, make sure that it is checked in the dialog.

Methods and properties of creatable objects included in a library can be instanced using the class identifier of the object, provided that the object library has been included in the VB project that attempts to use them.

Generally, you use New to instance objects that have an object library included in the current project, whereas you use CreateObject with Set to instance an externally creatable object that has not provided an included object library. (You use Set and GetObject to equate an object variable to an existing instance of an object.)

Referencing Office 97 Applications

To include the Office 97 object library in your VB application — which makes the Office toolbar and Bindery available to your applications — make sure Microsoft Office 8.0 Object Library is selected in the Project References dialog.

You can enable references to specific Office 97 applications in the same way. For example, to include the Word 8.0 object library, make sure that Microsoft Word 8.0 Object Library is selected. Figure 22-1 shows the Project References dialog with both the Office 97 and Word object libraries selected.

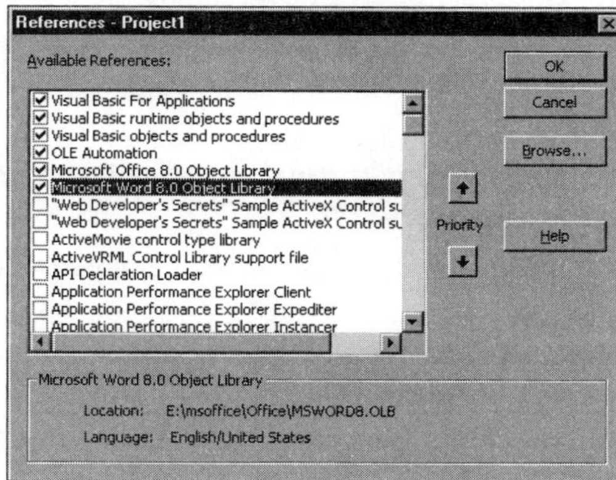

Figure 22-1: You can use the Project References dialog to include references to foreign application objects in your VB projects.

Once you have included a reference to the object library, you can use the Object Browser to find out about the exposed objects and members of the application that generated the library. For example, Figure 22-2 shows some of the members of Word's Document class.

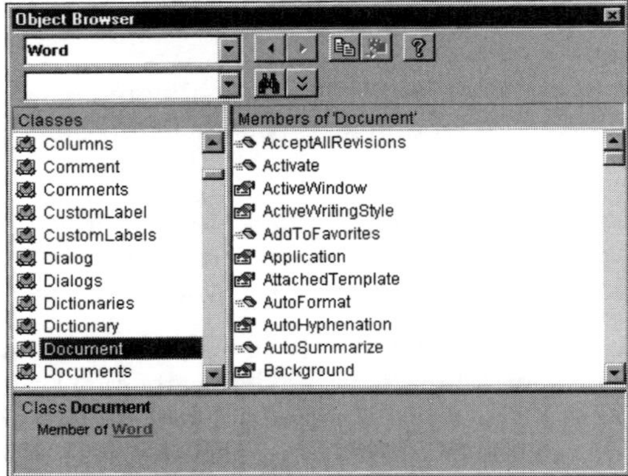

Figure 22-2: Once you have included a reference to an object library in your project, you can use the Object Browser to explore the exposed object hierarchy of the application that has been referenced.

Using Object Methods and Properties

Once an object has been instanced, you reference its methods and properties using the dot operator (.), as you would expect. For example, you could declare appXcel as a variable that will hold an instance of the Excel Application object:

```
Dim appXcel As Object
```

You could create an instance of the Excel application object, open a file in the instance, and change the caption of the instance (see Listing 22-1 and Figure 22-3).

Listing 22-1: Creating and manipulating an instance of Excel.Application

```
Private Sub cmdOpen_Click()
   Set appXcel = CreateObject("Excel.Application")
   appXcel.Workbooks.Open _
      filename:="H:\VB5Secrets\Ch22\Programs\book1.xls"
      'Change file location as needed
   appXcel.Caption = "Visual Basic 5 SECRETS"
   appXcel.Visible = True
End Sub
```

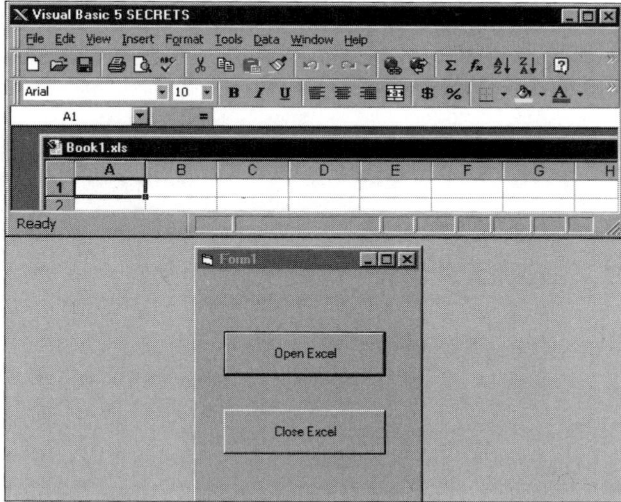

Figure 22-3: You can use an object's members to manipulate the object (here's a file being opened in Excel).

In addition to its Caption property, the Excel application object has a Quit property. You could call it, and then destroy the instance of the Excel application object:

```
Private Sub cmdClose_Click()
    appXcel.Quit
    Set appXcel = Nothing
End Sub
```

There is nothing terribly difficult about this process. Problems, however, do arise because object hierarchies are often neither clearly named nor well documented. This means that programming foreign application automation can involve a fair amount of trial and error.

Visual Basic for Applications

The major applications that are part of the Office 97 suite — including Access, Excel, and Word — include Visual Basic for Applications (VBA) as their common macro, or *scripting,* language. VBA in the Office 97 incarnation has become a tremendously powerful development environment in its own right. This is not your father's macro language.

Microsoft has licensed VBA to a number of important third-party vendors, meaning that VBA is well on its way to becoming the standard Windows scripting language. An even "liter" version of Visual Basic — Visual Basic Scripting Edition (VBScript) — is available for use with Web applications.

VBA is a subset of Visual Basic 5. You'll find the VBA editing environment extremely familiar, both conceptually and in appearance. Figure 22-4 shows the VBA macro programming environment, as invoked from Word 8.

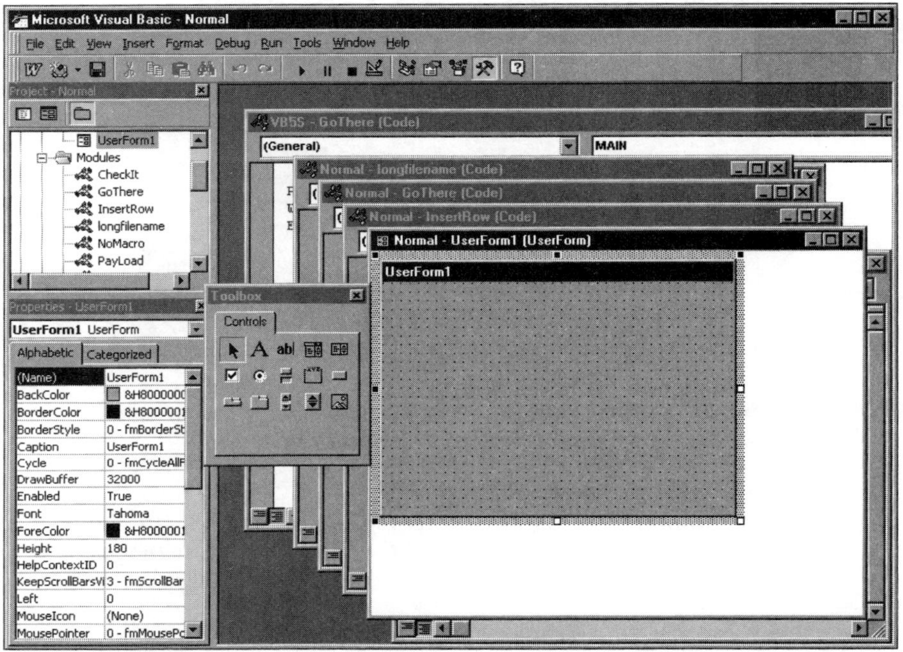

Figure 22-4: The Visual Basic for Applications (VBA) programming environment will be instantly familiar to VB programmers.

In the VBA environment, as implemented in the Office 97 applications, you can add forms, code modules, and class modules — but not UserControl modules. The Project Explorer, Toolbox, and Properties windows work exactly as they do in "regular," full-strength Visual Basic.

To understand exactly what parts of Visual Basic the VBA subset includes, you can open the Object Browser in VB5 and select VBA, as shown in Figure 22-5.

The members shown in the Object Browser as parts of VBA are the underlying language elements for Visual Basic for Applications 5.0 (contained in the library file ***Vba5.Dll***.)

Code written in VB5 is portable to VBA, provided that it doesn't make references outside the VBA language library. The obverse is also true: Code written in the VBA environments can be ported to Visual Basic 5, provided that it does not reference application-specific elements (such as an Excel worksheet or a Word document).

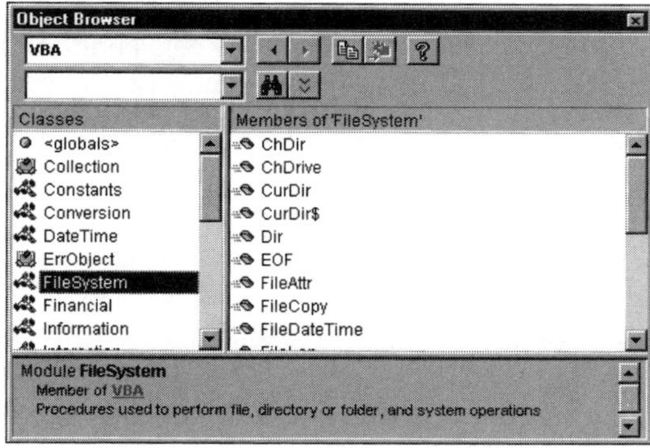

Figure 22-5: You can use the Object Browser to view the members of the VBA library.

The ability to go back and forth — with some limitations — between VBA and the "daddy," Visual Basic 5, is very powerful. You should be able to use this ability to go back and forth to leverage the usefulness of your code libraries. In addition, you should not overlook the new-found power of the VBA environment itself, which now implements such features as forms, class modules, and add-ins.

Object Hierarchies

Large-sized ActiveX applications usually have an application object at the top of their object hierarchy. This object provides access to other objects in its hierarchy (at least its own subobjects and collections). It provides properties and methods that affect the population of objects belonging to the application. Generally, you can instance these objects by using the CreateObject function without including a reference to the object library of the ActiveX application in your project.

Some objects present more than one top-level object that is externally instanceable. For example, Excel sheets are objects that can be accessed — and created — directly.

Usually, the name of the top-level object in an application is the name of the application, for example, Excel.Application and Word.Application. However, top-level objects do not have to be named this way. For example, the top-level object for an instance of the Visual Basic environment is VBIDE.VBE.

Subobjects are accessed through a stepping-stone sequence of object creation. The higher level object must be instanced before the subobject can be created or its properties used.

Often subobjects are actually collections of objects. To navigate these collections to reach the specific object you need to manipulate, you'll generally have to use methods supplied by the collections themselves. For example, the code shown in Listing 22-1 involves instancing the Excel application object, stored in a variable named appXcel. Then the Open method of the Excel application's WorkBooks collection is called:

```
appXcel.Workbooks.Open ...
```

In a similar fashion, you could create an Excel sheet in a variable named X, and then use the Add method of X's Button collection to place a button on the sheet:

```
Dim X as Object
Set X = CreateObject ("Excel.Sheet")
Dim Y as Excel.Button
Set Y = X.Buttons.Add (44,100,100,44)
Y.Caption = "My Button"
```

For information on working with collections, see Chapter 14, "Visual Basic and OOP."

For an example of an object hierarchy, you could turn to Chapter 29, "Creating a VB Add-In," which discusses VBIDE.VBE in detail.

The easiest way to determine the structure of an Office application's object hierarchy is to open the object's library in the Object Browser and click the help button (it displays a question mark) in the Browser's upper-right corner. Figure 22-6 shows the display of the Excel object hierarchy you can obtain as a result.

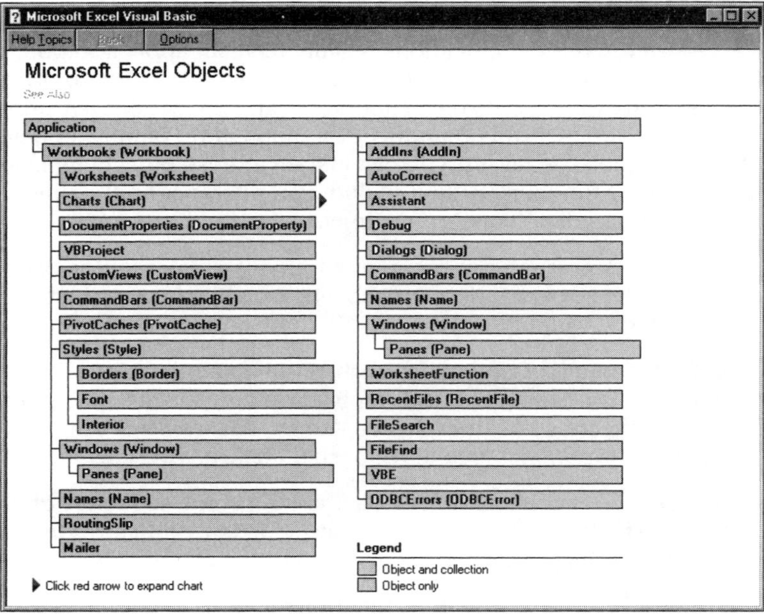

Figure 22-6: You can use Help from the Object Browser to obtain information about an application's object hierarchy (here is the Excel Application object).

Using Excel to Calculate Loan Payments

The demonstration project — saved on the CD-ROM as ***LoanCalc.Vbp*** — uses Excel as a server to quickly calculate loan payments on an amortized loan (see Figure 22-7).

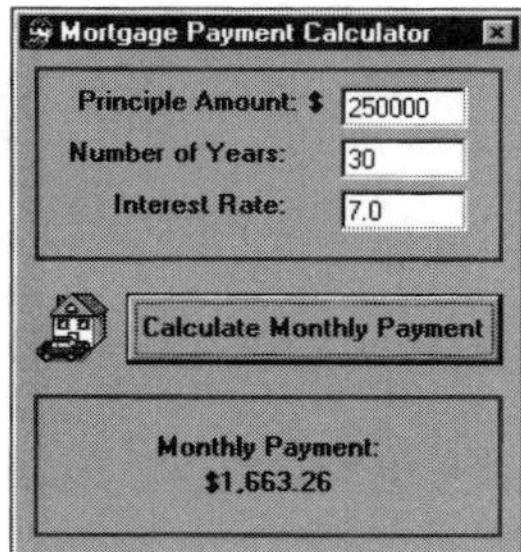

Figure 22-7: You can use Excel as an ActiveX automation component to do the "back office" work for a Visual Basic application.

The ***LoanCalc*** project consists of a form and a ***.Bas*** file code module. The code module contains the function that interacts with Excel. This way, if you want to reuse the function you just plug in the code module and call the function.

A function is used because any call to the objects and methods of an ActiveX automation server may fail. As a trivial example, the ActiveX component may not be properly installed — or may not be installed at all — on a target machine. Because ActiveX components are known to sometimes fail, it's a very good idea to encapsulate ActiveX server calls in a function that provides a return value indicating whether the operation succeeded. For example:

```
Public Function DoActiveXServerCall(FormalParameters) as Boolean
   DoActiveXServerCall = False
   'Check validity of FormalParameter
   'If it is no good, exit function
   'Create an instance of the server
   ....
   'Perform operations using server
   ...
   'Set instance of the server = Nothing
   DoActiveXServerCall = True
End Function
```

This function can then be called and its success checked in one fell swoop. The form that calls a function in a code module in this fashion is sometimes called an *interface* form.

```
Private Procedure cmdDoSomething_Click()
   If Not DoActiveXServerCall(Arguments) Then
      MsgBox "ActiveX automation call failed!"
```

```
    Else
        'Use ActiveX return values to update your form
    End If
End Procedure
```

The virtue of this approach is that, not only are you — and your users — warned if there has been a failure in server operations, but you automatically avoid taking any action unless the server call has succeeded.

Here's the code in the project's interface form (see Figure 22-7) that calls the Excel server object and — provided that the call is successful — populates the interface form with the result:

```
Private Sub cmdCalc_Click()
Dim Payment As Currency
    If Not CalcPay(CSng(txtAmount), Val(txtYears), _
        CSng(txtInterest), Payment) Then
        MsgBox "Go Home! We can't calculate this!", _
            vbCritical, ProgTitle
    Else 'Successful return!
        Image1.Visible = True
        Label3 = Format(Payment, "$#,##0.00;($#,##0.00)")
    End If
End Sub
```

The click event calls the CalcPay function, which in turn calls the server. If CalcPay fails, a message to that effect is displayed. If it succeeds, Label3 is used to display the result — properly formatted using the Format function. By the way, setting Image1's Visible property to True causes the icon of the house and car to be displayed (see Figure 22-7). ProgTitle is a global constant (defined in the code module) that is used when the project title is required.

The parameters passed to CalcPay are the user inputs converted using VB's predefined CSng and Val functions. Payment, a variable of type currency, is used to return the result of the function's calculation. Although this "return value" could have been combined with the function's return values to eliminate a parameter — perhaps sending back 0 or some negative number to indicate failure — it is generally unwise to combine more than one role per function parameter or return. It's best to use one variable to return a value and another (or the function's return value) to flag the success or failure of the function.

Listing 22-2 contains the complete code module and CalcPay function:

Listing 22-2: Using the Excel object to calculate loan amortization

```
Option Explicit
Public Const ProgTitle = "Mortgage Payment Calculator"

Public Function CalcPay(Amount As Currency, Years As Integer, _
    Interest As Single, Payment As Currency) As Boolean
    On Error GoTo HandleError
    Dim xlApp As Object
    ' the Excel object type
    Const hdExcelObject = "Excel.Application"
```

```
    Screen.MousePointer = vbHourglass
    CalcPay = False
    ' instance the Excel application object
    ' that will do the calculation!
    Set xlApp = CreateObject(hdExcelObject)
    ' Call Excel Pmt method
    Payment = xlApp.Pmt((Interest / 100) / 12, Years * 12, _
       -1 * Amount)
    xlApp.Quit
    Set xlApp = Nothing
    CalcPay = True
    Screen.MousePointer = vbDefault
    Exit Function
HandleError:
    'figure out what error occurred
    Select Case Err.Number
      Case 429
        MsgBox "Unable to create OLE Automation object" + vbCrLf + _
           "Make sure Excel (ver 5.0 or higher)" + _
           " has been properly installed.", vbCritical, ProgTitle
      Case Else
        MsgBox "Error #" + Str(Err.Number) + ": " + _
           Err.Description + ".", vbCritical, ProgTitle
    End Select
    Screen.MousePointer = vbDefault
End Function
```

You can see that the business end of the procedure — once the Excel automation server is up and running — takes exactly one line.

The first step is to declare xlApp as an object. Because this declaration is local to the scope of the CalcPay function, the instance of the server created should disappear when execution passes beyond the function. To make this point clear — as will be demonstrated in the Word document header example later in this chapter — if you want the server object to be available after the function has completed, you should declare the object that represents the instance of the server globally, not at the procedure level.

In this case, to play it safe, before the function returns it will shut down the instance of the Excel object using its Quit method and set the object variable to Nothing — always a good practice to make sure all the memory claimed has been released:

```
Set xlApp = Nothing
```

Here's the statement that creates the instance of the Excel OLE server object:

```
Set xlApp = CreateObject(hdExcelObject)
```

Note that I previously defined hdExcelObject:

```
Const hdExcelObject = "Excel.Application"
```

All that remains is the actual calculation, which is done using xlApp's Pmt method. Within Excel, Pmt is a worksheet financial function that returns the periodic payment for an annuity based on constant payments and a constant interest rate. To make this function work for a loan rather than an annuity, the sign on the total amount is reversed:

```
Payment = xlApp.Pmt((Interest / 100) / 12, Years * 12, _
      -1 * Amount)
```

Obviously, you could work backwards from the general formula for interest compounded annually to calculate this in VB without using Excel:

```
Total_Sum = Principle * (1 + Interest_Rate / 100)^Years
```

But why bother?

It's important to include error handling at least to the extent of displaying a message describing internal errors. If something goes wrong in the process of calling an automation server, you want all the clues you can get about what the problem is.

Inserting an Excel Custom Control

By the way, suppose you wanted to take this application a little further and display yearly spreadsheets of payments with amounts of principle and interest indicated. Of course, it's not hard to do this in Excel. You could use an OLE container control to display the resulting spreadsheets (see Chapter 21, "Creating Applications that Support OLE").

Another tack is to add Excel to your Toolbox as an "insertable object" using the Insertable Objects tab of the Components dialog, as shown in Figure 22-8. An Excel Sheet object will then be added to your Toolbox, as shown in Figure 22-9.

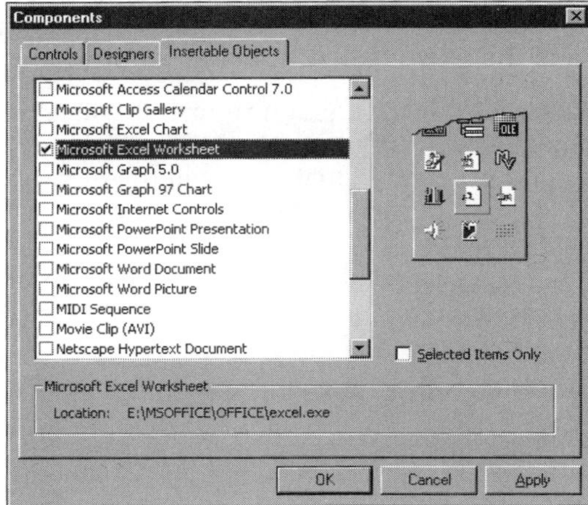

Figure 22-8: Before you can draw an insertable object on a form, you must enable it using the Insertable Objects tab of the Components dialog.

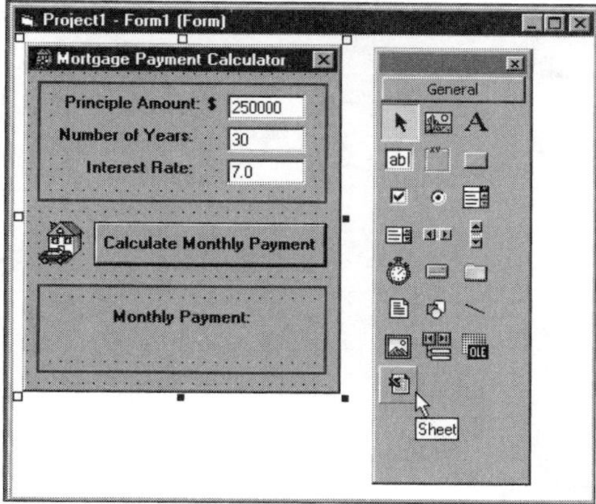

Figure 22-9: Insertable objects that have been added using the Components dialog will appear in your Toolbox.

You can then draw an instance of Excel on your form (see Figure 22-10). The functionality will work pretty much the same as if you had embedded it in the container control except that the container control properties, methods, and events will not be available. The worksheet does support in-place activation, but you must perform most other manipulation using the exposed Excel object.

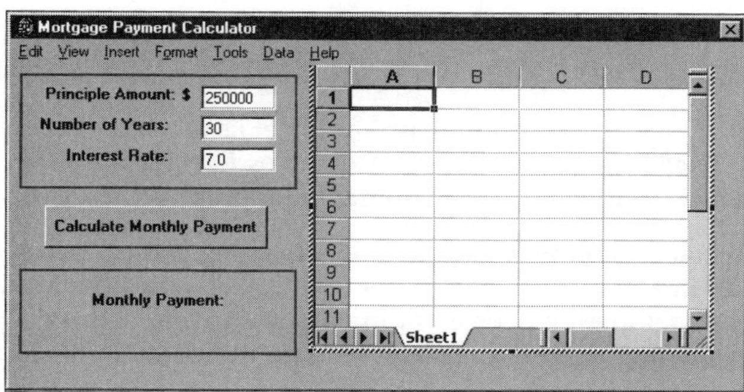

Figure 22-10: You can draw an Excel worksheet on a form as though it were any other control.

At design time, the list of properties for the inserted Excel object is quite short, as you can see in the Properties window depicted in Figure 22-11.

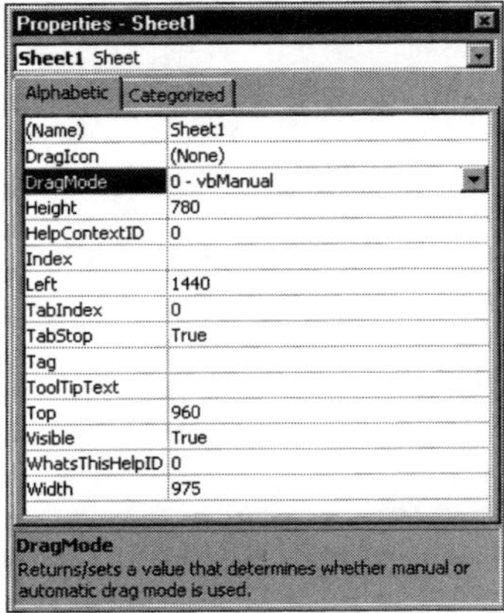

Figure 22-11: The Visual Basic Properties window does not contain many properties for the inserted Excel object.

Most properties are set in Excel itself, not in VB's design mode.

To access the settings for the properties of the inserted Excel object, right-click the control and choose Edit from the pop-up menu. This will start the Excel object in edit mode. It's interesting to notice that when you do this, Excel's menus are set to contend with — and replace most of — VB's menu items.

Using an Excel Server as a Spell Checker

There's a somewhat more complex use of Excel as an ActiveX automation server in the ***Spell.Vbp*** project. This project uses Excel's spell checking facilities to check, and correct, the contents of a RichTextBox control.

Like the loan calculation project, the spell checking project is divided into two pieces: an interface form and a function that handles the actual OLE service. This division enhances error checking and also allows you to use spell checking in any project simply by adding the code module and calling the function.

The interface form is quite simple, consisting of the RichTextBox control and a command button (see Figure 22-12).

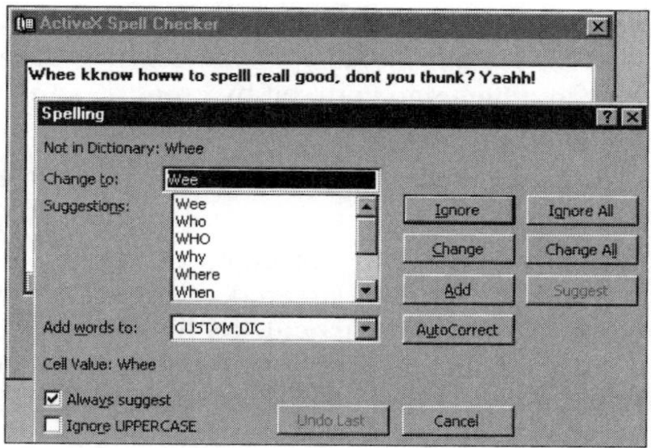

Figure 22-12: You can use Excel as an ActiveX automation server to check and correct the spelling of text entered in a Visual Basic control.

Here's the complete code from the interface form module:

```
Option Explicit

Private Sub cmdCheck_Click()
   If Not SpellCheck(Me.RichTextBox1) Then
      MsgBox "No can do: can't spell check today!", vbExclamation, _
         "No OLE"
   End If
   Me.SetFocus
End Sub

Private Sub Form_Unload(Cancel As Integer)
   End
End Sub
```

This code calls the SpellCheck function with the RichTextBox control as an argument and makes sure that focus is set on the interface form after the function returns.

SpellCheck itself involves a little more than the use of Excel in the loan calculation example, primarily for two reasons:

- The text in the VB control must be saved to disk. This text file is then read into Excel. Each word becomes a cell.
- Excel will not correctly handle commas and quotes placed in a cell. (The string "Hello, my dearest" becomes three Excel cells, the first of which is "Hello",".") For this reason, commas and quotes in the text to be checked must first be replaced with characters that Excel ignores, and then — after the spell check is complete — reinstated.

To save a file to disk, you must create a temporary file whose fully qualified name will not conflict with any other file. It's possible, although rather laborious, to construct such a filename yourself by creating a temporary directory and creating a file in the new directory. However, Windows provides an API function — GetTempFileName — that handles this for you in one step.

GetTempFileName creates a temporary file based on the three arguments passed to it: the directory where it will be created, a three-letter prefix for the file name, and an unsigned integer from which a hexadecimal string is created to form the rest of the filename. A fourth argument is a pointer to the filename; the return value of the function is not of particular interest.

As a practical matter, if you send a period as the first argument ("."), the file is created in the current directory, which is usually fine. You can use any three-letter prefix you like. The unsigned integer should always be 0; this tells the function to derive the hexadecimal string from the current system time.

Listing 22-3 shows the declaration for GetTempFileName and the wrapper function I use to encapsulate these details. The function need only be passed the first two arguments to return a unique temporary filename. (If the first argument is ".", the temporary file is created in the current directory.)

Listing 22-3: Getting a temporary file name

```
' used to create a temporary file that can be
' opened in the Excel object
Declare Function GetTempFileName Lib "kernel32" Alias _
    "GetTempFileNameA" (ByVal lpszPath As String, _
    ByVal lpPrefixString As String, ByVal wUnique As Long, _
    ByVal lpTempFileName As String) As Long

Public Function GetTempFile(Directory As String, _
    Prefix As String) As String
    Dim FileName As String
    FileName = String(256, 0)
    ' get a temporary filename
    Call GetTempFileName(Directory, Prefix, 0, FileName)
    ' trim off null terminator
    FileName = Left(FileName, InStr(FileName, Chr(0)) - 1)
    ' return the results
    GetTempFile = FileName
End Function
```

Here's the way this function is called from within the SpellCheck function:

```
    ' get a temporary filename in the current directory
    FileName = GetTempFile(".", "OLE")
```

As shown in Listing 22-4, the issue of Excel's handling of commas and quotes is taken care of with a string manipulation function that can be used first to replace the offending character with one that Excel ignores and then, at the end, to substitute the commas and quotes back in.

Listing 22-4: Substituting characters

```
Private Function StripText(InChar As Integer, _
   OutChar As Integer, InText As String) As String
   ' Replaces InChar with OutChar in InText
   Dim StartPos As Integer
   Dim FoundPos As Integer
   StartPos = 1
   FoundPos = InStr(StartPos, InText, Chr(InChar))
   While FoundPos > 0
      Mid(InText, FoundPos, 2) = Chr(OutChar)
      StartPos = FoundPos + 1
      FoundPos = InStr(StartPos, InText, Chr(InChar))
   Wend
   StripText = InText
End Function
```

You can see from the code that the StripText function accepts the arguments for the character that will be replaced — and its replacement — as ASCII numbers.

To start with, the SpellCheck function declares internal variables, variables to declare the Excel objects, Excel constants, and constants for use with the StripText function as shown in Listing 22-5:

Listing 22-5: Using the Excel object as a spell checker

```
Public Function SpellCheck(ThisControl As Control) As Boolean
   On Error GoTo HandleError
   Dim xlApp As Object
   Dim xlWorkBook As Object
   Dim xlWorkSheet As Object
   Dim FileName As String
   Dim FileName2 As String
   Dim ThisText As String
   Dim FileNum As Integer

   Const xlTextPrinter = 36
   Const xlWindows = 2
   Const xlDelimited = 1
   Const xlNone = -4142
   Const xlText = -4158
   Const xlTextWindows = 20

   'the Excel object type
   Const hdExcelObject = "EXCEL.APPLICATION"

   'constants for fixing text - ASCII codes
   Const hdCommaText = 44    'Comma
   Const hdCommaSub = 147    'Unused
   Const hdQuoteText = 34    'Quote
   Const hdQuoteSub = 148    'Unused
   Const hdTabText = 9       'Tab
   Const hdSpaceText = 32    'Space
   ...
```

The easiest way to find constant values for a foreign ActiveX server application is to use the Object Browser, as in Figure 22-13. Make sure that the object library in question has been included in the References dialog (which you open via the Tools menu).

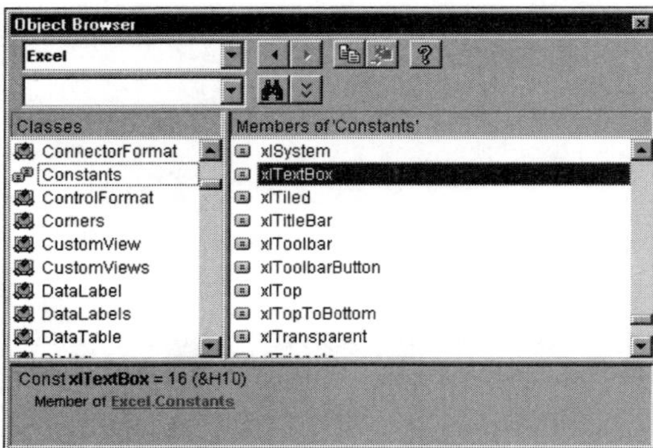

Figure 22-13: Using the Object Browser is the easiest way to get constant values for ActiveX automation server applications.

SpellCheck continues by setting its initial return value to False and using the TypeOf...Is statement to check that the control passed to the function to operate on is either a RichTextBox or text box control:

```
...
SpellCheck = False
If Not TypeOf ThisControl Is RichTextBox And _
   Not TypeOf ThisControl Is TextBox Then
   MsgBox "Internal Error: " + vbCrLf + _
      "The control you are checking is neither a text box " _
      + vbCrLf + "nor a RichTextBox!" + vbCrLf + _
      "Spell check will not work.", vbCritical, "OLE!"
   Exit Function
End If
...
```

Now, with the preliminaries out of the way, SpellCheck can really get to work. The cursor is set to the hourglass icon, the control's text read into an internal variable, and commas and quotes replaced with a placeholder:

```
...
Screen.MousePointer = vbHourGlass
ThisText = ThisControl.Text
ThisText = StripText(hdCommaText, hdCommaSub, ThisText)
ThisText = StripText(hdQuoteText, hdQuoteSub, ThisText)
...
```

A temporary filename in the current directory is obtained, and the text stored in the file:

```
...
FileName = GetTempFile(".", "OLE")
FileNum = FreeFile
Open FileName For Binary As #FileNum
Put #FileNum, , ThisText
'close the file
Close #FileNum
...
```

Next, the Excel application object that will do the spell checking is created and the text (as stored in the temporary file) is opened into it:

```
...
Set xlApp = CreateObject(hdExcelObject)
'open our file
xlApp.Workbooks.OpenText FileName, xlWindows, 1, xlDelimited, _
   xlNone, True, False, False, False, True, False, ""
'get the active sheet
Set xlWorkSheet = xlApp.ActiveSheet
'get the current workbook
Set xlWorkBook = xlApp.ActiveWorkbook
...
```

Here's the statement that does the actual spell checking:

```
...
xlWorkSheet.CheckSpelling
...
```

What remains is cleanup.

```
...
'get a second filename
FileName2 = GetTempFile(".", "OLE")
'Delete it
Kill FileName2
' ...but still use the name - save the worksheet
xlWorkSheet.SaveAs FileName2, xlTextWindows
' set the Saved property so Excel won't prompt us to save it
xlWorkBook.Saved = True

' quit Excel
xlApp.Quit

' get a free file number
FileNum = FreeFile
' open the file back up
Open FileName2 For Binary As #FileNum
' read the data into the file
ThisText = Input(LOF(FileNum), #FileNum)
' close the file again
Close #FileNum
' replace tabs with spaces
ThisText = StripText(hdTabText, hdSpaceText, ThisText)
' replace the comma substitute with commas
ThisText = StripText(hdCommaSub, hdCommaText, ThisText)
' replace the quote substitute with quotes
```

```
    ThisText = StripText(hdQuoteSub, hdQuoteText, ThisText)
    ' put the text back in the control
    ThisControl.Text = ThisText
    ' remove the object from memory
    Set xlApp = Nothing
    ' kill the temporary files
    Kill FileName
    Kill FileName2
    ' let user know function is done
    MsgBox "Spelling check is complete.", vbInformation, _
       "ActiveX automation!"
    ' Set function value to True
    SpellCheck = True
    Screen.MousePointer = vbDefault
    Exit Function
HandleError:
    ' figure out what error occurred
    Select Case Err.Number
      Case 429
        MsgBox "Unable to create OLE object with Excel." + _
           vbCrLf + "Make sure Excel (ver 5.0 or higher)" + _
           "has been properly installed.", vbCritical, "OLE Error"
      Case Else
        MsgBox "Error #" + Str(Err.Number) + ": " + Err.Description _
           + ".", vbCritical, "OLE Error"
    End Select
    Screen.MousePointer = vbDefault
End Function
```

Admittedly, this seems like a lot of fussing to get Excel to perform exactly as we'd like. It is. But, it works; see Figure 22-14. And, it's certainly much less effort than writing a functioning spell checking add-in program from the ground up. You don't even have to input a dictionary because Excel already comes with one! Once you have written the SpellCheck function, you can reuse it with any program you like, just by plugging the code module into the new project and calling SpellCheck. (As always with ActiveX automation servers, the caveat "provided that the server is properly installed on the target system" applies.)

Figure 22-14: Using Excel as an OLE server, you can easily correct any misspelled text.

Creating and Editing Word Documents

With Office 97 and Word 8, programmers no longer need to intimately learn the quirks of Word Basic. Word 8 comes equipped with VBA as its native macro language.

As an example, I'll show you how to use the Word.Application object hierarchy to create a document under the name supplied by the user. The sample program — saved on the CD-ROM as ***Word.Vbp*** — also places a header in the document, inserts the date, and adds text specified by the user.

The interface form uses two text boxes to receive input from the user regarding the filename for the Word document and the text to be inserted in the document, as illustrated in Figure 22-15.

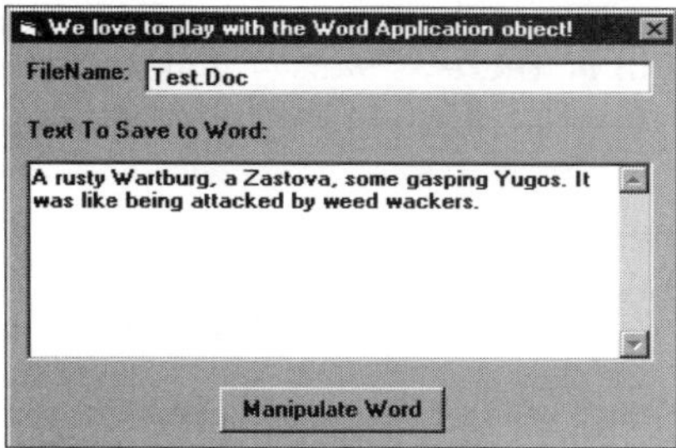

Figure 22-15: You can use the Word.Application object to manipulate Word documents from VB applications.

The Word.Basic Object

In Word 7, only one object was exposed: Word.Basic. Although this was the only object exposed, it was a powerful one: Its methods were the commands of the WordBasic macro language.

With the passing of Version 7 of Word and the idiosyncratic Word Basic variant of the Basic language, Word 8 has joined the other Office applications and implemented a standard application object structure. This hierarchy will be somewhat unfamiliar to those of you who have programmed the old Word object model. However, it is very close in flavor to the general object hierarchy model, meaning that it is much more robust and object-oriented than the Word.Basic object ever was.

You should also know that most legacy code written to handle Word 7's Word.Basic model will still work in Word 8.

Here's the code contained in the interface form:

```
Option Explicit
Private Sub cmdSave_Click()
   If Not ManipulateWord(txtSaveText, txtFileName.Text) Then
     MsgBox "Unable to manipulate Word", vbInformation, ProgTitle
   End If
End Sub

Private Sub Form_Load()
   Me.Caption = ProgTitle
End Sub

Private Sub Form_Unload(Cancel As Integer)
   End
End Sub
```

ProgTitle is a global variable used to reference the application's name declared in the Declarations section of the code module. The Word application object is declared Public there as well — making its scope global to the project — so that Word stays open when the function has finished executing.

If you wanted Word to close when the function completed execution, you'd remove the Word application object's Public variable declaration — which makes the object global to the project — and make the variable local to the function.

Here are the declarations:

```
Option Explicit
Public objWord As Object  'Move into the function to make Word
                          'close following execution

'program name
Public Const ProgTitle = "We love to play with the Word" + _
   " Application object!"
```

Here's the ManipulateWord function itself:

```
Public Function ManipulateWord(ThisControl As Control, _
   ThisFileName As String) As Boolean
   Dim objDoc As Object 'Variable to hold Word document object
   On Error GoTo HandleErr
   'set initial value
   ManipulateWord = False
   If Not TypeOf ThisControl Is RichTextBox And _
      Not TypeOf ThisControl Is TextBox Then
         MsgBox "Internal Error: " + vbCrLf + _
            "The control you are checking is neither a text box " _
            + vbCrLf + "nor a RichTextBox!" + vbCrLf + _
            "The Manipulate Word Function, will not work.", _
            vbCritical, ProgTitle
         Exit Function
```

```
    End If
    If ThisFileName = "" Then   'user left filename text box blank
        MsgBox "You must provide a filename" + _
            " so that text can be saved to WinWord.", _
            vbCritical, ProgTitle
        Exit Function
    End If
    Screen.MousePointer = vbHourglass
    'open up Word
    Set objWord = GetObject(, "word.application")
    'open a new document
    Set objDoc = objWord.Documents.Add
    Documents(objDoc).Activate
    ActiveWindow.WindowState = wdWindowStateMaximize
    'set the header information
    If ActiveWindow.View.SplitSpecial <> wdPaneNone Then
       ActiveWindow.Panes(2).Close
    End If
    If ActiveWindow.ActivePane.View.Type = wdNormalView _
       Or ActiveWindow.ActivePane.View.Type = wdOutlineView _
       Or ActiveWindow.ActivePane.View.Type = wdMasterView Then
          ActiveWindow.ActivePane.View.Type = wdPageView
    End If
    ActiveWindow.ActivePane.View.SeekView = wdSeekCurrentPageHeader
    Selection.Font.Bold = True        'turn on bold
    Selection.InsertAfter ProgTitle  'insert the program name
    Selection.InsertAfter Chr$(9)    'tab over once
    Selection.InsertAfter Format(Date, "mmmm d, yyyy")  'Insert Date
    Selection.Font.Bold = False       'turns bold back off
    'Close header pane
    ActiveWindow.ActivePane.View.SeekView = wdSeekMainDocument

    Dim button As Long
    Selection.InsertAfter vbCrLf  'insert a line break
    Selection.InsertAfter vbCrLf
    'put the text in the document
    Selection.InsertAfter ThisControl.Text
    'return success!
    ManipulateWord = True
    Screen.MousePointer = vbDefault
    Set objDoc = Nothing
    Exit Function
HandleErr:
    MsgBox "Error #" + Str(Err.Number) + ": " + _
       Err.Description + ".", vbCritical, ProgTitle
    Screen.MousePointer = vbDefault
End Function
```

When you run the ManipulateWord function from VB, it has no problem opening a new document with the desired name and entering the header and document text (see Figure 22-16).

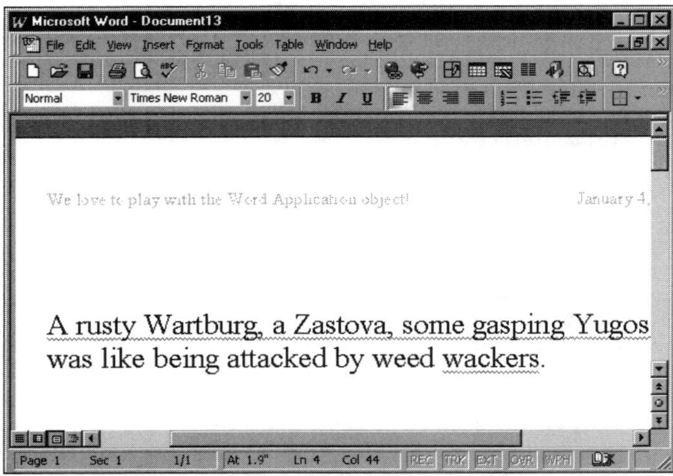

Figure 22-16: You can control everything about the appearance and contents of Word documents from Visual Basic.

Manipulating an Access Database

The next sample project, ***Access.Vbp***, uses the Access.Application object and contains two functions. GetReports retrieves the names of all reports associated with an Access database. PrintReports prints a copy of any report in the list. Figure 22-17 shows the project interface unit with the ubiquitous Northwind Trading Company database loaded. (The Northwind database is a sample that ships with Access. It's intended for use for practice and demonstration purposes. As the disclaimer screen for the database states, "The names of companies, products, people, characters, and/or data mentioned herein are fictitious and are in no way intended to represent any real individual, company, product, or event, unless otherwise noted." I guess that covers all the bases!)

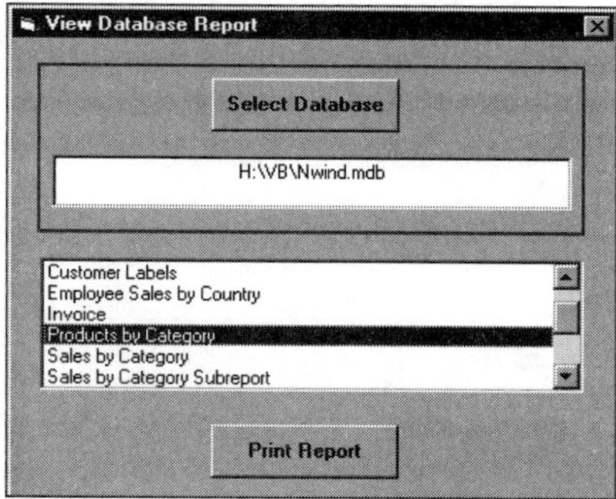

Figure 22-17: You can use ActiveX automation objects exposed by Access to list all the reports included in an Access database.

The code in the project's interface unit follows the usual ActiveX client pattern, with the addition of a call to the common dialog control to allow the user to select a database. (For information on using the common dialog control, see Chapter 7, "Windows Common Dialog Secrets.")

```
Private Sub cmdSelect_Click()
   On Error GoTo ErrHandle
   Dim OurFile As String
   CommonDialog1.CancelError = True
   CommonDialog1.DialogTitle = "Select a database, please!"
   CommonDialog1.Filter = "Access Database Files" + _
      " (*.Mdb)|*.mdb|All Files (*.*)|*.*"
   CommonDialog1.Flags = cdlOFNFileMustExist
   CommonDialog1.ShowOpen
   txtDBName = CommonDialog1.filename
   On Error GoTo 0
   If Not GetReports(txtDBName, lstReports) Then
      MsgBox "Unable to open the database file selected!", _
           vbCritical, ProgTitle
   End If
   Exit Sub
ErrHandle:
   If Err = cdlCancel Then
      MsgBox "Cancelled Out!", vbInformation, ProgTitle
   End If
End Sub

Private Sub cmdPrint_Click()
   If Not PrintReport(lstReports.List(lstReports.ListIndex)) Then
      MsgBox "Report Print Failed!", vbCritical, ProgTitle
   Else
      Me.SetFocus
   End If
End Sub
```

The interface module has a rather more elaborate unload event than I've used previously. This is because the Access object (and database) are expected to remain open after the database has been selected and until the form is unloaded:

```
Private Sub Form_Unload(Cancel As Integer)
   If Not objAccess Is Nothing Then
      objAccess.Quit
      Set dbs = Nothing
      Set objAccess = Nothing
   End If
   End
End Sub
```

In the code module, the Access object and an attached database are declared globally:

```
Option Explicit
Public Const ProgTitle = "View Database Report"
Public objAccess As Object
Public dbs As Object
```

The GetReports function uses the Exists function (explained in Chapter 16, "Optimizing Secrets") to do minimal checking on the purported database file passed to the function. The Exists function at least establishes whether it's an existing file (although not, of course, whether it's really an Access ***.Mdb*** database file). Here's the Exists function:

```
Public Function Exists(F As String) As Boolean
   Dim X As Long
   On Error Resume Next
   X = FileLen(F)
   If X Then
       Exists = True
   Else
       Exists = False
   End If
End Function
```

GetReports itself cycles through the documents in the Access database's Reports collection and adds their names to the list box control, as shown in Listing 22-6:

Listing 22-6: Retrieving Access Reports

```
Public Function GetReports(DbName As String, _
   ThisControl As Control) As Boolean
   On Error GoTo ErrHandle
   Dim IntRep As Integer
   GetReports = False
   If Not Exists(DbName) Then
      MsgBox "Internal Error: " + vbCrLf + _
         "The database file " + DbName + vbCrLf + _
         "does not exist.", vbCritical, ProgTitle
      Exit Function
   End If
```

```
    If Not TypeOf ThisControl Is ListBox Then
       MsgBox "Internal Error: " + vbCrLf + _
          "Control is not a list box", vbCritical, ProgTitle
       Exit Function
    Else
       ThisControl.Clear
    End If
    Screen.MousePointer = vbHourglass
    Set objAccess = CreateObject("Access.Application")
    With objAccess
       .OpenCurrentDatabase (DbName)
       Set dbs = .CurrentDb
       With dbs.Containers("Reports")
          For IntRep = 0 To .Documents.Count - 1
             If Left(.Documents(IntRep).Name, 4) <> "~TMP" Then
                ThisControl.AddItem .Documents(IntRep).Name
             End If
          Next IntRep
       End With
    End With
    GetReports = True
    Screen.MousePointer = vbDefault
    Exit Function
ErrHandle:
    MsgBox "Error #" + Str(Err.Number) + ": " +  _
       Err.Description + ".", _
       vbCritical, ProgTitle
    Screen.MousePointer = vbDefault
End Function
```

The PrintReport function starts where GetReports left off. Essentially, one line of code is required to print a report once the database it is part of is active in Access:

```
Public Function PrintReport(WhichReport) As Boolean
    On Error GoTo ErrHandle
    Screen.MousePointer = vbHourglass
    PrintReport = False
    If WhichReport = "" Then
       MsgBox "Internal Error: " + vbCrLf + _
          "Report String not passed.", vbCritical, ProgTitle
       Exit Function
    End If
    objAccess.DoCmd.OpenReport WhichReport ',acPreview for preview
    PrintReport = True
    Screen.MousePointer = vbDefault
    Exit Function
ErrHandle:
    MsgBox "Error #" + Str(Err.Number) + ": " + _
       Err.Description + ".", _
       vbCritical, ProgTitle
    Screen.MousePointer = vbDefault
End Function
```

You can preview rather than print the report by adding the optional constant argument acPreview (equal to 2) to the line of code that prints the report, following the report name:

```
objAccess.DoCmd.OpenReport WhichReport, acPreview
```

The results of adding the acPreview constant are shown in Figure 22-18. Again, the best source of information on the values of Access constants is the Object Browser (once the Microsoft Access 8.0 Object library has been included in available References).

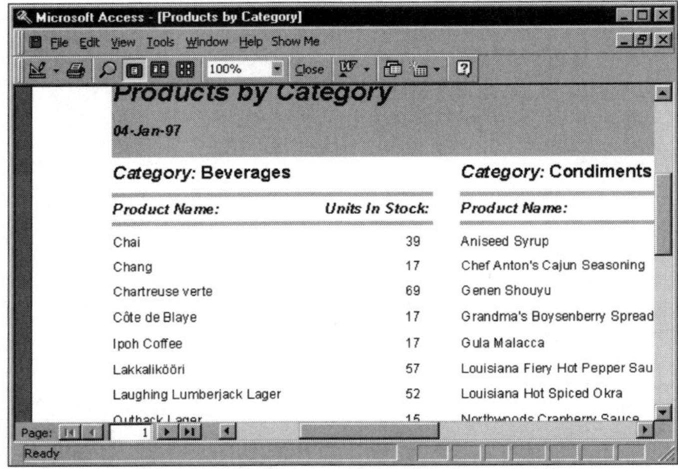

Figure 22-18: The sample Northwind Trading Company database report "Products By Company" is displayed in Access's Preview mode.

The DoCmd object is an Access object that exists to execute orders. See Access on-line help for a list of the DoCmd object's methods and what they do.

Summary

This chapter has explained how to navigate and control the objects of an OLE server application from Visual Basic. The topics covered included

- Understanding object libraries
- Creating instances of objects
- Navigating object hierarchies
- Controlling the scope of object references

- Structuring functions that call ActiveX components to handle errors and return success or failure of the ActiveX function
- Using Excel as an ActiveX automation server to calculate loan amortization
- Using Excel as an ActiveX automation server to spell check the user-supplied contents of Visual Basic controls
- Using the GetTempFileName API
- Creating a wrapper function around the GetTempFileName API
- Using a general parsing function that replaces one character in a string with another
- Controlling Word 8 and the Word.Application object from within Visual Basic
- Using Access as an ActiveX automation server to print the "Reports" associated with a database

Chapter 23

Creating ActiveX Applications

This chapter explores the other side of the looking glass. Chapter 21, "Creating Applications that Support OLE," and Chapter 22, "Controlling 'Foreign' Application Objects," demonstrated how to control ActiveX servers and implement OLE in your projects. This chapter shows you how to create ActiveX applications. Using the techniques I've covered in the previous two chapters, client applications — written by you or someone else — can then access and use the exposed objects of your ActiveX components.

This is very exciting material. You can write ActiveX components to encapsulate code that can be reused again and again by yourself or others, to extend the Visual Basic environment, to break up large programs into a series of smaller modules, to be used as libraries by OLE client applications such as Excel or Word for Windows, or to be used as development tools.

Visual Basic 5 SECRETS has already demonstrated a number of impressive uses for ActiveX applications. For example, in Chapter 10, "Programming the Registry in VB," I explained how to create an ActiveX application that encapsulated many of the Registry APIs.

The Object Formerly Known As OLE Server

ActiveX components are what used to be known as OLE server applications. It's important to understand that—as the terms are used here—an ActiveX component is not the same thing as an ActiveX control. ActiveX controls are, in fact, implemented as ActiveX components. This is another way of saying that ActiveX controls are one kind of ActiveX component.

ActiveX components can be implemented as out-of-process servers, meaning that they run in their own process space, in which case they are normally compiled as executable files with an ***.Exe*** file extension. Alternatively, they can be compiled as in-process dynamic link libraries, normally resulting in a compiled file with a ***.Dll*** extension. Think of an ActiveX component as "the object formerly known as OLE server."

Microsoft believes that the new terminology makes it easier to discuss interactions between objects without recourse to the "overworked" word server. And, as Microsoft puts it, "if you really want to, you can continue to use the old terminology. Just pronounce 'ActiveX component' as *oh-lay ser-ver*."

Personally, I sometimes find it easier to think of ActiveX components, and sometimes clients and servers. I'll try to keep the terminology as clear as possible in this chapter in relation to the context in which it arises.

Visual Basic add-ins are ActiveX applications containing specific class module procedures that are called by an instance of the VB environment acting as an OLE client. In Chapter 29, "Creating a VB Add-In," I'll demonstrate how to create an ActiveX application that is an add-in that changes the BackColor property of all controls on a form loaded in the VB environment.

Technically speaking, there is nothing inherently difficult about creating an ActiveX application. At a minimum, an ActiveX application must contain one class module with its Instancing property set so that objects based on the class are externally creatable.

Table 23-1 shows the meanings of the six possible settings for a class module's Instancing property. As you can see from the table, if the Instancing property of a class module included in an ActiveX project is set to anything other then 1-Private or 2-PublicNotCreatable, it can be externally created.

Table 23-1 Settings for the Instancing Property of a Class Module

Setting	*Meaning*
1 - Private	The class module is private (local in scope) to the project. It cannot be externally created. Other applications aren't allowed access to type library information about the class, and cannot create instances of it. Private objects are only for use within your application or component.
2 - PublicNotCreatable	Not externally creatable, but can be used externally once it has been created by the application or component.
3 - SingleUse	Allows other applications to create objects based on the class, but every object of this class that a client creates starts a new instance of your server.
4 - GlobalSingleUse	Similar to SingleUse, except that properties and methods of the class can be invoked as if they were simply global functions.
5 - MultiUse	Allows other applications to create objects based on the class. One instance of your application can provide any number of objects created in this fashion, regardless of how many applications request them. If your server is not running when the class object is created, the server is started.
6 - GlobalMultiUse	Similar to MultiUse, with one addition: Properties and methods of the class can be invoked as if they were simply global functions. It's not necessary to explicitly create an instance of the class first, because one will automatically be created.

However, saying that an ActiveX application need only include an externally creatable class module is a bit like saying that there is nothing to a VB application because it's easy to display a message box saying "Hello, World." In both cases, true enough, but there's a lot more to learn. (For background information on the class module Instancing property and how Visual Basic works with classes and collections, see Chapter 14, "Visual Basic and OOP.")

This chapter provides the information you'll need to successfully create ActiveX applications (and to fully understand the almost impenetrable jargon surrounding the subject). Topics covered in this chapter include

- Different kinds of ActiveX applications: in-process and out-of-process servers
- The class module instancing property
- Creating a class module that serves as a wrapper
- Creating object hierarchies
- Externally creatable objects
- Dependent objects
- Error handling in ActiveXs
- The References dialog and OLE version compatibility
- Collection classes
- Creating Application objects
- ActiveXs and registration
- Binding
- Passing parameters versus setting properties
- Creating in-process servers (ActiveX DLLs)

Different Kinds of ActiveX Applications

It's perfectly possible for applications to be both normal executables and ActiveX applications whose exposed objects can be used by client applications. For example, Excel can be started normally; its exposed objects can also be used behind the scenes by OLE clients. (Several examples in the preceding chapter showed how client applications could use Excel as a server to calculate loan amortization and spell check the contents of VB controls.) Applications that have these two aspects are the mild-mannered, disguised super heroes of the ActiveX world — Clark Kent as a normal application preparing workaday spreadsheets, Superman as a hidden developers' tool set to be used by other applications.

However, it's a fact of life that many applications created in VB5 will be one, or the other, but not both. As a practical matter, why go to the trouble of changing from Clark Kent to Superman in a phone booth unless there's a real need to do so? Applications that present both a full-fledged interface to users upon normal execution and exposed OLE objects for clients to access are twice the work to create.

The majority of ActiveX applications written in VB are intended to remain in the closet, used by client applications but never seen by the user.

> **Servers and Clients, Classes and Objects**
>
> No, servers, clients, classes, and objects are not "cabbages," nor "kings," whatever the Walrus might say. These words have simple meanings. A *class* is the blueprint—think of it as a stencil or cookie cutter—from which instances of the class are created. Each instance of the class is known as an *object*—hence the verb *to instance* (or instantiate) an object, meaning to create an object based on a class. In VB5, classes are defined using class modules.
>
> A *server* exposes (makes available) one or more objects for use by other applications. Applications that access these exposed objects are *clients*.

Because the majority of ActiveX applications do not present a visible interface, the default ActiveX project in VB5 includes a class module, but no form modules. Of course, you are free to add as many forms as you'd like to an ActiveX project.

Although Visual Basic automatically handles many of the housekeeping issues involved in ActiveX creation, as usual, there is a price to be paid for giving up control. In software terms, "giving up control" means not having complete access to low-level functionality.

You can create three kinds of ActiveX applications:

- Out-of-process servers, sometimes called cross-process servers, are separate VB5 executables that start with their own stacks in their own process space.
- In-process servers are ActiveX DLLs that offer services to client applications using the client's stack and process space. An in-process server will run more quickly than the comparable out-of-process server because no cross-process calls — calls to an application running in another thread — are involved. However, there are some limitations on what you can place in a VB5 ActiveX DLL. For details, see the section "Creating In-Process Servers (ActiveX DLLs)" later in this chapter.
- Remote servers are VB5 executables that run across a network.

The Class Module Instancing Property

Let's have a closer look at the class module's Instancing property, which, as I noted earlier, is crucial to the question of whether an application is technically an ActiveX. Every ActiveX application must include at least one class module whose Instancing property is set so that objects based on the class are externally creatable.

If a class module cannot be instanced (because the Instancing property has been set to 1-Not Creatable or 2-PublicNotCreatable), objects based on the class cannot be created externally by client applications.

You can still create the objects internally to the server and use them externally once they have been created if the Instancing property is set to 2-PublicNotCreatable.

You accomplish external creation using the Dim...As New, Set, and CreateObject statements and functions. External applications can manipulate objects that they can't directly create. In this case, the ActiveX application must itself provide a method (usually called Add and applying to an internal collection) for indirectly creating objects. Such objects are called *dependent*, and are discussed later in this chapter in the section "Dependent Objects."

If objects based on a class module are externally creatable (because the Instancing property of the class module is set appropriately), objects based on the class can be externally instanced by client applications. It's more usual to set Instancing to Creatable MultiUse than Creatable SingleUse. The difference is how many instances of an object the server can create. The Creatable MultiUse setting causes all copies of objects instanced from a class to be created from one running server. Creatable SingleUse, on the other hand, loads a separate copy of the ActiveX object into memory for each instance of the class that is created. Obviously, this is costly in terms of memory. In some situations, however, you should specify Creatable SingleUse despite the greater cost in resources: Because multiple instances of objects are controlled by entirely distinct ActiveX applications, one instance cannot block method calls of another instance (see "The Component Request Pending Dialog" later in this chapter).

Step-by-Step Guide to Creating an ActiveX Application

This section details the steps, and some of the options, involved in creating an ActiveX application — saved on the CD-ROM as ***ActiveX.Vbp*** — and a client, ***Client.Vbp***, that uses the classes the ActiveX application exposes.

The ActiveX application contains a class module named StringFunctions with a number of properties and three string manipulation methods that are functions developed earlier in *Visual Basic 5 SECRETS*. StringFunctions also contains a method that displays a form modally. Tables 23-2 and 23-3 show the methods and properties included in the StringFunctions class module.

Table 23-2 StringFunctions Class Methods

Method Name	*Description*	*Prior Discussion in* Visual Basic 5 SECRETS
CapFirstLetter	Capitalizes first letter of each word in a string	"String Manipulation" in Chapter 13, "Secrets of Good Programming Practice"
ReverseString	Reverses the contents of a string	N/A
StripText	Replaces each instance of a character in a string with another character	"Using an Excel Server as a Spell Checker" in Chapter 22, "Controlling 'Foreign' Application Objects"

The StringFunctions class module is designed so that properties are set rather than parameters passed (see "Properties Versus Parameters" later in this chapter).

Table 23-3 StringFunctions Class Properties

Property	*Description*
InReplace	Character to be replaced in StripText method
InText	Text string to be operated on
OutText	Text string after operations are complete
OutWith	Replacement character for the StripText method

In addition, there are two private variables used internally to convert InReplace and OutWith to one-character ASCII equivalents, named InChar and OutChar.

Here are the declarations for the class module:

```
Option Explicit
Public InText As String, OutText As String
Private InChar As Integer, OutChar As Integer
```

CapFirstLetter and ReverseString take no arguments and return no values; their input is the InText property and their output is the OutText property, as shown in Listing 23-1.

Listing 23-1: Capitalizing the first letter and reversing a string

```
Public Sub CapFirstLetter()
   Dim PosDel As Integer, DeLim As String
   DeLim = " "
   Mid(InText, 1, 1) = UCase(Mid(InText, 1, 1))
   PosDel = InStr(InText, DeLim)
   While PosDel <> 0
      Mid(InText, PosDel + 1, 1) = UCase(Mid(InText, PosDel + 1, 1))
      PosDel = InStr(PosDel + 1, InText, DeLim)
   Wend
   OutText = InText
End Sub

Public Sub ReverseString()
   Dim intCt As Integer
   Dim strNew As String
   For intCt = 1 To Len(Trim(InText))
      strNew = Mid(InText, intCt, 1) & strNew
   Next intCt
   OutText = strNew
End Sub
```

Here are the class properties that convert InReplace and OutWith to single ASCII codes for use with the StripText method:

```
Public Property Let InReplace(vNewValue As String)
   If vNewValue = "" Then vNewValue = " "
   InChar = Asc(vNewValue)
End Property

Public Property Let OutWith(vNewValue As String)
   If vNewValue = "" Then vNewValue = " "
   OutChar = Asc(vNewValue)
End Property
```

And here's the modified StripText method itself:

```
Public Sub StripText()
   Dim StartPos As Integer
   Dim FoundPos As Integer
   StartPos = 1
   FoundPos = InStr(StartPos, InText, Chr(InChar))
   While FoundPos > 0
      Mid(InText, FoundPos, 2) = Chr(OutChar)
      StartPos = FoundPos + 1
      FoundPos = InStr(StartPos, InText, Chr(InChar))
   Wend
   OutText = InText
End Sub
```

ActiveX Class Naming

It's particularly important to name classes and their properties, methods, and events in a clear fashion that users of your applications can easily understand. Microsoft suggests sticking to the following guidelines:

- ActiveX constants should start with a prefix based on the name of the server.
- Use entire words, or the entire first syllable of words, to name classes, methods, and properties. For example, use StringFunctions, not StrFuncs. Because there can be a number of different ways to abbreviate a given word, abbreviations can be confusing.
- Use mixed case single word identifiers — for example, ReverseString.
- Don't use Hungarian notation.
- Most important of all, try to refer to exposed objects and their methods and properties using terminology that makes sense to users of the objects.

Properties Versus Parameters

Formally speaking, you can pass parameters in a method call or alternatively make multiple property calls. Suppose you have a method DoSomethingToName in an instance of a class module, X. If DoSomethingToName takes as an argument OldName, does something to it, and returns an altered value, the traditional way to write this as a function is:

```
NewName = X.DoSomethingToName(OldName)
```

If you've defined OldName and NewName properties in the class module, you can rewrite DoSomethingToName as a procedure without parameters.

DoSomeThingToName would then input the OldName property and assign a value internally to the NewName property. You'd first set the OldName property, invoke DoSomeThingToName, and then use the value stored in the NewName property:

```
X.OldName = "I Love Lucy"
X.DoSomethingToName
txtMytext = X.NewName
```

As a practical example, consider the transformation of the StripText function (found in its original version in "Using an Excel Server as a Spell Checker" in Chapter 22). StripText originally accepted passed parameters. It was rewritten — in the version found in the StringFunctions class module in this chapter — to have no passed arguments. The transformed StripText function achieves its goals solely by reading and setting properties.

It's the accepted style to use properties rather than pass parameters when working with objects based on class modules because this makes the objects easier to use. However, each property setting for an out-of-process server exacts a performance penalty.

You can use the Optional keyword to allow a method call with or without parameters. If the parameters are not passed, the method sets the property. (For more on the use of the Optional keyword, see Chapter 4, "The Visual Basic Language.")

For example, I could define objects based on a Pizza class module:

```
Public Topping As String 'Define a property
...
Public Sub Bake (Minutes As Long, Optional Topping As Variant)
' If Topping was passed then set the Topping property using Me to
' reference the Pizza object
    If Not IsMissing(Topping) Then Me.Topping = Topping
...
```

Getting Ready to Run the Server

You tell Visual Basic to compile a program as an ActiveX component using the Component tab of the Project Properties dialog, and you're almost ready to do that with ***ActiveX.Vbp***. But first, one more thing to handle.

Starting from Sub Main

You should set ActiveX applications to start from Sub Main in a code module. Although you can certainly display forms from a server — and may even wish to display a form when the server starts in specialized situations — you should do this through creating (and destroying) explicit instances of forms (see the following section, "Displaying Forms in an ActiveX Application") rather than through the initial load of a form.

To add a Sub Main, use the Add Module item on the Project menu to add a regular code module to your project. Then add a Sub Main procedure — which can remain empty — to the module. Here's the entire regular code module — including the Sub Main procedure — for the demonstration ActiveX project:

```
Option Explicit
Public Const ProgTitle = "ActiveX application demo for VB5 SECRETS"

Public Sub Main()
    'Pro forma Sub Main for ActiveX Application
End Sub
```

Use the General tab of the Project Properties dialog to set the application to start from Sub Main.

Displaying Forms in an ActiveX Application

Forms that are displayed from objects based on class modules should be instanced using a variable, as explained in "Encapsulating VB Dialogs" in Chapter 3, "Event-Driven Programming," and in Chapter 14, "Visual Basic and OOP." For example, here's the method that displays an instance of Form1 in the StringFunctions class:

```
Public Sub DisplayForm()
    Dim X As New Form1
    X.Show
End Sub
```

If you wanted your server application to display a form upon startup, you'd add comparable code to the Sub Main procedure. Note that in-process ActiveX DLLs cannot display modeless forms (see the section "Creating In-Process Servers (ActiveX DLLs)" later in this chapter). Also, beware of adding modal forms to ActiveX applications if the form might not be unloaded. If this happens, the server will act as if it's perpetually busy, blocking other client calls to the server and causing the Component Request Pending Dialog to appear. (For further information see "Placing Code in Class Events" and "The Component Request Pending Dialog" later in the chapter.)

Setting the Project Options

You choose the settings that will make an application an ActiveX component — and provide the description that other applications can use to access it in the References dialog — using the Project Properties dialog. The settings for the demonstration ActiveX application are shown in Figures 23-1 and 23-2.

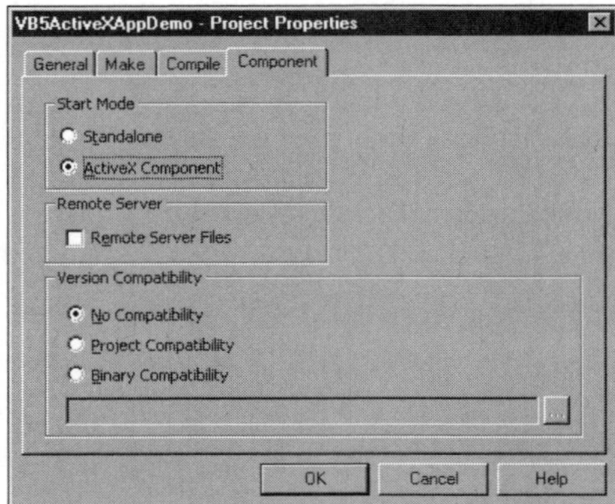

Figure 23-1: You use the Component tab of the Project Properties dialog to identify a project as an ActiveX component to the VB compiler.

Setting Start Mode to ActiveX Component rather than Standalone tells VB to keep the application going and wait for a request from a client; applications that are stand-alone execute and quickly terminate, depending on the code they contain.

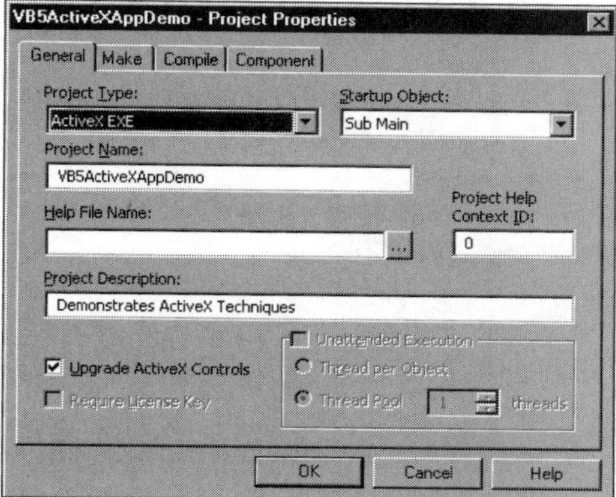

Figure 23-2: The project description that you provide on the General tab of the Project Properties dialog is used to identify the ActiveX application in the References dialog.

Using the General tab of the Project Properties dialog (shown in Figure 23-2), make sure that the Startup Object option is set to Sub Main (see the earlier discussion).

The project name you give the application, in this case VB5ActiveXAppDemo, will appear in the Object Browser.

The application description will also appear in the Object Browser. In addition, the description — in this case, "Demonstrates ActiveX Techniques" — is what appears in the References dialog when another application wishes to use the exposed classes of the ActiveX component (see "Setting References in the Client Project" later in this chapter).

Starting the ActiveX Application

To test the ActiveX component, you'll want to have it running in design mode while a client application is started in another instance of Visual Basic.

Make sure to run the ActiveX project using Start With Full Compile (rather than Start) from the Run menu. (The keyboard shortcut for Start With Full Compile is Ctrl+F5, as opposed to F5 for Start.)

This option fully compiles the project before running it. If you don't fully compile the ActiveX project, compile time errors may not be detected until after the component's objects are called by the client, making debugging more tedious.

Calling the ActiveX Component from a Client

Figure 23-3 shows the form used for ***Client.Vbp***.

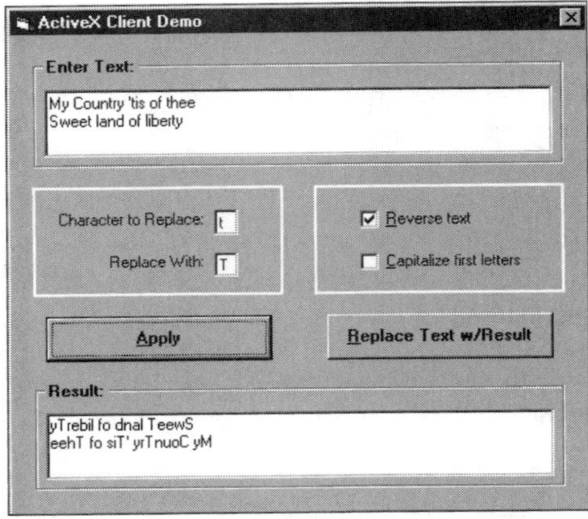

Figure 23-3: The client demonstration calls the exposed methods and properties of an instance of the StringFunctions class.

All the methods and properties of an instance of the class — except DisplayForm — are called from the Apply button. Listing 23-2 shows how these properties and methods are invoked.

Listing 23-2: Invoking the properties and methods of an ActiveX class

```
Private Sub cmdApply_Click()
   Dim x As New StringFunctions
   x.InText = txtManipulate
   x.InReplace = txtReplace
   x.OutWith = txtWith
   x.StripText
   If chkCap Then x.CapFirstLetter
   If chkReverse Then x.ReverseString
   lblResult = x.OutText
   Set x = Nothing
End Sub
```

Setting References in the Client Project

For the reference to the OLE class

```
Dim X as New StringFunctions
```

to work, the ActiveX application has to be available (and checked) in the References dialog (found on the Project menu), as shown in Figure 23-4.

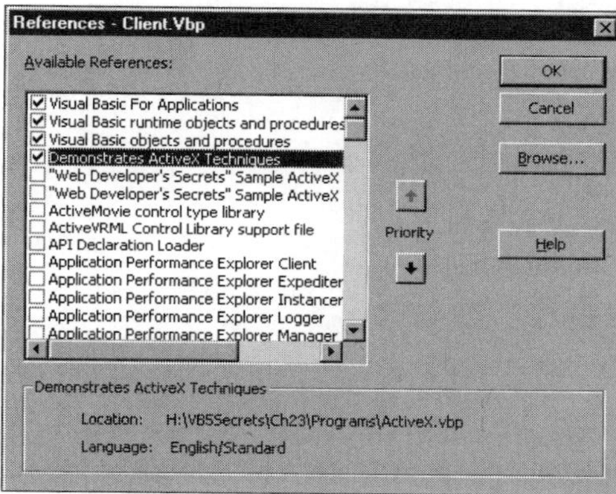

Figure 23-4: You can use the References dialog to connect a client to an ActiveX application.

As you will discover when you work with servers running in VB's design mode, the connection between server and client made by the References dialog can be quite fragile. You may have to stop and restart the server a number of times to get the reference to appear correctly in the client's References dialog.

For example, if the ActiveX application is not running — or if you change it — the client will no longer be connected to the server in the References dialog. A "User-defined type not defined" error message when you try to invoke class methods or properties is an indication of this problem.

When you open the References dialog from the client application in this case, you'll see a "MISSING" caption next to the ActiveX description in the dialog, as shown in Figure 23-5.

To get the client working again, you need to restart the ActiveX component (if necessary), deselect the reference to the missing ActiveX component in the client application's References dialog, click OK to exit the References dialog, open the References dialog again, find the new ActiveX component reference (it's probably listed alphabetically in the list in the References dialog), select it, click OK, and start the client project again.

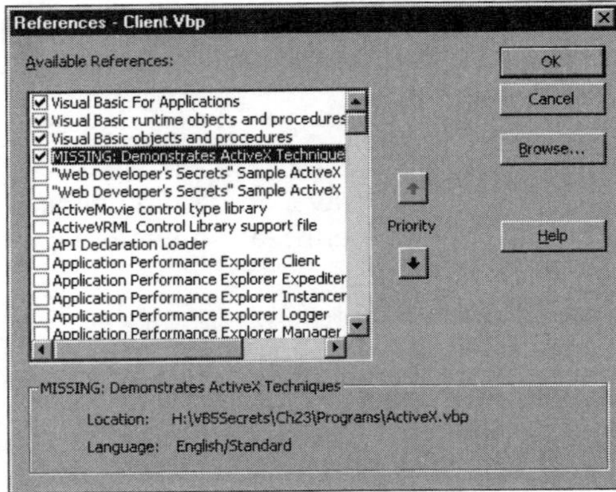

Figure 23-5: If an ActiveX application is no longer running in an instance of VB, or if it has been changed, the reference to it may no longer be available.

References — and taking advantage of the versioning facilities built into VB ActiveX components — are discussed later in this chapter under "Versioning an ActiveX Component."

Objects based on ActiveX class modules can be externally created without including them in the References dialog provided that the ActiveX component has been compiled. For information on using the CreateObject function to do this, see "Creating the Object Without the References Dialog" later in this chapter.

Using the Object Browser

Once you have successfully referenced the ActiveX object library in the client project using the References dialog, you can use the Object Browser to display class members, as shown in Figure 23-6.

Using the Procedure Attributes Dialog

You can use the Procedure Attributes dialog in the ActiveX component application to set the class member description (shown at the bottom of Figure 23-6. You open the Procedure Attributes dialog (shown in Figure 23-7) from the Tools menu. Make sure the member whose description and attributes you wish to enter (or edit) is selected in the Name list box.

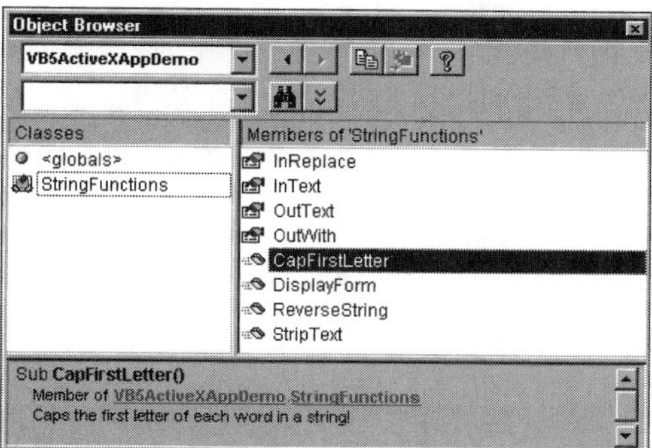

Figure 23-6: You can use the Object Browser in a client project to display the methods and properties of a referenced class module.

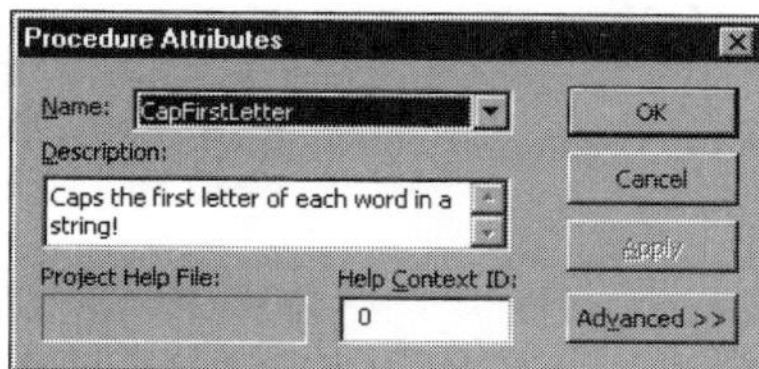

Figure 23-7: You can use the Procedure Attributes dialog to set member attributes, including the description that is displayed in the Object Browser.

If you open the Procedure Attributes dialog while the cursor is in a procedure in the Code Editor, that procedure will be selected in the Procedure Attributes Name list by default.

You use the Procedure Attributes dialog to set the Help Context ID for specific members as well as the description that appears in the Object Browser. (The text "Caps the first letter of each word in a string!" entered under Description in Figure 23-6 appears to describe the method as shown in Figure 23-7.)

Displaying a Form: The Client

It's easy to use an ActiveX application class method to display a server application form from a client, as shown in Figure 23-8. You can invoke the DisplayForm method (see its code listing in the earlier section, "Displaying Forms in an ActiveX Application") in the same way you invoke any other class method:

```
Private Sub Form_Click()
   Dim x As New StringFunctions
   x.DisplayForm
End Sub
```

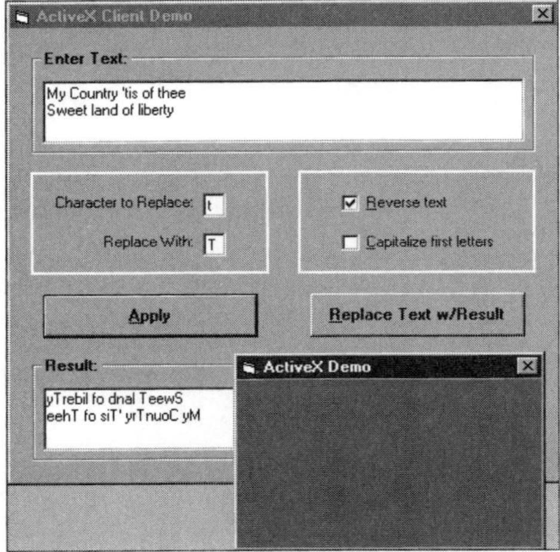

Figure 23-8: The server's ShowForm method is invoked from the client project to display a form.

Forms invoked in this fashion can be used for almost any conceivable purpose, although class methods and properties may have to be crafted to allow appropriate access.

Creating the Object Without the References Dialog

You can create objects without attaching them to the current project using the References dialog (the general way ActiveXs were connected to in the examples in Chapter 22). The syntax used is to dimension a variable as an object and then use the CreateObject function.

Before you can connect to an OLE application's object using CreateObject, the application must be compiled (otherwise you'd be trying to connect to an instance of the VB IDE). While the ActiveX application is running in design mode, VB takes care of registration of the component's OLE objects. When you compile the ActiveX application as a stand-alone, its objects are automatically registered.

In this context, it makes no difference whether you compile your application to p-code or native code.

Note that your setup routine should handle ActiveX registration on target machines automatically if you are distributing ActiveXs; see Chapter 36, "Setup Programs," and the sidebar, "Registering and Unregistering ActiveX Components," later in this chapter.

When using the CreateObject function, you refer to the ActiveX application by the project name entered in the General tab of the Project Properties dialog, not — as you might expect — by the executable filename. For example, if the ActiveX demonstration program were compiled as ***Seymour.Exe***, objects created based on its StringFunctions class module would be referenced as VB5ActiveXAppDemo.StringFunctions, because VB5ActiveXAppDemo was the name given to the Project internally in its Project Properties dialog. (This identifier is sometimes referred to as the application's ProgID.)

OLE objects belonging to the compiled ***Seymour.Exe*** are added to the Windows Registry when it is compiled. To try referencing the server's objects, use the CreateObject function. Next, make sure that the reference to the design time server demonstration has been removed from the References dialog in the client application. Finally, modify the first lines of the cmdApply Click event code:

```
Private Sub cmdApply_Click()
    Dim x As Object
    Set x = CreateObject("VB5ActiveXApp.StringFunctions")
    x.InText = txtManipulate
    x.InReplace = txtReplace
    x.OutWith = txtWith
    x.StripText
    If chkCap Then x.CapFirstLetter
    If chkReverse Then x.ReverseString
    lblResult = x.OutText
    Set x = Nothing
End Sub
```

By the way, there is nothing to stop you from using the References dialog to include a compiled ActiveX application you have created in a client application. In this case, you'd use the familiar

```
Dim X as New StringFunctions
```

syntax explained earlier. For information on the impact of the different ways of connecting to a server, see the section, "Binding," that follows.

Registering and Unregistering ActiveX Components

ActiveX applications can be registered in three ways:

- By compiling the application into an executable file.
- By running the compiled application for the first time.
- By running the compiled application with /Regserver as a command-line argument, for example:

```
C:\VB\Seymour.Exe /Regserver
```

Running an ActiveX application with the /Regserver flag causes the application to terminate immediately after registration is complete. Without the flag the application will keep on going.

In addition, as mentioned, ActiveX components should be registered automatically when they are installed on target machines. Installation programs such as the Microsoft Setup Wizard should take care of this for you. For more information, see Chapter 37.

Unregistering ActiveX components is also important. Simply deleting the executable file may get it off your hard drive but does not remove the entries from the Registry. To clean the entries from the Registry, before you delete the OLE application's executable, run it with the /UnRegserver switch, for example:

```
C:\VB\Seymour.Exe /UnRegserver
```

There is no reason to have pesky little test OLE application servers like Seymour cluttering up your Registry when you no longer need them!

By the way, it's a little known (and undocumented) secret that an efficient registration cleaning utility ships with the VB5 CD-ROM. Look for ***Regclean.Exe*** in the ***Tools\Regclean*** directory.

The GetObject Function

You can use GetObject, a companion function to CreateObject, when there is already a current instance of the object active or if you want to create an object with a file already loaded. The syntax for referencing an object connected with GetObject is the same as the syntax for referencing one created with CreateObject. However, you cannot use GetObject to reference an object based on a class created by running a project within the Visual Basic IDE.

Binding

A moment ago, you learned that objects based on Visual Basic ActiveX classes can be created in two ways. If you include a reference to the server in the client project using the References dialog, you can declare a variable as a new instance of one of the server's classes:

```
Dim X As New StringFunctions
```

Alternatively, you can declare the variable as an object, and use the CreateObject function to load a reference to a specific object based on a class using the Set statement:

```
Dim X As Object
Set X = CreateObject("VB5ActiveXAppDemo.StringFunctions")
```

What's the actual difference between the two ways of connecting a client to an instance of an ActiveX class? It comes down to an issue of *binding*. Binding will be familiar if you have worked in a fully object-oriented environment; it covers the topic of when events, properties, and methods are assigned to an object. In VB5, this concept is applied to OLE object references: When does VB actually evaluate the validity of property and method calls you make?

When you declare a variable as an object and then set a reference to an object in the variable using the CreateObject function, VB employs *late binding*. This means that the compiler cannot actually determine the validity of your method and property calls until your code is run. For example,

```
Dim X As Object
Set X = CreateObject("VB5ActiveXAppDemo.StringFunctions")
X.ThisMethodDoesntReallyExistHaHa
```

will compile just fine, although, of course, you'll get a runtime error message. To late bind, VB must include runtime code that checks the validity of method (and property) calls, obtains the ActiveX identifier needed to invoke the method, and raises errors. The process involves looking up functions in a virtual table to find their identifier. (This virtual table of an object and its functions is sometimes called a *vtable*.) If Visual Basic doesn't know exactly what object is being referenced, it doesn't know what vtable to use.

Late binding is, therefore, the most expensive (meaning slowest and most resource consumptive) way to reference ActiveX class objects. You might, however, want to use it anyhow in some cases. For example, you might not know until runtime what kind of object will be referenced by an object variable.

Early binding is accomplished when VB can detect what object methods and properties belong to at compile time. The compiled code then only needs to include the method invocation (the code required to do a vtable lookup and check for errors can be left out). This results in a considerable gain in performance over late binding.

To employ early binding, you must reference the ActiveX application in your client project by making sure that the server is selected in the References dialog.

A variable that is declared as a new instance of a referenced class included in the server, for example,

```
Dim X As New StringFunctions
```

can only contain an object of the StringFunctions class and VB will be able to detect ActiveX function identifiers (or whether a method or property, in fact, exists) at compile time. The following code

```
Dim X As New StringFunctions
X.ThisMethodDoesntReallyExistHaHa
```

will generate a compile time error. So who's laughing now?

Note that early binding is based on the server's unique class identifier (CLSID), which is a hexadecimal identifier supplied when the server is compiled. The class (or project) names aren't used because there could be more than one class with the same name but with different methods and properties. You can browse your Registry with Regedit to get an idea of what CLSIDs look like.

You'll find more information on CLSIDs and binding in Chapters 9, "Using the Windows Registry," and 14, "Visual Basic and OOP."

Placing Code in Class Events

Class modules have two events:

- **Initialize** Fired when an instance of an class is created
- **Terminate** Fired when the instance is destroyed

(These events are covered in more detail in Chapter 14.)

You can easily add code to display a message box to track when the events are fired, for example:

```
Private Sub Class_Initialize()
   MsgBox "Eeek! Performance anxiety: I've Been Initialized!", _
      vbExclamation, ProgTitle
End Sub

Private Sub Class_Terminate()
   MsgBox "Terminating is hard to do, yes it is!", _
      vbExclamation, ProgTitle
End Sub
```

The Initialize message box is displayed when you create the object based on the StringFunction class by clicking the Apply button, as shown in Figure 23-9.

When the instance of the class is destroyed — in this case by the scope passing out of the function that creates the instance — the Terminate message box is displayed, as you can see in Figure 23-10.

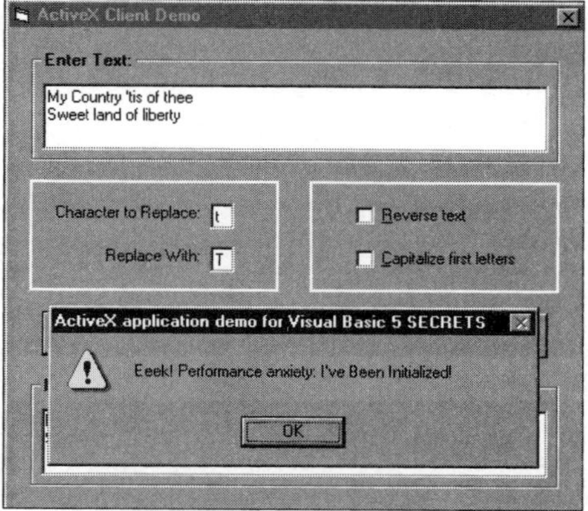

Figure 23-9: Client applications fire code that has been placed in a class module Initialize event when objects based on the class are created.

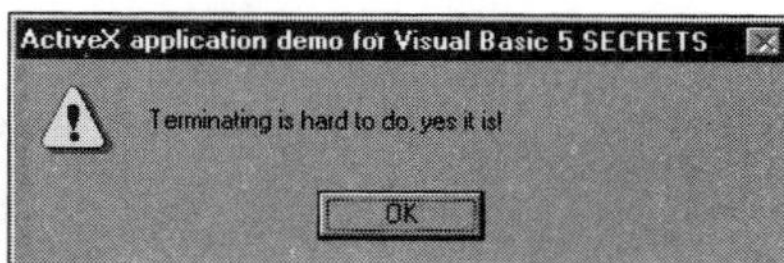

Figure 23-10: Client applications fire code that has been placed in a class module's Terminate event when the object based on the class is destroyed.

The Component Request Pending Dialog

If you try to invoke an object instance of the StringFunctions class before clicking OK in the message boxes shown in Figures 23-9 and 23-10, you'll probably get the pesky little Component Request Pending Dialog shown in Figure 23-11.

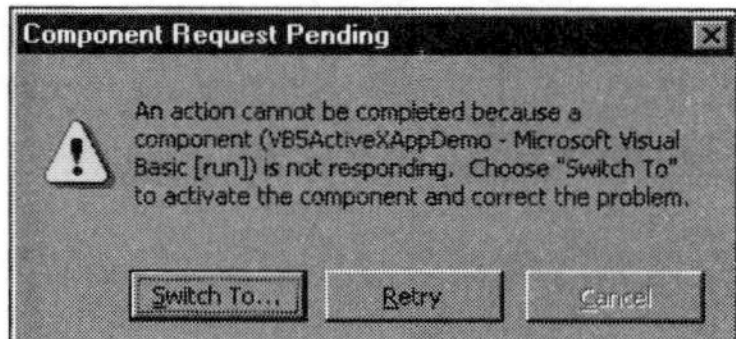

Figure 23-11: Trying to access a server while it is tied up generates the Component Request Pending dialog.

The Component Request Dialog was formerly known as the Server Busy dialog. If you spend any amount of time at all working with ActiveX components that are functioning as servers, you'll find that they do tend to become busy — and generate the Component Request Pending dialog — during the development process.

Because the message box generated by the MsgBox functions in the ActiveX class events is modal, the server is stalled, waiting for a response to the message box before it can do anything else. In this situation, neither of the available buttons depicted in Figure 23-11 — Switch To and Retry — will do any good. Retry will just keep on trying endlessly to no avail — bringing the Component Request Pending dialog back up — until someone clicks OK on the modal message box (which by now has probably disappeared). Switch To displays the Windows Task Manager. Unfortunately, the ActiveX component application (because it has no visible interface) will not be listed as one of the applications you can switch to and shut down.

The Component Request Pending dialog is generated by servers with such great frequency that, if you haven't encountered it yet in your dealings with ActiveX components, it's a sure bet that you will soon! Fortunately, you can set some options in the client application that make the Component Request Pending dialog a little more friendly.

For starters, there's no point in including a Switch To button that serves no purpose, and may confuse users. In Figure 23-11, notice that the Cancel button is disabled. Technically, the Cancel button is enabled when the Component Request Pending dialog is displayed because of a *server busy* condition — analogous to a busy telephone signal — and disabled when the Component Request Pending dialog is displayed because of a *request pending* condition — analogous to being put on hold with bad Christmas music playing.

The point is that a "request pending" condition might still go through — if the caller can bear to hold even though they are playing bad music. A call that returns a "server busy" condition will not go, period. It must be "dialed" again.

Functionally, because the Component Request Pending dialog is responding to a request pending condition and has its Cancel button grayed out, the dialog has one button the user can use, and this button does nothing, thus making it like a message box with an OK button (or, as dubbed by some wags, a Not OK button). Why not make the dialog appear more like what it is?

The client application's App object has a number of properties that you can use to customize the appearance of the Component Request Pending dialog. For example, if you place the following code in the client's form load event,

```
Private Sub Form_Load()
   App.OleRequestPendingMsgText = _
      "Hacker's Component Request Pending Dialog"
   App.OleRequestPendingMsgTitle = "Not OK"
End Sub
```

you'll get a Component Request Pending dialog like the one shown in Figure 23-12.

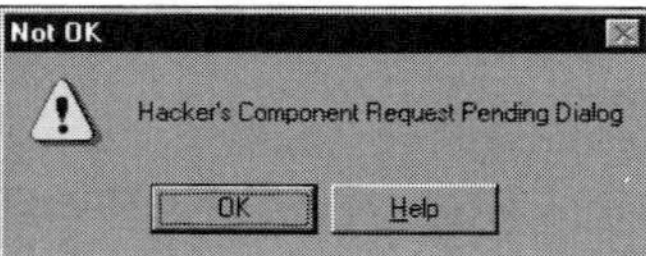

Figure 23-12: You can use the properties of the App object to customize the appearance of the Component Request Pending dialog.

In the real world, it might be somewhat more useful to suggest that the user contact in-house technical support, or whatever.

You can also change the appearance of the Component Request Pending dialog when the dialog is caused by the server busy condition rather than the result pending condition. In this case, the dialog will have a Cancel button as well as an OK button. The text and title are controlled with the App object's OleServerBusyMsgText and OleServerBusyMsgTitle properties.

You can also use the OleServerBusyTimeOut and OleRequestPendingTimeOut properties to change the default values before the Component Request Pending dialog is displayed. You can set these properties at runtime. This might be useful if your server is going to be occupied for long periods of time — for example, in loading a huge database. You could avoid needlessly causing the appearance of the Component Request Pending dialog.

In the case of the server busy condition, you can also bypass the Component Request Pending dialog completely by setting the app's OLEServerBusyRaiseError property to True and trapping for the OLE Server busy error (see the code that follows). (This is equivalent to having a user press Cancel in the Component Request Pending dialog.)

```
App.OleServerBusyRaiseError = True
...
On Error GoTo ErrHandle
Const OleServerBusyError = &H80010001
...
Exit Sub
ErrHandle:
   If Err = OleServerBusyError Then
      MsgBox "Quitting...", vbCritical, "OLE Error"
   Else
      'Handle other errors
   End If
   'Clean up code as necessary
End Sub
```

A Class Module that Is a Wrapper

It's easy to add a class module that serves as *wrapper* (interface) with standard code modules (or forms). You might wish to do this simply to turn existing code libraries into servers. In addition, there are some limitations on what you can place in class modules: If you try to place global constants or external function declarations in a class module, you'll get a compile time error like the one shown in Figure 23-13.

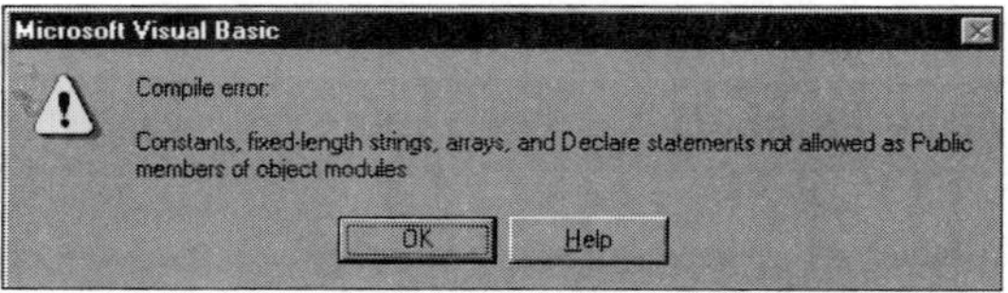

Figure 23-13: If you want to use global constants or external declarations, you need to place them outside of a class module.

As a demonstration, the server ***Wrapper.Vbp*** provides an interface with the File_Utilities code module developed in Chapter 16, "Optimizing Secrets." Two of the File_Utilities functions are wrapped: GetTempFile, which returns a temporary filename, and FixFile, which adds a backslash to the end of a file path if necessary. (See "Using an Excel Server as a Spell Checker" in Chapter 22 for a full explanation of the GetTempFile function.)

To call the wrapper from a client, you must give it the project name Wrapper and start it in ActiveX component mode — using Start With Full Compile — from Sub Main, as described earlier in the chapter.

The class module itself is named Files. Its Instancing property is set to 5-MultiUse. Here's the wrapper function that calls the FILE_UTILITIES code module:

```
Public Function GetTempFile(Directory As String, _
   Prefix As String) As String
   GetTempFile = FILE_UTILITIES.GetTempFile _
      (FILE_UTILITIES.FixPath(Directory), Prefix)
End Function
```

To call the ActiveX component, make sure that Wrapper has been selected in the References dialog (the client is saved as ***WrapCli.Vbp***). You'll find the ActiveX component listed in the References dialog with the description "Wraps File Utility Module."

It's easy then to call the Wrapper component, as shown in Figure 23-14:

```
Private Sub cmdGet_Click()
   Dim FileName As String
   Dim X As New Files
```

```
    FileName = X.GetTempFile(txtDirect, txtPrefix)
    Set X = Nothing
    If FileName = "" Then
       MsgBox "Unable to create a temp file!", vbCritical, "ActiveX!"
    Else
       MsgBox "Your Temp File Name Is: " & FileName, vbInformation, _
          "ActiveX!"
    End If
End Sub
```

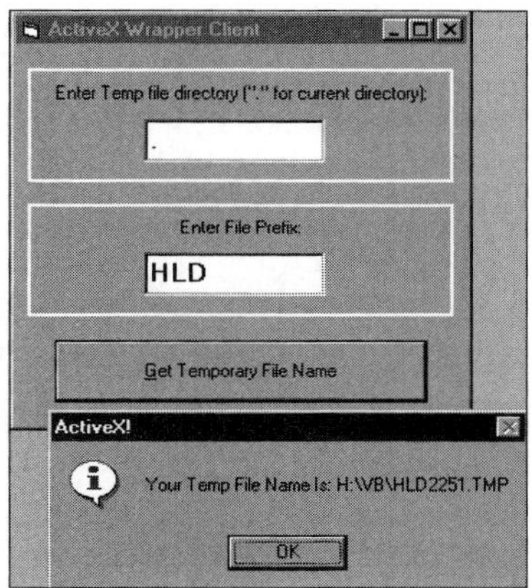

Figure 23-14: You can use ActiveX class modules to wrap existing code modules.

Error Handling in ActiveX Components

Untrapped errors in an ActiveX component, or errors that you intentionally generate using the Raise method of the Err object, are raised in the client application that invoked the component. (For more general information on the Err object and the Raise method, see Chapter 15, "Handling Errors.")

The implication of this is that it is not appropriate to deal with an error condition in an ActiveX component simply by displaying a message box. Server error handling must return information to the client so the client can decide what, if anything, to do about it.

For example, the Wrapper class module described in the previous section really should check that a valid prefix has been passed to the GetTempFile function. Without a valid prefix, the API call will fail, the ActiveX will fail, and a cryptic message will go back to the client (or no message at all if the thread simply stalls). You could add code that raises an error if a valid prefix isn't passed to the GetTempFile function:

```
...
Const hdNoPrefixError = 512
If Prefix = "" Then
   Err.Raise Number:=vbObjectError + hdNoPrefixError, _
   Description:="Client forgot to pass a prefix!", _
   Source:="Wrapper.Files"
End If
...
```

(Obviously, in real life you'd want to test for more than just the existence of the string: It should be three alphabetic characters long, and so on.)

vbObjectError is a predefined constant (with a value of -2,147,221,504). Error constants that you create in your servers should start at vbObjectError + 512. (They can go as high as vbObjectError + 65535.) It's important to document your error codes well for users of your ActiveX component objects. You should also include a description of the problem in the Err object's Description property when you raise the error and should include source information in the Source property in the ProgID form of *object.class*.

The client application can trap for specific errors and handle them. For example:

```
...
On Error GoTo ErrHandle
...
Exit Sub
ErrHandle:
   With Err
   If .Number = vbObjectError + hdNoPrefixError Then
      MsgBox "Error # " + CStr(.Number) + vbCrLf + _
         "Description: " + .Description + vbCrLf, vbCritical, _
         "Source: " + .Source
      End If
   End With
End Sub
```

Admittedly, this merely displays the message box shown in Figure 23-15. You might prefer to handle the error by supplying a prefix and trying again, or by setting the focus on the prefix text box.

Figure 23-15: An error that is raised in an ActiveX component can be trapped in a client application that invokes the component.

If you try to run the wrapper programs in uncompiled versions, the error will be trapped by VB's default handlers. Although VB will display an error number and error description, the box displayed in the VB environment won't match the one shown in Figure 23-15.

Versioning an ActiveX Component

ActiveX components are intended to be distributed as parts of other compiled applications. This leads to a potential problem if your ActiveX components change. Will the applications that are based around the component continue to work with the updated component? Hopefully, the server is being updated because developers who are using your server as components are so enamored of it that they are clamoring for new and improved features.

Fortunately, VB provides a feature to help with ActiveX component versioning issues. The trick is to enter the full path to the previous version of the ActiveX in the Compatible ActiveX field in the Component tab of the Project Properties dialog. VB keeps track of the ActiveX component's classes and members using an internal type library number. In Figure 23-16, ***Seymour.Exe*** is the compiled version of ***ActiveX.Vbp*** developed earlier in this chapter. Once you have a compiled version 1.0 of your project — such as ***Seymour.Exe*** — you should use it as the Compatible ActiveX component until you have a complete version upgrade of the server. In other words, you don't want to clutter the version tracking mechanism with a lot of interim builds. (For further information on the differences between Project Compatibility and Binary Compatibility options, and on avoiding Version trees, see the "Compatibility and Versioning" topic in the Visual Basic Professional documentation.)

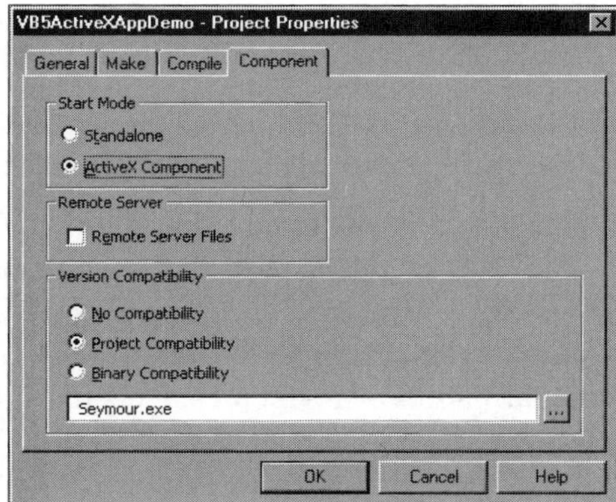

Figure 23-16: You use the Version Compatibility settings on the Component tab of the Project Properties dialog to help track versions of ActiveX components.

I've changed code in the demonstration ActiveX component's StringFunctions class module in a way that will surely *break* the ActiveX component — "break"meaning create an incompatibility between the new compiled version and a previous version. To break the new server, I've changed the CapFirstLetter sub to a function named ThisOldHouse and added a formal parameter. (This could represent a decision to pass parameters to the routine rather than setting properties. See "Properties Versus Parameters" earlier in this chapter.) Here's the new code for ThisOldHouse:

```
Public Function ThisOldHouse(InText As String) As String
    Dim PosDel As Integer, DeLim As String
    DeLim = " "
    Mid(InText, 1, 1) = UCase(Mid(InText, 1, 1))
    PosDel = InStr(InText, DeLim)
    While PosDel <> 0
        Mid(InText, PosDel + 1, 1) = UCase(Mid(InText, PosDel + 1, 1))
        PosDel = InStr(PosDel + 1, InText, DeLim)
    Wend
    CapFirstLetter = InText
End Function
```

In general, the actions that will break an ActiveX component are

- Changing the project name
- Changing the name of any public class module in the project
- Deleting a class module or setting its Public property to False
- Deleting, changing its scope to private, or changing the data type of any public variable, procedure, or Property procedure in a public class module
- Changing the name or altering the formal parameter list of any public procedure in a public class module

My changes to the CapFirstLetter procedure certainly constitute an example of the last of these no-nos. (Actually, if you think about it, this all makes perfect sense: The versioning system is trying to avoid a situation in which the client's call to a server's properties or methods are formally unmatched. This kind of versioning cannot check the internal logic of any changes you make.)

When I compile the modified server (by selecting Start With Full Compile), I get the incompatibility dialog shown in Figure 23-17.

The dialog shown in Figure 23-17 actually provides quite a bit of information about the problem and possible solutions. One possible solution is to accept the incompatibility (or incompatibilities), in which case clients that use your server will not work with the new version. (So be it? More upgrade fees? At least you can be responsible about notifying users of the server about the potential problem.)

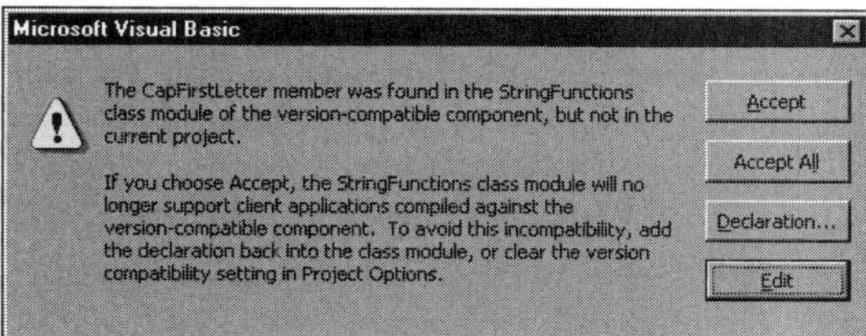

Figure 23-17: If a Compatible ActiveX application has been selected, you will be warned of incompatibilities when you try to compile new versions of the server.

If you don't want to accept the incompatibility, the Declaration button will display the original version that is incompatible with the revision, as shown in Figure 23-18. The Edit button will take you to the offending portion of source code.

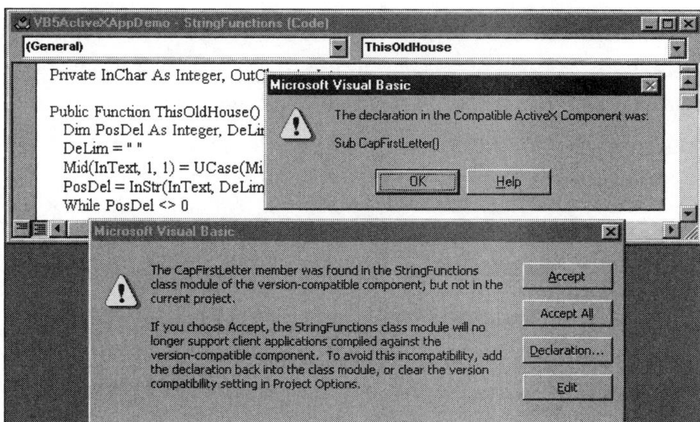

Figure 23-18: The incompatibility dialog will pinpoint the exact problem for you.

Creating an Application Object

The commercial ActiveX applications that were accessed in Chapter 22 each had a top-level Application object. Typically, Application objects contain information about an application as a whole as well as access to lower levels of an application's object hierarchy. There is no requirement to include an Application object in an ActiveX, but if you decide to do so, it should probably include at least the following properties:

- If the ActiveX has a user interface, a Caption property that sets and returns the caption of the server application's main window
- A read-only Name property
- A Path property that returns the path to the application's executable file
- A Version property that returns the VB version information that is compiled into an executable file

One thing that should not be implemented as part of an Application object is a method that closes the server. (Yes, yes, Igor, I know Excel has a Quit method, Igor. Down, Igor. Igor, do what Microsoft says, not what they do!) The reason for this is that, at least in theory, a well-behaved ActiveX does not control its own lifetime: only the client does. As long as a client holds a reference to a server object in scope, the server should continue. Shutting down a server internally risks leaving clients with references to objects that no longer exist. I've created a sample ActiveX with an Application object that implements the four application properties just listed as class properties. (The project is saved as ***App.Vbp***.) It's set to run in ActiveX component mode with a Project Name of Hacker. The project contains:

- A form, frmMain, that represents the main form of an ActiveX application.
- A code module that contains global constants and declarations and the *pro forma* Sub Main for startup as an ActiveX application.
- A public class module, named Application, that contains the Hacker.Application object. The class module's instancing property is set to 5-MultiUse. An instance of frmMain is shown in the module's Initialize event and unloaded in its Terminate event.

Here's the code module:

```
Option Explicit
Public Const hdAppName = "Hacker's ActiveX Component"
Public X As New frmMain

Public Sub Main()
   'Pro Forma Sub Main for ActiveX Component start!
End Sub
```

As shown in Listing 23-3, the Application class module contains the code for the Caption, Name, Path, and Version properties:

Listing 23-3: Creating an ActiveX Application object

```
Option Explicit

Public Property Get Caption() As String
   Caption = X.Caption
End Property
```

```
Public Property Let Caption(vNewValue As String)
   X.Caption = vNewValue
End Property

Property Get Name() As String
   Name = hdAppName
End Property

Property Get Path() As String
   Path = App.Path
End Property

Property Get Version() As String
   Version = App.Major & "." & App.Minor
End Property
```

X, the instance of frmMain used by the server, is displayed in the class module Initialize event, and is unloaded in its Terminate event:

```
Private Sub Class_Initialize()
   X.Show
End Sub

Private Sub Class_Terminate()
   Unload X
End Sub
```

I've compiled the project, using the Make tab of the Project Properties dialog, to set a version number of 4.2.

The next step is to create a client that can communicate with the demonstration application object. I've called the client project ***AppClient.Vbp***.

Of course, as usual, to use the Application ActiveX component on your system you'll have to first register it, either by compiling it or running the executable file.

If you make sure that Hacker's Application object is selected in the References dialog, you'll be able to use the Object Browser to display the Application properties, as shown in Figure 23-19.

The demonstration client for the application I've written uses late binding to create the server object, so you can remove Hacker's Application object from the list of enabled references if you'd like.

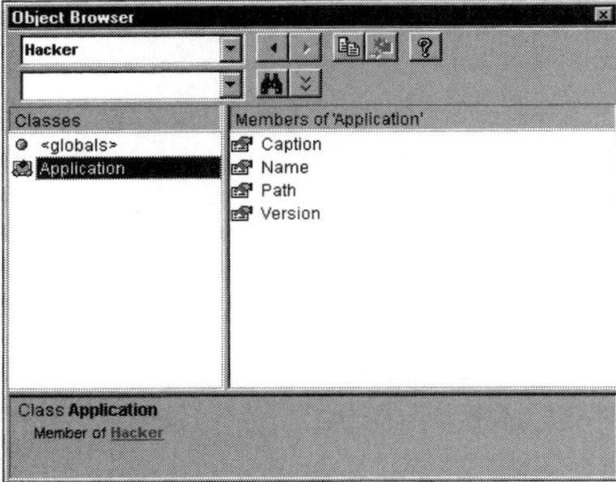

Figure 23-19: If Hacker's Application object is included in the list of available references, you can use the Object Browser to view the Application properties.

The demonstration client, shown in Figure 23-20, consists of a single form that creates a form-level variable to hold an instance of the ActiveX component object. Here's the form-level declaration and the form Load event code:

```
Option Explicit
Dim X As Object

Private Sub Form_Load()
   Set X = CreateObject("Hacker.Application")
   'populate the form based on server values
   lblName = X.Name
   lblPath = X.Path
   lblVersion = X.Version
   txtCaption = X.Caption
End Sub
```

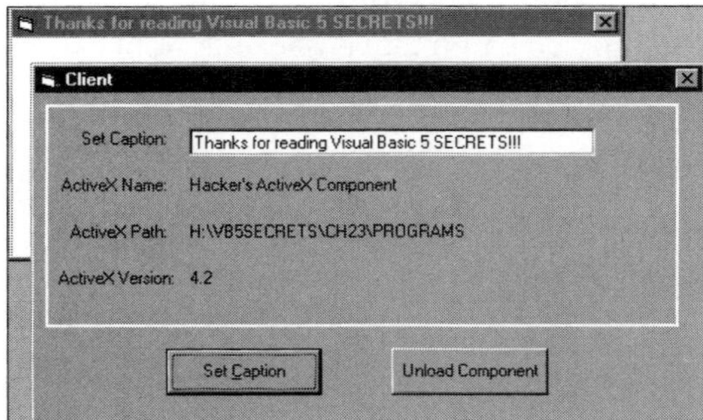

Figure 23-20: A client application can easily retrieve and set properties of the Hacker.Application object.

To make sure that the demonstration form has the focus, I've added a Me.SetFocus command to its Activate event (this causes an error if placed in the form's Load event):

```
Private Sub Form_Activate()
   Me.SetFocus
End Sub
```

The code that sets new ActiveX component form captions couldn't be simpler:

```
Private Sub cmdSetCap_Click()
   X.Caption = txtCaption
End Sub
```

I've added another button to the demonstration form (see Figure 23-20) that toggles between Unload Component and Load Component, depending on whether X contains an instance of the Hacker.Application object:

```
Private Sub cmdUn_Click()
   If Not X Is Nothing Then
      Set X = Nothing
      cmdUn.Caption = "Load Component"
   Else
      Set X = CreateObject("Hacker.Application")
      cmdUn.Caption = "Unload Component"
   End If
   Me.SetFocus
End Sub
```

Object Hierarchies

There are many ways you can organize objects, classes, and hierarchies within ActiveX applications. In this connection, however, you should understand two particularly important concepts: dependent objects and collection classes.

Dependent Objects

Dependent objects are objects contained within other objects. Client applications can manipulate dependent objects, but they cannot create them because the Instancing property of the dependent object's class module has been set to 1-Private or 2-PublicNotcreatable. If the client cannot directly create the dependent object, what is the mechanism for the creation of the dependent object?

In this case, the ActiveX component provides a method that creates the dependent object. Typically, this method is called Add or AddItem. The component creates the dependent object in the code for the method and returns a reference to the newly created dependent object to the client.

Collection Classes

A *collection* is an object that contains a set of related objects (see Chapter 14 for more information). A *collection class* is a class module that groups similar objects that are instances of another class.

A Virtual Pizza

For example, consider a pizza class that is externally instanceable. A collection object, Toppings, contains all the Topping objects for a given Pizza object. Objects of the Topping class are not externally instanceable and can only be created using the Pizza class's Toppings collection AddTopping method.

This object hierarchy requires three class modules. Going from the bottom of the hierarchy towards the top, these are:

- The Topping class module, which defines one pizza topping per instance
- The Toppings class module, which defines a collection object to contain Topping items
- The Pizza class module, which defines the whole pizza with a collection of Topping objects

You can see these class modules in the Project Explorer with the demonstration ActiveX component project, ***Pizza.Vbp***, open, as shown in Figure 23-21.

Figure 23-21: The class modules in the Pizza project serve as templates for the objects that will be based on those classes.

The Topping class contains one property, the name of the topping:

```
Public name As String
```

Because objects of the Topping class are dependent, Instancing for the class should be set so that the class is not externally creatable. Because instances of the class should be visible outside the scope of the ActiveX application, the Instancing property for the class should be set to 2-PublicNotCreatable.

Instances of the Toppings class are also dependent, meaning that the class module Instancing property is also 2-PublicNotCreatable. This class serves as a template for a collection of Topping items. It implements a private collection object:

```
Private ThisPizzaToppings As New Collection
```

The methods of the Toppings class are "wrappers" around the methods of the Visual Basic collection object (see the section "A Class Module that Is a Wrapper" earlier in this chapter). In other words, the Toppings methods encapsulate default collection object method calls. AddTopping adds a Topping item to the ThisPizzaToppings collection, using the collection object's add method, and passes back a reference to the new Topping item. The NumberToppings property wraps the collection Count property to return the number of items in the user-defined collection. The GetItem method calls the Item method of the ThisPizzaToppings collection to return an object reference to the indexed item in the collection:

```
Public Function AddTopping(ByVal name As String)
   Dim ThisTopping As New Topping
   ThisTopping.name = name
   ThisPizzaToppings.Add ThisTopping
   Set AddTopping = ThisTopping
End Function ' Return a reference to the new Topping object

Property Get NumberToppings() As Integer
   NumberToppings = ThisPizzaToppings.Count
End Property

Public Function GetItem(Which As Integer)
   Set GetItem = ThisPizzaToppings.Item(Which)
End Function ' Return a reference to the selected Topping object
             ' based on its collection index
```

Finally, the Pizza class module is an externally creatable class (its Instancing property is set to 5-MultiUse).

Pizza contains only one line of code:

```
Public Toppings As New Toppings
```

This means that every Pizza object created based on the Pizza class module will have its own Toppings collection based on the Toppings collection class.

An object based on the Toppings collection class can exist only as part of a Pizza object. A Topping object can only be created using the AddTopping method of the Toppings collection. These relationships are enforced by the instancing properties of the class modules.

Let's get ready to bake some pizzas! Roll up your sleeves; get out the dough! To use the ActiveX Pizza component, start it as an ActiveX application through a pro forma Sub Main in the normal server fashion.

The client project is named, logically, ***PizzaCli.Vbp***. Because I've connected the client to the server using early binding (the Dim X As New ... statement; see "Binding" earlier in the chapter), the first step is to make sure that the Pizza ActiveX component is selected in the References dialog.

The Pizza client creates an object of the Pizza class, which, in turn, instances an object of the Toppings collection class. The wrapped standard collection object methods of the Toppings collection class are used to implement the functionality displayed in Figure 23-22: adding a topping to the instance of the Toppings collection, and displaying the names of all the Topping objects in the collection.

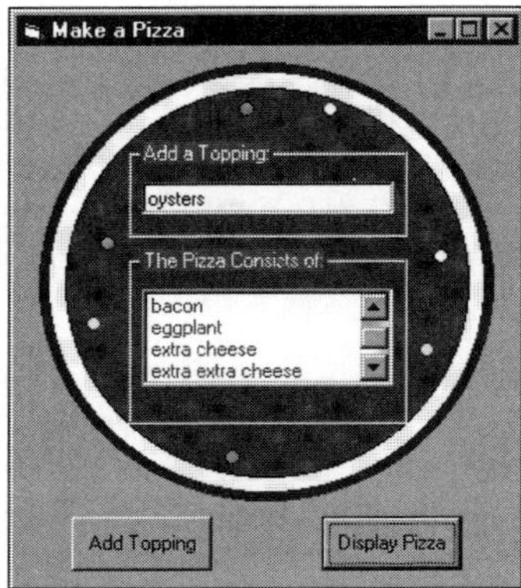

Figure 23-22: You can use the instancing properties of class modules to enforce object hierarchies.

The form module first instances an object of the Pizza class, and automatically creates a new Toppings collection for the class:

```
Option Explicit
Dim X As New Pizza
```

The "Add a Topping" procedure calls the AddTopping method of the collection class:

```
Private Sub cmdAdd_Click()
   X.Toppings.AddTopping txtTopping
End Sub
```

The "The Pizza Consists of" procedure uses the collection class NumberToppings property and GetItem method to add the names of all the toppings in the collection to a list box:

```
Private Sub cmdDisplay_Click()
   Dim K As Integer
   For K = 1 To X.Toppings.NumberToppings
      lstToppings.AddItem X.Toppings.GetItem(K).Name
   Next K
End Sub
```

Creating In-Process Servers (ActiveX DLLs)

You create in-process servers (ActiveX DLLs) by selecting ActiveX DLL for the Project Type on the General tab of the Project Properties dialog (as shown in Figure 23-23). Making an ActiveX DLL is in most respects pretty much like creating a stand-alone ActiveX component.

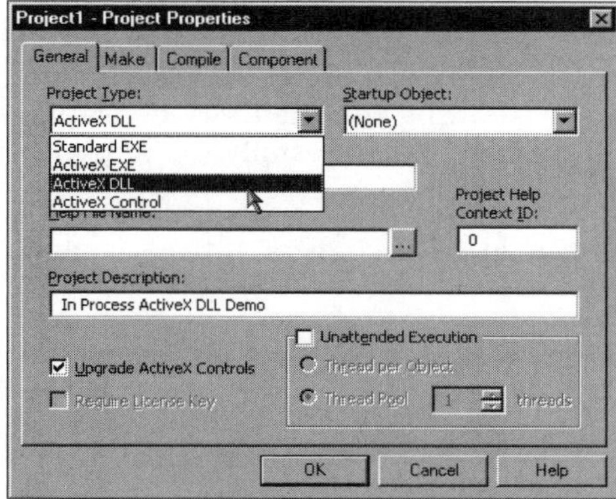

Figure 23-23: You use the ActiveX DLL option under Project Type to compile your project as an ActiveX DLL.

In-process servers cannot run in stand-alone mode. Because they run in the process of the application that invokes them, they are usually faster — and consume fewer resources — than out-of-process servers (such as ActiveX applications).

There are some restrictions on the contents of VB in-process servers. If you can live with these, in-process servers are a good choice for projects including:

- Visual Basic add-ins and Wizards
- Compiled modules intended to be called by OLE automation clients, such as Excel
- Breaking up large executables into several smaller modules

In-Process DLL Restrictions

The following restrictions apply to in-process ActiveX DLLs:

- They are 32-bit only and can only be used on 32-bit operating systems (Windows 95 and Windows NT).
- At least one class module with its Instancing property set to 5 - MultiUse is required.

- Modeless forms cannot be displayed.
- The End statement is not allowed in an in-process server and will cause a compile time error. (Note that End should not be used in an out-of-process server, either. The rule is that clients should determine the lifetime of servers.)

Summary

Creating ActiveX components is very exciting from a programming point of view. This chapter focused on showing you the tools, concepts, and tricks of the trade that you need to know to successfully roll out your own ActiveX applications.

In this chapter, I discussed the different kinds of ActiveX components and showed you how to

- Create an ActiveX application
- Instance objects based on classes
- Call ActiveX components from clients
- Set references in clients using the References dialog
- Use the CreateObject and GetObject functions
- Define classes that are externally creatable
- Create a collection class
- Work with object hierarchies and dependent objects
- Display forms in ActiveX applications
- Work with class module events
- Set ActiveX project options
- Register your ActiveX components
- Handle errors in your ActiveX components
- Customize the Component Request Pending dialog
- Use the ActiveX versioning tools
- Create an Application object
- Use early and late binding
- Have your object-oriented virtual pizza and eat it, too!

PART VI

Creating ActiveX Controls

Chapter 24: Understanding ActiveX Controls

Chapter 25: Creating the Control Interface

Chapter 26: Implementing Control Functionality

Chapter 27: Deploying VB ActiveX Controls on the Web

Chapter 24

Understanding ActiveX Controls

ActiveX controls are ActiveX components — the old term for ActiveX component was "OLE server" — that meet some additional criteria. For more information on ActiveX components, see Chapter 20, "Understanding ActiveX and OLE," and Chapter 23, "Creating ActiveX Applications."

What Are Controls?

Controls prepared for distribution are compiled ActiveX executables that normally have an ***.Ocx*** filename extension. They are not expected to run on their own. Rather, they interact with design time development environments in specific ways. When an application that uses an ActiveX control is executed, the control behaves in a very different way than at design time. The specifics of a control's runtime activities depend on the code that the developer has added to the control's members.

A control's *members* are defined as its properties, methods, and events. Our old friends — properties, methods, and events — are also termed the control's *interface*.

Bear in mind that you will probably interact with an ActiveX control in three modes:

- Designing the control in the VB environment
- Application design in VB, or some other IDE, using the control
- As part of a compiled, running application

You could think of this as "Me, my Developer, and my End Users."

ActiveX controls can be *hosted* by many development environments, including Visual Basic, Delphi, Visual C++, and Web development tools such as the ActiveX Control Pad. When a development environment hosts an ActiveX control, the control can be added to the environment's Toolbox for a particular project. In VB, you can add ActiveX controls to the Toolbox using the Components dialog, as shown in Figures 24-1 and 24-2.

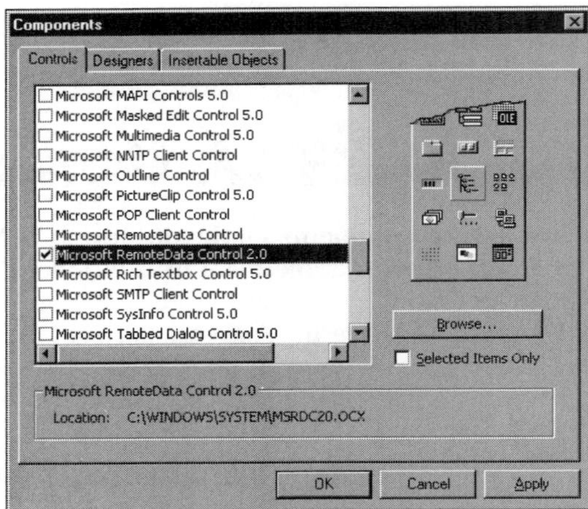

Figure 24-1: You can use the Components dialog to add an ActiveX control to your Toolbox (the RemoteData 2.0 control is shown selected for addition).

Figure 24-2: Once you have added a control to your project, it will appear in your Toolbox (here's the RemoteData 2.0 — MSRDC — control).

The project — ***.Vbp*** — file is used to keep track of which ActiveX controls have been added to a VB source project. For example, here are the first few lines of the project file for a project containing the RemoteData 2.0 control:

```
Type=Exe
Form=Form1.frm
Object={F6125AB1-8AB1-11CE-A77F-08002B2F4E98}#2.0#0; MSRDC20.OCX
Startup="Form1"
```

```
Command32=""
Name="Project1"
...
```

For more information on the internal format of VB project files, see "Inside Project Files" in Chapter 19, "Runtime Display Secrets."

Once you've added a control to the Toolbox, you can add it to any object that can serve as an ActiveX control *container* — also referred to as *hosting* a control.

The most common example of an object that can host a control is a form, but other objects — such as some controls — can also serve as control containers. For more information, see "Controls and Containers" later in this chapter.

You add controls to a container — for example, a form — in one of two ways:

- Double-clicking a control in the Toolbox adds it to the active object.
- Selecting the control in the Toolbox lets you "draw" it on any container object and modify it by selecting the control on the container using the Pointer tool (shown in Figure 24-3).

Figure 24-3: You can use the Pointer tool in the Toolbox to select an ActiveX control on a container and then modify it.

Once you have added a control to a project, as shown in Figure 24-4, you can access its members in project design mode.

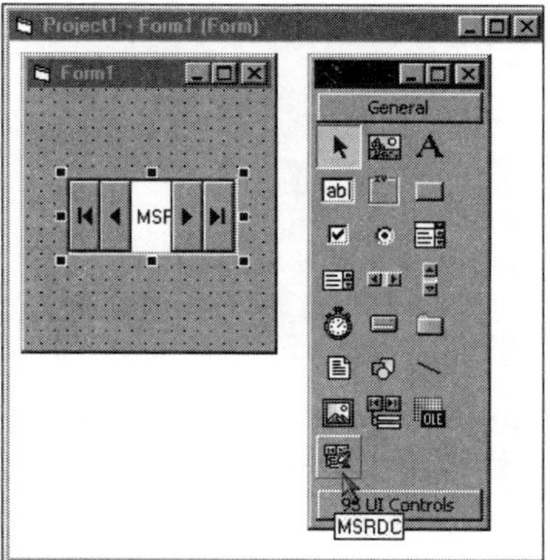

Figure 24-4: Once you've added controls to the Toolbox, you can add them to a project by placing them on a form or other container.

You can use the Properties window — shown in Figure 24-5 — to set control properties. Of course, you can also set and retrieve control properties in code at runtime.

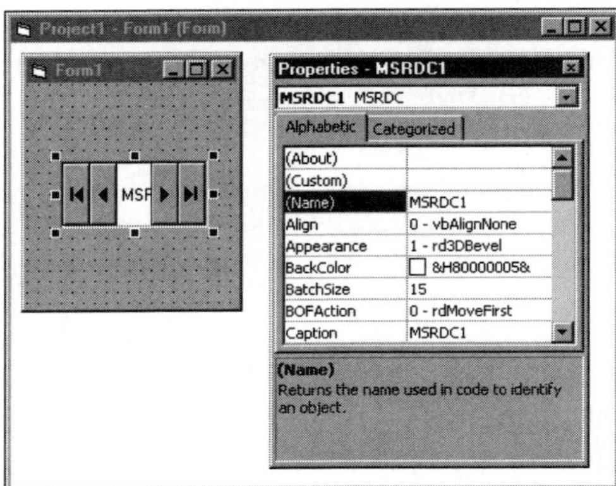

Figure 24-5: You use the Properties window to set the properties of an ActiveX control at design time.

You can only invoke control methods in code for runtime execution.

Control events are added to the project's event scaffolding so that you can add code to respond to the event. A MsgBox statement has been added to the RemoteData control's Validate event in Figure 24-6.

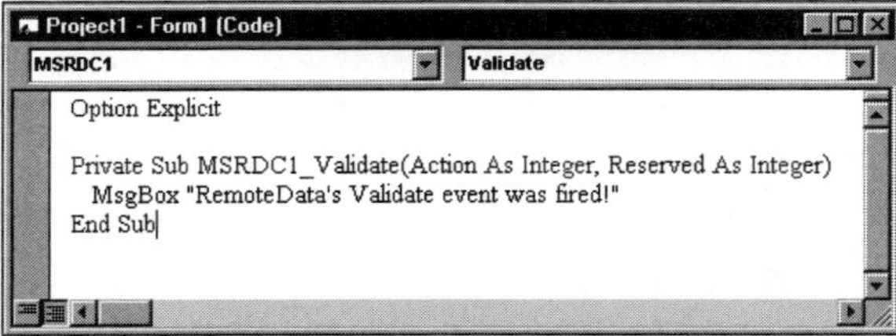

Figure 24-6: You can add code that responds to control events when they are fired.

It's important to distinguish events that a control fires from events received by a control. For an explanation of the distinction, see the section "Control Life Cycle" later in this chapter.

The design time control interface that has just been described is, of course, very familiar to all VB developers who have ever used third-party controls (which is almost all of them, since part of the point of a development environment like VB is its extensibility). You'll find information on creating interfaces for your own controls later in this chapter under "The Control Interface," and in Chapter 25, "Creating the Control Interface." Part VIII of this book, "Third-party Tools, Setup Programs, and Help Files," explains how to use some of the most exciting third-party ActiveX controls that are commercially available.

The new — and incredibly exciting — feature of Version 5 of Visual Basic is that you can create your own ActiveX controls — without leaving the VB environment.

These ActiveX controls will run in Web applications — provided that an Explorer browser equipped with the Visual Basic Virtual Machine (VM) is being used.

Visual Basic developers have been liberated. They can now compete with the "big boys" who create OLE-based ActiveX controls in VC++ without the complexities of C++.

ActiveX Control Projects

You can open a new ActiveX Control project by choosing New from VB's File menu and choosing ActiveX Control as the project type.

If Prompt for Project has been selected on the Environment tab of the Options dialog, you can start a new ActiveX Control project when you first start VB.

You can add an ActiveX Control project to an existing project (such as a Standard Exe project) by choosing Add Project on the VB File menu. Alternatively, you can add a Standard Exe project to an existing ActiveX Control project.

Once the two types of projects have been opened together in VB, a project group is formed, as shown in Figure 24-7.

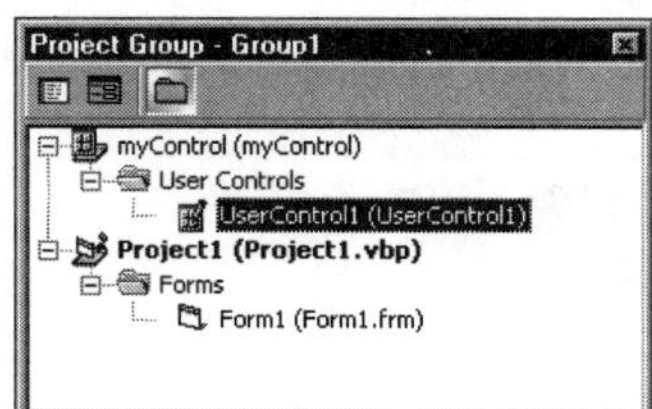

Figure 24-7: If you add a Standard Exe project to an ActiveX Control project, the two projects are combined into a Project group that is displayed hierarchically in VB's Project Explorer.

An ActiveX Control — for example, an ***.Ocx*** file — cannot be run by itself even after it has been compiled.

In theory, you could test your control by compiling it, opening a new VB project, and making the new control available by adding it using the Components dialog. Next, you would add the control to a form or other container, add test code, and run the new project to make sure your control worked.

In practice, it is far easier to create a project group containing your control's project and a standard executable project designed to test the control. Provided that the control project has been saved and correctly constructed internally, the new ActiveX control will appear in the Toolbox of the test project. It can then be added to a VB container.

For more information about project groups and about the different types of projects that are available in VB5, see "Working with Visual Basic Source Files" in Chapter 3, "Event-Driven Programming."

UserControls

A UserControl is an object that is to an ActiveX Control as a form is to a normal executable project. By default, each new ActiveX Control project is started with one UserControl object, just as each Standard Exe project is started with one form object.

You can use the standard VB tools such as the Properties window and Toolbox to change the appearance of the UserControl object, as shown in Figure 24-8. (Note that there is no requirement that ActiveX controls be visible at runtime.)

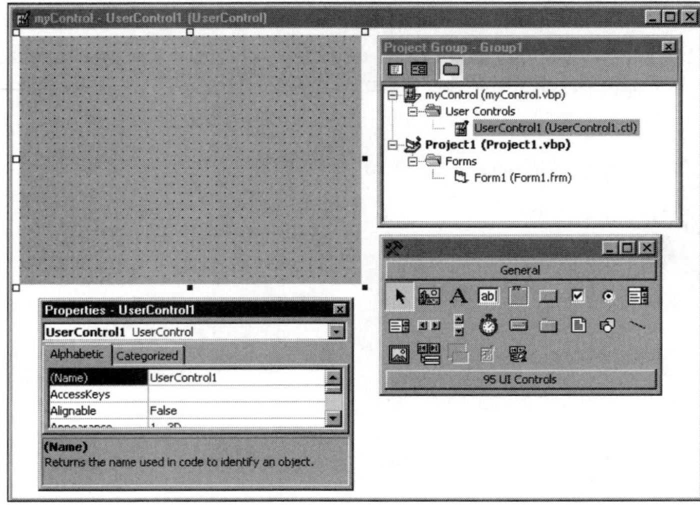

Figure 24-8: You can edit UserControl objects using the same tools you use to edit form objects.

ActiveX Control projects can contain other kinds of modules besides UserControls (***.Ctl*** files), included forms (***.Frm*** files), standard modules (***.Bas*** files), and class modules (***.Cls*** files). Understanding class modules, and how classes work in VB, is particularly important to effective control design.

Classes

Class modules — covered in detail in Chapter 14, "Visual Basic and OOP" — contain properties, methods, and events. Properties are implemented with Property procedures, or using variables. Methods are implemented using Public functions. Events are declared using the event keyword and then fired using RaiseEvent at the appropriate time. For example:

```
Event RedAlert (EnterpriseInDanger As Boolean, _
   WhoCausedIt As String)
...
If AppropriateCircumstances Then
   RaiseEvent RedAlert(True, "The Borg")
End If
```

Class modules do not have a screen representation *per se*; however, you will often want to add classes to components. In older versions of Visual Basic, class modules were used to encapsulate the internal functioning of an application. Each public class module you add to a control is the cookie-cutter template for an object that is part of your control.

The name you give a class module is combined with the name of your control to yield the class *progID,* or programmatic ID. For example, suppose you added a class module named myNewClass to the myTool control. The progID for the new class would be myTool.myNewClass.

The Instancing property of each class module defines how the class can be accessed. For ActiveX control projects, class module instancing must be either *Private* or *PublicNotCreatable*. Private means that outside applications cannot access type library information about the class and cannot create objects based upon it. PublicNotCreatable means that outside applications can only use instances of this class if your control has first created it. Objects based on the PublicNotCreatable class module are termed *dependent*, because they must be created by their parent component before they can be used. If you want external applications to be able to create dependent objects, you have to provide a component method — such as Add — that creates an instance of the dependent object.

Packaging ActiveX Controls

Another reason that you can create standard executables in VB5 has to do with the scope of the ActiveX controls included in your project.

If you'd like, instead of distributing your ActiveX control in a separate ***.Ocx*** file, you can include the source code in one executable by compiling the Project group rather than the control separately. The net effect of this approach is to make the ActiveX control private to the executable. As they sometimes say, the advantages of one are not the disadvantages of the other.

An ActiveX control in VB5 is contained in an ActiveX Control project containing at least one UserControl source code module (the source file is saved with a ***.Ctl*** extension). The question of whether to compile this project into an executable, or to compile it separately into an ***.Ocx*** file that must be distributed, is one of what is called *packaging*.

An ActiveX Control project can contain more than one UserControl module — and more than one ActiveX control.

Public *controls* are controls that can be used by other applications. They must be compiled in an ActiveX control project (and the Public property of the UserControl object must also be set to True). They are compiled into ***.Ocx*** files. You make a control *private* by setting the Public property of the UserControl object to False. After the project is compiled, private controls cannot be used by other applications. They can be used only within the project in which they were compiled. The Public property of a UserControl object cannot be set to True unless the UserControl is an ActiveX Control project. If one of the controls in an ActiveX Control project is only meant to be used by other controls within the project, you can set the Public property of the UserControl to False. External applications will not be able to use it but other controls in the project will.

Changing the Packaging

You can easily change the way a control you've created is packaged just by shifting the source files to a different type of project. For example, if you create some private controls that are part of a project and you want to allow other applications to use them, you can add the ***.Ctl*** files to an ActiveX control project, and compile it into an ActiveX control.

If you don't want to distribute a separate, compiled component, you can instead add the control's ***.Ctl*** file to the project for an application. When the application is compiled, the control is compiled into the executable.

The advantages of including a control as source code compiled into an executable are:

- You don't need to distribute an external ***.Ocx*** file.
- It's simpler to test and debug the control, because you only have to worry about the way it is used in your particular application; you don't have to worry about all possible uses for it.
- You don't have to worry about future distributions of an updated control breaking your application, because the control code is completely compiled into the executable.

Here are the disadvantages of including controls as source code:

- If you wish to update the control — or discover a bug in it that you need to fix — you can't just distribute the revised control. You must recompile the entire application, and redistribute the application.
- You may end up distributing the same code a number of times because multiple applications cannot share the control, and each application will require the source files that the control represents. This will lead to bigger applications that require more hard disk space on target systems.
- Version control becomes more difficult because source code used in separate applications inevitably gets changed. It may become hard to know what version of a control's source code is included in a given project.
- It's more difficult to share source code with other developers; this will require more support effort than distributing a compiled component with a standard interface.
- By distributing source code rather than a compiled ***.Ocx***, you give up control over your source code.

Control Life Cycle

It's important to understand that instances of your controls are constantly being created and destroyed. This is not the way form-based applications work. A typical form is only created and destroyed a handful of times during the course of an application.

The following events create and/or destroy controls:

- Opening or closing the container holding the control
- Adding or removing a control to a container
- Running a project that includes the control

Creating or destroying a control means creating or destroying the UserControl module containing the control's code — and all associated forms and modules.

Here's a sample control life cycle for a UserControl project that is uncompiled in the VB development environment.

First, the developer using the control adds it to a form. An instance of the form is created.

To add a control to a form when the control is included in a design mode ActiveX Control project, you must first close the control's UserControl designer.

The control's Initialize event is fired.

Next, one of two control events is fired. If the Initialize event was fired because a new instance of the control was placed on a form, the control's InitProperties event is fired. On the other hand, if the control is being instanced because a form that it was saved on is being reopened, the control's ReadProperties event is fired.

InitProperties saves the control's default properties while, if ReadProperties is fired instead, previously set property values are retrieved. The mechanism for storing and retrieving control property values — making sure they *persist* — is discussed later in this chapter in "The PropertyBag."

Next, the events that occur as the control is displayed on the screen are fired. These are:

- Resize, which causes the control to be resized according to the way it was sized when it was placed on the form
- Show, which displays the control
- Paint, which is fired after code in the control's paint event is executed

Suppose that you run the project containing the form that contains the control. The Visual Basic IDE closes the form. This fires the control's WriteProperties event, which saves the current values of the control's properties. Next, the control's Terminate event is fired. The instance of the control is destroyed.

A control is an object to which the concept of reincarnation in different manifestations can aptly apply!

As part of the process of creating a runtime instance of the form that contains the control, a runtime instance of the control is also created. The sequence of events that I've just described is initiated again. And, as you probably suspected, when the runtime form is closed and the IDE returned to design mode, the part of the sequence that involves the destruction of the control instance is fired. But wait.... Part of opening the form in design mode is firing the control instance creation events.

As Kurt Vonnegut might have said, "So it goes!"

In a moment, I'll show you how to add Debug.Print commands to a control's events so you can view this life cycle. But first, a word about control events.

Being a Control Voyeur

Would you like to be present at — and witness — the events that are part of the control life cycle? Sure you would. First, start a Standard Exe project in VB5. Use the Project Properties dialog to change the name of the project to TestProj. Use Add Project on the VB File menu to open an ActiveX Control project. Change the name of the control project to myControl. Choose Save Project Group from the File menu to save both projects and a project group file. Your project group will now look like the hierarchy displayed in the Project Explorer shown in Figure 24-9.

Events: Is it Better to Give or Receive?

I've already noted that events fired by a control are different from events received by the control. You can think of it this way: Events fired by the control are a chance for you to do something in response to the event while events received by the control are a chance for the control to do something.

In this regard, you'll notice that the event-handling framework for a control in VB's Code Editor is very different when the control is in its own project, and when it has been added to a container in a test project. In the former case, you'll see the control events described in this section. In the latter, you'll see the events fired by the control, including custom events such as RedAlert (used as an example earlier in this chapter).

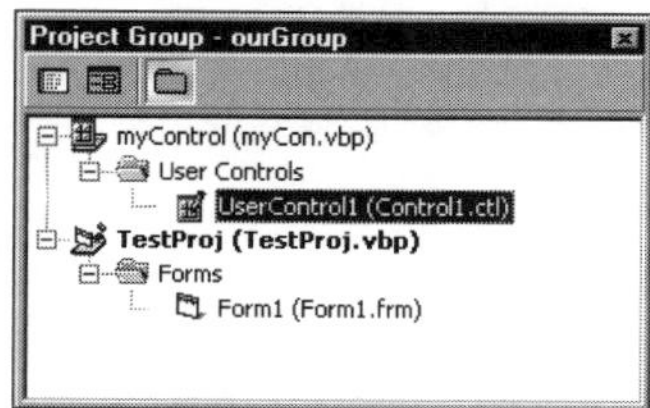

Figure 24-9: The Project Explorer makes it easy to understand complex project groups.

If you'd like, you can customize the UserControl contained in the myControl project, perhaps by changing its name to "Frodo" and its BackColor to red. Now open the Code Editor for the UserControl. Add code to respond to the key control life cycle events along the lines of that shown in Listing 24-1.

Listing 24-1: The Control life cycle

```
Private Sub UserControl_Initialize()
   Debug.Print "Wake me,  shake me! Initialize..."
End Sub

Private Sub UserControl_InitProperties()
   Debug.Print "For the very first time! InitProperties..."
End Sub

Private Sub UserControl_ReadProperties(PropBag As PropertyBag)
   Debug.Print "We are experienced! ReadProperties..."
End Sub

...

Private Sub UserControl_Terminate()
   Debug.Print "Life without me! Terminate..."
End Sub
```

```
Private Sub UserControl_WriteProperties(PropBag As PropertyBag)
   Debug.Print "Saving our properties! WriteProperties"
End Sub
```

When you have finished playing with your control, close the UserControl object. This will place the icon for the control in the Toolbox for TestProj in run mode, as shown in Figure 24-10. The figure shows the default UserControl Toolbox icon. In Chapter 25, I'll show you how to substitute your own custom icon for the default.

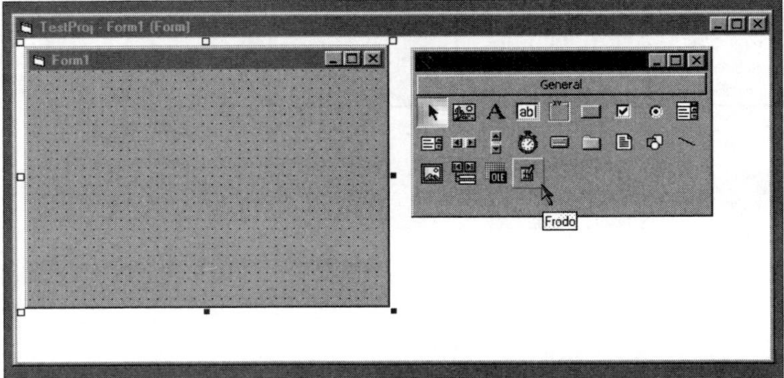

Figure 24-10: Once you've closed a UserControl object, the icon for the control it represents is activated in the Toolbox.

If you look at the TestProj Toolbox before closing the UserControl object, you'll find an icon for myControl. However, the icon is grayed out, indicating that the control is disabled and cannot be added to a container.

Double-click the control icon to add it to the form. Figure 24-11 shows the control, surrounded by "handles," placed on Form1. (The control looks radically different from the form because the control's BackColor property was set to a specific color.)

Figure 24-11: Once a control has been activated in the Toolbox, you can add it to a container (such as a form).

Make sure the Immediate window is open, so you'll be able to see the display generated by the Debug statements shown in Listing 24-1. Run the project. As shown in Figure 24-12, the control's Initialize and ReadProperties events are fired. (InitProperties is never fired in this sequence because the control has been set with property values other than the default.)

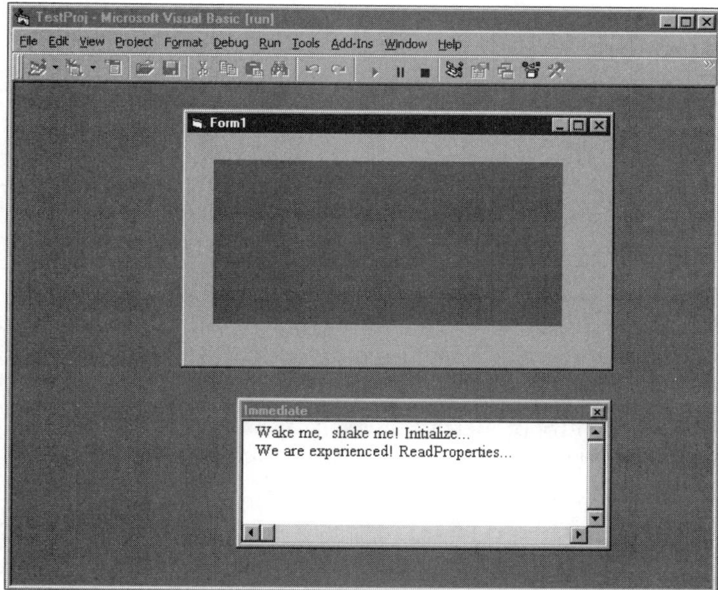

Figure 24-12: Running a form that contains a control fires control events creation events.

If you stop the running project, and open it again, you'll see that the control creation and destruction event sequence has been fired a number of times, as shown in Figure 24-13.

The PropertyBag

As you can see from examining the life cycle of a control, it's often important that control properties persist. To say that a control property has persistence means that its values stay the same even though the control has been destroyed and recreated. For example, if you add a control to a form, set its Name property to "Frodo," run the project containing the form, and close it, you still want the name of the control to be Frodo with the form open in design mode. The mechanism set up to provide property value persistence across invocations of a control is a UserControl object named the PropertyBag.

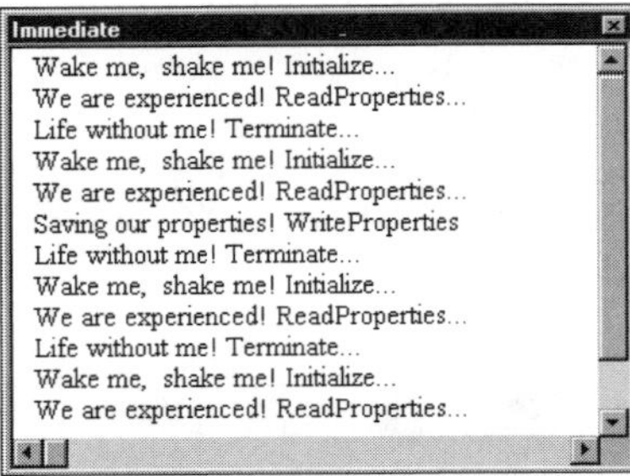

Figure 24-13: Closing a form that contains a control fires first control destruction events and, next, control creation events, as the control opens in design mode.

Using the methods of the PropertyBag object, the control can read or write its own properties. The ReadProperty method is used to retrieve a value for a property, while the WriteProperty method is used to save a property value.

A value of a control property can, itself, be an object. In that case, the PropertyBag object will attempt to make sure that subobject members persist.

Listing 24-2 shows sample invocations of the ReadProperty and WriteProperty methods of a control's PropertyBag object (appropriately placed in the control's ReadProperties and WriteProperties event handlers):

Listing 24-2: Using the PropertyBag object

```
Private Sub UserControl_ReadProperties(PropBag As PropertyBag)
   m_BackColor = PropBag.ReadProperty("BackColor", m_def_BackColor)
   m_ForeColor = PropBag.ReadProperty("ForeColor", m_def_ForeColor)
   m_Enabled = PropBag.ReadProperty("Enabled", m_def_Enabled)
   Set Font = PropBag.ReadProperty("Font")
   m_BackStyle = PropBag.ReadProperty("BackStyle", m_def_BackStyle)
   m_BorderStyle = PropBag.ReadProperty("BorderStyle", _
      m_def_BorderStyle)
   Debug.Print "We are experienced! ReadProperties..."
End Sub
...
Private Sub UserControl_WriteProperties(PropBag As PropertyBag)
   Call PropBag.WriteProperty("BackColor", m_BackColor, _
      m_def_BackColor)
   Call PropBag.WriteProperty("ForeColor", m_ForeColor, _
      m_def_ForeColor)
   Call PropBag.WriteProperty("Enabled", m_Enabled, m_def_Enabled)
   Call PropBag.WriteProperty("Font", Font)
   Call PropBag.WriteProperty("BackStyle", m_BackStyle, _
      m_def_BackStyle)
   Call PropBag.WriteProperty("BorderStyle", m_BorderStyle, _
      m_def_BorderStyle)
   Debug.Print "Saving our properties! WriteProperties"
End Sub
```

Controls and Containers

No control is an island unto itself. An instance of a control never exists by itself. It only has a life once it has been placed on a container. Classically, the container is a Visual Basic form, but it need not be. Controls can themselves be containers. An Internet Explorer window is an up-and-coming candidate for container of the hour.

You cannot run an ActiveX control application directly in Visual Basic. You must add a standard executable application to your project group, and add the control to a container in that application before you can test your control.

Some of the interface members that appear to users of your control to be part of your control actually belong to the container object that holds the control.

Your control is hosted by a container's *Extender* object. You can access the properties and methods of the container your control has been placed on through the Parent property of the container's Extender.

In addition, a UserControl's Ambient object contains property information that you can use to make your control consistent with its background.

Neither the Extender nor Ambient objects are available until a UserControl has been sited on a container. They are not available until InitProperties or ReadProperties has been fired, which is subsequent to the firing of the control's Initialize event.

Some ActiveX control features require support from the container it is placed on, and not every container supplies all possible feature support. Thus, depending on the container your control is attached to, some features may be disabled.

Visual Basic forms support the following features that are not supported by many other containers:

- Transparent control background
- The ControlContainer property
- Alignable controls
- Modeless forms displayed by your control

Using the Container's Extender Object

If you place an instance of your control on a container, such as a form, and view its properties with the Properties window, you'll find quite a few properties you didn't create. These are the Extender object properties provided by the container object, although to a user of your control, they appear to be a seamless extension of your control.

You can use the properties of the Extender object to set the properties of your control. For example, it's common to have the default value of the caption (or text) property of a control be the name given to the control by the container object. Usually, this is the name of the control followed by a number indicating the number of instances of the control that have been placed on the container.

Table 24-1 lists the extender properties that all containers are supposed to provide according to the ActiveX control specification.

Table 24-1 Mandatory Container Extender Properties

Property	*Data Type*	*Access*	*Meaning*
Name	String	Read	The name the user assigns to the control instance
Visible	Boolean	Read/Write	Indicates whether the control is visible
Parent	Object	Read	Returns the object that contains the control, such as a Visual Basic form
Cancel	Boolean	Read	True if the control is the cancel button for the container
Default	Boolean	Read	True if the control is the default button for the container

The truth is that not all containers provide even these properties. You should use error trapping in code to make sure that any extender properties referred to actually exist whenever using a control's container's Extender object.

Many containers provide extender properties beyond those listed in Table 24-1 — for example, Left, Top, Width, and Height properties.

To manipulate the visibility of your control at runtime — or to allow a developer using your control to do so — do not use the extender object's visible property. Instead, use the UserControl object's InvisibleAtRuntime property.

You should know that if your control and its container's extender object have properties with the same name, the extender property will take precedence.

The Ambient Object's UserMode Property

You should know about the UserMode property of the Ambient object that allows an instance of your control to determine whether it's running at design time (UserMode = False) or at runtime.

The mnemonic for keeping straight in your head what the value of UserMode means is that at design time, the person working with your control is a *developer*, not an end user. Since the control is not in "user" mode, UserMode = False.

For example, you could create a different container caption for developers and end users in a control's resize event, as shown in Listing 24-3.

Listing 24-3: The Ambient object's UserMode property

```
Private Sub UserControl_Resize()
   If Ambient.UserMode Then
      Extender.Parent.Caption = "myTool says," + Chr(34) + _
         "Hi, end user!" + Chr(34)
   Else
      Extender.Parent.Caption = "Developer, thanks for" + _
         " all the fish and for using myTool!"
   End If
End Sub
```

Figure 24-14 shows an instance of myControl added to a form in design mode; Figure 24-15 shows the same control and form in run mode.

Figure 24-14: You can use the Ambient object's UserMode property to set the properties of the Extender object of the container for a control in the VB design environment...

Figure 24-15: ...and to set Extender properties of the parent object differently at runtime.

The Control Interface

Once the control has been added to a container, its *interface* can be explored. The interface of a control is defined as its exposed properties, methods, and events. In Chapter 25, I'll show you in detail how to design and implement control interfaces. In the meantime, here is a recap of the key control interface concepts.

An ActiveX control *exposes* its available properties, methods, and events in a standard manner. This means that any application — from Visual Basic to Excel to Web scripting languages — that speaks this standard can use the exposed interface to communicate with and manipulate the ActiveX control.

Properties are used to set or retrieve values stored with the control.

Methods are functions that, when executed, cause the control to do something.

Events are code procedures (known as "event handlers") that an object causes to be executed ("fired") under certain conditions. They represent opportunities for users to add their own code to projects containing controls you created.

Licensing

It's important to understand that ActiveX controls will ultimately be used in one of two ways:

- By a developer when creating applications that use the control
- By the end user

These modes are radically different. Developers need access to the interface of your control so they can use it; end users do not need — and should not generally have — this access. The end user just needs the control module to play its part in the functionality of the application as a whole.

There is a business issue involved here. Normally, the developer of a control distributes the control to other developers who use it at design time as a code module in their applications. These other developers then redistribute the control with their applications to the world at large. As a control developer, you probably do not want the world at large to be able to access your design time interface (at least, not without paying for the access).

Visual Basic contains a mechanism that allows a control to determine whether it is in design mode or run mode. You can use this mechanism to create controls that require a license file to run in design mode (but do not require the file in run mode). Control deployment issues are covered in greater detail in Chapter 27, "Deploying VB ActiveX Controls on the Web."

Requiring a License for Developer Use

If you create an ActiveX control that does something important — in other words, a version of myControl that developers are actually willing to pay for — you should probably implement a licensing scheme so that developers must license use of the control.

There are some complexities involved with this issue, because developers who use your control may themselves create controls that include yours as a component part. If you have required a design time license for your control, and these subdevelopers have introduced a licensing scheme themselves, for the new control to open on target "end developer" systems, developer licenses will have to be present in the target Registry for both the subdeveloper's control and your control. Ultimately, this may not prove satisfactory to end developers. But for now, here is how it is supposed to work.

You can elect to include a licensing key for design time use by making sure that Require License Key is checked in the General tab of the Project Properties dialog before you make your ***.Ocx*** file (as shown in Figure 24-16).

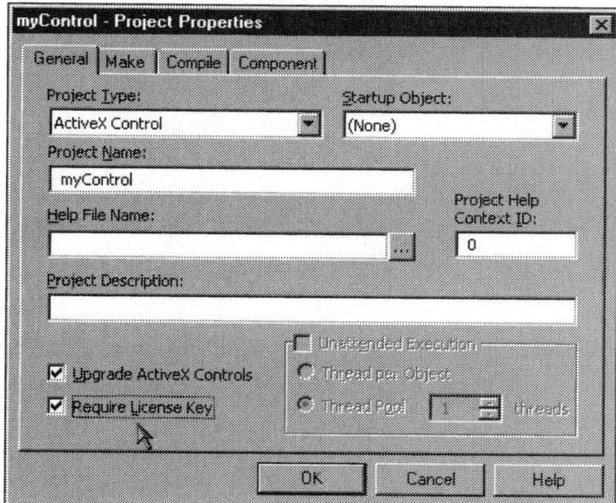

Figure 24-16: You can use the Project Property dialog to require a license key for your compiled ActiveX control.

After you've compiled your control, run the VB Application Setup Wizard. The resulting Setup program, when executed, will transfer the license key to another computer's Registry, allowing your controls to be used in design mode for development. The Setup Wizard is covered in more detail in Chapter 36, "Setup Programs."

Simply copying your ***.Ocx*** file to another computer and then registering it will not transfer the license key. Without the license key, the control will only work in runtime mode, and cannot be used by developers at design time! If a developer has a copy of your control, but not the Registry key, the control cannot create instances of itself in the development environment.

Visual Basic creates a file with a ***.Vbl*** suffix that contains the Registry key that licenses your control. When you use the Setup Wizard to create an installation routine for your ***.Ocx***, the ***.Vbl*** file is automatically included in the routine.

Summary

The ability to create full-fledged ActiveX controls using Version 5 is an extremely important step forward for Visual Basic developers. ActiveX controls are specialized ActiveX component applications, which were explained in detail in Part V, "Using ActiveX." This chapter began where Part V left off, and showed you how to use ActiveX concepts to understand the nature and life cycle of ActiveX controls.

Topics covered included

- ActiveX controls and the VB environment
- ActiveX control projects
- UserControl objects
- Packaging ActiveX controls
- The ActiveX control life cycle
- Key control events
- The PropertyBag object
- Control containers
- The Container's extender object
- The Ambient object
- Control licensing

Chapter 25

Creating the Control Interface

A control's interface consists of its members — properties, events, and methods — as explained in Chapter 24, "Understanding ActiveX Controls."

Generally, the process of creating a control involves three phases:

- Creating the appearance of the control
- Defining the control's interface
- Implementing the logic required by the interface

The appearance of a control — how the control appears at design time and at runtime — should *not* be confused with the control's interface. A control's interface was defined in detail in Chapter 24.

You can create the appearance of a control in one of two ways:

- By placing existing controls on the new control and manipulating the properties of the UserControl object and the controls it contains. Designing the appearance of a control in this way is pretty much like designing the appearance of a form.
- By using graphics methods in the control's Paint event.

ActiveX controls constructed using the latter approach are called *user-drawn* controls, and will be explained in Chapter 26, "Implementing Control Functionality." Visual Basic provides an ActiveX Control Interface Wizard, which greatly simplifies the task of building a control's interface. I'll explain how to use it in the next section, and then I'll show you how to manually duplicate the interface code the Wizard creates. Next, I'll demonstrate how to add some flourishes such as Property Pages and About Boxes to your control interfaces.

The ActiveX Control Interface Wizard

The ActiveX Control Interface Wizard provides you with a jump-start on creating the interface for a control.

If you are going to create the appearance — as opposed to the interface — of your control by adding existing controls to the UserControl object and manipulating the properties of the contained controls and the UserControl, this is easiest to do before you run the Interface Wizard.

The ActiveX Control Interface Wizard is a Visual Basic add-in. Before you can use it, you must make sure that it is selected in VB's Add-In Manager, as shown in Figure 25-1. You open the Add-In Manager by choosing it from the Add-Ins menu.

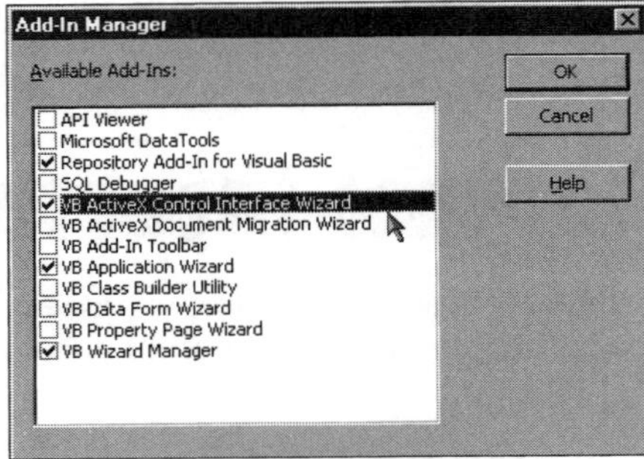

Figure 25-1: Before you can run the ActiveX Control Interface Wizard, you must make sure that it is enabled in the Add-In Manager.

To show you how to use the Control Interface Wizard, I'll demonstrate how to create an ActiveX control that looks like a text box, and behaves like the common old text box, with a few new custom members in its interface.

Setting Up the Control

The UserControl source file is saved on the companion CD-ROM as ***SelText.Ctl***. The ActiveX Control project is saved as ***SelText.Vbp***. Table 25-1 shows the source file names for project and module files related to the SelectText control.

Table 25-1 SelectText Control Filenames (*SelText.Ocx*)

Filename	***What it Contains***
SelText.Ctl	ActiveX control module source code
SelText.Vbp	ActiveX control project
Custom.Pag	Custom property page source code module
FrmAbout.Frm	Control AboutBox
Test1.Frm	Test form
Test1.Vbp	Test standard executable project
Secrets.Bmp	Toolbox icon
SelText.Vbg	Project group containing the control and test projects
SelText.Ocx	Compiled ActiveX control

Figure 25-2 shows this project group structure in the Project Explorer (note that the property page source module has not yet been added to the control project).

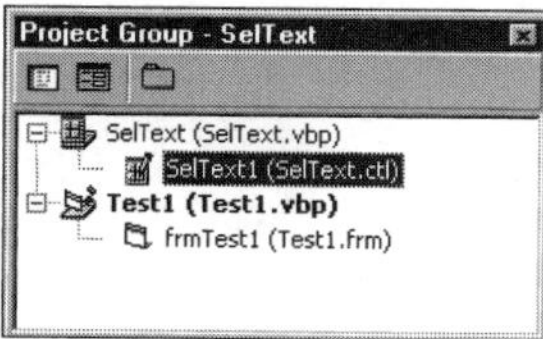

Figure 25-2: You can use the Project Explorer to view the structure of your projects.

The idea behind the SelectText control is nothing fancy. It should behave in most ways like a normal text box, except that it will automatically select all text in the box when the user clicks within the control. The SelectText control will implement the custom members shown in Table 25-2.

Table 25-2 Custom Members in *SelText.Ctl*

Member Name	*Type*	*Data Type*	*Default Value*
ClickEnabled	Property	Boolean	False
SelectText	Method	N/A	N/A
onSelectText	Event	N/A	N/A

Table 25-3 explains how these members will operate.

Table 25-3 Functionality of *SelText*'s Custom Members

Member Name	*What it Does*
ClickEnabled	If ClickEnabled is set to True, all text in the SelectText control is selected when the control receives a click event.
SelectText	Selects all text in the control when the method is invoked.
onSelectText	Fired when a SelectText selection occurs

You can draw the text box (and other constituent controls that make up your particular ActiveX control) either before starting the Wizard or after the Wizard has completed. (If you need to use the Wizard to modify your control, you can always run it later by selecting a control.)

It's important to realize that the Wizard does not implement members, except via the process of *delegation* — where one control inherits properties, methods, or events from *constituent* controls. (Constituent controls are controls used to create the appearance and interface of another control.) This means that you are responsible for adding code that makes your user-defined members — meaning, custom members — work. Code added by the Wizard is essentially template-like in nature.

Here's the difference between events your control receives and events that it triggers. (Events that a control causes are said to be *raised* by the control.) You can place code in the event-handler framework of your control to respond to events it receives; event-handler framework code is created for the use of developers using your control so they can respond to events it raises.

First, create the appearance of the SelectText control by drawing a normal text box on the UserControl object. Use the Properties window to remove the default text property — Text1 — from the constituent control. (Later in this chapter, under "Making the Control Work," I'll show you how to add your own default Text or Caption properties to a control.)

Make sure that the SelectText UserControl object itself is not too big. Figure 25-3 shows a good size. Because the default dimensions of the ActiveX control when it is added to a container are determined by the size of the UserControl object, normally you don't want to overdo this.

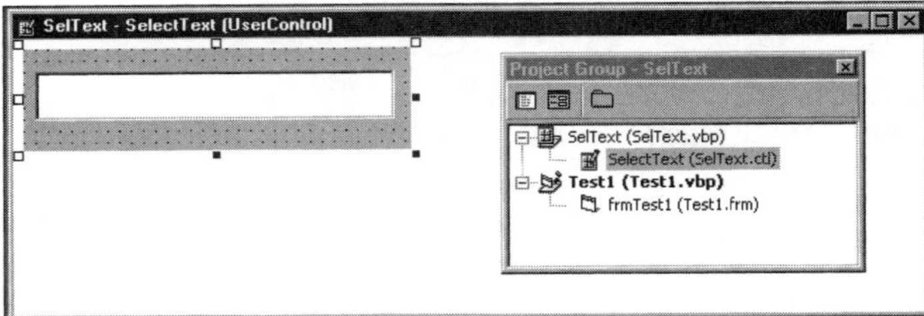

Figure 25-3: The size of the UserControl object determines the default size of the ActiveX control when it is placed on a container.

The SelectText control is supposed to look exactly like a text box. (All together now, one more time, "the appearance is the same, but the interface is different.")

To make the constituent text box the same size as the entire UserControl, add the code shown in Listing 25-1 to the UserControl's Resize event:

Listing 25-1: Sizing a constituent control to occupy the entire UserControl client area

```
Private Sub UserControl_Resize()
   Text1.Move 0, 0, ScaleWidth, ScaleHeight
End Sub
```

The UserControl Resize event is fired every time the control is created (or moved). You'll find that much of the generic code relating to control initialization and functionality is placed in this event.

Adding a Toolbox Icon for Your Control

You can add a custom Toolbox icon for your control using the ToolboxBitmap property of the UserControl object. When your control is selected, you can use the Properties window to set this property (the example uses a bitmap called ***Secrets.Bmp***, which is shown in Figure 25-4).

Ideally, Toolbox bitmaps should be about 26 pixels high and 26 pixels wide. Conventional icons of 32 pixels by 32 pixels are the wrong size and should not be used for this purpose. Also, you should ignore documentation that suggests a substantially smaller bitmap. I've found that bitmaps larger than 26 × 26 pixels get squashed when used for this purpose, and smaller bitmaps look a little lost.

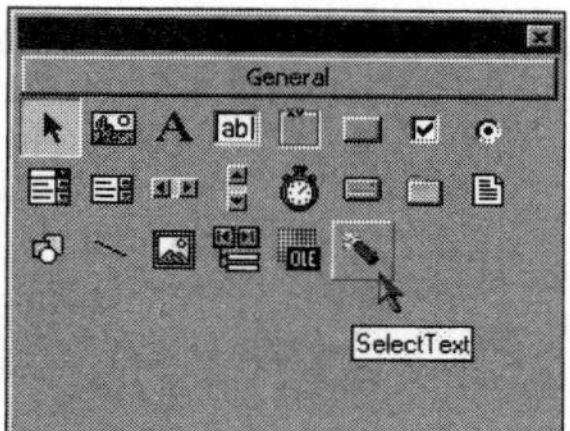

Figure 25-4: The right size for custom Toolbox bitmaps is roughly 26 × 26 pixels, like the SelectText bitmap of a firecracker shown here.

Running the Wizard

Enough of these preliminaries! Let's rock and roll! It's time to run the Control Interface Wizard by choosing it from the Add-Ins menu.

The first panel the Wizard displays summarizes what the Wizard does. You can elect not to see this screen when running the Wizard in the future, using a check box included on the panel.

You use the next panel — shown in Figure 25-5 — to select stock interface members. By default, the Wizard preselects standard members for your control (these appear in the Selected Names list box shown in Figure 25-5 when the panel opens).

Although you can use this panel to remove the standard members, in most cases you will want to leave the preselected standard members in the Selected Names list.

You can also use the Select Interface Members panel to add other commonly used members from a list of likely candidates. I've chosen to add the SelLength, SelStart, and SelText properties shown in Figure 25-5.

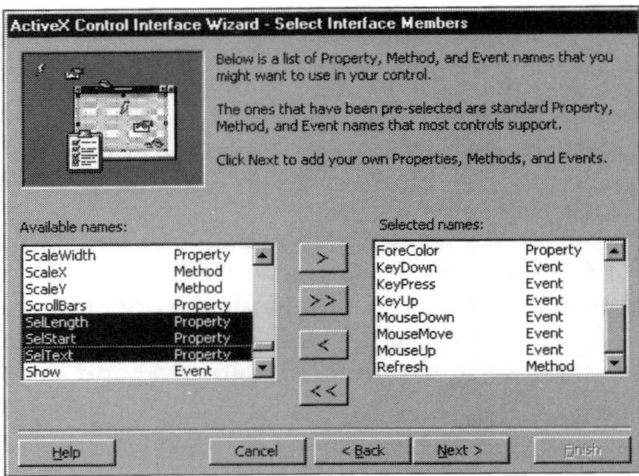

Figure 25-5: The Interface Wizard starts your control off with standard members and allows you to add other stock member names to your interface.

Generally, the intention when adding a standard member is to implement it through delegation of a control that will be constituent to your control.

The next Wizard panel allows you to add custom — user-defined — interface members. Figure 25-6 shows the Add Custom Member dialog, which appears when you click the New button on the Create Custom Interface Member panel. The Add Custom Member dialog allows you to name user-defined properties, events, and methods.

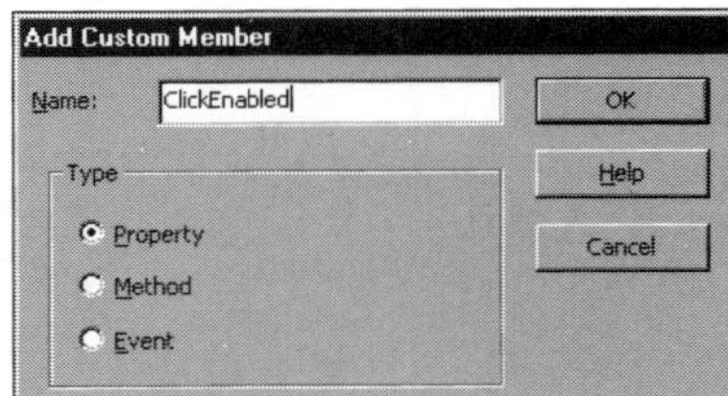

Figure 25-6: You can use the Add Custom Member dialog to create custom properties, events, and methods.

You can use the My Custom Members list in the Create Custom Interface Members panel, shown in Figure 25-7, to delete and edit member names, as well as create new custom member names. For example, if you decided you didn't like onSelectText as an event — maybe you really meant to define a method rather than an event, or maybe onReachingaGooglePlex would have been a more descriptive name — you can change it using the Edit Custom Member dialog shown in Figure 25-8, which you access by clicking the Edit button in the Create Custom Interface Members panel.

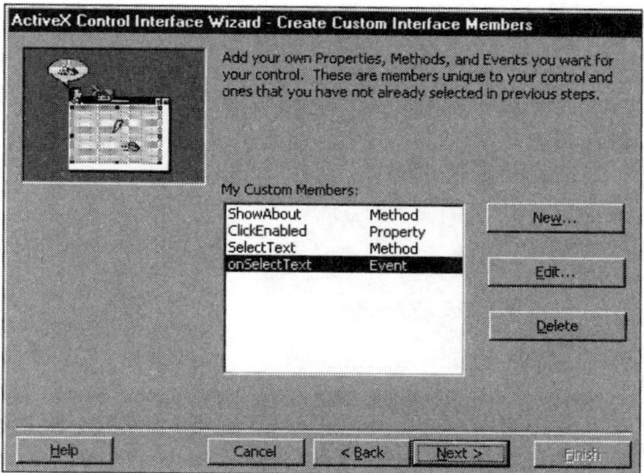

Figure 25-7: You use the Create Custom Interface Members panel to name the user-defined properties, methods, and events included in your control.

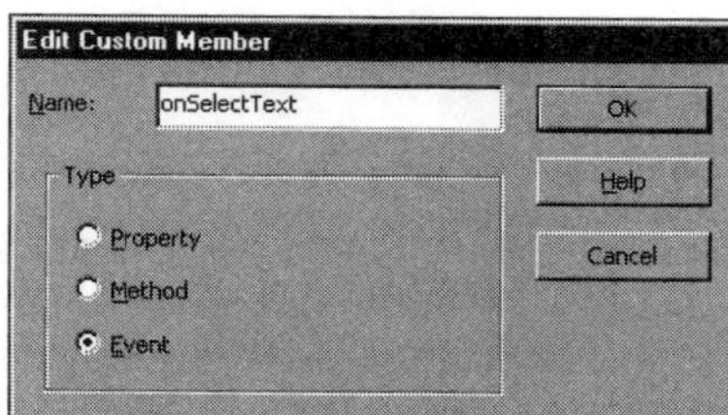

Figure 25-8: You can easily edit custom members using the Edit Custom Member dialog.

You use the next Wizard panel, Set Mapping (Figure 25-9), to map the functionality of members of your control to members of constituent controls. For example, if you map the UserControl Change event to the Change event of a constituent text control, the text control takes over the job of firing the UserControl's Change event.

Next, the Set Attributes panel, shown in Figure 25-10, helps you to set the attributes for each of your custom members. You use this panel to set the data type, the default value, whether the member can be saved and retrieved at design time and/or at runtime access, descriptive text that will appear at the bottom of the Properties window, and arguments if applicable.

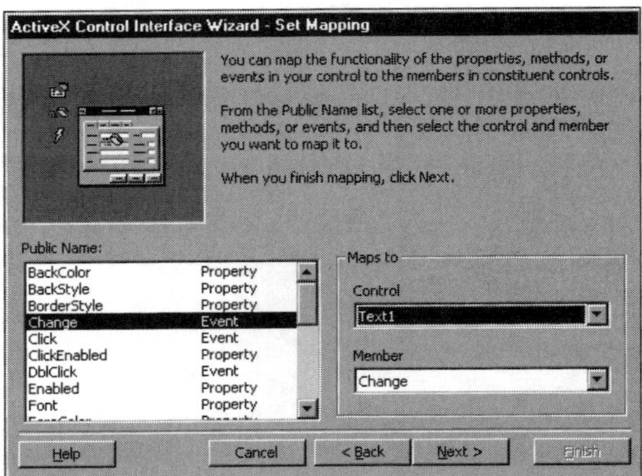

Figure 25-9: You can use the Set Mapping panel to map the functionality of your control's members to the members of constituent controls.

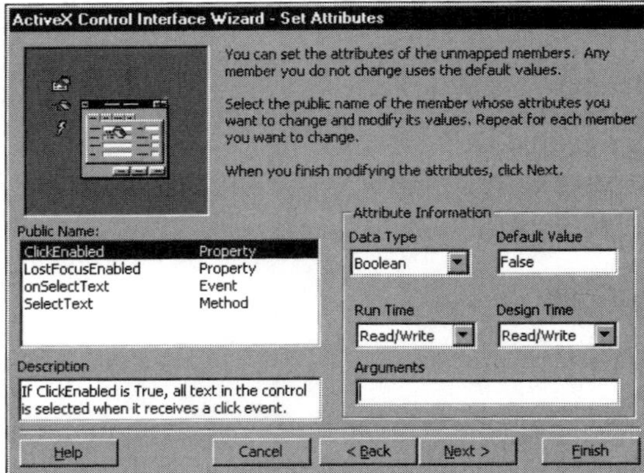

Figure 25-10: You can use the Set Attributes panel to set attribute information for custom control members.

Although custom members don't need arguments, methods and events will often, in fact, have parameters.

To create the template code for your control based on your choices within the Wizard, click Finish. (Note that you can always come back and run the Wizard again if you prefer to make changes to your control using the Wizard interface rather than directly in the Code Editor.)

As a final act of charity to the struggling developer, the Interface Wizard displays a summary To Do list of required steps for completing the debugging of your control interface, as shown in Figure 25-11. You can save and print the list for reference (a sample is saved on the companion CD-ROM as ***Ctlwiz.Txt***.)

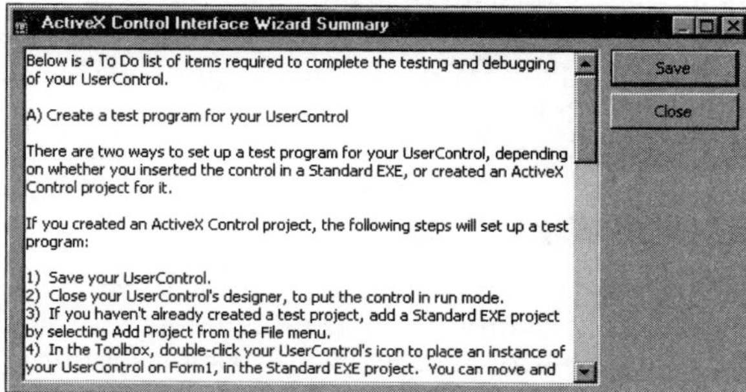

Figure 25-11: The Control Interface Wizard generates a summary report — that you can save for future reference — listing the remaining steps required to debug your control's interface.

Generally, you will have to take the following steps:

1. Save your control.
2. Close the control's *designer* — the window used for changing the appearance of the control. This places the control in run mode.
3. If the control is not already part of a project group containing a test project, add a standard executable project, using Add Project on the File menu. Save the combined projects as a project group (***.Vbg***) file. The standard executable project is used to test your control in both design and run modes.
4. Double-click your control's icon in the Toolbox to add it to the standard project's default form. If you haven't specified a Toolbox bitmap for the control as explained earlier, it will use a default icon.
5. Select your control on the form, and open the Properties window. Make sure you can see, and change, any properties you added to the control.
6. Change the value of one of your custom properties and close and open the form. Make sure that the changes to the value of your property were retained.
7. Open the Code window for your control, and make sure that any custom events you added to the control appear in the right-hand (Procedure) drop-down list in the Code window.

8. At this point, you may want to go back to the control (rather than the instance of the control that is on the form) to add code and tweak existing code to make the control functional. Note that you should delete the instance of the control that is on the form, and add a new instance once your modifications are complete.
9. Add some simple test code with the control on the form in design mode. For example, add MsgBox or Debug.Print statements to any events to make sure they are fired appropriately. Invoke methods to make sure they actually execute. Run the project, and make sure all is in order.

Verifying the Interface

Most of the steps in preceding list — which, essentially, were listed on the report supplied by the Control Interface Wizard upon its completion — involve verifying that the control interface works as it's supposed to.

Here's how you might do that using the SelectText control as an example. With the UserControl closed, add a SelectText control to the test form. Open the Properties window and check whether all the stock properties selected on the Wizard's Select Interface Members panel are listed. Next, verify that the custom properties you added using the Create Custom Interface Members are present and accounted for, and that they have the data type and default value selected in the Set Attributes panel. Figure 25-12 shows the custom property member ClickEnabled in the Properties Window.

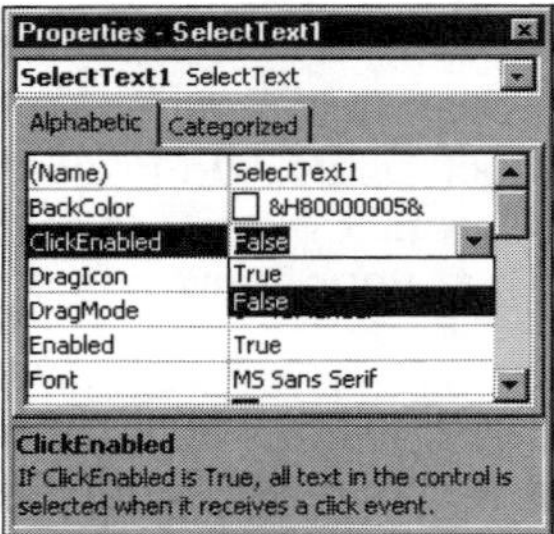

Figure 25-12: Custom properties should show up with the data type, default value, and description that were assigned using the Control Interface Wizard.

You should check that changes to custom property values persist, which is key to the functioning of a control. To do this, change the value of a custom property. For example, you could change the value of ClickEnabled from False to True. Destroy the instance of the SelectText control — for example, by closing the form it is on. Open the form to instance it again, and make sure that ClickEnabled is still set to True in the Properties window.

Next, make sure that custom control events have, in fact, been added to the event handler framework present in the test project's form module. Remember, events that are members of the control are fired by the control and give the user a chance to respond to them. They are not received by the control.

Figure 25-13 shows the Code Editor open with the onSelectText custom event handler displayed.

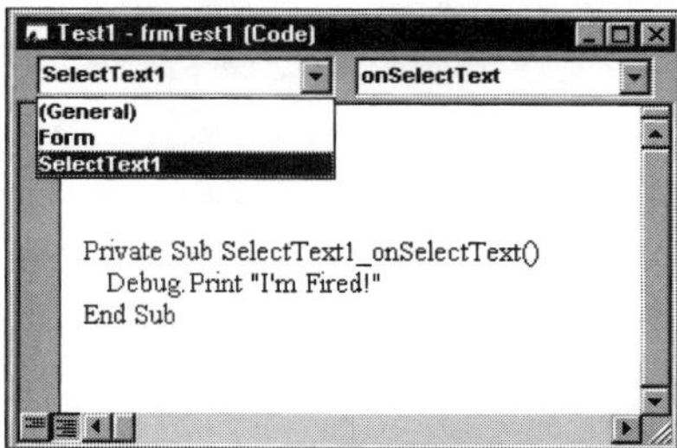

Figure 25-13: It's important to check that custom control events have been added to the test project's event handler structure.

Finally, it makes sense to check that custom control methods are actually invoked. To test this, you first have to reopen the UserControl module containing the control, and add a little code to the method procedure:

```
Public Function SelectText() As Boolean
   Debug.Print "SelectText method invoked"
End Function
```

If you didn't add some code to display a message to the method function, you'd have no way of knowing whether the method had been invoked.

Save and close the UserControl module. Return to the test project and delete the old instance of the SelectText control from the form. Add a new instance from the Toolbox.

You can now proceed to the form's Code Editor to add some test code to determine whether the control's method is appropriately invoked. Figure 25-14 shows a test method invocation being added to the form's click event. It's a very good sign that the custom SelectText method appears in the Properties/Methods drop-down list.

Here's the form click handler that calls the custom method:

```
Private Sub Form_Click()
   SelectText1.SelectText
End Sub
```

If you run the project and click the form, the Immediate Window will, indeed, display the message indicating that the control's custom method was called (see Figure 25-15).

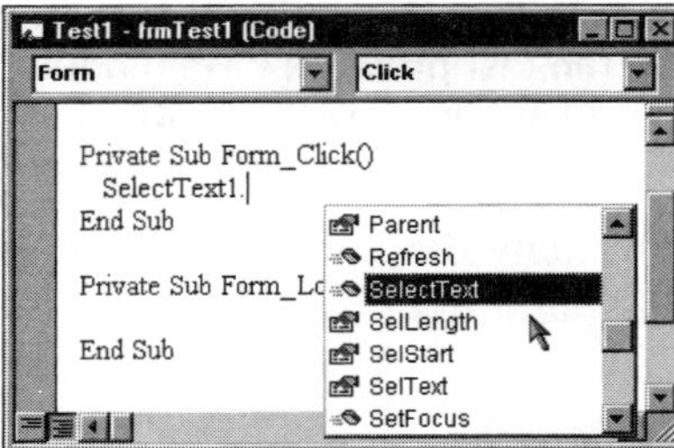

Figure 25-14: To test a custom control method, add a simple line of code that invokes it.

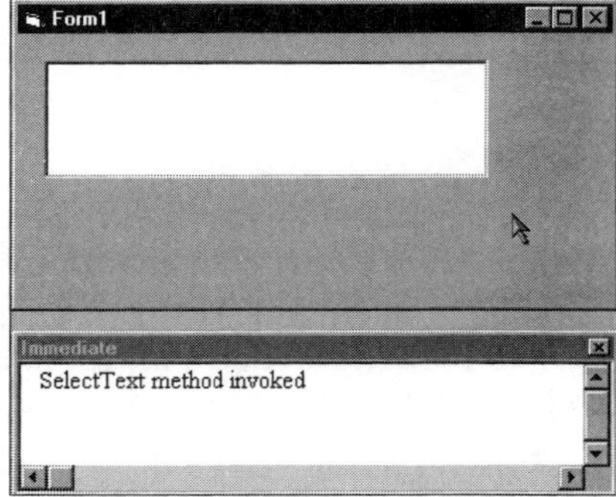

Figure 25-15: You must make sure that custom methods belonging to a control are actually invoked.

Brava! Bravo! A standing ovation! The tests show that the Interface Control Wizard has done its job well, and the control's interface is now complete. Of course, the control doesn't really do anything yet, but we'll get to that later.

What the Wizard Does

Remember the Wizard in the Wizard of Oz? The great and powerful Oz. Of course, in the end, the Wizard proved to be merely another fallible mortal — and Dorothy didn't need him, anyway. Once you understand what the ActiveX Control Interface Wizard does, you may come to feel the same way that Dorothy did. That is, who needs Wizards, anyway?

The Interface Wizard adds code to the UserControl module, based on your inputs. Let's have a detailed look at the code it adds.

First, the Wizard adds a constant definition for the default value of each custom property method, as shown in Listing 25-2.

Listing 25-2: Default property values

```
Const m_def_ClickEnabled = False
```

Next, as you can see in Listing 25-3, variables are declared for each custom property.

Listing 25-3: Property variables

```
Dim m_ClickEnabled As Boolean
```

Each event — including both custom events and stock events — is declared next, as shown in Listing 25-4.

Listing 25-4: Event declarations

```
Event Click()
Event DblClick()
Event KeyDown(KeyCode As Integer, Shift As Integer)
Event KeyPress(KeyAscii As Integer)
Event KeyUp(KeyCode As Integer, Shift As Integer)
Event MouseDown(Button As Integer, Shift As Integer, X As Single, _
   Y As Single)
Event MouseMove(Button As Integer, Shift As Integer, X As Single, _
   Y As Single)
Event MouseUp(Button As Integer, Shift As Integer, X As Single, _
   Y As Single)
Event Change()
Event onSelectText()
```

You'll notice that there is no difference in the way custom and stock events are declared.

Each property that is a member of the control's interface is given a matching Property Get and Property Let procedure. If a constituent control has mapped the property, the constituent's property is assigned to the UserControl in the Property Get procedure and the UserControl's property assigned to the constituent control in the Property Let procedure.

If an object rather than a variable is being set — for example, the font object — the Property Get procedure is paired with a Property Set procedure (rather than a Property Let procedure).

The PropertyChanged method is invoked in the Property Let procedures. This notifies the container that a control property value has changed. The control can then take appropriate action — such as synchronizing property values.

Listing 25-5 shows some property implementations.

The OLE_COLOR type used, in the BackColor and ForeColor property procedures, is defined in the OLE Automation library. You must use the Project References dialog to include the OLE Automation library in the project for these property procedures to run without generating a compile time error.

Listing 25-5: Property implementations

```
Public Property Get BackColor() As OLE_COLOR
   BackColor = Text1.BackColor
End Property

Public Property Let BackColor(ByVal New_BackColor As OLE_COLOR)
   Text1.BackColor = New_BackColor
   PropertyChanged "BackColor"
End Property

Public Property Get ForeColor() As OLE_COLOR
   ForeColor = Text1.ForeColor
End Property

Public Property Let ForeColor(ByVal New_ForeColor As OLE_COLOR)
   Text1.ForeColor = New_ForeColor
   PropertyChanged "ForeColor"
End Property

Public Property Get Enabled() As Boolean
   Enabled = Text1.Enabled
End Property

Public Property Let Enabled(ByVal New_Enabled As Boolean)
   Text1.Enabled = New_Enabled
   PropertyChanged "Enabled"
End Property

Public Property Get Font() As Font
   Set Font = Text1.Font
End Property

Public Property Set Font(ByVal New_Font As Font)
   Set Text1.Font = New_Font
   PropertyChanged "Font"
End Property

Public Property Get BorderStyle() As Integer
   BorderStyle = Text1.BorderStyle
End Property

Public Property Get SelText() As String
   SelText = Text1.SelText
End Property

Public Property Let SelText(ByVal New_SelText As String)
   Text1.SelText = New_SelText
   PropertyChanged "SelText"
End Property

Public Property Get SelStart() As Long
   SelStart = Text1.SelStart
End Property
```

```
Public Property Let SelStart(ByVal New_SelStart As Long)
   Text1.SelStart = New_SelStart
   PropertyChanged "SelStart"
End Property

Public Property Get SelLength() As Long
   SelLength = Text1.SelLength
End Property

Public Property Let SelLength(ByVal New_SelLength As Long)
   Text1.SelLength = New_SelLength
   PropertyChanged "SelLength"
End Property

Public Property Get Text() As String
   Text = Text1.Text
End Property

Public Property Let Text(ByVal New_Text As String)
   Text1.Text = New_Text
   PropertyChanged "Text"
End Property

'Custom properties follow
Public Property Get ClickEnabled() As Boolean
   ClickEnabled = m_ClickEnabled
End Property

Public Property Let ClickEnabled(ByVal New_ClickEnabled As Boolean)
   m_ClickEnabled = New_ClickEnabled
   PropertyChanged "ClickEnabled"
End Property
```

The Wizard provides code, shown in Listing 25-6, that implements delegate events:

Listing 25-6: Delegated events

```
Private Sub Text1_Change()
   RaiseEvent Change
End Sub

Private Sub Text1_Click()
   RaiseEvent Click
End Sub

Private Sub UserControl_DblClick()
   RaiseEvent DblClick
End Sub

Private Sub Text1_KeyDown(KeyCode As Integer, Shift As Integer)
   RaiseEvent KeyDown(KeyCode, Shift)
End Sub
```

```
Private Sub Text1_KeyPress(KeyAscii As Integer)
   RaiseEvent KeyPress(KeyAscii)
End Sub

Private Sub Text1_KeyUp(KeyCode As Integer, Shift As Integer)
   RaiseEvent KeyUp(KeyCode, Shift)
End Sub

Private Sub Text1_MouseDown(Button As Integer, Shift As Integer, X As
Single, Y As Single)
   RaiseEvent MouseDown(Button, Shift, X, Y)
End Sub

Private Sub Text1_MouseMove(Button As Integer, Shift As Integer, X As
Single, Y As Single)
   RaiseEvent MouseMove(Button, Shift, X, Y)
End Sub

Private Sub Text1_MouseUp(Button As Integer, Shift As Integer, X As
Single, Y As Single)
   RaiseEvent MouseUp(Button, Shift, X, Y)
End Sub
```

Next, the custom control properties are initialized with their default values, as shown in Listing 25-7.

Listing 25-7: Initializing properties

```
Private Sub UserControl_InitProperties()
   m_ClickEnabled = m_def_ClickEnabled
End Sub
```

As Listing 25-8 shows, a routine is added that will read persistent property values from storage using the PropertyBag object.

Listing 25-8: Loading property values from storage

```
Private Sub UserControl_ReadProperties(PropBag As PropertyBag)
   Text1.BackColor = PropBag.ReadProperty("BackColor", &H80000005)
   Text1.ForeColor = PropBag.ReadProperty("ForeColor", &H80000008)
   Text1.Enabled = PropBag.ReadProperty("Enabled", True)
   Set Font = PropBag.ReadProperty("Font")
   Text1.SelText = PropBag.ReadProperty("SelText", "")
   Text1.SelStart = PropBag.ReadProperty("SelStart", 0)
   Text1.SelLength = PropBag.ReadProperty("SelLength", 0)
   Text1.Text = PropBag.ReadProperty("Text", "")
   m_ClickEnabled = PropBag.ReadProperty("ClickEnabled", _
      m_def_ClickEnabled)
End Sub
```

Values that are read must also be written. The Wizard adds a routine that writes property values using the PropertyBag, as shown in Listing 25-9.

Listing 25-9: Writing property values to storage

```
Private Sub UserControl_WriteProperties(PropBag As PropertyBag)
   Call PropBag.WriteProperty("BackColor", Text1.BackColor, _
```

```
        &H80000005)
    Call PropBag.WriteProperty("ForeColor", Text1.ForeColor, _
        &H80000008)
    Call PropBag.WriteProperty("Enabled", Text1.Enabled, True)
    Call PropBag.WriteProperty("Font", Font)
    Call PropBag.WriteProperty("SelText", Text1.SelText, "")
    Call PropBag.WriteProperty("SelStart", Text1.SelStart, 0)
    Call PropBag.WriteProperty("SelLength", Text1.SelLength, 0)
    Call PropBag.WriteProperty("Text", Text1.Text, "")
    Call PropBag.WriteProperty("ClickEnabled", m_ClickEnabled, _
        m_def_ClickEnabled)
End Sub
```

That's absolutely all there is to it! You'll want to understand the code the Wizard has created. Even if you use the Wizard to get you started on a control, it's often easier to modify code by hand rather than run the Wizard again when you need to change the interface application.

Wizards! Piffle! This, if necessary, you can do for yourself.

Making the Control Work

Making the control work means implementing the interface. This implies adding code to the SelectText control that adds functionality to its two custom properties, custom method, and custom event. But first, let's set up the SelectText control so it displays an appropriate default Text property.

Adding a Default Text Value

If you added a plain vanilla Text control to a form, the control would be initialized with a default Text property of Text1, the name of the control. It's easy to use the Extender object to add a comparable default value feature for your control's Text (or Caption) property. (For a detailed explanation of the Extender object, see the section, "Controls and Containers," in Chapter 24.)

Our sample control is named SelectText. The default name provided for the first instance of the control is SelectText1. "SelectText1," then, is the string that should appear as the default value for SelectText1.Text, as shown in Figure 25-16.

To implement this, you first need to add a variable to hold the value of the control's text property. (If a delegated Text property had not been added to the control using the Wizard, you would also have to add appropriate Property procedures manually.)

Next you'll have to add code to SelectText's UserControl_InitProperties() event to let its Text property be the default name of the control. For this particular control, because its entire visible presence is the constituent Text control, you'll also need to add code that changes the Text1.Text as well. (Without it, the default text value in the Properties Window would change, but not the text displayed on the control.)

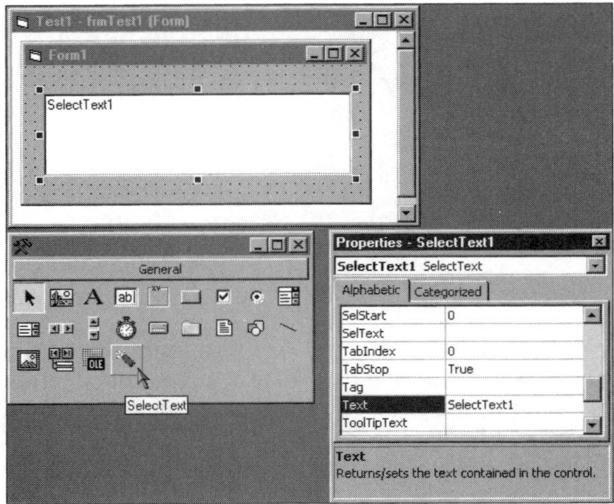

Figure 25-16: You can use the properties of the container's Extender object to set default values for your control's properties.

Listing 25-10 shows how to change the default Text property to the control's name.

Listing 25-10: Changing the default Text property to the control's name

```
'Property Variables:
...
Dim m_Text As String
...
'Initialize Properties for User Control
Private Sub UserControl_InitProperties()
   ...
   m_Text = Extender.Name
   Text1.Text = m_Text
End Sub
```

You'll also need to add a line of code in the UserControl module to the Text Property Let procedure to make sure that the text value displayed on the constituent text control is updated when the user changes the value of the text property for the SelectText instance in the Properties window:

```
Public Property Let Text(ByVal New_Text As String)
   m_Text = New_Text
   Text1.Text = m_Text 'Added for dynamic display change
   PropertyChanged "Text"
End Property
```

Implementing the SelectText Method

A custom control method that has been added to the control's interface is simply an empty function. For example:

```
Public Function SelectText() As Boolean

End Function
```

You can add any code you'd like to the function to implement the method.

Because we'll be invoking the logic that selects the contents of the control from a number of places, it makes sense to create a new procedure to handle the actual work, as shown in Listing 25-11.

Listing 25-11: The SelectText method

```
Public Function SelectText() As Boolean
   DoItToTheText
End Function

Private Sub DoItToTheText()
   Text1.SelStart = 0
   Text1.SelLength = Len(Text1.Text)
End Sub
```

The logic of this text selection procedure was discussed in the section "Finding Files on Disk" in Chapter 16, "Optimizing Secrets."

To test that this method works, invoke it from the test form. For example:

```
Private Sub Form_Click()
   SelectText1.SelectText
End Sub
```

If you now run the test project, enter some text in the SelectText control, and click the form, all text in the form will be selected, as shown in Figure 25-17.

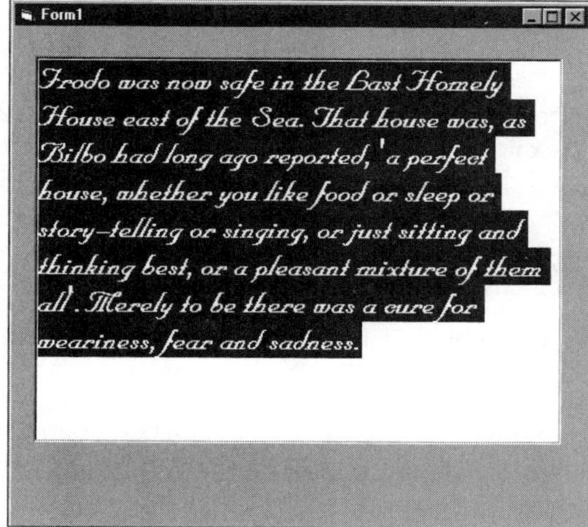

Figure 25-17: You can implement control methods using standard Visual Basic statements and procedures.

The SelectText control shown in Figure 25-17 accepts multiple lines of text. This was achieved by setting the Multiline property of the constituent Text control to True.

Implementing the onSelectText Event

You're responsible for making sure that custom events are fired when you want them to be in your controls. Visual Basic is not, unfortunately, a mind reader, and cannot take care of this for you.

You use the RaiseEvent statement to fire an event. (Events, of course, must also be declared in the UserControl module.) Because the onSelectText event should be fired every time DoItToTheText is invoked, it makes sense to raise the event from within that procedure. It also makes sense to check that the Text control actually contained some text for selection before firing it.

Listing 25-12 contains the revised code:

Listing 25-12: Raising a custom event

```
Private Sub DoItToTheText()
   If Text1.Text <> "" Then
      Text1.SelStart = 0
      Text1.SelLength = Len(Text1.Text)
      RaiseEvent onSelectText
   End If
End Sub
```

To test that onSelectText event is actually fired when it's supposed to be, code must be added to the test project's event-handler structure:

```
Private Sub SelectText1_onSelectText()
   Debug.Print "I'm Fired!"
End Sub
```

Now, open the Immediate window and run the project. When you call the SelectText method — by clicking the form — the text is selected and the Immediate window shows that onSelectText was fired (see Figure 25-18).

Implementing Custom Properties

The custom property ClickEnabled is already implemented — in the sense that its Boolean value persists across control creation and destruction, and the property appears in the Properties window. The trick is to do something with the property. This involves calling the DoItToTheText routine from the control's Click events, respectively, but only if the appropriate property is True.

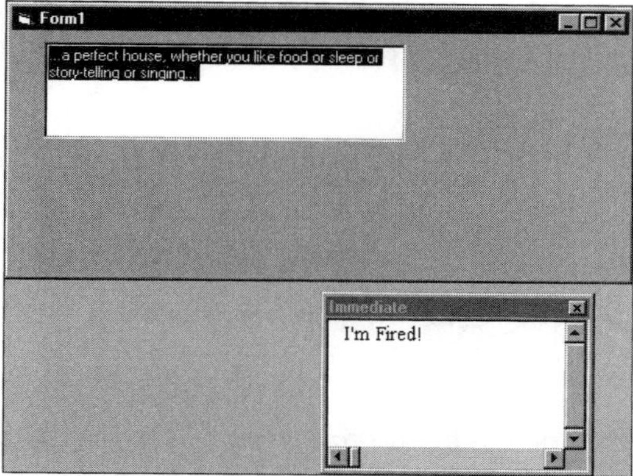

Figure 25-18: You use the RaiseEvent statement to fire an event from the control that is received by the project containing the control.

Here's code in the UserControl's Text1_Click handler that accomplishes this goal:

```
Private Sub Text1_Click()
   If ClickEnabled Then
      DoItToTheText
   End If
   RaiseEvent Click
End Sub
```

Obviously, it's easy enough to test that this works by adding the revised control to the test form, running the test project, adding some text to the SelectText control, and clicking it. It does work — but only if you first set the ClickEnabled property to True.

Recap

To summarize, you must add the following pieces of code to a UserControl's code for a property to show up and perform as expected in the control's interface (for example, Properties window):

1. Define a constant as the default property value, for example:

   ```
   Const m_def_MessageText = "Do you really want to click me?"
   ```

2. Declare a variable of the appropriate type for the property, for instance:

   ```
   Dim m_MessageText As String
   ```

3. Write Property Get and Property Let procedures for the property per the preceding examples.

4. Add ReadProperties and WriteProperties Property Bag method calls using the methods of the UserControl object, as shown a moment ago.

This seems to me not much more difficult than using the Wizard.

Although the Interface Wizard pretty much handles the details of creating custom properties for you, it does no such thing for methods and events. A UserControl method is simply a public function. The Wizard does add the code framework for the function, along the lines of:

```
Public Function ShowMessage() As Variant
...
End Function
```

It's up to you to take care of adding the code that makes the method tick. (The return type the Wizard creates for the function depends on what you entered in the Set Attributes dialog.)

As far as events go, the Interface Wizard adds an event declaration depending on events you have included in the Select Interface Members and Create Custom Interface Members dialogs:

```
'Event Declarations:
...
Event MouseDown(Button As Integer, Shift As Integer, x As Single,_
   Y As Single)
...
Event onShowMessage()
```

This serves to add an event-handling framework for declared events when the control is added to a container (such as a form). Parameters that are displayed in the Code window for the event handler depend on the arguments listed in the declaration, which you can also establish in the Set Attributes dialog of the Wizard.

It's up to you to implement within the UserControl code module anything that triggers the event. (When the event is fired, the code entered by developers using your control in the event-handler framework is executed.)

To fire an event, use the UserControl's RaiseEvent method:

```
RaiseEvent onShowMessage
```

To Wizard or not to Wizard: The choice is yours! Either way, you'll want to have a good grasp of the underlying code implementation of a UserControl.

The Property Page Wizard

Property pages are an alternative interface that you can make available to developers who use your controls. They are accessed via a button in the value field of the (Custom) property that appears towards the top of the list of properties in the Property window, as shown in Figure 25-19.

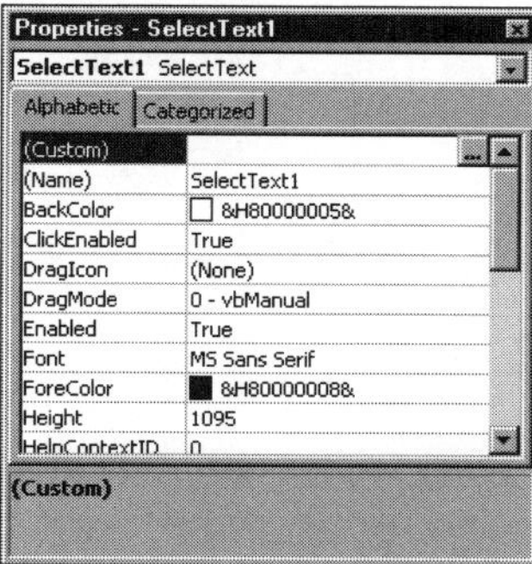

Figure 25-19: You can access property pages by clicking the ellipsis in the value field of the Custom property in the Properties window.

As a developer who has used ActiveX controls, you are probably familiar with property pages and their appearance; they consist of a tabbed set of dialogs, with one page per tab. Each page allows users of the control to set properties using conventional controls (rather than using the sometimes awkward Properties window).

The source code for each property page associated with a control is stored in a ***.Pag*** file. These files are ASCII text files similar in structure to normal Visual Basic form module files (***.Frm*** files). This means that they contain internal references to encapsulated controls and their properties that — in theory — could be edited using a text editor.

You modify property pages just the way you modify forms: using the Toolbox, the Properties window, and the Code Editor.

Each property page file becomes a node in the Property Pages folder under the control's project, as displayed in the Project Explorer (see Figure 25-20).

You can add property pages to a control in two ways:

- By running the Property Page Wizard
- By choosing Add Property Page from the Project menu with the control selected

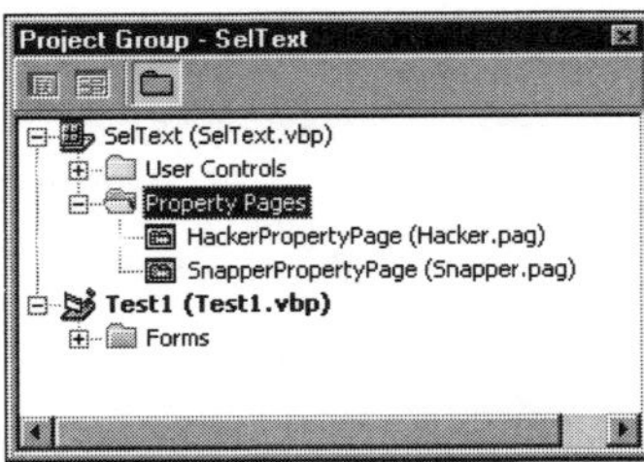

Figure 25-20: Property pages are stored in ***.Pag*** files, which are displayed as nodes of a UserControl project in the Project Explorer.

Running the Property Page Wizard

Before you can run the Property Page Wizard, you must enable it using the Add-In Manager.

To start the Property Page Wizard, make sure your UserControl object is selected. The first panel of the Wizard lets you add the property pages you'd like. The Wizard will generate property pages for each named page that is checked in the Select Property Pages dialog (shown in Figure 25-21). By default, StandardColor and StandardFont pages will be created; if you don't want them, be sure to unselect them.

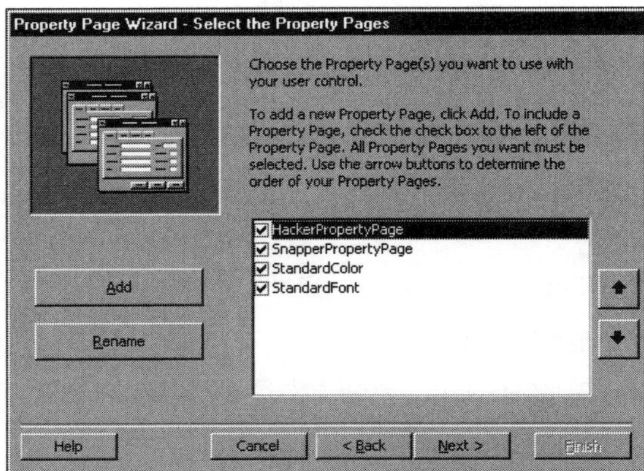

Figure 25-21: You can use the Wizard's Select the Property Pages dialog to easily add custom property pages.

The next step is to add the properties you want to the appropriate pages, as shown in Figure 25-22.

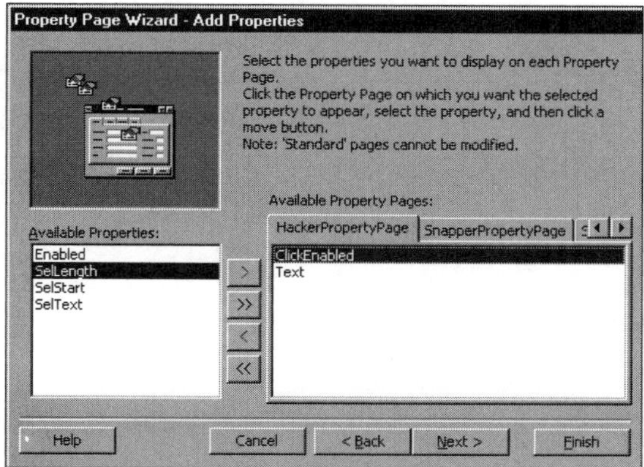

Figure 25-22: You can use the Add Properties dialog to assign any available property to any available property page.

Based on the information you have provided, the Wizard generates your property page (or pages). A report of what you still must do to make the property pages functional is generated as its final step. Typically, this will consist of checking the code the Wizard has generated for comments labeled "TO DO" and following the directions contained in the comments. (For simple property pages, there may even be nothing further to do.)

Often, you'll want to modify the appearance of the property pages generated by the Wizard. For example, the property page shown in Figure 25-23 had a text field that was originally captioned "Text." "Enter text that sings..." is much more interesting.

You can use the property page's designer to change the appearance of the property page — just as you would with a normal form.

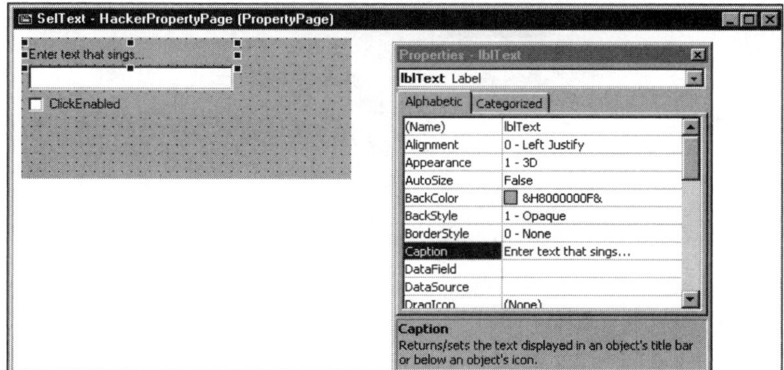

Figure 25-23: You can change the appearance of a custom property page using its designer, in the same way that you would alter a form.

When you close the property page's designer (and the control's, if it is open) and open the form containing the control, you'll find a (Custom) item at the top of the Properties window for the control. When you click the button in the value field for this item, you'll see the custom property page you have created, as shown in Figure 25-24.

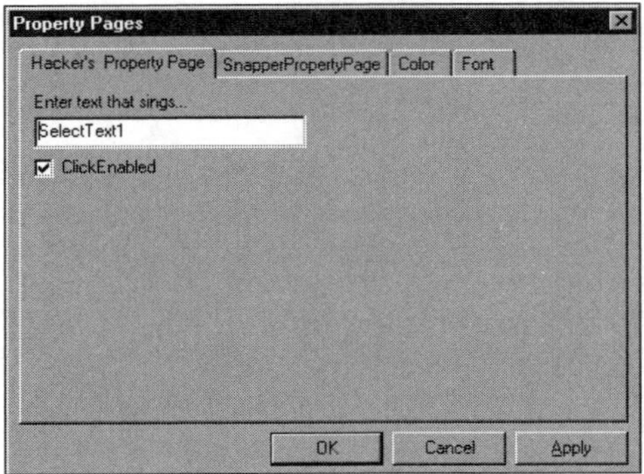

Figure 25-4: Property pages you have added to your control are accessed from the top item in the Properties window and are organized as a tabbed dialog.

The Standard Font property page, automatically generated by the Wizard, is wonderfully functional, and quite nifty (see Figure 25-25).

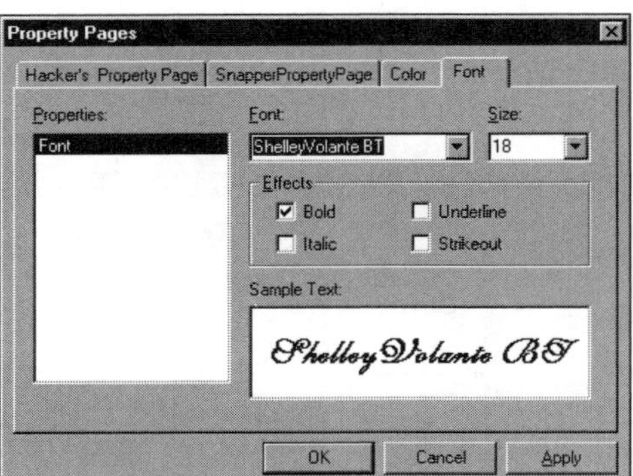

Figure 25-25: The Wizard automatically generates the Standard Font property page.

Adding Property Pages Manually

To add a property page manually, first add a new property page to your project using Add Property Page from the Project menu. Next, add controls and manipulate the properties of the controls and the property page using the page's designer. This works just like designing a form. Figure 25-26 shows a custom property page (saved as ***Custom.Pag***) being designed.

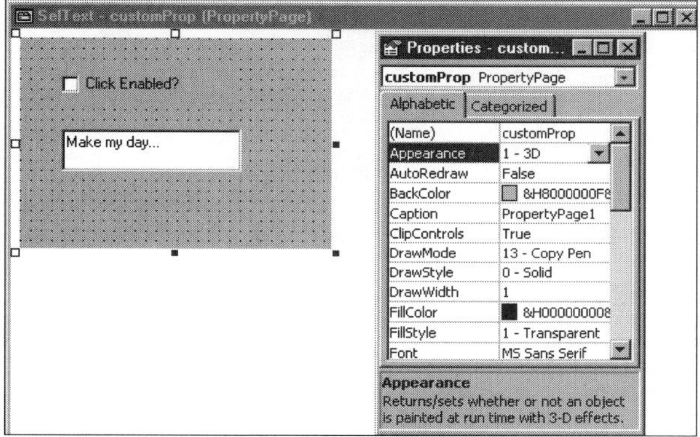

Figure 25-26: You design the appearance of a custom property page just like you design a form.

The next step is to connect the property page to the control. You do this using the Connect Property Pages dialog, shown in Figure 25-27.

To access this dialog, select your UserControl and double-click the PropertyPages property in the Properties window.

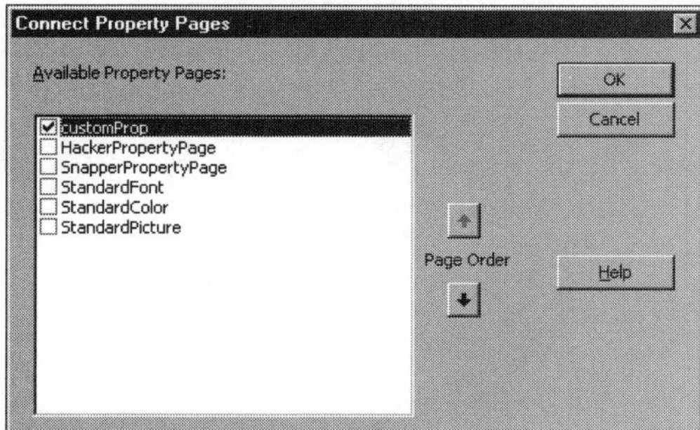

Figure 25-27: You use the Connect Property Pages dialog to connect custom property pages to a control.

Finally, you must add some code to the new property page to make it functional. The code added to the property page's module to make it functional is not terribly extensive (see listing 25-13). You'll have to modify it depending on the names of the controls on your property pages — and the names of the UserControl properties they relate to.

Listing 25-13: Code required to make a custom property page functional

```
Option Explicit
Private Sub chkClickEnabled_Click()
   Changed = True
End Sub

Private Sub txtText_Change()
    Changed = True
End Sub

Private Sub PropertyPage_ApplyChanges()
   SelectedControls(0).ClickEnabled = _
      (chkClickEnabled.Value = vbChecked)
   SelectedControls(0).Text = txtText.Text
End Sub

Private Sub PropertyPage_SelectionChanged()
   chkClickEnabled.Value = (SelectedControls(0).ClickEnabled _
      And vbChecked)
   txtText.Text = SelectedControls(0).Text
End Sub
```

Figure 25-28 shows the custom property page and the UserControl properties that can be changed using it.

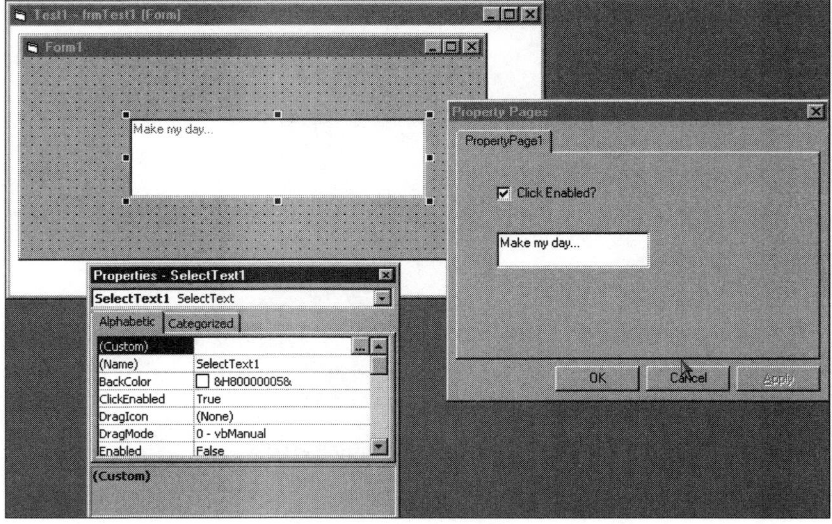

Figure 25-28: It's not hard to wire a custom property page so that it is fully functional.

Adding an About Dialog to Your Control

You can easily add a custom About box to your control. Developers using your control can open this dialog at design time by clicking the button in the value field of the About property in the Properties window. You can use the About box to provide contact, copyright, authorship, and "vanity plate" information about your control.

First create your About form, and add it to the ActiveX control project. (In the example, this form is named dlgAbout. You may remember it as the About box containing an Easter egg from Chapter 19, "Runtime Display Secrets.")

Be sure to add the About form to the control project, not the test project that is part of the same project group. Otherwise, the form object will not be in scope within the control.

Next, open the Code window for the UserControl object, and add the following procedure:

```
Public Sub ShowAbout()
    dlgAbout.Show vbModal
    Unload dlgAbout
    Set dlgAbout = Nothing
End Sub
```

With the Code window still open, choose Procedure Attributes from the Tools menu. Click the Advanced button to expand the Procedure Attributes dialog, as shown in Figure 25-29.

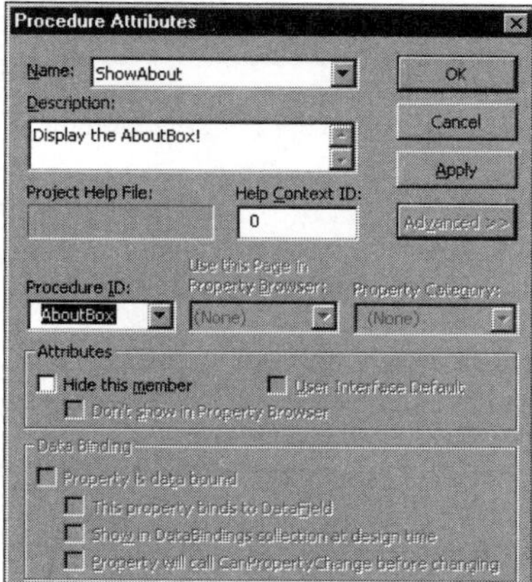

Figure 25-29: You can use the Procedures Attributes dialog to assign a procedure that shows an About box to an identifier that causes it to display in the Properties window.

Make sure that ShowAbout is selected in the Name list box, and assign it to the AboutBox Procedure ID.

If you'd like, you can add a fanciful description such as "Display the AboutBox!" This description will appear in the Properties window when the About box is selected.

You can assign the same About box to as many controls as you'd like within a project.

If you open the form in the test project in design mode and go to the Properties window with the SelectText control selected, you'll see an About field in the Properties window. Clicking the button on the right of the About field displays the About box, as shown in Figure 25-30.

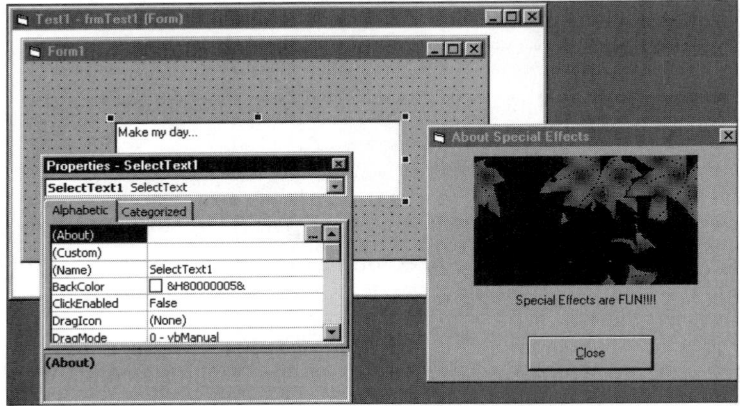

Figure 25-30: It's easy to add a professional touch to your controls with an About box.

Summary

This chapter has shown in detail how to create and implement the interface for a simple but sturdy custom control, SelectText. SelectText is based on a constituent control, meaning that much of its interface is delegated to the Text control that was placed on it in design mode.

Topics covered in this chapter included

- Designing the appearance of a control
- Running the ActiveX Control Interface Wizard
- Setting up a control project

- Constituent controls and delegation
- Adding a control Toolbox icon
- Verifying a control interface
- Control interface code
- Making the control work
- Adding default property values
- Implementing custom properties
- The Property Page Wizard
- Manually adding property pages
- Adding an About box to the control

Chapter 26

Implementing Control Functionality

Chapter 24, "Understanding ActiveX Controls," explained the key concepts you'll need to know to create your own controls, and Chapter 25, "Creating the Control Interface," explained how to construct the interface for a control based on a constituent Text control.

This chapter takes up where Chapters 24 and 25 left off. I'll cover a smorgasbord of more advanced topics of control construction, including:

- Adding enumerated types to a control's interface
- Adding custom dialogs to the Properties window
- Basing a control on several constituent controls
- Runtime and design time functionality
- User-drawn controls
- Understanding UserControl objects

Along the way, I'll provide some examples of interesting controls.

The Sticky Frame Control

Perhaps you'll recall the "Locking Users Onto a Control" example in Chapter 11, which demonstrated the use of the GetDesktopWindow, GetWindowRect, and ClipCursor APIs to restrict the cursor within the area of a control.

In "Extending an Existing Control" in Chapter 14, the example was recycled to show how to use class modules to create a delegated Frame control. In another words, the built-in Frame control was *wrapped*, along with a class module, to create a pseudo new Frame control with Stick and UnStick methods. The techniques demonstrated in Chapter 14 were not dependent on the ability to create true ActiveX controls.

Clearly, it's a far better solution to create a whole new ActiveX control, StickyFrame. To use it in a project, all you need do is add it from the Toolbox. The ActiveX mechanism takes care of creating and destroying instances of the control. This means that — unlike in the Chapter 14 demonstration — we don't have to worry about coding Create and Destroy methods for the control.

The source code for the control is saved in a module named ***Sticky.Ctl*** in a project group named ***Sticky.Vbg***. Figure 26-1 shows the project group structure for the StickyFrame control and test project in Project Explorer.

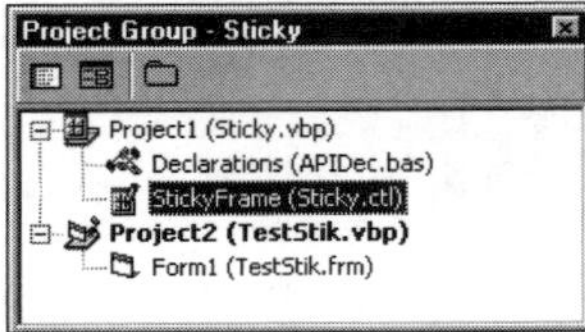

Figure 26-1: You can view the project hierarchy for the StickyFrame control project group in Project Explorer.

The first step is to add a Frame control to the StickFrame UserControl object, as shown in Figure 26-2.

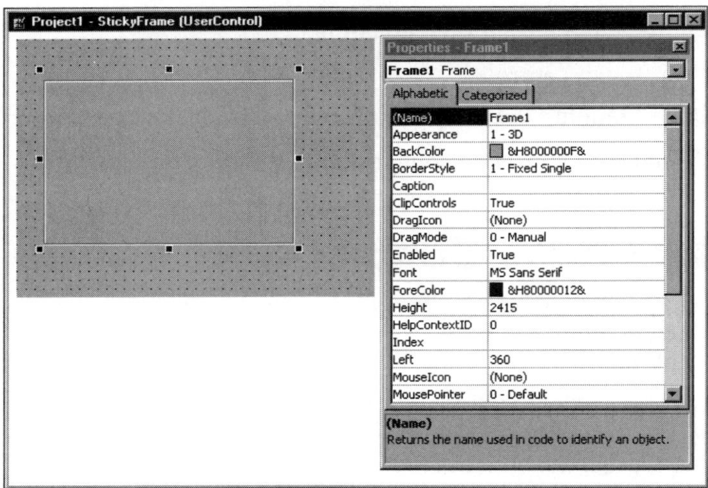

Figure 26-2: Because the StickyFrame is based on a Frame control, you must add the Frame control to the StickyFrame UserControl object.

To make sure that the StickyFrame will be sized like its constituent Frame control, add appropriate code to the StickFrame UserControl Resize event:

```
Private Sub UserControl_Resize()
   Frame1.Move 0, 0, ScaleWidth, ScaleHeight
End Sub
```

Because the StickyFrame is supposed to behave like a regular frame — with the addition of a couple of methods — most of the members of the Frame control should be mapped into the StickyFrame UserControl.

You can use the Properties window list of properties for the Frame control, partially shown in Figure 26-2, to gather a list of constituent control properties that should be mapped. In addition to the properties shown in the Properties window, you should be sure to map an hWnd property for the frame constituent control. GetWindowRect requires a handle to a "window" as a parameter, so the Stick method will not work without it.

It's up to you whether you like to create the code containing the StickyFrame interface — and constituent control mapping — manually or using the ActiveX Control Interface Wizard. (See Chapter 25 for explanations of both courses.) Whichever way you choose to generate it, you need an internal code structure including Property procedures and control persistence routines.

Members are declared, for example:

```
Event Click()
```

Property procedures are added, with constituent mapping as appropriate:

```
...
Public Property Get BorderStyle() As Integer
   BorderStyle = Frame1.BorderStyle
End Property

Public Property Let BorderStyle(ByVal New_BorderStyle As Integer)
   Frame1.BorderStyle() = New_BorderStyle
   PropertyChanged "BorderStyle"
End Property
...
Public Property Get hWnd() As Long
   hWnd = Frame1.hWnd
End Property
...
```

Because the Frame's hWnd — or, window handle — property is read only, it is implemented with a Property Get procedure that is not matched with a Property Let (or Set) procedure.

Property persistence and the control life cycle is handled:

```
'Load property values from storage
Private Sub UserControl_ReadProperties(PropBag As PropertyBag)
   ...
   Frame1.BorderStyle = PropBag.ReadProperty("BorderStyle", 1)
   ...
End Sub
...
'Write property values to storage
Private Sub UserControl_WriteProperties(PropBag As PropertyBag)
   ...
   Call PropBag.WriteProperty("BorderStyle", Frame1.BorderStyle, 1)
   ...
End Sub
```

It would be nice to have the StickyFrame initialize with the name of the instance of the ActiveX control as the value of its caption property — for example, StickyFrame1, as shown in Figure 26-3.

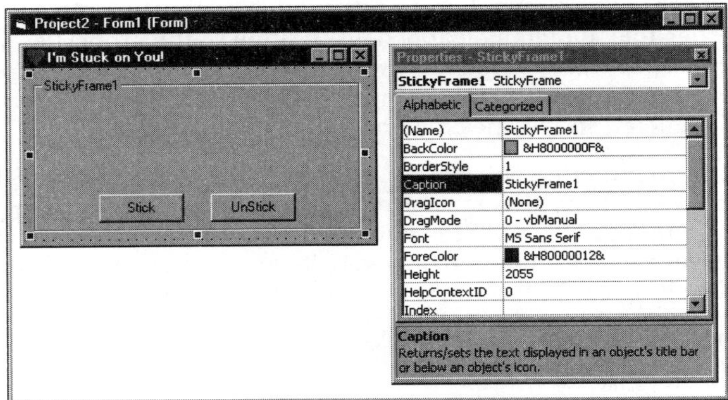

Figure 26-3: ActiveX controls should, by default, have the initial value of the control's caption (or text) property be the control's name.

To make this so, add code to the UserControl's InitProperties event that assigns the value of the Extender.Name property to the constituent caption:

```
Private Sub UserControl_InitProperties()
   Frame1.Caption = Extender.Name
End Sub
```

It's time to implement the control methods, Stick and UnStick.

First, add the module containing API types and declarations (***APIDec.Bas***) to the UserControl project.

Declare a local in scope to the UserControl variable of the Windows RECT type. This variable will hold the dimensions of the rectangle that the cursor is restricted to.

Also, declare a private Boolean variable (named Stuck) for keeping track of whether the cursor has been restricted. It should be initialized to False when the instance of the UserControl is created — meaning, in its Initialize event:

```
Private FrameRect As RECT
Private Stuck As Boolean

Private Sub UserControl_Initialize()
   Stuck = False
End Sub
```

The implementation of the Stick and UnStick methods themselves is quite straightforward:

```
Public Function Stick() As Boolean
   Stick = False
   GetWindowRect Me.hwnd, FrameRect
   ClipCursor FrameRect
   Stuck = True
   Stick = True
End Function

Public Function UnStick() As Boolean
   Dim ScreenRect As RECT, ScreenHandle As Long
   UnStick = False
   ScreenHandle = GetDesktopWindow
   GetWindowRect ScreenHandle, ScreenRect
   ClipCursor ScreenRect
   Stuck = False
   UnStick = True
End Function
```

It's good practice to provide return values for your methods that indicate whether they have succeeded. Users are not required to check the return value, but they have the option of doing so if they wish.

It's a good idea to build a fail-safe provision into this control, to make sure the cursor is not locked when the control is destroyed — even if the user has forgotten to invoke the UnStick method. This code should go in the UserControl's Terminate event:

```
Private Sub UserControl_Terminate()
   If Stuck Then
      Me.UnStick
   End If
End Sub
```

To test the control, save it and close it. Add the new StickyFrame control to a form in the test project. Add two buttons, cmdStick and cmdUnStick, to the StickyFrame. It's very simple to call the StickyFrame's methods:

```
Private Sub cmdStick_Click()
   StickyFrame1.Stick
End Sub

Private Sub cmdUnStick_Click()
    StickyFrame1.UnStick
End Sub
```

If you run the project, once cmdStick has been clicked — and the StickyFrame's Stick method invoked — the cursor is locked on the control until the UnStick method is called (see Figure 26-4). It's really pretty easy to create new controls, such as the StickyFrame, that extend the capabilities of existing controls.

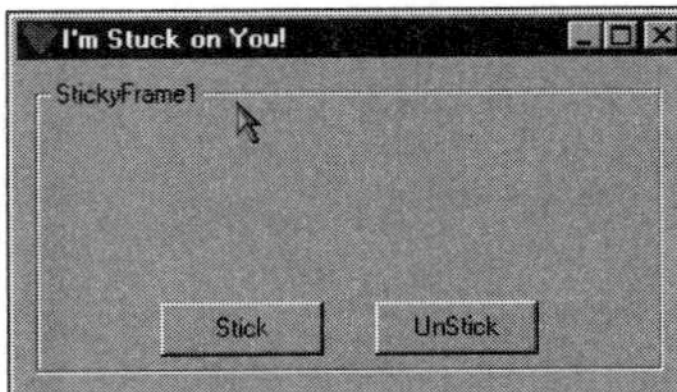

Figure 26-4: The cursor is held in bondage by the StickyFrame control.

Enumerated-Type Properties

If you play with the interface of the StickyFrame control — by entering values in the Properties window with the control selected — you'll find that some of the custom control properties don't work quite as you might like.

A good case in point is the BorderStyle property, which is used to determine whether a frame has a border. In a regular old Frame control, BorderStyle has two possible values, 0-None or 1-Fixed Single. The developer using the control can select between the two using a drop-down list in the Properties window.

However, the StickyFrame control does not present the same interface in the Properties Window. BorderStyle simply accepts any integer value that the user cares to enter. If the user enters anything other than 0 or 1, a runtime error results, as shown in Figure 26-5.

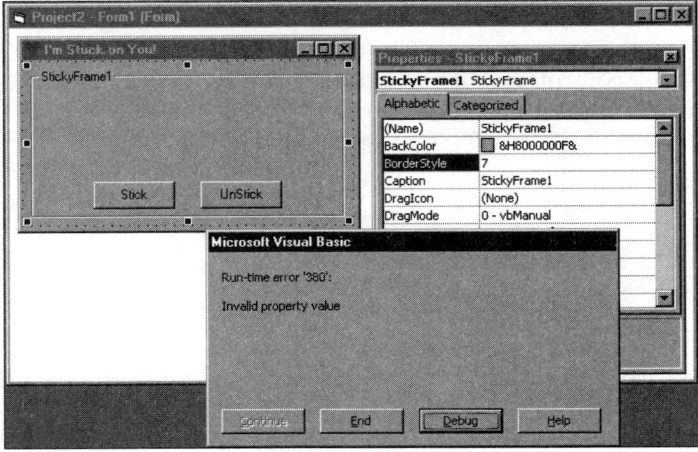

Figure 26-5: If you enter anything other than 0 or 1 as a value for the StickyFrame BorderStyle property, you'll get a runtime error.

Enumerated Types

You declare enumerated types at the module level using the Enum statement. Enumerated types consist of a set of members, each of which can be assigned a constant long value. For example:

```
Enum WildAnimals
   Lions = 0
   Tigers = 1
   Bears = 2
End Enum
```

The error depicted in Figure 26-5, Error 380, means that an invalid property value was entered. Obviously, it's preferable that users not be able to cause these kinds of errors. In order to prevent it, you have to know how to present a drop-down list box of choices.

Here are the StickyFrame Property procedures, including delegation from the constituent Frame control, as prepared by the ActiveX Control Interface Wizard:

```
Public Property Get BorderStyle() As Integer
   BorderStyle = Frame1.BorderStyle
End Property

Public Property Let BorderStyle(ByVal New_BorderStyle As Integer)
   Frame1.BorderStyle() = New_BorderStyle
   PropertyChanged "BorderStyle"
End Property
```

The problem here is with the As Integer type declarations. An enumerated type is required instead.

An enumerated type, containing the two possible BorderStyle values, should be declared as Public in the UserControl Module:

```
Public Enum Bord
   None = 0
   FixedSingle = 1
End Enum
```

Next, adjust the BorderStyle Property procedure Get types so they retrieve and save Bord constants rather than integers:

```
Public Property Get BorderStyle() As Bord
   BorderStyle = Frame1.BorderStyle
End Property

Public Property Let BorderStyle(ByVal New_BorderStyle As Bord)
   Frame1.BorderStyle() = New_BorderStyle
   PropertyChanged "BorderStyle"
End Property
```

Save the modified UserControl module, place an instance of the control on a form, and have a look at the control's BorderStyle property in the Properties window. As shown in Figure 26-6, BorderStyle must now be entered from the drop-down list defined by the enumerated type Bord.

Figure 26-6: By using enumerated types, you can make sure that developers using your controls must choose property values from a drop-down list.

User-Defined Enumerated Properties

It's easy to create user-defined properties that will be displayed in drop-down lists in the control's Properties window. For example, suppose you had a ClawsAndPaws property with a value that the user would supply from a drop-down list. You would first define the enumeration for the drop-down list:

```
Public Enum WildAnimals
   Lions = 0
   Tigers = 1
   Bears = 2
End Enum
```

Next, the property would be implemented in the UserControl module in the normal fashion with Property procedures (I've omitted the persistence references to the ClawsAndPaws property in the UserControl's InitProperties, ReadProperties, and WriteProperties events):

```
'Default Property Values:
Const m_def_ClawsAndPaws = 2 'Bears
'Property Variables:
Dim m_ClawsAndPaws As Long
...
Public Property Get ClawsAndPaws() As WildAnimals
   ClawsAndPaws = m_ClawsAndPaws
End Property
```

```
Public Property Let ClawsAndPaws(ByVal New_ClawsAndPaws As
WildAnimals)
    m_ClawsAndPaws = New_ClawsAndPaws
    PropertyChanged "ClawsAndPaws"
End Property
```

The ClawsAndPaws property would then be displayed as a drop-down list in the Properties window, as shown in Figure 26-7.

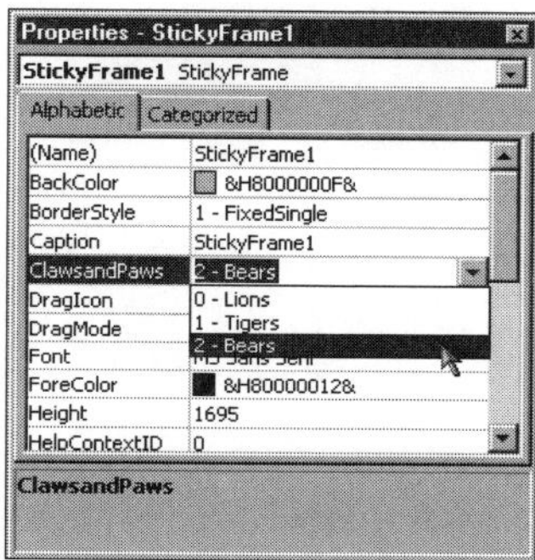

Figure 26-7: User-defined properties can be displayed as an enumerated list.

Setting a Default Property

The default property of a control is the one that is implied when no property has been explicitly used. For example, the Text property is the default property of the Text control. Therefore, the statement

```
Text1 = "The more it SNOWS-tiddely-pom"
```

is identical in effect to

```
Text1.Text = "The more it SNOWS-tiddely-pom"
```

Both statements assign the same string to the Text1.Text property.

Your control's default property should be the property most likely to be set in code by users of your control.

You use the Procedure Attributes dialog, which you can open from VB's Tools menu, to set the default property (or method). Figure 26-8 shows the StickyFrame control's Caption property being set as the default for the StickyFrame control using the Procedure ID list.

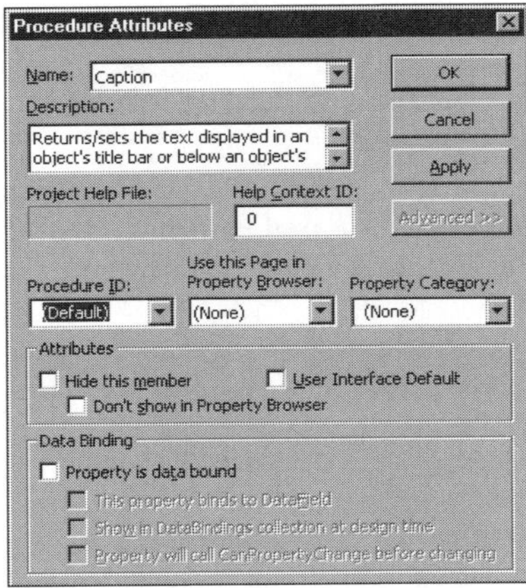

Figure 26-8: You use the Procedure Attributes dialog to set a property or method as the default.

If a member is already assigned as the default, you must assign it to (None) using the Procedure ID drop-down list before you can assign another member as the Default Procedure ID.

The Object Browser, shown in Figure 26-9, displays the default member of a class. In the figure, you can tell that Caption is the default member of the StickyFrame class because of the small round ball above and to the left of the Caption member icon (in full color, it is blue).

By the way, the Procedure Attributes dialog is opened by choosing it from the context menu when a member is selected in the Object Browser.

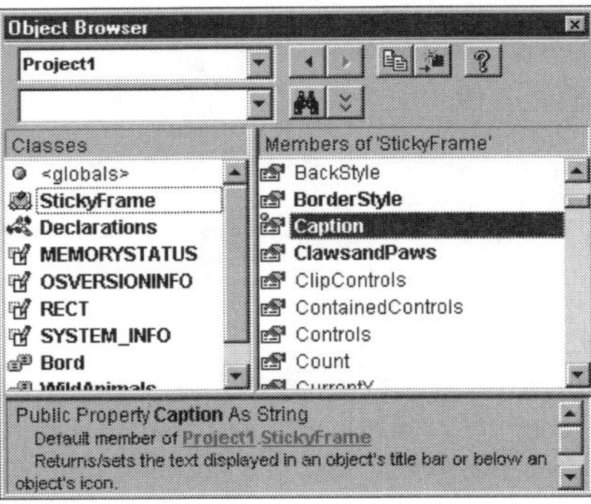

Figure 26-9: The default class member is marked with a blue ball in the Object Browser.

Once the default member has been set, you can omit explicit references to it in code. For example:

```
Private Sub Form_Load()
   StickyFrame1 = "The more it SNOWS-tiddely-pom"
End Sub
```

sets the caption property of the StickyFrame control, with the results shown in Figure 26-10.

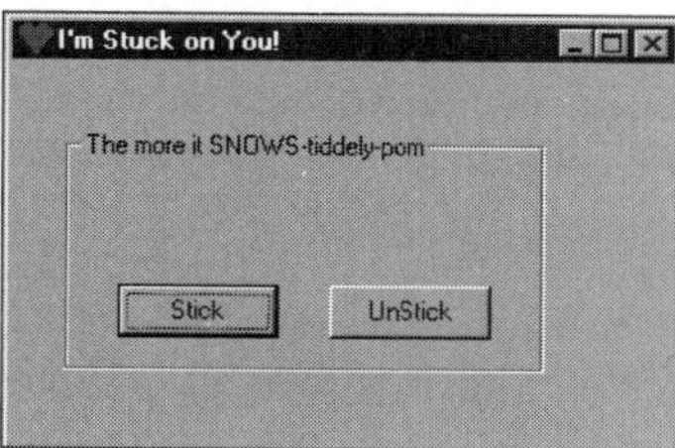

Figure 26-10: You can omit explicit references to a control's default member.

Creating a User Interface Default Property

When a new control instance is placed on a container, Visual Basic chooses a property to highlight in the Properties window. This is the last property that was highlighted in the Properties window, provided that the new control has that property. Otherwise, Visual Basic uses the property the developer selects as the *user interface default.*

If the developer doesn't specify a user interface default, Visual Basic picks one itself, roughly speaking, based on the order in which members were added to the control.

The user interface default — obviously, this is a different default than the default control property — is also the procedure that is selected when the Code Editor is opened for a UserControl.

The user interface default should be the property that developers using your control will most often set. For example, the Interval property is the user interface default for the Timer control.

To set the a property as the user interface default, use the Procedure Attributes dialog. With the property selected in the Name drop-down list, check the User Interface Default box. Figure 26-11 shows the ClawsAndPaws property being selected as the User Interface Default.

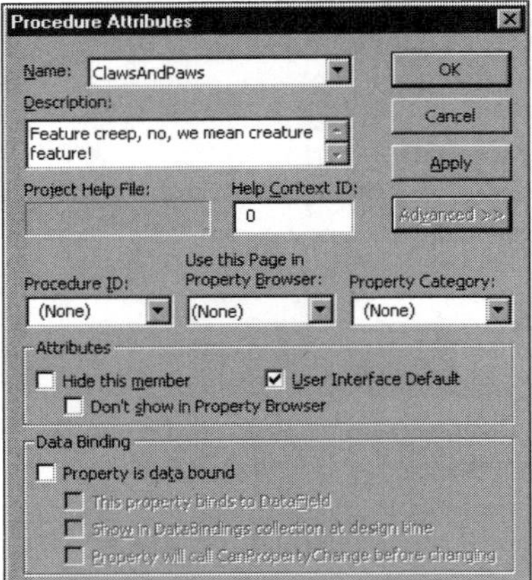

Figure 26-11: You use the User Interface Default check box to set a property as the user interface default.

Once a property has been assigned as the user interface default, if you open a new instance of the control, the user interface default is highlighted in the Properties window, as shown in Figure 26-12.

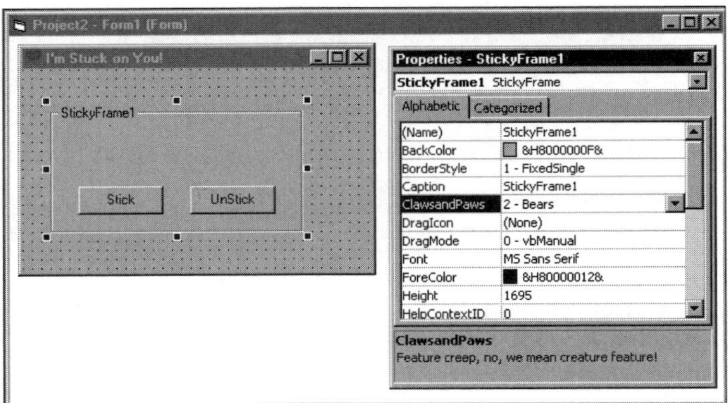

Figure 26-12: The user interface default is highlighted when a new instance of the control is opened and its properties displayed in the Properties window.

Adding Custom Property Dialogs

In some cases, a property is too complex to set using the Properties window. For example, a property might itself be an object, such as the Font object, with properties of its own. To handle this situation, you can click the Font properties ellipsis button to open an associated property page, as shown in Figure 26-13.

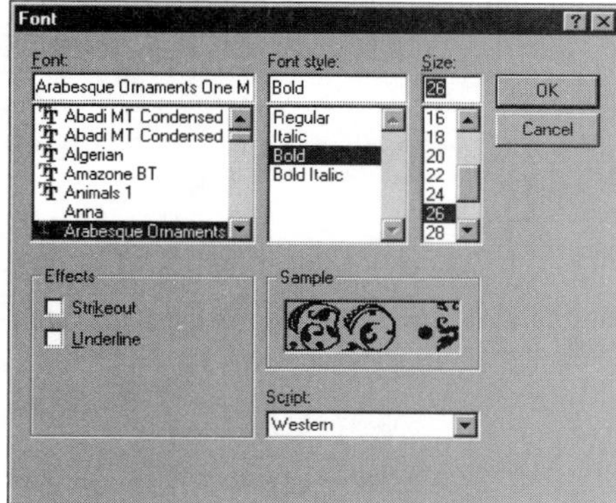

Figure 26-13: The Font property is, itself, an object with its own properties.

A property might even consist of a collection of objects, such as a collection of buttons for a Toolbar, or nodes for a TreeView.

If you declare a property of type Font, OLE_COLOR, or Picture, the property will automatically be associated with a StandardFont, StandardColor, or StandardPicture property page.

To associate a property with a custom property page, first create the property page (*.Pag*) file. I've added a sample custom property page named CreatureFeature, and saved as ***Creature.Pag***, to the StickyFrame control project.

Next, open the Procedure Attributes dialog. You can use the Use this Page in Property Browser drop-down list to connect a property with a custom property page. (Figure 26-14 shows how to associate the CreatureFeature property with the CreatureFeature custom property page.)

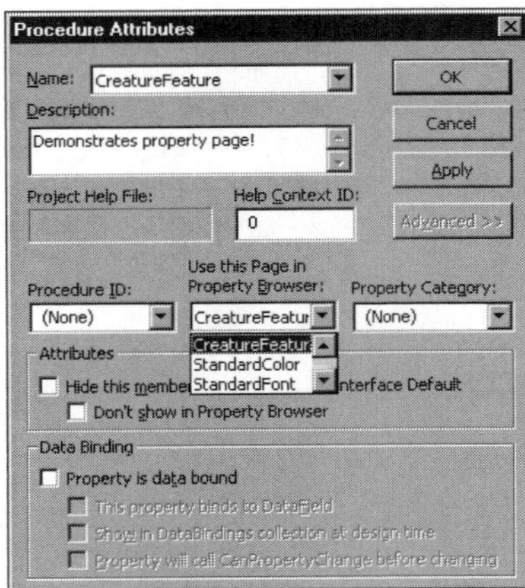

Figure 26-14: The Use this Page in Property Browser drop-down list in the Procedure Attributes dialog connects a property with a property page.

Now, when you open the Properties window and an instance of the StickyFrame control, the CreatureFeature property is represented by an ellipsis in its value column, as shown in Figure 26-15.

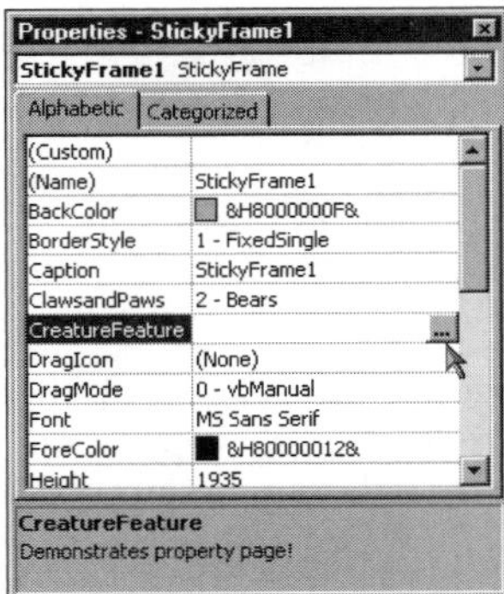

Figure 26-15: An ellipsis in the value column of the Properties window means that a custom property page is associated with the property.

If you click the ellipsis, the custom property page opens, as shown in Figure 26-16.

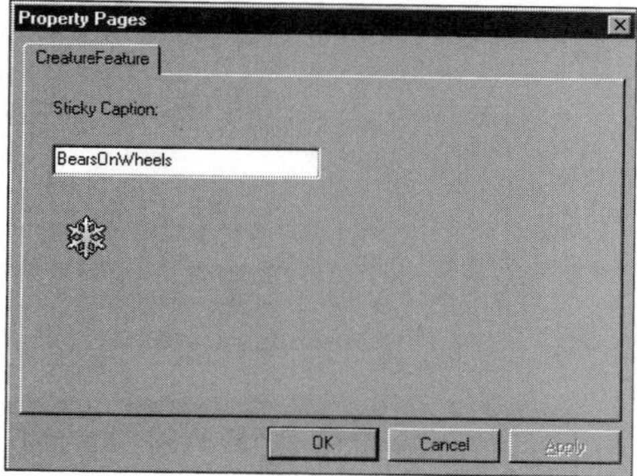

Figure 26-16: You can design a custom property page in any way you'd like.

Of course, you'll have to take care of synchronizing changes made to properties shown on a custom property sheet with the control (see "Adding Property Pages Manually" in Chapter 25 for more information).

It's perfectly legal to associate a number of properties with the same custom property page. In fact, this is a good way to organize related properties.

Grouping Categories by Property

A new feature of VB5 is that the Properties window has two tabs, one showing all of a control's properties, and the other organizing the properties into categories. You can organize your control's properties by assigning them to one of the existing categories, or to new categories that you've created.

It's a good idea to organize your properties into categories because Visual Basic places all unassigned properties in the Misc category.

It will probably come as no surprise that you use the Procedure Attributes dialog to categorize properties. You can use the Property Category drop-down list to assign a property to an existing category. Alternatively, you can create your own category by entering it in the Property Category list box (the category Animals is shown in Figure 26-17).

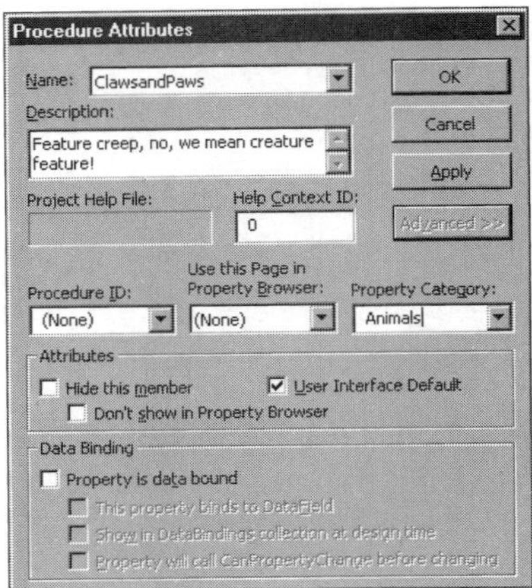

Figure 26-17: You use the Property Category drop-down list to assign properties to existing categories and to create new categories.

To assign several properties to the same custom category, you'll have to manually enter the name of the category — such as Animals — each time. Custom categories are not added to the drop-down list.

Once properties have been assigned to categories using the Property Category list, they appear as categorized in the Properties window, as shown in Figure 26-18.

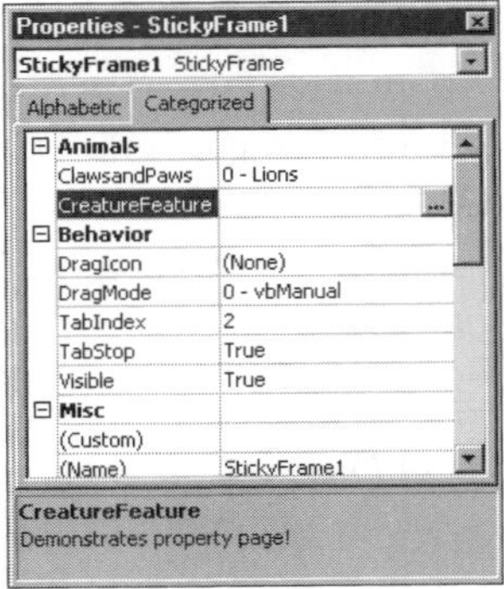

Figure 26-18: Categorized properties appear together on the Categorized tab of the Properties window.

Runtime and Design Time Properties

You may wish to create control properties that are read-only at runtime and can be set at design time. To do this, create a custom property in the normal fashion, and test the value of the UserMode property of the Ambient object in the Property Let or Property Set procedure. (For more information on working with the ambient object, see "The Ambient Object's UserMode Property" in Chapter 24.)

Listing 26-1 shows the UserControl implementation of a read-only at runtime property named ImReadOnlyAtRunTime.

Listing 26-1: A read-only at runtime property

```
...
Dim m_ImReadOnlyAtRunTime As String
...
Public Property Get ImReadOnlyAtRunTime() As String
   ImReadOnlyAtRunTime = m_ImReadOnlyAtRunTime
End Property

Public Property Let ImReadOnlyAtRunTime(ByVal New_ImReadOnlyAtRunTime _
   As String)
   If Ambient.UserMode Then
      Err.Raise Number:=31013, _
         Description:= _
         "Property is read-only at run time."
   End If
   m_ImReadOnlyAtRunTime = New_ImReadOnlyAtRunTime
   PropertyChanged "ImReadOnlyAtRunTime"
End Property
...
```

If you preferred, of course, you could implement it so that the property was read-only at runtime without raising an error.

Creating Runtime-Only Properties

You can create a property available only at runtime by writing property procedures that do not write properties when the UserMode property of the Ambient object is False.

Listing 26-2 contains an example of a runtime-only property:

Listing 26-2: Creating a runtime-only property

```
Public Property Get ImRunTimeOnly() As String
   If Ambient.UserMode Then
      ImRunTimeOnly = m_ImRunTimeOnly
   End If
End Property
```

```
Public Property Let ImRunTimeOnly(ByVal New_ImRunTimeOnly As String)
   If Ambient.UserMode Then
      m_ImRunTimeOnly = New_ImRunTimeOnly
      PropertyChanged "ImRunTimeOnly"
   End If
End Property
```

If you had caused the property to fail at design time by raising an error (rather than just doing nothing), VB would not display it in the Properties window. As it is, an ImRunTimeOnly property does indeed show up in the control's interface, but values entered for it in the Properties window do not persist.

To remove the property from the design time interface, check the Don't Show in Property Browser box in — you guessed it — the Procedure Attributes dialog, as shown in Figure 26-19.

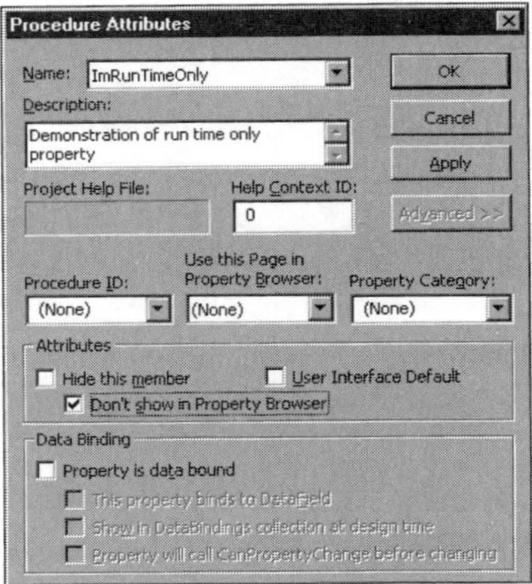

Figure 26-19: If you check Don't Show in Property Browser in the Procedure Attributes dialog, a member is not displayed in the Properties window.

Note, however, that as long as Hide this Member remains unchecked (see Figure 26-19), the property will still be displayed in the Object Browser, as shown in Figure 26-20.

You might wish to verify that ImRunTimeOnly behaves properly at runtime. It's easy to add code to the test project that will verify this when it is run:

```
Debug.Print StickyFrame1.ImRunTimeOnly
StickyFrame1.ImRunTimeOnly = "Frodo Baggins is a Hobbit"
Debug.Print StickyFrame1.ImRunTimeOnly
```

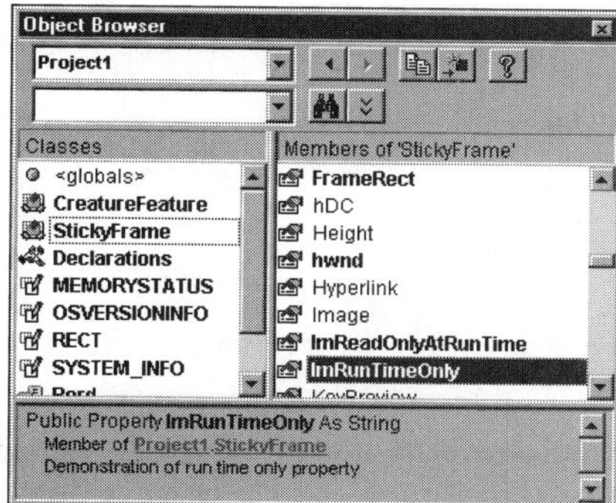

Figure 26-20: Even properties that have been removed from the design time interface of a control can be displayed in the Object Browser unless Hide this Member was selected as a procedure attribute.

Basing a Control on Several Constituent Controls

It's pretty common to base a new control on several constituent controls. (This is known as keeping the good stuff and throwing away the rest....) For example, you could combine a Label control and a Shape control to make a round label control. (The project group containing the control and a test project is saved on the CD-ROM as ***Circ.Vbg***; the source file for the circButton UserControl module is ***CircleB.Ctl***.)

If the UserControl responded to click events within the circle area of the shape, it could be used essentially like a round button. To set this up, add a shape control, named Shape1, and a label control, named Label1, to a UserControl. Set the properties for Shape1 and Label1 as shown in Tables 26-1 and 26-2.

Table 26-1 Shape1 Properties

Property	*Value*
BorderStyle	0-Transparent
FillColor	&H000000FF (Red)
FillStyle	0-Solid

Table 26-2 Label1 Properties

Property	*Value*
Alignment	2-Center
BackStyle	0-Transparent
ForeColor	&H00FFFFFF (White)

Next, add code to the UserControl's Resize event to size the shape to take up the entire area of the circButton control, and to center the label vertically and make it the width of the circButton:

```
Private Sub UserControl_Resize()
   Shape1.Move 0, 0, ScaleWidth, ScaleHeight
   Label1.Move 0, (ScaleHeight _
      - Label1.Height) / 2, ScaleWidth
End Sub
```

You should implement the usual delegated constituent members in the normal way.

A problem comes up with the click event. It's easy enough to delegate click events fired by the label control so they are processed by the circButton:

```
Private Sub Label1_Click()
   RaiseEvent Click
End Sub
```

This raises a circButton click event whenever the user clicks Label1. But, ideally, the circButton click event should also be raised when the user clicks the shape control as well. Shapes, with only the implementation they were born with, do not raise click events.

The code shown in Listing 26-3, in the UserControl's MouseUp event, uses a technique known as *hit testing*.

Listing 26-3: Hit testing for a click event

```
Private Sub UserControl_MouseUp(Button As Integer, _
   Shift As Integer, X As Single, Y As Single)
   If Point(X, Y) = Shape1.FillColor Then
      RaiseEvent Click
   End If
End Sub
```

Provided that you don't place any other constituent controls on the UserControl with the same FillColor as Shape1, this should work fine.

To test it, add the circButton control to a form, along with some appropriate code:

```
Private Sub circButton1_Click()
    Form1.Caption = "In the circle!"
End Sub

Private Sub Form_Click()
    Form1.Caption = "Out of the circle!"
End Sub
```

If you run the program, you'll see that the circButton control fires a click event when the user clicks within the constituent shape control — and not outside it — as shown in Figure 26-21.

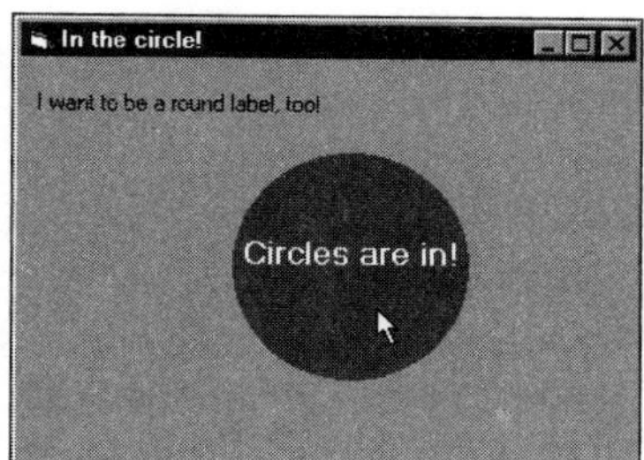

Figure 26-21: Controls can easily combine the characteristics of constituent controls.

User-Drawn Controls

A *user-drawn* control is one that handles drawing its appearance itself — and does not depend on constituent controls for the way it looks. Generally, the only place you need to put drawing code is in the UserControl's Paint event. Paint event code can consist of the graphics methods of the UserControl object, or, if necessary, calls to the Windows API.

You should know when to draw your control, what state it's in (for example, clicked or unclicked), and whether you should draw a focus rectangle. (With controls made up of constituent controls, most of these details are handled for you.)

When the container repaints the area where your control is located, the UserControl object will receive a Paint event.

If your control has to change the way it looks based on user actions, such as when the user clicks the control, you can raise the Paint event by calling the UserControl's Refresh method.

A Confetti Control

As an example of how user-drawn controls work, here's how you would create a Confetti control, pictured at runtime in Figure 26-22. The Confetti control module is saved as ***Confetti.Ctl***, and the ActiveX control project that includes it is part of the ***Cnfetti.Vbp*** project group (which also includes a test project).

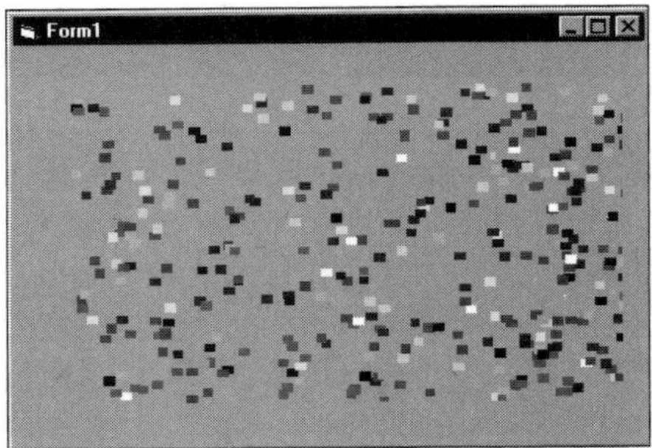

Figure 26-22: You can create user-drawn controls that handle their own screen appearance.

The Confetti control is very simple. It drops randomly colored confetti on its screen representation for the number of times specified in its Iterations property. This happens every time its Paint event is raised — for example, when resized or initialized — or its Refresh method is invoked.

A developer can force the triggering of the Paint event by calling the Confetti's Refresh method. In addition, it has an Enabled property, so the developer using the control can decide whether she wants this potentially obnoxious display always running. I also added code to make sure the control was in runtime mode before doing its thing.

Listing 26-4 shows the entire code for the UserControl module, and absolutely all that is involved in creating this control:

Listing 26-4: A "Confetti" control

```
Option Explicit
'Default Property Values:
Const m_def_Iterations = 5000
Const m_def_Enabled = True

'Property Variables:
Dim m_Iterations As Long
Dim m_Enabled As Boolean
```

```
Public Property Get Iterations() As Long
   Iterations = m_Iterations
End Property

Public Property Let Iterations(ByVal New_Iterations As Long)
   m_Iterations = New_Iterations
   PropertyChanged "Iterations"
End Property

Public Property Get Enabled() As Boolean
   Enabled = m_Enabled
End Property

Public Property Let Enabled(ByVal New_Enabled As Boolean)
   m_Enabled = New_Enabled
   PropertyChanged "Enabled"
End Property

Function Refresh()
   UserControl_Paint
End Function

Private Sub UserControl_InitProperties()
   m_Iterations = m_def_Iterations
   m_Enabled = m_def_Enabled
End Sub

Private Sub UserControl_ReadProperties(PropBag As PropertyBag)
   m_Iterations = PropBag.ReadProperty("Iterations", _
      m_def_Iterations)
   m_Enabled = PropBag.ReadProperty("Enabled", m_def_Enabled)
End Sub

Private Sub UserControl_WriteProperties(PropBag As PropertyBag)
   Call PropBag.WriteProperty("Iterations", m_Iterations, _
      m_def_Iterations)
   Call PropBag.WriteProperty("Enabled", m_Enabled, m_def_Enabled)
End Sub

Private Sub UserControl_Paint()
   Dim I As Integer, X1 As Integer, Y1 As Integer, Color As Long
    If Enabled Then
       If Ambient.UserMode Then 'runtime only!
          Randomize
          For I = 1 To Iterations
             X1 = Rnd * ScaleWidth
             Y1 = Rnd * ScaleHeight
             Color = QBColor(Rnd * 15)
             Line (X1, Y1)-(X1 + 85, Y1 + 65), Color, BF
          Next I
       End If
    End If
End Sub
```

That's it! Now, when you add the control to a container and run the project, it will confetti away — provided that the control's Enabled property is set to True.

The graphics methods used in the Confetti control's Paint event were explained under "Special Effects" in Chapter 19, "Runtime Display Secrets."

UserControls Are Not Forms

UserControls are not forms. Some of the events you may be used to from working with forms never happen to a UserControl object. For example, there is no Activate or Deactivate event, because controls are not activated and deactivated (but forms are). In addition, the familiar Load, Unload, and QueryUnload events are missing from the lifestyle of a UserControl.

The UserControl object's Initialize and ReadProperties events provide the functionality of a form's Load event. The main difference between the two is that when the Initialize event occurs, the control has not been sited on its container, so the container's Extender and Ambient objects are not available. The control has been sited when InitProperties or ReadProperties occurs.

The UserControl event most like a form's Unload event is Terminate. The constituent controls still exist at this point, although you no longer have access to the container, because your control has been unsited.

The WriteProperties event cannot be used in the place of Unload, because it occurs only at design time.

UserControl objects don't have QueryUnload events because controls are just parts of a form. Theirs is to do or die, and not to wonder why. It's not up to a control to decide whether the form that contains it should close. A control's duty is to destroy itself when it's told to, no questions asked.

UserControls don't have to be visible at runtime. (For example, consider the Timer control.) Just set the UserControl's Visible property to False.

UserControl methods can be used to manipulate the appearance of objects other than themselves — for example, the appearance of their containers.

Summary

Creating your own ActiveX controls is a tremendously exciting and fulfilling experience.

This chapter discussed many topics that you'll want to understand when you start implementing controls.

Topics covered in this chapter included:

- The StickyFrame control
- Using enumerated properties
- User-defined enumerated properties
- The Procedure Attributes dialog
- Setting a default property
- Setting the user interface default property
- Custom property dialogs
- Property categories
- Creating read-only properties
- Creating runtime-only properties
- Basing a control on several constituent controls
- User-drawn controls
- The Confetti control
- UserControls and forms

Chapter 27

Deploying VB ActiveX Controls on the Web

Once you have used VB5 to create an ActiveX control, it can be used by any application that can provide a container that will host ActiveX controls. It is particularly exciting to be able to use VB5 ActiveX controls in Internet — public — and intranet — private — Web applications.

But not all ActiveX control containers are created equal. As a container, a Web page works somewhat differently than a VB form. For a Web application that includes an ActiveX control to work, the ActiveX control must be set up on the local machine that is browsing the Web application. Internet control setups work somewhat differently than normal control setups.

This chapter explains how to use the ActiveX controls you have created in VB on the Web.

Installing Controls Across the Web

The Internet is a public Web — meaning a vast network of computers connected via the TCP/IP and HTTP protocols that are accessible to everyone with appropriate access software. Each node on this network — nodes are also called Web servers — generates content using HTML (and extensions to HTML such as embedded ActiveX controls). Browsers are client applications that can decode the HTML generated by a Web server and present it in a page layout fashion.

An intranet web is conceptually exactly the same thing as the public Web — the Internet — except that access to it is controlled (and private).

The *extranet* is a new kind of web, namely a private web — or intranet — that is made available to the public, but only in a few specific contexts. For example, an overnight delivery business might make a few of its intranet interfaces available to the public so they could track their deliveries. The company would have transformed its intranet into an extranet.

Whatever the kind of web used — extranet, intranet, or the public Web — applications that include ActiveX controls all work the same way. Therefore, to keep the material in this chapter simple, I'll only discuss Web applications. But, bear in mind that the same techniques apply equally to intranets and extranets.

Browsers that "Understand" ActiveX

You can think of a Web application as a client/server application in which the browser is the client. Executable content such as ActiveX controls are located on the server until they are accessed by a client browser.

But not all browsers "understand" ActiveX. For an application that includes an ActiveX control to run correctly, it must be accessed by Microsoft's Internet Explorer, version 3.0 or later.

In addition, the NCompass ActiveX plug-in for Netscape's Navigator allows users to "play" ActiveX while running Navigator. You can download the plug-in and learn more about it at *http://www.ncompass.com*.

However, the NCompass ActiveX plug-in does not really support all ActiveX features. It's best to assume that Web applications you create that include ActiveX controls will require users to browse with Internet Explorer.

Take a simple application placed on a Web server that includes HTML codes to control the appearance of the Web page, an ActiveX control, and VBScript commands that manipulate the exposed members of the control depending on the user's input. For this application to work in the client browser, the ActiveX control must be installed on the client system.

I'll explain the steps involved in an Internet control download and installation. However, to better get the gist of what's involved with Internet setups, it's important to review the requirements for a normal control installation.

Normal Setup

Before you can install a control on a system, the control and all support files — such as the Visual Basic runtime library, or license files — must be present on the target system. Support files must be located where the system can find them, normally in the ***Windows\System*** directory or in the directory containing the control. Finally, the control must be registered on the system. You can do this by running ***Regsvr32.Exe***. For example:

```
Regsvr32 C:\Windows\Occache\Confetti.Ocx
```

If the control has been properly installed and registered, you can now add it to a container. For example, you could use the VB Components dialog to add it to your VB Toolbox. From the Toolbox, you could add it to a VB form.

The Visual Basic Setup Wizard is a separate application that you can use to create a stand-alone control setup that will automate these steps. Later in this chapter, I'll explain how to use the Setup Wizard to create an Internet download; for general information about using the Setup Wizard, see Chapter 36, "Setup Programs."

You may wish to manually remove a control from your system. To get references to a control out of your Registry, it's not enough merely to delete the control. You should also run the Regsvr32 utility with its /u flag ("u" is short for "unregister"). For example:

```
Regsvr32 /u C:\Windows\Occache\Confetti.Ocx
```

Web Setup

In concept, Web setups work similarly. You identify an ActiveX control in the HTML code that makes up a Web page using <OBJECT> and </OBJECT> tags and the control's CLSID — a unique object identifier. If the control has already been installed on the target system, an instance of it can be created when the browser processes the <OBJECT> tag.

If the ActiveX control has not yet been installed on the target system, you must first download and run a program that installs it. You use the Codebase parameter of the <OBJECT> tag to point to the location of compressed installation programs on the server. These are saved in the ***.Cab***, or *cabinet*, format.

Similarly, you must download system files required by the ActiveX control — such as the VB runtime, or virtual machine, ***Msvbvm50.Dll***. Unless you specify otherwise, these files will be downloaded from Microsoft's Web sites.

When an instance of an ActiveX control is created in a Web application, the <PARAM NAME> attributes — pairs of named properties and related values — are passed to the control's InitProperties event using the standard PropertyBag object. <PARAM NAME> attributes are the standard *property equals value* pairs that are normally associated with controls. For example:

```
<PARAM NAME="Enabled" VALUE="0">
```

Unlike what happens when you place an ActiveX control on a Visual Basic form and close the form, HTML pages don't save design time information. Therefore, a control on an HTML page always acts as though it's being created for the very first time. (Maybe it's also humming a Madonna song....)

When the HTML is processed by a browser, a control on the page receives the Initialize, InitProperties, Resize, and Paint events — but not ReadProperties.

To open a control with a persistent custom property value that is not the default, you should add <PARAM NAME=...VALUE=> pairs to the control's object tag. For example, the default value of the custom Enabled property of the Confetti control is True. If you wanted an instance of the control to be created with Enabled set to False, you would add to the attribute and value pairs that belong to the <OBJECT> tag:

```
<OBJECT ...>
   <PARAM NAME="Enabled" VALUE="0">
</OBJECT>
```

Running the Application Setup Wizard

The easiest way to create a Web setup for your ActiveX controls is to run the Application Setup Wizard. (The Application Setup Wizard is a separate program found in the Visual Basic 5 programs folder under the Start button. It is discussed in more detail in Chapter 36, "Setup Programs.") The Setup Wizard will generate an installation routine (***.Cab*** file), and sample HTML code which you can adopt for your own uses. To use the Setup Wizard to create a Web setup for an ActiveX control, you must point it at the control project and make sure that Create Internet Download Setup is selected, as shown in Figure 27-1.

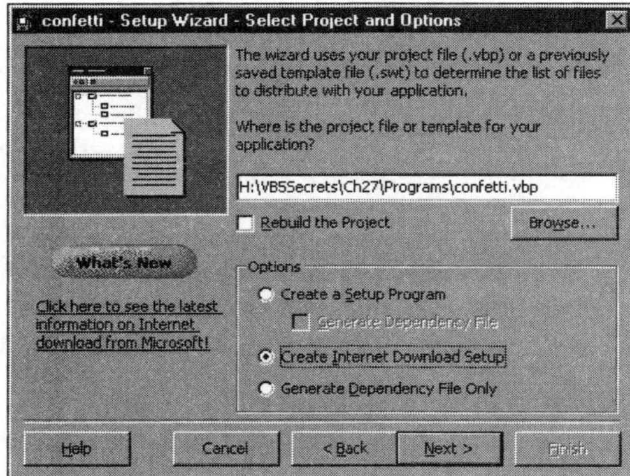

Figure 27-1: To set up your control for download across the Web, make sure that Create Internet Download Setup is selected.

You will not be able to use a setup routine that has been written for Internet component download for normal setup purposes. An Internet component download setup is intended for runtime usage, and is, therefore, radically different from a conventional setup program, which is intended for design time use.

You will also need to specify a location for the ***.Cab*** software installation file that the Wizard will create, and any supporting files that are required. ***.Cab*** files — cabinet files — are compressed in the standard Microsoft delivery format. For example, you'll find that your Windows 95 or NT CD-ROM mainly contains ***.Cab*** files. It's a good idea to place all the ***.Cab*** files in one directory on your Web site, for ease of administration. Figure 27-2 shows the Wizard's Internet Distribution Location dialog. This location could be the root directory or in the hierarchy of your Web server. Or, you could copy the files to the appropriate locations at a later point.

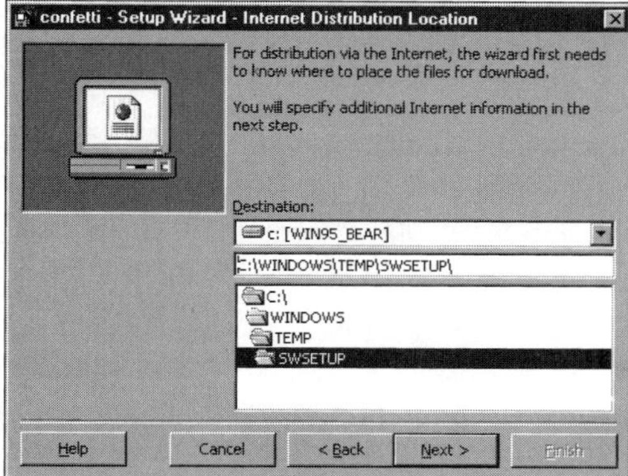

Figure 27-2: You must specify the target destination for your control setup files.

Figure 27-3 shows the Internet Package dialog, which follows the Distribution Location dialog. You use this dialog to specify whether Visual Basic's runtime files should be downloaded from Microsoft's site or from an alternate location (if they are required).

Figure 27-3: The Internet Package dialog allows you to specify a support download file location (the default is from Microsoft).

Unless you are in an intranet setting with no outside Web access, you should download the ***.Cab*** files from Microsoft (which is the default setting). Using Microsoft's site ensures that your users will get the latest versions of Microsoft-supplied support files, and that the correct version for the target browser's operating system will be sent.

The following are the most commonly required support files, which have been digitally signed by Microsoft and are freely downloadable from the Microsoft web site:

- ***Msvbvm5b.Cab***, VB5 Virtual Machine, required for all VB5 built controls and applications
- ***CmCtlb32.Cab***, VB5 common controls, including TreeView, ListView, and so on
- ***Cmdlgb32.Cab***, VB5 common dialog control

If you are developing an intranet application, you should set up one standardized URL for support download to avoid versioning problems and administrative headaches.

Assuming that your component is safe for initialization and scripting, you should mark it as safe by clicking the Safety button in the Internet Package dialog and checking the appropriate boxes in the Safety dialog (shown in Figure 27-4).

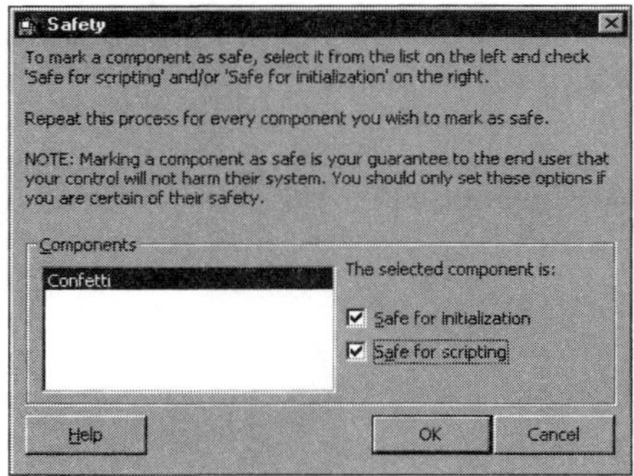

Figure 27-4: You can use the Safety dialog to mark your controls as safe for initialization and safe for scripting.

Making Controls Safe for Scripting

Making controls safe for scripting is one of those topics that sounds rhetorical, like making the world safe for democracy, but there are some serious issues you should consider.

The basic principle is that someone scripting your control should not be able to use to it to read or write specific files or Registry entries across the Web. (By specific files or Registry entries, I mean ones selected by the person who is doing the scripting.) If a malicious person could gain these kinds of access through a Web ActiveX control, theoretically nothing on the systems that downloaded the control would be secure from that person.

Because ActiveX controls downloaded across the Web do not come with whatever reassurance shrink-wrapped consumer packaging may provide, several mechanisms have been devised to reassure users.

Digital signatures create a path to you (through the company that authorized your certificate). You can incorporate your signature when you use Setup Wizard to create an Internet setup for your control component.

Obviously, if you go into commercial deployment of ActiveX controls on the Web, you'll need to obtain digital certificates — to placate potential customers, if for no other reason. In the meantime, the ActiveX SDK contains various test digital certificates you can use when debugging component downloads, as well as tools for obtaining your own certificate. The URL for the ActiveX SDK download is *http://www.microsoft.com/intdev/sdk/*.

You can mark your control as safe for scripting, which tells users that you believe there's no way a script on an HTML page can use your control to cause harm to their computers, or to obtain information they haven't supplied willingly.

A control that permits a Web page designer to do any of the following is probably not safe for scripting:

- Create a file with a name supplied by a script
- Read a file from the user's hard drive with a name supplied by a script
- Insert information into the Windows Registry (or into an ***.Ini*** file), using a key (or filename) supplied by a script
- Retrieve information from the Windows Registry (or from an ***.Ini*** file), using a key (or filename) supplied by a script
- Execute a Windows API function using information supplied by a script
- Create or manipulate external objects using programmatic IDs (for example, "Excel.Application") that the script supplies

The line between safe and unsafe isn't necessarily obvious. For example, a control that uses the SaveSetting method to write information to its own Registry key doesn't disqualify itself for safe scripting by doing so. On the other hand, a control that allows the Registry key to be specified (by setting a property or invoking a method) is not safe.

A control that uses a temporary file may be safe for scripting. If the name of that temporary file can be controlled by a script, the control is not safe for scripting. Allowing a script to control the amount of information that goes into a temporary file will make the control unsafe for scripting, because a script could continue dumping information into the file until the user's hard disk overflowed.

As a final example, a control that uses API calls is not necessarily unsafe for scripting. Suppose, however, that the control allows a script to supply data that will be passed to an API, and doesn't guard against oversize data overwriting memory, or invalid data corrupting memory. Such a control is not safe for scripting.

As an indication of the seriousness of scripting safety, note that VBScript itself does not include methods to access the Registry, save files, or create objects.

You can mark your control safe for initialization, which lets users know you believe there's no way an HTML author can harm their computers by feeding your control invalid data when the page initializes it.

When you use the Application Setup Wizard to create your Internet setup, you indicate that your control is marked in this fashion. If you don't, Internet Explorer by default will refuse to download your component.

Even if you mark your control as safe, the default setting in Explorer is to reject unsigned ActiveX components. To override this default, select the Security tab in Explorer's Options dialog, click Advanced, and deselect the High Security setting.

Files Created by the Setup Wizard

Before completing its work, the Wizard lists the files that it has determined are required by your ActiveX control, as shown in Figure 27-5. This is your chance to add additional files that may have escaped the Wizard's notice, such as a ReadMe or data file.

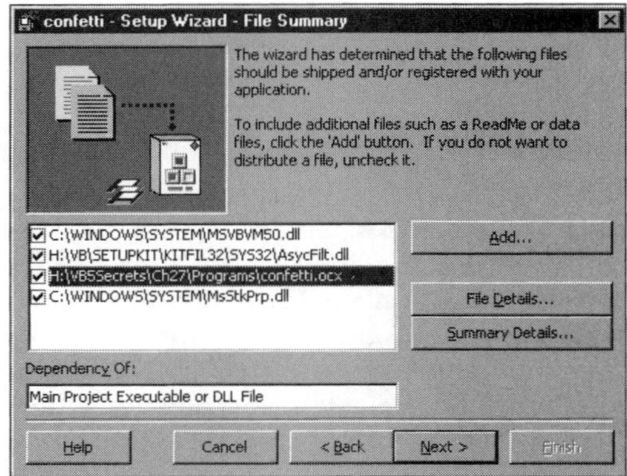

Figure 27-5: The File Summary lists the files that are required by your control and lets you add other files to the list.

One of the files shown in Figure 27-5, ***MsStkPrp.Dll***, is used to display property pages in environments other than VB.

When you select Next, based on the files included in the File Summary dialog, the Wizard completes its work and creates a number of files (and a folder). These are

- A ***.Cab*** file containing your control in the location you specified. In the example, it's called ***Confetti.Cab***.
- A sample HTML file containing the <OBJECT> tag with CLSID reference for the confetti control. In the example, this is named ***Confetti.Htm***.
- A ***Support*** folder containing the input files for ***Confetti.Cab***. The ***Support*** folder contains the control, ***Confetti.Ocx***; a setup information file, ***Confetti.Inf***; and a project file for creating the ***.Cab*** file, ***Confetti.Ddf***.

For more information on creating ***.Cab*** files, check out *http://www.microsoft.com/workshop/java/CAB-f.htm*.

Using the Control on the Web

Here's the partial contents of ***Confetti.Htm*** as generated by the Setup Wizard:

```
<HTML>
   <OBJECT ID="Confetti" WIDTH=320 HEIGHT=240
      CLASSID="CLSID:2FDDA94E-5E8D-11D0-B8E9-0080C6026268"
      CODEBASE="confetti.CAB#version=1,0,0,0">
   </OBJECT>
</HTML>
```

If you open this HTML page in Explorer, every time the Confetti ActiveX control's paint event is fired because the page it is on is resized, you'll get the confetti effect with iterations set to the default, 10,000, as shown in Figure 27-6.

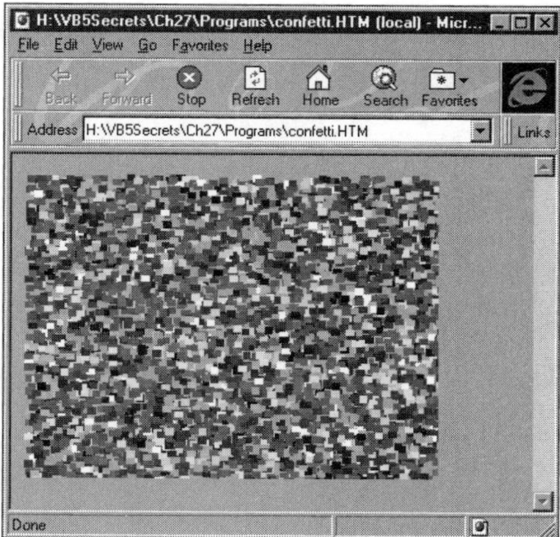

Figure 27-6: The Application Setup Wizard generates a functional sample HTML page using your control, complete with an <OBJECT> tag and CLSID.

Each ActiveX control you create will have its own CLSID, which is theoretically unique to that control in the whole wide universe. To prevent multiple CLSIDs being created for the same control, make sure to select Binary Compatibility in the VB5 Project Properties dialog for your project before "making" your control.

This behavior on the part of the Confetti ActiveX control in the sample HTML page generated by the Wizard is actually totally obnoxious. For one thing, the user loses control of Internet Explorer while the Confetti control does its thing. For another, maybe the developer doesn't want the control to fire on page load (which fires a resize event), and maybe the user should be able to control the amount of confetti (iterations).

You can use applications such as FrontPage 97 (Figures 27-7 and 27-8), ActiveX Control Pad (Figure 27-9), or just-plain-vanilla Notepad to add appropriate property values and VBScript commands.

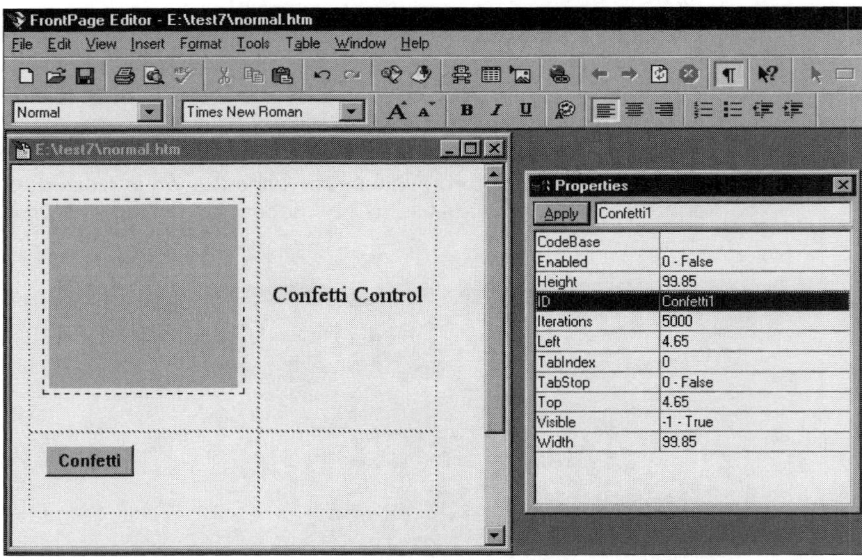

Figure 27-7: You can use the FrontPage 97 Editor to position and set properties of controls you have created.

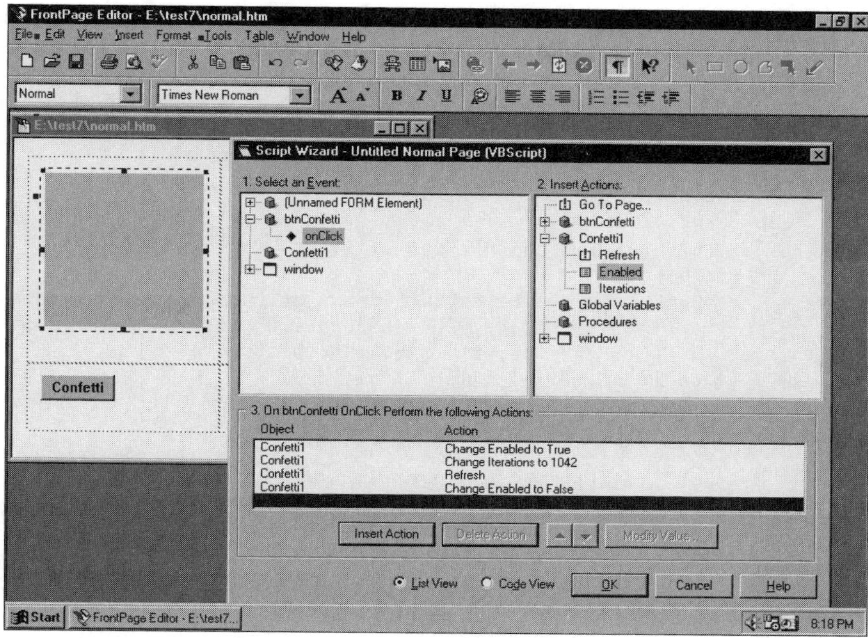

Figure 27-8: You can also use the FrontPage 97 Editor to generate on-the-fly scripts using the exposed members of your control.

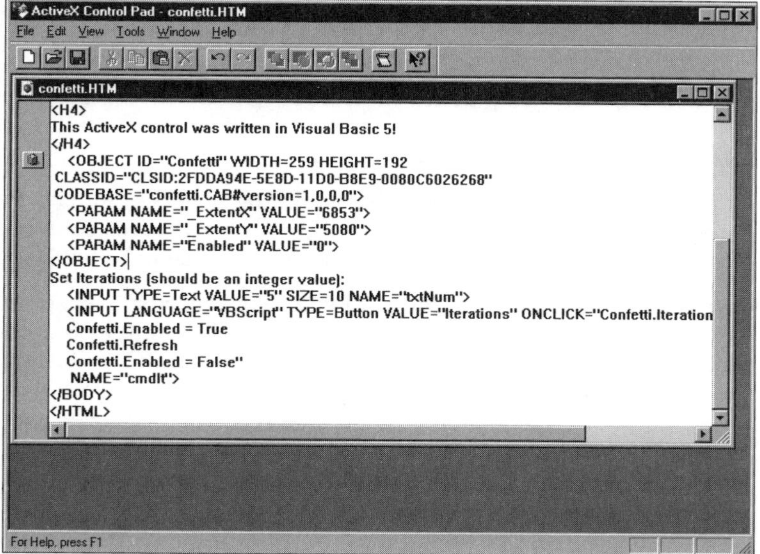

Figure 27-9: You can use ActiveX Control Pad to edit HTML and VBScript directly, as well as to manipulate the properties of custom ActiveX controls that you have created.

Using one of these ActiveX Web editing tools, you might modify the page containing the reference to the Confetti ActiveX control as follows:

```
<HTML>
   <TITLE>
      Confetti ActiveX Control
   </TITLE>
   <BODY>
   <H4>
   This ActiveX control was written in Visual Basic 5!
   </H4>
   <OBJECT ID="Confetti" WIDTH=259 HEIGHT=192
      CLASSID="CLSID:2FDDA94E-5E8D-11D0-B8E9-0080C6026268"
      CODEBASE="confetti.CAB#version=1,0,0,0">
      <PARAM NAME="_ExtentX" VALUE="6826">
      <PARAM NAME="_ExtentY" VALUE="5080">
      <PARAM NAME="Enabled" VALUE="0">
   </OBJECT>
   Set Iterations (should be an integer value):
   <INPUT TYPE=Text VALUE="5" SIZE=10 NAME="txtNum">
   <INPUT LANGUAGE="VBScript" TYPE=Button VALUE="Iterations"
   ONCLICK="Confetti.Iterations = txtNum.value
      Confetti.Enabled = True
      Confetti.Refresh
      Confetti.Enabled = False"
   NAME="cmdIt">
   </BODY>
</HTML>
```

The key aspect of this script is that it sets the initial value for the custom property Enabled to False. This is done as part of the <OBJECT> tag:

```
<PARAM NAME="Enabled" VALUE="0">
```

The Confetti control's paint event is not fired on the Web page until the user clicks the input button, causing the control's Refresh method to be invoked with the number of iterations supplied by the user.

To test that the ActiveX download — and the script — actually works, I can unregister the control and then connect to a Web server containing this page. It works in the client browser, as you can see in Figure 27-10.

Note that if you have your copy of Explorer's security level set to High, this Web page may appear to load, but the interactive content will have been broken. To load active content with the default high security setting, you'll need to digitally sign your code.

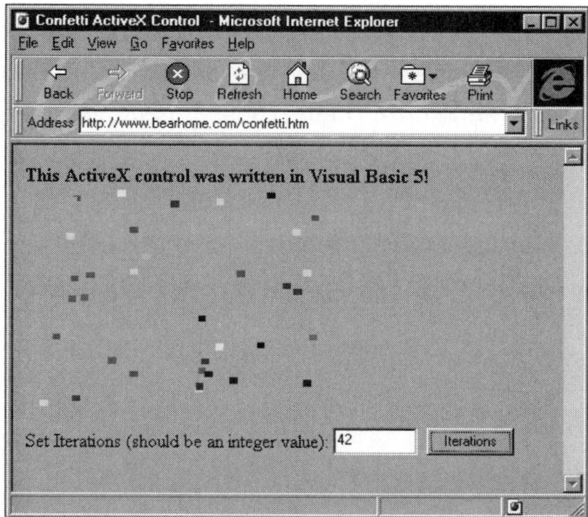

Figure 27-10: You can use VBScript in HTML applications to control the behavior of custom ActiveX controls created in VB5.

Licensing and the Web

Many of the issues involved with requiring a license file to use an ActiveX control — in design or run mode, or both — were discussed in Chapter 24, "Understanding ActiveX Controls."

Licensed controls can be used on Web pages along with Internet Explorer. Both the control and the license key must be available to be downloaded to the browser accessing the Web page.

The downloaded license key is not added to the Registry. Instead, the browser asks the control to create a runtime instance of itself, and passes it the downloaded license key. The Web site that uses the control must be able to supply both control and license. If the license is not available, control creation will fail, and the browser will receive a standard control creation error.

You can use a program named ***Lpk_tool.Exe***, located in the ***Tools\Lpk_Tool*** directory of your VB5 CD-ROM, to create a license package file for any controls that require licensing. The license package file is then referenced in the HTML code prior to the <OBJECT> tag that creates an instance of the ActiveX control. This reference will be along these lines:

```
<OBJECT CLASSID="clsid:5220cb21-c88d-11cf-b347-00aa00a28331">
   <PARAM NAME="LPKPath" VALUE="LPKfilename.LPK">
</OBJECT>
```

Summary

ActiveX controls you create in VB5 can easily by deployed on the Web. You can use ActiveX controls, and script their exposed members, to easily add executable content to your Web applications.

This chapter has explained

- ActiveX controls and browsers
- Basic Web terminology
- Normal control setup
- Web control setup
- Cabinet (***.Cab***) files
- Using the <OBJECT> tag
- Using <PARAMETER NAME> pairs to set default initialization values for custom properties
- Files generated by the Setup Wizard
- Marking controls as safe
- Scripting controls on the Web
- Licensing on the Web

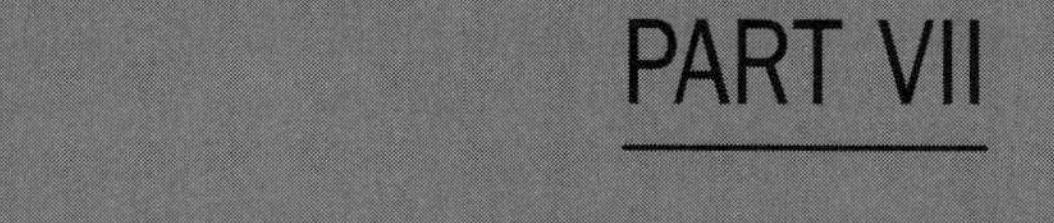

PART VII

Extending the VB Environment

Chapter 28

Creating Internet Applications in VB

This chapter discusses two exciting techniques you can use to extend the capabilities of VB5 programs. The first part of the chapter explains how to add Internet capabilities to your VB applications. The second part explains how to create ActiveX document applications — special kinds of programs that include both document content and programming content. They can be designed to "play" in an Internet Explorer window or in the Office 97 Binder.

Internet-Related Controls

The Professional and Enterprise Editions of Visual Basic 5 ship with three ActiveX controls that you can use to extend your VB applications by adding Internet-related technology.

These controls are

- The WebBrowser control, which incorporates much of Internet Explorer's functionality
- The Internet Transfer control, which encapsulates three Internet protocols
- The WinSock control, which allows the user to connect to a remote machine and exchange data

Adding Internet Features to Controls

One important way to add Internet capabilities to your VB5 applications is to write these capabilities into the controls you create. (For more information on creating controls, see Part VI, "Creating ActiveX Controls.")

ActiveX controls created using Visual Basic 5 can support a variety of Internet-related features. (These features generally require that the control's container be Internet Explorer to work.) For example, UserControl objects can support asynchronous downloading of property values, such as Picture properties that may contain bitmaps. Through the Hyperlink property of the UserControl object, they can also request that a browser jump to a URL, or navigate through its history list.

If you normally design your controls to read and write property values using a PropertyBag object, these values will not persist between different loads of a Web page. You may want to design your control to support both normal loading of property values from a PropertyBag, which is not supported by browsers, and asynchronous downloading of property values.

The WebBrowser Control

Once you add the WebBrowser control to a form, you can quite easily add Web browsing capabilities to your applications. A sample project that contains the necessary code is saved on the companion CD-ROM as ***Browser.Vbp***.

You can use the VB Application Wizard to generate a form containing the browser control that is pretty much along the lines of the demonstration project.

The first step towards adding the control and implementing Web browsing in your project is to add the control to your Toolbox using the Controls tab of the Components dialog. As shown in Figure 28-1, you'll find it listed as Microsoft Internet Controls.

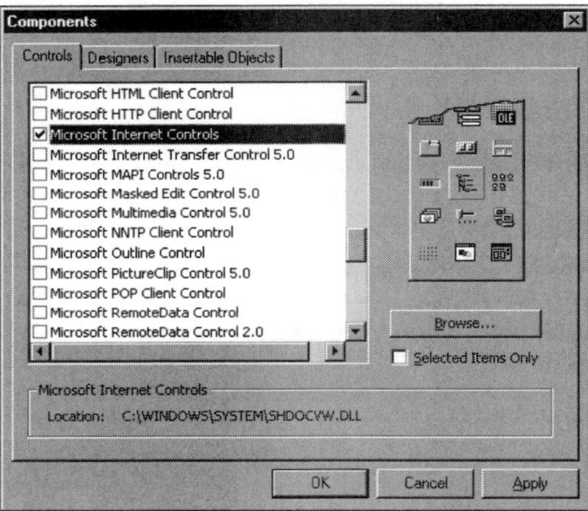

Figure 28-1: To add the Web Browser control to your Toolbox, enable Microsoft Internet Controls in the Components dialog.

To explore the members exposed by the WebBrowser control, select the SHDocVwCtl library in the Object Browser, as shown in Figure 28-2.

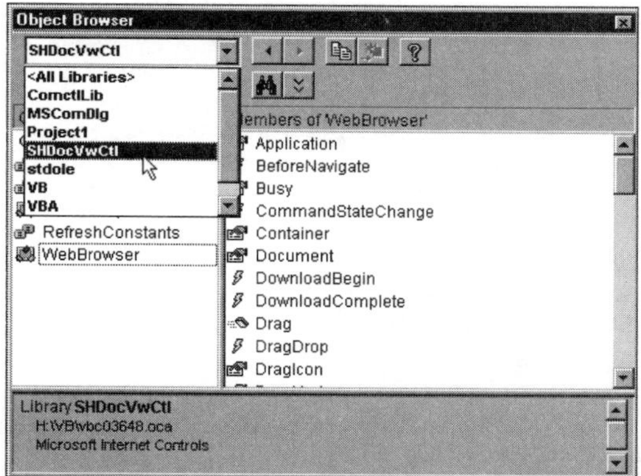

Figure 28-2: Once you've added the WebBrowser control to your project, you can view its members by selecting the SHDocVwCtl library in the Object Browser.

Browser.Frm in the sample project contains — in addition to the WebBrowser control — a Timer, a ComboBox, and a Toolbar control. When the browser form loads, the WebBrowser control needs to be sized and given a starting address:

```
Public StartingAddress As String
Private Sub Form_Load()
   On Error Resume Next
   Me.Show
   tbToolBar.Refresh
   Form_Resize
   StartingAddress = "http://www.bearhome.com"
   cboAddress.Move 50, lblAddress.Top + lblAddress.Height + 15
   If Len(StartingAddress) > 0 Then
      cboAddress.Text = StartingAddress
      cboAddress.AddItem cboAddress.Text
      'try to navigate to the starting address
      timTimer.Enabled = True
      brwWebBrowser.Navigate StartingAddress
   End If
End Sub
```

The form resize code handles sizing the WebBrowser:

```
Private Sub Form_Resize()
   cboAddress.Width = Me.ScaleWidth - 100
   brwWebBrowser.Width = Me.ScaleWidth - 100
   brwWebBrowser.Height = Me.ScaleHeight - _
      (picAddress.Top + picAddress.Height) - 100
End Sub
```

It's the job of the Timer control — once it has been enabled — to keep trying by firing its Timer event at short intervals until the WebBrowser connects to the specified address:

```
Private Sub timTimer_Timer()
    If brwWebBrowser.Busy = False Then
        timTimer.Enabled = False
        Me.Caption = brwWebBrowser.LocationName
    Else
        Me.Caption = "Working..."
    End If
End Sub
```

Assuming a working Internet connection and a valid address, this should work quite nicely. Figure 28-3 shows the WebBrowser control in the sample project with a Web page loaded.

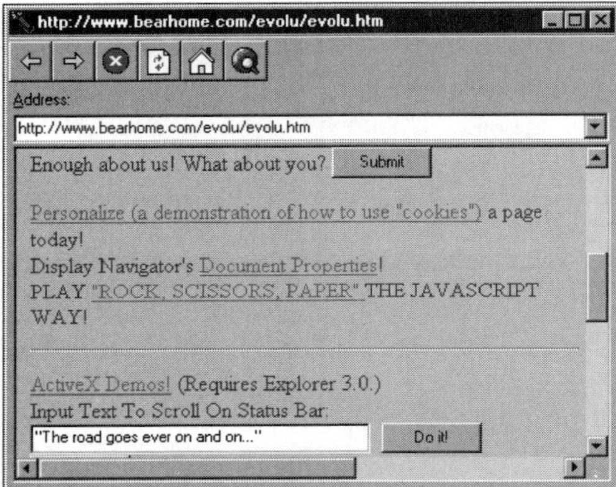

Figure 28-3: It's easy to use the WebBrowser control to connect your projects to the Web.

As the VB Application Wizard sets up a browser, the Toolbar buttons, when clicked, invoke methods of the WebBrowser object. For the most part, this works well. However, Home — which calls the GoHome method — and Search — which invokes the GoSearch method — are "hard-wired" into Microsoft Internet Explorer settings.

This makes more sense that it appears to at first, because the WebBrowser control is essentially an interface between your applications and the Internet Explorer object automation library.

The net effect, however, is that if you want to control the effects of the Home or Search commands, you cannot use the built-in methods. You can substitute your own URLs using the control's Navigate method.

Here's the revised Toolbar code:

```
Private Sub tbToolBar_ButtonClick(ByVal Button As Button)
    On Error Resume Next
    timTimer.Enabled = True
    Select Case Button.Key
        Case "Back"
```

```
            brwWebBrowser.GoBack
        Case "Forward"
            brwWebBrowser.GoForward
        Case "Refresh"
            brwWebBrowser.Refresh
        Case "Home"
            brwWebBrowser.Navigate StartingAddress 'GoHome
        Case "Search"
            brwWebBrowser.GoSearch
        Case "Stop"
            timTimer.Enabled = False
            brwWebBrowser.Stop
            Me.Caption = brwWebBrowser.LocationName
    End Select
End Sub
```

The Internet Transfer Control

You can add the Internet Transfer Control to your Toolbox using the Components dialog. The class name for this control as it appears in the Properties window is Inet. It appears in the Object Browser as InetCtlsObjects.Inet. Inet's purpose is to make it easier for your applications to perform Internet file transfers using common Internet protocols. Figure 28-4 shows the Custom Property Page dialog for an instance of the control. You select a protocol from the enumerated types shown in the Protocol drop-down list.

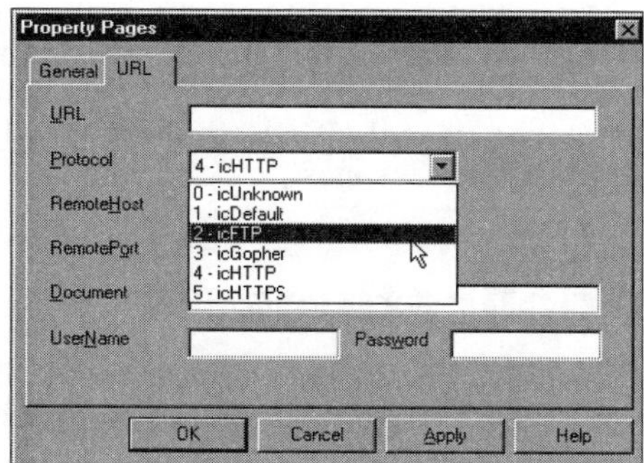

Figure 28-4: You use the Internet Transfer Control to implement file transfers using standard Internet protocols.

The WinSock Control

You add the WinSock control to your Toolbox by selecting Microsoft Winsock Control 5.0 in the Components dialog. Once you've added this control to your project, you can view its object library in the Object Browser (its name is MSWinsockLib).

The WinSock control, invisible to the user, provides an easy way to use TCP (transfer control protocol) and UDP (user datagram protocol) network services. By setting properties and invoking methods of the control, you can easily connect to a remote machine and exchange data in both directions. This is intended to help you create network client/server applications.

TCP Connections

TCP allows you to create and maintain a connection to a remote computer. Using the connection, both computers can stream data between each other. If you are creating a client application, you must know the server computer's name or IP address (RemoteHost property), as well as the port (RemotePort property) on which it will be "listening." After supplying values for these properties, you can invoke the control's Connect method. If you are creating a server application, set a port (LocalPort property) on which to listen, and invoke the Listen method. When the client computer requests a connection, the ConnectionRequest event will occur. To complete the connection, invoke the Accept method within the ConnectionRequest event. Once a connection has been made, either computer can send and receive data. To send data, invoke the SendData method. Whenever data is received, the DataArrival event occurs. Invoke the GetData method from within the DataArrival event to retrieve the data.

How UDP Works

UDP is a connectionless protocol. Unlike computers using TCP, computers using UDP do not first have to establish a connection. To transmit data, first set the client computer's LocalPort property. The server computer then only needs to set the RemoteHost to the Internet address of the client computer, set the RemotePort property to the same port as the client computer's LocalPort property, and invoke the SendData method to begin sending messages. The client computer then uses the GetData method within the DataArrival event to retrieve the sent messages.

ActiveX Document Applications

ActiveX documents are a new kind of Visual Basic application that you can create. You can use ActiveX document projects to create complex applications that are entirely contained in a host, such as Internet Explorer.

ActiveX document applications consist of ActiveX component automation servers and "documents." These documents call the automation server behind the ActiveX document application in precisely the same way that Word documents call the exposed automation objects in the Word document server, ***Winword.Exe***.

.Vbd document files, created when you compile an ActiveX document application, use OLE structured storage so that data in the document can be accessed and manipulated via standard OLE interfaces — just as Word and Excel documents do. In other words, an ActiveX document application consists of two conceptually distinct parts: ActiveX components that function as an OLE automation server, and documents that are designed to interact with the server.

Compiling a Visual Basic document application creates both a document (a ***.Vbd*** file) and a corresponding ActiveX server (a ***.Dll*** or ***.Exe*** file). The ***.Vbd*** file is to the ActiveX server as a ***.Doc*** file is to ***Winword.Exe***.

ActiveX document applications require a host application to run, much as ActiveX controls require a container. Possible ActiveX document application hosts include Microsoft's Internet Explorer, Microsoft Office 97 Binder, and the Visual Basic 5 IDE.

You can use the CreateToolWindow function to create a dockable tool Window in the Visual Basic IDE that could contain an ActiveX document application — such as, for example, an enhanced resource editor.

Creating an ActiveX Document Application

To create a new ActiveX document application, select ActiveX Document EXE or ActiveX Document DLL from the New Project dialog. Selecting an EXE project results in an out-of-process automation server, while selecting a DLL project produces an in-process server.

Document applications compiled as DLLs are likely to run much faster than document applications compiled as EXEs, but they are subject to more constraints. For example, you can't open a modeless form in a DLL application.

A default ActiveX document project contains a UserDocument object, in the same way that a Standard EXE project is based on a form, and a control project is based on a UserControl.

Controls are placed on the UserDocument, and modules and code are added to the project to achieve its desired functionality.

When the ActiveX document project is compiled, in addition to the file containing the automation server, ***.Vbd*** files are created for each UserDocument in the application.

Many of the techniques involved in creating ActiveX document applications are related to those used in creating ActiveX controls. (See Part VI for more information.) You'll also need to understand ActiveX automation techniques, discussed in Chapter 22, "Controlling 'Foreign' Application Objects," and Chapter 23, "Creating ActiveX Applications."

.Vbd Files

Once an ActiveX Document application has been compiled, the ***.Vbd*** files created by the compilation are opened by a host application, such as Internet Explorer.

Each ***.Vbd*** file contains a reference to the class identifier of its automation server. It is also used by the application to store persistent data related to the document.

Once the ***.Vbd*** file has been generated, you can rename the extension if you like. For example, if you renamed ***ActXDoc.Vbd*** to ***ActXDoc.Bad***, it would still be perfectly functional.

Implementing ActiveX Documents

Figure 28-5 shows a sample ActiveX document application open in Internet Explorer.

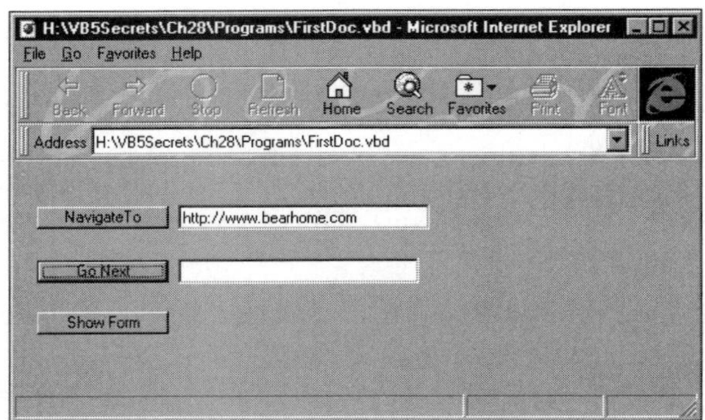

Figure 28-5: ActiveX document applications can be hosted by Internet Explorer.

When the user clicks the Go Next button, Internet Explorer moves to a second ActiveX document, as shown in Figure 28-6. The second document is based on a second UserControl module included in the ActiveX document project.

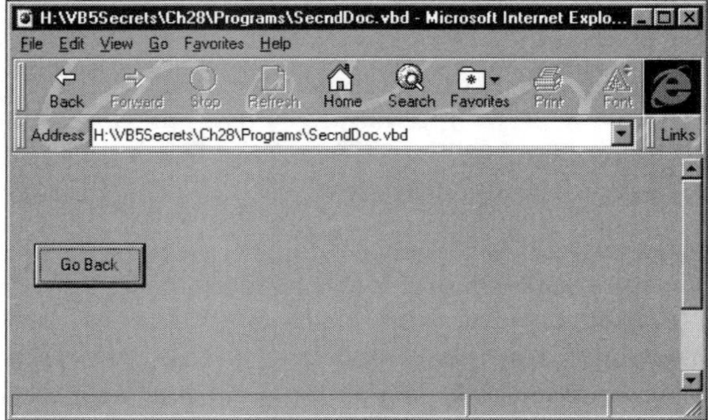

Figure 28-6: You can navigate been ActiveX documents in an ActiveX document host (such as Explorer).

Converting Existing Applications

Conceptually, ActiveX document applications are closer to ActiveX control applications than to normal projects. For one thing, both ActiveX documents and ActiveX controls must work with a container, or host. However, if you do want to convert an existing standard project, you may have some good candidates. (Note that ActiveX document applications cannot include the OLE container control.) The ActiveX Document Migration Wizard is a Visual Basic add-in that helps to convert standard projects into ActiveX document projects.

If the host for the ActiveX document application is Internet Explorer, you can use the NavigateTo method of a UserDocument's Hyperlink object to get from one document to another. For example:

```
UserDocument.Hyperlink.NavigateTo "file://C:\Sparerib\Second.Vbd"
```

Here's the code in the first document's Go Next click event:

```
Private Sub cmdGoNext_Click()
   Dim strPath As String     ' String to be parsed
   Dim strAbsPath As String ' Result of parsing
   Dim intI As Integer       ' Character position counter

   ' Return the path of the current ActiveX document
   strPath = Trim$(UserDocument.Parent.LocationName)

   ' Find the position of the last separator character.
   For intI = Len(strPath) To 1 Step -1
      If Mid$(strPath, intI, 1) = "/" Or _
         Mid$(strPath, intI, 1) = "\" Then Exit For
   Next intI
   ' Strip the name of the current .vbd file.
   strAbsPath = Left$(strPath, intI)
   ' Set the global variable to Me, allowing
   ' the SecndDoc document to get any public
   ' properties, or call any public functions.

   Set gFirstDoc = Me 'Declared in code module

   ' Navigate to the second ActiveX document.
   UserDocument.Hyperlink.NavigateTo _
      strAbsPath & "SecndDoc.vbd"
End Sub
```

This routine assumes that the two ActiveX documents are located in the same directory.

Going back to the first document is simple:

```
Private Sub cmdGoBack_Click()
   UserDocument.Hyperlink.GoBack
End Sub
```

ActiveX documents can also be added to Microsoft's Office 97 Binder, as shown in Figure 28-7.

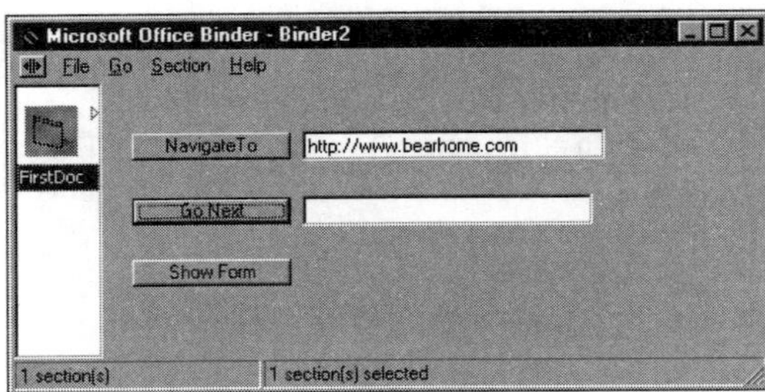

Figure 28-7: You can add ActiveX documents to a Binder.

To add an ActiveX document to a Binder, choose Add from File on the Binder's Select menu. Select the appropriate ActiveX document file. (Unless the extension has been changed, this will be a ***.Vbd*** file.)

You can use the object structure of other applications' objects that are added to a Binder from within an ActiveX document application. First, add the Microsoft Binder 8.0 Object library to your ActiveX project, as shown in Figure 28-8. Next, access the Binder's object hierarchy through the UserDocument.Parent.Parent property.

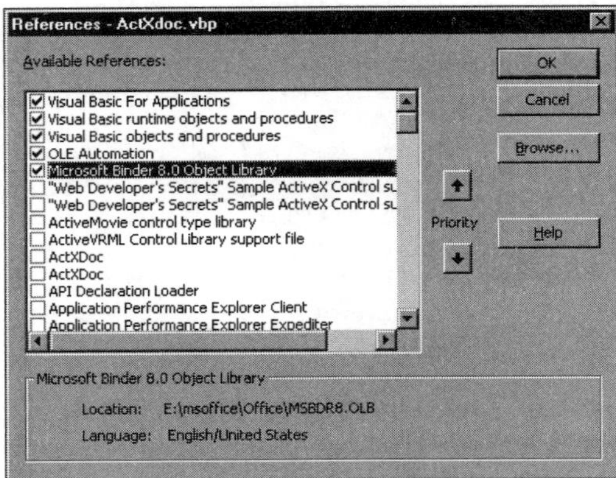

Figure 28-8: You can add the Binder object library to your VB project using the References dialog.

Determining the Container

You can programmatically determine an ActiveX document's container by using the TypeName statement with the Parent property of the UserDocument:

```
Dim strWhat As String
StrWhat = TypeName (UserDocument.Parent)
```

Table 28-1 shows three possible return strings. (Note: these *are* case sensitive!)

Table 28-1 Container Return Strings

Container	***String***
Binder	Section
Explorer	IwebBrowserApp
VB5 IDE Tool window	Window

The sample ActiveX document project saved on the CD-ROM as ***Contain.Vbp*** determines its container in Listing 28-1.

Listing 28-1: Determining an ActiveX Document host programmatically

```
Private flgShow As Boolean 'Module level
...
Private Sub UserDocument_Show()
   If Not flgShow Then
      Dim strContainer As String
      strContainer = TypeName(UserDocument.Parent)
      Select Case strContainer
         Case "IWebBrowserApp"
         'Supported container, no problem
         Case "Section"
            MsgBox "I'm not for the binder!"
         Case Else
            MsgBox "Please use Internet Explorer!",,strContainer
      End Select
   flgShow = True
   End If
End Sub
```

This code goes in the UserDocument Show event, which occurs when the ActiveX document is sited on a container.

Because the Show event is fired again whenever the ActiveX document is shown — and to avoid erratic results — a module-level flag is added to the routine. This makes sure that the container is only tested when the ActiveX document is first sited, not when it is subsequently shown.

The ActiveX document, ***Contain.Vbd***, that includes this code is sited without incident in Internet Explorer. However, it is less happy with Microsoft Office Binder, as shown in Figure 28-9.

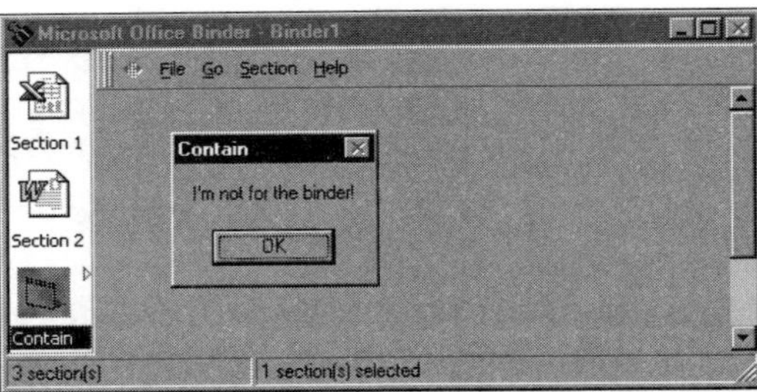

Figure 28-9: You can test the UserDocument's parent to determine the ActiveX document host.

Summary

This chapter explained how to add Internet features into your applications using Microsoft's Internet controls. In addition, it discussed how to create ActiveX document applications. This is a big topic, and one that will be increasingly important to developers in the future. ActiveX documents use OLE compound storage and a related automation server.

Topics covered in this chapter included

- Using the WebBrowser control to add Web capabilities to your applications
- Understanding how the Internet Transfer controls and Winsock controls work
- Understanding ActiveX document applications
- The ***.Vbd*** file
- ActiveX documents and navigation
- Hosting ActiveX documents
- Adding an ActiveX document to an Office 97 Binder
- Determining an ActiveX document's container programmatically

Chapter 29

Creating a VB Add-In

Visual Basic add-ins are ActiveX server components that interact with instances of the Visual Basic development environment. Generally, the purpose of an add-in is to make a complex or tedious development task easier. Therefore, the "users" of add-ins are likely to be developers. To these users, an add-in appears to be a seamless part of the Visual Basic development environment.

Add-ins are a remarkable and exciting way to extend the capabilities of the Visual Basic IDE. For example, you could build add-ins to set the appearance of all forms in a project or to parse and optimize code in a project. You can use the full capabilities of Visual Basic to interact with the project loaded in the current instance of the VB development environment.

The Visual Basic Integrated Development Environment is abbreviated as VBIDE. VBIDE.VBE refers to an object that contains the current instance of the Visual Basic design environment. (For more information on members that the VBIDE object exposes, see "Members of the Root Object" later in this chapter.)

It is quite possible to create a Visual Basic add-in in languages and environments other than VB — for example, in Visual C++ or Delphi32. The only requirement is that the language must be capable of creating ActiveX components (OLE servers) that can communicate with instances of the Visual Basic IDE object (VBIDE.VBE). For a detailed explanation of ActiveX server components, see Chapter 23, "Creating ActiveX Applications."

This chapter explains how to create add-ins using Visual Basic. The fact that you can create add-ins using Visual Basic itself, and need no knowledge of languages other than VB, opens the doors to all kinds of exciting possibilities.

Programmers can create add-ins to customize their own working VB environment and to automate complex development chores. In addition, you should not overlook the possibility of distributing and reselling any add-ins you have written.

This chapter will explain

- What an add-in is
- How to use the Add-In Manager
- Add-ins that ship with VB
- The Add-In toolbar
- How to create a custom add-in
- Advanced add-in techniques

What Is an Add-In?

Add-ins are specialized OLE server programs — written in VB5 or another language — that are in two-way communication with the Visual Basic IDE. You can use add-ins to:

- Automate repetitive tasks
- Standardize object properties across a project or form
- Build forms and applications from a standardized framework
- Guide the user in a Wizard-like fashion through almost any task that can be accomplished in the IDE
- Much more. The sky is the limit — use your imagination!

Because add-ins can detect events fired by VBIDE.VBE instances, they can react in an intelligent fashion to what the user is doing. For example, an add-in can easily respond when the user clicks a menu item or opens a form.

Kinds of Add-Ins

There are four kinds of Visual Basic 5 add-ins:

- The just-plain-vanilla add-in, referred to simply as an add-in. Add-ins perform tasks within the Visual Basic IDE, often in response to events fired by user actions. These tasks may or may not be apparent to the user.
- The Wizard, which is an add-in implemented using a "Wizard" interface. Wizards are usually used to guide users through complex but linear tasks that can be profitably divided into separate steps.

  VB5 provides the Wizard Manager — itself an add-in — to help create add-ins. Chapter 30, "Building a Wizard," explains in detail how to create an add-in Wizard. (Using VB to create a Wizard for use outside the VBIDE was covered in Chapter 8, "Windows User Interface Controls.")
- A *utility* is a program that is an ActiveX component executable that can run as a VB add-in and can also run externally to the VBIDE.
- A *builder* is a type of add-in that is used to set properties of a control (or properties that a group of controls have in common). In VB5, the functionality of a builder add-in has largely been superseded by custom property pages.

You start most add-ins by specifically selecting them from a menu or toolbar. However, there is no requirement that a VB5 add-in be started in this way. A VB5 add-in can lurk in the background waiting for an event such as an object resize event to be fired. An add-in need not be visible on the screen, and the results of running the add-in don't have to be visual. For example, an add-in could reset a Timer control when a new project loads.

Using the Add-In Manager

The Add-In Manager is a utility that is part of the Visual Basic IDE that lets you enable available add-ins. To start the Add-In Manager, choose it from the Add-Ins menu. The dialog that appears, as shown in Figure 29-1, lets you add (make available) or remove (disable) available add-ins. As explained in a moment, add-ins that are included in ***Vbaddin.Ini*** — and properly registered as ActiveX components — will appear (but not necessarily be available) in the list in the Add-In Manager.

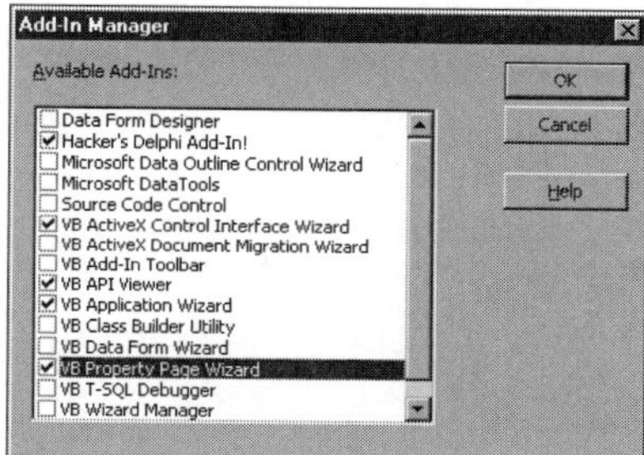

Figure 29-1: The Add-In Manager is where you add or remove available add-ins.

The add-ins listed in the Add-In Manager — both those that are enabled and those that are not — have been registered with Visual Basic. Registering an add-in with VB involves adding an entry to the file named ***Vbaddin.Ini***, which is located in the ***Windows*** directory. Entries in ***VBaddin.Ini*** are of the form ProgId = 0, meaning the add-in is not enabled, or ProgId = 1, meaning the add-in is enabled. Figure 29-2 shows Notepad displaying the ***Vbaddin.Ini*** file that corresponds to the Add-In Manager shown earlier in Figure 29-1. Later in this chapter, I'll show you how to add your own add-ins to the ***Vbaddin.Ini*** file.

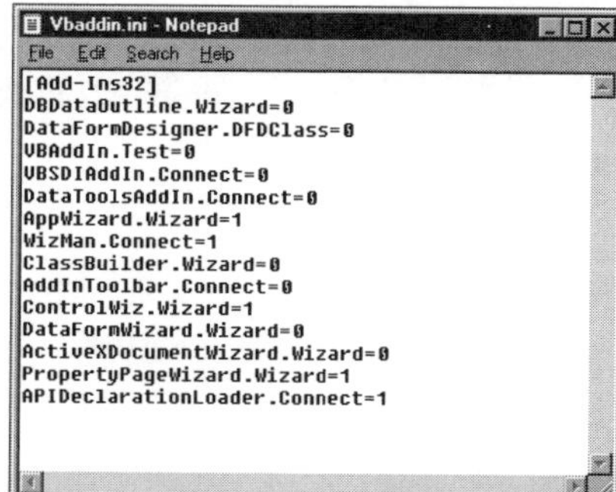

Figure 29-2: The contents of the ***Vbaddin.Ini*** file will correspond to the add-ins listed in the Add-In Manager.

Add-ins that have been successfully registered with Windows as ActiveX components and enabled in the Add-In Manager usually appear as menu items on the Add-Ins menu. Typically, the user starts an add-in by clicking the menu item displayed in the Add-Ins menu, as shown in Figure 29-3. Depending on the add-in design, at this point you can either activate a submenu system or load a form or perform some other action.

Active add-ins do not have to start execution through the Add-Ins menu. You can easily place an add-in on any Visual Basic menu.

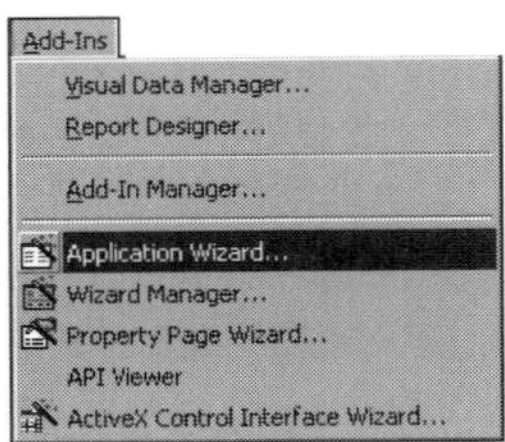

Figure 29-3: Here the Add-Ins menu includes a number of add-ins: Visual Data Manager, Report Designer, Application Wizard, Wizard Manager, Property Page Wizard, API Viewer, and the ActiveX Control Interface Wizard.

Add-Ins that VB Always Installs

The add-ins that appear above the Add-In Manager item on the menu — the Visual Data Manager and the Report Designer — have been placed there by Visual Basic itself and the user cannot configure them using the Add-In Manager.

The Visual Data Manager, shown in Figure 29-4, allows you to create new Microsoft Access databases, examine or map databases in a variety of other formats, create SQL queries, and perform a variety of database-related tasks.

The Report Designer add-in interfaces with Crystal Reports for Visual Basic, which is shown in Figure 29-5. Crystal Reports is a powerful tool for creating custom reports, forms, and lists from existing databases.

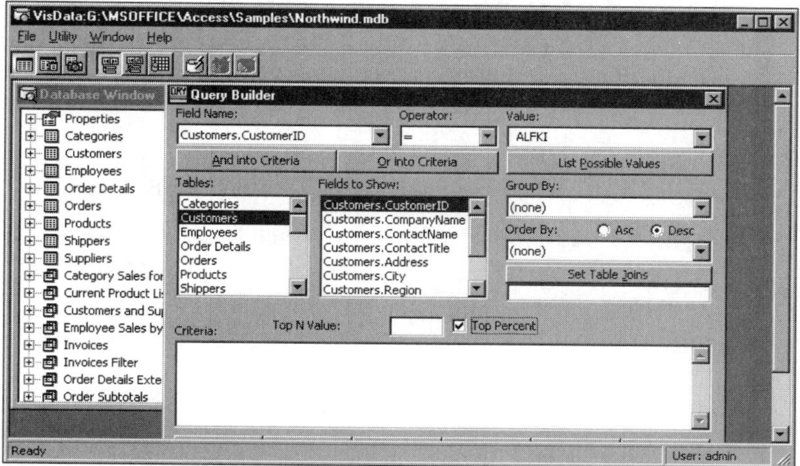

Figure 29-4: You use the Visual Data Manager add-in to create and manipulate databases.

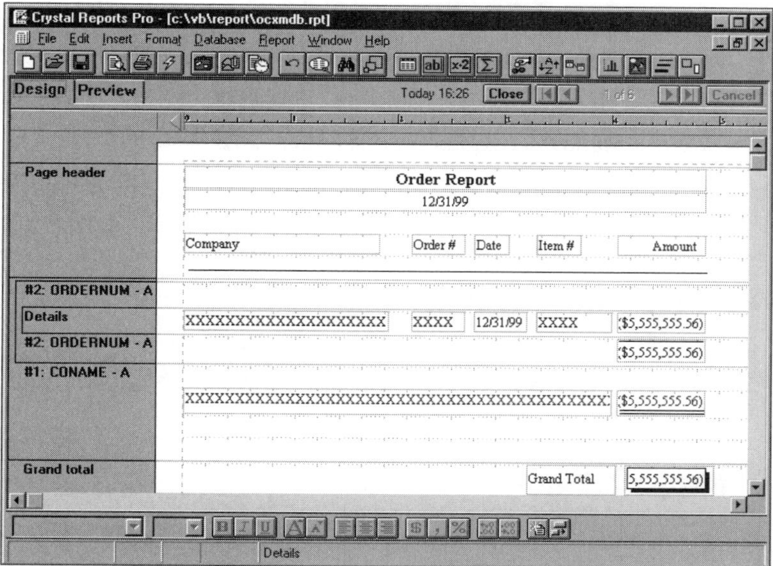

Figure 29-5: The Crystal Reports Designer add-in enables you to create reports, forms, and lists.

Other Add-Ins that Ship with VB

Beneath the Add-In Manager item on the Add-Ins menu are menu items for optional add-ins that have been enabled. VB5 ships with a number of add-ins that add items to this menu if they are enabled. Other items on this menu are custom add-ins such as ones you write yourself or obtain from other software developers. It's almost certain that you already have some familiarity with many of the add-ins supplied with VB. These include:

- ActiveX Control Interface Wizard, which helps you design the interface for ActiveX controls (see Chapter 25, "Creating the Control Interface")
- ActiveX Document Migration Wizard, which helps to convert forms in a project to ActiveX documents (see Chapter 28, "Creating Internet Applications in VB")
- Add-In Toolbar (see the next section)
- API Viewer, which provides an interface between VB and the API Viewer application
- Application Wizard, which helps construct the initial framework for standard executable VB projects
- Class Builder Utility, which helps to design class module members
- Data Form Wizard, which helps you create a form with objects bound to a local or remote data source
- T-SQL Debugger, used to help test and debug stored SQL statements
- Wizard Manager (explained in Chapter 30)

Many of these add-ins are extremely important on their own account, and appear to users below the advanced level to be a part of Visual Basic itself.

The Add-In Toolbar

If VB Add-In toolbar is enabled in the Add-In Manager, a toolbar with buttons for available add-ins is added to the VB environment, as shown in Figure 29-6.

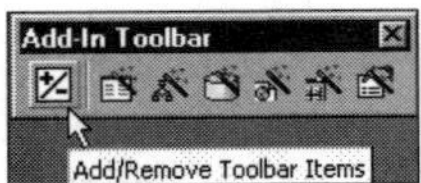

Figure 29-6: The Add-In toolbar displays buttons that activate available add-ins.

As explained later in this chapter, you can add code to your custom add-ins that automatically adds a button to the Add-In toolbar and opens the Add-In toolbar if it is not already enabled.

The leftmost button on the Add-In toolbar opens the Add/Remove Toolbar Items dialog (shown in Figure 29-7), which allows users to configure the toolbar.

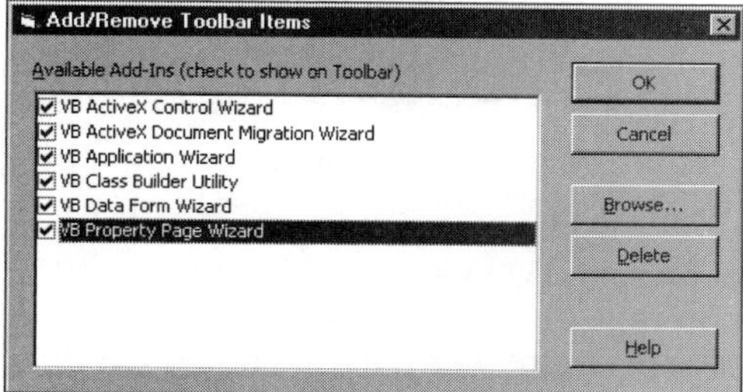

Figure 29-7: Users can easily configure the Add-In toolbar by adding or removing specific add-ins in the Add/Remove Toolbar Items dialog.

VBIDE Object Concepts

The VBIDE (Visual Basic Integrated Development Environment) object encapsulates exposure of its child objects and their properties, events, and methods belonging to instances of the Visual Basic environment.

This exposure of objects, properties, events, and methods lets you perform many tasks:

- Initialize and shut down add-ins
- Add new menu items to the VBIDE, and respond when the user selects the menu item
- Manage the creation, opening, and closure of files associated with the current VB project
- Manipulate forms and their controls in the current project
- Respond to user actions

Working with add-ins requires an understanding of three different kinds of objects:

- The root object
- A Visual Basic instance variable
- The IDTExtensibility Interface

The root object represents an instance of the Visual Basic environment (including all related program source files). It is referred to using a Visual

Basic instance variable. For example, the following declaration assigns the current instance of the VB environment to the global variable gMyVBInstance:

```
Global gMyVBInstance As VBIDE.VBE
```

Members of the Root Object

Members of the root object are referred to using the dot operator and a Visual Basic instance variable.

You can use the Object Browser to view the members of the VBIDE object, as shown in Figure 29-8. To do this, make sure that Microsoft Visual Basic 5.0 Extensibility is selected in the References dialog. Then open the Object Browser, and select VBIDE in the topmost drop-down list box.

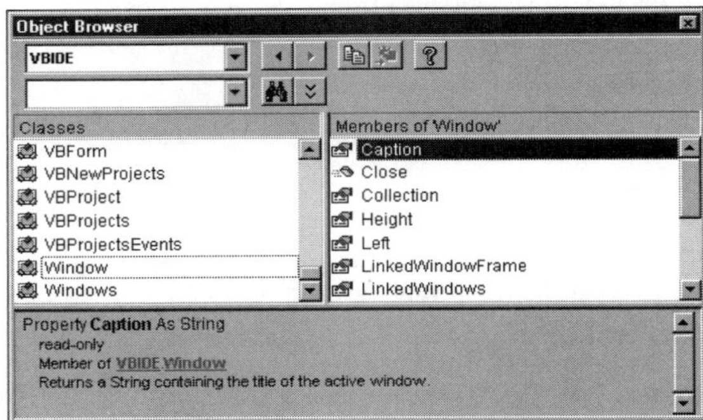

Figure 29-8: You can use the Object Browser to view the members of the VBIDE object, provided that the Microsoft Visual Basic 5.0 Extensibility library has been enabled.

The VBIDE.VBE extensibility model includes objects that fall in the following categories:

- Extend the user interface, including command bars, windows, and code panes. The term "command bar" as used in the extensibility object model means VB toolbars and menus.
- Manipulate projects.
- Manipulate forms.
- Respond to events.
- Manipulate code.
- User add-ins.

You can find an overview diagram of the extensibility object model that helps make the relationships involved clear in the VB5 Books Online documentation in "The Extensibility Model Object" in the *Component Tools Guide*.

User Interface Extensibility

Objects that extend the user interface include the CommandBars, Windows, and CodePanes collections. These collections are used for such tasks as:

- Adding a new button or command to an existing toolbar or menu
- Creating an entirely new menu or toolbar for an add-in
- Opening, closing, moving, or altering the size of user interface windows
- Using the CodePanes collection and CodePane object to display code and determine what code a user has selected

Manipulating Projects

The VBProjects collection allows you to manipulate VB projects in many ways, including:

- Selecting one project out of several to operate on, or selecting several for group project operations
- Removing all projects from the Visual Basic environment, and starting a new project
- Adding new projects to the current Visual Basic session
- Notifying your add-in or reacting appropriately when particular projects are loaded or unloaded
- Displaying project names — for example, in a combo box
- Changing project options

Manipulating Forms

Objects belonging to the VBForm object allow you to programmatically manipulate the designers for a form, control, property page, or ActiveX document to achieve tasks including:

- Adding a designer
- Adding code or controls
- Hiding or displaying a designer
- Positioning controls
- Changing the properties of a designer

Responding to Events

The VBIDE.VBE Events collection helps you respond to events that occur in the instance of Visual Basic. You may also need to add handling for events that occur in other VBIDE object collections, including:

- VBProjects
- VBComponents
- VBControls

Manipulating Code

The members of the VBE CodeModule object allow you to programmatically control and manipulate code in Visual Basic.

Using these objects, you could perform many tasks, including:

- Selecting, adding, or deleting lines of code
- Searching and/or replacing occurrences of specific strings

Using Add-Ins

The AddIns collection allows you to connect and disconnect add-ins, and to access exposed objects belonging to individual add-ins.

IDTExtensibility Methods

The IDTExtensibility interface contains methods that must be invoked by a Visual Basic add-in. These methods are:

- OnConnection, which occurs when an add-in is connected to the Visual Basic IDE
- OnDisconnection, which occurs when an add-in is disconnected from the Visual Basic IDE, either programmatically or through the Add-In Manager
- OnStartUpComplete, which occurs when the startup of the Visual Basic IDE is complete
- OnAddInsUpdate, which occurs when changes to the ***Vbaddin.Ini*** file are saved

Although these are methods to the IDTExtensibility interface, they appear to the VB programmer to operate like events. For example, the OnConnection method is called automatically when an add-in is connected to Visual Basic. This can be responded to programmatically as if an event has been fired.

I'll explain the process of creating an add-in in detail in the next section. For now, in the context of the IDTExtensibility interface, you should know that each add-in must contain a class module. The class module must use the Implements statement in its Declarations section to include the IDTExtensibility interface and access its events:

```
Implements IDTExtensibility
```

In addition, the class module must contain routines for each of the IDTExtensibility methods.

Empty routines are deleted when a VB project is compiled. It's important you add something, even if it is only a comment, to each of these four Subs so they are not deleted during the compilation process. Add-ins without subroutines corresponding to all four of the IDTExtensibility methods will not function properly. For example:

```
Private Sub IDTExtensibility_OnAddInsUpdate(custom() As Variant)
    'Comment is placeholder so routine is not deleted during
    'compilation
End Sub
```

Creating a Simple Add-In

It's easiest to understand the process of creating an add-in in the context of an example. The example project is saved on the companion CD-ROM as ***Vb5s.Vbp***. It contains a class module — as all add-ins must — as well as a code module and a form. The project structure can be displayed in the Project Explorer, as shown in Figure 29-9.

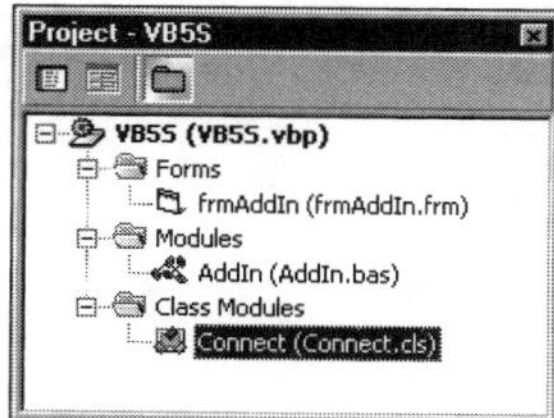

Figure 29-9: All add-in projects must contain at least one class module.

Much of the template code for a simple add-in is available as a template project. To open a project based upon the supplied add-in template, select Addin from the New Project dialog, as shown in Figure 29-10.

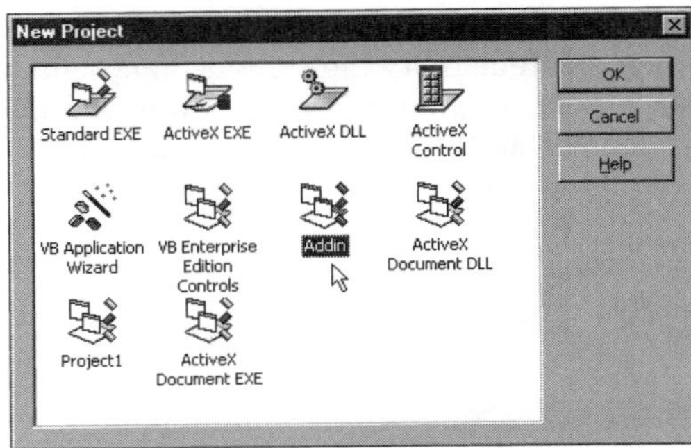

Figure 29-10: You can open a template project you can use for creating custom add-ins by selecting Addin from the New Project dialog.

All add-ins must include the library for the Microsoft Visual Basic 5.0 Extensibility object. In addition, as will usually be the case, if you'd like to have your add-in place menu items on VB menus, or add buttons to toolbars, you'll need to include a reference to the Microsoft Office 8.0 Object Library. Figure 29-11 shows references to both libraries enabled using the Project References dialog.

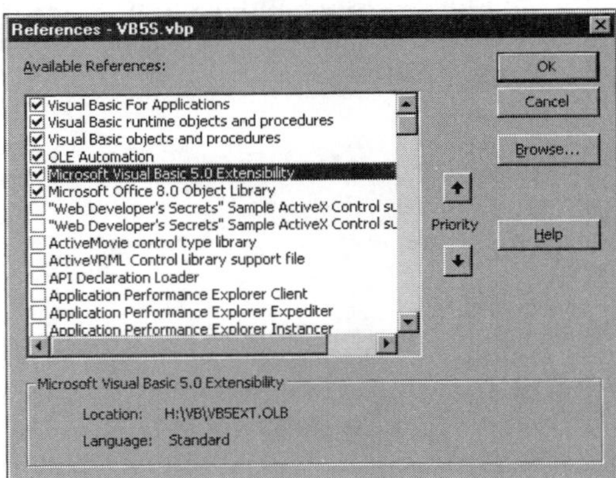

Figure 29-11: You should add the Microsoft Visual Basic 5.0 Extensibility Object and the Microsoft Office 8.0 Object Library to your add-in project using the References dialog.

The default name used to register your add-in with Visual Basic is the ProgID — or, *programmatic identifier* — for the class module containing the IDTExtensibility procedures — in other words, the project name, as set in the Project Options dialog, followed by the dot operator, followed by the name of the class module.

Because the sample project is named VB5S, and the class module is named Connect, the add-in's identifier is VB5S.Connect. As I'll explain in moment, you'll need to construct a ***Vbaddin.Ini*** entry that reflects this, for example:

```
VB5S.Connect=1
```

An add-in's ProgID is the way it is identified by default in the Add-In Manager.

Although computers — and Visual Basic — may speak ProgIDs fluently, your run-of-the-mill human developer does not. It is, therefore, a good idea to internally identify your add-in in a clearer way, so users will understand its entry in the Add-In Manager.

To set the description that VB will use in the Add-In Manager, open the add-in project in the Object Browser and select the class module containing the connection code. Using the right-mouse context menu, choose Properties for the class module to open its Member Options dialog. As shown in Figure 29-12, enter the description that users will see in the Add-In Manager dialog.

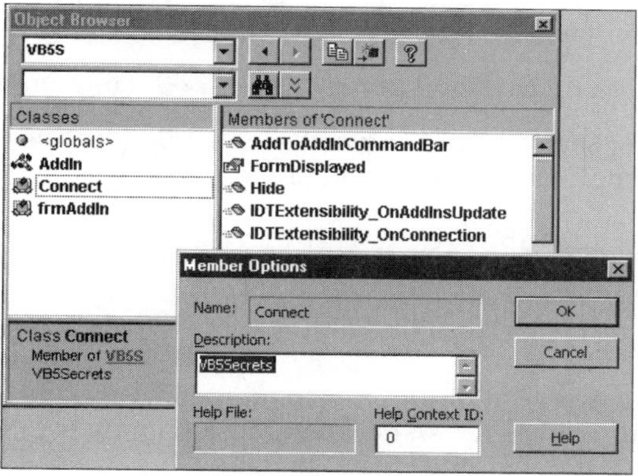

Figure 29-12: You use the Member Options dialog of the class module containing the IDTExtensibility code to change the description of an add-in that will appear in the Add-In Manager.

Compiling an Add-In

You will not be able to test an add-in until it has been compiled, registered on the target machine, and registered with Visual Basic. (The act of compiling the add-in, of course, automatically handles registering it on the machine on which it is compiled.)

Add-in projects must be compiled as ActiveX components, meaning as ActiveX DLLs or ActiveX EXEs. In "old-speak," this statement would have been that add-ins are compiled as in-process (***.Dll***) or out-of-process (***.Exe***) OLE servers. You use the Project Type drop-down list on the General tab of the Project Properties dialog to determine which way a project will be compiled.

It's most common to compile add-ins as ActiveX DLLs. As a general rule, in-process components — ActiveX DLLS — are faster than out-of-process components (ActiveX EXEs).

The primary reason you might want to compile an add-in as an ActiveX EXE is to allow the add-in to run independently of an instance of the Visual Basic IDE.

Manually Registering and Unregistering Add-Ins

Compiling an ActiveX component application automatically registers the application with the system it is compiled on. However, it is an unfortunate fact of life that debugging and testing a program means going back a number of times and correcting any problems.

You'll also need to make sure that add-ins are registered on the systems of users to whom you distribute them. Setup utilities, including the Application Setup Wizard, will usually take care of generating the required code for you. (See Chapter 36, "Setup Programs," for more information.) However, it makes sense to know how to do this manually — in case you have to talk a user through registering or unregistering one of your ActiveX components.

Here's how to manually register and unregister ActiveX components.

You register and unregister in-process components (***.Dll*** files) using ***Regsvr32.Exe***. For example, to register an in-process server:

```
Regsvr32 MyServ.Dll
```

To unregister the server:

```
Regsvr32 /u MyServ.Dll
```

You register and unregister out-of-process components (***.Exe*** files) using a command-line switch. To register an out-of-process component:

```
MyServ.Exe /regserver
```

To unregister it:

```
MyServ.Exe /unregserver
```

Registering with VB

Add-ins must also be registered with Visual Basic before they appear in the Add-In Manager. This registration consists of adding a line to the [Add-Ins32] section of the ***Vbaddin.Ini*** file. Usually you accomplish this by calling the WritePrivateProfileString API in the setup program for the add-in after it has been registered with the system.

You can use the subroutine AddtoINI( ) in the ***AddIn.Bas*** code module in the VB5S add-in project to add the line to ***Vbaddin.Ini***. Listing 29-1 shows the code:

Listing 29-1: Registering an add-in with VB

```
Declare Function WritePrivateProfileString& Lib "Kernel32" _
   Alias "WritePrivateProfileStringA" (ByVal AppName$, _
   ByVal KeyName$, ByVal keydefault$, ByVal FileName$)

Sub AddToINI()
   Dim ErrCode As Long
   ErrCode = WritePrivateProfileString("Add-Ins32", _
      "VB5S.Connect", "0", "vbaddin.ini")
   If ErrCode Then
      Debug.Print "Add-in successfully added to Vbaddin.Ini!"
   Else
      Debug.Print "Oops. No can do! Not registered in Vbaddin.Ini."
   End If
End Sub
```

For your own add-ins, you should substitute the add-in's ProgID for the one used in the example ("VB5S.Connect").

For testing purposes, you can enter a call to this routine in the Immediate window. As shown in Figure 29-13, the Debug message indicates whether the call to WritePrivateProfileString succeeded.

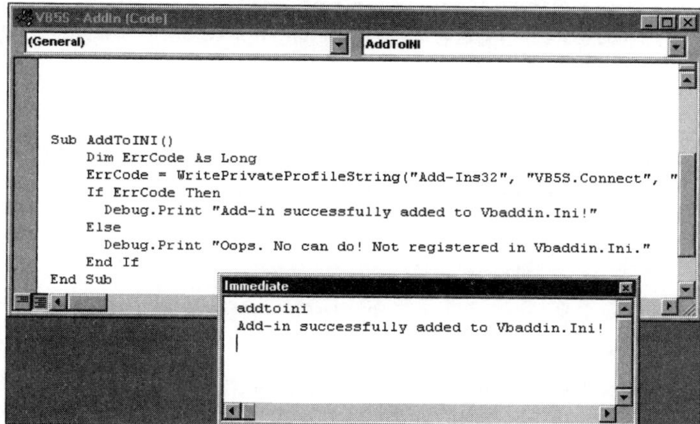

Figure 29-13: You can execute the routine that registers an add-in with VB directly from the Immediate window.

Here's the [Add-Ins32] section of the ***Vbaddin.Ini***, with the registration line added by the code from Listing 29-1.

```
[Add-Ins32]
...
VB5S.Connect=0
```

The Connection Class Module

Code in the ***Connect.Cls*** class module handles the four IDTExtensibility methods that must be present in every add-in. Here are the declarations for the module:

```
Implements IDTExtensibility

Public FormDisplayed          As Boolean
Public VBInstance             As VBIDE.VBE
Dim mcbMenuCommandBar         As Office.CommandBarControl
Dim mfrmAddIn                 As New frmAddIn
Public WithEvents MenuHandler As CommandBarEvents
```

The IDTExtensibility OnConnection procedure adds the add-in to VB, as shown in Listing 29-2.

Listing 29-2: The IDTExtensibility OnConnection procedure

```
Private Sub IDTExtensibility_OnConnection(ByVal VBInst As Object, _
   ByVal ConnectMode As vbext_ConnectMode, _
   ByVal AddInInst As VBIDE.AddIn, custom() As Variant)

   On Error GoTo error_handler
   MsgBox "I'm in the IDTExtensibility_OnConnection sub", _
      vbInformation, "Connecting..."
   'save the Visual Basic instance passed to the procedure
   Set VBInstance = VBInst
   If ConnectMode = vbext_cm_External Then
      'Used by the wizard toolbar to start
      Me.Show
   Else
      Set mcbMenuCommandBar = AddToAddInCommandBar _
         ("VB5 Secrets AddIn")
      Set Me.MenuHandler = _


   VBInst.Events.CommandBarEvents(mcbMenuCommandBar)
   End If

   If ConnectMode = vbext_cm_AfterStartup Then
      If GetSetting(App.Title, "Settings", _
         "DisplayOnConnect", "0") = "1" Then
          ' set this to display the form on connect if desired
          ' based on registry settings
          ' Me.Show
      End If
   End If
Exit Sub
error_handler:
   MsgBox Err.Description
End Sub
```

A ConnectMode constant is passed as a parameter to the OnConnection procedure. As shown in Figure 29-14, you can use the Object Browser to determine the possible values of the members of vbext_ConnectMode (and what they mean).

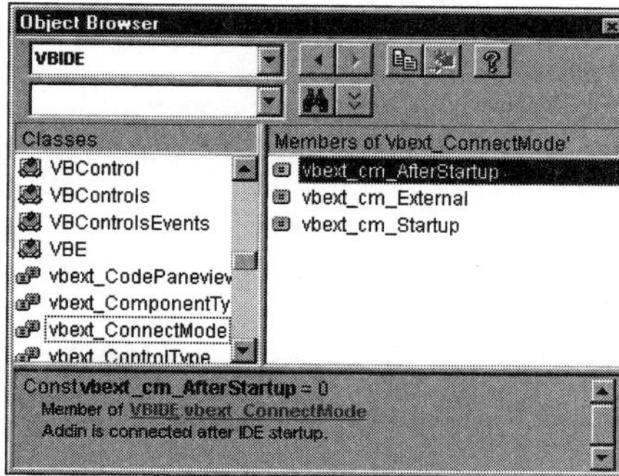

Figure 29-14: You can select the VBIDE object in the Object Browser to help determine the meanings of the constants that are possible values of its classes, collections, and members.

Once the add-in has been enabled in the Add-In Manager, as shown in Figure 29-15, the add-in's IDTExtensibility OnConnection procedure is fired when the user clicks OK in the Add-In Manager.

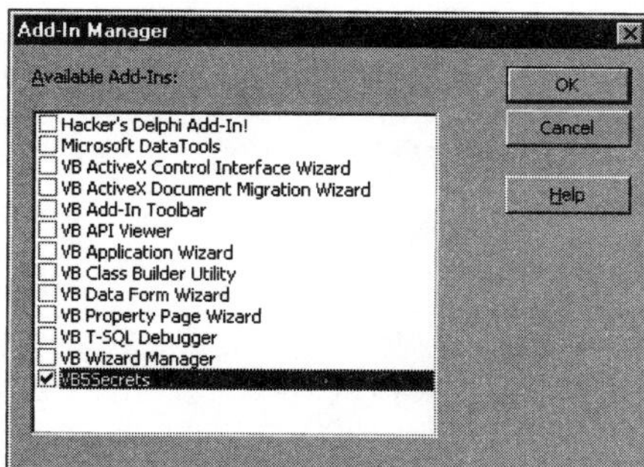

Figure 29-15: An add-in's OnConnection routine is fired when the add-in is enabled in the Add-In Manager and the Add-In Manager is closed because the user clicked OK.

Provided that the add-in is enabled, its IDTExtensibility OnConnection procedure is also fired when an instance of Visual Basic itself is started.

Figure 29-16 shows the message box displayed by the OnConnection procedure to demonstrate that it is engaged.

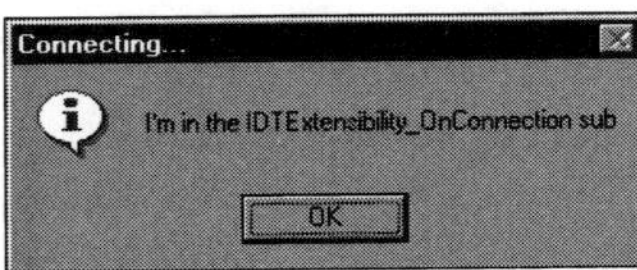

Figure 29-16: If you add message box statements to the IDTExtensibility procedures, you can get a feeling for when these procedures are invoked.

Within the IDTExtensibility OnConnection procedure, an item for the new add-in is added to the Visual Basic Add-Ins menu. This is accomplished by invoking the AddToAddInCommandBar function:

```
Set mcbMenuCommandBar = AddToAddInCommandBar _
   ("VB5 Secrets AddIn")
```

Listing 29-3 contains the AddToAddInCommandBar function, also from the Connect class module, which can be customized to suit the needs of your add-in:

Listing 29-3: Adding an add-in menu item

```
Function AddToAddInCommandBar (sCaption As String) _
   As Office.CommandBarControl
   Dim cbMenuCommandBar As Office.CommandBarControl
   'command bar object
   Dim cbMenu As Object
   Set cbMenu = VBInstance.CommandBars("Add-Ins")
   If cbMenu Is Nothing Then
      'no Add-Ins menu
      Exit Function
   End If
   'add it to the command bar (menu)
   Set cbMenuCommandBar = cbMenu.Controls.Add(1)
   'set the caption
   cbMenuCommandBar.Caption = sCaption
   Set AddToAddInCommandBar = cbMenuCommandBar
End Function
```

The CommandBar object contains other CommandBar objects that can act as either buttons or menu commands. In other words, if the CommandBar object were named for what it really contains, it would be called the “CommandBarandMenuObjectHolder.”

When the IDTExtensibility OnConnection procedure calls the AddToAddInCommandBar function, an item — captioned with the parameter passed to the function — is added to the Add-Ins menu, as shown in Figure 29-17, using the Add method of the CommandBars object.

Figure 29-17: You can use the CommandBars object to create a menu item for your add-in.

A procedure named MenuHandler was declared as WithEvents in the Declarations section of the Class module:

```
Public WithEvents MenuHandler As CommandBarEvents
```

The new command bar (or menu item) object has been assigned to the variable mcbMenuCommandBar:

```
Set mcbMenuCommandBar = AddToAddInCommandBar _
     ("VB5 Secrets AddIn")
```

The following line of code in the IDTExtensibility OnConnection procedure tells VB where to send events generated by the new menu item:

```
Set Me.MenuHandler = _
   VBInst.Events.CommandBarEvents(mcbMenuCommandBar)
```

You'll need to add a corresponding procedure to the Connect class module to handle events that are fired when users click on the new menu item:

```
Private Sub MenuHandler_Click(ByVal CommandBarControl _
   As Object, handled As Boolean, CancelDefault As Boolean)
   MsgBox "My menu was clicked!"
   Me.Show
End Sub
```

When the user clicks the add-in's menu item, the MenuHandler Click procedure displays a message box indicating that it was fired, as shown in Figure 29-18, and executes any other code you have placed in it.

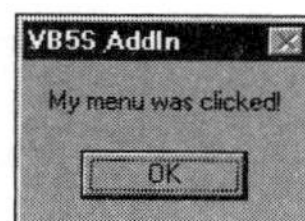

Figure 29-18: You can add a message box to the add-in menu item's click handler to make sure that it is really fired.

The handler for the add-in's menu item click event is where you'd normally place code that fulfills the destiny of the add-in. Here's where you would display a form (or perform a task if the add-in does not have a visible display).

The statement at the end of the MenuHandler procedure, Me.Show, invokes the Connect class module's Show procedure, which displays an instance of the form that is included in the VB5S add-in project:

```
Sub Show()
   On Error Resume Next
   If mfrmAddIn Is Nothing Then
      Set mfrmAddIn = New frmAddIn
   End If
   Set mfrmAddIn.VBInstance = VBInstance
   Set mfrmAddIn.Connect = Me
   FormDisplayed = True
   mfrmAddIn.Show
End Sub
```

An instance of the frmAddIn is displayed. As shown in Figure 29-19, it has an OK and a Hide button.

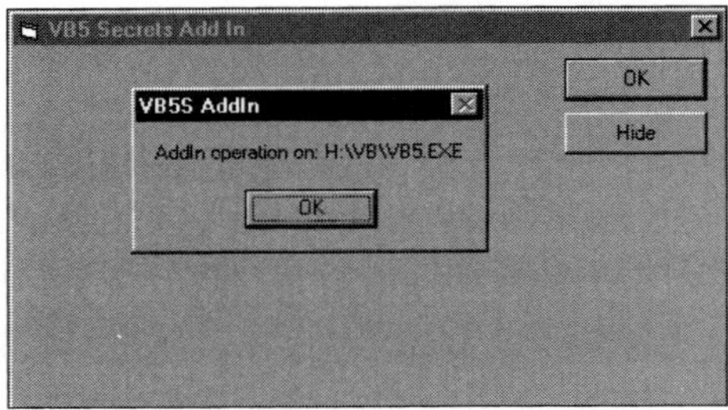

Figure 29-19: Usually, you'll want to display a form when the user clicks your add-in's menu item.

Clicking the OK button displays the value of the FullName property of the current instance of VB:

```
Private Sub OKButton_Click()
   MsgBox "AddIn operation on: " & VBInstance.FullName
End Sub
```

Clicking the Hide button invokes the Connect class module's Hide procedure, which calls the Hide method of the form instance:

```
Private Sub cmdHide_Click()
   Connect.Hide
End Sub

Sub Hide()
   On Error Resume Next
   FormDisplayed = False
   mfrmAddIn.Hide
End Sub
```

The IDTExtensibility OnStartupComplete procedure can be used to display an instance of the add-in's form when the Visual Basic IDE finishes loading. Even if you don't want to use the procedure, you should place a comment in it as a placeholder, as I explained earlier in this chapter, so the empty procedure is not deleted by the compiler:

```
Private Sub IDTExtensibility_OnStartupComplete(custom() As Variant)
    'Me.Show
    'I'm a placeholder!
End Sub
```

The IDTExtensibility OnAddInsUpDate procedure is fired when changes to the ***Vbaddin.Ini*** file are saved. You can use this procedure to automate connecting add-ins, as I'll show you in a moment in "Programmatic Connections." However, most of the time you'll want to leave it empty, except for a placeholder:

```
Private Sub IDTExtensibility_OnAddInsUpdate(custom() As Variant)
    'I'm a placeholder!
End Sub
```

The IDTExtensibility OnDisconnection procedure is fired when the add-in is removed from VB. This is where your clean-up code should go:

```
Private Sub IDTExtensibility_OnDisconnection(ByVal RemoveMode _
    As vbext_DisconnectMode, custom() As Variant)
    On Error Resume Next
    MsgBox "I'm in the IDTExtensibility_OnDisconnection sub", _
        vbInformation, "Disconnecting..."
    'Delete the command bar entry (e.g., menu item)
    mcbMenuCommandBar.Delete
    'Shut down the add-in form if it is loaded
    Unload mfrmAddIn
    Set mfrmAddIn = Nothing
End Sub
```

The message box included in the OnDisconnection procedure (see Figure 29-20) is shown when the user disables the add-in and clicks OK in the Add-In Manager, or when an instance of VB shuts down with the add-in connected.

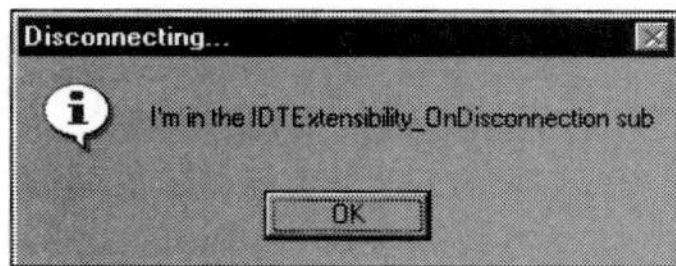

Figure 29-20: The IDTExtensibility OnDisconnection procedure is fired when the add-in is disconnected.

Programmatic Connections

Sometimes users get lazy! They just don't want to go into the Add-In Manager and connect an add-in. Here's how you can accommodate them by automating the process of connecting a specific add-in. To users, this may make the add-in seem even more an integral part of the VB environment.

First, I've added a call from the IDTExtensibility OnConnection procedure to a class procedure named AutoConnect. AutoConnect cycles through the add-ins in the add-ins collection for the current instance of VB. When it finds the add-in to automatically connect — based on the value of its ProgID — it sets the Connect property for that add-in to True, as shown in Listing 29-4.

Listing 29-4: Creating a programmatic add-in connection

```
Sub AutoConnect()
   Dim X As Object
   For Each X In VBInstance.Addins
      'Go through the add-ins in the collection
      If X.ProgId = "VB5S.Connect" Then
         'Set the connect flag to true for "our" add-in
         X.Connect = True
      End If
   Next X
End Sub
```

You'll also need to add a line of code to the hitherto empty IDTExtensibility OnAddInsUpdate event:

```
Private Sub IDTExtensibility_OnAddInsUpdate(custom() As Variant)
   VBInstance.Addins.Update
   'Call the UpDate method of the Addins collection
End Sub
```

This calls the UpDate method of the Addins collection, which causes the instance of VB to reread the ***Vbaddin.Ini*** file.

A final step is to edit the ***Vbaddin.Ini*** to set the add-in to connected. You could do this manually, or in code using WritePrivateProfileString:

```
VB5S.Connect=1
```

Provided that the ***Vbaddin.Ini*** entry has been set to 1, the next time an instance of VB is started, VB will notice that its entry has been set to connected, reread the list of add-ins from the file, and connect the add-in.

To programmatically disconnect an add-in, reverse the process, setting the Connect property of the add-in to False.

Creating an Add-In: The Required Steps

Here's a recap of the steps you must take to create an add-in:

1. Start a new project for the add-in's ActiveX component application. The project should include a class module to contain the add-in connection code as well as any source code and forms that are required to make your add-in functional. You should plan to compile your add-in as an in-process ActiveX component (***.Dll*** file) or as an out-of-process ActiveX component (***.Exe*** file). As an example, the project saved as ***Very.Vbp*** (and named Very) contains a class module for the connection code named Simple.
2. Choose References from the Project menu. Make sure that Microsoft Visual Basic 5.0 Extensibility and Microsoft Office 8.0 Object Library are checked.
3. Expose the IDTExtensibility interface to the class module using the statement

   ```
   Implements IDTExtensibility
   ```

   in the Declarations section of the class module. The four methods of the IDTExtensibility interface — OnAddinsUpDate, OnConnection, OnDisconnection, OnStartUpComplete — will appear in the class module's Procedure and Object drop-down boxes. These IDTExtensibility interface methods can be used like events that are fired in the class module.
4. Use the Object Browser to give the add-in a description that will appear in the Add-In Manager. The default is the ProgID. (If the project is named Very, and the class module Simple, the ProgID is Very.Simple.) A descriptive name is much nicer, and also pretty simple. In the Object Browser, select the add-in class module — by definition, the one that contains the IDTExtensibility event code. Select properties from the context menu to open the Member Options dialog for the class module and, in the Description box, enter the add-in name as you wish it to appear on the VB Add-In Manager (see Figure 29-21).

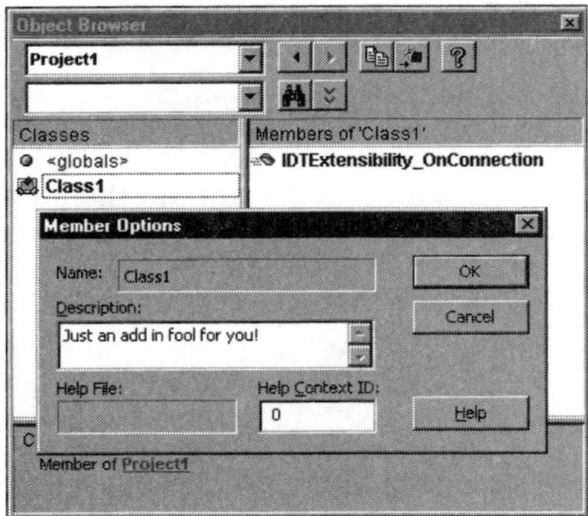

Figure 29-21: You can use the Member Options dialog for the class module containing the IDTExtensibility interface code to change the description of an add-in as it appears in the Add-In Manager.

5. Add code to the IDTExtensibility_OnConnection and IDTExtensibility_OnDisconnection procedures to handle connecting and disconnecting the add-in, as described in the previous section. Here's the minimum code required — admittedly, it doesn't do much — in the Simple class module:

```
Public VBInstance As VBIDE.VBE

Private Sub IDTExtensibility_OnAddInsUpdate(custom() As Variant)
   'placeholder
End Sub

Private Sub IDTExtensibility_OnConnection(ByVal VBInst As Object, _
   ByVal ConnectMode As VBIDE.vbext_ConnectMode, _
   ByVal AddInInst As VBIDE.AddIn, custom() As Variant)
   Set VBInstance = VBInst
End Sub

Private Sub IDTExtensibility_OnDisconnection(ByVal RemoveMode _
   As VBIDE.vbext_DisconnectMode, custom() As Variant)
   'Placeholder
End Sub

Private Sub IDTExtensibility_OnStartupComplete(custom() As Variant)
   'Placeholder
End Sub
```

6. Compile the add-in project using the Make command on the File menu. This will register it with your system. Note that you'll have to take care of registration in the installation routine (or provide installation instructions) if you distribute your add-in to others.

7. Register your add-in with Visual Basic by adding a reference to it in the [Add-ins32] section of ***Vbaddin.Ini***. ***Vbaddin.Ini*** is, of course, an old-style (Windows 3.*x*) private profile string. You can use the WritePrivateProfile API to enter the required information in ***Vbaddin.Ini***.

   The form of the entry is add-in *ProgID*=0 or *ProgID*=1. 0 indicates that the add-in is not enabled in the Add-In Manager; 1 means that it is.

   The add-in's ProgID is its project name as entered on the General tab of the Project Properties dialog followed by a period and the name of the class module containing the IDTExtensibility connection code.

   Here's a sample ***Vbaddin.Ini*** entry for an add-in that is not enabled in the Add-In Manager:

   ```
   [Add-Ins32]
   Very.Simple=0
   ```

   If the "Just an add in fool for you" add-in were checked in the Add-In Manager, as shown in Figure 29-22, the section would change:

   ```
   [Add-Ins32]
   Very.Simple=1
   ```

   As with registering the ActiveX component containing the add-in with Windows, there is no automatic way to register the product with VB when you distribute it. You have to take care of this as part of installing the add-in.

8. The user makes the add-in available — and adds it to the VB Add-Ins menu — by checking it in the Add-In Manager (see Figure 29-22).

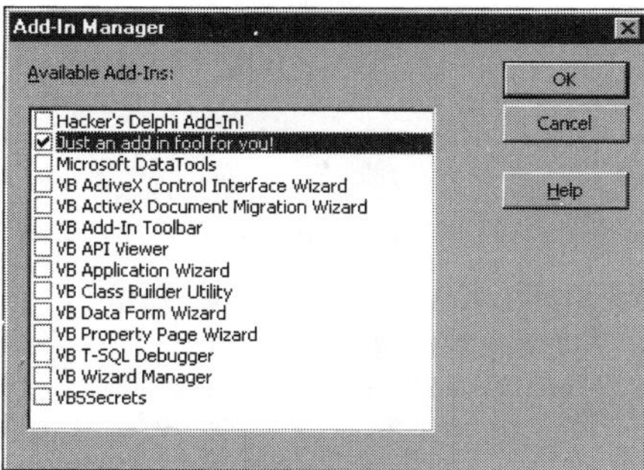

Figure 29-22: The add-in text in the Add-In Manager reflects the Class description entered using the Object Browser and the Member Options dialog.

ProgID and the Project Name

The project name used to create the add-in's ProgID is the name you have given the project in the Project Name field on the General tab of the Project Properties dialog, *not* the name with which the project was saved (for example, not ***Anything.Vbp***).

I won't say, "That's all there is to creating an add-in," because, obviously, there is some complexity involved — particularly in the first step, programming the thing in the first place. But once you get the hang of how to create add-ins, you'll find that it is more straightforward than it first seems.

The Change Colors Add-In

The remainder of this chapter demonstrates how to create a fully functional add-in called the Change Colors add-in. This add-in lets users click once to change either the BackColor or ForeColor property (or both) of all controls that have BackColor or ForeColor properties. The add-in will change the properties of controls on all open components that have designers in all projects that are loaded in the instance of Visual Basic.

Forms and UserControls are examples of components that have designers.

This add-in is potentially a real convenience when designing complex forms with many controls that you want to have the same color scheme. You could easily change the color scheme for all controls in a project by running the Change Colors add-in.

To change control properties, the program has to navigate the VBIDE.VBE object hierarchy. This means reaching down from the current instance of VB to all the projects that are loaded, to all the open components with designers, and so on, as I'll explain in detail. You can use the navigation strategy applied in the code as a chance to understand this important structure better.

The add-in works well as written, but you could also introduce bells, whistles, and refinements. If you want, go to town and have fun! You can do many more things with add-ins and the VBIDE object than are demonstrated in this chapter.

Change Colors works as follows: When you choose it from the Format menu in VB, you see a dialog that lets you choose the BackColor or ForeColor properties to apply to the form's controls. You use the Common Dialog control, in its ShowColor mode, to actually select the colors.

You can put menu items for your add-ins anywhere you'd like in the VB menu structure. The Format menu seemed appropriate for Change Colors because other Format items have to do with changing the appearance of controls and components.

The Change Colors add-in project is saved on the companion CD-ROM as ***Colors.Vbp***. I compiled it to native code as an ActiveX DLL. For the add-in to appear in the Add-In Manager, it must be registered with VB. This means adding a line to the ***Vbaddin.Ini*** file as described earlier in this chapter.

You can edit the ***Vbaddin.Ini*** file manually:

```
Colors.AddIn=1
```

Alternatively, you can invoke the AddToIni procedure (provided in the ***Colors.Vbp*** project for this purpose) from the Immediate window. (AddToIni is part of the ***Add2Ini.Bas*** module.)

You'll need to provide a way to create the ***.Ini*** file entry on any target systems to which an add-in is distributed.

Once you've compiled the project and added the entry to ***Vbaddin.Ini***, you can enable the Change Colors add-in in the Add-In Manager, as shown in Figure 29-23.

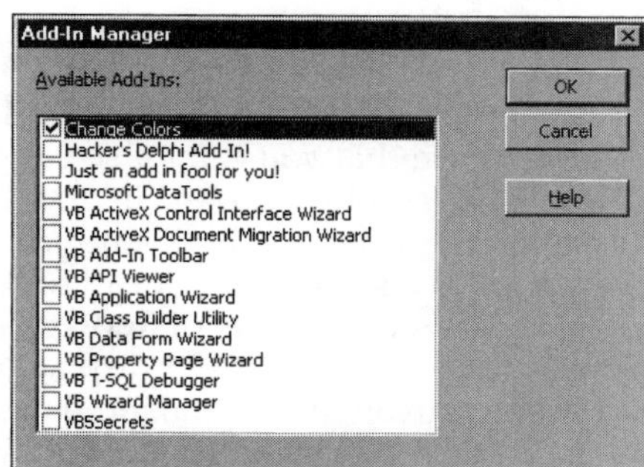

Figure 29-23: You can enable the Change Colors add-in from the Add-In Manager.

Once it has been enabled, you can select it from Visual Basic's Format menu, as shown in Figure 29-24.

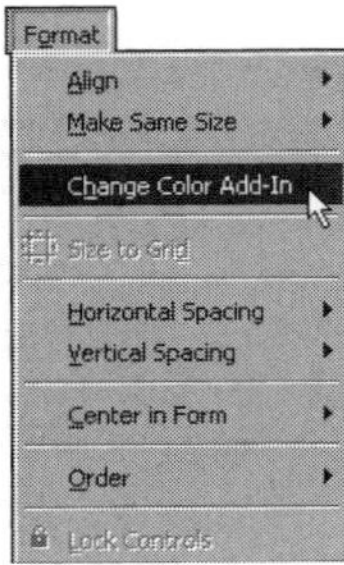

Figure 29-24: You can place an item that can be used to start an add-in on any Visual Basic menu (here it's on the Format menu).

Making Change Colors Work

This section describes how the actual Change Colors add-in is put together — meaning, how to do the work of changing all those controls. I'll get back to the mechanics of inserting the add-in in the VB environment later. First, I'll create the form, frmSetColor, which I'll use to let users specify the colors and properties they want changed (for example, ForeColor and/or BackColor). Figure 29-25 displays this form (at runtime) as I have designed it. There is a Common Dialog control added to the form that you cannot see at runtime, and an invisible label named RetVal. RetVal returns status information when the form is instanced, as explained in Chapter 3, "Event-Driven Programming." When the Apply button is clicked, the value of RetVal is the VBA constant vbOK; when Cancel is clicked, the value of RetVal is vbCancel. This form uses picture box controls for the selection and display of colors. Ideally, I would use command buttons instead, but command buttons don't have a ForeColor property and their BackColor property doesn't display. With a label on top of a picture box, I can simulate a command button displaying ForeColor and BackColor properties.

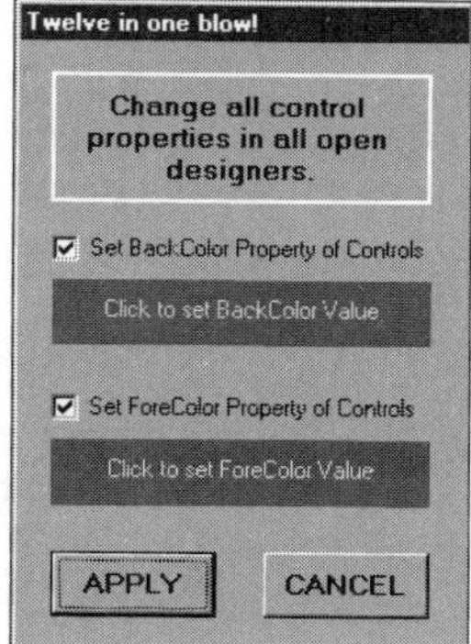

Figure 29-25: The Change Color add-in user options form allows users to change the color properties of all controls in open designers.

Programming frmSetColor

First, the form should be initialized in its load event:

```
Private Sub Form_Load()
   Dim fcolor As Long
   Dim bcolor As Long
   With Screen
      Left = (.Width - Width) / 2
      Top = (.Height - Height) / 2
   End With
   chkForeColor.Value = 1        ' Apply to ForeColor Properties
   chkBackColor.Value = 1        ' And to BackColors
   fcolor = vbYellow             ' initialize to yellow
   bcolor = vbRed                ' initialize to red
   SetPicts fcolor, bcolor
End Sub
```

The SetPicts procedure — called from the form load event and when the user changes the color selection — sets the color values of the picture boxes (which are simulated buttons as I just described) based on passed parameters.

```
Private Sub SetPicts(ByVal fcolor As Long, ByVal bcolor As Long)
   pctBackColor.BackColor = bcolor
   pctForeColor.BackColor = bcolor
   lblBackColor.ForeColor = fcolor
   lblForeColor.ForeColor = fcolor
End Sub
```

When the user fires the click event of one of the picture boxes to change the color settings, the ChooseColor procedure is called:

```
Private Sub pctBackColor_Click()
   ChooseColor "B", lblBackColor.ForeColor, pctBackColor.BackColor
End Sub

Private Sub pctForeColor_Click()
   ChooseColor "F", lblForeColor.ForeColor, pctBackColor.BackColor
End Sub
```

To complete the button simulation, clicking the labels on top of the picture boxes should have the same effect as clicking the picture box itself. To accomplish this, add a call to the picture box handler from the label handler:

```
Private Sub lblBackColor_Click()
   pctBackColor_Click
End Sub

Private Sub lblForeColor_Click()
   pctForeColor_Click
End Sub
```

ChooseColor itself simply initializes the Common Dialog control with the current color value, calls the common dialog using the ShowColor method, and returns the value the user selects, provided that Cancel wasn't pressed, as shown in Figure 29-26. (Common dialogs are covered in Chapter 7, "Windows Common Dialog Secrets.")

Figure 29-26: The ChooseColor routine uses the Common Dialog control to allow the user to select a color.

A branching control structure (as described in Chapter 4, "The Visual Basic Language") is used to determine which picture box click event-handler called the procedure.

```
Private Sub ChooseColor(Which As String, ByVal fcolor As Long, _
   ByVal bcolor As Long)
   CommonDialog1.CancelError = False
   On Err GoTo ErrHandler
```

```
    If Which = "B" Then
       CommonDialog1.Color = bcolor
    Else
       CommonDialog1.Color = fcolor
    End If
    CommonDialog1.ShowColor
    If Which = "B" Then
       bcolor = CommonDialog1.Color
    Else
       fcolor = CommonDialog1.Color
    End If
    SetPicts fcolor, bcolor
    Exit Sub
ErrHandler:
    Exit Sub
End Sub
```

That's the entire code logic encapsulated in frmSetColor, although — as I'll show you in a moment — there is a bit more to it. The decision logic in frmSetColor is actually controlled by the class module that instances it following the firing of the Change Colors add-in.

In other words — and I'll get around to the mechanics of this eventually, I promise — when the user clicks the add-in's menu item, a procedure named AfterClick in the ShowForm class module is called (ShowForm is saved as ***Color.Cls***).

Bear in mind that the class module containing the IDTExtensibility connection code — it is named AddIn and saved as ***Nextion.Cls*** — declares clsShowForm as a new instance of the ShowForm class:

```
Dim clsShowForm As New ShowForm
```

The event fired when the user clicks the add-in's menu item is handled in the MenuHandler_Click procedure in the AddIn class module:

```
Private Sub MenuHandler_Click(ByVal CommandBarControl As Object, _
    handled As Boolean, CancelDefault As Boolean)
    clsShowForm.VBIDE = VBInstance
    clsShowForm.AfterClick
End Sub
```

This code assigns the current VB instance to a ShowForm class module variable, VBIDE, and calls the AfterClick procedure.

Here are the general declarations for the ShowForm class module:

```
Option Explicit
Dim X As New frmSetColor
Dim ThisVBInstance As VBide.Application
```

X will be used to instance frmSetColor for user preference entry. ThisVBInstance will be used to store the VBide property value once it has been passed by the menu handler in the AddIn class module.

In this case, I don't need the matching Property Get procedure. I only need Property Let VBide, which is what allows the AddIn module to store the value of the instance of VB in ShowForm's module-level VBInstance variable:

```
Public Property Let VBide(vNewValue)
   Set ThisVBInstance = vNewValue
End Property
```

(Because the Property Get VBide is empty, you can delete the framework code for it.)

ShowForm's AfterClick code instances frmSetColor, populates it with default values, and calls SetFormsAndControls if the user clicks the Apply button.

```
Public Sub AfterClick()
   Dim Active, SetF, SetB As Boolean
   X.Show vbModal
   If X.RetVal = vbOK Then
      SetF = False
      SetB = False
      If X.chkForeColor.Value = 1 Then
         'Apply to ForeColor Properties
         SetF = True
      End If
      If X.chkBackColor.Value = 1 Then
         'And to BackColors
         SetB = True
      End If
      SetFormsAndControls SetF, SetB, _
         X.lblBackColor.ForeColor, X.pctBackColor.BackColor
   End If
   Unload X
End Sub
```

The statement If X.RetVal = vbOK determines whether Apply was clicked using the invisible label RetVal (this technique is explained in Chapter 3, "Event-Driven Programming").

Exploring the VBIDE.VBE Hierarchy

The actual work of changing the control properties for all control on components that are open in designers in all projects that are loaded in the current instance of VB is handled by SetFormsAndControls (see Listing 29-5). SetFormsAndControls is a private member of the ShowForm class, and is called when the Apply button is clicked.

Listing 29-5: Changing the properties of all controls

```
Private Sub SetFormsAndControls(ByVal YesToFore _
   As Boolean, ByVal YesToBack As Boolean, _
   ByVal frcol As Long, ByVal bkcol As Long)
   Dim AllProjects As VBProjects
```

```
    Dim ThisVBProject As VBProject
    Dim TheCurrentComponent As VBComponent
    Dim ThisControl As VBControl

    On Error Resume Next
    '*** Control might not have BackColor or ForeColor property!
    '*** If not found, just go on.
    Set AllProjects = ThisVBInstance.VBProjects
    For Each ThisVBProject In AllProjects
       For Each TheCurrentComponent In ThisVBProject.VBComponents
          If TheCurrentComponent.HasOpenDesigner Then
             For Each ThisControl In _
                TheCurrentComponent.Designer.VBControls
                If YesToBack Then
                   ThisControl.Properties("BackColor") = bkcol
                End If
                If YesToFore Then
                   ThisControl.Properties("ForeColor") = frcol
                End If
             Next ThisControl
          End If
       Next TheCurrentComponent
    Next ThisVBProject
    Set AllProjects = Nothing
    Set ThisVBProject = Nothing
    Set TheCurrentComponent = Nothing
    Set ThisControl = Nothing
End Sub
```

The logic of this routine cycles through collections that are part of the VBIDE.VBE hierarchy to arrive at the objects in which we are interested. At the top level is the variable AllProjects, which is set to the VBProjects collection for the VBIDE.VBE instance. Each VBProject item in the VBProjects collection is examined. The VBComponents collection of a VBProject represents modules in a project.

Each component in the VBComponents collection is examined. The variable TheCurrentComponent represents a component. If the HasOpenDesigner property of TheCurrentComponent is True, it means that the component is a container, such as a form or UserControl module, capable of hosting controls. Furthermore, its designer is open.

Each control in the TheCurrentComponent.Designer.VBControls collection is looked at, and if appropriate, its properties are saved.

Adding Connection Code

Listing 29-6 contains the code in the AddIn class module that handles connecting the Change Colors add-in to the VB environment (by definition, the class module containing the IDTExtensibility procedures).

Listing 29-6: Connecting Change Colors

```
Implements IDTExtensibility

Public FormDisplayed         As Boolean
Public VBInstance            As VBIDE.VBE
Dim mcbMenuCommandBar        As Office.CommandBarControl
Dim clsShowForm              As New ShowForm
Public WithEvents MenuHandler As CommandBarEvents

Private Sub IDTExtensibility_OnAddInsUpdate(custom() As Variant)
   'Placeholder
End Sub

Private Sub IDTExtensibility_OnConnection(ByVal VBInst As Object, _
   ByVal ConnectMode As VBIDE.vbext_ConnectMode, ByVal AddInInst _
   As VBIDE.AddIn, custom() As Variant)
   On Error GoTo error_handler
   Set VBInstance = VBInst
   Set mcbMenuCommandBar = AddToAddInCommandBar _
      ("C&hange Color Add-In")
   Set Me.MenuHandler = _
      VBInst.Events.CommandBarEvents(mcbMenuCommandBar)
   Exit Sub
error_handler:
   MsgBox Err.Description
End Sub

Private Sub IDTExtensibility_OnDisconnection(ByVal RemoveMode _
   As VBIDE.vbext_DisconnectMode, custom() As Variant)
   On Error Resume Next
   mcbMenuCommandBar.Delete
   Unload clsShowForm
   Set clsShowForm = Nothing
End Sub

Private Sub IDTExtensibility_OnStartupComplete(custom() As Variant)
   'Placeholder
End Sub

Function AddToAddInCommandBar(sCaption As String) _
   As Office.CommandBarControl
   Dim cbMenuCommandBar As Office.CommandBarControl
   Dim cbMenu As Object
   On Error GoTo AddToAddInCommandBarErr
```

```
    Set cbMenu = VBInstance.CommandBars("Format")
    If cbMenu Is Nothing Then
        'not available so we fail
        Exit Function
    End If
    'add it to the command bar
    Set cbMenuCommandBar = cbMenu.Controls.Add(before:=3)
    cbMenuCommandBar.BeginGroup = True
    'set the caption
    cbMenuCommandBar.Caption = sCaption
    Set AddToAddInCommandBar = cbMenuCommandBar
Exit Function
AddToAddInCommandBarErr:

End Function

Private Sub MenuHandler_Click(ByVal CommandBarControl As Object, _
    handled As Boolean, CancelDefault As Boolean)
    clsShowForm.VBIDE = VBInstance
    clsShowForm.AfterClick
End Sub
```

This works in pretty much the same way as the connection examples provided earlier in this chapter and explained in "Creating an Add-In: The Required Steps."

Note that you can position an item for your add-in on any VB menu you'd like:

```
Set cbMenu = VBInstance.CommandBars("Format")
```

You can locate it on the menu in any position as you please (in the example, above the third item):

```
Set cbMenuCommandBar = cbMenu.Controls.Add(before:=3)
```

It's also quite easy to include a separator before the item:

```
cbMenuCommandBar.BeginGroup = True
```

When all is said and done, connection is fairly easy to handle once you have the mechanics down. For that matter, surfing the objects and collections that make up the hierarchy of the VBIDE.VBE sea is rather fun!

Once you have your connection code in place, have compiled your add-in, added it to ***VBaddin.Ini***, and enabled it in the Add-In Manager, you can use it to zap many controls simultaneously, as shown in Figure 29-27.

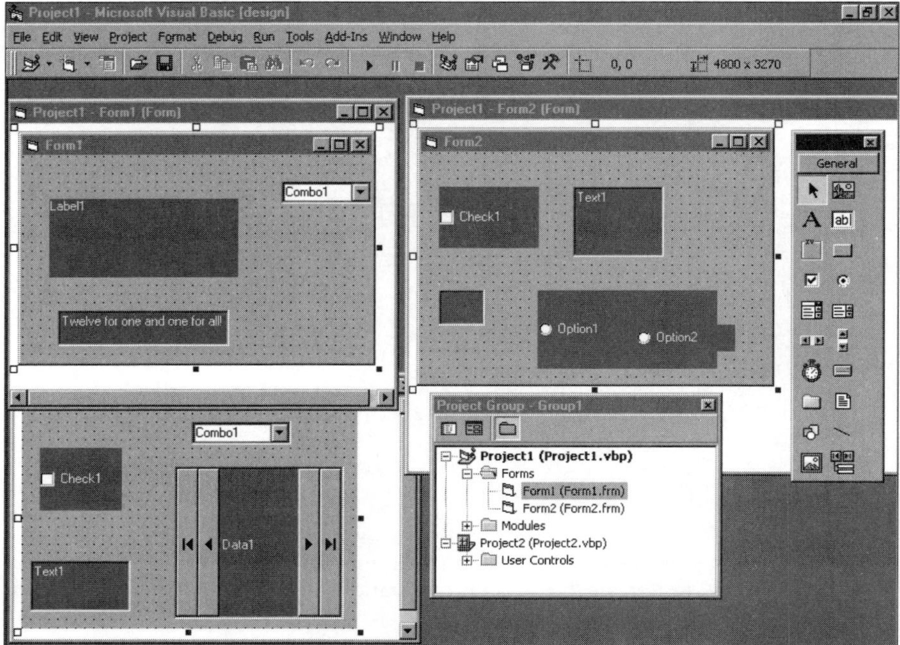

Figure 29-27: The Change Colors add-in efficiently changes the properties of any control it finds.

Summary

This chapter covered the fascinating topic of add-ins — ActiveX component applications that use the exposed items of the VBIDE.VBE object to modify the current instance of the Visual Basic IDE. After reading the chapter, you should have the information you need to create your own sophisticated add-in. Topics covered included

- Understanding add-ins
- Kinds of add-ins
- The Add-In Manager
- Add-ins that ship with VB
- The Add-In toolbar
- Visual Basic's VBIDE.VBE object hierarchy
- Accessing and manipulating members of the hierarchy
- Implementing IDTExtensibility methods
- Creating a simple add-in

- Component registration
- Registering with VB
- Connection class module code
- Programmatic connections
- Creating add-in menu items
- Required steps for an add-in
- The Change Colors add-in

Chapter 30

Building a Wizard

The Wizard Manager — sometimes quaintly called the *Wizard Wizard* — is a Visual Basic add-in that makes it easier to create Wizards, which are themselves add-ins. (For more information on add-ins, see Chapter 29, "Building a VB Add-In.")

The Wizard user interface does not work well in every situation. You should only use a Wizard interface in your application if you are sure that it is appropriate. Wizard interfaces work best to help users accomplish tasks that can readily be separated into discrete topics, with each topic corresponding to a Wizard panel.

In Chapter 8, "Windows User Interface Controls," I explained how to create a Wizard that is a normal executable application. In contrast, Wizards created using the Wizard Manager are in-process ActiveX components (compiled as ***.Dll*** files) or out-of-process ActiveX components (compiled as ***.Exe files).***

Wizards that are in-process ActiveX add-ins must be run from within VB while Wizards that are out-of-process ActiveX add-ins can be designed to run from ActiveX client applications — such as the Office 97 applications.

The primary purpose of the Wizard Manager is to help developers manage panel display issues. If you've created your own Wizards — or followed the example in Chapter 8 — you'll realize that these can be pretty complex, as Wizards typically consist of a single form. Wizards created using the Wizard Manager name this form frmWizard.

The illusion of movement between panels is created through manipulating the Visible properties of the controls on the form. In addition to helping with this sleight of hand, the Wizard Manager provides you with working template code that deals with creating a functional add-in (see Chapter 29 for more information on what this involves).

Running the Wizard Manager

The Wizard Manager ships with the Professional and Enterprise Editions of VB, but by default, it is not enabled. To enable the Wizard Manager, select it in the Add-In Manager, as shown in Figure 30-1.

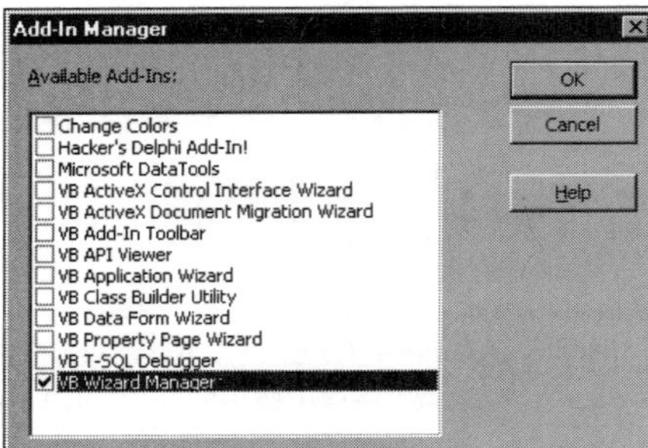

Figure 30-1: You can enable the Wizard Manager using the Add-In Manager.

Once the Wizard Manager has been enabled, an item for it appears on VB's Add-Ins menu, as shown in Figure 30-2.

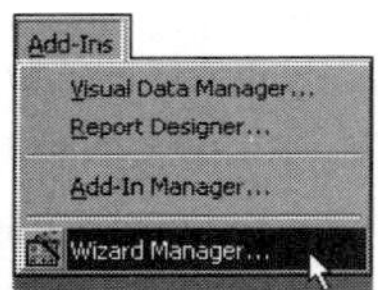

Figure 30-2: When the Wizard Manager is enabled, it places an item for itself on VB's Add-Ins menu.

You start the Wizard Manager by clicking the Wizard Manager item. Provided that you do not already have a Wizard project open, you'll be asked if you want to create a new Wizard project (see Figure 30-3).

Figure 30-3: The Wizard Manager will offer to create a new Wizard project for you.

The project that the Wizard Manager creates contains the Wizard form — frmWizard. It also includes a code module, a class module to handle add-in connectivity, and a resource file (***Wizard.Res***) to store strings and bitmaps that will be used to customize the Wizard.

Figure 30-4 shows a template Wizard project in Project Explorer, along with the Wizard Manager interface.

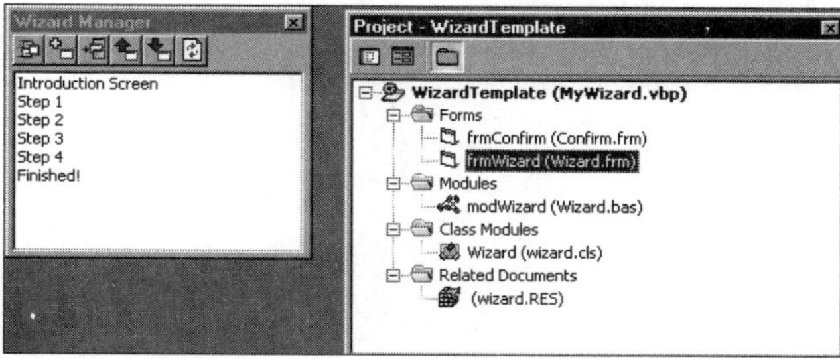

Figure 30-4: A template Wizard project contains a Wizard form, code and class modules, and a resource file.

The Wizard Manager Interface

The Wizard Manager interface has two purposes. First, it lists all the panels in the Wizard project, as shown in Figure 30-5. When a panel is selected, it appears in the designer for frmWizard, as shown in Figure 30-6.

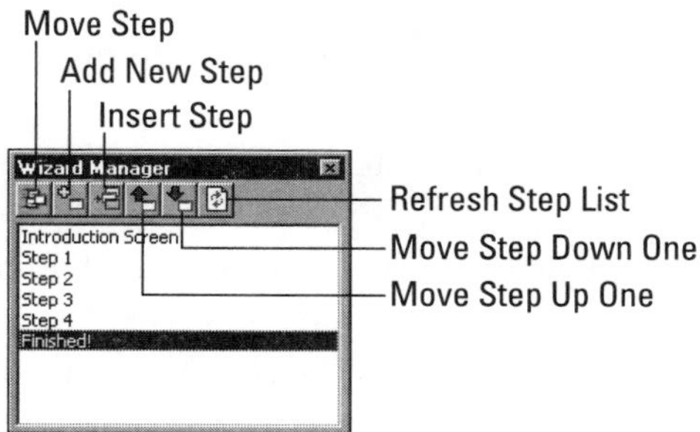

Figure 30-5: The Wizard Manager interface helps you to navigate between panels.

Wizards panels are not true panels in any sense. frmWizard actually contains an array of frames. The current Wizard virtual "panel" is the member of that array in position on the form to be visible. Each panel is also referred to as a Wizard *step*.

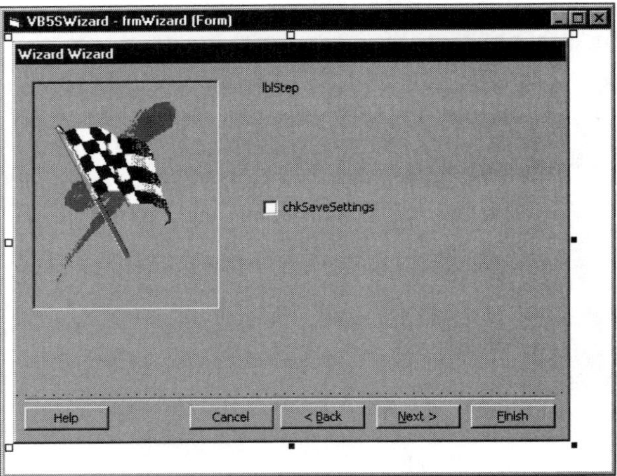

Figure 30-6: Selecting a Wizard panel in the Wizard Manager causes it to be displayed in frmWizard's designer.

The Wizard Manager also provides six toolbar buttons (see Figure 30-5):

- The Move Step button moves the currently visible Wizard panel out of the Wizard's visible screen frame. You should usually click this button after you have completed your Wizard. Otherwise, the last panel you worked on — such as Finished! — will display when the Wizard starts.
- The Add New Step button adds a new virtual panel to the Wizard, before the Finished! panel, but after all other steps.
- The Insert Step button creates a new step before the currently selected step.
- The Move Step Up One button moves the selected panel up one step in the Wizard.
- The Move Step Down One button moves the selected panel down one step in the Wizard.
- Refresh Step list refreshes the list of steps to reflect changes made to it.

Wizard Basics

You don't really have to understand a great deal about the project that the Wizard Manager has created — or about how the Wizard Manager functions — to create a customized working Wizard.

Using the Resource File

Most of the strings that the Wizard displays are loaded from the resource file that accompanies the project. This file is created by the Wizard Manager with the name ***Wizard.Res***.

You'll find more information on using external resource files in Chapter 16, "Optimizing Secrets," and Chapter 18, "Managing MDI Applications and Menus."

You can edit resource files using the utilities provided on the VB5 CD-ROM in the ***Tools\Resource*** directory, but the programs provided are not very user friendly. You are much better off using a full-fledged resource editor, such as the one that is part of Microsoft's Developer Studio. Developer Studio is an integral part of a number of Microsoft development environments, including Visual C++ and Visual J++.

You can use Developer Studio to edit the String Table contained in ***Wizard.Res***, as shown in Figure 30-7.

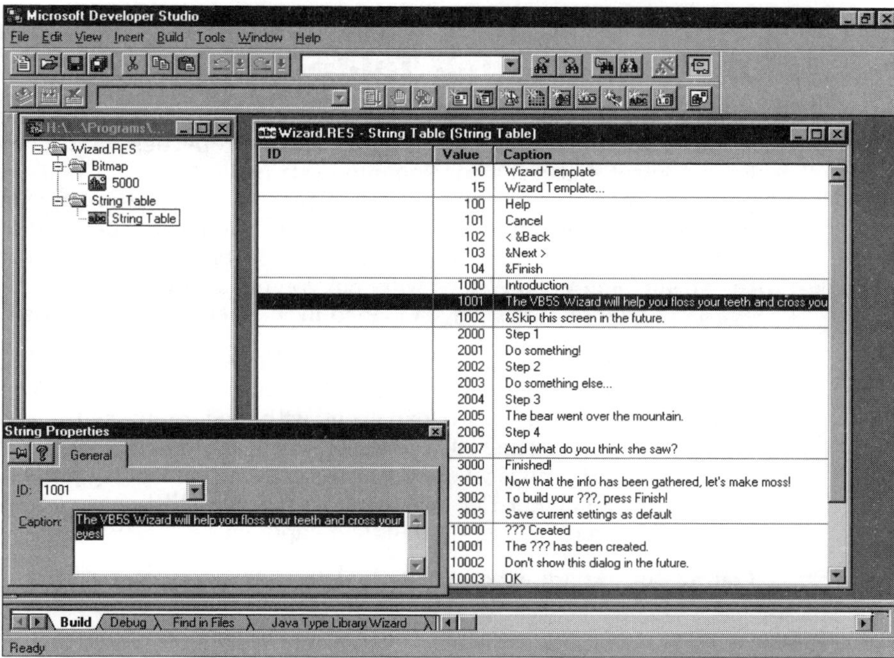

Figure 30-7: You can edit the String Table in ***Wizard.Res*** using Developer Studio.

Changes that you make to the strings will be reflected in your custom Wizard, once it is compiled and run (see Figure 30-8).

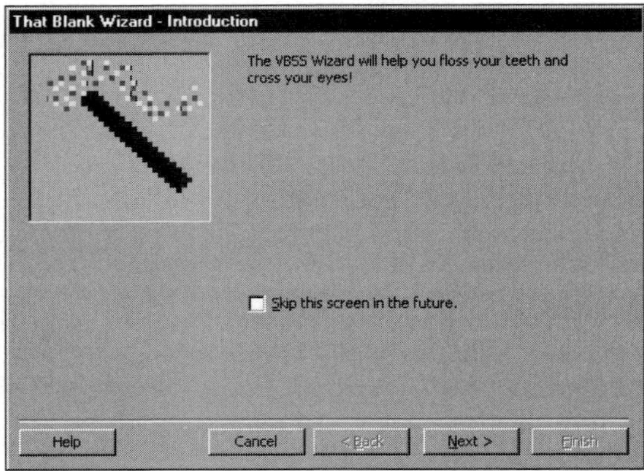

Figure 30-8: Values you enter in the resource file's String Table will be displayed by the Wizard once it is compiled and run.

Retrieving String Table Values

The Wizard uses some pretty snappy code to correctly retrieve String Table values, and assign them to the right control properties. Here's how it works. Each control that has a corresponding string in the String Table has its tag property set to the ID of the string. (For more information on using a control's tag property, see Chapter 8.) For example, a label control on the Wizard Introduction Screen has its tag property set to 1001. 1001 is the ID for the string "The VB5S Wizard will help you floss your teeth and cross your eyes!" Therefore, this string is loaded in the label before the Wizard is shown.

A procedure named LoadResStrings in the ***ModWizard.Bas*** module handles the actual work of placing strings with controls that have tag values. LoadResStrings is called from the frmWizard load event, with the form passed as an argument. As you can see in Listing 30-1, LoadResStrings attempts to load all Wizard form and control text strings where the corresponding control tag property can be evaluated to a number. Because menu strings do not have a tag property, they are loaded based on IDs stored in their captions.

Listing 30-1: Loading control and menu strings

```
Sub LoadResStrings(frm As Form)
    On Error Resume Next
    Dim ctl As Control
    Dim obj As Object
    'set the form's caption
    If IsNumeric(frm.Tag) Then
        frm.Caption = LoadResString(CInt(frm.Tag))
    End If

    'set the controls' captions using the caption
    'property for menu items and the Tag property
    'for all other controls
```

```
    For Each ctl In frm.Controls
        If TypeName(ctl) = "Menu" Then
            If IsNumeric(ctl.Caption) Then
                If Err = 0 Then
                    ctl.Caption = LoadResString(CInt(ctl.Caption))
                Else
                    Err = 0
                End If
            End If
        ElseIf TypeName(ctl) = "TabStrip" Then
            For Each obj In ctl.Tabs
                If IsNumeric(obj.Tag) Then
                    obj.Caption = LoadResString(CInt(obj.Tag))
                End If
                'check for a tooltip
                If IsNumeric(obj.ToolTipText) Then
                    If Err = 0 Then
                        obj.ToolTipText = _
                            LoadResString(CInt(obj.ToolTipText))
                    Else
                            Err = 0
                    End If
                End If
            Next
        ElseIf TypeName(ctl) = "Toolbar" Then
            For Each obj In ctl.Buttons
                If IsNumeric(obj.Tag) Then
                    obj.ToolTipText = LoadResString(CInt(obj.Tag))
                End If
            Next
        ElseIf TypeName(ctl) = "ListView" Then
            For Each obj In ctl.ColumnHeaders
                If IsNumeric(obj.Tag) Then
                    obj.Text = LoadResString(CInt(obj.Tag))
                End If
            Next
        Else
            If IsNumeric(ctl.Tag) Then
                If Err = 0 Then
                    ctl.Caption = LoadResString(CInt(ctl.Tag))
                Else
                    Err = 0
                End If
            End If
            'check for a tooltip
            If IsNumeric(ctl.ToolTipText) Then
                If Err = 0 Then
                    ctl.ToolTipText = _
                        LoadResString(CInt(ctl.ToolTipText))
                Else
                    Err = 0
                End If
            End If
        End If
    Next
End Sub
```

Customizing the Wizard

To customize your Wizard you should:

- Change the values of the ***Wizard.Res*** String Table to reflect the needs of your Wizard, as described earlier.
- Use the Wizard Manager to add panels, delete panels, or rearrange the order of panels in the Wizard.
- Use the Wizard Manager to view different panels of the Wizard. For each panel, add controls and adjust control properties as needed. Be sure to add string IDs to the tag properties of new controls and corresponding String Table entries, as described earlier.
- Change constants in the ***Wizard.Bas*** code module to reflect your Wizard. For example:

  ```
  Global Const WIZARD_NAME = "VB5SWizard"
  ```

- Add code to the cmdNav click event (found in the frmWizard module) to accomplish the Wizard's goal when the user clicks the Finish button. The position where this code should be located is indicated with a comment:

  ```
  Case BTN_FINISH
     'wizard creation code goes here
  ```

Doing the Add-In Thing

Before anyone can use the Wizard you've created, you'll need to follow the steps required to compile and register it as an add-in. (See Chapter 29 for detailed information on these steps.)

You might wish to change the location of the VB menu item that is added for your Wizard (it is on the Add-Ins menu). The code that handles this is in the AddToAddInCommandBar procedure.

It's probably a good idea to customize the name that will be used for your Wizard in the Add-In Manager. You can do this using the Member Options dialog for the class module containing the IDTExtensibility code, as shown in Figure 30-9. (As set up by the Wizard Manager, this class module is named ***Wizard.Cls***.)

The Wizard project should be compiled as an ActiveX component. This means that the Project Type should be set to ActiveX DLL or ActiveX EXE on the General tab of the Project Properties dialog, as shown in Figure 30-10.

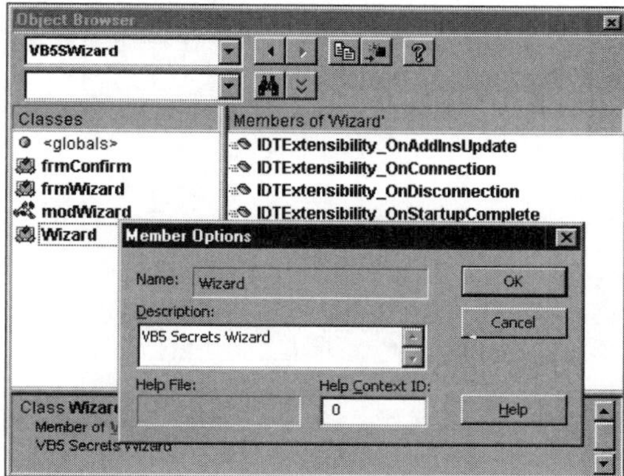

Figure 30-9: You can use the Member Options dialog to change the way the Wizard is named in the Add-In Manager.

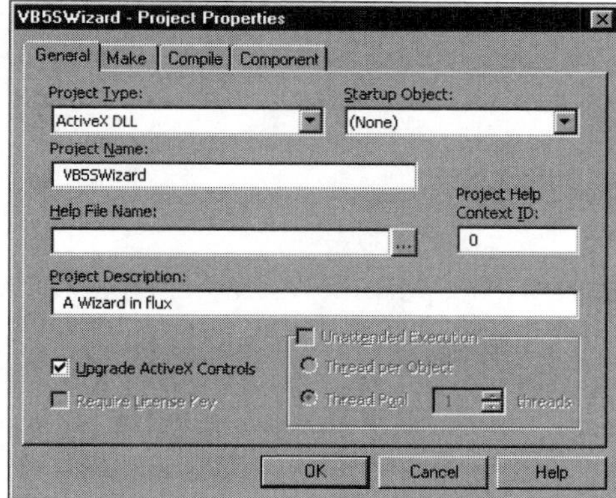

Figure 30-10: Your Wizard should be compiled as an ActiveX component.

Once the Wizard has been compiled, you'll need to register it with Visual Basic by adding an entry to ***Vbaddin.Ini***.

Wizard.Bas contains a procedure, ***AddToINI***, which you can use to automate this process.

If you call AddToINI from the Immediate window, it will add the entry to the initialization file, returning a 1 if it succeeds, as shown in Figure 30-11.

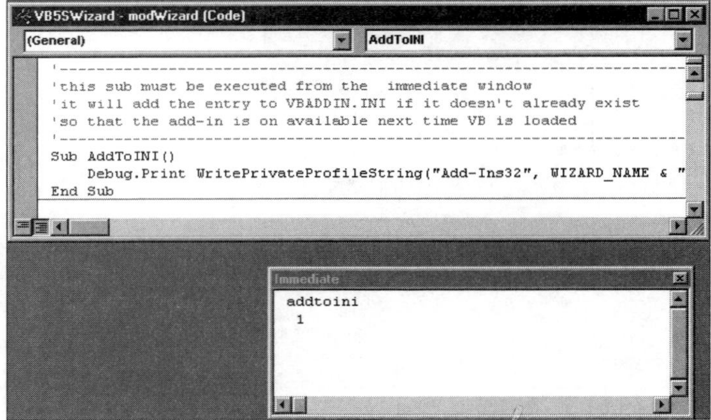

Figure 30-11: You can invoke the AddToINI routine from the Immediate window to add the required entry to ***Vbaddini.Ini***.

Of course, you could always manually add an entry to ***Vbaddini.Ini*** reflecting the Wizard's ProgID:

```
VB5SWizard.Wizard=0
```

Framed Again

Each Wizard step is actually a frame, part of the fraStep( ) frame array. Only one member of the frame array is visible at a time.

Before your Wizard has been compiled, making sure that the right frame is visible when you move from one Wizard step to another, is the job of the Wizard Manager. Although both the Wizard Manager and the Wizard add-in that it is used to generate function in the Visual Basic design time environment, you can think of this as a design time versus runtime distinction. When creating your Wizard (design time), the Wizard Manager handles manipulating the frame array. After your Wizard has been compiled into an add-in, this manipulation is handled by code internal to your Wizard.

You have access, of course, to the internal code that handles frame manipulation when your Wizard is running, as described in a moment. But the internal workings of the Wizard Manager are a "black box," because its source code is not available. One thing is certain: the Wizard Manager does what it does by operating on objects in the VBIDE.VBE hierarchy. (For more information on VBIDE.VBE, see Chapter 29.)

After your Wizard has been compiled into an ActiveX component, manipulation of the frame array is handled by a procedure named SetStep, called from the cmdNav click event. (This code is included in *your* Wizard!)

The cmdNav click event is fired every time the user clicks one of the Wizard's buttons. Here is the full procedure:

```
Private Sub cmdNav_Click(Index As Integer)
   Dim nAltStep As Integer
   Dim lHelpTopic As Long
   Dim rc As Long

   Select Case Index
      Case BTN_HELP
         mbHelpStarted = True
         lHelpTopic = HELP_BASE + 10 * (1 + mnCurStep)
         rc = WinHelp(Me.hwnd, HELP_FILE, HELP_CONTEXT, lHelpTopic)
      Case BTN_CANCEL
         Unload Me
      Case BTN_BACK
         'place special cases here to jump
         'to alternate steps
         nAltStep = mnCurStep - 1
         SetStep nAltStep, DIR_BACK
      Case BTN_NEXT
         'place special cases here to jump
         'to alternate steps
         nAltStep = mnCurStep + 1
         SetStep nAltStep, DIR_NEXT
      Case BTN_FINISH
         'wizard creation code goes here
         Unload Me
         If GetSetting(APP_CATEGORY, WIZARD_NAME, _
            CONFIRM_KEY, vbNullString) = vbNullString Then
            frmConfirm.Show vbModal
         End If
   End Select
End Sub
```

The only difference between the Back and Next button being clicked is that in one case the current step counter is decremented, and in the other it is incremented. Also, SetStep is called with an argument that indicates the Wizard direction.

Here is the portion of the SetStep procedure that handles moving to a new step:

```
'move to new step
fraStep(mnCurStep).Enabled = False
fraStep(nStep).Left = 0
If nStep <> mnCurStep Then
   fraStep(mnCurStep).Left = -10000
End If
fraStep(nStep).Enabled = True
```

This is really pretty awesome! The frame that represents the current step is placed in the visible area, by setting its Left property to 0. All other frames are moved "out of the picture" by setting their Left property to -10000, way out of the visible portions of the Wizard form.

You can think of this as a process where steps that are not in use are kept in a kind of storage. This storage is out of sight, and, as they say, "Out of sight, out of mind."

Form dimensions and location coordinates are expressed in twips. (For more on units of measure and screen manipulation, see Chapter 19, "Runtime Display Secrets.") The dimensions used to manipulate the frame array used in the Wizard code are also twips.

Any position that is less than zero will not be visible to users. Each element of the frame array is 7155 twips wide (as indicated by the control's Width property). This means that when the frame element's Left property is set to -10000, its right edge will be positioned at -2845 twips — well off the visible screen.

You should picture a stack of Wizard frames, one on top of the other — all to the left of the visible frame, and all invisible to the user.

Summary

Don't you just love the phrase "Wizard Wizard?" This chapter has explained how to use the Wizard Wizard, more often called the Wizard Manager. Whatever name it goes by, the Wizard Manager is an add-in that is a busy backstage impresario that helps you to create your own Wizard add-ins.

Topics covered in this chapter included

- Running the Wizard Manager
- The Wizard Manager interface
- Loading a Wizard's text strings from an external resource file
- The correspondence between Wizard control tag properties and String Table IDs
- Customizing the template Wizard
- Compiling a Wizard as an add-in
- How the Wizard manipulates its frames

PART VIII

Third-Party Tools, Setup Programs, and Help Files

Chapter 31

Overview of Third-Party Tools

Third-party tools are a great way to quickly extend the power and capabilities of Visual Basic. In this chapter, you'll find

- A discussion of why you should use third-party tools
- Lists of selected currently available 32-bit ActiveX controls (and other tools) by vendor, including contact information

Why Use Third-Party Tools?

Experienced developers use third-party tools because:

- It saves time. If the functionality you need already exists, why take the time to re-create it?
- It saves money. You don't have to value your own efforts as worth much per hour to realize that a control that replaces time spent coding quickly pays for itself.
- ActiveX controls extend the capability of what Visual Basic can do.
- ActiveX controls from major third-party vendors — such as those listed later in this chapter — have been professionally created and extensively tested. They are reliable and help to give your applications professional polish.

If you need a particular capability that is not built into the tools available with Visual Basic, there is probably a third-party tool out there in the marketplace that will do the job for you. Why reinvent the wheel? Someone else has already done the work for you. All you need to do is load the ActiveX control onto your system by running its setup program, add it to your VB Toolbox, and pop it on the form where you need it. *Voila!* An instant tool that does the job.

Drawbacks to Using Third-Party Products

You should consider some potential drawbacks to using third-party products before promiscuously adding numerous custom controls to a project. Because you can achieve much of the functionality of third-party controls with a little extra effort in "just plain vanilla" VB — using the techniques I've explained in *Visual Basic 5 SECRETS* — you should carefully weight the pluses and minuses of using third-party products.

Potential drawbacks to using third-party products include:

- The initial cost of the additional product, and the cost of any necessary distribution licenses.
- The need to keep up with changing versions of numerous products as they are updated.
- The need to distribute additional files with your application (and, therefore, to create more complex installation routines).
- Version control issues as third-party vendors update their products.
- Technical support problems because using additional tools leads to more possible places where things can go wrong. The more tools in use, the harder it can be to determine the cause of a "bug."

Although these problems can be serious, you can to some degree ameliorate the risks involved by using quality third-party products from vendors who stand behind their tools — such as those listed in this chapter. In addition, there are no reasons not to use tools that are intended to enhance your working environment rather than to be distributed as part of your software. Because these products are used "in the privacy of your own home," and are not distributed with software you create, the list of potential problems — other than the cost of the software and learning curve — does not apply.

Visual Basic Add-Ins

With Visual Basic Version 5, you can now create add-ins that interact with the VBIDE (see Chapter 29, "Creating a VB Add-In"). Add-ins created by third-party vendors constitute an important way to enhance the power and capabilities of your programming environment.

Third-Party Products

If you are creating a project that needs a specific functionality not built into Visual Basic, there's probably a third-party tool out there in the software marketplace that will do it for you.

What follows is a list of selected vendors whose products I have found particularly helpful, their addresses, phone and fax numbers, Web URLs if available, and a brief description of some of the many fine tools that they publish.

Blue Sky Software Corporation

7777 Fay Avenue, Suite 201
La Jolla, CA 92037
800-571-9767 (Phone)
619-551-2486 (Fax)

http://www.blue-sky.com

RoboHelp 4.0 is the leading tool for creating modern Windows Help files. It is described in Chapter 35, "Help Files." Using RoboHelp, you can create Windows Help files and HTML documentation from one source.

Information about products, ActiveX controls, and utilities from Blue Sky is available on the *Visual Basic 5 SECRETS* companion CD-ROM.

Crescent Division of Progress Software Corporation

14 Oak Park
Bedford, MA 01730
800-352-2742 (Phone)
617-280-4025 (Fax)

http://crescent.progress.com

Crescent publishes many fine development toolkits, including:

Crescent Internet ToolPak allows you to access the Internet from Visual Basic applications without low-level coding or a knowledge of Internet protocols.

NetPak Pro is a collection of OCXs that allows you to add Netware and Windows 95 networking functions to your projects.

PDQComm is a complete communications library that you can add to your Visual Basic applications.

QuickPak Pro is a library of professional routines, modules, and forms that perform a variety of functions from string manipulation to creating 3D effects for forms and controls.

Desaware

1100 East Hamilton Avenue, Suite 4
Campbell, CA 95008
408-377-4770 (Phone)
408-371-3530 (Fax)

http://www.desaware.com

SpyWorks is an advanced Visual Basic toolkit that allows you to access low-level Windows functionality, including subclassing and Windows message trapping.

StorageTools is an OLE control that allows you to add OLE structured storage to your VB programs. This product also includes a Registry control that allows easy access to the Windows 95 Registry and the Registration Database.

VersionStamper-VB is a control that allows you to keep track of version information of applications you distribute.

FarPoint Technologies

133 Southcenter Court, Suite 1000
Morrisville, NC 27560
800-645-5913 (Phone)
919-460-7606 (Fax)

http://www.fpoint.com

FarPoint is a leading maker of industrial strength controls.

ButtonMaker lets you create unique graphical command buttons at design time (and these ain't just rectangles!), as shown in Figures 31-1 and 31-2. A demonstration of ButtonMaker is available on the *Visual Basic 5 SECRETS* companion CD-ROM.

Figure 31-1: ButtonMaker lets you create buttons that are way out of the ordinary, like this "button" button, which functions exactly like a regular command button.

Figure 31-2: You can load multiple graphics on a ButtonMaker button, thus creating buttons that appear to be animated.

Daily PlanIt is a customizable daily planner designed to help developers create scheduling applications.

ListPro is the ultimate data viewer, a combination of a combo box and a list box.

Spread is a powerful spreadsheet control that is basically the industry standard.

Tab Pro is an OLE custom control that allows you to create custom virtual index cards, file folders, or notebooks.

ImageFX

3021 Brighton-Henrietta Road
Rochester, NY 14623-2749
716-272-8030 (Phone)
716-272-1873 (Fax)

http://www.imagefx.com

ImageFX is a leading developer of multimedia tools and applications. Their products include:

FractalFX is a fractal image toolkit.

FXTools is a comprehensive ActiveX imaging and multimedia toolkit. You'll find an exciting demonstration version on the *Visual Basic 5 SECRETS* companion CD-ROM.

FXPic 4.0 is an image decompression tool for use with multimedia applications.

VectorFX adds vector image support to Windows applications. For example, you could use VectorFX to display native CorelDraw (***.Cdr***) files in your applications.

InstallShield Corporation

1100 Woodfield Road, Suite 108
Schaumburg, IL 60173-9946
800-374-4353 (Phone)
847-240-9120 (Fax)

http://www.installshield.com

InstallShield publishes leading industrial strength installation programs (as well as DemoShield, a program used for creating demonstrations of software).

Mabry Software, Inc.

P.O. Box 31926
Seattle, WA 98103
800-99-MABRY (Phone)
206-632-0272 (Fax)

http://www.mabry.com

Mabry publishes ActiveX toolkits, including:

Internet Pack gives applications access to the Internet, including direct access to Windows sockets.

Mega Pack contains 22 controls, such as bar code generators, alarms, and formatted labels.

Midi Pack gives easy access to MIDI files and devices. MIDI (Musical Instrument Digital Interface) files are designed to let computers and synthesizers communicate with each other.

You'll find demonstration versions of the Mabry tool packs on the *Visual Basic 5 SECRETS* companion CD-ROM.

MicroHelp

4211 JVL Industrial Park Drive, N.E.
Marietta, GA 30066
770-645-2121 (Phone)
770-516-1099 (Fax)

http://www.microhelp.com

MicroHelp is a respected publisher of products for serious developers. You'll find many demonstrations of MicroHelp's products on the *Visual Basic 5 SECRETS* companion CD-ROM. MicroHelp products include:

Communications Library is a robust communications tool.

Fax Plus is an easy way to build faxing into your application.

OLETools is an incredible, must-have library of 54 OCXs whose functionality ranges from specialized 3D text input boxes to a dice control that lets you create games.

Sax Software

950 Patterson Street
Eugene, OR 97401
541-344-2235 (Phone)
541-344-2459 (Fax)

http://www.saxsoft.com

Sax Setup Wizard creates sophisticated setup programs for your applications.

Sax Basic Engine Pro is a custom control that lets you integrate macro language support into your applications.

Webster is a full-featured World Wide Web browser that you can integrate into your Visual Basic projects.

Sheridan Software Systems, Inc.

35 Pinelawn Road
Melville, NY 11747
516-753-0985 (Phone)
516-753-3661 (Fax)

http://www.shersoft.com

Calendar Widgets is a library of ActiveX controls that facilitates date and time management and display.

Data Widgets is a set of bound ActiveX controls that helps you design front ends for database applications.

Designer Widgets is an ActiveX library containing four tools that range from a dockable toolbar to a notebook control that comes complete with cover and binder rings.

TVObjects Corporation

29 Emmons Drive
Princeton, NJ 08540
1-800-85-VBNET

http://www.tvobjects.com

VBnet is a Visual Basic add-in that allows you to seamlessly migrate VB projects to the Web.

Applet Designer is a utility that helps you create Java applets from within Visual Basic.

VideoSoft

5900 Hollis Street, Suite T
Emeryville, CA 94608
510-595-2400 (Phone)
510-595-2424 (Fax)

http://www.videosoft.com

VSFlex, VS-Ocx, and VSView are ActiveX libraries that contain many powerful features, as described in detail in Chapter 33, "VideoSoft's VS-Ocx, VSView, and VSFlex."

WhippleWare

20 Cedar Street
Charlestown, MA 02129
800-241-8727 (Phone)
617-241-8496 (Fax)

http://www.whippleware.com

VB Compress Pro is an excellent tool that optimizes Visual Basic source projects by removing duplicate and obsolete code.

Summary

From A-Z, there are many fine purveyors of ActiveX products that extend the capabilities of Visual Basic at a relatively low cost. Much of the success of Visual Basic as a development environment has come because the third-party products community has energetically worked to create tools with the additional features that programmers need. It can only work to your benefit to take advantage of the imagination, innovation, and hard work of these third-party vendors.

This chapter gives an overview of why you might consider using third-party tools to:

- Enhance the power of your working copy of the Visual Basic environment
- Avoid wasting time creating code that has already been written
- Extend the range of what applications you write in Visual Basic can do

Chapter 32

Creating Special Effects with FXTools

The Professional Edition of FXTools created by the developers at ImageFX consists of eight 32-bit ActiveX controls designed to quickly add super special effects to your Visual Basic 5 projects.

By setting a few properties, you can speedily add professional-quality effects to images, text, sound, and video files. Some of the great effects supported by these controls include

- *FXImage* supports numerous image file formats and lets you incorporate such professional effects as wipes, double wipes, dissolves, pushes, pulls, sparkles, slides, and transitions.
- *FXLabel* works like a VB label control but also lets you add 3D font styles, colored shadows, colored 3D borders and bevels, and animation effects such as wipes, splits, transitions, and wand effects.
- *FXShape* emulates the VB shape control but also includes 16 built-in shapes — such as pentagon, triangle, and star — colored drop shadows, embedded images, and animation effects.
- *FXRtext,* the rotate control, lets you rotate TrueType fonts at any angle as well as add 3D borders, different text-fill and background styles, colored shadows, and animation effects.
- *FXMtext,* the moving text control, lets you quickly create text that moves in predefined paths, has colored shadows, and has 3D font styles. You can also create user-defined motion paths.
- *FXSnd* manages up to 32 channels of individual or simultaneous playback of ***.Wav*** files without programming MCI strings. It also plays ***.Mid*** sounds and lets you set sound mixing quality, including bass, treble, and loudness.
- *FXTimer* is a handy timer control that lets you generate single and timed periodic events, and set the accuracy of the timer in milliseconds.
- *FXVid* lets you play selected portions of a video file (as well as the complete file), and add transition, animation, and dissolve effects without having to program MCI strings.

In this chapter, I'll show you how to use the FXImage, FXMtext, and FXSnd controls to quickly add nifty effects to your projects. The demonstration project is located on the companion CD-ROM in the Chapter 32 folder as ***FXTools.Vbp***. I've also created an executable, ***FXTools.Exe***, that you can run to view the effects discussed here.

To run the executable version, you'll first need to register the FXTools ActiveX controls using the techniques explained in Chapter 20, "Understanding ActiveX and OLE." Note that to open the project included on the CD-ROM in the VB5 design time environment, you'll have to buy the product to obtain the appropriate license files.

Using FXSnd

The first thing you'll notice when you run the demonstration project is that a sound, ***Sparkle.Wav***, is played. Using the FXSnd control is easy. All you have to do is drop the control on a form, set the FileName property to the location of a sound file, and then change AutoPlay to True. That's it! (This assumes, of course, that you have the FXTools controls and have loaded them into VB5 using the Components dialog that you access via the Project menu.)

If you want to play, pause, resume, stop, and so on a sound at a different point in an application — for instance, when a button is pushed or a particular form loads — you should set the AutoPlay property to False, and should set the Command property in code.

FXMtext

The second thing you'll notice when running the demonstration application is that some text at the lower-left corner of the form moves up to the top. This is rather similar to a scrolling marquee on a Web page. (You'll need to add the FXMtext control to your VB Toolbox using the Components dialog that you access from the Properties menu.)

To add moving text, draw an FXMtext control on a form, and then click Custom in the Properties window. The Property Pages dialog for the FXMtext control will open, as shown in Figure 32-1.

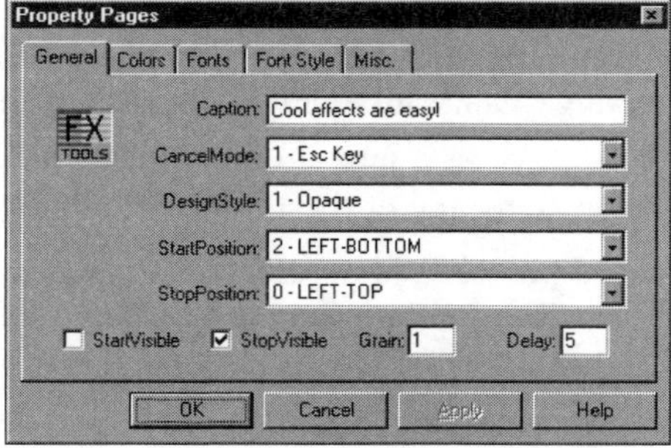

Figure 32-1: The Property Pages dialog for the FXMtext control makes it easy to add moving text to a project.

On the General tab, type a line of text in the Caption text box, and then set the StartPostion and StopPosition properties to define the path of the moving text. In the case of the demo application, StartPosition is set to 2-Left-Bottom and StopPosition is set to 0-Left-Top. In addition, using the StartVisible and StopVisible check boxes at the bottom of the tab, you can set whether the text will be visible before it starts moving and after it has finished moving.

To add a 3D effect to the moving text, change to the Font Style tab in the Property Pages dialog, as shown in Figure 32-2. Use the Font3D drop-down list box to select a 3D effect for the moving text. That's all there is to it! When you run the application, the text will move from the StartPosition to the StopPosition as specified.

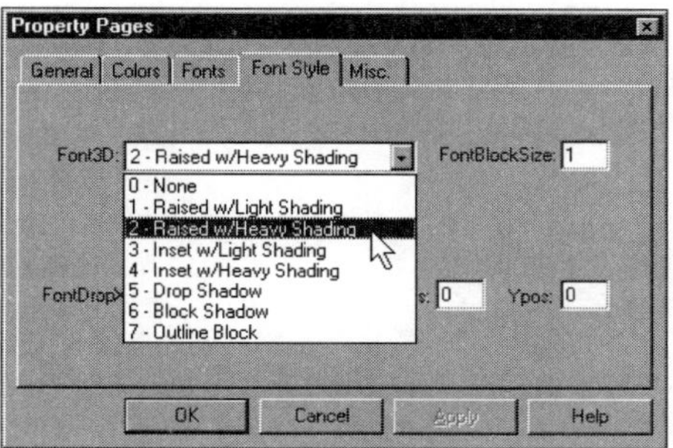

Figure 32-2: Use the Font Style tab of the Property Pages dialog to set the type of highlighting and shadowing that your moving text will have.

If you wanted to make the text move when a specific event occurred, not when the form loaded, you would need to set the MoveMode property from its default, 0-Automatic, to 1-Manual and set the text's original x and y coordinates using the Xpos (horizontal position) and Ypos (vertical position) properties at design time. Then, you would set the new coordinates for the text and make the text move in code like this:

```
Private Sub cmdMove_Click()
   With FXMtext1
      .Xpos = 100      'new horizontal text position in pixels
      .Ypos = 100      'new vertical text position in pixels
      .Action = MoveText
   End With
End Sub
```

Using FXImage

The main part of the demo application on the *Visual Basic 5 SECRETS* CD-ROM deals with graphical effects that you can quickly create using the FXImage control. I'll cover four effects:

- Setting a simple main effect, in this case a horizontal squash
- Making the background of an odd-shaped graphic transparent
- Adding a transitional gradient effect to a transparent graphic
- Creating a triple pass dissolve that shows three different dissolves, one after the other

Creating a Main Effect

The quickest effect you can create using the FXImage control is a single main effect. To get started, add the FXImage control to the VB Toolbox using the Components dialog that you access via the Properties menu. Then draw an FXImage control on a form.

Open the control's Property Pages by clicking Custom in the Property window. The dialog shown in Figure 32-3 will open.

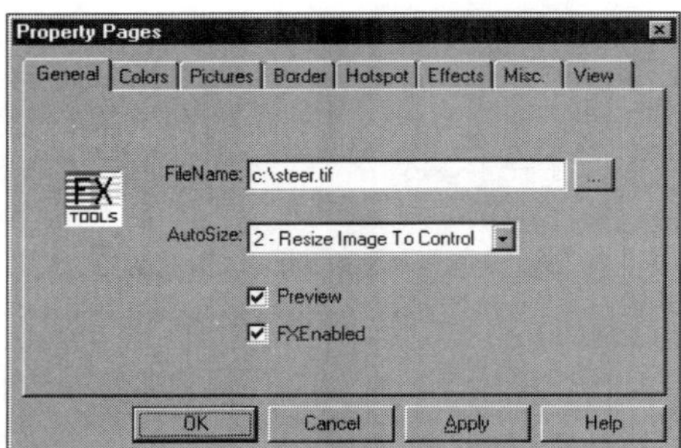

Figure 32-3: The FXImage control's Property Pages dialog lets you set many effects.

On the General tab, set the location of the graphic in the FileName text box. Then set the AutoSize property to crop the image to the size of the control, resize the image to the control, resize the control to the image, or tile the image inside the control. Make sure the Preview property is checked. This lets you view the effect you've created at design time. Also, you can use the FXEnabled property, whose default value is True, to toggle the effect on and off.

Next, move to the Misc. tab page and set the CancelMode property to any keyboard setting that you prefer. I tend to set it to the Esc key. This property cancels all effects that are pending or occurring for the control and immediately repaints it. This is important when experimenting with time delay and grain settings (more about these properties in a minute), because the combination of a long delay and a small grain setting can make an effect very, very slow.

Click the Effects tab. This tab is where you set the effects action, and it can look a bit daunting at first (see Figure 32-4).

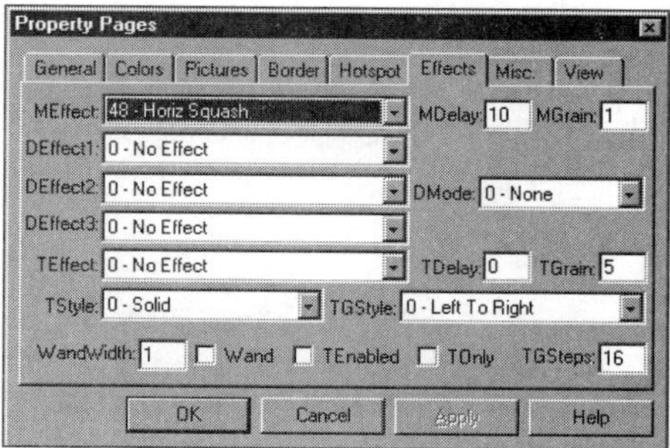

Figure 32-4: You use the FXImage Property Pages dialog Effects tab to set hundreds of different special effects.

If you look at Figure 32-4, you'll notice that the properties on the Effects tab are divided into different groups, using prefix letters — "M" for main, "D" for dissolve, "T" for transition dissolve, and "TG" for transition gradient.

For this example, I'm going to set the main properties, MEffect, MDelay, and MGrain. There are over 100 MEffect settings from which you can choose — from a left to right wipe, to a swirl in, to an image stretch from the bottom to the top. Because the image in the demo program is divided into left and right halves with a black/white effect, I've used a horizontal squash, which makes the two halves appear from the left and right sides and move toward the center of the control simultaneously, as shown in Figures 32-5 and 32-6.

Figure 32-5: When the horizontal squash is doing its thing, the image is split into halves and each half moves toward the center from the edges.

Figure 32-6: After the effect is complete, the image is plain to see.

You can speed up the main effect or slow it down by changing the MDelay property. MDelay sets the time delay between redraws in milliseconds. The sister property to MDelay is MGrain. MGrain is the smallest increment or image area used when an effect is displayed. You can set MGrain from 1 to 256. The smaller the value, the smoother the effect, but the longer it takes. So, the size of the control and the settings for MDelay and MGrain determine how fast an effect works. If MDelay is set to a large number and MGrain is set very small, at 1 or 2, an effect can be very slow.

Making an Image Transparent

FXImage lets you make the background of an image transparent. In the sample application, I've used an irregular image with a white background (see Figure 32-7) and set its background to match that of the form (see Figure 32-8).

Figure 32-7: A bitmap with an irregular edge has a background that is very apparent.

Figure 32-8: When the bitmap is loaded into an FXImage control and the Transparent property is set, the bitmap's background matches that of the form on which it's placed.

Here's how this works. Draw an FXImage control on a form and load an image using the Picture property. Change the Transparent property to True, and then set the TransparentColor property to the *exact* color of the image's background. This tells FXImage to substitute the color of the background that the control is on with that color.

The Preview mode does not work with transparencies, so you'll have to run the project to see the effect you've created.

Creating a Transition

In this third example, I'll use the properties prefixed with a T to create a super transition effect. Draw an FXImage control on a form and load an image into the control. Set the background of the image so that it is transparent, as described in the previous section. (Because a transparent image is involved, the Preview mode won't work, so you'll have to run the project to see the effect you've created.)

Next, open the Property Pages dialog for the FXImage control by choosing Custom in the Properties window. Move to the Effects tab and turn your attention to the properties prefixed with a "T" (see Figure 32-9).

As with the main effect, there are over 100 transition effects to choose from when setting the TEffect property. In this case, I selected 22-Explode, which will make the effect explode from the center of the form. Next, I set the TStyle property to 8-Gradient. This will create a blend of two colors when the explode effect occurs (these two colors are set by the TGColor1 and TGColor2 properties).

From there, I set the TGStyle property to 14-Ellipse to Center. TGStyle sets the style of a transition gradient. Instead of an ellipse, I could have chosen a blend of colors from left to right or right to left, top to bottom or bottom to top, and so on. (There are 15 settings from which to choose.)

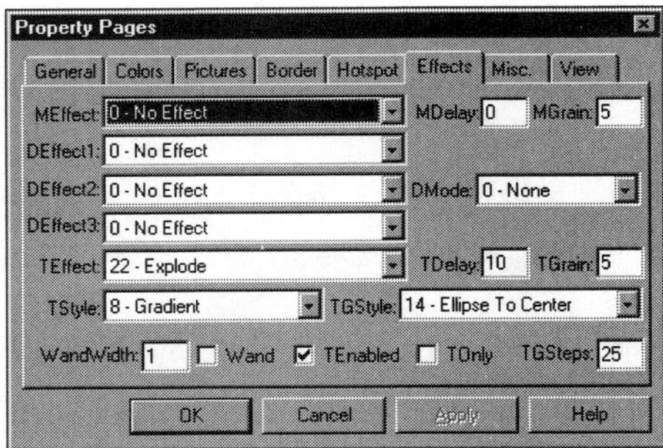

Figure 32-9: The FXImage control properties prefixed with a "T" create transition effects.

A *gradient* is a blend of colors from a start color to a finish color; the intermediate colors created as the blend proceeds are called *steps*. FXImage includes a TGSteps property, so you can set the number of steps that will occur as one color transitions to another. In the demo app, I set this property to 25.

Finally, I experimented with the TDelay and TGrain properties, finding the right amount of time delay in proportion to the "grains" that redraw after the time delay. These properties are identical to MDelay and MGrain, except that they effect transitions.

You'll have to click the Transition button in the demo program to see the transition at work, but you can see the gradient effect behind the transparent image in Figure 32-10.

Also, if you take a look at Figure 32-9, you'll notice that there are two more properties prefixed with a "T" — TEnabled and TOnly. TEnabled turns the transition effect on and off, depending upon a True or False setting, respectively. If TOnly is set to True and TEnabled is set to True, only transitional effects will occur; main effects and dissolve effects will be disabled.

Figure 32-10: The background gradient really sets off the transparent image.

Creating a Triple Dissolve

This final set of effects is just as easy to create as the others I've already discussed. To create any kind of dissolve — single, double, or triple — you need to use the properties prefixed with a "D."

To start, add an FXImage control to a form and load an image into the control. Set the Preview property to True, so you can see the effects you are creating at design time. Open the FXImage Property Pages dialog by selecting Custom from the Properties window, and then move to the Effects tab. Use the drop-down list box next to DMode, as shown in Figure 32-11, to select the number of dissolve effects that will occur one after the other. For the demo application, I've selected 3-Triple Pass.

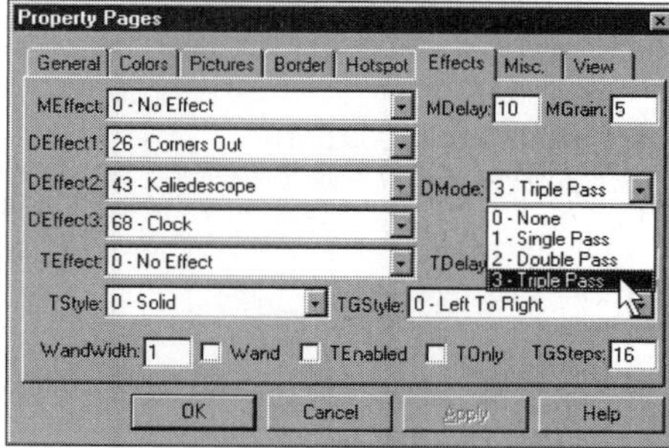

Figure 32-11: Use the DMode property on the Effects tab of the Property Pages dialog to set the number of dissolve effects that will occur.

From there, use the DEffect1 drop-down list to set the first dissolve effect, the DEffect2 drop-down list to set the second dissolve effect, and DEffect3 to set the third. Each drop-down list supplies over a hundred dissolve effects to choose from, so experiment with different combinations.

To set the time delay and grain size for the dissolve effects, use the MDelay and MGrain properties. Because I was creating a triple dissolve, I didn't want the effects to take too long, so I set MDelay to 10 and MGrain to 5.

And that's it! A figure here won't really show you the effects I've created, so click the Dissolve button in the demo application to see it run.

Summary

FXTools, created by the folks at ImageFX, is a set of eight super ActiveX controls that let you use your imagination to add amazing effects to your projects. FXTools is an incredible third-party tool that makes adding multimedia to applications simple, fast, and fun!

In this chapter, I showed you how to

- Add sound to a form using FXSnd
- Start an effect in code
- Create moving text with FXMtext
- Use FXImage to create a main effect
- Set time delay and grain size
- Make the background of an image transparent using FXImage
- Add a transition effect that includes a gradient
- Create a triple dissolve

Chapter 33

VideoSoft's VS-Ocx, VSFlex, and VSView

VideoSoft has created several ActiveX libraries that are important to the Visual Basic developer because they contain tools that are unique and powerful. Granted, you perhaps could re-create the functionality that these tools provide after a ton of sweat and hard work, but why bother? The work's already been done for you.

The three VideoSoft OCX libraries covered in this chapter — VS-Ocx, VSFlex, and VSView — have plenty to offer. These three libraries contain nine controls whose capabilities range from sophisticated text and data parsing controls to a printer object that can format text to a tool that automatically resizes all controls proportionately when the user resizes a window.

The *Visual Basic 5 SECRETS* companion CD-ROM includes fully functional demonstration versions of each of these ActiveX controls. These demonstration versions are completely identical to the commercial version that you can buy except that when an application using one of them starts to run, a banner states that a demo version of the control is being used, as shown in Figure 33-1.

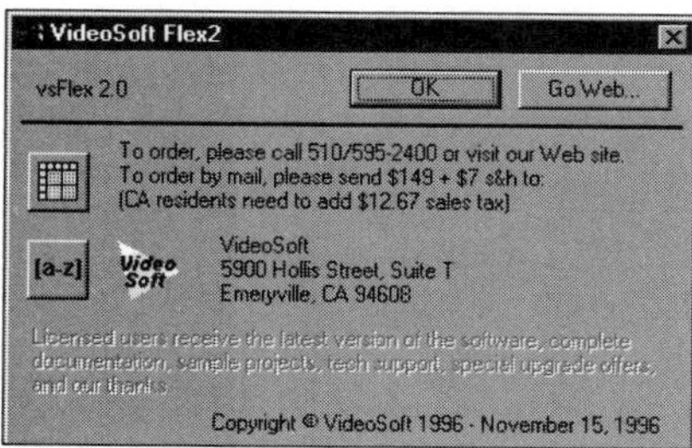

Figure 33-1: The demonstration VideoSoft controls included on the *Visual Basic 5 SECRETS* companion CD-ROM display a banner when they are opened in the design environment.

To run the projects that accompany this chapter, you should first install the VideoSoft controls from the *Visual Basic 5 SECRETS* companion CD-ROM.

The demonstration versions on the *Visual Basic 5 SECRETS* CD-ROM are VS-Ocx 5.0, VSFlex 2.0, and VSView 2.0. As you may know, the Microsoft FlexGrid Control, included with the Professional and Enterprise Editions of VB5, is essentially VideoSoft's Version 1.0 of VSFlex.

In this chapter, I will delve into these three ActiveX libraries and show you:

- What each of the tools these OCXs contain can do
- How to quickly put them to use

In the spirit of *Visual Basic 5 SECRETS,* let's just jump right in and head for the action. This chapter is divided into two major sections. The first, "Using the Right Tool for the Job," describes the powerful VideoSoft tools contained in these custom control libraries. Two of these tools, Awk and FlexArray, are featured in quick demo applications. The second section, "A VideoSoft Demo," develops a project that puts to work three more tools: InForm, Elastic, and IndexTab.

Using the Right Tool for the Job

The three VideoSoft ActiveX libraries each contain several tools that are Very Useful Indeed, as the inimitable Winnie-the-Pooh would say. If you add all three ActiveX controls to a Visual Basic project using the Components dialog, nine tool buttons are added to your Toolbox, as shown in Figure 33-2.

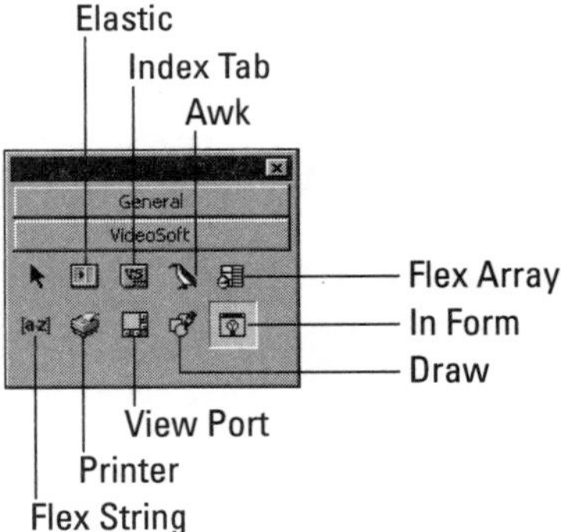

Figure 33-2: These nine tool buttons are added to the Visual Basic Toolbox when you add the three VideoSoft ActiveX controls — VS-Ocx, VSFlex, and VSView — to a project

In woodworking, knitting, cooking, scuba diving, or software development, it pays to use the right tool for the job. Let's see what each of these tool buttons does.

VS-Ocx

This VS-Ocx library contains three tools that comprise the first three tools in the top row of Figure 33-2 — Elastic, IndexTab, and Awk.

Elastic

Elastic is a great tool that you can use to replace commonly used Visual Basic controls such as panels, frames, command buttons, picture boxes and image controls, and labels. Now, why would you want to do that, you ask? This is where the beauty of Elastic comes in: If a form is resized by the user, any "Elastic controls" or regular Visual Basic controls contained in an Elastic control automatically resize, proportionately.

Also, Elastic is very flexible in its border presentation. You can set several properties — BevelInner, BevelInnerWidth, BevelOuter, BevelOuterWidth, and BevelOuterDir — that let you create custom borders for your projects.

IndexTab

Yes, I know that I've already discussed two tab controls back in Chapter 8, "Windows User Interface Controls." So, why another? Well, the VideoSoft IndexTab control offers some interesting visual features that both the Visual Basic and Sheridan tab controls don't.

The first thing you should know is that the IndexTab's Caption property is very important; you won't get anywhere without it. The Caption property creates the tabs and simultaneously sets the text that goes on each tab. For instance, if you wanted to set up three tabs — named Frodo, Bilbo, and Samwise — you would have to enter

```
Frodo | Bilbo | Samwise
```

in the Caption property's settings box, as shown in Figure 33-3. This "piping" reminds me of the way the Filter property is entered in the ShowOpen and ShowClose versions of the common dialog.

If you prefer, you can enter the caption for the IndexTab using its Custom Property page dialog.

Using the FrontTabColor property in conjunction with the BackTabColor property, you can set up a multicolor tab control with a selected tab that is, for instance, light gray, and with unselected tabs that are dark gray.

With the CaptionStyle property, you can create a 3D raised or lowered look for the tab text. The Style property lets you select from ten different tab styles — Slanted, Chamfered, CutCorners, and more. And the Template property offers five interesting preset tab page templates that quickly create a custom look. The settings include 1-Redmond, 2-Scotts Valley, 3-Cambridge, 4-Berkeley, and 5-Chicago. I'm sure you can guess which one of these has the "Windows 95 look." (Hint: It's not Redmond, and it is the major mid-Western city that was the code name for the prerelease version of Windows 95.)

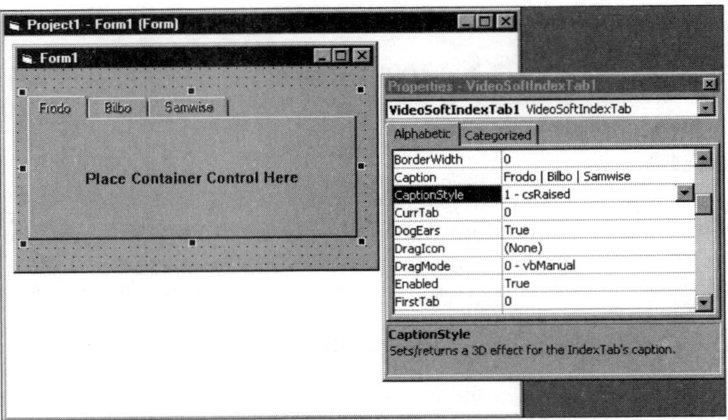

Figure 33-3: You can use the Caption property of the VideoSoft IndexTab control to create and name three tab pages.

Awk

The final tool contained in VS-Ocx is Awk, a text parsing tool that quickly scans text strings and files, and manipulates their contents. (By the way, the name "Awk" is derived from the Awk language, which was developed under the UNIX operating system to handle text parsing.) For instance, using Awk you can examine text validity of a file with a comparison check, create reports, or retrieve items.

Here's a quick example: Suppose that you want to count the words contained in a text file. You could build a procedure that moves through a text file, parsing out words and nonword characters (such as +, =), and count the words by detecting spaces and hard returns. Or, you could use VideoSoft's Awk tool and four lines of code. (This sample application is available on the companion CD-ROM as ***Awk.Vbp***.)

First, you have to add VS-Ocx to your project using the Components dialog to load the Awk tool in the VB Toolbox. Then, add a rich text box, three command buttons — one to open the text file, one to get Awk counting words, and one to end the demo — the Awk control, and a Common Dialog control.

This initial piece of code is what I call the "preliminaries." Using the Open command button's click event, add code that uses the Common Dialog control to open a text file. Also, load the file into both the RichTextBox and Awk controls using their Filename properties.

```
Private Sub cmdOpen_Click()
   With CommonDialog1
      .CancelError = True
      On Error GoTo ErrHandler
```

```
        .Flags = cdlOFNFileMustExist
        .Filter = "Text Files _
           (*.txt)|*.txt|Rich Text Files (*.rtf)|*.rtf"
        .DialogTitle = "Open a Text File for Word Counting"
    End With
    CommonDialog1.ShowOpen
    RichTextBox1.filename = CommonDialog1.filename
    VideoSoftAwk1.filename = CommonDialog1.filename
    On Error GoTo 0
    Exit Sub
ErrHandler:
    If Err = cdlCancel Then
       MsgBox "You didn't choose a file!"
    End If
End Sub
```

Now comes the fun part. With that groundwork out of the way, it takes only four lines of code to start the Awk scan of the text file, set the NumWords property to zero, count the words using Awk's NF property, and then send up the result in a message box.

```
Private Sub cmdCount_Click()
   Screen.MousePointer = vbHourglass
   VideoSoftAwk1.Action = 0   'Setting the Action property causes
                              'the Awk to start scanning
End Sub

Private Sub VideoSoftAwk1_Begin()
   NumWords = 0     'Begin is fired when Awk starts scanning
End Sub

Private Sub VideoSoftAwk1_Scan()
   NumWords = NumWords + VideoSoftAwk1.NF  'NF = number of fields
                                           'Fired once per line
...
End Sub

Private Sub VideoSoftAwk1_End()  'Fired when Awk finishes scanning
   Screen.MousePointer = vbDefault
   MsgBox "The number of words in this text file is: " _
      + Format(NumWords, "###,###")
End Sub
```

That's all there is to it! Because the Awk's Scan event is fired once per line, you can easily display the code line by line in the Debug window using Debug.Print while Awk is scanning the text file:

```
Private Sub VideoSoftAwk1_Scan()
    NumWords = NumWords + VideoSoftAwk1.NF
    Debug.Print VideoSoftAwk1.L   'prints each line in the Debug
                                  'window as it is scanned by Awk
End Sub
```

I've placed a sample text file called ***Test.Txt*** on the CD-ROM for you to use; of course, you could also use any text file you wish to play with this demo applet. Figure 33-4 shows the results of this project.

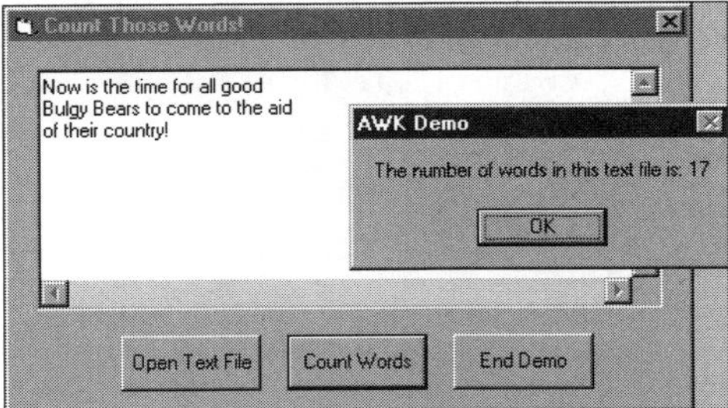

Figure 33-4: The Awk tool makes counting the words in a text file really simple and fast! You could easily modify this application to parse each line of text or to parse specific sections of text.

VSView

As its name implies, the VSView OCX provides tools that are visual in nature. The four tools included in this custom control library are Printer, ViewPort, Draw, and InForm.

Printer and ViewPort

The first two tools — Printer and ViewPort — are complementary and work well together. ViewPort gives you extra space on forms by adding scroll bars. In essence, these scroll bars provide a "virtual space" that extends the actual dimensions of the form. You use ViewPort in conjunction with the VideoSoft Printer tool when you want print preview capabilities.

The Printer tool is not just another printer object. Besides using it to print preview or print documents, you can use the Printer tool to format text, graphics, and the page that the text and graphics are printed on. Among other things, you can use the Printer tool to set:

- Page margins
- A border around the page
- Page headers and footers
- Whether the text will be printed in tables or columns (and how many)
- Fonts, line spacing, text color, justification, and more

The Printer tool would be very handy for a corporate project where data was pulled in from different sources with different formatting. You could use the Printer tool to create a consistent printing format.

Draw

The next VideoSoft tool, Draw, lets you create graphics — maps, charts, diagrams — in code. You can then view these graphics on the screen, print them, or send them to the Clipboard, thereby making them available to other applications such as Word or Excel.

The two properties that you need to get going with this tool are Action, which specifies what action — drawing, printing, or copying — the Draw tool will take, and Draw, which lets you quickly create lines, rectangles, and ellipses by specifying X1, Y1, X2, and Y2 property coordinates.

InForm

The InForm tool lets you customize the *nonclient* area of a form — those parts of the form that the Visual Basic developer cannot usually alter: the caption bar, window borders, and caption bar buttons. This is not a tool for someone who wants to design applications that look like everyone else's. A form that doesn't look like everyone else's is shown in Figure 33-5. By the way, the window shown in Figure 33-5 is *very* colorful, as you can see if you open the ***Vsview.Vbp*** project (located on the companion CD-ROM and described later in this chapter)!

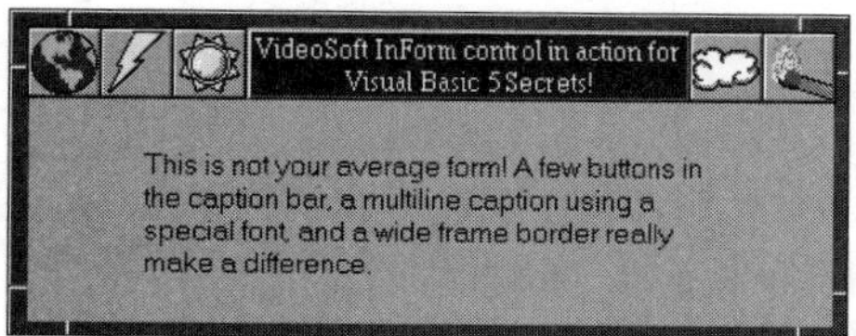

Figure 33-5: The InForm control makes it easy to create a distinctive look with a multiline caption, custom buttons in the caption bar, and a wide frame around the form's border.

With the InForm control, you can create a frame around the window and set its thickness and color. You can customize the caption bar to include up to six buttons — three on the left and three on the right — and the caption itself is not limited to the system font or a single line of text. Also, you can set the caption with a 3D raised or lowered effect.

VSFlex

VSFlex is an ActiveX with muscle. (Yes, the name was begging for that bad pun; I couldn't help myself!) The two controls contained within the ***.Ocx*** file — FlexArray and FlexString — both deal with text manipulation.

FlexArray

The FlexArray tool is designed to work alone or work with another grid control. You can use it to sort and group tabular data; edit, format, and merge spreadsheet cells; and rearrange data by moving columns and rows. Figure 33-6 displays a FlexArray table that contains grouped data whose columns can be moved to change data emphasis.

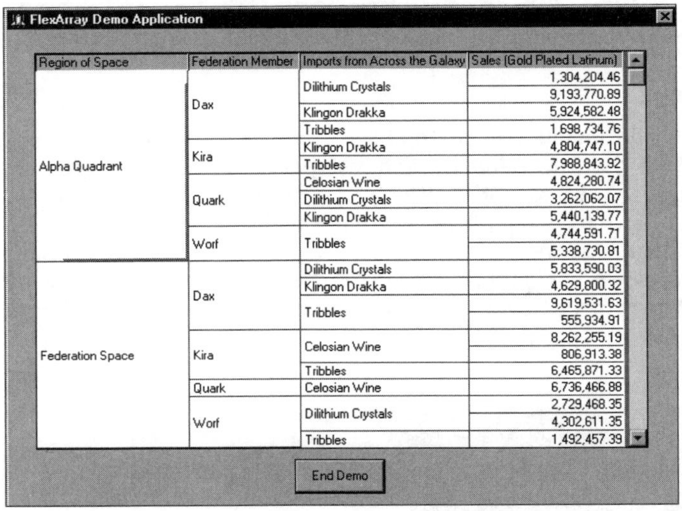

FlexArray Demo Application

Region of Space	Federation Member	Imports from Across the Galaxy	Sales (Gold Plated Latinum)
Alpha Quadrant	Dax	Dilithium Crystals	1,304,204.46
			9,193,770.89
		Klingon Drakka	5,924,582.48
		Tribbles	1,698,734.76
	Kira	Klingon Drakka	4,804,747.10
		Tribbles	7,988,843.92
	Quark	Celosian Wine	4,824,280.74
		Dilithium Crystals	3,262,062.07
		Klingon Drakka	5,440,139.77
	Worf	Tribbles	4,744,591.71
			5,338,730.81
Federation Space	Dax	Dilithium Crystals	5,833,590.03
		Klingon Drakka	4,629,800.32
		Tribbles	9,619,531.63
			555,934.91
	Kira	Celosian Wine	8,262,255.19
			806,913.38
		Tribbles	6,465,871.33
	Quark	Celosian Wine	6,736,466.88
	Worf	Dilithium Crystals	2,729,468.35
			4,302,611.35
		Tribbles	1,492,457.39

End Demo

Figure 33-6: You can use the FlexArray control to quickly organize data into a very clearly formatted table.

The table shown in Figure 33-6 displays data in a hierarchical fashion that moves across the table from left to right. The leftmost column displays the region where items were sold, the second column displays the Federation members who sold items in that region, the third column shows what each person sold (dilithium crystals, tribbles, and so on), and the final column displays the sales of each item (expressed in gold-plated Latinum bars).

You could rearrange the table by dragging the Federation Member column, for example, to the leftmost position. Then, the table's macro topic would be the Federation members doing the selling, what regions they sold in, what they sold there, and how much.

You can play with this actual table, because it is in a demonstration application saved on the companion CD-ROM as ***Flex.Vbp***.

The way the FlexArray table is manipulated is really very neat. The only control needed on the form is a FlexArray. Its properties should be set as shown in Table 33-1.

Table 33-1 FlexArray Property settings

Property	Setting
Cols	4
FixedCols	0
FixedRows	1
FormatString	Region of Space | Imports from Across the Galaxy | Federation Member | Sales (Gold Plated Latinum)
MergeCells	2-Restrict Rows

The FormatString property sets up the column headers. As with the IndexTab control's Caption property discussed earlier, each header is delineated with a pipe character (|). When entering the long string that makes up the FormatString property, you must put a blank space before the first header or the header's first letter will be chopped off.

Now that the preparation is all set, let's wire the FlexArray application.

To have a table that can be sorted, you must first have data. Using the Form's Load event, I call two functions — GetString and GetIndex — that randomly generate data for the table. (Normally, of course, you would be retrieving data from a database.) Then, using the FlexArray's MergeCol property, you can merge the columns containing identical information. Finally, another procedure, SortInfo, is called to sort the data and place it in the proper columns.

```
Private Sub Form_Load()
   Dim X As Integer
      'create data for demo app
      With vsFlexArray1
         For X = .FixedRows To .Rows - 1
            .TextArray(GetIndex(X, 0)) = _
               GetString(0) 'space the final frontier
            .TextArray(GetIndex(X, 1)) = _
               GetString(1) 'imports from across the galaxy
            .TextArray(GetIndex(X, 2)) = _
               GetString(2) 'federation member
            .TextArray(GetIndex(X, 3)) = _
               Format(Rnd * 10000000, "###,###,###.00")_
               'sales (gold plated latinum)
         Next X
            'merge columns to organize data
            .MergeCol(0) = True
            .MergeCol(1) = True
            .MergeCol(2) = True
      End With
   SortInfo     'procedure to sort data and
                'place it in the proper columns
End Sub
```

The heart of the application is really the SortInfo procedure. With only three FlexArray properties, the entire set of data can be sorted in ascending order:

```
Private Sub SortInfo()
   With vsFlexArray1
      .col = 0     'set active column
      .ColSel = .Cols - 1
      .Sort = 1    'generic ascending sort
   End With
End Sub
```

Then, to let the user move the columns around to re-sort the data, the FlexArray's MouseDown and MouseUp events are used like this:

```
Private Sub vsFlexArray1_MouseDown(Button As Integer, _
   Shift As Integer, X As Single, Y As Single)
   vsFlexArray1.Tag = ""
   If vsFlexArray1.MouseRow <> 0 Then
      Exit Sub
   End If
   vsFlexArray1.Tag = Str(vsFlexArray1.MouseCol)
   MousePointer = vbCustom
End Sub

Private Sub vsFlexArray1_MouseUp(Button As Integer, _
   Shift As Integer, X As Single, Y As Single)
   MousePointer = vbDefault
   With vsFlexArray1
      If .Tag = "" Then
         Exit Sub
      End If
      .Redraw = False
      .ColPosition(Val(.Tag)) = .MouseCol
      SortInfo
      .Redraw = True
   End With
End Sub
```

That's all that this demo application requires. The FlexArray tool and its properties take care of business for you. Try it out and see which Federation member has been selling the most tribbles in the Romulan Neutral Zone.

VSFlex Version 2 has numerous enhancements over the earlier version of this control. For details, see the ***Readme.Txt*** file placed in the VSFlex samples directory when you install the control.

FlexString

You use FlexString to parse complex text stings and to incorporate pattern matching — for instance, search-and-replace functionality — into your projects. Each line of a text string is placed into the tool's Text property at runtime, and is then compared to the string assigned to the Pattern property. To assist with the text matches that are found, the MatchCount property returns the number of matches, and the MatchIndex property can be used to scan through individual matches.

A VideoSoft Demo

This demonstration project will use the Elastic, InForm, and IndexTab tools to quickly produce a *very* original form. Check out how the Elastic proportionately stretches any controls contained on it at runtime. Also, play with the demo application to see the different templates that come built into the IndexTab, and watch InForm's multiline caption as you stretch the window. The project is available on the companion CD-ROM as ***Vsview.Vbp***.

After adding the VS-Ocx and VSView controls to a new Visual Basic project, double-click the Elastic tool to drop an Elastic on the default form. Using the Properties window, set the Elastic's Align property to 5-Fill Container, and then load a picture into the Picture property (a firecracker icon, ***Misc39a.Ico***, found in the Visual Basic ***Graphics\Icons\Misc*** directory is used for the project on the CD-ROM). Then set the PicturePos property to 10-Tile to create a background wallpaper of the picture. Make sure to leave the AutoSizeChildren property at 0-None until later when you have all the controls sized and shaped as you want them. (I'll tell you why in a moment.)

Next, add an InForm control to the form. Even though this tool changes the nonclient area of the form, the graphical representation of the control is only a small button filled with the InForm icon that is visible only at design time. The effects that the InForm tool produce on the form are only available at runtime. So, you need to experiment with the control, changing the InForm properties and then running the project to see what you've done.

To make the form work correctly with the InForm control, you should set the form's BorderStyle property to 0-None. Otherwise, a ghost set of Windows 95 minimize, maximize, and close buttons that have no functionality will appear on top of the buttons that InForm places in the caption bar. Set the InForm's BarColor and CapColor properties, and then set the ButtonsLeft property to 3 and ButtonsRight to 2, creating five buttons on the InForm caption bar. At this point, move down the Properties window until you reach the PicLeft and PicRight properties to add pictures to each button.

The buttons added to the caption bar by an InForm tool use index numbers starting from the outside edges of the form and moving inward, as shown in Figure 33-7.

To load an icon into the leftmost button, use the PicLeft0 property. Then move on to the button to the right of that one and load an icon into PicLeft1. You should also load PicLeft2 with an icon. Now, move over to the buttons that will appear to the right of the caption. Because ButtonsRight has been set to 2, you only have to load two buttons' properties, PicRight0 and PicRight1, with icons.

PicLeft*x*						PicRight*x*
0	1	2	Caption	2	1	0

Figure 33-7: Using the VideoSoft InForm control, you can add up to six buttons on the form's caption bar. These buttons are labeled with index numbers starting at the outside edges of the form and moving toward the center.

Moving to the border of the InForm control, change its CustomFrame property to True. Then change the CapMultiLine property from False to True. Because the caption will be long, splitting it into two lines will look good. To make the caption high enough that the user can view the second line, change the BarHeight property from its default of 0 to 35 (BarHeight uses pixels as its unit of measure).

Next add an IndexTab control on top of the firecracker-tiled Elastic. Size it just the way you want it, and also added two command buttons, cmdApply and cmdClose, below the IndexTab control.

After using the IndexTab control's Caption property to set up two tabs, drop an Elastic onto the first tab page. The Elastic automatically resizes itself to fill the client area of that tab page. Next, right-click the second tab to bring it to the front. Add an Elastic to act as a container on this tab page, also. From there, you can add the controls that you will need — two sets of option buttons and a text box — to play with the IndexTab and Elastic properties.

Once the controls are sized and located exactly where you want them, return to the Elastic covering the form to set its AutoSizeChildren property to 7-Proportional. As mentioned, we left this property alone until all controls were shaped and placed on the form as desired. Here's the reason for this: If you set the AutoSizeChildren property to anything but 0-None, any controls on an Elastic cannot be resized or moved. If you try, they will just spring stubbornly back to their original positions.

Writing the code for this application is straightforward. You need to create two private procedures, SetTabTemplate and SetElasticProp, to take care of setting the IndexTab's Template property. They should be called from the Apply button's Click procedure using an If...Then loop and the value of the selected tab's CurrTab property:

```
Private Sub cmdApply_Click()
   If frmVideoSoft.vsTab.CurrTab = 0 Then
      SetTabTemplate
   Else
      SetElasticProp
   End If
End Sub
```

```
Private Sub SetTabTemplate()
    Dim i As Integer, k As Integer, WhichOption As Integer
    For k = 0 To 5
        If optStyle(k) Then WhichOption = k
    Next k
    With frmVideoSoft.vsTab
        .CaptionStyle = csFlat
        .New3D = False
        Select Case WhichOption
            Case 0
                .Template = tpRedmond     '1
            Case 1
                .Template = tpScotts      '2
            Case 2
                .Template = tpCambridge   '3
            Case 3
                .Template = tpBerkeley    '4
            Case 4
                .Template = tpChicago     '5
            Case 5                        'Custom IDG Style
                .BackTabColor = vbRed
                .CaptionStyle = csRaisedLight
                .New3D = True
                .Position = tpBottom
                .Style = 5   'chamfered corners plus 3D
        Case Else
            MsgBox "We shouldn't be here!"
        End Select
    End With
End Sub

Private Sub SetElasticProp()
    Dim k As Integer, WhichOpt As Integer
    pnlForm.FloodPercent = CSng(txtFlood)
    For k = 0 To 3
        If optFloodDir(k) Then WhichOpt = k
    Next k
    pnlForm.FloodDirection = WhichOpt + 1
End Sub
```

The FreezeElastics Property

FreezeElastics, a design-time-only property, can also be used to disable Elastics alignment. Suppose you have a command button contained in an Elastic that you want to resize and move. If the FreezeElastics property is set to False, you won't be able to change the button — it will just snap back to its original position and size. However, if you set FreezeElastics to True, you can move and resize any controls contained within that Elastic. When you're finished, set FreezeElastics back to False to lock the controls in place on the Elastic.

The InForm buttons are activated using two procedures, ClickLButton and ClickRButton, which both use a Button argument as a parameter. As with the PicLeft and PicRight properties, the Button argument corresponds to the button index displayed in Figure 33-7. You can use an InForm property, FreeMemory, to display the system's free memory when the button with the lightning bolt icon (second from the left in Figure 33-8) is pressed. That code is as follows:

```
Private Sub vsInForm1_ClickLButton(Button As Integer)
   Dim MyMemory As Long
   ...
   Select Case Button
      ...
      Case 1    'lightning button
         With vsInForm1
            MyMemory = .FreeMemory
            MsgBox "Free System Memory is " & _
               Format(MyMemory, "###,###") & _
               " KB", vbInformation, ProgTitle
         End With
      ...
```

And that's it! Play with the application and see what the Elastic, InForm, and IndexTab controls can do quickly for you (take a look at Figure 33-8)!

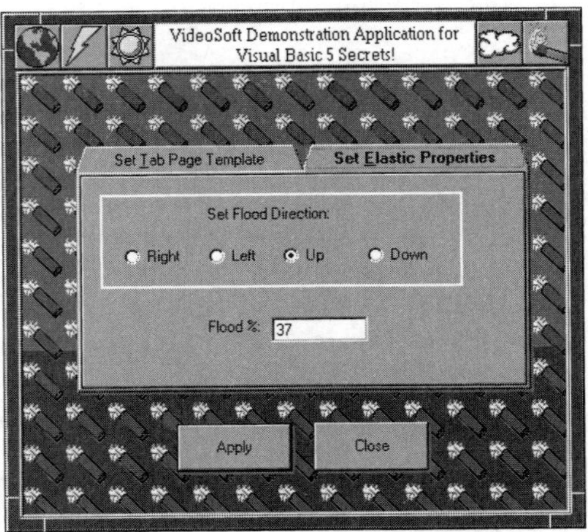

Figure 33-8: You can use the VideoSoft ActiveX controls to create many interesting and useful effects.

Summary

VideoSoft is the creator of several custom control libraries that you can use to rapidly expand the power of Visual Basic. In this chapter, I took a brief look at the three VideoSoft ActiveX libraries: VSFlex, VS-Ocx, and VSView. I introduced each of the tools these libraries contain, explaining what they can do. The tools discussed included

- FlexString
- FlexArray
- Elastic
- IndexTab
- Awk
- Printer
- ViewPort
- InForm
- Draw

Several of these tools were explained by using them in sample applications:

- Using VS-Ocx's Awk tool and three lines of code, we parsed a text file and counted the number of words it contains.
- With VSFlex's FlexArray tool, we quickly generated a sorted data table that can be reorganized at runtime simply by dragging and dropping columns.
- Using the Elastic, IndexTab, and InForm tools from the VSView and VS-Ocx libraries, we created a *very* distinctive window with a multiline caption bar, custom caption bar buttons, and controls that automatically resize proportionately when the window is resized.

Chapter 34

MicroHelp ActiveX Controls

May I say "Wow!" The trial version ActiveX tools and demonstration programs supplied by MicroHelp (available on the *Visual Basic 5 SECRETS* CD-ROM) really knock my socks off!

There's a gamut of goodies for you to try out:

- Encryption X-ponents 1.0 is a set of ActiveX controls and exposed security and encryption objects. The security controls work much like a Visual SourceSafe schema with administrator and user Active X controls. The encryption portion of the tool set offers a choice of four encryption algorithms. You can incorporate these encryption ActiveX controls into your applications.
- Fax Plus 2.0 is a set of three ActiveX controls that allows you to add faxing capabilities to your projects.
- Explorer X-ponents is a set of four tools that let you quickly add icons with ToolTips to the tray on the Windows 95/NT status bar and create a fully functional Explorer window. (See "Adding an Icon to the Windows 95 Tray" in Chapter 11 for information about doing this on your own.)
- OLETools 5.0 is an amazing compendium of 54 ActiveX controls that range from game tools to parsing controls and enhanced common controls, such as labels, text boxes, and command buttons.
- MicroHelp Zip is a complete utility for managing file archives. Using MHZip, you can create archives, unzip files, zip files, create self-extracting zip files, and make backups of files and drives.
- VBViewer 2.0 lets you add a viewer to your projects that lets users open and look at files of any format. For example, you could use this control as an adjunct to graphics utilities in your programs.

Let's take an exploratory look at a few of the ActiveX controls included in the OLETools collection, one of the most powerful and extensive ActiveX control collections on the market.

OLETools

The OLETools library, which contains 54 tools, is the "War and Peace" of ActiveX controls. (Perhaps the only other library of third-party tools comparable to OLETools in its range and quality is Crescent's QuickPak Pro.) If you need something, it's likely to be in this collection.

OLETools contains controls that cover a wide range of functions, from a 3D check box, button, gauge, and dial to dice and playing card controls to Registry and calendar controls. Each one of the 54 tools comes packaged in its own ***.Ocx*** file, so you only need to add the MicroHelp tools that you want to use. This lets you keep projects that use OLETools to a minimal size.

If you added every tool that comes in the OLETools library to a project, your Toolbox would expand to include the buttons displayed in Figure 34-1.

Figure 34-1: The MicroHelp OLETools library includes 54 separate tools that you can add individually to your Visual Basic Toolbox.

Here's a sampling of the custom controls that come with OLETools.

Mh3dButn

Mh3dButn is a souped up version of the standard VB command button. With it, you can create buttons with a custom 3D appearance, multiline captions, and multiple bitmaps. For instance, you could create a button that displays a green check mark next to the OK caption. Figure 34-2 shows the a demo application that makes good use of this special command button.

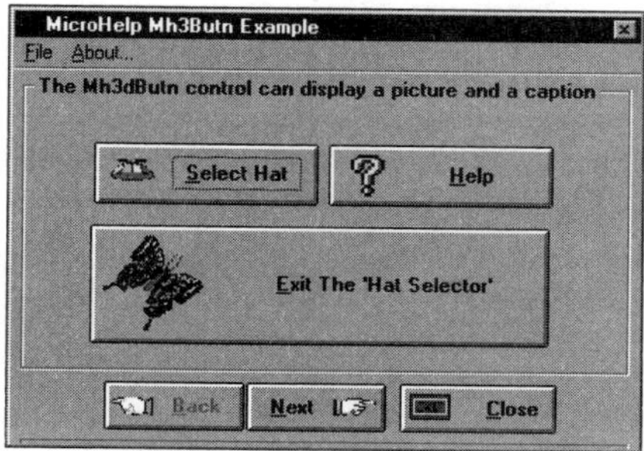

Figure 34-2: MicroHelp's 3D command button makes clicking fun!

Mh3dFile

Mh3dFile is an enhanced version of the Visual Basic file list box control. You can customize the control's 3D appearance, the font used for display, set it for single or multiple file selection, and add a caption. Mh3dFile can also search the items contained in the control for a string or part of a string. Figure 34-3 shows the 3D file list box control in action.

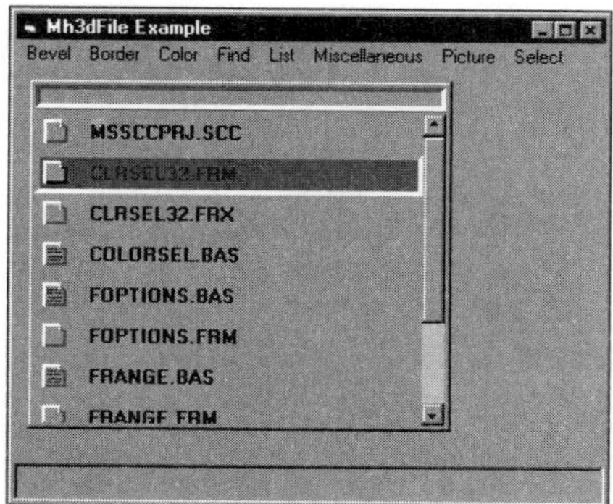

Figure 34-3: You can customize the 3D file list box control to look any way you want. You can also use it to search for strings.

MhIni/Registry

You can use the MhIni/Registry control to easily allow your users to create, edit, and remove *.Ini* and Registry settings. The sample application available on the companion CD-ROM performs both *.Ini* file manipulation and Registry manipulation. Figure 34-4 shows this demo application at work.

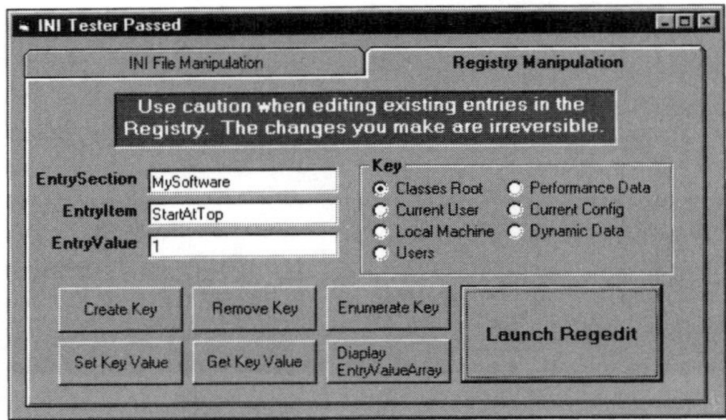

Figure 34-4: The MhIni/Registry control lets you quickly add Registry and ***.Ini*** file manipulation to your programs.

MhCard

The MhCard control quickly gets you started on any game application. This control lets you display any card from the standard 52-card deck of playing cards. In addition, you can set the graphic that is displayed on the card backs. Figure 34-5 displays a shuffled deck and a dealt card.

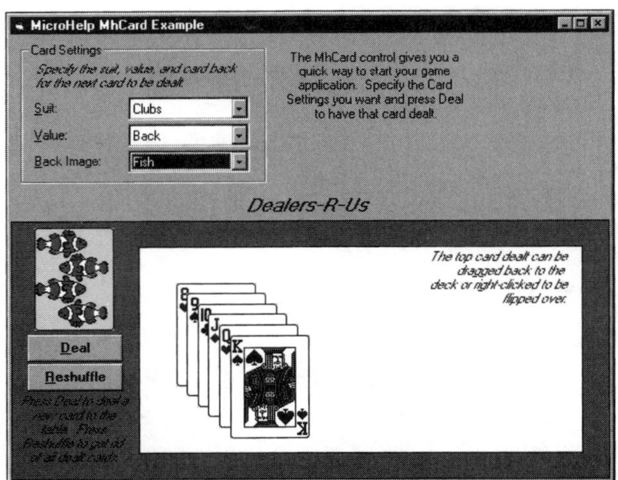

Figure 34-5: It's easy to add a deck of cards to any project using MicroHelp's MhCard control.

MhHistograph

MhHistograph is a special picture box that mimics the display of a plotter. MhHistograph lets you create charts that plot data along a time line and moves virtual plotting paper forward as it draws its points. Figure 34-6 shows the histograph control plotting a graph.

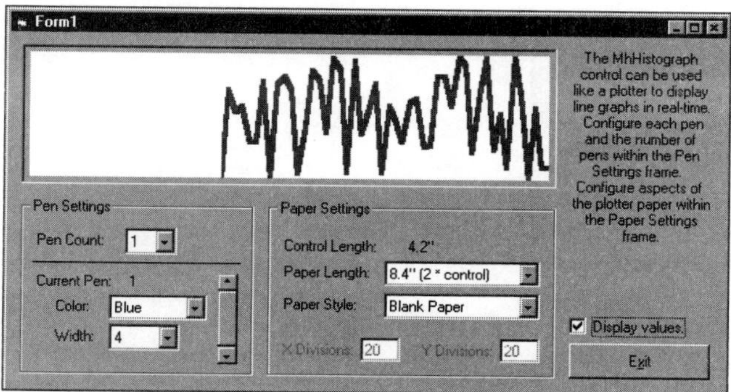

Figure 34-6: You can easily add a graphical plotter to any application using the MhHistograph control.

Summary

The MicroHelp products discussed in this chapter quickly add powerful functionality to your Visual Basic projects. It would take a great deal of time and effort to duplicate the features they implement.

This chapter described MicroHelp's controls, including:

- Encryption X-ponents 1.0
- Fax Plus 2.0
- Explorer X-ponents
- MicroHelp Zip
- VBViewer 2.0

In addition, I took a look at OLETools, MicroHelp's extensive collection of ActiveX controls.

Chapter 35

Help Files

We all need help sometimes. No matter how clear a program interface may be, there's always a user who needs an explanation of a particular feature. Or there's always the user who refuses to read the manual and relies on the on-line help file. A fully compiled, context-sensitive help system is an absolute must for any polished, professional application.

This chapter takes an in-depth look at help files, including the following topics:

- 32-bit Windows help features
- A step-by-step description of how to create help files using your favorite word processor and Help Compiler Workshop — a set of programs provided by Microsoft on the Visual Basic 5 CD-ROM
- How to connect a help file to Visual Basic

Creating and compiling a 32-bit Windows help file is really very easy once you see how all of the component files fit together. This chapter first discusses 32-bit Windows help features, and then moves right on to creating a compiled help file complete with jumps, pop-ups, graphics, and hot spots.

32-Bit Windows Help Features

With the advent of 32-bit Windows, virtually every aspect of the user interface, including the help system, received either a facelift, a complete reworking, or both. Some of these features include:

- A tab page metaphor lets the user look up topics on a Contents tab, search for items using an Index tab, or find topics using keywords on a Find tab.
- Shortcut buttons let the user move directly to an application command. For instance, if the user has launched help to find out how to install a new piece of hardware in 32-bit Windows, a shortcut button in the Adding Hardware topic takes her directly to the Add New Hardware Wizard.
- Users can access a context-sensitive menu at any time by right-clicking in the help window. With this menu, the user can make an annotation, copy or print a topic, change the help window's font size, make the window stay on top, or change the help window to system colors (if the help file designer has used another color scheme).
- Users can access context-sensitive or "What's This?" help using either the right mouse button or the ? button found at the upper-right corner

of a window. This is a pop-up window that displays a precise bit of information regarding a particular feature found in a window or dialog.

From the developer's point of view, there are several features that changed behind the scenes, including the ability to:

- Create custom tabs.
- Set default fonts and display up to 24-bit color depth.
- Create transparent bitmaps whose background color matches that of the window in which it is displayed
- Add buttons anywhere in a help topic.
- Transparently link ***.Hlp*** files together.
- Position secondary windows absolutely.
- Add multimedia (***.Avi***) files to any help topic. The multimedia files can be compiled directly into the ***.Hlp*** file so you don't have to include the files separately with the program installation.

How to Make a Help File

A help file — with its topics, references, jumps, and pop-ups — can be just as complex as a Visual Basic program. Consequently, it pays to come up with a solid help project architecture before you start creating a help project.

Planning a Help Project

First, you have to consider the application for which you are designing the help project and come up with help topics.

At this stage, I have found that old-fashioned index cards can be very handy. I use them to organize information — for instance, by writing one help topic on each card — and then arrange them alphabetically.

Next you need to come up with a game plan for the help project. This includes:

- Defining the audience for your product. Is it a game for children? Or is it an application for expert users? The language and content for these two help projects would be entirely different.
- Planning the contents of the help project. This includes topics such as designing the help menu in the actual application, creating contents screens that describe the program, and coming up with keywords and index topics.
- Creating a help topic structure.
- Deciding which controls in the application are going to be context-sensitive.

- Designing the actual help topics. This includes writing the topics, adding graphics and multimedia files, and using colors. (You could use blue text to emphasize something — just don't go overboard with colors and special effects!)

File Types for Creating a Help File

After you plan the help project, it's time to get down to the actual business of creating the files that go into a compiled help file. There are several types of files used to create a compiled 32-bit Windows help file, as listed in Table 35-1.

Table 35-1 Types of Files You Can Use to Create 32-Bit Windows Help Files

File Extension	*File Type*	*Description*	*Necessary for 32-Bit Windows Help?*
.Rtf	Help topic	Contains the text for the help file and the codes necessary to link topics. Can also contain actual graphics or calls to graphic files.	Yes
.Cnt	Help contents	Contains the hierarchical numbering of help topics that creates items found on the Contents tab when help runs.	Yes
.Hpj	Help project	Similar to a private profile file with section headers. This file contains a list of text and graphics files needed for the help file, macro names, secondary window definitions, and optional instructions.	Yes
.Bmp, .Wmf	Graphic	Needed only if you reference a graphic in the ***.Rtf*** file instead of embedding it there.	No
.Shg	Hypergraphic	An enhanced graphic with one or more hot spots created using ***Shed.Exe.***	No
.Mrb	Multiple-resolution bitmap	A special bitmap compiled by ***Mrbc.Exe*** that contains more than one version of the bitmap at different screen resolutions.	No
.Avi	Multimedia	These files are referenced in the ***.Rtf*** file using {mci ***FileName***}.	No

The sample help file compiled in this chapter is going to be created for the Mortgage Calculator application, ***LoanCalc.Vbp,*** from Chapter 22, "Controlling 'Foreign' Application Objects." The improved application and its associated files — including various help project files, bitmaps, and the actual Word file used to create the help topic file — are available on the companion CD-ROM in the Chapter 35 directory.

In this chapter, I'll create several of the file types listed in Table 35-1, in the following order:

1. Help topic file (***.Rtf***)
2. Hypergraphic file (***.Shg***)
3. Contents file (***.Cnt***)
4. Help project file (***.Hpj***)

The help topic file will be created in a word processor that supports Rich Text Format. The hypergraphic will be created with a Hotspot Editor, ***Shed.Exe***, and the contents and help project files will be created using Microsoft's Help Compiler Workshop.

Help Compiler Workshop

Help Compiler Workshop is provided on the Visual Basic 5 CD-ROM in the ***Tools\HCW*** folder. You'll need to install the Workshop with the ***Setup.Exe*** file found in that folder.

The Workshop contains several applications:

- Help Workshop (***Hcw.Exe***) helps you quickly create the project (***.Hpj***) and contents (***.Cnt***) files.
- Help Compiler (***Hcrtf.Exe***) is a help compiler that works in conjunction with ***Hcw.Exe***.
- Help Author's Guide (***Hcw.Hlp***) is a help file that provides complete information about designing a help project, from initial conception through compilation.
- Hotspot Editor (***Shed.Exe***) is a graphics editor that helps you create bitmaps with multiple hotspots that activate pop-ups or links.
- Multiple Resolution Bitmap Compiler (***Mrbc.Exe***) is a compiler that combines bitmaps of different resolutions into one multiple resolution bitmap.
- Dialog Box Help Editor (***Dbhe.Exe***) uses Microsoft Word for Windows to quickly create context-sensitive help.

If you want, you can still use the old command-line Help compiler, ***Hc.Exe***, to create 32-bit Windows help files even though it is not included on the Visual Basic 5 CD-ROM. Besides creating the topic file in a word processor, you would need to create the help project and contents files in a simple text editor such as Notepad.

However, if you use the new Help Workshop application to create the help project and contents files, the old DOS-based compiler will not be able to compile the files.

Once you have planned a help project, you first need to create a help topic file.

How to Code a Help Topic File

You can create a help topic file in any word processing program that can save files in Rich Text Format (***.Rtf***). For the sample help file for this chapter, I used Word for Windows.

Coding a help topic file is easy once you get the hang of it. The help project uses special control codes for specific tasks, some of which are displayed in Table 35-2.

Table 35-2 Control Codes Used in the Help Project File

Control Code	***Formal Name***	***Description***
# (footnote)	Context String	Defines a context string that uniquely identifies a help topic.
$ (footnote)	Title	Defines the help topic title (optional).
K (footnote)	Keyword	Defines a keyword that the user employs when searching for a topic.
+ (footnote)	Browse sequence number	Defines a sequence that determines what order the user browses through topics (optional).
* (footnote)	Build tag	Defines a tag that specifies topics compiled conditionally by the Help compiler.
Double-underlined or ~~Strikethrough~~ text	Jump	Appears in the compiled help file as green, single-underlined text, indicating to the user that she can click it to jump to another topic.
Single-underlined text	Definition (pop-up)	Shows up in the compiled help file as green, dashed-underlined text. When the user clicks it or presses Enter, a pop-up window appears.
Hidden Text	Context string	Specifies the context string that will appear for the topic when the user clicks the text immediately preceding it.

For a complete list of control codes, open “Topic footnotes” in the Help Author’s Guide.

Using Table 35-2 for reference, take a look at Figure 35-1. This figure shows the help topic file ***Mortgage.Rtf*** (or you can open the actual file found on the companion CD-ROM).

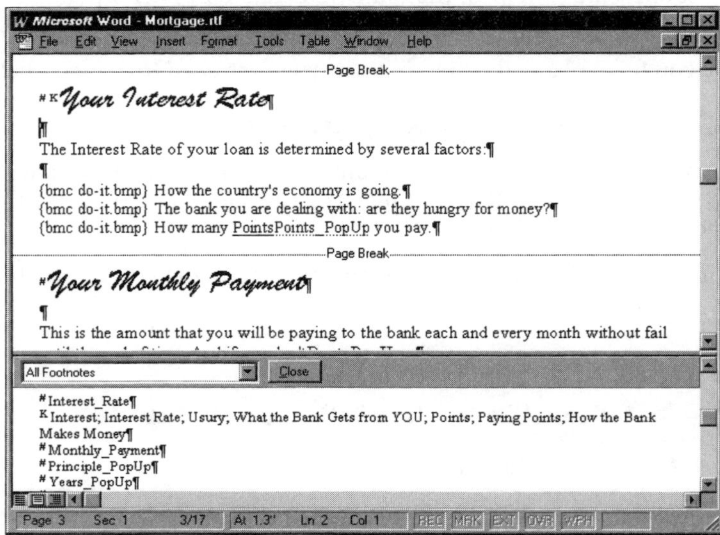

Figure 35-1: Here is the help topic file ***Mortgage.Rtf*** in Word for Windows, showing the help topics at the top of the window and the footnote control codes at the bottom.

Figure 35-1 shows two help topics: “Your Interest Rate” and “Your Monthly Payment.” Topics must be divided by hard page breaks and each topic must have a unique context string.

Here’s how to create a topic with context string: At the beginning of the line, insert a footnote using the # character. In the footnote area, type the name of the context string. In the case of the “Your Interest Rate” topic, the context string is Interest_Rate. Return to the main window and type in the help topic. That’s it.

If you want to add a help topic title, move your insertion point to just after the # footnote marker and add a footnote using the $ character. Down in the footnote section enter a title, for instance, Mortgage: Interest Rate.

To add keywords that will reference the “Your Interest Rate” topic, place the insertion point just after the # footnote and add a footnote using K. Down in the footnote section, as shown in Figure 35-1, enter keywords like this:

```
Kinterest; Interest Rate; Usury
```

Notice that semicolons separate the keywords.

Linking Topics with Jumps and Pop-Ups

Once you have your help topics entered, you can add jumps and pop-ups. Jumps are green, single-underlined text that appear in the compiled help file. Clicking a jump "jumps" the user to another, related topic. Pop-ups (or definitions) are green, dashed-underlined text in help files. Clicking such text or pressing Enter produces a pop-up window containing a definition of the underlined text.

You create jumps and pop-ups using hidden text and underscores. To create a jump, select the word or words you want to use to indicate the jump and double-underline or ~~strikethrough~~ the text. Directly next to that text (don't put in any spaces!), change the font attribute to Hidden, and then type the context name without using spaces. (The center of Figure 35-1 contains the context string Points_PopUp. Notice that it is underlined with dots — Word's indication that this text is hidden.)

To create a pop-up, select the word or words you want to use to indicate the pop-up and single-underline the text. Place the hidden context name right next to the underlined words as you would for a jump. The center of Figure 35-1 contains the pop-up Points, with its hidden text context string Points_PopUp just to its right.

Adding Graphics to the Topic File

It's easy to add graphics to any help file, although you have to make a choice: You can refer to a graphic using code or (when using Word for Windows) you can actually embed it in the document, by choosing Picture from the Insert menu. The good news about embedding a graphic in the document is that you don't have to distribute the individual graphic file with your application. The bad news is that the ***.Hlp*** file will, of course, be bigger, and if you need to edit the graphic, you will have to re-embed it. On the other hand, if you reference the graphic, you can call it any number of times in the help file and edit it externally, but you have to distribute the individual graphics file.

Graphics files can get rather large, but Microsoft has managed to make that a nonissue for help files. The maximum size for a compiled help file is 2GB!

You can use several commands when referencing a ***.Bmp*** or ***.Wmf*** file, as shown in Table 35-3.

Table 35-3 Commands for Referencing Graphics Files in Help Topic Text

Command	*Description*
bmc	Aligns the graphic as a character on the baseline of the type
bml	Aligns the graphic at the left margin and wraps the text along the graphic's right edge
bmr	Aligns the graphic at the right margin and wraps the text along the graphic's left edge

Figure 35-1 shows ***Do-it.Bmp*** referenced three times using the bmc command. Figure 35-2 shows the finished appearance of the help file topic.

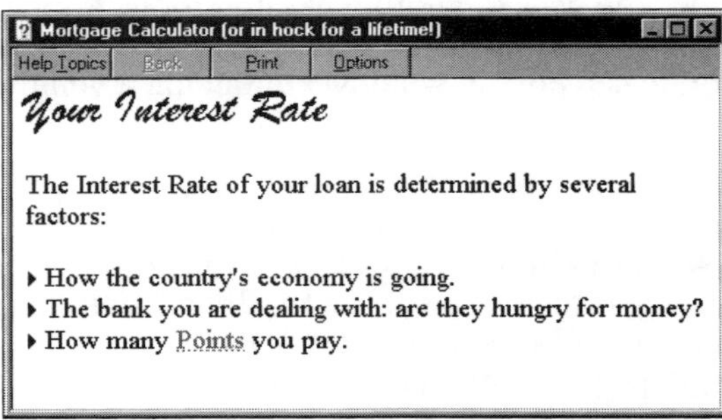

Figure 35-2: This help topic references a triangular-shaped bitmap three times using the bmc command.

You can also add a t parameter to any of the commands listed in Table 35-3. For instance:

```
{bmlt MyGraphic.Bmp}
```

The t creates a "transparent" bitmap, telling Help Workshop to substitute the bitmap's background color with the background color of the window in which it is displayed. However, this parameter only works with 16-color bitmaps.

There are several bitmaps — such as a bullet, em dash, and shortcut arrow — included with Help Workshop that you can reference in a topic file. For a complete list of these graphics, see "Bitmaps supplied by Help Workshop" in the Help Author's Guide.

Creating Hypergraphics with Hot Spots

Using the Hotspot Editor that comes with the Help Workshop, you can jazz up your help project with hypergraphics. Hotspot Editor (***Shed.Exe***) lets you quickly create graphics with *hot spots* — sometimes called *hypergraphics*. A hot spot is a visual hyperlink. Figure 35-3 shows a hypergraphic being created in the Hotspot Editor.

To create a hypergraphic, launch the Hotspot Editor and choose Open from the File menu to load a graphic file. Use the mouse pointer to draw a rectangle where you want the hot spot to appear. When you do, an Attributes dialog will open. Enter the context string (created in the help topic file) to which this hot spot will be linked and set the type of hot spot you want: jump or pop-up. Click OK to close the Attributes dialog, and then choose Save As from the File menu to save the hypergraphic as a ***.Shg*** file.

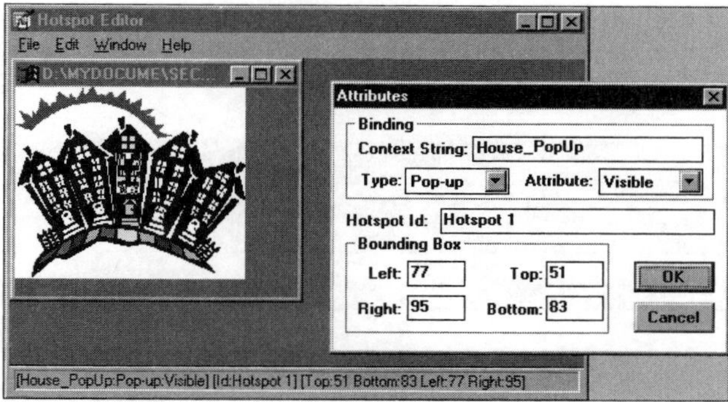

Figure 35-3: You can use the Hotspot Editor, ***Shed.Exe***, to create hypergraphics — graphics with hot spots.

You can reference any hypergraphic you create as you would any other bitmap in the help topic file using one of the commands listed in Table 35-3.

Once you have finished creating the help topic file, it's time to launch the Help Workshop application and create the contents (*.**Cnt***) and help project (*.**Hpj***) files.

Using Help Workshop to Create a Contents File

You use the contents (*.**Cnt***) file to generate the Contents tab found in a 32-bit Windows help window. This tab contains graphic images — the closed/opened books and pages containing question marks — and contents items.

After launching Help Workshop, choose New from the File menu. A New dialog box opens, letting you create a help project or help contents file, as shown in Figure 35-4.

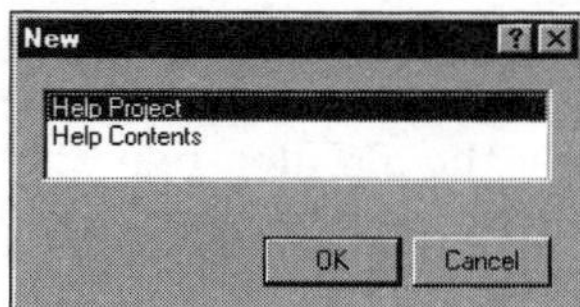

Figure 35-4: To create a new help project or help contents file, choose New from the File menu, and then make your selection in the New dialog box that appears.

Select Help Contents, and then click OK. Help Workshop opens a contents file screen like the one shown in Figure 35-5 (but without any of the entries).

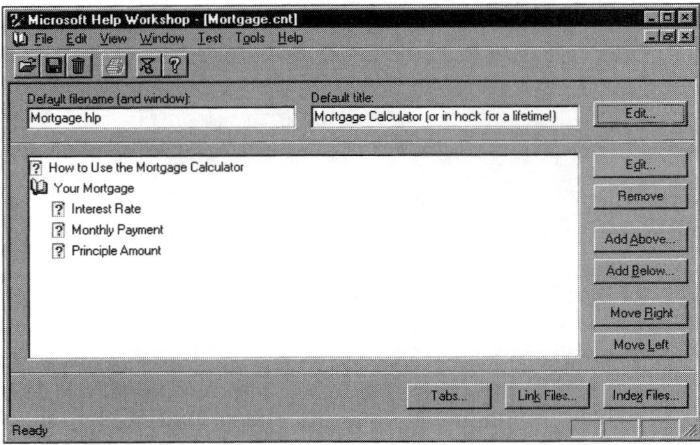

Figure 35-5: The contents file screen that Help Workshop opens will help you quickly create a contents file.

To get going with the contents file, start at the top of the window and click the Edit button to the right of the Default Filename and a Default Title fields. A Default Help Information dialog opens. In this dialog enter:

- The default name for your help file, for instance, ***Mortgage.Hlp***
- The default title for your help file, for example, Mortgage Calculator

Next, click the Add Below button. This opens the Edit Contents Tab Entry dialog shown in Figure 35-6. Select either the Heading option button — to create a header with a book icon next to it — or the Topic option button — to create a topic with a question mark page next to it. If you select the Heading option, enter a title for the heading, and then click OK to close the dialog. If you select the topic option, enter the title for a topic and the topic ID that you assigned for that topic in the ***.Rtf*** file; then Click OK. Continue adding headings and topics until you have added the items you need for your help project.

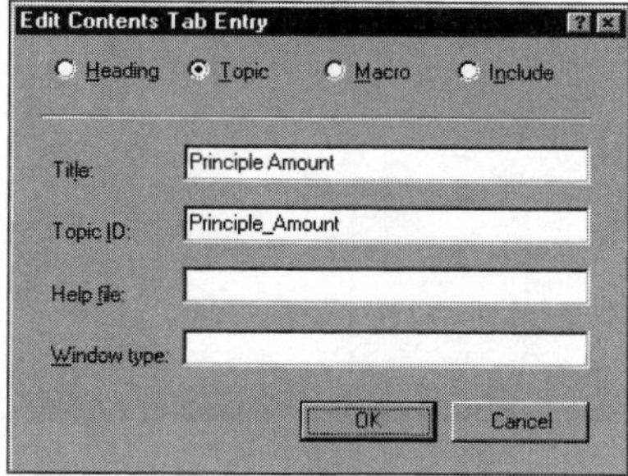

Figure 35-6: The Edit Contents Tab Entry dialog lets you quickly enter Contents tab topics and headers.

A contents file is really just a plain vanilla text file saved with the ***.Cnt*** extension. If you opened the contents file, ***Mortgage.Cnt***, created by the Help Workshop, you would see what is shown in Figure 35-7.

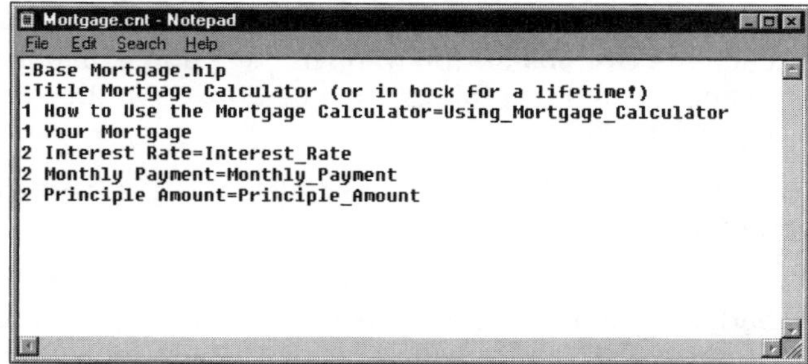

Figure 35-7: The contents file for the demonstration help file, ***Mortgage.Cnt***, sets the contents items found on the Contents tab page when ***Mortgage.Hlp*** is compiled and run.

Creating the Help Project File

When you are finished adding items to the contents file, save it and then choose New from the File menu to open the New dialog and create a help project (***.Hpj***) file. After you select Help Project in the New dialog, the Help Workshop interface changes to help you create a ***.Hpj*** file, as shown in Figure 35-8. (The Help Workshop window for a new ***.Hpj*** file would be empty.)

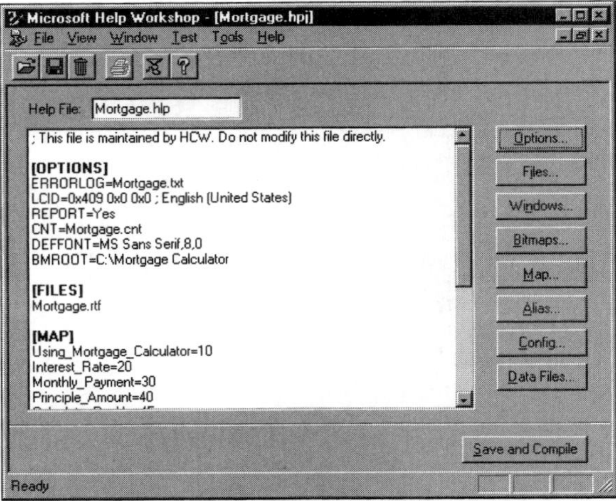

Figure 35-8: The Help Workshop user interface may seem a bit confusing at first, but once you've created help project and contents files, you'll get the hang of it.

To get going, click the Options button to open the Options dialog box shown in Figure 35-9. There are several things you need to set on the various tabs to build the help project file:

- On the General tab, set the default topic, help file title, and copyright information for the help file.
- On the Files tab, set the default name of the help file (for example, ***Mortgage.Hlp***), the name and folder location of an error log text file (for instance, ***Mortgage.Txt***), and the location of the help topic (***.Rtf***) file and the contents file (***.Cnt***) you created earlier.
- On the Fonts tab, set the default font for the windows in your help file.
- On the Compression tab, set the amount of compression — none, maximum, or custom — that will be applied to the compiled help file.

Next, click the Bitmaps button to open the Bitmap Folders dialog. Use the Browse button in this dialog to tell Help Workshop where the bitmaps referenced in the help topic (***.Rtf***) file are located.

The next button to click is Map; this opens the Map dialog shown in Figure 35-10. Use this dialog to set the topic IDs you created in the topic file equal to a positive integer. For instance, in Figure 35-10, Interest_Rate is equal to 20.

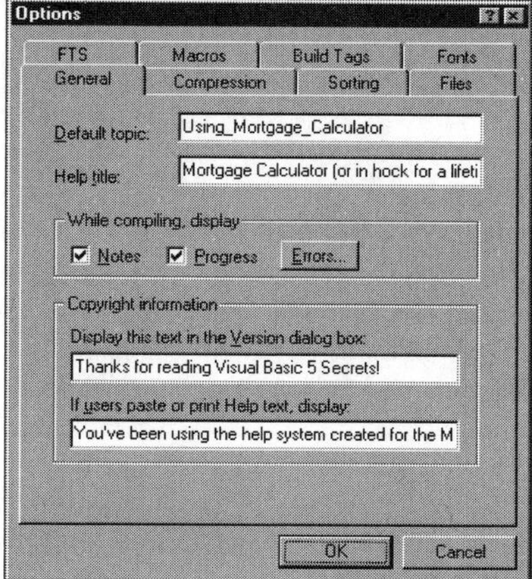

Figure 35-9: You use the Options dialog to set many necessary parameters for a help project file.

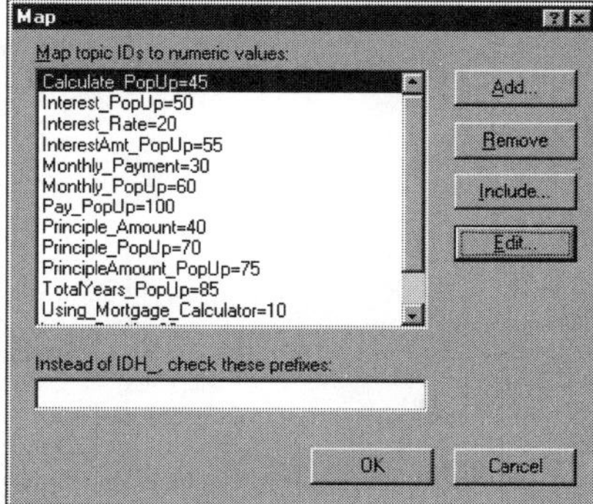

Figure 35-10: You use the Map dialog to assign integer values to topic IDs. These numbers are used to call context-sensitive help directly from an application.

Adding Macros to Your Help Project

You can add macros to a help project that perform many tasks, including adding and removing custom buttons and menus, changing the function of menu items and buttons, launching applications from within the help file, and making ***.Dll*** calls. Macros can also be called when the help file initially opens, when the user enters a topic, or from a hot spot. A number of macros come built into the help compiler ready for you to use; for a complete list of these macros, consult the "Macro quick reference" topic in the Help Author's Guide.

Just like the contents file created earlier, the help project file is a plain vanilla text file that you can view in any text editor, as shown in Figure 35-11.

```
Mortgage.hpj - Notepad
File Edit Search Help
; This file is maintained by HCW. Do not modify this file directly.

[OPTIONS]
ERRORLOG=Mortgage.txt
LCID=0x409 0x0 0x0 ; English (United States)
REPORT=Yes
CNT=Mortgage.cnt
DEFFONT=MS Sans Serif,8,0
BMROOT=C:\Mortgage Calculator
HLP=Mortgage.hlp

[FILES]
Mortgage.rtf

[MAP]
Using_Mortgage_Calculator=10
Interest_Rate=20
Monthly_Payment=30
Principle_Amount=40
Calculate_PopUp=45
Interest_PopUp=50
InterestAmt_PopUp=55
Monthly_PopUp=60
Principle_PopUp=70
```

Figure 35-11: The help project file created in Help Workshop is a plain text file that you can view in a text editor.

There are all sorts of bells and whistles you can add to a help project using Help Workshop — such as generating a full text search index, setting conditional compilation for specific help topics, and creating foreign language versions of a help file. To find out more about Help Workshop's full range of capabilities, check out "What's New in Version 4.0" on the Contents page of the Help Author's Guide.

That's all you need to do to create the help project file. The next step is compiling the files you've created into one help (*.Hlp*) file, dealing with errors, and getting Help Workshop to automatically test jumps and pop-ups.

Compiling and Testing the Help File

Now that all the components have been gathered for this Mortgage Calculator help file, let's compile it! Compiling a help file with the Help Workshop is much easier than it used to be when running the old command-line compiler. You just click the Save and Compile button in the lower-right corner of the Help Workshop window (see Figure 35-8). When Help Workshop completes the compilation, it opens a log screen that describes the file that has been compiled and mentions whether there were any errors, as shown in Figure 35-12.

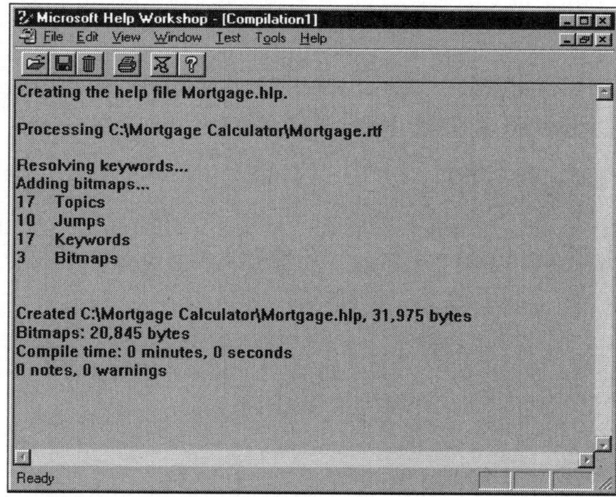

Figure 35-12: When a help project is compiled, Help Workshop displays a log that shows information about the compilation and any errors that occurred.

Help Workshop offers three types of error messages when it compiles a help file:

- Notes for problems that do not affect the way the help file works
- Warnings for problems found in a help file even though these problems do not stop the compilation
- Errors that keep the help file from compiling

After compiling a help file, you can use the items on Help Workshop's Test menu to test a contents file and all pop-ups and jumps, send macros to see how they will perform in the help file, and call a WinHelp API as if it were called from another program.

Another Help Workshop feature — Help Author — supplies additional debugging and authoring information. When Help Author is checked on the File menu:

- The help window title bar displays the help topic number instead of the help title.
- You can press Ctrl+Shift+right or left arrow key to step through the topics in your help file.
- Specific information is displayed about problems in the help project or contents files.
- You can right-click any help topic to display information about the current topic, or you can left-click any hot spot to display the hot spot's topic ID or any macro associated with the hot spot.

Connecting a Help File with a Visual Basic Project

Creating the Mortgage Calculator help file took a while, but connecting it to the Mortgage Calculator application is quick and easy.

The first step is to connect your project to a specific help file. You do this either by choosing Properties from the Project menu and entering a help file on the General tab of the Project Properties dialog, or by setting the HelpFile property of the App object in code, for example:

```
App.HelpFile = "Mortgage.Hlp"
```

Next, for each form in the project that you want connected, select the form and change both the WhatsThisButton and WhatsThisHelp properties to True. Then select each control that will have context-sensitive help and set its WhatsThisHelpID property to the proper context ID number that was set in the Map dialog when ***Mortgage.Hpj*** was created. (It's really handy to have a printout of the ***.Hpj*** file to refer to.) For instance, if you select lblPrinciple, you should set its WhatsThisHelpID property to 70 — the context ID number for Principle_PopUp.

After you have set all the controls' WhatsThisHelpID properties, it's time to add the code that will activate the context-sensitive help when the user either right-clicks the control or uses the What's This? button in the upper-right corner of the window. You need to use the MouseDown event for the various controls, check that the right mouse button has been clicked, and use the ShowWhatsThis method. However, instead of typing *control*.ShowWhatsThis inside the MouseDown event of every control, you can create a private procedure — GetHelp — that uses the control's name as a parameter and is passed to the ShowWhatsThis method.

For example, here is the code for the lblPrinciple MouseDown event and GetHelp:

```
Private Sub lblPrinciple_MouseDown(Button As Integer, _
    Shift As Integer, X As Single, Y As Single)
    If Button = vbRightButton Then
        GetHelp lblPrinciple
    End If
End Sub

Private Sub GetHelp(C As Control)
    C.ShowWhatsThis
End Sub
```

One final touch for this application would be to add a small menu that contains a "Help" title and the menu item "How to Use the Calculator." To activate this menu item, you have to drop a common dialog control on the form and add the following lines of code to the menu item's Click event:

```
Private Sub mnuCalcHelp_Click()
    CommonDialog1.HelpFile = "Mortgage.Hlp"
    CommonDialog1.HelpCommand = cdlHelpContents
    CommonDialog1.ShowHelp
End Sub
```

And that's it! All you need to do is compile an executable of this project and run the application from the ***.Exe*** file. This is because, when you are working on a program in design mode and run a project, the project will look for the ***.Hlp*** file in the current — Visual Basic — directory, rather than in the project's own directory.

As a rule of thumb, most 32-bit Windows Help files are located either in the application's directory or in the ***Windows\Help*** directory. However, Chapter 16, "Optimizing Secrets," demonstrated a routine that will hunt down a specific file. You could use this routine to track help files associated with an application.

The help file for the Mortgage Calculator is hooked up and working, as shown in Figure 35-13.

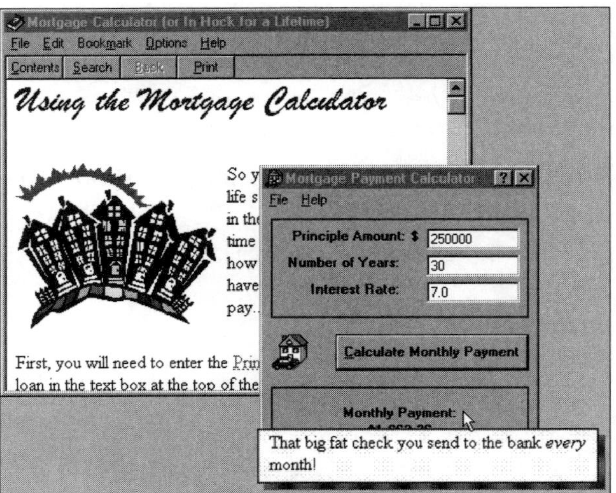

Figure 35-13: The Mortgage Calculator help file really looks professional.

If you click on the hypergraphic that we created earlier, you can see that the pop-up works just fine, as displayed in Figure 35-14.

Third-Party Help Tools: RoboHelp

A number of products on the market make it much easier to create help files — and connect them to VB projects. The premier product in this category is Blue Sky Software Corporation's RoboHelp.

RoboHelp is constructed as an extension to the Word for Windows environment. Using RoboHelp, you can create a hard copy manual and a Windows help file in one pass. RoboHelp's new HTML plug-in also lets you simultaneously create World Wide Web pages.

Essentially, RoboHelp allows you to add help file features visually without having to compile a help project to view its appearance. Tools included in RoboHelp make it particularly easy to link Visual Basic projects to your help file.

If you are creating help files of any complexity, it makes sense to use an authoring tool such as RoboHelp rather than to follow the raw help file generation process outlined in this chapter. (Of course, to the extent that you understand the process as it works without aids, you will be a better user of products like RoboHelp.)

Figure 35-14: The hypergraphic's hot spot displays an appreciative pop-up when clicked!

Summary

Every complete Visual Basic application should ship with a well-designed and polished help system. It "helps" if your help system is also snappy, visually appealing, and genuinely helpful.

Figuring out how to create a help system the first time is not easy. That's the purpose of this chapter: to present the process of creating a full-fledged help project clearly, one step at a time. Once you understand the process, you'll find it easy to create help files and connect them to your Visual Basic projects.

Topics covered in this chapter included

- 32-bit Windows help features
- Planning a help project
- What files make up a compiled help file
- Coding a help topic (*.Rtf*) file
- Linking help file topics
- Adding graphics to help files
- Using the Hotspot Editor (***Shed.Exe***)
- Using Help Workshop to create contents (*.Cnt*) and help project (*.Hpj*) files
- Compiling a help project
- Testing and debugging a help file
- Connecting a help project to a Visual Basic project
- Setting the WhatsThisHelpID property
- Using third-party tools

Chapter 36

Setup Programs

All things come to a close, even *Visual Basic 5 SECRETS*. And because, in the end, we've come round full circle, there seems no better place than the final chapter of this book to discuss beginnings: your program's installation program (also called a setup program or procedure).

To put this another way, from a good beginning comes a good end. If your program is not distributed with a reliable installation procedure, it will not do the job it was created to do. The first impression left by your installation program is likely to be a lasting impression. Furthermore, flaws in an installation program can undermine the functionality of your entire application.

This chapter covers the following topics:

- Using the Visual Basic Application Setup Wizard
- The Visual Basic Setup Toolkit
- Inside the Setup1 project

This chapter explains some setup features that are new to the Application Setup Wizard in Version 5 of Visual Basic. These features include the ability to create dependency (***.Dep***) files, and the ability to package an application for installation over the Internet.

The Visual Basic Application Setup Wizard

The Application Setup Wizard is a separate application that is started from the Visual Basic project group on the Windows Start menu. Its purpose is to guide you through the process of creating installation routines.

The setup program that the Wizard creates for you is compiled from the Setup Toolkit project, ***\Setupkit\Setup1\Setup1.Vbp***, which is installed under the Visual Basic folder. Later in this chapter, I'll show you how to customize your setup programs by modifying the ***Setup1.Vbp*** source project. But be warned: Once you have changed this project, all installation programs created by the Application Setup Wizard will reflect the changes you have made. It's wise, therefore, to make a copy of the entire directory containing ***Setup1.Vbp*** before modifying the project.

Using the Application Setup Wizard supplied with Visual Basic, you can easily prepare installation programs adequate for many situations.

If the default setup program created by the Application Setup Wizard doesn't fulfill your needs, you can customize the Setup1 Visual Basic project that is used by the Wizard. There are also a number of excellent third-party setup generation tools on the market that are easy to use and generate superb customized installation programs. InstallShield, from InstallShield Corporation, is considered the leading industrial strength third-party installation utility.

Installation Details Handled by the Application Setup Wizard

The Application Setup Wizard parses a project (*.Vbp*) file that it is pointed at and inputs a number of panels' worth of information from you to determine:

- Whether the Wizard will create a setup program, package an application for Internet download, or merely create a dependency file
- Which files need to be distributed with your application
- Data access drivers that should be included with the project
- The target destination and media for the setup files
- ActiveX components required by the application
- Remote ActiveX servers required by the application
- Whether the application should be installed as an executable, an ActiveX component, an ActiveX document application, or an ActiveX control

Once the information is gathered, the Application Setup Wizard:

- Prepares a text file, ***Setup.Lst***, that lists all files the application requires, including ActiveX components, controls, DLLs, and so on. This file is in private profile format. In other words, it is a good, old-fashioned ***.Ini*** file with headings and keywords. Information can be retrieved from it by the Setup1 project accordingly, which will use it to copy files to the appropriate places, register ActiveX components and controls as required, and create links and Start menu entries.
- Creates a dependency (***.Dep***) file, if that option was selected (see "Dependency Files," later in the chapter).
- Compresses the application files and calculates the number of disks required for a distribution.
- For Internet installations, creates an Internet package and sample HTML code.
- Copies *bootstrap* files — those necessary to initially run the setup program — to the target destination (such as distribution media). It also copies compressed files required by the application to the target destination (and splits them across multiple disks if required).

Note that if you create your own installation procedure — or modify the Setup1 project used by the Application Setup Wizard as described in a moment — you must be sure to take care of each of these steps (if they apply to your application).

Automatic Uninstallation

Windows 95 interface compliance includes distributing an automatic uninstaller with your application. ***St5unst.Exe*** is an application removal utility that is part of the Visual Basic Setup Toolkit and is included with distribution media by the Application Setup Wizard, which copies it to the Windows directory of target machines.

The bootstrap setup program and Setup1 prepare a log file that contains complete information about changes the installation makes to the target system. If the installation is successful, the application is added to the list of programs in the Add/Remove facility in the Control Panel. Removing the program causes ***St5unst.Exe*** to use the log file entries in an attempt to reverse changes made by the setup programs.

When the prepared installation procedure actually runs on a target machine — for example, from a floppy disk — the first bootstrap file, ***Setup.Exe***, is run, followed by other programs included in the [BootStrap] section of ***Setup.Lst***. These files include the Visual Basic files needed to make ***Setup.Exe*** (itself a VB program) run and ***Setup1.Exe***, which is compiled from the Setup1 project and customized for the specific application installation by the Application Setup Wizard. (Note that you can rename this file as long as the new name is referenced in ***Setup.Lst***.)

The bootstrap executable, ***Setup.Exe***, is copied to the target Windows directory. ***Setup.Exe*** then reads configuration information from the copy of ***Setup.Lst*** that has been placed in the Windows directory. Normally, its next step is to invoke ***Setup1.Exe***, which proceeds with copying the actual application files to a destination specified by the user.

Point and Go: The Application Setup Wizard

Operation of the Application Setup Wizard is truly straightforward. Start it by selecting Application Setup Wizard from the Visual Basic project group on the Windows Start menu. After an introductory panel, you are prompted to tell the Wizard the project for which you want to prepare an installation program, as shown in Figure 36-1. You also use this panel to select between a standard setup program, an Internet setup, and merely creating a dependency file.

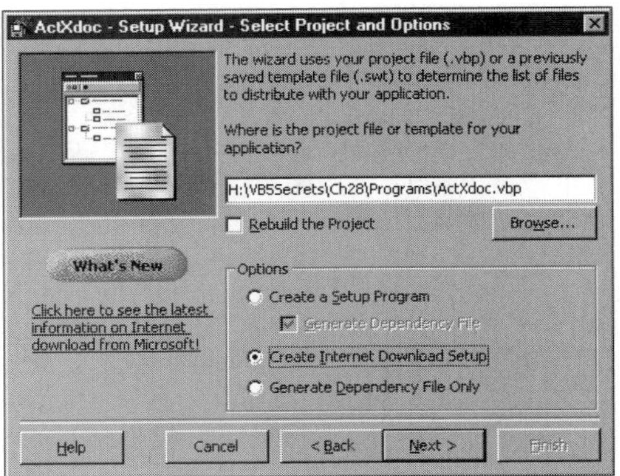

Figure 36-1: You use the first panel of the Application Setup Wizard to select a Visual Basic project (***.Vbp***) file and to determine the type of setup routine the Wizard will create.

The Application Setup Wizard guides you through several panels, each requesting information required to prepare the installation program. A penultimate panel, shown in Figure 36-2, allows you to manually add files that your application needs (or to manually delete files that you believe the Wizard has erroneously added).

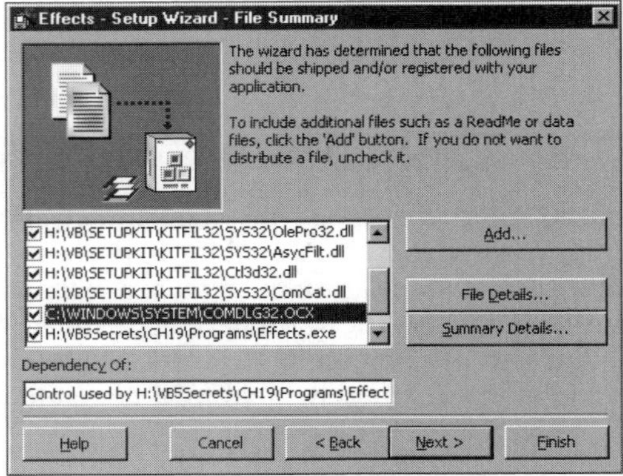

Figure 36-2: You use the penultimate panel of the Application Setup Wizard to add and delete files required for the distribution.

The final Wizard panel (see Figure 36-3) allows you to save a Setup Wizard template (***.Swt***) file based on the information you've provided to the Wizard.

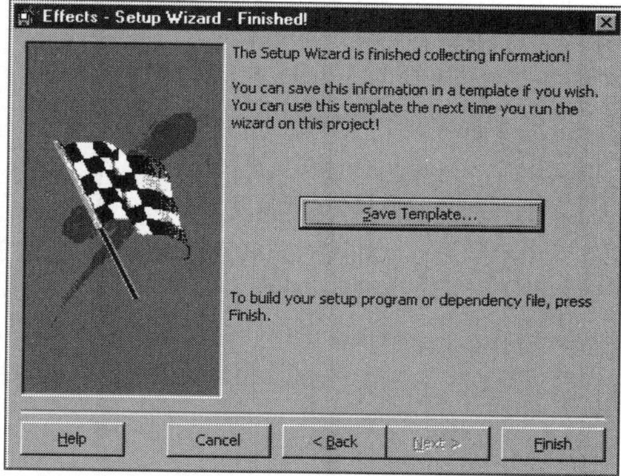

Figure 36-3: The final Wizard panel allows you to save a Setup Wizard template (***.Swt***) file based on your Wizard entries.

Clicking Finish causes the Wizard to prepare ***Setup.Lst***, compress the selected files, and copy the required files to the distribution media or target directory.

If you run the resulting plain vanilla installation program generated by the Application Setup Wizard, you'll see that the Wizard has created a perfectly respectable generic setup program, as shown in Figure 36-4. Note that the shaded words in the upper-left corner of the setup screen are, by default, the application title entered in the EXE Options dialog of the target project with the word "Setup" appended. You can easily change this default display by editing ***Setup.Lst***, as I'll show you shortly.

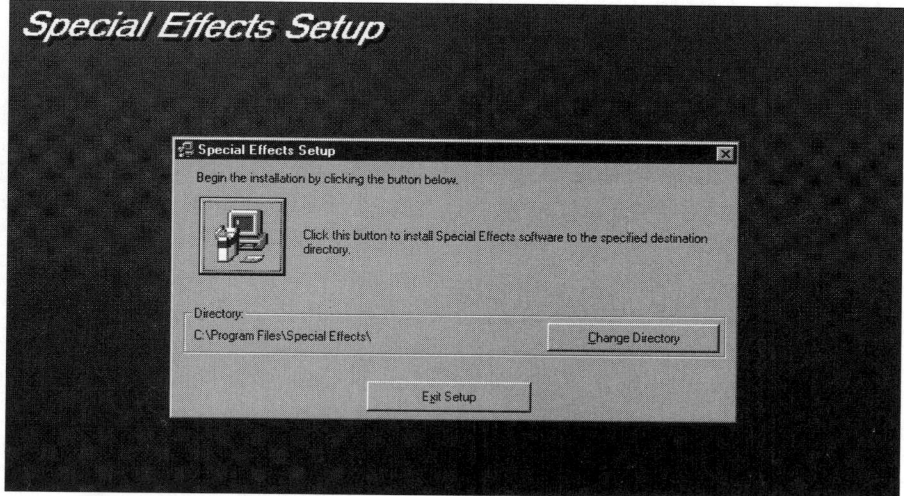

Figure 36-4: The Application Setup Wizard creates a very nice generic setup program.

Dependency Files

A dependency (*.Dep*) file is intended to provide information about the runtime requirements of an application, component, or control.

You can use the Application Setup Wizard for the sole purpose of creating a *.Dep* file; or you can elect to have a *.Dep* file created along with your setup program. *.Dep* files created by the Wizard are placed in the same directory as the component or project for which it was created.

.Dep files can be created for components and for projects. Additionally, dependency information for Visual Basic itself can be found in the *Vb5dep.Ini* file.

Component Dependency Files

Component dependency files are used to determine dependency information about controls or other components. It's a good idea to provide a *.Dep* file for any controls or components that you intend to distribute. A typical *.Dep* file lists all the dependent files — that is, files required for the component or control to operate properly. In addition, the *.Dep* file contains version information and Registry information. For example, here is the partial contents of *Comdlg32.Dep*, the dependency file for the common dialog control.

```
[ComDlg32.ocx]
Dest=$(WinSysPath)
Register=$(DLLSelfRegister)
Version=5.0.36.9
Uses1=ComCat.dll
Uses2=
CABFileName=ComDlg32.cab
CABDefaultURL=
CABINFFile=ComDlg32.inf
```

The *Vb5dep.Ini* File

Vb5dep.Ini is used to provide the Setup Wizard with a list of all files required by Visual Basic (dependencies). *Vb5dep.Ini* also includes a list of all references used by VB and information that the Setup Wizard may require about the system on which VB is installed (for example, the media size of removable drives).

In previous versions of Visual Basic, the file serving this purpose was named *Swdepend.Ini*.

When Visual Basic is installed on a system, it creates a *Vb5dep.Ini* file, which is placed in the *\SetupKit\Kitfil32* directory.

Here is the portion of ***Vb5dep.Ini*** that lists VB runtime dependencies:

```
[VB Runtime]
Dest=$(WinSysPath)
Uses1=MSVBVM50.dll
Uses2=StdOle2.tlb
Uses3=Ctl3d32.dll
Uses4=ComCat.dll
Uses5=AsycFilt.dll
```

Project Dependency Files: Putting It All Together

When the Application Setup Wizard generates a setup program for a project, it places dependency information in the ***Setup.Lst*** file.

Note that you can elect to use the Setup Wizard solely to create a dependency file for a project, component, or control.

The Wizard parses the project to discover dependencies and references. It also reads ***Vb5dep.Ini*** and any ***.Dep*** files provided by components and controls included in the project. The combined dependencies are used to generate the list of files and references required to install your application, ***Setup.Lst***.

Internet Setups

The Setup Wizard will generate an installation routine, including a compressed project file in Internet format (a Cabinet ***.Cab*** file), and sample HTML code that you can adapt for your own uses.

If you use the Setup Wizard to create a Web setup, make sure Create Internet Download Setup is selected on the first panel.

It's a good idea to place all the ***.Cab*** files intended for Web use in one directory on your Web site, for ease of administration.

Figure 36-5 shows the Wizard's Internet Distribution Location dialog. This location could be the root directory, or in the hierarchy, of your Web server, or any other location that you like.

Figure 36-6 shows the Internet Package dialog, which follows the Distribution Location dialog. You use this dialog to specify whether Visual Basic's runtime files should be downloaded from Microsoft's site or from an alternative location. (If the target system already has the current VB runtime files — or, as they are sometimes called in the Web context, the Visual Basic Virtual Machine — they will not be downloaded.)

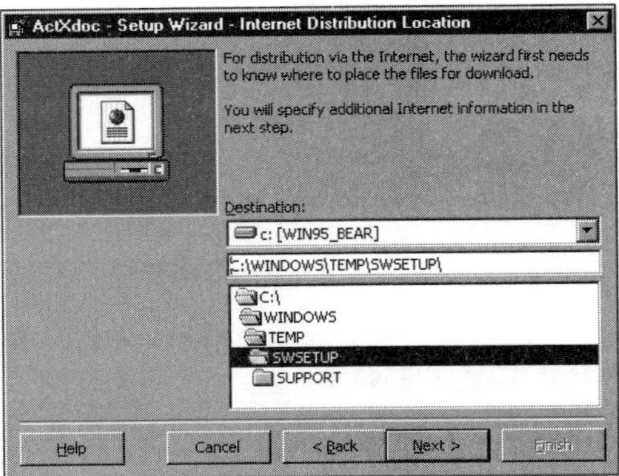

Figure 36-5: You must specify the target destination for your control setup files.

Unless you are in an intranet setting with no outside Web access, you should download the ***.Cab*** files from Microsoft (which is the default setting).

Figure 36-6 also shows the Safety dialog, which you can use to mark your component projects as safe for initialization and scripting. For more information about Web applications and security concerns, see Chapter 27, "Deploying VB ActiveX Controls on the Web."

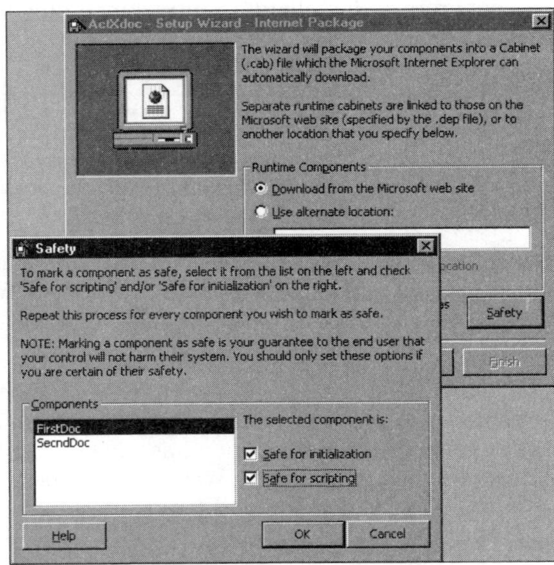

Figure 36-6: The Internet Package dialog allows you to specify a support download file location (the default is from Microsoft) and to access the Safety dialog.

The Setup Toolkit

The Setup Toolkit includes the files shown in Table 36-1.

Table 36-1 Files Included in the Visual Basic Setup Toolkit

File(s)	*Comment*
Setup.Exe	Bootstrap program that starts the installation process.
Setup.Lst	Text file, in private profile format, listing all files to be included in the distribution.
Setup1.Vbp	Visual Basic source code for ***Setup1.Exe***, which is used to actually do most of the installation work. ***Setup1*** can be customized as you'd like. Also note that ***Setup1.Exe*** can be renamed, provided that the name is changed in ***Setup.Lst***. The ***Setup1*** project includes a code module, ***Setup1.Bas***, with routines that perform most of the tasks required for setup (see the section "Modifying the Setup1 Project" later in this chapter).
Vb5stkt.Dll	Library for the use of ***Setup1.Bas***. Includes routine for expanding files that are compressed with ***Compress.Exe***.
St5Unst.Exe	Application removal utility.
CliReg32.Exe	Remote OLE automation client registration utility (Enterprise Edition only).
Compress.Exe	File compression utility.
Makecab.Exe	Cabinet file compression utility (used for Internet setups).
Vb5dep.Ini	Visual Basic dependency file.

You can make some quick and nifty changes to your setup program simply by editing ***Setup.Lst***. For example, the display banner and default destination shown in Figure 36-4 are "Special Effects Setup" and ***Program Files\ Special Effects***, respectively. You can edit the [Setup] section of ***Setup.Lst*** to change these defaults. For example:

```
[Setup]
Title=Don't worry, be happy
DefProgramGroup=Special Effects
DefaultDir=$(ProgramFiles)\Fun
Setup=setup1.exe
AppExe=Effects.exe
AppToUninstall=Effects.exe
AppPath=
```

would create a banner display reading "Don't worry, be happy Setup" and a default program destination of ***Program Files\Fun***, as shown in Figure 36-7. (The absolute location of the ***Program Files*** directory depends, of course, on the target system's configuration.)

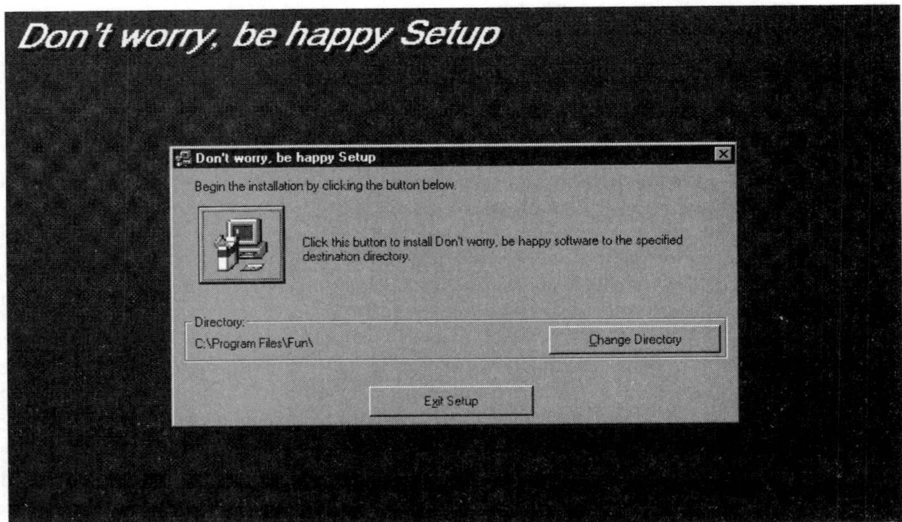

Figure 36-7: You can easily modify the behavior and appearance of the setup program by editing ***Setup.Lst*** in a text editor.

Modifying the Setup1 Project

As I noted in the description of the Visual Basic Application Setup Wizard, the Wizard customizes installations to meet the needs of specific applications by modifying the entries in ***Setup.Lst*** that are used by the ***Setup1.Vbp*** project. This project is located in the ***VB\Setupkit\Setup1*** directory. There is nothing to stop you from making your own modifications, although I strongly suggest that you make a backup copy of this project before experimenting.

In some cases it works well to create a customized version of Setup1, compile it, and then let the Application Setup Wizard automatically generate your distribution media. Of course, if you'd prefer, you can plan the entire distribution yourself by determining the necessary files, compressing them, copying the compressed files to distribution locations, and preparing a ***Setup.Lst*** file manually.

If you decide to try modifying the Setup1 project, you'll be glad to know that Microsoft has provided extensive comments to guide you.

The place to start is the Form Load event for frmSetup1. This procedure contains the code that performs the installation, primarily by calling ***Setup1.Bas*** routines that operate on data supplied by ***Setup.Lst***.

For example, the statement

```
CopySection strINI_FILES
```

calls the CopySection routine in ***Setup.Bas***, which attempts to copy all the files listed in a section of ***Setup.Lst***.

You could easily add a dialog requesting user input to the Form Load event.

To modify the appearance of the setup program, you could change the way frmSetup1 looks. You can apply any of the graphics techniques explained in Chapter 19, "Runtime Display Secrets," to this form.

Setup.Bas itself contains numerous utility routines that involve manipulating files and the Windows environment. Because these procedures are intended for widespread distribution and are written by the authors of Visual Basic — in other words, Microsoft — and are well commented, to boot, it's well worth your while to study them.

Summary

Installation programs are important both because they give users their first impression of your application and because a good setup routine can help to ensure that your program runs properly. The Visual Basic Application Setup Wizard provides a sturdy and easy-to-use way to generate installation routines. The Application Setup Wizard uses a bootstrap to run a compiled Visual Basic project that handles the work of setting up an application. You can modify the source code contained in this project to customize the look and feel of the setup program, and how it operates.

Topics covered in this chapter included

- Information gathered by the Application Setup Wizard
- What the Wizard does
- The concept of bootstrapping
- Automatic uninstallation
- Dependency (***.Dep***) files
- Creating Internet setups
- Using the Application Setup Wizard
- The contents of the Setup Toolkit
- Modifying ***Setup.Lst*** files
- Customizing ***Setup1.Exe***

Appendix A

Contents of the CD-ROM

The companion CD-ROM contains all the Visual Basic source projects developed in *Visual Basic 5 SECRETS*. It also includes utility code modules. Source code projects and modules are organized by chapter.

A number of leading vendors of third-party Visual Basic products have agreed to supply material for the CD-ROM. Each vendor's product has been placed in its own directory. In most cases, the vendors have supplied their own setup programs, which you should run to install the product on your system. In a few instances, you'll need to copy a zipped file to your hard drive and unzip it before you can run the product's installer. (You'll find further information about these vendors and their products in Chapter 31, "Overview of Third-Party Tools.")

Here are the third-party goodies you'll find on the CD-ROM:

- **From Blue Sky Software Corporation:** HTML-based white papers containing information about RoboHelp 4, WinHelp Office 4, and other Blue Sky programs; the SmartHelp ActiveX control, which helps with creating context-sensitive help; the WinHelp Inspector utility; and Blue Sky's *Windows 95 Help Style Guide*.
- **From Desaware:** A help file containing information about Desaware's exciting new products designed specially for Visual Basic 5. Hypertext links in the help file allow you to download the current trial versions of these products from Desaware's Web site.
- **From FarPoint Technologies:** Demonstration versions of Visual Basic 5 versions of FarPoint's professional tools, including a program that demonstrates ButtonMaker, a control that lets you create unique graphical command buttons at design time. The ButtonMaker demo includes two fun games. These games — completely created using the ButtonMaker control — involve finding your way through booby-trapped mazes. FarPoint has also included time-limited trial versions of some of their other products.
- **From ImageFX:** A complete demonstration of the Professional Edition of FXTools, a set of imaging and multimedia components.
- **From Mabry Software:** Trial version of Mabry's Internet, Mega and Midi Packs.

- **From MicroHelp:** A trial version of OLETools, a premier collection of powerful OCXs that perform tasks ranging from string manipulation to multimedia playback. MicroHelp has also included demonstration versions of some of their other products, including Explorer X-ponents, Encryption X-ponents, Fax Plus 2, and their Zip compression ActiveX control.
- **From Sax Software:** Demonstrations of the Sax Setup Wizard, Version 2 of the Sax Webster Control, and the Sax Basic Engine Pro, a control that lets you integrate macro language support into your applications.
- **From TVObjects Corporation:** A demonstration version of Applet Designer for VB5, a product that allows you to create Java applets from VB source projects.
- **From VideoSoft:** Evaluation versions of VS-Ocx 5.0, VSView 2.0, and VSFlex 2.0. These important additions to any programmer's toolkit — described in detail in Chapter 33 — are fully functional except that, when a project containing them loads, they display a banner indicating that an evaluation version is being used.

INDEX

Numbers and Symbols

A

(continued)

D

E

F

(continued)

G

H

I

N

O

(continued)

P

Q

R

T

U

V

W

X

Z

NOTES

NOTES

NOTES

NOTES

CD-ROM Installation Instructions

You can begin using the Visual Basic 5 SECRETS CD-ROM in the familiar way:

Place the disc in your CD-ROM drive and then close the drive.

Open the README file for further instructions.

For more information on installing and using the software on the CD-ROM, see Appendix A.

IDG BOOKS WORLDWIDE, INC.
END-USER LICENSE AGREEMENT

Read This. You should carefully read these terms and conditions before opening the software packet(s) included with this book ("Book"). This is a license agreement ("Agreement") between you and IDG Books Worldwide, Inc. ("IDGB"). By opening the accompanying software packet(s), you acknowledge that you have read and accept the following terms and conditions. If you do not agree and do not want to be bound by such terms and conditions, promptly return the Book and the unopened software packet(s) to the place you obtained them for a full refund.

1. **License Grant.** IDGB grants to you (either an individual or entity) a nonexclusive license to use one copy of the enclosed software program(s) (collectively, the "Software") solely for your own personal or business purposes on a single computer (whether a standard computer or a workstation component of a multiuser network). The Software is in use on a computer when it is loaded into temporary memory (i.e., RAM) or installed into permanent memory (e.g., hard disk, CD-ROM, or other storage device). IDGB reserves all rights not expressly granted herein.
2. **Ownership.** IDGB is the owner of all right, title, and interest, including copyright, in and to the compilation of the Software recorded on the CD-ROM. Copyright to the individual programs on the CD-ROM is owned by the author or other authorized copyright owner of each program. Ownership of the Software and all proprietary rights relating thereto remain with IDGB and its licensors.
3. **Restrictions on Use and Transfer.**

   (a) You may only (i) make one copy of the Software for backup or archival purposes, or (ii) transfer the Software to a single hard disk, provided that you keep the original for backup or archival purposes. You may not (i) rent or lease the Software, (ii) copy or reproduce the Software through a LAN or other network system or through any computer subscriber system or bulletin-board system, or (iii) modify, adapt, or create derivative works based on the Software.

   (b) You may not reverse engineer, decompile, or disassemble the Software. You may transfer the Software and user documentation on a permanent basis, provided that the transferee agrees to accept the terms and conditions of this Agreement and you retain no copies. If the Software is an update or has been updated, any transfer must include the most recent update and all prior versions.

4. **Restrictions on Use of Individual Programs.** You must follow the individual requirements and restrictions detailed for each individual program in Appendix A, Contents of the CD-ROM. These limitations are contained in the individual license agreements recorded on the CD-ROM. These restrictions may include a requirement that after using the program for the period of time specified in its text, the user must pay a registration fee or discontinue use. By opening the Software packet(s), you will be agreeing to abide by the licenses and restrictions for these individual programs. None of the material on this disk(s) or listed in this Book may ever be distributed, in original or modified form, for commercial purposes.

5. **Limited Warranty.**

   (a) IDGB warrants that the Software and CD-ROM are free from defects in materials and workmanship under normal use for a period of sixty (60) days from the date of purchase of this Book. If IDGB receives notification within the warranty period of defects in materials or workmanship, IDGB will replace the defective CD-ROM.

   (b) **IDGB AND THE AUTHOR OF THE BOOK DISCLAIM ALL OTHER WARRANTIES, EXPRESS OR IMPLIED, INCLUDING WITHOUT LIMITATION IMPLIED WARRANTIES OF MERCHANTABILITY AND FITNESS FOR A PARTICULAR PURPOSE, WITH RESPECT TO THE SOFTWARE, THE PROGRAMS, THE SOURCE CODE CONTAINED THEREIN, AND/OR THE TECHNIQUES DESCRIBED IN THIS BOOK. IDGB DOES NOT WARRANT THAT THE FUNCTIONS CONTAINED IN THE SOFTWARE WILL MEET YOUR REQUIREMENTS OR THAT THE OPERATION OF THE SOFTWARE WILL BE ERROR FREE.**

   (c) This limited warranty gives you specific legal rights, and you may have other rights which vary from jurisdiction to jurisdiction.

6. **Remedies.**

   (a) IDGB's entire liability and your exclusive remedy for defects in materials and workmanship shall be limited to replacement of the Software, which may be returned to IDGB with a copy of your receipt at the following address: Disk Fulfillment Department, Attn: Visual Basic 5 SECRETS, IDG Books Worldwide, Inc., 7260 Shadeland Station, Ste. 100, Indianapolis, IN 46256, or call 1-800-762-2974. Please allow 3–4 weeks for delivery. This Limited Warranty is void if failure of the Software has resulted from accident, abuse, or misapplication. Any replacement Software will be warranted for the remainder of the original warranty period or thirty (30) days, whichever is longer.

   (b) In no event shall IDGB or the author be liable for any damages whatsoever (including without limitation damages for loss of business profits, business interruption, loss of business information, or any other pecuniary loss) arising from the use of or inability to use the Book or the Software, even if IDGB has been advised of the possibility of such damages.

(c) Because some jurisdictions do not allow the exclusion or limitation of liability for consequential or incidental damages, the above limitation or exclusion may not apply to you.

7. **U.S. Government Restricted Rights.** Use, duplication, or disclosure of the Software by the U.S. Government is subject to restrictions stated in paragraph (c) (1) (ii) of the Rights in Technical Data and Computer Software clause of DFARS 252.227-7013, and in subparagraphs (a) through (d) of the Commercial Computer — Restricted Rights clause at FAR 52.227-19, and in similar clauses in the NASA FAR supplement, when applicable.

8. **General.** This Agreement constitutes the entire understanding of the parties and revokes and supersedes all prior agreements, oral or written, between them and may not be modified or amended except in a writing signed by both parties hereto which specifically refers to this Agreement. This Agreement shall take precedence over any other documents that may be in conflict herewith. If any one or more provisions contained in this Agreement are held by any court or tribunal to be invalid, illegal, or otherwise unenforceable, each and every other provision shall remain in full force and effect.